T0313959

Contraband

CONTRABAND

*Louis Mandrin and the Making
of a Global Underground*

MICHAEL KWASS

Harvard University Press

Cambridge, Massachusetts
London, England
2014

Library of Congress Cataloging-in-Publication Data
Kwass, Michael.
Contraband : Louis Mandrin and the making of a
global underground / Michael Kwass.
pages cm
Includes bibliographical references and index.
ISBN 978-0-674-72683-3 (hardcover : alk. paper)
1. Mandrin, Louis, 1725–1755. 2. Criminals—France—Biography.
3. Smugglers—France—Biography. 4. Smuggling—France—History—
18th century. 5. France—Commerce—History—18th century. 6. France—
Economic conditions—18th century. 7. France—Social conditions—
18th century. I. Title.
HV6248.M278K93 2014
364.1'336092—dc23
[B]   2013032888

For Laura, Max, and Isabel

Contents

Figures

Contraband

Introduction

A HIGH-RANKING CUSTOMS OFFICIAL stationed in a remote frontier town agrees to meet a trafficker from across the border. The smuggler, one of countless men, women, and children who run an illegal psychoactive substance from their impoverished country into the richest and most powerful nation in the hemisphere, has intimated through a third party that he is prepared to cut a deal: in exchange for a new life and clean conscience, he will rat out his boss, a notorious underworld kingpin the police have been tracking for months. Eager to take down the leader of a violent criminal gang, the customs agent brushes aside warnings from colleagues and agrees to a rendezvous at dusk on the banks of a river tracing the serpentine boundary between the two countries. At the appointed hour, as the official walks through a violet-studded meadow toward the river, shots ring out. One pierces his forearm. Another grazes his thigh. The third enters his body above the right hip and rips through his abdomen. Hemorrhaging, the wounded agent is whisked to a nearby military outpost, but to no avail. He dies the following evening, another casualty in a contraband war that has been raging for decades. Rumors fly that the author of the deadly ambush was none other than the legendary kingpin himself: Louis Mandrin.

This is a disturbingly familiar story. A customs agent investigates a transnational drug ring that feeds a wealthy nation of consumers. Violence erupts at the border as police do battle with armed traffickers. Shoot-outs and killings are so common that authorities do not hesitate to characterize the conflict as a war. Although intellectuals deplore the violence and call for decriminalization, courts continue to dispatch petty dealers to an ever-expanding prison system. All the while, the flow of illicit substances continues unabated, driven by intense consumer demand.

This border killing did not take place in present-day El Paso, Juárez, or Tijuana, but in the middle of the eighteenth century on the outskirts of Pont-de-Beauvoisin, a bustling gateway to southeastern France. Indeed, when we stop to consider the peculiar historical circumstances that conspired to produce this cold-blooded assassination, much of what initially seemed familiar becomes strange. The customs agent, Pierre Robert Le Roux de La Motte, was not a public official. He worked for a private company known as "the Farm," which contracted the right to collect taxes for the king of France. The river was not the Rio Grande but the Guiers, a shallow stream that divided the mighty French kingdom from the mountainous province of Savoy, ruled loosely from across the Alps by the king of Sardinia. The smuggler who set the rendezvous (and probably one of the shooters) was twenty-two-year-old Louis Jarrier aka "the Piedmontese," one of scores of Savoy-based traffickers who served in Mandrin's gang. Strangest of all, the substance that Mandrin and his band smuggled—and over which La Motte was killed—was not marijuana, cocaine, or heroin but a new drug from America: tobacco.

Taken from the war between Farm and smuggler, such an episode of violence accords ill with what historians call the "consumer revolution" of the eighteenth century. Before the factories of the Industrial Revolution were built, Europeans of the middling classes and, to some extent, even members of the laboring classes freed themselves from the grip of scarcity to initiate a buying spree of historic proportions. Between 1650 and 1800, they filled their homes with beds, dressers, mirrors, and pottery; expanded their wardrobes to include white linens and brilliant calicoes; sported new personal accessories such as fans, umbrellas, and pocket watches; sipped exotic hot beverages (tea, coffee, and chocolate), heavily sweetened with sugar; and smoked, chewed, and snorted prodigious quantities of tobacco. Their ancestors would have been amazed. Propelled by new products, marketing innovations, shorter fashion cycles, and a dramatic expansion in world trade, modern consumption was born.[1]

Although historians have long pointed out that the rise of European consumption depended in part on the exploitation of slave labor in the New World and the use of armed trading in Asia, they have been slower to examine the violence, coercion, and turmoil that accompanied trade in the metropole. Merchants there are portrayed exchanging merchandise in perfect tranquility as consumers happily accumulated goods. In France, however, the violence unleashed by Farm agents and smugglers, the brutal crackdown on the underground economy by the criminal justice system, and the clamorous public controversy over the repression of illicit trade suggest a darker image of eighteenth-century commerce and consumption. Empire, globalization, and the consumer revolution they helped spawn may have had a more turbulent effect on the economic and political life of metropolitan Europe than is often believed.

How we understand the consumer revolution is of utmost importance to the larger story of the birth of the modern Western world. For generations, that story has turned on the eighteenth century, when the prevailing winds of history appear to have shifted irrevocably from tradition to change. While the cultural origins of the modern West have long been located in the Enlightenment (1680–1800), a momentous intellectual movement in which thinkers like Voltaire attempted to vanquish superstition and free the individual from the oppressive constraints of the past, its political roots are often traced back to the French Revolution (1789–1799), a watershed event in which the people of a nation toppled an oppressive regime to forge a new order based on universal democratic principles. Although contemporary historians are rightly suspicious of grandiose narratives of Enlightenment and Revolution, they still cling to the idea of the eighteenth century as a pathway to modernity. If they no longer find origins of modernity exclusively in the ideas of great philosophers or the actions of famous revolutionary leaders, it is because they have turned to an array of new social and cultural practices that flourished in the hothouse environment of rising consumption. The widening circulation of goods and the proliferation of public sites of consumption—cafés, restaurants, salons, bookshops, theaters, public gardens—helped to soften rigid social hierarchies, generate a public sphere of critically minded citizens, and produce modern understandings of self and society.[2] For Daniel Roche, a pioneer in the field, the birth of consumption in France was essential to a larger cultural transformation whereby the traditional values of a stationary economy ceded to the egalitarianism and individualism of modern commodity culture.

In arguing that the modernizing effects of consumption were positive, Roche and others take on a venerable intellectual tradition that, since the days of the consumer revolution itself, has blamed expanding consumption for numbing the political sensibilities of modern man. "The people recognize themselves in their commodities," lamented Herbert Marcuse, one of the last century's fiercest critics of capitalism; "they find their soul in their automobile, hi-fi set, split-level home, kitchen equipment. The very mechanism which ties the individual to society has changed, and social control is anchored in the new needs which it has produced."[3] The materialism of modern consumer society, Marcuse warned, impeded critical thinking and prevented human beings from reaching their full social and political potential. Roche explicitly challenges that line of criticism, contending that "despite a deeply entrenched intellectual tradition, commodities did not necessarily foster alienation; in fact, they generally meant liberation. . . . The expansion of consumption was not purely negative." The dizzying cycles of eighteenth-century fashion weakened tradition's purchase on society and encouraged "a new state of mind, more individualistic, more hedonistic, in any case more egalitarian and more free."[4]

Inserting the consumer revolution into the grand narrative of modern history is a worthy enterprise but risks reconstructing, along materialist lines, an older teleological (some would say Whiggish) interpretation of the age. Certainly, eighteenth-century thinkers and taste makers—from philosophers and economists to luxury artisans and fashion retailers—touted the civilizing and emancipatory effects of burgeoning trade and consumption. But should we take them at their word? Is there not a danger in accepting at face value their own interpretations of the commercial changes going on around them? I do not urge a return to a Marcusian position that holds all acts of superfluous consumption to be inherently alienating, regardless of what consumers themselves believe. People of all sorts derive great meaning from consumption, and those meanings (emancipatory and otherwise) must be taken seriously if we are to understand the historical development of consumer culture. However, for the field to advance, for consumption to take its rightful place in history, we must do more than simply document the rise of trade, count the growing number of goods, and consult taste makers for the cultural significance of it all. We must place consumption in a broader global, political, and social context—the kind of context that can explain why smugglers were gunning down customs agents along the French-Savoyard border.

A global perspective is most sorely needed in French history.[5] If historians of France have been notoriously slow to incorporate the wider world into the nation's history, scholars of French consumption have been particularly hesitant to venture into the rough-and-tumble world of global production and exchange. One reason for this, paradoxically, is that the archives documenting French material life are so rich. French archives are filled with after-death inventories, probate records that list in exquisite detail all the movable goods an individual possessed at the moment of his or her death. Without exhaustive research on such precious documents, we would never have known that consumption climbed in eighteenth-century France, much as it did in England. Probate inventories put French consumption on the map.[6] And yet, for all their wonderfully colorful detail, they are problematic, not only for the oft-cited reason that wealthier families were more prone than poorer ones to have them drawn, but because such documents offer a narrowly circumscribed snapshot of the world of goods. Inventories reveal little about where goods came from, who produced them, and what path they took before reaching consumers. The image of material culture they project fails to capture the boisterous and often violent world of production and exchange that brought goods to market in the first place.

Second, the historiography of the French consumer revolution does not sufficiently engage eighteenth-century politics. In the decades before the French Revolution, France was plagued with food riots, tax rebellions, workplace disputes, religious controversies, constitutional struggles, and tumultuous public debate. Was there a connection between the proliferation of commodities and such prerevolutionary strife? Astoundingly, this question is rarely posed.[7] What seems an obvious line of inquiry has been eclipsed by the preoccupations of two dominant scholarly traditions. The *Annales* school of social history, which privileged long-term continuities in economy and society over short-term political events, did not encourage historians to explore connections between consumer culture and politics. As grand master Fernand Braudel observed, the school's break with traditional event-based history worked "to the advantage of economic and social history, and to the detriment of political history."[8]

Scholarship on the French Revolution has not been much help either. Marxists once claimed that the Revolution was the work of a dynamic bourgeoisie that, emboldened by economic and social change, seized political power in 1789 to supplant feudalism with capitalism. Revisionists and their heirs replied that no coherent bourgeoisie existed in the eighteenth century, that commercial capitalism was not sufficiently developed to act as an agent of revolutionary change, and that the Revolution was in fact the product of new political discourse, rituals, and ideas.[9] The turn toward revolutionary political culture produced a rich body of literature, but there is mounting concern that the pendulum has swung too far from the question of capitalism and the everyday experiences of material life. Fundamental economic problems have been pushed aside, resulting in a "separation of economic history from cultural and political history [that] is positively harmful to both."[10] It is time to reverse this process of fragmentation; to reintegrate economic, political, and cultural histories of the period; and to reconsider the conditions under which the old regime state collapsed.

Social history must be more fully incorporated as well. Optimistic views of consumer revolution that highlight improving material conditions (and the modern forms of consciousness they engendered) stand in apparent contradiction to the findings of social historians who emphasize the century's persistent poverty, wage stagnation, chronic unemployment, land fragmentation, desperate migration, and rising criminality. Multitudes lived precarious lives, eking out a living in city streets or on small patches of land. How is one to reconcile these two images of the period, both of which are founded on unimpeachable evidence? How does one account for cheerful depictions of ordinary people consuming more and more goods *and* dismal portrayals of bereft peasants and artisans taking to the road? Any analysis of consumption must account for the fact that eighteenth-century France witnessed "an acceleration in both upward and downward social mobility."[11]

This book does not pretend to resolve all of these methodological and historiographical problems. But by delving into the underground economy of eighteenth-century France, it shows how the convergence of three formidable historical forces—globalization, consumption, and state formation—destabilized the old regime and contributed to the outbreak of revolution. Hence, more than simply putting consumption in a wider context, this book illuminates links between global, national, and local transformations that are too often treated in isolation.

Early modern globalization is an essential piece of the story.[12] In common parlance, "globalization" refers to two distinct phenomena that are often mistakenly conflated: neoliberalism and the integration of world markets. Since 1980, neoliberalism has been on the ascendant. The Soviet Union collapsed, the communist-ruled economy of China was partially liberalized, Western monetary policy tacked toward fighting inflation rather than unemployment, and nations like Britain and the United States deregulated industry and finance while curbing the power of labor.[13] Even in the tense aftermath of the global financial crisis of 2008, austerity triumphed over Keynesianism to remain the order of the day. Meanwhile, the integration of global markets has given the impression that the nation-state is in steep decline. We imagine money, goods, people, and information zipping across borders at lightning speed, as social connections between near and far multiply. Indeed, the vision of a single world economy has become so pervasive that it is now the object of intense controversy: conservatives fear its cultural dislocations, neo-liberals extol its open markets, and leftists worry about its corrosive effects on the welfare state.

And yet, despite an undeniable surge in global trade at the turn of the twenty-first century, neoliberal dreams of peace, prosperity, and state retreat have not been realized. Walls between peoples continue to be erected; battles over currencies, markets, and natural resources flare; wars rage and the public debts that result from them roil; piracy disrupts shipping on the high seas; and territorial states continue to act in power-ful and authoritarian ways both domestically and internationally.[14] Perhaps most strikingly, the rise of world trade has ushered in a global crime wave of unprecedented proportions that has, in turn, provoked severe yet unevenly applied state repression. Since the fall of communism and the liberalization of financial and commodity markets, the volume of illegal arms, drugs, money, counterfeit goods, and intellectual prop-erty flowing across national borders has skyrocketed. At the end of the twentieth century, the world's "gross criminal product" edged above the $1 trillion mark, representing as much as 15 to 20 percent of all global turnover.[15] Moreover, in the case of illegal drugs, a $500 billion global business, the combination of fervent consumer demand, thriving illicit markets, and unusually harsh repression has produced extraordinarily high levels of incarceration in the United States. The U.S. "war on drugs," declared by President Richard Nixon in 1971, currently nets 1.7 million arrests and 250,000 incarcerations annually, boosting the nation's rate of imprisonment, now the highest in the world. Of the 2.3 million U.S. citizens locked in jail or prison, 500,000 are drug offenders. The number of African American men imprisoned for drug violations is so disproportionately high as to invite comparisons to the devastating injustices of Jim Crow. Meanwhile, south of the border, the former president of Mexico, Felipe Calderón, declared his own war on drug cartels, which has yielded a staggering death toll of 60,000 (and counting). The police force is riddled with corruption. Military repression has led to charges of human rights violations. The flood of narcotics into the United States continues undiminished.[16]

That contemporary globalization has not been able to transcend war, border conflicts, crime, and repression puzzles many observers, but it should not surprise anyone familiar with the early modern world. In the seventeenth and eighteenth centuries, when oceanic trade links between Asia, Africa, Europe, and the Americas proliferated to create worldwide commercial circuits, government policies were anything but liberal, and trade was anything but free. Indeed, the growth of early modern world trade was bound up inextricably with the rise of powerful European fiscal-military states that could tax and borrow on a scale large enough to engage in modern global warfare. As rival European rulers competed for military, diplomatic, and economic hegemony, they intervened in a fast-rising global economy to gain access to, and control over, transcontinental flows of goods. Projecting their dynastic and national rivalries onto the wider world, they built formidable navies; chartered overseas trading companies (the ancestors of today's multinational corporations); founded and fought over ultramarine colonies; subsidized the transatlantic slave trade and the New World plantation complex; instituted all manner of prohibitions, monopolies, tariffs, and navigation laws; ran up enormous public debts; and taxed just about anything that moved. It was this bewildering jumble of state policies that Adam Smith rejected as the "mercantile system" in book IV of *The Wealth of Nations.* Yet, contrary to Smith's claim that mercantilism was less productive than free trade, recent research demonstrates that aggressive and exploitative imperial policies deeply enriched the polities of metropolitan Europe.[17]

This book takes the globalization of this period for what it was, an economic system marked indelibly by vigorous and often violent European state intervention. But more than providing an overview of that system, it considers a little-studied yet profoundly important consequence of it: the spectacular growth in illicit markets. Plumbing the depths of the underground economy, the following chapters tell the tale of the dark side of globalization.

In France, that tale begins with the mighty Louis XIV. In the late seventeenth century, the Sun King made two bold interventions that attempted to control the consumption of global imports but unintentionally encouraged the growth of underground commerce, inflaming French politics down to the Revolution. First, seeking to bolster the state's fiscal power, he looked west, to the Atlantic world, and established a state tobacco monopoly. One of several psychoactive products to flourish during the consumer revolution, New World tobacco was widely regarded as a potent medicinal remedy and a miraculous catalyst of social interaction. It was also addictive. In 1674, capitalizing on soaring home demand for the weed, the crown declared a state monopoly and promptly subcontracted it to a private company, the General Farm, which marketed millions of pounds of slave-produced American tobacco to the subjects of France. In the hands of the Farm, the monopoly was to become the largest institution of its kind in the world, akin to the mammoth State Tobacco Monopoly Administration that operates in China today.

Soon after monopolizing Atlantic tobacco, Louis XIV turned east to erect a protectionist shield against the influx of textiles from Asia. Lightweight, vivid, and, to the amazement of European consumers, colorfast, Indian cottons became enormously popular in the seventeenth century. During this so-called calico craze, the inflow of inexpensive yet high-quality Indian cloth threatened French textile manufacturers, who aggressively lobbied the government for protection. In 1686, the monarchy answered their pleas by banning all importation of the cloth. Policed by the General Farm, the prohibition was to last seventy-three years, only to be replaced by a heavy tariff.

These two measures differed in their aims: the tobacco monopoly sought to exploit home demand for a cheaply produced colonial import, whereas the calico ban attempted to stifle it. But their effect was the same, insofar as they stimulated the development of a massive transcontinental parallel economy that operated beyond the reach of the state, even as it fed on state fiscal and economic structures. There had long been illicit trade in France, principally in salt, but the addition of two new global commodities galvanized the black market. Eager to supplement their meager incomes with an occasional foray across the border, legions of traffickers shuttled sacks of tobacco and calico into France and sold them clandestinely in towns and villages. Although the majority of traffickers worked alone or in pairs, some joined organized gangs, the precursors of today's drug cartels, to run large quantities of contraband deep into the interior. Beneath the rock of capitalism was a bustling underworld of antlike traders operating beyond the law: indigent peasants, underemployed artisans, vagabond peddlers, poorly paid soldiers, down-and-out deserters, and small-time fugitives from justice. By supplying large quantities of cheap contraband to eager consumers, these poor men, women, and children, criminals in the eyes of the state, stoked the flame of French consumption.

If the development of the underground economy was an unintended by-product of globalization and state formation, it nonetheless had far-reaching political consequences. The criminality and violence associated with illicit markets posed a serious challenge to states whose very policies produced them. Faced with a rapidly developing trade in illegal tobacco and calico, the French crown introduced a sweeping overhaul of the criminal justice system. In an effort to capture, convict, and punish smugglers, it hardened the penal code, strengthened the paramilitary wing of the General Farm, established extraordinary courts of law, and expanded a nascent prison system. As a result, tens of thousands of traffickers were dispatched to galleys and labor camps, forerunners of the modern penitentiary. But the monarchy was soon to learn that criminalizing smuggling was not like criminalizing murder or theft, the punishment of which corresponded to everyday understandings of such acts as moral transgressions. Traffickers refused to internalize the degrading criminal status imposed on them and resisted repression vigorously. Although many avoided confrontation by hugging the shadows of the trade, increasing numbers engaged the Farm in violent confrontation. Individuals resisted arrest, crowds attacked Farm guards, and gangs ambushed customs posts in what contemporaries described as nothing less than a war between Farm and trafficker. No benign consumer revolution this: the trade in highly regulated commodities like tobacco and Indian cloth generated cycles of repression and revolt that disrupted public order, destabilized border provinces, and, combined with other forms of collective action, shook the monarchy well before the French Revolution.

That this vicious cycle of repression and rebellion unfolded in the age of Enlightenment, a period of robust critical thinking and expanding media, had profound political repercussions. Popular writers, engravers, and singers depicted the battle against the Farm in words, images, and songs that allowed large audiences to experience the vicarious thrill of underground violence—much as American crime movies and Mexican *narcocorridos* do today. At the same time, Enlightenment philosophers, economists, and legal theorists took up the cause of the underground, lambasting state policies and institutions. As they thrust a subversive political agenda into the public sphere, reformers condemned the monopolies and prohibitions that produced the crime of smuggling and warned that a "despotic" fiscal-judicial complex would engulf the monarchy if fundamental institutional changes were not forthcoming. The historical significance of this reform movement should not be underestimated. In 1789, as the monarchy reeled from an excess of debt, the convergence of popular and elite opposition to the state would spark the French Revolution.

From a macrohistorical perspective, it is possible to see that the simultaneous rise of global trade, the fiscal-military state, and European consumption produced turmoil not only in the colonies but also in the very heart of the metropole. To discern how such large-scale processes played out locally in France, however, it is useful to descend to the microhistorical level. To that end, this book reconstructs the career of Louis Mandrin, the famous French smuggler who, as we have seen, reportedly hired Louis Jarrier to assassinate Pierre Robert Le Roux de La Motte on the banks of the Guiers River in 1755.

Mandrin is a legend in French popular culture. Much like Robin Hood, Jesse James, or other iconic "social bandits," Mandrin is mostly remembered through fictional re-creations that stretch back to the golden age of crime literature in the late nineteenth century.[18] The memory of Mandrin came alive in this era of near-universal literacy and mass culture, as French readers anxious about moral decay and urban crime inhaled detective novels, serial crime dramas, and sensationalized crime reports *(faits divers)* on the front page of newspapers.[19] Sanitizing picaresque representations of the bandit forged under the old regime and recycled long after the Revolution, Jules de Grandpré published a highly successful serial novel in 1885, *Le Capitaine Mandrin,* which cast the smuggler as a swashbuckling romantic hero, part Robin Hood, part private detective, and part heartthrob. Smuggling and rebellion in this account took a back seat to crime scenes, love affairs, and family melodramas. Arthur Bernède facilitated Mandrin's transition to the silver screen in the twentieth century with his own cloak-and-dagger yarn of the *justicier* (righter of wrongs) who nobly battled the social ills of the old regime, escaped punishment, and lived happily ever after. Adapted for the screen in 1924, 1947, and again in 1962, Bernède's novel turned Mandrin into a sword-fighting matinee idol who never failed to rescue the damsel in distress. Mandrin's image underwent yet another transformation during the social movements of the late 1960s, when activists claimed the smuggler as a symbol of a radical popular will. Leftist singer and actor Yves Montand recorded several versions of Mandrin's funeral dirge, while French TV aired a six-part series about the rebel in 1972.[20]

Today, Mandrin's memory is utterly commodified. In what the tourist industry quaintly calls "Mandrin country," his name appears on restaurant signs, craft beer, and organic chicken as a badge of rustic authenticity, a piece of *terroir* to be consumed. But the political meaning of the legend has not been completely snuffed out. The latest cinematic iteration, a 2011 film by Rabah Ameur-Zaïmeche called *Les Chants de Mandrin,* attempts to breathe new radicalism into memories of the trafficker, whom the director first encountered in grade school after emigrating from Algeria in 1968. For Ameur-Zaïmeche, whose previous films dealt with immigration, trafficking, and police in contemporary France, Mandrin represents all those who are treated as "outlaws in [their] own country."[21]

This book digs below the fictional representations that have accumulated over the last century and half to excavate the historical Mandrin—the young man who was born in the small town of Saint-Étienne-de-Saint-Geoirs in 1725 and quit the family business to run contraband into France.[22] A study of the historical Mandrin not only provides a unique point of entry into the underground economy but also makes it possible to see how, long before the dime novels of the belle époque, his legend was fabricated in the eighteenth century. A potent and multivalent symbol of the shadowy underworld from which he came, his myth, too, is worth examining for what it reveals about the politicization of popular culture in the decades before the French Revolution.

In recounting the tale of Louis Mandrin and his comrades, my purpose is twofold. Mandrin's story humanizes abstract arguments about globalization, states, consumption, and rebellion by adding flesh and bone (and blood) to what may otherwise appear as vast, impersonal forces of history. His border crossings, armed trading, extortion, and apotheosis as a legend reveal the drama inherent in the economic and political transformations of the global eighteenth century.

Mandrin was more than a mere reflection of his times, however. His career also lays bare a microscopic world of attitudes and gestures that remain unseen from distant vantage points. Zooming in on a single individual makes it possible to see how he responded to the world in which he found himself, what choices he made during his short but volatile life, and what cultural and material resources he deployed to make his way amid desperately challenging circumstances. Was the aim of his commercial endeavors simply to enrich himself, or did they have political overtones, too? Any assessment of a smuggler from the lesser ranks of society must acknowledge the extent to which large-scale social processes and rigid normative systems limited the freedom of the poor and marginalized in the eighteenth century; a peasant could no less choose to become an aristocrat than a woman a minister of state. But within the limits of such constraints lay a measure of latitude best observed at the microscopic level. By focusing on the interstices between power structures, the microhistorian bears witness to the strategies, negotiations, and appropriations of ordinary people as they struggled to make their own lives and perhaps, in the process, challenged the order of things. Giovanni Levi, the master of the genre, suggests that it is in this oxymoronic realm of heavily constrained freedom, where the mental faculties of the individual confront mighty but not quite omnipotent social structures and norms, that the decisions of daily life are taken. To observe how ordinary men and women operate strategically within this arena is to see how history is made from below.[23]

In Mandrin's case, we are obviously dealing with an extraordinary "ordinary" person. He was in many ways an atypical smuggler. But the life of an atypical individual can be equally if not more illuminating of the society in which he or she is embedded than that of the ever elusive "average" person.[24] Mandrin's violent methods of marketing contraband set him apart from many of his colleagues, but they also dramatized the broader dynamics of the parallel economy. Exploiting an already rebellious popular culture, he improvised a set of commercial techniques that directly challenged the power of the Farm and excited public debate about the legitimacy of institutions at the heart of the French fiscal state. Only microhistory can capture the performative dimension of his career, through which he expressed himself to spectators and royal authorities alike. And only microhistory can reveal how writers and other interlocutors in popular culture invested meaning in his rebellions to forge a symbol of political defiance.

No single scale of observation—macro, micro, or any level in between—has a monopoly on historical reality. The best we can do is to shift between them—playing with scale itself—in the hope of grasping a more complete understanding of the past.[25] In this spirit, the following chapters will shuttle between large-scale, long-term processes that affected much of humanity, medium-scale evolutions in European states and societies (principally, though not exclusively, French), and small-scale, even minuscule, instantaneous events in the life of a single human being. Shifting between such perspectives makes it possible to see connections not only between worldwide exchanges, empires, and individual lives but also between the very categories of economic, political, and cultural history by which scholars divide the past. Bridging the global, the national, and the local as well as the economic, the political, and the cultural, this book aims to explore the full force and impact of the eighteenth-century underground economy.

1

The Globalization of European Consumption

THE YEAR: 1745. CARTER'S GROVE, VIRGINIA. Marcellus toils in a low-lying field on the banks of the James River. Captured in West Africa, shipped across the Atlantic, and purchased by a wealthy colonial planter, he and some twenty other slaves labor ceaselessly to cultivate tobacco. Under the watchful eye of an overseer whose salary rises and falls with the harvest, they clear land, prepare seedbeds, transplant seedlings, weed, prune, and reap, producing thousands of pounds of sweetly scented leaf each year. The product of their grueling labor is packed into large wooden hogsheads that are wedged into ships and sailed downriver to the mouth of the Chesapeake Bay, before reaching the open Atlantic. After arriving in the British Isles, the tobacco will probably be reexported to France, where consumers grind it into powder and snort it.[1]

1 November 1739. Pondicherry, India. Some 8,600 miles from Carter's Grove, Ananda Ranga Pillai sits in his home on the Coromandel coast, scribbling in his diary. Having distinguished himself as an entrepreneur, he is now the chief agent for the French East Indies Company at Pondicherry. A fastidious chronicler, Pillai notes the day's events: two company ships—the *Fleury* and the *Triton*—set sail for France laden with hundreds of bales of cloth produced by highly skilled Indian weavers. The fabric is of astounding variety; silky muslins are packed next to brilliant calicoes and yards of blue and white Guinea cloth. Slipping from Pondicherry, the ships will ply the deep waters of the Indian Ocean before rounding the Cape of Good Hope and heading north to the Atlantic port of Lorient on the rocky Breton coast of France. There, some fabric will be unloaded, sold at auction, and ultimately hawked to fashion-conscious Europeans. The rest will be taken to the west

coast of Africa where, not far from Marcellus's birthplace, it will be exchanged for slaves, who will in turn be jammed into cargo holds and transported across the Atlantic to the Americas.[2]

22 June 1754. Millau, France. Louis Mandrin and a score of heavily armed smugglers ride into a small town in the southern province of Languedoc. To the astonishment of the subdelegate, the only representative of royal authority in town, they occupy the market square and, in broad daylight, peddle contraband tobacco and Indian cloth "more publicly than one sells spangles and rosary beads." After taking in more than a thousand *écus,* they treat the town to a military review and promptly decamp, leaving villagers craving more. One local catches up with the gang in the next town to ask for another four louis' worth of cloth, but he is too late. The stock is depleted, so he settles for some cheap weed instead.[3]

At first glance, it may not be apparent how these three men—Marcellus, a slave on the western edge of the Atlantic; Pillai, a merchant on the east coast of the Indian subcontinent; and Mandrin, a smuggler from a landlocked province in France—are related. But their lives and those of countless others were linked by trade in two new global commodities: tobacco and calico.[4] Although the tobacco that Mandrin smuggled was not entirely Virginian and the Indian cloth his band peddled was not in fact from India, the underground economy on which he thrived was an unintended creation of the French monarchy's interventions in the rapidly expanding markets of the Indian and Atlantic oceans. As Mandrin crossed the smuggler-infested borderlands of France, Savoy, and Switzerland, he was participating in a world economy that stretched from the shores of the Chesapeake to the Bay of Bengal. He was also participating in a European consumer culture that was fast incorporating colonial goods from distant continents. To understand how this young smuggler from rural Dauphiné came to challenge one of the most powerful regimes in the world, we first need to know how his underground dealings were connected to a fast-rising global economy that spurred new consumer practices in the heart of Europe.

Consumer Revolution

Scarcity was the norm in medieval and early modern Europe. Apart from monarchs, nobles, and wealthy merchants, who dined on game, wore fine apparel, and lived in relative comfort, most people—whether rural peasants or urban artisans and laborers—lived precarious lives. Many struggled just to survive, eating little more than bread and gruel, covering themselves with coarse woolen clothes, and taking shelter in simple cottages or single rooms. Thriving towns did exist, of course, but until the seventeenth and eighteenth centuries, their trade had only a limited effect on the overall agrarian economy, which grew at a glacial pace when it grew at all. At bottom, this was a peasant society in which only the privileged few had access to anything beyond what we would consider the barest essentials.

And yet, historians have discovered that from about 1650 to 1800, before the coming of the Industrial Revolution, ordinary western Europeans began to acquire goods on an unprecedented scale. Not only did the nobility increase its already prodigious consumption but also middling professionals, wholesale merchants, skilled artisans, better-off farmers, and domestic servants began to consume a wider variety of commodities. They filled their homes with wooden furniture (beds, chairs, dressers, and wardrobes) and decorative housewares (cookware, pottery, clocks, mirrors, and curtains). They bought more clothes (coats, suits, shirts, breeches, gowns, and stockings) and sported novel accessories (umbrellas, snuffboxes, and pocket watches). They ingested more food and drink (white bread, sugar, brandy) and splurged on cultural objects and events (books, paintings, the theater). During the last century of preindustrial Europe's long history, the material world of middling and, to some extent, lower classes gradually filled.[5]

Society had not become so saturated with goods as to warrant the term "mass consumption," for a sizable group of the desperately poor and chronically undernourished remained excluded from the efflorescence of consumption.[6] But the material world had certainly become full enough to give many people the impression that they were living in a new age. Indeed, the proliferation of consumer products at many levels of society prompted a vigorous debate over the moral and political implications of "luxury," a word subject to intense scrutiny in the eighteenth century. On one side, moralists worried about the violation of Christian interdicts against the pursuit of earthly pleasure, the usurpation of social status by commoners who consumed above their station, and the corruption of civic virtue that seemed to always follow in the destructive wake of luxury. On the other side, apologists of luxury claimed that its spread was merely the benign effect of long-term material progress. What moralists condemned as dangerous luxuries were, according to apologists, reasonable conveniences that would be perceived as simple necessities by future generations.[7]

Why levels of consumption began to rise in the first place is a perplexing question. Consumer growth cannot be attributed to the Industrial Revolution, since mechanized factory production began to appear only at the tail end of the period. If anything, the consumer revolution and the global trade that sustained it helped produce its better-known successor, not the reverse.[8] More plausibly, a combination of multiple cultural and economic factors produced the surge in consumption. First, fashion became increasingly commercialized as the proliferation of newspaper advertisements, fashion journals, retail shops, and peddlers stoked the desire to consume.[9] Second, although wages were not rising in this period, households seem to have been working harder. Men toiled longer and more intensively, while women and children entered the labor market in droves. The resulting rise in the supply of market labor may have offset stagnant wages to increase family purchasing power. Although some families worked harder just to stay afloat, others seem to have deliberately taken on more paid labor in order to buy more things.[10] Third, trade and manufacturing within Europe expanded. Agriculture became increasingly specialized and oriented to the market, towns grew faster than the rate of population growth to boost urban demand, and commercial transport within and between countries markedly improved.

Finally, the globalization of trade broadened the material world of Europe. Although most of the durable and semidurable goods consumed in Europe were produced there, some of the most successful commodities of the period were imported from distant overseas continents. Indeed, European practices of consumption changed dramatically after new channels of global trade were opened, as the abbé Raynal boldly proclaimed in the opening passage of his momentous *Histoire philosophique et politique, des établissements et du commerce des Européens dans les deux Indes:*

> There has never been any event as important for the human race in general and for the peoples of Europe in particular, as the discovery of the new world and the passage to the Indies around the Cape of Good

Hope. It was then that began a revolution in commerce, in the power of nations, in the mores, industry, and government of all peoples. It was at this moment that men in the most distant countries became necessary to one another: the produce of equatorial regions were consumed by those in polar climes; northern industry was transported to the south; the cloths of the Orient dressed the west, and everywhere men exchanged their opinions, their laws, their customs, their medicines, their illnesses, their virtues and their vices. Everything has changed and must go on changing.[11]

Raynal was exaggerating, of course. The value of intra-European and intra-Asian trade remained much higher than that of intercontinental trade throughout the early modern period. And the wealthiest Europeans had for centuries enjoyed access to South and East Asian luxuries by way of land and water routes (such as the Silk Road) that ran from as far as Java and China to the Levant in the eastern Mediterranean to southern Europe. However, after the "discovery" of the New World in 1492 and the opening of a direct sea route around the Cape of Good Hope to Asia in 1501, long-distance maritime trade routes multiplied to encircle the globe, linking the Americas, Europe, Asia, and Africa as never before. "For the first time in human history regular commercial contact connected the world's continents directly," creating new patterns in the flow of transcontinental goods.[12]

From the sixteenth to the eighteenth century, a truly global circuit formed after the discovery of silver deposits in what is now known as Mexico, Peru, and Bolivia. Mined by an exploited labor force of indigenous Americans, Africans, and mixed-race Creoles, western European merchants shipped heavy cargoes of silver from Central and South America to Europe, where the precious metal added liquidity to a species-starved economy. Circumventing the Venetian and Mamluk middlemen who controlled European imports of Asian spices, merchants then transported silver from Europe to South and East Asia, where they traded it for spices, raw silk, cotton textiles, porcelain, and tea, which they sailed around the Cape of Good Hope back to Europe to sell at great profit to eager consumers.[13] The links among continents did not stop there. Although many Asian imports were consumed in Europe, much of the Indian cotton cloth that arrived in Europe only grazed the continent's Atlantic shores before being reexported to the west coast of Africa, where discerning African rulers, merchants, and consumers coveted it as much as their European counterparts. As a French writer observed of the African trade, "a beautiful *indienne* will always fetch more than another more costly cloth, either because the variety of colors is more to the taste of Negroes, or because the lightness of the cloth is more suited to these hot climates."[14] Little wonder, then, that among the many goods British and French merchants bartered for African captives at the height of the Atlantic slave trade in the eighteenth century, when some six million people were forced to leave Africa, Indian cloth was the single most valuable item, worth far more than the alcohol, guns, and trinkets so often associated with the trade.[15] Purchased with calico, captive Africans were shipped to American plantations, where they were compelled to produce large quantities of tropical commodities (sugar, tobacco, chocolate, and coffee) for European consumers, who reaped the benefits of falling commodity prices that came with large-scale colonial exploitation. Based on this unprecedented forced migration, the American plantation complex assured that commerce across the Atlantic would by the eighteenth century dwarf that between Europe and Asia. To the extent that mercantile channels between the Atlantic and Indian oceans grew in number and volume, however, it is possible to speak of a process of early modern globalization in which world trade was increasingly integrated (Figure 1.1).[16]

We are only beginning to take the full measure of the impact of colonial goods on European consumption.[17] If the trade in rare luxury products such as spices and silk dominated early Eurasian trade—indeed, it was the holy grail of Asian spices that lured Columbus to America in the first place—that of a handful of semiluxury (or even "populuxe") commodities from Asia and the Americas outstripped their predecessors in the seventeenth and eighteenth centuries. Not that precious luxury goods destined for elites disappeared from the trade, but during the later stage, huge volumes of imported goods were consumed by Europeans of all sorts. The numbers speak for themselves. By the late eighteenth century, Europeans were annually consuming 125 million pounds of imported tobacco, 120 million pounds of coffee, 40 million pounds of tea, 13 million pounds of chocolate, and half a billion pounds of sugar.[18] They were also buying millions of pieces of Indian cloth and boatloads of Chinese porcelain.[19]

The spectacular growth of these commodities and manufactures profoundly transformed the economic and cultural landscape of Europe. Europeans of the upper and middling classes changed how they took their meals, what they ate and drank, how they dressed themselves and decorated their homes, and how they socialized with one another. Having once argued that the rationalist philosophy of the eighteenth century heralded the arrival of the modern world, scholars of the Enlightenment now suggest that there was something distinctively modern in the period's consumer culture. Embedded in changing practices of consumption were a host of emerging values and aspirations—comfort, domesticity, novelty, respectability, individuality, authenticity, cleanliness, utility, simplicity, privacy—many of which are still with us today. In an age when the Enlightenment ideal of earthly happiness was gaining purchase, consumer values reflected a new perspective on the relationship between human beings and the material world. As Roy Porter affirmed, "The Enlightenment's novelty lay in the legitimacy it accorded to pleasure, not as occasional binges, mystical transports or blue-blooded privilege, but as the routine entitlement of people at large to pursue the senses (not just purify the soul) and to seek fulfillment in this world (and not only in the next)."[20]

Among the most important global commodities of the early modern period, tobacco and calico—the two goods traded by Mandrin's armed gang—played central roles in these transformations. Produced on opposite sides of the planet, they converged on Europe to define an emerging consumer culture in which men and women, city-dwellers and country folk, aristocrats and farmers all participated to a greater or lesser degree. Where, how, and by whom were these goods produced? What meanings did consumers ascribe to them, and how did those meanings relate to the wider culture of consumption that was taking shape? Narrowing our focus to the social lives of tobacco and calico makes it possible not only to trace their sprawling geographical trajectories but also to observe the cultural meanings attached to them as they moved from sites of production to those of consumption, generating intense consumer demand in the process.

West to East: New World Tobacco

Europeans had for centuries ingested products such as alcohol and local herbs that affected their mental states, but with the expansion in global trade, consumers were exposed to an array of new and powerful psychoactive substances. Between 1650 and 1800, tobacco, coffee, tea, and

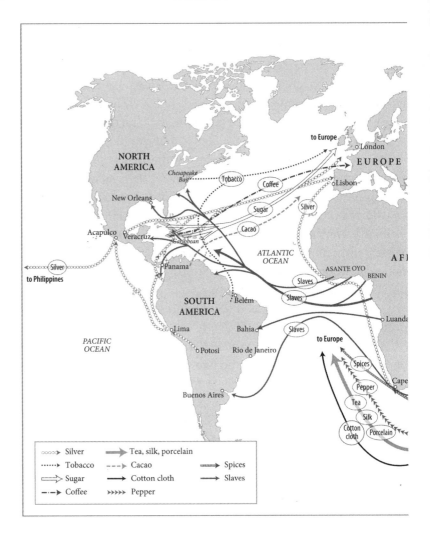

chocolate—the three beverages taken with heaps of Caribbean sugar—
became staples of European cultural life. So swiftly did such goods disseminate and so entrenched did they become that one historian has
posited that a "psychoactive revolution" lay at the heart of the broader
consumer revolution.[21]

One obvious explanation for the spectacular rise of these commodities is their addictive properties. Tobacco, coffee and tea, and chocolate
contain, respectively, nicotine, caffeine, and theobromine, mind-altering

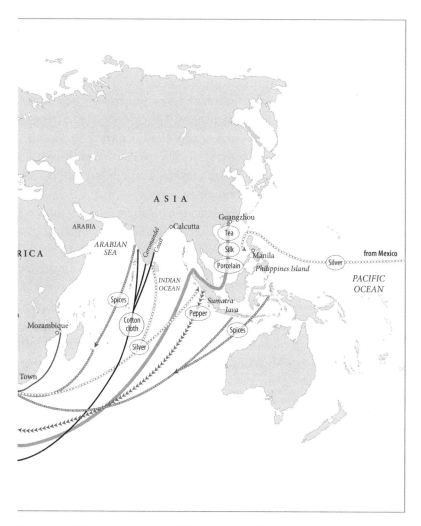

Figure 1.1. World trade, circa 1750: select goods and routes.

chemicals that in Europe would spread beyond the rarefied world of medicine to which they first belonged to become items of recreational consumption. "Once their pleasurable and consciousness-altering properties became known, they escaped the therapeutic realm and entered that of popular consumption." As broader segments of the population were exposed to these drugs, "regular users needed larger doses to experience the original effect, which meant that the volume of sales was likely to increase."[22] This was particularly true of tobacco, which became the most widely consumed psychoactive colonial product of the eighteenth century. Nicotine, an alkaloid that acts on brain receptors to increase levels of dopamine, is both a stimulant and a relaxant that induces states of alertness, euphoria, and calmness. Insofar as it raises dopamine levels, however, it is also extremely addictive, as any smoker who has grown accustomed to an after-dinner cigarette (or two) can attest. Snorting or smoking tobacco carries an even higher risk of addiction than shooting heroin because the tobacco delivery systems provide the brain with a series of tiny pleasure rushes (rather than one big rush) to produce powerful associations between tobacco and pleasure.[23]

Physical addiction is only one explanation for the success of tobacco, however. At the very least, its psychoactive effects must be placed in a broader cultural context that accounts for the significance that consumers themselves attributed to the plant. And here we bump up against a complicated historical problem. To assess the cultural meaning of goods imported into Europe from overseas, it is important to consider what they meant in their indigenous environments and how those meanings were rejected, modified, or appropriated as they entered metropolitan Europe. This is no easy task. Whereas some historians emphasize a process of "commodity indigenization" by which the meaning of imports were reframed to accord with the culture into which they flowed, others stress that the meanings attached to imports in their native environments continued to adhere after they were imported, serving to enhance their appeal.[24] Perhaps it is best not to see this problem in such starkly binary terms, for both processes were often at work in the complex cultural biographies of colonial goods. As Igor Kopytoff explains, such biographies "can show what anthropologists have so often stressed: that what is significant about the adoption of alien objects—as of alien ideas—is not the fact they are adopted, but the way they are culturally redefined and put to use."[25] What is striking in the case of tobacco and, as we shall see, calico is how Europeans redefined many of their indigenous meanings to mesh with the developing consumer culture of the day.

Some of the meanings Europeans invested in tobacco in the seventeenth and eighteenth centuries can be traced back to the New World. Indigenous to America, tobacco was a staple of the Amerindians, for whom it was charged with great religious, cultural, and social significance. In Amerindian religion, it played important roles in myths about the creation of the world and was offered up to hungry gods who, in exchange for the precious tribute, were believed to bestow their favor upon agriculture, hunting, war, trade, and reproduction. Tobacco was also used to induce spiritual hallucinations that brought human beings closer to the supernatural order and facilitated communication with spirits. Shamans, for example, took tobacco to enter a trance state by which they traveled to the spirit world for knowledge and advice.[26] Given such sacred associations, it is hardly surprising that tobacco was used for healing. Healers not only blew smoke over bodies to diagnose illness but applied leaf to treat a host of ailments from toothaches to chest pains to wounds.[27] Finally, Amerindians smoked tobacco for the purposes of marking social ceremonies: rulers expressed their hospitality during councils and assemblies by serving guests pipefuls of pulverized leaves, merchants celebrated departures and homecomings with ceremonial smoking, and men participated in community festivals and dances while drawing on tobacco pipes.[28]

The first Europeans to see tobacco were Christopher Columbus and his men, who in 1492 encountered Native Americans on the island of San Salvador. In an exchange of gifts, Columbus recounted, the islanders brought him "dry leaves," a present he would also receive in the Bahamas and on Cuba, where sailors witnessed men and women "with a firebrand of weeds in their hands to take in the fragrant smoke to which they are accustomed."[29] Such encounters became common as the first generations of Spanish, Portuguese, English, Dutch, and French explored and settled in the New World in the sixteenth and early seventeenth centuries. Although colonists sought gold, spices, and neglected souls, not tobacco, western Europeans rapidly took to the leaf, ingesting it in the same manner as the Amerindians. Soon, the leaf was trickling back across the Atlantic in the sea chests of merchants, sailors, and clergy who had smoked in America and wanted to bring tobacco home for personal use or to distribute as gifts to friends and acquaintances. Having been brought to the shores of Europe, tobacco slowly diffused through much of the continent. Well-connected Atlantic merchants shared tobacco with other traders and nobles, who introduced it into European royal courts. Jean Nicot, French ambassador to the court of Lisbon in 1659–1660, who admired a species of tobacco growing in the Portuguese king's gardens, sent specimens of it to the cardinal of Lorraine, who gave a sample of snuff to the queen of France, Catherine de Medici. Returning to his natal kingdom, Nicot was delighted to learn that the increasingly popular tobacco plant, heretofore called "pétun," was now dubbed "herbe à Nicot."[30] In addition to courtiers, clergymen who had spent time in the New World were vanguard consumers. Tobacco spread quickly through the church, provoking heated debate about the morality of its use among priests. Lower down the social scale, sailors who had seen something of the Americas smoked tobacco in the crowded taverns of European ports, spreading the custom to urban artisans, laborers, migrants, and soldiers. Soldiers in turn exposed local populations to the wonders of the leaf as they marauded across Europe during the Thirty Years' War (1618–1648).

As tobacco migrated to Europe, so, too, did its Amerindian cultural meanings. Its association with sociability heightened its appeal in Europe at a time when middling and upper classes were developing their own interests in sociability, first as a courtly virtue and then as a principle of Enlightenment. As Molière, a shrewd observer of fashion, wryly remarked in the opening scene of *Don Juan,* snuff had the uncanny ability to transform ordinary men and women into urbane *"honnêtes gens"* who appreciated the art of conversation: "Don't you see how affable people become as soon as they take a pinch, how delighted they are, wherever they may be, to give it away left and right?"[31] "An open snuffbox is a public right to which no one can be refused access," one anonymous writer excitedly declared.[32] Thus aristocrats at Versailles shared tobacco from elegant silver boxes that became themselves objects of collection.[33] Tobacco was offered as a gesture of politeness in less exalted circles, too. During a grand display of fireworks on the Quai du Louvre in 1739, several bourgeois women proffered a pinch of snuff to out-of-towner Pierre Prion while striking up a conversation.[34] Smoking, which became a masculine activity, was likewise associated with vibrant social interaction. Respectable professionals and merchants smoked in coffeehouses as they discussed business or politics, while peasants and artisans puffed in village taverns as they played cards and drank wine, beer, and brandy.[35] The virtues of such plebian sociability were extolled by Paris engraver Nicolas Guérard in *Fraternal Charity* (Figure 1.2), which depicted a compassionate commoner blowing smoke into the empty pipe of a less fortunate crony. (That a beggar could be expected to own his own pipe suggests how far down the social hierarchy the practice of smoking had spread.)

For the laboring classes, tobacco's social uses conveniently dovetailed with its psychoactive properties. The same substance that helped forge friendships and solidarity also staved off hunger, thirst, and cold,

SI TOUT SUPERFLUX SE DONNOIT NUL MALHEUREUX ON NE VERROIT.

Valentin, dans son Peu, trouve du superflux,
Pour ayder l'Indigent, qu'il voit dans la misere,
Et Luc dans le Beaucoup, de ses gros revenus,
Loing dy trouver superflux pour bien faire,
Tout son Beaucoup, se tourne en necessaire,
Car malgré ses gros biens, il depence encore plus.

A Paris chez Nicolas Guerard Graveur
rue St Jaques proche St Yves. C.P.R.

CHARITE FRATERNELE

Donné moi du Tabac dit Jean à son Compere.
Ma foi Compere Jean, j'ai ma Pipe et rien plus,
Mais si tu veut la fumer toute entiere,
Tien la voila, n'en fait point de refus.

Compere Paul, garde ton necessaire.
Suffit pour moi du Superflux,
Quel est mon Superflux, tien Paul c'est la fumée
Qui se perd par le bout de la Pipe allumée.

Figure 1.2. *Fraternal Charity.* Bibliothèque Nationale de France, Réserve
QB-201 (75).

a miraculous effect for soldiers, peasants, and artisans who could not depend on a steady supply of calories and were often exposed to the elements. In this respect, tobacco was not unlike sugar and other colonial "drug-foods" that Sydney Mintz describes as "sating—and, indeed, drugging—farm and factory workers" in eighteenth-century England.[36] Millions of European laborers took tobacco to subdue the relentless pangs of hunger that afflicted them.

Although Old World consumers emphatically rejected the Amerindian cosmology and tobacco's place within it—this was one cultural meaning that did not cross the Atlantic—Europeans did appropriate the belief that New World tobacco had special healing properties. Indeed, Jean Nicot sent a specimen to the cardinal of Lorraine in the first place because he believed tobacco to be a marvelous herbal remedy for physical ailments; in 1561, he prescribed snuff for Catherine de Medici's chronic migraines. But it was Nicolas Monardes (1519–1588), a doctor living in Seville, who more than any other European legitimated the use of tobacco for medical purposes. Monardes carved out an important place for tobacco in the world of European medicine by incorporating it into humoral theory, a basis of medical science since the ancient Greeks. According to this theory, good health was determined by the proper balance of the four humors—blood, black bile, phlegm, and yellow bile—which were associated, respectively, with four basic qualities—hot, cold, wet, and dry. Improperly balanced humors sickened the human body, which could be restored to health only with the recovery of humoral equilibrium. Fortunately, certain herbs could be counted on to restore this balance and, thanks to Monardes, tobacco became known as one of them. According to the Spaniard's widely read history of New World plants, tobacco, which he classified as hot and dry, cured as many as twenty common ailments (from chest pain and asthma to stomachaches and toothaches) by expelling excessively moist humors. Although some clerics insisted that tobacco was the devil's weed because it was used by pagans in the New World, Monardes's positive medical assessments prevailed, holding sway into the age of Enlightenment, when psychoactive colonial products overtook locally grown herbal remedies.[37]

In the seventeenth and eighteenth centuries, tobacco expanded well beyond the therapeutic realm to become what we would today call a recreational drug. In its recreational context, the leaf seemed an endless source of pleasure, entertainment, and diversion, as Guérard's witty engraving, *Fashionable Pastime*, illustrates (Figure 1.3). The engraving

Figure 1.3. Fashionable Pastime. Bibliothèque Nationale de France, Réserve QB-201 (75).

depicts a nobleman reclining in an armchair as he grates a "carrot" of tobacco into snuff. If, according to the caption, the powder "awakens the mind and purges the brain"—a medicinal effect—it also served as an object of obsessive personal entertainment, keeping the fashionable gentleman busy doing nothing. "Because with you [snuff] one has always something to do, / If you know how to entertain, you also know how to keep a person busy; / Every moment one must grate, / Open, fill, close his snuffbox, / Snort, sneeze, wipe, blow / Faster and faster, / Start all over again." Tobacco was understood not only to heal but also to amuse by keeping its consumer in an oxymoronic state of active idleness. Such obsessive behavior did not always meet with approval, of course. "Pleasure" becomes "habit," and "habit" becomes "necessity," bemoaned one critic.[38] German physician Friedrich Hoffman urged that smoking tobacco "should be permitted more as a medicine than for pleasure," but he was writing against the cultural tide.[39]

For all these reasons—psychoactivity, sociability, health, and recreation—tobacco consumption soared in the two centuries that followed the publication of Monardes's protobacco treatise. By the late eighteenth century, a wholly new article of popular consumption was born, as Europeans from all walks of life chewed, smoked, and, most of all, snorted an estimated 125 million pounds of imported tobacco annually.[40] Although historians have generally explained the growth of early modern consumption in terms of social emulation—common folk imitated the middling classes, middling classes aped the nobility, and the nobility took cues from the king—the spread of tobacco in early modern Europe followed no simple top-down trajectory.[41] Having entered both elite and popular networks in the sixteenth century, it took off among all social groups and both sexes in the following centuries to become the most pervasive colonial commodity in Europe.

Initially, to feed growing demand, peasants in the Netherlands, Alsace, and southwestern France in the early seventeenth century began to cultivate tobacco, which, thanks to the Columbian biological exchange, had taken firm root on European soil. However, European production was soon overtaken by that of plantations mushrooming in the Caribbean and along the eastern seaboard of the Americas. Spanish, Portuguese, Dutch, British, and French colonists rushed to take up tobacco production in the Americas in the hope of striking it rich, but not all were successful. Over the seventeenth century, British and French planters in the Caribbean abandoned tobacco for sugar and coffee, leaving British North America (and, in a lesser role, Portuguese Brazil) as the center of New World production. Chesapeake Bay became the greatest supplier of tobacco in the world, tripling its production between the 1720s and 1770s to reach over 100 million pounds annually.[42] Until the American Revolution, tobacco was North America's most valuable export.

The massive production that kept Europeans rolling in leaf at lower and lower prices came at an extraordinarily high human cost. Tobacco cultivation was labor intensive. In addition to sowing seedbeds and transplanting seedlings, plants had to be "topped" and "suckered" (their tops cut off and secondary shoots removed), and then cut and cured. Finally, leaves had to be stripped from their stalks, stems removed, and tobacco stuffed into barrels for transport across the Atlantic. In the Chesapeake colonies of Virginia and Maryland, this year-round labor was first performed by planters' family members and indentured Irish or English servants, but from the 1680s, as the price of indentured servants rose, planters started buying slaves from Africa, in particular from the Bight of Biafra on the western coast. Owing to both natural increase and the constant arrival of new captives, the population of slaves mounted quickly in the Chesapeake to reach approximately 165,000 souls in 1755, half of whom belonged to the wealthiest 10 percent of white planters.[43] As the Chesapeake colonies evolved into full-blown slave societies, small plots gave way to large plantations worked by gangs of slaves under the close supervision of overseers who did not hesitate to use whips and restraints to maintain high volumes of production.[44] The changing labor conditions in the Chesapeake, which reflected a broader reordering of the Atlantic world, serve as a reminder that certain commodities essential to the consumer revolution were soaked in the blood and sweat of slaves. In the case of tobacco, colonial exploitation only deepened as European consumption grew.

East to West: Indian Calicoes

If the surge in the European consumption of tobacco sprang from a rapidly growing Atlantic slave economy, that of cotton calico depended on gaining access by sea to a much older Asian trade zone centered on the Indian subcontinent. Indeed, long before and well after the arrival of the first European vessels, India was the greatest textile producer in the world, its renowned cloth gracing markets from the islands of Southeast Asia to Islamic Persia to the Swahili ports of East Africa. It has been estimated that in 1750 the littoral of the Asian subcontinent produced as much as a quarter of the world's textile output, much of it for export. "India clothed the world."[45] Thus, when European traders first approached Indian textile merchants in the early seventeenth century, they were marginal figures in a market that already touched many parts of the globe. They did not dream of reorganizing the region's system of labor and production, as their counterparts would do in the Americas. Rather, they established fortified trading enclaves on the coast and, with occasional military assistance, tapped into existing commercial structures. Eventually, Britain took imperial control of Bengal in 1765, but prior to that, European countries had to compete in well-established, thriving Asian markets. If the Europeans enjoyed a slight technological advantage at arms, it was not decisive. What allowed them to make inroads into Indian trade was the durability of state-sponsored companies that practiced "armed trading" and used the know-how of skilled Indian laborers and merchants to exploit metropolitan demand for Asian imports.[46]

Although Europeans came late to this global market, they wasted no time building their trade. In the seventeenth century and on the heels of the Portuguese, many northwestern European governments established joint-stock "East India" companies, precursors to modern-day multinationals, and granted them monopolies over maritime trade with Asia. At first, the two most profitable companies—the Dutch East India Company (1602–1799), which overtook the Portuguese in the early seventeenth century, and the English East India Company (1600–1858), which would overtake the Dutch in the eighteenth century—purchased cotton fabric on the western Gujarat plains and east coast of India in order to exchange it for spices (pepper, cloves, cinnamon, nutmeg, and so on) in the southeast Asian archipelago, which they in turn sold on European markets. But the companies soon discovered that they could make greater profits by importing the cloth directly into their home countries and selling it to Europeans or reexporting it to Africa and the New World. In 1664, jealous of the commercial success of his rivals, especially the Dutch, a "nation of herring mongers" who were plundering what he believed to be the most lucrative sector of the global economy, Colbert retaliated by establishing the French Indies Company.[47] A top-heavy creation of the state, this "Versailles of commerce" joined the fray in the Indian Ocean trade, extracting cloth from the seaboard of the subcontinent, chiefly the southeastern Coromandel coast, and sailing it around the Cape of Good Hope to Lorient in Brittany.[48]

In exchange for silver from Central and South America, for there was little else Europeans could offer Asian merchants, the Dutch, English, and French companies placed major orders for Indian cotton cloth. To extract textiles from the subcontinent, companies hired Indian brokers to act as their intermediaries with local producers. Brokers retained merchants, who provided financial advances to weavers, who used the working capital to buy large quantities of raw materials and support themselves while completing orders. Long experienced at adapting their products to the particular tastes of far-flung markets, Indian textile artisans were quick to tailor their cloth to European sensibilities. European companies guided them, sending specific written instructions regarding the size, shape, color combinations, designs, and borders that were likely to sell best in the year ahead. As early as 1643, the directors of the English East India Company were instructing agents to alter the color scheme of the cloth they purchased in India. Indian painters and printers had always placed white patterns on colored backgrounds, but when agents asked producers to invert this design (so that colored patterns appeared against white backgrounds), demand for the product soared. Soon the company was sending patterns on which Indian painters and printers freely elaborated, yielding a final product that, neither entirely English nor wholly Indian, blended Hindu, Islamic, Chinese, and European design elements. The French company produced similar hybrids, such as an "oriental" handkerchief with a fable by La Fontaine at its center. Unlike tobacco, an Amerindian plant that migrated across the Atlantic in something close to its precommodified indigenous form, calico imports were a hybrid commodity from the outset, the result of a company-mediated dialogue between European consumers and skilled Indian weavers.[49]

In the late seventeenth century, what began as a trickle from east to west became a flood, as the import of handwrought Indian piece goods surged past spices to become the main object of company trade. In fashion-conscious western Europe, an "Indian craze" took hold of consumers who, for the next century, could not get enough of the fabric. Together, the English and Dutch in the 1680s imported more than a million pieces of Indian textiles annually, most of it cotton fabric; the French, head-quartered in Pondicherry, brought in an additional 300,000 pieces by the 1730s.[50] Meanwhile, European producers began to make their own imitation *indiennes*, as manufactories sprouted in Marseille, London, Amsterdam, Geneva, and elsewhere, a phenomenon we explore in Chapter 2. At first composed of simple monochrome designs, the knockoffs were of lesser quality than the genuine article but cheaper and so in high demand among middling- and lower-class consumers. Real or imitation, a new object of consumption was born.[51]

At first, calicoes were used exclusively to decorate domestic interiors. Swept up in a broad cultural shift toward domesticity, a virtue enshrined by many Enlightenment writers, European consumers used calicoes to make their homes more intimate, private, and comfortable.[52] Indian covers, curtains, and valances rendered the bed, by far the most expensive piece of furniture in the home, a warm, private, and visually striking centerpiece. In an age when many urban folk ceased sharing mattresses with relatives and came to have a bed of their own, drawing decorative curtains around a high frame created a new intimate space in the heart of the household, a sort of house within the house. Indian cloth was also used to make fashionable window curtains, wall hangings, and upholstery for chairs and couches.

Having covered their interiors with the fabric, Europeans of both sexes experimented with wearing it. At the forefront of fashion consumption, women sported Indian jackets, skirts, and blouses and adorned themselves with myriad cotton accessories, such as aprons, cloaks, hoods, sleeves, headdresses, petticoats, and pockets. Stylish men wore Indian morning gowns and nightshirts in the informal privacy of their homes and added splashes of color with Indian shirts, cravats, and cuffs when out on the town; the handkerchief became a particularly popular accessory, thanks to the spread of messy habits like coffee drinking and tobacco snorting. By 1708, Daniel Defoe could trace the stealthy progress calico had made: "it crept into our houses, our closets and bed-chambers; curtains, cushions, chairs and at last the beds themselves were nothing but Calicoes or Indian stuffs. In short, almost everything that used to be made of wool or silk, relating to the dress of women or the furniture of our houses, was supplied by the Indian trade."[53]

The sudden demand for calico can be partly explained by its exotic appeal. Whereas in the Middle Ages Europeans were inclined to construe difference in terms of time (imagining a past Golden Age, state of nature, land of Cokayne, and so on), in the early modern period, as acquaintance with the wider world grew, Europeans increasingly thought of the exotic in terms of space.[54] In this imaginary of the foreign, India was part of a fascinating but vaguely construed Orient that stretched from the Ottoman Empire to India, China, and Japan. In France, consumers exhibited a strong predilection for exotic chinoiserie (Chinese-style porcelain and lacquered furniture) and turquerie (Ottoman-style furniture, clothing, and coffee drinking), both of which evoked eastern luxury and ultimately fed into the whimsical rococo style of the mid-eighteenth century.[55] Madame de Pompadour, the favorite of Louis XV, bedecked her magnificent Bellevue château with Ottoman-style furniture, the finest Indian upholstery, and a series of paintings by Carle van Loo portraying life in a Turkish seraglio.[56] In a different register, calicoes exuded exoticism through their elaborate floral motifs such as blossoming trees, which mixed Persian and Chinese elements to tap into a growing European fascination for botany and sculpted landscapes in the late seventeenth century. As collectors across western Europe, including Louis XIV, enhanced their gardens with rare species, the demand for flower-patterned cloth intensified. "Floral designs," writes one textile historian, "were the hallmarks of East Indian textiles, with calicos, chintzes, muslins, and percales bedizened with sprays of blossom and verdant trees-of-life interspersed with exotic fauna" (Figure 1.4).[57]

But we should be careful not to overemphasize the role of the exotic. Indian cloth may have possessed the allure of the Orient, but trading companies tamed its alien qualities by adding familiar styles that rendered the cloth palatable to skittish metropolitan buyers, hence the detailed instructions company officials sent to producers. In the end, the companies were selling "European ideas of what eastern design ought to be."[58]

Beyond the thrill of the exotic, calico appealed to European consumers because it spoke to their evolving tastes and aspirations. By far the most distinctive aspect of the cloth was its brilliant color. Colored cloth had long been invested with deep symbolic meaning in Indian society: it conveyed not only social and political status but holiness and purity as well. Rich and vibrant colors were to be worn exclusively by certain

Figure 1.4. Chintz underskirt from Coromandel coast, India, circa 1750. Victoria and Albert Museum, IS. 19-1950.

castes, professions, and holy people.[59] This cultural framework encouraged Indian artisans to develop sophisticated methods of dyeing that would bowl over Europeans. In Europe, bright colors had for centuries been worn only by the privileged few, who stood out like peacocks against a background of drab commoners clad in somber shades of black, gray, and brown. As vivid Indian imports (and lower quality knockoffs) poured into the market, the color of European clothes passed from dull earth tones to dazzling reds and pinks and flamboyant blues and yellows. Elite women were in the vanguard of this trend, but it touched both sexes and almost all social classes, constituting "a veritable transformation of sensibilities." Centuries-old customs of dress were challenged as "the Enlightenment brought all the colors of the rainbow within reach of ordinary people."[60] No wonder consumers were excited.

Better still, Europeans marveled at the *fastness* of the color of Indian cloth, which did not fade with exposure to light or, crucially, repeated washing. Employing a technique wholly unknown to Europeans (but which they would eventually copy), Indian producers used iron or aluminum mordants to fix colors to cotton, a vegetable fiber extremely difficult to dye, to create an insoluble, colorfast, and washable material.[61] Again, Indian cultural sensitivity to ideas of pollution and purity encouraged the development of industrial technology that permitted frequent washing. The arrival of such cloth on European shores coincided serendipitously with an emerging Enlightenment culture that placed a premium on cleanliness as a sign of health, virtue, and respectability.[62] As one Briton asked in the 1730s, "Is there a wench above sixteen who does not find herself more acceptable to others when she looks clean, than when she is obliged to wear Woolen, which never looks so clean; or when dirty, can it so easily be made clean?"[63]

In this environment, a truly washable fabric was a godsend. "The cloth from the Indies draws its value and its price from the liveliness, endurance, and adherence of the colors with which they are painted, which is such that, far from losing their brilliance when one washes them, they become only more beautiful," enthused the encyclopedist Louis de Jaucourt.[64] According to the municipal officers of Toulon, townswomen prized calicoes because of the fastness of their color. "The extreme poverty which reigns in this city and the low price of indiennes and painted Indian cloths that can be washed like linen have engaged nearly all the women and girls to make use of them."[65] Consumers became "accustomed to the sharp colors of the toiles peintes," explained an official from Languedoc, "and the ease of maintaining the colors by soaping them; they hate to see when cottons and siamoises [linen or silk floss imitations of calicoes] come back from the laundry completely changed."[66]

Finally, cotton calicoes were coveted because they were light and comfortable. Personal comfort had never been a very important consideration in the production of European clothing, which was designed primarily to convey social status or, among common people, to facilitate work. However, during the Enlightenment, Europeans put more and more stock in the idea of comfort, in regard to not only the home but also apparel. With respect to fabric, this transition manifested itself in the waning of stiff broadcloths and woolens and the waxing of soft and airy cottons. Think of the loose-fitting dressing gowns that many men of letters donned for their portraits. By the late eighteenth century, even the Parisian working classes had abandoned much of their wool for cotton: 20 percent of the wardrobe of male wage earners and 57 percent of that of their female counterparts now consisted of that organic fabric.[67] Light cottons were especially convenient in summertime, but even in winter, men and women found a source of comfort in an additional layer of cotton underwear below their heavy wool clothes.

In 1755, economist François Véron de Forbonnais marveled at the variety of men and women who participated in the fashion for *indiennes*.[68] Reserved for "the luxury of a small circle of opulent people," the highest quality cloth graced the court where, as petitions to the royal council of commerce attest, ladies wrapped themselves in polychrome chintz dresses with exquisite hand-painted floral motifs.[69] The "middle classes"—Forbonnais's term—also dressed their young and decorated their residences with the new cloth, eschewing splendor in favor of "cleanliness and elegance." Indeed, merchants, professionals, and artisans in the Breton port of Nantes elaborately adorned their homes and their wives with the fabric.[70] Finally, the economist explained, "the lowest quality calicoes comprise the ordinary clothing of commoner women in the towns," as well as that of inhabitants of the "sugar islands" in the French West Indies. In Avignon, even the poor experimented with Indian dressing gowns, aprons, petticoats, and headscarves.[71] Calicoes were also reexported to the west coast of Africa, where local rulers traded captives for indigo-dyed "Guinea cloth," and to the Americas, where colonists increasingly donned cotton.[72]

Consumers at the lower end of the social scale had access to calico because it was less expensive than traditional European silks and fine linens (even if lower-quality linens were equally cheap). This price disparity between Indian cloth and high-quality European fabric stemmed not, insists one historian of India, from some stereotypical labor force of impoverished Indian weavers who were more deeply exploited than their European counterparts. Rather, a thriving agricultural sector on the subcontinent kept food prices down, which reduced money wages and allowed workers to produce cloth on highly competitive terms for the European market.[73] Even after pocketing a substantial markup, East India companies could sell fabric at relatively low prices, encouraging the diffusion of the cloth across a broad segment of society. Thus, if Molière, in 1671, could poke fun at Monsieur Jourdain, the archetypal bourgeois social climber, for coveting an Indian dressing gown because "people of quality" were known to wear them in the morning, a century later such an act of sartorial usurpation was no longer a joke.[74] The social parameters of calico widened considerably, evincing a fundamental change in European material culture.

The meteoric rise of tobacco and calico reflected the dynamic globalization of European consumption in the late seventeenth and eighteenth centuries. Cultivated by plantation slaves in the Americas, tobacco inundated the Old World to feed a habit that Europeans have yet to kick. An addictive Amerindian substance that was incorporated into European practices of healing, sociability, and recreation, tobacco eclipsed European-grown herbal remedies to become one of the most widely consumed transcontinental imports of the period. Calico enjoyed an astounding success, too. Produced by skilled Indian weavers and shipped to Europe by armed trading companies, calico flooded European textile markets. Millions of European consumers actively decorated their interiors and their own bodies with this exotic, vivid, colorfast, and lightweight fabric. In both cases, European consumers modified the meanings imparted to the goods in their indigenous environments to integrate them into an emerging consumer culture. And in both cases, the products diffused through Europe laterally along multiple social levels, defying simplistic trickle-down models of consumption.

Heightened European demand for global goods explains why Mandrin was peddling tobacco and calico in the market square of Millau in 1754. But it does not explain why he required an armed gang to do so or why the subdelegate was so shocked to see him hawking such merchandise in public. Why, in other words, was Mandrin a smuggling kingpin and not simply a merchant? This question leads us ineluctably into the realm of politics. For if tobacco and calico generated an ordinate amount of consumer demand, they did not do so without attracting the attention of European rulers. In the seventeenth and eighteenth centuries, several European polities, including France, established elaborate regulatory apparatuses to control tobacco and calico, bringing the full weight of the state to bear on their trade and consumption. Mandrin's illustrious career suggests that such efforts were not perfectly successful.

2

The King Intervenes

THE GLOBALIZATION of Western European consumption from 1650 to 1800 did not take place in a political vacuum. On the contrary, during the very same period in which trade globalized and consumption surged, the European "fiscal-military state" was born—an awesome beast that could tax and borrow on an unprecedented scale to field mighty armies on the continent or deploy blue-water navies around the world.[1] Fiscal-military states fundamentally shaped the global commerce that was transforming consumption. Projecting fierce European rivalries onto the larger world, bellicose rulers competed for access to, and control of, transcontinental flows of valuable colonial goods. They issued navigation laws, created monopolistic trading companies, founded colonies, imposed high tariffs on foreign imports, and waged military war on commercial enemies and commercial war on military enemies. All of this was in an era of rapidly expanding world trade. The dual processes of state formation and globalization were inextricably intertwined in the early modern period.

The interventions of European states in the global economy were driven by two basic frameworks of political-economic thought and action. One was fiscalism, the desire to raise state revenues for funding war and war debt. Well aware that international power depended on state finance, rulers desperately searched for ways to raise money through loans and taxes. The other political-economic framework was mercantilism, the belief that states should aggressively promote national wealth by supporting domestic industry and encouraging favorable balances of trade, thereby capturing the gold and silver bullion that generated or at least signaled national prosperity.[2] Colonies were considered essential to achieving this goal. In a world believed to contain finite wealth, "each of the powers looked upon its colonies as suppliers of raw materials and markets for manufactures of the 'mother country' alone, with foreign interlopers to be excluded by force if necessary." Because the unilateral embrace of free trade was not a viable option in this polycentric war-torn era, mercantilist intervention remained the order of the day.[3]

The policies that followed from fiscalism and mercantilism dramatically enhanced the muscle and reach of early modern states. However, as the French case will illustrate, they also had the unintended consequence of stimulating the growth of underground markets that expanded steadily to accommodate illegal trade in regulated overseas imports. In the shadows of an emerging global economy, a parallel illicit economy would thrive.

Fiscalizing Consumption: The Tobacco Monopoly

During the period in which tobacco became a popular consumer good, European states were engaged in what can best be described as a fiscal arms race. As English economist (and former tax collector) Charles Davenant noted in 1695, "war is quite changed from what it was in the time of our forefathers[,] when in a hasty expedition and a pitched field, the matter was decided by courage. . . . [N]ow the whole art of war is in a manner reduced to money." The prince "who can best find money to feed, cloath and pay his army," rather than the one who "has the most valiant troops, is surest of success and conquest."[4] Money became increasingly important as more battles were fought on the high seas and in distant colonies as well as on European soil, and as armies ballooned, requiring more intensive training and elaborate supply networks. As the costs of war skyrocketed, European rulers, notably those of continental superpowers France and Britain, scrambled to find new means of raising revenue to pay for current wars and to service mounting public debts generated by previous ones. Although historians have emphasized (to the point of caricature) the different ways by which absolutist France and constitutionalist Britain went about raising treasure, the paths of the two kingdoms converged in one crucial respect: both fiscalized consumption. That is, both attempted to capture the fiscal power of rising consumption by taxing consumer products. During the late seventeenth and eighteenth centuries, as France and Britain did battle in a second Hundred Years' War, the two states dramatically shifted their tax structures from direct taxes on persons and property to indirect taxes on goods. As state revenues shot up, keeping pace with high rates of demographic and economic growth in France and surpassing those rates in Britain, the fiscal burden fell increasingly on items of popular consumption.

Britain epitomized this trend. Over the eighteenth century, British customs duties (on imported tea, sugar, wine, foreign spirits, and tobacco) and excise taxes (on beer, malt, domestic spirits, and salt) pushed revenue to staggering heights. By the reign of George III, indirect taxation had grown to 80 percent of total tax revenues, providing ample funding for Britain's debt and catapulting the nation to great-power status. This rise in indirect taxation was not merely a reflection of British commercial growth, as vigorous as that growth was. It was the result of a deliberate policy to generate higher revenues by creating new kinds of indirect taxes and raising rates on those that already existed. While it is true that such taxes fell on merchants and producers in the first instance, they were overwhelmingly passed on to ordinary consumers in the form of higher prices. Indeed, regressive consumption taxes struck the laboring classes with such force that it is not too much of an exaggeration to say that the debt of the British Empire was carried on the backs of metropolitan middling and poor consumers, especially beer drinkers! The "consumer society" that historians of England have so diligently excavated was increasingly exploited by the state as a supremely valuable source of revenue.[5]

In France, consumption was fiscalized as well. Not that its shift toward indirect taxes was as dramatic as Britain's, but given France's comparatively large agricultural sector, the move toward trade and consumption taxes was nonetheless impressive.[6] Although Louis XIV created new direct taxes during the second half of his reign, the proportion of revenue derived from indirect taxes jumped from roughly a quarter of the budget in the first half of the seventeenth century to about half in the eighteenth century.[7] By 1788, indirect-tax revenue, including revenue from the royal domain, amounted to no less than 270.5 million livres tournois (hereafter lt) or 57 percent of the budget, most of it coming from a tax on private contracts and an assortment of levies on salt, alcoholic beverages, tobacco, and customs duties that fell disproportionately on poor and middling consumers.[8] Direct taxes for the same year added up to 163 million livres or 34.5 percent of the budget. It is clear that France increasingly found in consumption taxes a resource with which to wage war and fund war-generated debt.[9] Thus, not only did France, like Britain, experience a boom in foreign and colonial trade and a related surge in consumption during the eighteenth century but the French monarchy, like the English parliament, was learning to harness consumption's fiscal power.[10]

The process by which consumption was fiscalized was glaringly apparent in the case of tobacco. States intervened in the Atlantic tobacco trade either by imposing customs taxes on imports or creating monopolies. In England, as soon as it became clear that tobacco was a commercially viable crop in the New World, parliament imposed heavy customs taxes on its import; in 1685, tobacco customs were set at the rate of 100 percent of the precustoms price. Such duties could be levied without fear of scaring off importers because the navigation acts of the seventeenth century forced English ships that carried tobacco and a handful of other "enumerated" colonial goods to transport their cargo directly to the mother country, where it was taxed on arrival. This was consistent with the mercantilist principle that national ships should funnel colonial goods directly to metropolitan centers rather than allowing foreign ships to transport those goods to foreign countries. However, British lawmakers, who hoped to turn London and other English ports into global entrepôts on the model of Amsterdam, inserted an important loophole in the navigation acts that drastically scaled back customs taxes on certain reexported products. If British merchants reexported tobacco they brought to the mother country, they would receive substantial rebates on the customs duties they had initially paid. Such "drawbacks," as the rebates were called, allowed English colonial tobacco to compete favorably in the continental European market. A merchant who imported Virginian tobacco into Bristol, for example, could reexport the merchandise to Holland or France and "draw back" the import duties he had advanced. While this system of imposing customs taxes generated revenue, parliament was clearly more interested in encouraging a colonial reexport trade to continental Europe, which would promote a favorable balance of trade. Fully 85 percent of Chesapeake tobacco was reexported in this fashion.[11]

At first, France followed a similar model. In 1621, the monarchy established a customs tax on tobacco and, eight years later, restructured the tax to favor its newly acquired Caribbean islands: high duties were placed on imports of foreign tobacco, while leaf from French colonies was exempted.[12] Under Louis XIV's powerful finance minister, Jean-Baptiste Colbert, however, France changed course by scrapping the customs duties to create a royal monopoly in their stead. Here, Spain served as the model, having established a lucrative tobacco monopoly as early as 1636. Portugal, France, Austria, and many German and Italian states would all follow suit and found their own state monopolies.[13] When the French crown decreed its monopoly on 27 September 1674, it acknowledged the general trend: "The use of tobacco having become so common in every State that it has prompted most of our neighboring Princes to make of this commerce one of their principal revenues, we believed that we would be able to establish a like commerce in our provinces through the distribution and sale of Tobacco."[14]

A royal monopoly on tobacco was "all the more reasonable," the Sun King explained in the preamble, given the "extraordinary expenses of the current war [against Holland]" and the fact that tobacco was not "necessary for . . . the maintenance of life." While the reference to the Dutch War should not have surprised anyone—almost all new French taxes since the fifteenth century had been given public justification by the need to fund costly yet somehow unavoidable wars—the description of tobacco as a nonessential consumer good represented a curious rhetorical departure for the French monarchy.[15] Implicit in this description of tobacco was an invidious comparison to the gabelle, the infamous royal salt monopoly that provoked major revolts in the seventeenth century. In the early modern period, salt was a good of absolute necessity and widely understood as such. The precious mineral sustained the human body, nourished farm animals, and preserved fish and meat. Since the fourteenth century, French kings had shamelessly exploited this necessity for fiscal purposes. In the regions of the grande gabelle in northern France, where more than half the French population resided, the monarchy not only monopolized the sale of salt, setting its prices far above market value, but also forced subjects to buy a fixed allotment of state salt every year. Little wonder the gabelle was the most loathed tax in French history.[16]

The tobacco monopoly would be different, the declaration insisted, because the monarchy was not exploiting a good that one needed to subsist. On the contrary, it was selling a nonessential commodity, a luxury, that would be made available to all through the monopoly. Because consumers would purchase tobacco of their own volition, as they did all luxury goods, they could hardly consider the monopoly oppressive. The monarchy drove this point home though subsequent legislation, never failing to point out that tobacco revenues "resulted only from voluntary and superfluous consumption."[17] Not surprisingly, ministers and tax officials at the highest levels of the monarchy touted this fiscal logic, claiming that, far from satisfying a "natural need," tobacco was "only an object of caprice and fantasy."[18] Sébastien Le Prestre de Vauban, Louis XIV's famous military engineer, believed that those who volunteered to pay the tobacco tax did so as a self-imposed "penalty for their luxury."[19] Jean-Louis Moreau de Beaumont, esteemed member of Louis XV's finance council, stressed that the tobacco levy was "a purely voluntary tax for the people: if [tobacco] has in some way become a need, they are themselves the authors of this new necessity. Can the King find a less onerous resource to provide for the expenses of his State? . . . Should he not desire to see this part of his Domain make all the progress of which it may be susceptible?"[20] Jacques Necker, Louis XVI's finance minister, heartily agreed, proclaiming in his summa on finance that "the tax on tobacco is the gentlest and most imperceptible of all contributions, and it is rightly ranked among the most skillful fiscal inventions."[21] Present at the birth of the monopoly, this argument underpinned all major apologies for the taxation of tobacco down to the French Revolution.

The success of the monopoly hinged on its ability to procure, process, and distribute tobacco from the Americas, quash tobacco cultivation at home, and guard against smuggling and fraud. To handle these operations, the crown leased the institution to the United General Farms in 1681. It had long been the practice of French finance ministers to subcontract the collection of indirect taxes to private financiers who, in exchange for making lump-sum payments up front, enjoyed the right to gather revenue and pocket any profits they made beyond the lease price. To modern eyes, tax farming appears to be an archaic and dangerous alienation of public power, but to cash-strapped French kings, it offered substantial advantages. Not only did tax farming guarantee steady streams of revenue without the financial risks and bureaucratic hassles of direct administration but, more important, it provided the monarchy with an extraordinarily useful credit mechanism, as tax farmers amassed capital from noble and bourgeois families to advance huge loans to the king, the interest from which could simply be deducted from the price of the lease. The lines of credit that monarchs tapped through tax farming were remarkably deep. In the middle of the eighteenth century, the Farmers General who composed the consortium of financiers at the head of the United General Farms bankrolled Louis XV to the tune of 68 million lt in long-term and 60 million lt in short-term debt.[22] Lenders of the first order, the Farmers General became a mainstay of French court capitalism, a "permanent lobby" lodged at the very center of an elaborate court-based system of clientelism through which state creditors were rewarded with lucrative offices, positions, contracts, and interest payments.[23] Thus, more than simply extracting resources, fiscalizing consumption redistributed wealth up the social hierarchy from consumers to a narrow (yet growing) class of creditors that included, most conspicuously, the Farmers General.

Save for a rupture between 1697 and 1730, "the Farm," as it came to be known, ran the tobacco monopoly from 1681 to 1791. Although critics berated it for corruption and inefficiency, the Farm was arguably the most modern institution of the old regime, a vanguard of bureaucratic professionalism credited with the invention of such forward-looking managerial policies as the modern pension system.[24] A colossus, it dwarfed every other institution in France, public or private, except for the royal army. At its apex stood forty Farmers General, the "40 columns of the State" as Cardinal Fleury called them, rich and cultivated patrons of the arts who integrated themselves into the upper reaches of the nobility through strategic marriage alliances.[25] Based in their splendid right-bank headquarters in the hôtels de Longueville (Figure 2.1) and Bretonvilliers, which, housing several hundred administrators and clerks, was the largest office complex in Paris, the Farmers consulted with finance ministers, ran the central committees that kept the institution humming, and corresponded with the all-important directors in the field.

Every year, several Farmers toured the company's forty-two provincial directions, each headed by a single well-paid director whose job was to oversee the collection of indirect taxes in his jurisdiction. Residing in the provincial capital, the director was responsible for conducting local tours of his own, bringing cases of fraud and smuggling to trial, managing Farm personnel, and submitting accounts to Paris. To help in this daunting task, he counted on a small staff of officers: two or three

Figure 2.1. Farm headquarters at the Hôtel de Longueville. Bibliothèque Nationale de France, VA-227-Fol.

controllers who tracked the storage and sale of salt and tobacco and followed the flow of revenue in the area, a receiver-general through whom all the direction's money passed, and two or three inspectors who oversaw the accounts of tobacco retailers, reported cases of fraud to the appropriate legal authorities, and handled the recruitment and operations of the Farm's brigades. Directors, receivers, and inspectors all had numerous lower-level clerks working for them, but the largest branch of the Farm was undoubtedly the army of guards that patrolled Paris and the provinces on the lookout for smugglers. Of the 28,839 employees who worked for the Farm in 1774, 21,188 of them were armed guards.[26] Although the number of quill-pushing bureaucrats in the Farm was astonishing by early-modern standards, the bulk of the Farm's manpower was to be found in paramilitary brigades. This armed force, the largest of its kind in Europe, constituted the bulwark of the monopoly.

In taking on the tobacco monopoly, the Farm faced challenges that went far beyond its experience with salt. The salt monopoly had always been a relatively local affair, as the mineral was extracted from mines and salt flats within the kingdom and sold to French subjects or exported to northern Europe. The tobacco monopoly, by contrast, drew the crown into a sprawling Atlantic economy that involved peoples from four continents and several empires. Although tobacco was known to grow in Europe, the Farm looked to its original home in the Americas for its supply. From a practical perspective, it made sense to instill in consumers a taste for overseas tobacco, because lesser quality European-grown leaf, such as that cultivated in Holland, was much easier to smuggle into France. Better to hook French subjects on an overseas import they could not easily obtain. Mercantilist principle also deemed that mother countries should, if possible, import raw goods from their own colonies rather than from rival nations. Accordingly, the monarchy at first procured tobacco from its Caribbean colony of Saint Domingue (now known as Haiti) and then from Louisiana. But from the 1720s, defying mercantilist principle and the wishes of French colonial planters, the monopoly spurned the colonies and began purchasing tobacco from Britain, whose merchants delivered cheap, top-quality Chesapeake Bay leaf to French agents in Britain. As the largest single purchaser in the British market—what economists call a monopsonistic buyer—the Farm was able to drive wholesale prices down to rock-bottom levels, which widened its profit margins. By the eve of the Revolution, 90 percent of Farm leaf was grown in the Chesapeake.[27] This sharp turn toward British colonial product can only be interpreted in one way: when it came to tobacco, the French monarchy put fiscality first. In this characteristically French slippage from mercantilism to fiscalism, revenue took priority over empire building. Even in the midst of war, the Farm preferred to buy tobacco from France's archenemy than to pay more for lesser leaf from its own colonies.[28]

It was mostly Chesapeake tobacco, then, that was shipped (via Britain) to the Farm's ten or so manufactories in France.[29] Anticipating the factories of the nineteenth-century Industrial Revolution, the scale of some of these plants was breathtaking. In an age when most workshops still consisted of a master and a few journeyman, the kingdom's tobacco manufactory at Morlaix, Brittany, employed more than a thousand workers, many of them women and children, who processed hundreds of thousands of pounds of tobacco a year. Inside the Morlaix plant, low-wage workers opened thousand-pound hogsheads, sorted the leaves stuffed inside, spun them into long rolls, and then seasoned, pressed, and cut the rolls into what were known as "carrots," sticks of tobacco wound tightly with a special string so that they could stand up to rasping.[30] The string, which would disappear as the carrot was grated, also served as the distinctive mark of official Farm tobacco. The carrots and

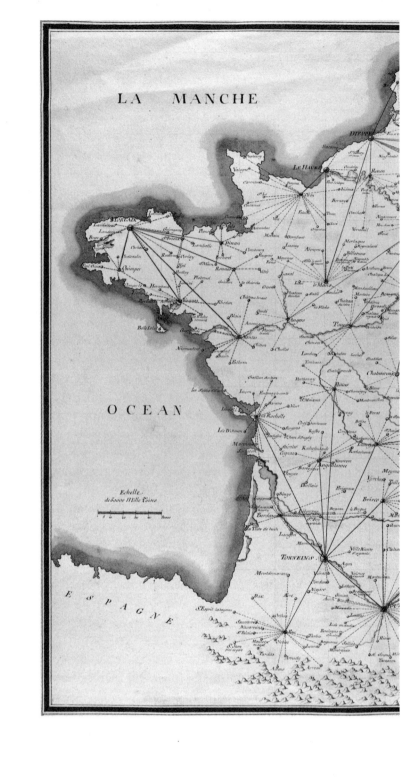

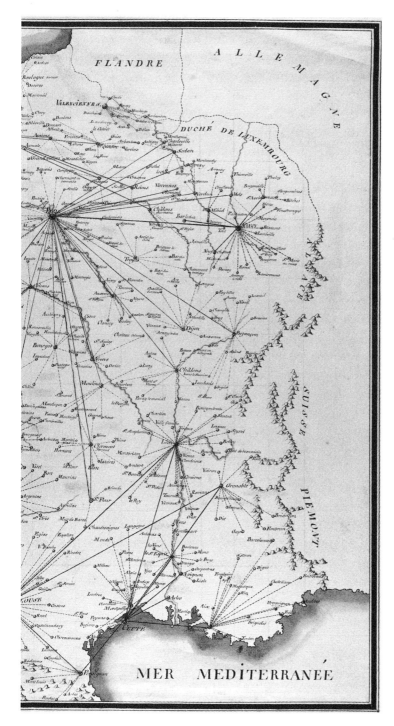

Figure 2.2. Distribution of Farm tobacco in France. Lavoisier Manuscript Collection, no. 4712. Division of Rare and Manuscript Collections, Cornell University Library.

other types of leaf processed in state factories were transported to forty-odd "directions" throughout the kingdom, each of which had two or three distribution centers.[31] The distribution centers supplied 566 warehouses, which in turn provided the tobacco to over 10,000 licensed retailers in cities, towns, and villages throughout France. Unlike the gabelle, the tobacco monopoly spanned nearly the entire territory of the realm (Figure 2.2).[32]

State retail shops, the capillaries of the distribution system, served as the principal point of purchase for consumers. Knowing almost instinctively that the key to tobacco marketing was exposure, Farmers urged warehousers to make the weed readily available to people in their jurisdiction through a multitude of local outlets. As the royal council explained, consumers "did not want to incur the costs of going two or three leagues to get an ounce or half pound of tobacco."[33] Thus, warehousers planted tobacconists in every nook and cranny of the kingdom and kept a close eye on how much they sold: those who exceeded their monthly quotas received bonuses; those who came up short were suspected of fraud and investigated.[34] Scales at their side, tobacconists sprung up in rural villages and urban neighborhoods across France. In Paris, whose voracious residents provided the monopoly with a large share of its revenues, 1,200 state retailers were hawking tobacco as early as 1708; that number would rise further as more and more café owners doubled as tobacconists.[35] In the countryside, tobacco outlets were installed in almost every burg of the monopoly zone. The tiniest, most isolated villages had retailers. No fewer than three sellers served the 240 households of Valdrôme, a rural parish situated some twenty miles from the nearest town. Even minuscule hamlets like Orel, with no more than a hundred households, were not spared.[36] If the Farm was going to compete with smugglers, it had to pair its armed guards with a retail network that reached deep into rural France.

The strategy of blanketing the kingdom with state tobacco retailers paid off handsomely. As annual household consumption of tobacco grew from negligible quantities to about three pounds (six for Paris), annual revenue climbed from 500,000 lt in the monopoly's early years under Colbert to over 30 million on the eve of the French Revolution, a sixty-fold increase.[37] Already by the middle of the eighteenth century, what began as a minor financial experiment had come to occupy a major place in the kingdom's tax system, contributing upwards of 20 percent of indirect tax receipts and over 7 percent of total state revenue.[38] Of all the different revenue branches, observed Moreau de Beaumont, "none has made progress as rapidly and substantially as tobacco. . . . Although the most recent, [it] has nevertheless become one of the most consider-able." Jacques Turgot, Louis XVI's finance minister who, as a free-trade economist, detested monopoly on principle, could not help but admire the "astonishing progress" of tobacco revenues over the years. Of all the departments, "this is the one that merits the most favor, and it is in the national interest to make it prosper."[39] A source of seemingly in-finite bounty, the monopoly represented the cutting edge of the monar-chy's project to fiscalize consumption.

Protecting Industry: The Calico Prohibition

Tobacco was not the only global commodity that caught the eye of European states. Indian cloth, which was pouring into European markets by the late seventeenth century, also attracted attention. Although its importation was a smashing success insofar as the English, Dutch, and French East India companies were able to turn handsome profits on its sale, that very success threatened wool, linen, and silk producers al-ready established on European soil. They now clamored for protection. One way to understand this conflict between trading companies and domestic textile producers is to see it as the unraveling of an incoherent mercantilist framework. State-sponsored European trading companies were justified on "mercantilist" grounds that governments should ag-gressively support their merchants' overseas trade, especially if it cut into that of commercial rivals. This is precisely what Colbert intended when he created the French East India Company in 1664. We must "obtain Asian commerce for the kingdom," he wrote, "and prevent the English and Dutch from profiting from it alone as they have done until now."[40] At the same time, however, the Asian trade violated other max-ims of mercantilism, which dictated that rulers ought to protect na-tional industry from foreign competition and promote the accumula-tion of bullion. Here the importation of calico ran into trouble, for in no way could the cloth be construed as a raw good to be finished at home. It was a foreign industrial product that competed directly (and favor-ably) with domestic rivals. Further, it was difficult to justify shipping boatloads of American silver, considered to be real tangible wealth, to the shores of India. Spending silver to import a semiluxury good like Indian cloth contradicted basic mercantilist principles and threatened to undermine vital textile industries at home.

But this conflict was about more than abstract economic doctrine. A coalition of interested parties formed in opposition to the Indian cotton trade as soon as it began to thrive. In France, pressure to restrict the inflow of *indiennes* became particularly intense in the 1680s. Alarmed by the sudden competition, textile manufacturers in Lyon, Nîmes, Tours, and, above all, Normandy strenuously lobbied royal officials for protection from the juggernaut of cheap, fashionable textiles arriving from the East and now produced in Europe as well. Claiming that the kingdom could not absorb all this new fabric without severely damaging existing industries, traditional manufacturers pleaded with officials to save their supposedly failing enterprises. As a certain Sieur Chauvel from Dieppe on the Norman coast complained to the Marquis de Seignelay, Colbert's son and successor, the imports of the East India Company "entirely ruined our manufactures of silk, of wool, and of linen." French consumers flocked to the low-priced imports "while all the products of our manufactures have remained unconsumed."[41] Did not the monarchy have an obligation to assist the home textile industry, the most important industrial sector of the economy, in its hour of need?

Further, officials feared for public order if workers in traditional textile industries were laid off. Underemployment was a chronic problem in the old regime, and the crown constantly worried about emigration or, worse yet, riots. Such anxieties were especially acute in the aftermath of the revocation of the Edict of Nantes (1685), which forced thousands of Protestant workers and highly skilled technicians into exile, throwing the textile industry into disarray. In this dismal economic atmosphere, calicoes proved a useful scapegoat. When two or three hundred unemployed textile workers assembled on the doorstep of the intendant of Rouen in February 1685, the intendant consulted with a local merchant, who blamed the menacing crowd on the recent arrival of a calico-laden ship. The influx of calico had dampened sales of worsted wool, he explained, depriving merchants of the means to pay workers. Although the intendant managed to defuse the situation, brokering a deal by which merchants would rehire workers at lower wages, there was no telling when other disorders might break out.[42] In England, London weavers pillaged East India Company warehouses in 1680, rioted in 1697, and attacked calico shops and even calico-clad people in June and July of 1719.[43]

Many royal officials, including the Marquis de Louvois, the influential Director of Domestic Commerce and Manufacture, sympathized with the plight of French industrialists and the workers for whom they claimed to speak. Indeed, most men of state believed that sinking large quantities of French bullion into an "Asian abyss" to import finished goods ran counter to the common wisdom that France should conserve its bullion, use its own raw materials for production, and export—not import—luxuries.[44] Of course, the directors of the French East Indies Company countered such arguments, claiming on behalf of consumers that it was better to import finished cloth from India than pay higher prices for Dutch or English cottons. Why allow France's enemies to profit from the trade? Nor did company directors accept that the export of silver would have such catastrophic economic consequences. Was it not obvious that manufacturers were exaggerating how much silver was leaving France in an effort to garner support for their cause? Although such counterarguments were perfectly logical and contained more than a grain of truth, the directors had few allies inside or outside the government. One potential group of supporters, French calico printers who copied Asian originals and were no doubt concerned about the possibility of a universal ban, were viewed as commercial upstarts in an otherwise well-entrenched textile industry and in no position to peddle influence in the halls of state. (They may have also been hoping for a ban on imports alone, which would have given their own businesses a boost.) Meanwhile, French consumers, who stood to lose from any protectionist measures, might have joined the company in common cause, but, like the workers on the other side of the conflict, they lacked any formal means to express their interests in such weighty political matters. Consumer activism in this period was generally confined to informal collective action on life-and-death issues of food provisioning and, as we shall see, assisting smugglers in their struggles against the Farm.

At the end of the day, after all the petitioning and influence peddling, Louvois and the traditional textile producers who had his ear prevailed. The royal council issued an *arrêt* on 26 October 1686 prohibiting the import of calicos from India and banning the production of facsimiles on French soil. The preamble carefully laid out the reasons for such drastic action:

> The King has been informed that the great quantity of cotton fabrics painted in the Indies or counterfeited in the Kingdom . . . have not only given rise to the conveyance of many millions outside the Kingdom, but have also caused the reduction of Manufactures long established in France for Stuffs of Silk, Wool, Linen, Hemp, & provoked at the same time the ruin & desertion of Workers who, no longer finding employment nor subsistence for their families due to the cessation of their work, have left the Kingdom.[45]

To reverse this decline, the decree ordered all merchants who imported painted or printed Indian fabrics into France to cease doing so immediately and commanded all domestic manufacturers of calicoes to stop production and destroy their print molds. Indian cloth could continue to be reexported (that is, imported into France to be exported to a foreign country), but it was in no way to penetrate the domestic market. In 1692, a decree extended the prohibition from production and exchange to consumption. Henceforth, anyone caught purchasing, wearing, or decorating with *indiennes* would be liable to heavy fines and the immediate confiscation of the material. To ensure that the cloth did not enter the French market, Louis XIV entrusted none other than the General Farm with the power to enforce the prohibition. The same institution that guarded the tobacco and salt monopolies, collected the excises on alcohol, and manned the kingdom's customs posts was now tasked with policing the calico ban and protecting the interests of entrenched textile producers. The ban was to be directly linked to the monarchy's fiscal apparatus.

Thus "royal authority endeavored to build a dyke against this torrent of cloth from the Indies, which inundated Paris and the provinces," explained Jacques Savary des Bruslons.[46] Controversial in its day and still hotly debated today, the 1686 decree ushered in a long era of prohibition in France.[47] For seventy-three years, the production, sale, and consumption of a major French consumer good was deemed illegal. When the ban was lifted in 1759, it was replaced by a stiff 25 percent duty on imported printed fabrics. The "dyke" would not be fully dismantled for another quarter century.[48]

The French prohibition was but the forerunner of a wave of protectionist legislation to sweep the continent in what was the first pan-

European movement to block a major Asian import. Indian calicoes were banned in England (1701 and 1721), Catalonia (1717 and 1728), and Prussia (1721). In France, the ban was nearly total. In England, the original import ban was extended to domestic production and consumption of printed cloth in 1721, but significant exceptions were made for printed linens and fustians and for printed cottons produced for export. In Catalonia, the ban on Indian imports was widened to European imports in 1728, but the crown never blocked domestic production, hoping to encourage a national import-substitution industry. In Prussia, as in Spain, bans were designed to shield national production from the importation of rival Indian calicoes. Even in the age of mercantilism, when national territory was increasingly delineated by lines of customs barriers and invested with economic meaning, this series of prohibitions constituted an extreme form of protectionism. While from the last quarter of the seventeenth century it was common to protect home industries with heavy customs tariffs, it was highly unusual to impose outright bans.

A Global Underground

Historian Maxine Berg has recently argued that the trade barriers thrown up to block Asian imports from entering Britain stimulated the production of British imitations, which encouraged innovation and paved the way for the Industrial Revolution.[49] Her fascinating thesis is undoubtedly correct: after Parliament banned Asian imports, a nascent cotton industry rose up to meet surging home demand, eventually mechanizing its production to become *the* leading sector of British industrialization. Thus, European calico printing represents "the missing link" between early modern world trade and late modern industrial production.[50] But that is only part of the story. In France (and Britain as well, for that matter) the regulation and taxation of transcontinental imports produced another significant if unintended consequence: they produced a robust parallel economy that exploited the fiscal and commercial borders the state had imposed.

We know that contraband was rife in the Americas. Imperial economic regimes designed to benefit the mother country—whether the Spanish fleet system, the English navigation acts, or the French *exclusif*—established trade boundaries between empires that, in practice, proved to be porous in the extreme. In the eighteenth century, the Caribbean constituted the eye of an illicit storm that ran the length of the eastern seaboard of the Americas. "[W]herever there were ports, from New France to Buenos Aires and from Chile to Brazil, illicit trade occurred," often "dwarfing" legal commerce.[51] Inhabitants of the colonies profited from the shadow economy by illegally importing captives of African descent, basic foodstuffs, and a host of finished consumer goods while illegally exporting precious metals and a variety of slave-produced agricultural products. Hence, a wide array of commodities—from slaves, silver, sugar, and rum to cacao beans, coffee, and tobacco—circulated outside the formal economy structured by metropolitan commercial law to be exchanged freely across empires.

Although smuggling, like piracy, is most commonly associated with the "masterless" denizens of the New World, it intensified in the more heavily policed Old World, too, as fiscal and mercantilist measures produced black markets in colonial goods that, in Europe, galvanized the preexisting underground economy.[52] In mid-eighteenth-century England, most spectacularly, between 3 and 3.5 million pounds of Chinese tea was smuggled into ports annually, almost three times as much as that imported legally by the East India Company.[53] Historians of French smuggling have long focused on local commodities such as salt, which formed the core of the early modern contraband trade, but from the late seventeenth century, the tobacco monopoly and calico prohibition triggered massive waves of contraband, in effect globalizing the metropolitan illicit economy in the final century of the old regime.[54] We will have occasion in subsequent chapters to examine the colorful and often tragic figures who populated this widening underground economy. Here it will suffice to sketch the basic outlines of the global underground, tracing the main channels through which illicit goods coursed from producers in the Americas, Asia, and Europe to consumers in France.

In the tobacco trade, every link in the chain of production and exchange from the New World plantation to the local French consumer was riddled with fraud. At the site of production on the lush banks of the Chesapeake, warehouse workers and dockworkers dipped into the supply line, helping themselves to handfuls of leaf as a customary right. Some of the tobacco they loaded onto ships did not pass directly to Britain, as the law required, but was smuggled to foreign colonies or to the British West Indies, whence it was repackaged and smuggled into

England aboard ships carrying sugar.[55] The tobacco that did sail directly (and therefore legally) from the Chesapeake to Britain was received by dockworkers on the other side of the Atlantic who, like their American colleagues, socked away leaf as they unloaded hogsheads onto the quay.[56] British customs officials, meanwhile, took kickbacks for underweighing imports ("hickory puckery"), which reduced the duty levied on tobacco, and for overweighing reexports ("puckery hickory"), which maximized tax rebates to merchants who shipped tobacco from Britain to the Continent. Many merchants who claimed drawbacks for reexports did not, however, send their tobacco abroad. Instead, their ships sailed out of British ports toward the open waters of the English Channel only to circle back and unload their cargo onto isolated stretches of British coast or to land the merchandise in Dunkirk or one of the independent Channel Islands before sending it back clandestinely to Kent or Sussex. Land smugglers then whisked the weed into the domestic black market, so ensuring that more than a third of the tobacco consumed in Britain in the middle of the eighteenth century was contraband.[57]

The remaining American leaf that sailed across the channel and did not return to Britain was safely delivered to the French Farm or other continental merchants. That which passed into the hands of the French Farm was placed under heavy surveillance, but some of it still managed to escape official channels and leach into the black market. Workers at gigantic Farm processing plants purloined the herb, believing, like British dockworkers on both sides of the Atlantic, that this was a perquisite of their job. So convinced were they of this right that when the Farm cracked down on such abuses at the manufactory in Dieppe, workers rebelled, threatening to beat up scabs brought in to replace them.[58] Local retailers who sold official Farm tobacco, moreover, weighed it down with water, cut it with contraband, or mixed it with a host of cheap additives— "foreign bodies" in the terminology of authorities—from tulipwood shavings and sifted ash to pulverized brick and plain old dirt. In Paris, the problem of retailers cutting their tobacco was so severe that the chief of police appointed two master apothecaries to analyze suspect leaf. In one of the first crime labs in modern history, they examined, weighed, burned, washed, and poured vitriolic acid on samples of confiscated tobacco. More often than not, the results of such scientific experimentation led to the conclusion that the tobacco in question was adulterated. No wonder Antoine Lavoisier, the father of modern chemistry and dedicated Farmer General, considered retailers "the true enemies of the tobacco farm."[59]

The Chesapeake tobacco sold to non-Farm continental merchants posed the principal danger to the monopoly. Merchants in the free French port of Dunkirk and the ports of the Netherlands shipped contraband tobacco to all quarters of the French monopoly zone, from the coast of Languedoc in the south to the littoral of Brittany and Normandy in the west. Supply ships hovered off the mainland as small craft ran tobacco ashore, where locals picked it up and hauled it inland for distribution. From the Channel Islands of Jersey and Guernsey, traffickers stowed contraband in small craft and sailed or rowed it to the nearby coasts of Normandy and Brittany. The most heavily trafficked gateway into the territory of the French monopoly, however, lay to the northeast of the kingdom where an enormous transshipment corridor formed from the United Provinces and Austrian Netherlands down through Alsace, Franche-Comté, Switzerland, and Savoy. This international region was perfectly suited for smuggling tobacco into the French monopoly zone. Not only did precious Virginian leaf flood this corridor via Dunkirk and the Netherlands but local homegrown tobacco, an eminently market-oriented crop, had long been cultivated in the area as well. By the middle of the eighteenth century, a fertile crescent of tobacco production—second in the world only to the Chesapeake—had risen along the Rhine from Utrecht through Alsace to the pays de Vaud in Switzerland.[60]

The fiscal geography of this region heavily encouraged illicit trade. Enmeshed in the lands of transshipment were several peripheral French provinces recently attached to the kingdom, notably Artois (1659), Flanders (1668), and Alsace and Franche-Comté (1678). Protected by privileges spelled out in the treaties by which they were patched onto the realm, these provinces remained outside the jurisdiction of the tobacco monopoly. In 1719, French finance minister John Law banned the cultivation of tobacco throughout France, including the southwestern generalities of Bordeaux and Montauban and parts of Provence and Normandy where cultivation had been previously allowed, but Law's otherwise universal prohibition did not apply to the peripheral northeastern provinces, which continued to produce their own tobacco. The French customs border ran not between these provinces and foreign countries but between these provinces and the territory of the monopoly in the heart of France—hence the use of clumsy official labels such as "provinces reputed foreign" and "provinces following the example of foreign countries"[61] (Figure 2.3). Further complicating the fiscal geography of this region were numerous sovereign enclaves (the Duchy of Lorraine, the Three Bishoprics, the principalities of Montbéliard and Dombes), which, despite French diplomatic pressure, were only slowly integrated into the monopoly. Much like Indian reservations in the United States today, such niche polities became vital conduits in the contraband trade. Although French officials wished to clean up the jumble of enclaves that obscured the frontier, the project to establish a uniform national-territorial border was not fully realized until the French Revolution. In the meantime, fiscal extraterritoriality would continue to foster underground trade.[62]

Consequently, an enormous reservoir of cheap, locally grown tobacco formed just beyond the eastern border of the French tobacco monopoly. Lacking the fine "scent and solidity" of the Virginian purchased by the Farm, European-grown tobacco was widely understood to be of lesser quality than its American-grown counterpart. The Dutch and Flanders leaf was the best of the European crop, the Alsatian was respectable, and the Swiss and Comtois was of such poor quality that only locals who could not afford better consumed it in its pure form.[63] However, European homegrown tobacco was mixed with superior American leaf by large manufactories in Dunkirk, Amsterdam, St. Omer, Strasbourg, and several Swiss towns (Berne, Lausanne, Morges) to produce a low-priced but good-quality blend that was ideal for smuggling into the French interior. Some intercontinental blends pierced the fiscal border from the north, passing through the Austrian Netherlands into Picardy and Champagne; others entered from the east, saturating Burgundy, the Lyonnais, and Dauphiné. It took a mere fortnight to ship tobacco down the Rhine from Amsterdam to Strasbourg and then carry it by road to the Swiss pays de Vaud, conveniently located just east of the French border and north of the southern transshipment province of Savoy. Switzerland became such a formidable contraband depot that when Farmer General Claude Dupin went undercover to investigate a tobacco manufactory in Vevey on Lake Léman, the owner assumed he was a merchant bankrolling trafficking expeditions. Smugglers all along the northern and eastern frontier, from small-time peddlers to well-organized gang leaders,

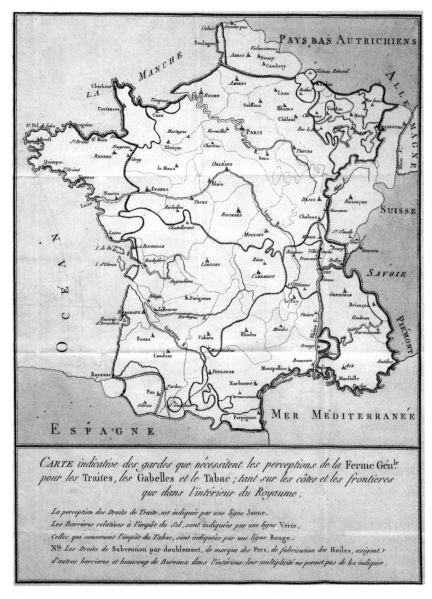

Figure 2.3. The Tobacco Border. The border is marked by the most peripheral dark line. Provinces outside the tobacco border (Artois, Alsace, and Franche-Comté) are identifiable by their respective capitals (Arras, Strasbourg, and Besançon). Courtesy of Special Collections, Spencer Research Library, University of Kansas Libraries.

drew from this reservoir to run the Euro-American hybrid into the monopoly, where it fetched prices many times higher than that for which it was purchased.[64]

Such contraband not only drenched the border provinces along the eastern edge of the French monopoly zone but flowed into the core of the kingdom, spreading as far as Normandy, the Paris basin, Auvergne, and Languedoc. In 1732, the intendant of Dauphiné noted that smugglers were shifting their purchases according to the tastes of consumers in Languedoc, who no longer desired unblended Franche-Comté tobacco. Instead, traffickers bought their inventory from Genevan merchants who purchased blended tobacco in Strasbourg, the provincial capital of Alsace. The sudden influx into Geneva of 300,000 pounds of tobacco from Strasbourg, he surmised, accounted for the dangerous rise of smuggling bands traversing his province.[65] A few years later, Dupin estimated that, while smugglers imported directly only a small proportion of the 8 million pounds of (presumably blended) tobacco Alsace produced each year into the French interior, roughly half flowed legally into Franche-Comté, Montbéliard, Switzerland, and Savoy, whence much of it was smuggled into the far reaches of the monopoly zone. Franche-Comté alone furnished traffickers with 1.5 million pounds a year.[66] In 1749, the crown attempted to slow imports of colonial tobacco into Alsace by levying customs dues on it, in essence establishing a border between Alsace and the rest of Europe, but the Strasbourgeois, who were able to delay, modify, and ultimately circumvent the law, continued to blend colonial and Alsatian tobacco throughout the century, producing an abundance of product for the contraband trade.[67]

Between the New World leaf siphoned off from official supply lines, that which was shipped to coastal France, and the blends flowing in by land from the north and east, vast quantities of illicit tobacco poured into France. Precisely how much is difficult to say. In 1770, economist Guillaume-François Le Trosne estimated that 40 percent of French tobacco was supplied by the underground, an estimate that squares with the findings of Farmer General Dupin, who concluded that 38 percent of the tobacco consumed in the department of Châlons was illicit. But these estimates were probably high. A physiocrat with an ax to grind against the Farm, Le Trosne was prone to exaggeration. Dupin's estimate seems accurate, but the area he was studying was near the contraband-soaked eastern border. A more reliable estimate comes from the pen of the well-informed François Véron de Forbonnais, economist and advisor to finance minister Silhouette, who in 1758 calculated that a third of the tobacco consumed in France was contraband, an estimate widely adopted by historians. Although it is impossible to know the volume of illicit commerce with any precision—such are the vagaries of working on underground markets—the rough estimate of one third suggests the magnitude of the trade.[68]

Just as the tobacco monopoly failed to prevent contraband leaf from entering France, the 1686 calico ban did not stop the influx of calicoes from India. Not only did the prohibition-free Netherlands continue to import the cloth, some of which was smuggled across the border into France, but the French company was allowed to carry on with its profitable reexport trade, which leaked into forbidden domestic markets. Channeled through the Breton port of Lorient, the French reexport trade was closely monitored by the General Farm. Ships arriving at Lorient were met by Farm launches that accompanied them to their moorings. After boarding the vessels to attach seals to the cargo, agents watched them dock at the quay and unload the merchandise, which was deposited in a heavily guarded warehouse to be inventoried jointly by the subdelegates of Nantes and Lorient and directors from the Farm and India Company. Once recorded, the calico remained in the locked facility until it was auctioned off to wholesale merchants from Nantes, Paris, and Geneva, who reexported the cloth outside of France.

Despite such elaborate security procedures, a portion of the calico that touched the Breton coast of France was siphoned off into the domestic shadow economy. Prior to entering the mouth of Lorient harbor, crews unloaded calico onto small craft and rowed or sailed it to remote points along the rocky Breton shore. Company sailors also stowed their own personal *pacotilles,* stashes of contraband they were tacitly allowed to take back from India and sell upon their return. The use of company ships for such private illicit trade was so common that sailors took out loans before voyages for the single purpose of stocking up on their own supplies of cloth. Fabric that could not be carried as *pacotilles* was buried in other kinds of cargo to avoid detection at the docks. Even calico locked in company warehouses mysteriously disappeared under the blind eyes of corrupt officials.[69] Once such contraband branched off from the official market, it found its way to local ports and spread inland from Rennes and other Breton towns to Normandy, the Loire Valley, and the Paris basin. On occasion, the inward diffusion was facilitated by high-ranking officials who could not resist dipping illegally into the reexport market. The intendant of Brittany instructed his subdelegate in Nantes to send him "eight or ten beautiful cravats" as well as pieces of embroidered cloth for some of his female friends in Paris.[70] In the 1750s, rumor had it that the finance minister himself, Jean-Baptiste de Machault d'Arnouville, was secretly financing the expenses of the royal court with money from the illicit trade in Company cloth.[71]

The stream of contraband diverted from the Indian reexport market was, however, nothing compared to the European-based trade in illicit knockoffs (Figure 2.4). Whereas today we associate Asia with the mass production of counterfeit Western goods (think fake "Nike" sneakers and designer handbags made in China), in the eighteenth century it was the *Europeans* who manufactured facsimiles of fashionable *Asian* products, particularly Indian calico. When France, England, Spain, and Prussia banned imports of calico, European manufacturers in areas beyond the reach of prohibitionist regimes stepped up their efforts to produce imitations. In England, where despite the prohibition on imports, the domestic printing of white Indian cloth, local linen, and cotton-linen mixtures was permitted, import substitution—the replacement of regulated or taxed imports with domestically manufactured goods—encouraged the growth of a national cotton industry whose eventual mechanization would usher in the Industrial Revolution.[72] In France, import substitution occurred as well. But because the French ban applied to importation *and* domestic production, such import substitution took place entirely within the confines of the black market.

Europe's first calico manufactories arose in the ancient Mediterranean city of Marseille, where, as early as the 1670s, city merchants began hiring Armenians who knew how to imprint color on white cotton cloth "as done in the Levant and Persia."[73] When prohibition hit in 1686, the free port of Marseille was the only French city exempted from its strictures, and its calico market continued to develop. Not only did city merchants clandestinely distribute genuine Indian cottons that were supposed to be reexported to other parts of the world, they churned out innumerable bolts of their own copies, smuggling both genuine and ersatz products into Aix, the distribution center for southern France. The Marseille-Aix axis introduced an estimated 100,000 pieces of calico a year into France, 80 percent of them fraudulent. From Aix the cloth spread south to Toulon,

Figure 2.4. Calico knockoffs. Although produced by special permission in Paris, these crude knockoffs are comparable to low-end illicit calicoes. *Le Journal Oeconomique,* June 1755 (144–146). Bibliothèque Nationale de France.

east to Fréjus, and west to the Beaucaire fair and the Comtat Venaissin. Throughout the south, common folk snapped up cheap local fabric while elites splurged on authentic material.[74]

The greatest influx of calicoes came from east of the perimeter of the French prohibition zone, where tobacco bound for the underground also accumulated. Several cities with no restrictions on production were situated dangerously close to the French interior, including Strasbourg and Mulhouse (an independent city-republic enclaved in Alsace), as well as Basle, Neuchâtel, and Geneva (all located in present-day Switzerland). In the Swiss cities, the industry had taken root as early as the late seventeenth century. After the revocation of the Edict of Nantes in 1685, French Protestants from the southern provinces of Provence, Dauphiné, and Languedoc, where the calico trade had spread from Marseille, flocked to Switzerland to continue their craft in exile. The intention of the revocation was not to root out calico manufacturers—government officials could not have known at the time that Protestants were disproportionately involved in the trade—but that was certainly the edict's effect as Protestant textile workers fled the kingdom.[75] A year later, the ban on Indian cloth sent more waves of workers and manufacturers to Switzerland and, consequently, a formidable trade developed across the border. The overlapping Protestant and calico diasporas, dubbed respectively (and retrospectively) the "Protestant" and "Indian cloth internationals," generated a thick web of commercial relations that spanned from London, Amsterdam, and Geneva to Marseille, Aix, and Montpellier. When the calico ban was lifted in 1759, many Swiss Protestants migrated back to France to establish workshops.

The trade in Geneva and Neuchâtel illustrates the kinds of networks through which knockoffs passed to reach the French interior. In Geneva, a good-sized city at mid-century, the calico business boomed to become the town's first modern industry.[76] Unlike the putting-out system by which merchants traveled the countryside supplying raw wool to cottagers who spun it into yarn and then shuttled the yarn to weavers, calico merchants bought plain white cotton cloth at Lorient or from Swiss producers and delivered the raw material, dyes, and mordants to laborers assembled in gigantic workshops beyond the reach of the city's guilds. Like tobacco manufactories, these workshops resembled the future factories of the Industrial Revolution in their scale and division of labor (and have thus been characterized as "protofactories"), although they did not possess the same degree of mechanization as the textile mills of the nineteenth century.[77] Calico was fabricated in large buildings where hundreds of employees toiled to complete all phases of production. Under a single roof, cotton was washed, stretched, and printed or painted and then pressed, smoothed, and sanitized. As much as 20 percent of the manual labor force of Geneva, some two to three thousand men, women, and children, worked in one of several calico plants to produce enormous quantities of cloth that were sold either legally in Switzerland, Savoy, and Italy or illegally in France. To supply the French underground, Genevan merchants hired smugglers to move the material to the nearby cities of Lyon and Grenoble or run it deeper into the kingdom to Provence and Languedoc. Towns as far as Montpellier were well stocked with Swiss-made "Indian" cloth.

A different pattern of diffusion emanated from Neuchâtel, home to the calico firm Fabrique-Neuve. Working in partnership with the greatest calico merchants in Europe, Pourtalès and company, Fabrique-Neuve employed 700 laborers and distributed its product to southern Germany, the provinces of eastern France that lay outside the prohibition zone such as Alsace and Franche-Comté, and the cities of Nancy and Bar-le-Duc in Lorraine. From pivot points along the French customs border, calico was smuggled into the provinces of Champagne and Burgundy and taken as far as Paris and Versailles. The roads extending west from Bar-le-Duc were lined with carts illegally trundling bundles of calico to the French capital.[78]

In sum, then, two different kinds of calico flowed illegally into France: "genuine" Indian cloth, which seeped in from the legitimate reexport market, and European facsimiles, the bulk of the contraband trade. All told, an estimated 16 million lt worth of calico was illegally consumed in metropolitan France every year during the ban.[79] After the ban was lifted in 1759, a domestic calico industry boomed in the hexagon, as Swiss firms transplanted themselves onto French soil.[80] Smuggling did not cease, however, because the ban was replaced by a 25 percent tariff that still made it worthwhile to circumvent customs. In fact, replacing the ban with a high import duty may have encouraged smuggling, since untaxed Swiss calico could easily infiltrate an open domestic market by passing for legal French-made cloth.

In an era of intense European military and commercial rivalry, Louis XIV and his successors made two particularly bold interventions in the world economy. Eagerly looking west, across the Atlantic to the Americas, they established a state monopoly on tobacco and marketed millions of pounds of aromatic Chesapeake Bay leaf to French consumers. Anxiously gazing east, beyond the Levant to South Asia, they built a formidable protectionist wall, prohibiting the importation, production, and consumption of vivid Indian cloth. In the long run, both policies largely succeeded in their aims. The tobacco monopoly further fiscalized French consumption, providing the French fiscal-military state with additional revenue with which to fund wars and war-generated debt. And the calico prohibition protected national textile producers, defending a critical sector of the domestic economy against overseas and foreign competition.

At the same time, however, both interventions had the unintended effect of globalizing black markets. Stimulating the growth of parallel markets in import substitutes for official state tobacco and banned overseas cloth, the French monopoly and prohibition activated a dramatic expansion in the geographic reach of the French underground, which now took in New World tobacco, in both its pure and hybrid forms, and Indian cotton, in both its original and copied designs. Whether genuine, imitation, or, as with blended tobacco, a mixture of both, "New World" tobacco and "Indian" calico pooled in a vast reservoir from the Netherlands to Savoy, whence smugglers ran them into the French interior and peddled them to avid consumers.

Twenty miles west of that contraband reservoir lay Saint-Étienne-de-Saint-Geoirs, the small French town where Louis Mandrin was born in 1725. After a series of calamities ruined his family's legitimate business, he abandoned his village, followed the river of contraband upstream, and crossed the border into the foreign kingdom of Sardinia. There, he would join a gang of hardened traffickers and plunge into the underground before resurfacing with a vengeance in his native kingdom.

3

The Making of a Smuggler

From the summer of 1754 to the spring of 1755, Louis Mandrin organized a series of outrageously daring smuggling expeditions that would make him the most famous criminal of his day. Although little is known about the formative years of his career, we catch an early glimpse of him on an August evening in 1753 strolling across the border from France into Savoy, the southern tip of the contraband corridor that stretched up to the North Sea. No description of what he looked like that summer evening exists, but police bulletins issued little more than a year later described him in the following terms:

> Louis Mandrin of St. Étienne de St. Geoirs in Dauphiné, around 30 years old, five feet four inches tall, well proportioned, long curly blond hair that he wears in a ponytail, he is dressed rather nicely, he wears a chapeau festooned with gold trim.

> Louis Mandrin of St. Étienne de St. Geoirs in Dauphiné, election of Romans, around thirty years old, five feet four inches tall [and] well proportioned, shoulders a bit broad, white, marked with some red spots, and a little pocked with smallpox, sharply cleaved gray eyes, brown eyebrows, same color hair that he usually wears in a ponytail or simply tied with a ribbon, large forehead, aquiline nose, small mouth, cleft chin. Last August the said Mandrin wore a gray wool coat with copper buttons called Pinchbeck and a chapeau with festooned gold trim.[1]

Lacking formalized methods of description, police bulletins in the middle of the eighteenth century were highly subjective—was his hair blond or brown?—but an eyewitness corroborated Mandrin's penchant for fine apparel, remarking that while most smugglers in his gang were "poorly dressed" in simple Savoyard clothing, he wore "a gray wool coat, a red velvet jacket with little squares, a silk handkerchief around his neck, a stolen chapeau with gold trim, [and] a wide belt to which was attached a hunting knife . . . and a pair of pistols."[2]

In early August 1753, as Mandrin ascended the Francis I Bridge that arched across the Guiers River dividing the town of Pont-de-Beauvoisin into its French and Savoyard halves, he did not yet possess the festooned hat on which observers would invariably comment, but it is safe to say that he was a young man of twenty-eight, not too tall but "well proportioned," probably nicely dressed, and certainly well armed. At the bridge's apex, he walked past the stone marking the border between the two kingdoms and descended to the eastern riverbank (Figure 3.1). After setting foot on Savoyard soil, he stopped at the first shop on the right and glared at a man sitting at the door. "Are you on the side of Monsieur de la Motte and Mongirod?" he asked menacingly. The shopkeeper, a certain Sieur Pierre who had lived in this border town all his

Figure 3.1. Francis I Bridge over the Guiers in Pont-de-Beauvoisin. Victor Cassien and Alexandre Debelle, *Album du Dauphiné*, 4 vols. (Grenoble: Prudhomme, 1835–1839; reprinted in Grenoble: Éditions des 4 Seigneurs, 1967), I, planche 32, 162–163.

life and observed Mandrin "for some time," was well aware of the meaning behind this question. He knew that the men to whom Mandrin alluded worked for the General Farm in French Pont-de-Beauvoisin: La Motte as a high-ranking controller and Mongirod as captain of the brigade. And he knew that a rash of deadly skirmishes in which Mandrin had been involved had broken out along the border in recent weeks.

Wanting no part in the conflict, Pierre answered Mandrin's question judiciously, too judiciously for his own good. The shopkeeper affirmed that Mandrin was entitled to conduct his affairs any way he wished but that he "did not meddle in anything" or "take anyone's side." The reply infuriated Mandrin, who saw no place for neutrality in the battle against the Farm. After a heated exchange of words, Mandrin set upon the shopkeeper, brandishing a pocketknife in one hand and a pistol in the other. Pierre dashed into his shop to get his musket, but the levelheaded woman inside persuaded him not to go back out. Mandrin stood his ground, pistol in hand. Only when it was clear that Pierre was not going to reappear did he let the affair drop and continue on his way. He would have ample opportunity in the days ahead to rough up allies of the General Farm.[3]

Mandrin's act of aggression on that August evening reflected widespread hostility to the Farm. Consumption taxes were loathed everywhere in early modern Europe, but in France, where they were collected by tax farmers, they generated particularly strong resentment. Tax farming created the not altogether false impression that tax revenues were being diverted from their legitimate destination, the royal treasury, into the pockets of greedy financiers. Because royal finances were cloaked in secrecy, speculation about tax farmers skimming off the top ran rampant, cultivating the perception of them as bloodsuckers preying on a defenseless population. Tax farming was, however, only part of the problem. Perhaps more disturbing still to French subjects was that certain consumption taxes were not really taxes at all, but monopolies on popular consumer goods. The English did not love their excise taxes, but excise men dealt with but a few merchants and producers, not the consuming public at large; merchants paid the duties and passed what they could on to consumers by raising prices. In France, by contrast, consumers bought salt and tobacco in state retail shops run by the Farm and protected by Farm police. Monopoly revenue was collected at widely exposed points of purchase rather than partially hidden points of production. Indeed, it would be difficult to imagine a more conspicuous form of raising taxes than establishing monopolies on consumer goods and entrusting their management to financiers who ran them for a profit with the assistance of a large semiprivate paramilitary force. The antipathy generated by such an arrangement only encouraged smuggling and the violence associated with it.

Beyond popular resentment of the Farm, however, Mandrin had personal reasons for hating the Farmers General. To fully comprehend why he became a knife-wielding, pistol-packing smuggler who attacked men like Pierre for their refusal to take part in the battle against the Farm, we must begin at the beginning. We must begin with his family.

A Fallen Merchant

Louis Mandrin was not born into a life of crime, nor was he pushed into it by abject poverty. He came from "one of the oldest and best families of Saint-Étienne," a small town in the border province of Dauphiné.[4] Like the patriarchs who preceded him, he was expected to take his father's business in hand and safeguard the family's good name, prominently established in this rural burg over the course of several generations. At his birth on 11 February 1725, no one could have predicted that the first son of local notable François-Antoine Mandrin would stray so far from the path marked out for him. Were it not for a premature death, the vagaries of war and peace, and the pitfalls of French court capitalism, he might have led a quiet, respectable, wholly unremarkable life.

The intendant of Dauphiné could well have been describing Mandrin's birthplace when he wrote that the people of this remote province were "in general very poor, having few resources for commerce." "Weighed down at various times by many calamities, their land subjugated to onerous dues, they live in great misery."[5] Misery was certainly no stranger in Saint-Étienne. A rustic town of some 1,300 souls tucked in the valley of St. Geoirs, whose wooded hills sloped upward toward the Alps, Saint-Étienne was composed mainly of illiterate peasants who eked out an existence on the land by growing wheat, rye, and oats and raising mules, cows, pigs, and goats. The village was also home to a smattering of artisans: a couple of bakers and tavern keepers, some cobblers and tailors, and a few masons, carpenters, and blacksmiths.[6]

But we should not dismiss Saint-Étienne out of hand. It was situated in the fertile plaine de Bièvre, a grain belt from which food was exported to the prosperous city of Grenoble, capital of the province. In addition to the laborers who constituted the majority of its population, Saint-Étienne boasted a number of relatively secure landowners and merchants who were educated and comfortably ensconced at the summit of small-town life. This was the social echelon into which Louis Mandrin was fortunate enough to have been born. Not only did his mother, Marguerite Veyron-Churlet, come from a well-off merchant family, but his father, François-Antoine, was a landowner, horse dealer, and merchant who, like most village traders of the day, bought and sold a little bit of everything—fabric, clothing accessories, hardware, tools, jewelry, wax, wine, eau-de-vie. It is quite possible that Mandrin *père* dabbled in contraband as well, but the complete absence of a paper trail suggests that if he did so, he was not sufficiently active to draw the attention of French authorities. Legally or illegally, he acquired what merchandise he could at local markets and fairs and turned it over for a profit. If the great commercial cities of the wider region (Lyon, Geneva, Turin, Marseille) were beyond his reach, his travels along the rugged byways of Dauphiné were fruitful enough to support one of the best families in town.

The Mandrins had resided in Saint-Étienne since 1617. Their shop was on the ground floor of an impressive three-story structure built by a noble family in the sixteenth century and sold to the Mandrins in 1644 for the tidy sum of 1,260 lt. Like its original owners, the house was invested with noble status, which exempted its inhabitants from taxes and militia service. The finely appointed residence stood at the center of town, right across the street from the market. On market days, when Louis was not busy helping his father in the shop, he must have played in the square as men and women haggled over grain, vegetables, livestock, dairy products, and more. This boy was no stranger to commerce.[7]

Under ordinary circumstances, Louis Mandrin ought to have taken the helm of the family business, found a local woman to wed, produced gainful offspring, and assumed an honorable place among the village elders until death and interment in the sacred soil of the church cemetery. But caught in the treacherous undertow of downward social mobility that lurks even in the best of times, he instead presided over the precipitous decline of his family. Denied legitimate paths to respectability, he abdicated his position as head of household and sought refuge in the underground economy. Literate, well traveled, and familiar with the ways of commerce, he would soon reappear, like some wayward phoenix, on the other side of the border—and on the other side of the law.

As for many children, Mandrin's misfortunes began with the premature death of a parent. François-Antoine Mandrin, his father and custodian of the family business, expired in 1742 at the age of forty-three and so thrust seventeen-year-old Louis, the eldest of eight children, into the position of head of household. Barely old enough to take the reins of the family, Louis carried on the trade, frequenting local fairs and traveling to large commercial centers such as Puy-en-Velay. He bought land, leased the family meadows, traded livestock, and built stables. As head of a substantial household, he took his place among other notables in town meetings.

It was to fulfill his promise as a duty-bound heir and successful merchant that Louis engaged in a major commercial venture in 1748, a risky endeavor that would haunt the rest of his days. Why he took on such a scheme in the first place is not quite clear. His biographers, pointing to a tempestuous land dispute and a bloody bout with a creditor, claim that he was desperate to revive a languishing business.[8] It is equally plausible that in taking on this enterprise Louis was acting out of ambition, hoping to gain entry into the fabulously lucrative world of war finance. In any case, he staked his fortune on an army contract to provision French troops in northern Italy. France had been engaged in the War of Austrian Succession since 1740, and its tens of thousands of soldiers operating east of Nice required food.[9]

Mandrin had some experience in this line of work. A year earlier, when the army requisitioned six mules from his hometown, the municipal assembly charged "sieur Louis Mandrin . . . merchant of St. Étienne" with the task of delivering them to Romans, about sixty miles to the southeast.[10] He successfully completed the mission and pocketed a modest sum for his efforts. The new venture was meant to unfold on a much grander scale. Rather than fulfilling a minor military requisition, he committed himself to a commercial contract with an established bank, Archimbaud, Dubois, and company of Lyon, which subcontracted military supply services from the Farmers General. (The Farmers had a hand in army provisioning as well as tax collection.) The contract stipulated that Mandrin would supply the troops of the maréchal de Belle-Isle in the Italian Alps. To finance the venture, he pooled money with two associates, Pierre Jacquier, a merchant from Saint-Hilaire, and Claude

Brissaud, from his hometown of Saint-Étienne, to acquire ninety-seven pack mules that were to be loaded with food and taken to the soldiers.

This was not some half-baked scheme. The families of some of the kingdom's wealthiest financiers had started out as army provisioners, most notably the famed Pâris brothers, who hailed from the town of Moirans, just down the road from Saint-Étienne.[11] Sons of a merchant tavern keeper who made his fortune supplying bread to the army during the Nine Years' War (1688–1697), the elder brothers (Antoine and Claude) had continued their father's work during the War of the Spanish Succession (1701–1713) and invested their profits in status-boosting royal offices. Trained in the business, the younger brothers (Joseph and Jean) embarked on careers in finance that carried them all the way to the court of Versailles, where they enjoyed the protection of none other than the Marquise de Pompadour, Louis XV's powerful mistress. From a rustic village in Dauphiné to the splendid halls of Versailles: here was a local success story of such spectacular proportions that one cannot help but wonder whether Mandrin had it in mind when he set out for Italy. At the very least, he must have been aware of the immense profits to be had through military supply. Although his father may not have dared to take on an enterprise of this scale, it was not unreasonable for a young merchant with some experience to undertake such an endeavor in hopes of receiving a substantial return on his investment. Windfalls were common in the high-stakes world of court capitalism, where nobles, financiers, and merchants wheeled and dealed in government contracts and loans.

In May 1748, the three partners set out with their ninety-seven mules, traveling down the Rhône Valley and eastward to Nice, whence Mandrin soldiered on alone to deliver rice, flour, and bread to a chain of camps along the mountainous coast. Then disaster struck. Just when it looked like the venture was going to pay off, the worst that can befall an army contractor befell Louis Mandrin: peace broke out. With the European powers expected to sign the treaty of Aix-la-Chapelle (21 January 1749), the maréchal de Belle-Isle abruptly discharged his soldiers. No commanding officer was willing to pay for provisions now that the war was coming to an end. Faced with the grim commercial prospect of peace, Mandrin had no choice but to abort the enterprise and head home with his mules. On the journey back to Saint-Étienne, the already unfortunate situation became an unmitigated catastrophe as mule after mule fell ill. With scores of mules afflicted, Mandrin cut his losses and sold a number of them on the poorest of terms. Others died on the long trek home. By the time he arrived at the gates of his natal village, Mandrin was leading a paltry pack of sixteen mules, out of the original ninety-seven, of which his partners would claim eleven.

The venture was a financial calamity. The first contract, of 1747, had stipulated that Mandrin would be reimbursed if any of the mules were to die, but no such clause existed in the Italian contract. Only in cases where mules had been killed by the enemy or drowned while crossing rivers would the merchants be compensated. Moreover, the money they were owed by supply officers for provisions that had been successfully delivered was not forthcoming. Mandrin petitioned the Farmers General who oversaw the contract, but his request was denied. The war was over, and royal finances were stretched thin, leaving supply merchants to fend for themselves. This was always the great risk in military contracting. Jean Pâris had avoided a similar fate at the end of the Nine Years' War by sending his sons to Paris to collect his debts. With the help of a cousin in the cloth trade, the brothers made contacts within the finance ministry and were able to recuperate what they were owed. But Mandrin had no inside connections to the clubby world of Parisian finance. His debts went unpaid and his losses unreimbursed. What might have been a prosperous career was cut short by the end of a war and the merciless crony capitalism of the French fiscal state.[12]

An Apprenticeship in Crime

In the aftermath of the ill-fated Italian venture, the Mandrin family business foundered, and the brothers descended into a local criminal underworld. The family's turn to the illicit was not all that unusual, for crime was ubiquitous in eighteenth-century France. Roughly a quarter of the population lived without food security, and such precariousness produced widespread delinquency, especially among young single men. High unemployment and low wages sent workers scrambling to make ends meet in a makeshift economy of seasonal migration, begging, theft, and smuggling.[13] This was the hardscrabble world into which the Mandrin brothers sank after Louis's ruinous foray into war provisioning. Yet, as Mandrin's sartorial predilections indicated, the brothers stood out from the majority of unfortunates in the makeshift economy for having once enjoyed the privileges of education, property, and elevated social status. In the wake of financial ruin, the scion of this formerly reputable family began consorting with a whole new element. Louis's parents had been "quite decent and respectable," lamented one local parish priest, "[b]ut this quick-witted young man had, in his youth, the misfortune to hang around with lost people."[14]

It is impossible to date the family's initial turn toward crime, but we know that by 1753 the law was catching up to them. In that single year, brothers Louis, Pierre, and Claude Mandrin were charged with serious offenses. They had had prior run-ins with the law—in 1749, a judge sentenced them to a stiff fine for plundering the barn of one of their tenants—but such petty theft was child's play compared to the criminal activities they now undertook. First, Pierre and Claude hatched a plot to rob the church of Saint-Étienne. Although theft was by far the most common crime in eighteenth-century France, church robbery was anything but banal. As tiny islands of wealth in a vast sea of poverty, churches made tempting targets, but stealing from the house of God was punished severely as a wicked act of sacrilege.[15] Undaunted, the brothers' accomplice, Ennemond Diot, a mattress maker from Irigny, entered the town church on the afternoon of 3 January 1753. After waiting for parishioners to leave, he broke into two money chests, one "for the souls of purgatory" and the other for church repairs. The caper might have come off but for a sacristan still on the premises who spotted the stranger. Diot was arrested and promptly sentenced to life in the galleys. Pierre and Claude escaped capture but were tried in absentia and found guilty. Determined to prevent word of his brothers' ignominious convictions from spreading through the community, Louis asked the priest of Saint-Étienne to refrain from announcing the verdicts from the pulpit. When the cleric ignored his plea and informed the whole town, Louis took revenge by uprooting the priest's saplings and vines and harassing the townspeople who had assisted the prosecution.

The same year Pierre and Claude were convicted of robbery, Louis and Pierre were charged with counterfeiting, a capital crime because it violated one of the most basic rights of the monarchy, that of striking coinage. Spending little time in his natal town, Louis evaded arrest, but Pierre was captured and hauled before a criminal court. On the basis of a single letter of denunciation from the curé of Brion, the court found him guilty and sentenced him to hang. On 21 July 1753, Pierre was executed on the place de Breuil in Grenoble. His older brother would not forget.

Louis had another run-in with the law that year, this time for murder. The violent case began when a young man named Benoît Brissaud was called up for militia service in the nearby parish of Izeaux. Like many peasants in Dauphiné, where resistance to conscription was deeply ingrained, Brissaud failed to show up for duty.[16] That would have been the end of the story but for a repressive law governing the royal militia: any man selected for service could exempt himself by capturing a known draft dodger. This was the law that prompted Pierre Roux, a recent conscript, to pursue Benoît Brissaud in an effort to free himself from the obligation to serve. Brissaud's father, Claude, who had been one of Mandrin's associates in the Italian venture, must have asked Louis for protection when he learned that Roux was after his son. Although Mandrin and Brissaud had been embroiled in a lawsuit over their failed enterprise, Louis agreed to help (probably after working out some kind of financial arrangement). On 30 March 1753, Mandrin, Benoît Brissaud, and two other Saint-Étienne natives, Antoine Sauze and Pierre Fleuret, confronted the Roux brothers on the outskirts of town. In a ruthless assault, Mandrin's posse bludgeoned the Rouxes with their rifles, killing Joseph and leaving François for dead (Pierre presumably escaped). Sauze and Brissaud were subsequently arrested while Mandrin and Fleuret (the latter appropriately nicknamed "Always Running") took flight. All four were put on trial for the murder of the brothers Roux.

Like theft, violence was part of everyday life in early modern Europe: defenseless children were beaten at home; intoxicated laborers brawled in taverns; rival youth gangs clashed at rural fairs; and proud nobles dueled in town and country.[17] Raised in an honor society that prized family reputation, men of all social ranks were easily offended and quick to take revenge. And yet, although physical scuffles were common enough that many assailants were never formally charged, outright murder like that of the brothers Roux was rare and vigorously prosecuted. Hence, on 21 July 1753, the same day Pierre Mandrin was executed for counterfeiting, the parlement of Grenoble sentenced Benoît Brissaud to be hanged and Pierre Fleuret and Antoine Sauze to the galleys. Louis Mandrin received the most severe sentence of all: death by the wheel. He was to be led by the executioner "to the said place du Breuil to have there on the scaffold, which will be erected to this effect, his arms, legs, thighs, and back broken and then to be put on a wheel, his face turned toward heaven, to remain there as long as it will please God to let him live."[18] Mandrin would later come face-to-face with the executioner, but for the moment he evaded capture, dodged the wheel, and, with nothing to lose but the death sentence hanging over his head, burrowed deeper into the criminal underground.

To church robbery, counterfeiting, and murder must be added one more crime of the brothers Mandrin: smuggling. In the years after the Italian debacle, Louis assumed a central role in a transnational smuggling ring based across the border in Savoy. The origins of this operation remain obscure but not impossible to discern, as indirect evidence points to a web of borderland traffickers. Joseph "the Blond" Jourdan, who had helped contrive the church robbery, was convicted of smuggling in 1754. Pierre Mandrin, arrested and temporarily incarcerated for smuggling, later claimed that he moved to Conflans in Savoy, a haven for traffickers, when his family fell on hard times in 1751. Joseph Patouille, an associate of Brissaud and Fleuret, the men who had helped murder the Roux brothers, lived in Conflans at the same time as Pierre.[19]

On the lam since his murder conviction, Louis Mandrin appears to have moved across the border to the contraband hub of Pont-de-Beauvoisin, where he joined forces with one Jean Bélissard aka "le Pays" (or the "home country"), an experienced trafficker about five years his senior. Born in Brion, Dauphiné, just a few miles from Mandrin's natal village, Bélissard served in the Sardinian army during the War of Austrian Succession, always good training for the underground, and then in the militia of Bressieux, home to Joseph "the Blond" Jourdan, church robber and convicted smuggler. At some point after the war, Bélissard and Mandrin, the two border-hopping Dauphinois, teamed up with several others to smuggle out of Savoy. We can see this band in action on 4 July 1753, in Mandrin's first recorded act of violence against the General Farm. On that summer day, during a return run from the Dombes, an enclave north of Lyon, Mandrin, Bélissard, and sixteen others stumbled across two Farm guards just outside of French Pont-de-Beauvoisin. According to the official report, the gang ordered the men to drop their weapons. Outnumbered, the guards did as they were told, fell to their knees, and begged for mercy. The smugglers fired off a round of shots, wounding at least one of the guards, who pleaded for a moment "to commend himself to God." Unmoved, gang members fired again, killed both men, and stripped the corpses of valuables.[20]

A few weeks later, on 23 July, two days after Pierre Mandrin was hanged for counterfeiting and Louis Mandrin sentenced in absentia to the wheel, Bélissard and a gang of eight or nine men stormed across the bridge from Savoy to the French side of Pont-de-Beauvoisin to rescue a captured comrade, Gabriel Degat aka "Curly," who, recently nabbed for smuggling, was tied up in the stables of La Motte, the highest-ranking Farm official in town. Bound by an unwritten code of honor that enjoined traffickers to rescue their own, Bélissard's band flew across the Guiers, guns blazing. In a feat of astonishing audacity, the men attacked the guards posted at La Motte's stables, secured the release of their comrade, and fought their way back over the bridge to Savoy. When the dust settled, crowds formed on the banks of the river to tally the damage: two French agents dead and one wounded; no smugglers hurt. Having returned safely to Savoy, the band spent the rest of the day taunting the guards across the river. When a French soldier dared to cross the bridge, Curly took his revenge by assaulting him with a heavy wooden log.[21]

French officials were aghast. The intendant of Dauphiné and the bishop of Valence feared that Bélissard's incursion into France that day portended higher levels of violence in the conflict between Farm and smuggler. Just days after the street battle in Pont-de-Beauvoisin, Mandrin would traverse the Francis I Bridge into Savoy and harass Pierre the shopkeeper for his neutrality amid growing conflict.

Savoy: The Wild East

Surveying the province that was to be his new home, Mandrin must have been aware of the Alpine region's peculiar political and economic status. Savoy, it bears repeating, was not part of France in the eighteenth century. Lying east of the French border, the province belonged to the kingdom of Sardinia, a patchwork monarchy that encompassed the duchy of Savoy, Piedmont in northwestern Italy, Nice in what is today the southeastern corner of France, and the Mediterranean island of Sardinia. Because the original core of this monarchy, Savoy, was alpine, landlocked, and poor, its people have long been characterized as isolated and immobile, even backward. A generation of local research suggests, however, that Savoyards were far more active than once thought.[22] Tons of merchandise moved through this province, which stood at the crossroads of two ancient trade routes: one running north-south to link the Netherlands with Italy via the Rhine Valley and Geneva and the other east-west, joining Italy and Spain via the south of France. Caravans of mule-drawn carts, brimming with goods from Holland, Britain, and Switzerland, rolled down from the north and snaked through the Savoyard Alps, bound for points southwest (Grenoble, Lyon, and by extension, Aix, Beaucaire, and Marseille) and southeast (Turin, Milan, and beyond). While finished products flowed downward into Savoy, agricultural goods, raw textiles, and leather traveled northeast from French Dauphiné into Savoy and on to Geneva or Turin. (See Figure 5.1.)

Savoyards were hardly content to sit and watch this commerce go by. Every autumn before the first fall of snow, tens of thousands of men and women—upwards of 10 percent of the population—descended from the mountains to journey far and wide in search of employment. They ventured west to Dauphiné, south to Italy and Provence, and north to Switzerland, Alsace, and the Holy Roman Empire. With little more than a provisional passport (usually a letter of identification from a parish priest), they used networks of family and friends to find jobs as agricultural workers in the Rhône Valley, textile laborers in Lyon, and domestic servants, water carriers, construction workers, and errand-goers in any town that would have them. In conjunction with this seasonal migration, legions of Savoyard peddlers with packs on their backs and, if lucky, mules at their sides, established long-distance trade networks, hawking bits of merchandise at fairs, in front of churches, or door-to-door in areas where urban markets had yet to penetrate. Trudging across this multinational—nay, "global"—corner of Europe, they sold everything from fabric and accessories to pots and pans to spices and remedies.[23] Entangled in this migration was a large contingent of smugglers, many of whom were scarcely distinguishable from the merchants, cart drivers, and peddlers with whom they shared the road and who often operated on the fringes of the law themselves.

As Mandrin would discover, Savoy was a smugglers' paradise. In economics jargon, it was an ideal "supply state" from which to provision the hungry "market state" of France.[24] To the north, Savoyards had easy access to Swiss markets in tobacco and calico, goods that were monopolized and prohibited in France but circulated widely—and cheaply—in Geneva and the Swiss pays de Vaud. Smugglers could haul all the calico and tobacco they wanted across the frontier into Savoy at little cost, because the border between Savoy and Geneva was wide open (thanks to the 1603 Treaty of Saint-Julien). Once back home, Savoy-based traffickers stockpiled their wares, secreted them across the porous French border to the west, and dashed home again, their purses bulging with coin. Opportunities abounded for anyone willing to risk a quick run across the frontier.

Savoyard authorities did not seem to mind that the province pulsed with contraband. Occasionally, under pressure from France, ministers in Turin sent orders to have violent traffickers arrested, but such commands were largely ignored by local officials, many of whom were themselves complicit in the traffic. Bélissard was arrested in Savoyard Pont-de-Beauvoisin only to escape from the Chambéry prison, no doubt with the help of his guards. Smugglers were confident that in Savoy they could conduct business with impunity.

Owing to a pervasive "borderland mentality" whereby national identity fluctuated, illicit commerce irrigated the local economy, and fiscal and customs law commanded little respect, smugglers knew they could count on locals to provide credit, horses, lodging, food and drink, and safe places to stash coin.[25] Savoyards from all walks of life were keenly aware of the extent to which the cash-starved region benefited from the illicit riches that smugglers brought back with them to spend on everything from stocks of inventory to food, drink, and lodging to the hiring of local wage laborers ("domestics") for contraband excursions. "All of Savoy is for them," wrote the French consul in Geneva of the traffickers. "They spend prodigiously with a generosity and abundance that wins the hearts and minds of the people, who find in such lavish expenditure a resource against their poverty." In this notoriously poor mountain province, the freewheeling spending of traffickers injected a desperately needed infusion of cash. And the allegiance of the few who were not won over by such largesse was gained though fear. The smugglers "spread a lot of money around, which they spend even more easily than they earn. Some [Savoyards] are drawn by the lure of profit and accept them, others fear the violence perpetrated by these scoundrels." Whether from pecuniary interest or fright, no one was about to get in their way, including the Sardinian army. "There is in all of Savoy only one regiment of Dragoons . . . and it does not make the slightest move" against them. Mandrin and his lieutenant spent eight days in Carouge and no one attempted to arrest them, though nothing "would have been easier if the Governor of Savoy had given orders."[26]

On top of all this, Savoy was saturated with arms and men who knew how to use them. Peasants in the eighteenth century routinely carried knives in their pockets and walking sticks at their side. But they also had access to an array of military surplus (pikes, maces, battle-axes, swords, and muskets), especially in war zones like Savoy, which was an active military theater in the first half of the eighteenth century. During and after the War of Austrian Succession (1740–1748), French and Spanish forces filled the province with guns that, thanks to discharged soldiers and deserters who kept or sold them upon returning to civilian life, spilled into the population at large. At mid-century, any Savoyard wishing to arm himself with more than a walking stick had ready access to an abundance of firearms. The French Farm was not only outnumbered. It was outgunned.[27]

In such an environment, legions of smugglers—amateur and professional, French and Savoyard, armed and unarmed—plied their trade along the French-Savoyard border. It is impossible to know with certainty how many peasants took an occasional hop across the frontier with some tobacco on their backs or how many peddlers buried a bit of calico in their saddlebags to turn a quick profit. As for the professionals engaged in the dangerous high-volume trade, often former soldiers, deserters, or fugitives from justice, the intendant of Dauphiné calculated in the 1730s that 400 traffickers were operating across the border in armed gangs of forty to sixty.[28] Their numbers would rise in the decades that followed.

Mandrin thrived in the "wild east" of Savoy. A moving target (for historians as well as the Farm), he had more than one base of operations. Before the glory days of his expeditions in 1754–1755, the fallen merchant could be found in the rough-and-tumble border town of Pont-de-Beauvoisin. A bustling burg at the crossroads of Geneva, Grenoble, Lyon, and Turin, Pont-de-Beauvoisin was really two towns in one. The Guiers, a shallow river that traced the crooked border between France and Savoy, divided the settlement into two politically distinct towns. Although the narrow Francis I Bridge connected the riverbanks, binding the communities into a single parish with a shared church, the political border shaped the lives of both in dramatically different ways. On the western bank, French Pont-de-Beauvoisin served as a strategic outpost of the mightiest kingdom on the continent of Europe. Fortified with far more state offices and military units than interior towns of the same size, it possessed a subdelegate who reported directly to the intendant of Dauphiné, a corps of mounted police, a military garrison, and a bureau of the General Farm, complete with a high-ranking controller and a brigade of guards.[29]

On the eastern bank, in stark contrast, Savoyard Pont-de-Beauvoisin was ruled with a blind eye by the court of Turin. With the tacit approval of authorities, who tolerated smugglers as long as they did not aggress against local residents, the town became a haven for gun-toting smugglers of tobacco, calico, and other taxed or regulated goods.[30] Trafficking was the lifeblood of the Savoyard side of town, which crawled with illicit traders from small-fry who ate and drank at taverns such as the White Cross and Notre Dame (Mandrin's favorite haunt) to town notables who directed smuggling operations like Mafia dons.[31] François Cretet, a local merchant-banker with ties to the Savoyard senate, was knee-deep in the underground calico trade, "informing [smugglers] of everything" and watching over the spoils of Mandrin's associate, Jean Bélissard.[32] Launched by illicit trade, the Cretet clan would spawn such prominent descendants as the comte de Champmol, who rose to the position of state minister under Napoleon and whose remains still rest in the Pantheon.[33]

At the height of his career, after garnering a measure of wealth and fame, Mandrin seems to have spent less time in Pont-de-Beauvoisin and more in Carouge and at a rural estate, the château de Rochefort. The small town of Carouge had much to offer. The smuggling chief lodged at the Silver Lion, whose proprietor, a certain Gauthier, graciously supplied him with food, money, and arms and took care of his mail. (If you knew the secret password "Toiry," Gauthier would treat you, too, as one of his own.) Conveniently situated in northern Savoy, Carouge was a quick sail across Lake Léman from the Swiss pays de Vaud, where tobacco processers provisioned Mandrin's gang and many other traffickers. It was also but a short hop to Geneva, where Mandrin deposited much of his fortune with the Bérard brothers, Huguenot textile traders who probably dabbled in contraband before becoming major players in the legitimate calico industry after the ban was lifted in 1759.[34] Besides Carouge, Mandrin frequented the château de Rochefort, which, located due east of

Pont-de-Beauvoisin, was owned by Honoré Piolenc de Thoury, a magistrate in the parlement of Grenoble whose father-in-law, the Marquis de Chaumont, like Cretet, held some of the smuggler's treasure.[35] Not far from the border, the château served as a country retreat where Mandrin could rest between smuggling campaigns.

Louis Mandrin was not born to be a criminal kingpin. A casualty of his father's sudden death and his own ruinous venture into war provisioning, he descended into a violent criminal underworld before finding his footing as a smuggler. Crossing the border into Savoy, the southern edge of a transnational reservoir of contraband, he established a mobile base of operations and would, in a few short years, become the star of the underground. Not only would Mandrin lead gangs of mounted traffickers hundreds of miles into the French interior, taking on the forces of order mustered against him, amassing riches beyond imagination, and winning the admiration of the European public, but, unlike most smugglers who hugged the shadows of the underground, he would openly dramatize—and politicize—the illicit trade that sustained him. Before we consider how this fallen merchant distinguished himself from garden-variety smugglers to become a legendary political symbol, however, it is worth exploring in greater depth the shadow economy in which he flourished and over which he was said to have ruled.

4

The Shadow Economy

MANDRIN INHABITED a vast underworld of smuggling. The yawning gap between the French monarchy's far-reaching claims to tax, monopolize, and prohibit the flow of consumer goods and its limited ability to enforce those claims resulted in the growth of a sprawling shadow economy.[1] In the eighteenth century, over a million men, women, and children from all walks of life worked in this parallel economic universe: nobles and clergy wheeled and dealed behind the scenes, merchants provisioned traffickers beyond the border, peasants funneled contraband across the frontier into towns, and urban dealers hawked illicit wares in bars, cafés, and rented rooms.[2] Meanwhile, untold numbers of consumers snatched up whatever contraband they could lay their hands on. Given the vast proportions of the shadow economy, just about everyone must have known an illegal smuggler, dealer, or consumer, if they were not one themselves.

Who exactly were these underground traders? What kinds of commercial networks did they form, and how did they circumvent the Farm to move illicit goods across borders into the hands of consumers? From a bird's-eye view, we have surveyed how fiscalism and mercantilism, embodied, respectively, in the tobacco monopoly and calico prohibition, produced large flows of contraband into France. It is now time to plunge deeper into the underground to behold the myriad souls engaged in this illicit trade and the bewildering variety of techniques they used to evade the law while moving large quantities of contraband from producer to consumer. As we shall see, their dangerous work made otherwise prohibited or highly taxed goods widely available to the public, thus contributing to the growth of French consumption.

The Things They Carried

All kinds of things were smuggled in the eighteenth century. Almost any good that moved into or across eighteenth-century France was subject to customs taxes, and almost any good that was taxed became an object of smuggling. The list of items that avoided duties to end up on the French black market was therefore very long indeed: coffee, tea, chocolate, sugar, and pepper; wine and spirits; soap, oil, and dyes; combs, buttons, buckles, pins, and needles; hats, handkerchiefs, ribbons, and stockings; cloth of silk, cotton, linen, and wool; watches and rings; gold and silver; hardware and cutlery; meat and flour; playing cards; porcelain; leather; and arms. By one estimate, as much as 45 percent of the goods entering France from England did so illegally.[3] However, the presence of customs taxes only partially explains the high volume of contraband coursing through the commercial veins of France. More important were government monopolies and prohibitions that restricted the sale of certain goods to create scarcities in high-demand products. Royal monopolies, which set prices at levels much higher than those resulting from customs or excise taxes, generated thriving black markets, as did prohibitions that ran counter to consumer demand. Indeed, four of the most widely trafficked goods in France—books, calico, salt, and tobacco—were subject either to bans (in the case of the first two) or state monopolies (in the case of the last two).

We know a great deal about book smuggling in prerevolutionary France, thanks to the illuminating work of Robert Darnton and others.[4] The Catholic Church, the parlements, and the French monarchy all possessed the power to ban "bad books" in the eighteenth century, but only the monarchy had anything close to an administration that could follow up bans with a measure of enforcement. Working through the Royal Publishing Office, city police forces, and printers' guilds, the crown attempted to prevent the circulation of all printed material it deemed subversive to the authority of church and state or offensive to public morality. It also reduced the number of provincial presses in hopes of nudging the remaining large firms out of the black market into legitimate trade. But that did not stop printers and booksellers from supplying customers with prohibited or pirated works. On the contrary, beyond France's eastern border, in many of the same lands that produced tobacco and calico, particularly the Low Countries in the first half of the eighteenth century and Switzerland from the 1770s, foreign francophone presses printed an array of banned and pirated books that were smuggled past authorities to booksellers in the kingdom. The poorly policed provinces were swamped with forbidden and counterfeit works, some of which made their way into the capital, where readers eagerly awaited the latest shipments. Darnton estimates that, apart from specialized professional and liturgical works, popular chapbooks, and almanacs, perhaps half the literature sold in France by 1770 was illicit, having been produced by foreign publishers or underground presses within the kingdom. The ubiquity of subversive literature, he contends, sapped the legitimacy of the old-regime state and cleared the way for revolution.

It is no wonder that forbidden books have attracted the historiographical spotlight, given their political significance as carriers of new "philosophical" ideas. But illegal books were merely the tip of an illicit iceberg in the eighteenth century. Underground markets in salt were far more pervasive than those in books, and the smuggling of the big three—salt, tobacco, and calico—was subject to much more severe repression. Although these goods did not carry the same ideological weight as printed texts—snorting contraband snuff was not quite like reading a banned book—they nonetheless became highly politicized commodities that undermined the authority of the Farm and ultimately challenged French fiscal institutions on a grand scale.

Salt had been the mainstay of the underground since King Philip VI established a royal monopoly on it in the fourteenth century. Reorganized by Colbert three centuries later, the salt tax was based on a division of the kingdom into five official regions (Figure 4.1). In the zone of the grandes gabelles, the northern core of the kingdom in which roughly half of the French population resided, every subject was legally obliged to buy a fixed allotment of salt (half a minot or roughly fifty pounds) every year. In the four other regions (*petites gabelles, salines, quart-bouillon,* and the exempt lands), salt was either moderately taxed or not taxed at all. The result was a jumble of jurisdictions with stark variations in price— perfect conditions for smuggling. The most striking price differential was that between Brittany, a western province endowed with salt marshes and guaranteed exemption from the monopoly when attached to the kingdom in 1532, and Maine, a province in the inner grandes gabelles zone. Privileged Bretons paid 1.5 lt to 3 lt for a minot of salt that cost their

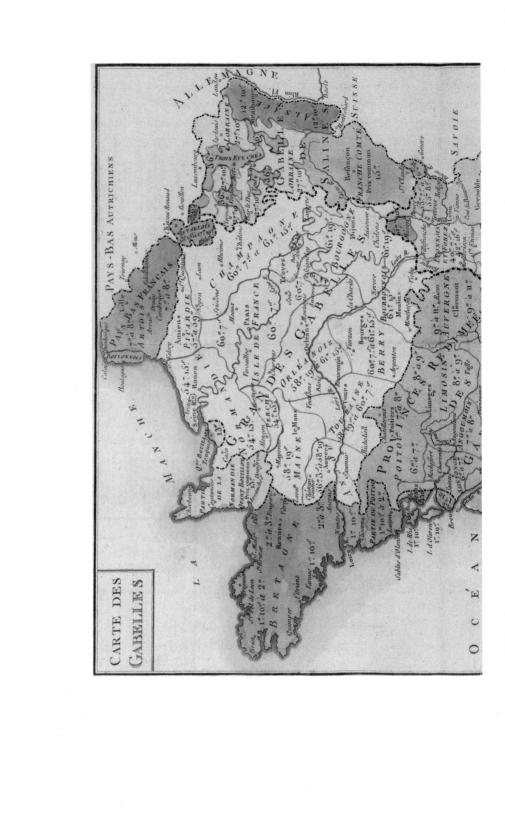

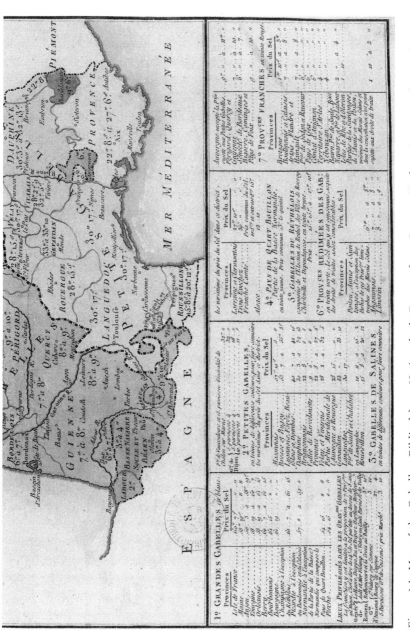

Figure 4.1. Map of the Gabelles. Bibliothèque Nationale de France, from Jacques Necker, *Compte rendu au roi* (Paris, 1781).

unprivileged eastern neighbors in Maine 58lt, twenty to forty times more. Little wonder that this was one of the most heavily trafficked— and heavily policed—borders in the kingdom. Every year, hundreds of salt smugglers, a mere fraction of the thousands operating in the area, were hauled before local law courts.[5] Other internal customs borders drew salt traffickers as well.[6]

In the late seventeenth century, as we have seen, the creation of the tobacco monopoly and promulgation of the ban on Indian cloth globalized the French black market. As objects of contraband, the two products had much to recommend them. They had much higher value-to-weight ratios than salt; that is, they were far more valuable, pound for pound, than what had long been the principal item of French contraband. And they elicited growing consumer demand, whereas the demand for salt seems to have remained relatively stable over the course of the last century of the old regime. As a result, the shadow economy underwent a marked expansion as new traffic in leaf and cloth (and print) joined the older traffic in salt. It was this new highly lucrative trade that lured Mandrin and countless others into the shadow economy.

The Smugglers

If large quantities of salt, tobacco, calico, and other goods circulated clandestinely throughout France, they did not move on their own. A testimony to human ingenuity, determination, and desperation, legions of men, women, and children threw contraband on their backs, stuffed it into saddlebags, and loaded it onto carts as they took to the roads and footpaths that crisscrossed international and provincial borders. The diversity of smugglers was striking: aging widows shared the road with young bachelors, landless peasants jostled with wealthy tradesmen, domestic servants cut deals with rowdy outlaws, unarmed civilians made way for gun-toting soldiers, rustic provincials colluded with wily Parisians, Frenchmen teamed up with foreigners. The illicit economy was large and porous enough to absorb almost anyone wishing to take part in it.

Of course, the vast majority of traffickers were peasants, who comprised 85 percent of the French population.[7] Plagued in the eighteenth century by such unfavorable economic conditions as rising prices, stagnant wages, and the "pulverization" of land under increasing demographic pressure, the lower ranks of the peasantry, particularly those who possessed little land and were therefore net buyers rather than sellers of grain, eked out an existence in which smuggling constituted a critical resource.[8] If long-term economic trends created the general conditions that drove rural folk into the underground, their movement was paced by the structural rhythms of economic life. Peasants worked hard but unevenly, their labor rising and falling with the agricultural cycle. During slack seasons, they took to trafficking, which provided income that could make the difference between subsistence and starvation. Beyond such structural forces, sudden spikes in grain prices during short-term subsistence crises pushed throngs onto the road with contraband on their backs. Waves of peasant smugglers, for example, plied the fiscal borders in the dearth-plagued years of 1709, 1740–1741, and 1770.[9] To be sure, most smugglers were not homeless vagabonds—many were ordinary men and women rooted in their communities with families to feed—but they were poor and on the move in an unforgiving economy.

Against this bleak background of chronic underemployment and precariousness, the potential gains from smuggling could not help but catch the eye of the beleaguered, especially those who happened to live in the borderlands. According to a 1774 internal Farm memo, a salt smuggler earned upwards of twenty lt for transporting a single fifty-pound load of salt. Tobacco smugglers pocketed even more, purchasing leaf outside the territory of the monopoly for twelve sols a pound and selling it inside for as much as thirty-six sols, a 200 percent profit. If a man carried fifty pounds of tobacco on his back, he stood to make as much as sixty lt, more than many rural laborers and provincial artisans earned in three or four months of licit work.[10]

It is no wonder, then, that men like Antoine Garnier, a "poor peasant who has a young wife and four little children," took to the contraband trade in 1728. The extreme misery that had befallen him, explained the Ladies of Mercy of Montpellier, "obliged him to go buy tobacco in Comtat with the intention of re-selling it in the Vivarais, in order to maintain the subsistence of his family."[11] Having spent his last sou purchasing thirty pounds of weed in the tobacco-rich papal enclave, he was nabbed in the middle of the night on 29 November crossing the Rhône into his home province. Had Garnier made it across the river that night, he could have kept his family afloat for a few more months, but his fate and that of his family now rested in the hands of royal officials. This Vivarais peasant was hardly alone. One local jailer at the other end of the kingdom, in Hainault, was amazed at the impecuniousness of a smuggler who was locked in prison for six months: "This man is so poor that he has to set aside some of his bread ration to send to his wife and children whom he has to feed."[12] Asked by magistrates why he smuggled, this prisoner would have probably responded the way most peasants did, by invoking any one of a number of personal calamities, from ruinous natural disasters to mortally ill family members to starving children. Interrogated as to why he and his partners in crime carried contraband, a certain Hubert replied in terms both poetic and poignantly pragmatic: "because hunger chases the wolf, and agents on patrol cannot be everywhere."[13] Implicit in such statements was an appeal to a basic right to subsistence that superseded the positive law of the state.

At the same time, the push of poverty was joined by the pull of profit. Rural folk did not universally fit the stereotype of the backward-looking, land-obsessed peasant, for many in the eighteenth century exhibited extraordinary flexibility and entrepreneurial energy to improve their material lives.[14] De Vries has recently gone so far as to argue that the lower classes of northwestern Europe actively sought additional work outside the household to earn cash for the purchase of new consumer goods.[15] For these laborers, extra wages meant extra spending money, which they used to buy fashion accessories, novelties, and home furnishings. As a part-time profession that could potentially yield quick profits, smuggling was precisely the kind of work that attracted covetous plebeians. When Savoyard Marcel Martin returned to his village after a successful smuggling run in 1761, he went on a buying spree, purchasing "a number of beautiful horses, a gold watch, [and] various pieces of silverware"—eighteenth-century "bling."[16] Smugglers were also known to blow their windfalls on food and drink in village taverns, which, on top of regular business expenditures such as buying inventory and renting horses and mules, pumped fresh money into the local economy. Although the great majority of peasants failed to smuggle their way out of poverty, a minority made enough money to indulge themselves, making their own small contribution to the aggregate lift in eighteenth-century consumption.

After the peasantry, the group that most thoroughly filled the ranks of the shadow economy was composed of mobility professionals—peddlers, coachmen, merchants, cart drivers, and bargemen—as well as the inn and tavern keepers who served them.[17] Often from Savoy and Auvergne, peddlers threw packs or wooden boxes on their backs or loaded mules to travel far and wide, offering an array of goods at prices that undercut those set by stationary shopkeepers. Beyond hawking legitimate items such as hardware, fabric, books, leather goods, and spices, peddlers boosted their profits by selling contraband on the side. The peddler who visited the home of Isaac Garde of Magat in the winter of 1733 did not find the master at home but persuaded his children to buy two yards of calico and three ounces of tobacco. This kind of door-to-door sale was so common that when overzealous Farm agents went after Garde for possession, the intendant of Dauphiné called them off and restored the man's good name.[18]

Coach drivers also ran contraband on the side. On 5 July 1710, Jacques Bizoüard, the driver of the Besançon-Dijon coach, whose route crossed the fiscal frontier between Franche-Comté and Burgundy, was arrested at a checkpoint when guards inspected his trunk and found three pounds of tobacco powder wrapped in a paper package and ten more pounds in a crate.[19] Bizoüard's colleagues on the routes from Lyon, Dijon, and Strasbourg to the capital were also known to traffic. As one veteran of the royal mail service divulged, "Of all the mail carriers along various routes there is not one who, more or less, does not smuggle some light merchandise."[20]

Carters piled contraband onto their horse-drawn carts, burying it beneath legal cargo. Many worked for bosses on the far side of the border. On 19 October 1765, Thomas Boyard from Flanders was driving a heavily laden cart and six horses through Picardy when stopped by Farm guards near Amiens. The driver was happy to hand the guards his papers, which indicated that he was bound for Paris with thousands of eggs in tow. Yet, as the guards discovered upon closer inspection, the eight large baskets in the cart were in fact filled with tobacco. Boyard, it turned out, was working for the Cauneken brothers of Amsterdam, who had paid him to drive 3,411 pounds of tobacco, covered with a thin layer of eggs, from Artois to the French capital.[21]

The most entrepreneurial truckers worked for themselves. When he could pull himself away from his studies, Jean-Baptiste Vast, a medical student living on rue de la Harpe in Paris, carted leaf from Artois to Paris. His supplier in Arras, a merchant named Dufour, provided Dutch, St. Vincent, and common tobacco in exchange for promissory notes. Dufour would have preferred to be paid in cash, given the "nature of the merchandise," but he was willing to accept notes so long as they were backed by a creditworthy financial agent. "My heart tells me I have nothing to fear," wrote Dufour, "but prudence tells me that I must ask that your notes be underwritten by a known endorser." Having found a respectable underwriter, the Chevalier de Gantès, Vast regularly bought hundreds of pounds of tobacco in Arras, which he packed into large wooden tubs, covered with a thick layer of salted butter, and transported in a horse-drawn cart back to Paris, where he sold the merchandise by the pound. He cleared a small fortune. Given that he purchased tobacco for twenty-four sols a pound and sold it for fifty, and that his loads were as heavy as 400 pounds, he earned over 500 lt per trip, more than most Frenchmen made in a year. This entrepreneurial medical student must have lived like a king . . . until he was busted at a Paris customs gate in 1772.[22]

Exhibiting great ingenuity, some drivers built false compartments into their coaches. Philippe François, a small landowner from Flanders who had installed several such compartments in his cabriolet, was driving to Paris on the evening of 4 November 1774 when he was stopped at the Saint-Denis customs gate at the northern edge of the city. Asked if he had anything to declare, he replied no, but guards could not help but notice that the sides of the carriage were unusually thick. They inspected the vehicle and discovered secret compartments in which some 347 white-paper packages of snuff, weighing a total of 320 pounds, had been packed.[23] A more elaborate scheme was organized by smuggler Joseph Despalles, who, from his perch in the enclave of Montbéliard, regularly hired drivers to usher his gilded berlin from Franche-Comté to Paris. On 2 May 1762, Farm agents stopped three of his drivers at the Ronchamp customs office and found 1,300 pounds of tobacco buried in false compartments.[24]

In addition to transportation workers, their closely linked siblings, inn and tavern keepers, played a pivotal role in the underground economy.[25] At the center of small-town life, tavern keepers (like their sometime rivals, parish priests) mediated between local communities and the outside world, giving them ample opportunity to profit from illicit trade. At a minimum, they provided a public space in which contraband changed hands freely as merchants, peddlers, stagecoach passengers, mail drivers, and other itinerants mixed with locals, played cards, and drank. Tavern keeper Magdeleine Bocquet took in smuggling gangs; stabled and nourished their horses; supplied the men with food, drink, and a room in which to rest; and looked the other way when they stashed contraband in the woods outside her establishment.[26] Other tavern keepers were more directly involved in the underground, lending money to smugglers; hiding illicit goods in their attics; making introductions among merchants, traffickers, and guides; passing bribes to Farm agents; and selling illegal tobacco to their customers. Pierre-Joseph Mairesse ran a smuggling ring out of the Silver Chain, a tavern situated in the town of Wignhies in the province of Hainault. From his bar, he recruited band members, convoked meetings, and plotted contraband runs. The proceeds he earned from smuggling tobacco must have overwhelmed what he took in serving cheap drinks and meals to locals.

Although peasants, mobility professionals, and a smattering of artisans, textile workers, and soldiers made up the bulk of smugglers, the clergy and the nobility—the two estates that dominated old-regime society—did not hesitate to indulge in the black market. Ever alive to the call of profit, the kingdom's spiritual leaders were hardly above putting their sacred property in the service of the shadow economy. Monasteries and convents, which Farm brigades hesitated to inspect, routinely broke the law by growing tobacco in their gardens, while abbeys and churches served as contraband depots and clearinghouses.[27] "Having done everything to hide their contraband tobacco, sometimes in the woods, sometimes behind boulders," the magistrates of the parlement of Rennes observed, "smugglers suddenly became aware of another means that they think is safer, which is to carry their tobacco during the night into churches, where they sell it to those who want to buy it; they could only do this with the collaboration of rectors, churchwardens, sacristans, and those who have the keys to the churches." Indeed, on 6 April 1699, four Farm guards entered the Breton parish church of Erquy at eleven at night and found "many individuals with candles, who were hidden behind the pillars of the church." Interrupted in their shadowy dealings, the flickering figures grabbed their muskets and fired six shots at the intruders, wounding two and chasing the others from the house of God. The two brigadiers who had dodged the shots returned the next morning to find a hundred pounds of abandoned tobacco, which they promptly confiscated.[28]

Although clerics rarely transported contraband themselves, some did run their own smuggling businesses. In Paris, the abbé du Garanet kept a depot of tobacco and calico in his house and sold the goods through a network of some two dozen peddlers. In Normandy, the parish priest of Saint-Vaast stored a load of 492 pounds of contraband tobacco in his presbytery. Did he hawk the profane herb after distributing the sacred host on Sundays?[29]

Nobles, too, played a role of some importance. Most commonly, they provided cover for an army of domestic servants—gatekeepers, carriage drivers, stable boys—who used their masters' châteaux to stockpile contraband. Domestic servants have recently been singled out for their important role on the demand side of the consumer revolution; acting as cultural intermediaries, they spread clothing fashions from town to country and from noble households to plebeian ones.[30] But domestics also participated on the supply side of the revolution as underground warehousers and retailers who exploited their access to secure spaces in which goods could be stored. Claude François Lefevre, the thirty-two-year-old servant of the Comtesse de l'Aigle, collaborated with domestics from other aristocratic households to ship tobacco from Dunkirk, Strasbourg, and St. Omer to Madame la Dauphine's residence in Versailles, a hub of contraband that drew tobacco and calico (and books) from all points and poured them into Paris. Using a large berlin, he transported as much as 2,400 pounds at a go, bribing a high-ranking Farm officer at Peronne to ignore the carriage as it rolled through customs into Picardy. Once the leaf was safely deposited in the Versailles stables, Lefevre sold it to clandestine retailers who peddled it in Rouen and Paris.[31]

Even magistrates charged with enforcing royal law protected domestics engaged in underground trade. In Neuilly, a fashionable western suburb of Paris, Joseph Pithon, concierge of Pierre Arnauld de la Briffe, a president of the parlement of Paris, the highest court in the land, stockpiled 1,500 pounds of tobacco in the magistrate's private theater.[32] In Aix, domestics in the pay of the parlement's magistrates were suspected of storing contraband calico in their masters' houses and, in one case, in the palace of justice itself. François Boyer de Bandol, one of the presidents of the Aix court, allowed his domestics to sell contraband from his country estate, knowing that authorities would not dare inspect his property: "he is highly ranked as it is," remarked one intimidated royal official, "and the office of president increases his rank still more."[33] In Montpellier, two merchants were charged with selling calicoes out of an apartment owned by a magistrate in the city's tax court.[34] And in Grenoble, parlementaires protected traffickers who crossed their estates and lent money to merchants who traded in contraband. Mandrin himself had dealings with these magistrates, for he was known to lodge at a château in Savoy that belonged to Honoré Piolenc de Thoury, a president *à mortier* of the very same court that had convicted him of murder two years prior.[35]

The exact relationship between nobles and their trafficking underlings was not always clear. Did nobles simply look the other away or were they actively involved in the illicit commerce? A case from Normandy suggests that some gentlemen were actually running the show from behind the scenes. In the town of St. Lo, a nobleman named Adigard imported fraudulent tobacco from the Channel Islands of Jersey and Guernsey, milled it in his manor house, and had his valet and a local dressmaker fill thousands of paper packets with snuff, which were then delivered under the cover of night to a corrupt local tobacco receiver with whom he split the profits. The receiver frequently dined at the nobleman's manor, making deals in "hushed tones" so the domestics did not hear.[36]

In Dauphiné and Savoy where Mandrin roamed, landed gentlemen routinely abetted smugglers. Besides affording peasants time off to run illegal goods, they provided traffickers with access to their land, boats for river crossings, and critical supplies.[37] When the leader of a band crossed the Dauphinois village of Uriage, "the lord of the place, Monsieur de Langon, furnished him with much needed refreshments."[38] Alexis Magallon de La Morlière, the valiant young officer sent to rid the kingdom of Mandrin, cursed the "many gentlemen, particularly those along the border," who encouraged their "vassals" to protect the armed bands that crossed their lands. Whenever the king sent army officers to clean up the area, the "gentlemen and notables of the frontier" won them over "through kindnesses, flattery, and hospitality."[39] Singled out for particular scorn was a certain Monsieur de Saint-Albin, son-in-law of Commander Marcieu, who "at all times moved smugglers into Dauphiné from his château near the Guiers, a quarter league from Pont de Beauvoisin." Saint-Albin "earned very considerable sums from this trade [and] presently conspires ... with many members of the parlement who have, like him, worked at this honorable profession."[40]

Although the clergy and nobility were deeply implicated, the typical smuggler was a peasant in his twenties or thirties (fully adult but young enough to bear heavy loads for long distances) who hailed from the same borderlands in which he plied his trade, was armed at best with a heavy walking stick, and smuggled on his own or in a very small group.[41] The profile of any given smuggler, however, depended in large part on what he was carrying. Because salt was extraordinarily cheap in many peripheral provinces, the cost of access to its trade was low, especially if the merchandise was simply carried on one's back rather than on carts or horses. As a result, salt trafficking remained a relatively artisanal form of underground commerce in which peasants, women, and children predominated. In the direction of Laval, ground zero for the illicit salt trade from Brittany to Maine and Anjou, almost 60 percent of those hauled into the local court were women. They were generally unarmed, worked individually or in pairs (sometimes with family members), and carried a little over twenty pounds of salt per trip.[42] Paid less than men and locked out of many professions, early modern women often sought recourse in peripheral markets, which boosted their autonomy even as their legal status declined in many respects. The underground salt market offered women irresistible commercial opportunities.[43] By contrast, male salt smugglers were more likely to operate in gangs, to use horses and carts for transport, and to carry firearms. In fact, the accused brought before the commission of Saumur, a high court that handled cases of salt smuggling involving gangs and violence, were 70 percent male.[44] In the east and north, where the smuggling of tobacco was more pronounced than that of salt, a similar pattern manifested itself. Men were far more likely to be involved in large-scale tobacco smuggling, whereas women engaged in the smaller-scale salt trade. In the north, where the commission of Reims judged major cases dealing mostly with tobacco, fully 93 percent of the accused were men.[45]

In sum, the underground economy touched all social classes and both sexes. In the lower echelons of the profession, petty smugglers of peasant origin ventured on foot to supplement their paltry incomes.

Female salt traffickers epitomized this level of trade. The upper levels of the shadow economy were filled by better organized male smugglers—often transportation professionals or soldiers—who used carts or went about on horseback, traded in tobacco and calico, carried weapons, and joined gangs. This was precisely the professional milieu in which Mandrin insinuated himself as a young man.

Gangs

In addition to lone peasants or artisans (or students!) hauling contraband for wages or profit, more and more smugglers banded together into large gangs in the eighteenth century. The first major bands began to form during the second half of Louis XIV's reign, when the economy languished and the demands of the War of Spanish Succession (1701–1714) swelled the ranks of the army and kept prices of state salt and tobacco high. Whole companies of soldiers and deserters engaged in trafficking during these chaotic years. But the stress of war does not explain the rapid proliferation of bands after the Treaty of Utrecht. In the 1720s and 1730s, following a sharp 20 percent rise in the price of Farm tobacco and a marked expansion in Farm police, a symbiotic relationship developed between Farm and smuggler that generated ever more gangs. As the Farm deployed greater numbers of guards to patrol the border, smugglers hungry for profit assembled in larger groups to overpower them. As smugglers joined together in ever larger formations, however, the Farm established more and more brigades to stop them, and so on in what scientists call a positive feedback loop.[46]

As a result of this tit-for-tat dynamic, which can still be seen in contemporary drug wars, organized gangs became a regular feature of the shadow economy. In northeastern France, court records reveal that thirty-eight large bands were in operation in the second half of the eighteenth century, not including those that evaded detection.[47] In the southeast, the intendant of Dauphiné estimated in the 1730s that around 400 smugglers were active in twenty-five to thirty different bands, the largest of which, the band d'Orange, was composed of seventy men, all "armed to the teeth."[48] Whisking calicoes and tobacco from Switzerland and Savoy to Provence and Languedoc, such bands could traverse Dauphiné at will without having to fear interference from intimidated Farm agents. The finance minister printed lists of wanted smugglers and distributed them to the region's intendants, but the problem, he admitted, was that once bands crossed the border into the French customs zone, they quickly sold their tobacco, stashed their weapons, and dispersed for the return trip, making it exceedingly difficult for authorities to catch them red-handed.[49] By the time Mandrin formed his own band in 1754, gangs of smugglers had roamed moonlit French borderlands for decades.

As we shall see, fictional accounts portrayed gangs as strange underworld societies that spoke incomprehensible slang and performed alien rites. In practice, smuggling bands were not quite so esoteric, but the most hardened did share a distinctive martial culture of camaraderie built on drinking, blasphemy, and life on the road. Like soldiers of the period, they adopted colorful nicknames that indicated places of origin (the Spaniard, the Provençal, Piémont, Nîmes), physical traits (Fatty, Curly, the Blond, Pug-Nose, the Hunch-Back), military rank or function (the Colonel, Cavalryman, the Captain, the Grenadier, the Gunner), personal character (Shameless, Lucifer, the Noble, Ready-to-Drink, Lucky), or mere fancy (Parrot, Carnival). Gang members also derived a sense of masculine honor from bragging about their disposal of Farm agents or about time served in the galleys. Undergirding this martial culture was the family unit, which shored up solidarity as the trade was handed down from father to son or older to younger brother or as family alliances were forged through marriage. Louis Mandrin's younger brother Claude took as his bride a woman from another Savoyard smuggling clan, the Colonniers aka the Coconiers. Authorities monitored the wedding, which was attended by several big-name traffickers, but no disturbances were reported.[50]

The average band was relatively small (ten or fewer members) and traveled on foot, but averages mask the extreme variety.[51] Some counted as few as five members; others amassed over a hundred. Some were composed of amateurs from the same village; others took in full-time professionals from distant regions. Some shuttled goods on foot in short hops across the border; others ventured deep into the interior on horseback. Some carried firearms, which they did not hesitate to use if they crossed paths with Farm brigades; others went unarmed and sought to avoid agents at all costs. Some collaborated with corrupt Farm officials; others worked on their own. All exploited the border as a resource, exposed themselves to the risk of death or capture, profited handsomely from the trade, and delivered cheap illegal merchandise to consumers.

To gain insight into gangs like the one Mandrin would head, it is worth looking at the structure of three large bands that operated in northeastern France: the Maurepas band, a village salt gang; the Wignhies band, a roving tobacco gang; and Rathier's pack of calico smugglers.[52] The Maurepas band was a classic village-based gang, the most common in the north.[53] At its height in the 1750s, it was composed of some fifty friends, neighbors, and relatives, almost all from Maurepas, a Picard village with a population of no more than several hundred that was located just north of the Somme River, the front line of the French customs zone. Proximity to the fiscal frontier encouraged Maurepas's day laborers, weavers, and artisans to engage in smuggling on a part-time basis, traveling every few weeks to the Cambrésis region of Artois to load up on inexpensive salt (and sometimes tobacco). On foot and armed with walking sticks, each carried about seventy pounds of contraband south to the Somme, which they crossed together for fear of running into a Farm patrol. On the far side of the river, they disbanded to sell their goods in nearby villages without penetrating far into the kingdom's interior. Some of the men were independent smugglers, buying and selling their own wares for profit but crossing the river with the others for safety; they earned good money, about six lt profit per trip. Others were paid laborers known as valets, the proletarians of the underground who carried other men's merchandise for a daily wage of thirty sols; they took the same risks as independents but were excluded from the lion's share of the profits. Two of the band's leaders, Pierre Saunier (aka Mirliton) and Jean-Baptiste Bourgier, served as scouts, walking fifteen minutes ahead of the pack to make sure the way was clear. In case the scouts were ambushed by Farm guards, valets carried their merchandise with the rest of the gang.

The key to this band's success was Farm corruption and the use of *passeurs* on the Somme, peasants who lived on the river, knew its every bend and current, and could ford smugglers and their goods across the water on the blackest of nights. Guilian Degrés, a married day laborer and father of three from the river settlement of Etinéant, served as a *passeur* for the Maurepas gang. Because boats had to be chained up at night and were closely watched by the Farm, Degrés constructed two small rafts from reeds, loaded each with two men (or a man and a bundle of contraband), tied them to a rope, and pulled them across the river. Once men and cargo had crossed, he and his assistant, Pierre

Eloy, a villager with a loose tongue and a penchant for drink, destroyed the rafts and threw their remains in the river to dispose of all evidence. (Further south in Dauphiné, smugglers used a portable set of ropes and pulleys to move merchandise across the Rhône).[54] For such work, Degrés charged a high fee (three to five lt for every two bundles passed) but sometimes experienced difficulty collecting it. For a night's work of passing forty-five members of the Maurepas gang and their goods in August 1752, he and two assistants should have taken in a total of 170 lt. But because some members of the band refused to pay, they received only 120 lt—still a hefty sum for a day laborer, even when divided three ways.

Degrés also had to share his earnings with the local Farm guards with whom he colluded. Indeed, bribery was essential to the entire operation. Degrés collaborated with Nicolas Sery, a guard at the post of Bray-sur-Somme and one of the most corrupt border agents on the river. Sery had been responsible for enticing Degrés into the underground in the first place. "Tempted by the lure of earnings and urged on by the need to provide subsistence to his family," Degrés later confessed that Sery had "seduced" him into a life of crime. The two men had perfected an almost foolproof system of fraud by which Degrés would lead contraband crossings while Sery was on duty. All profits were split between them. At the urging of his wife, who could not stomach the risk, Degrés tried to walk away from his shady dealings, or so he later claimed under interrogation, but he could not give up "earning money with so much ease and security."[55] With help from *passeurs* like Degrés and the complicity of officials like Sery, the Maurepas gang thrived for years.

If the Maurepas band was a typical village salt gang that smuggled on foot, without firearms, and within a narrow radius of the border, the Wignhies gang represents the professional tobacco band.[56] But for its size, which ranged from eight to eighteen men, it resembled Mandrin's dangerous pack in many respects: it smuggled tobacco (never salt); its membership consisted of full-time as well as part-time smugglers, some of whom hailed from places well beyond the village where it was based; it journeyed great distances in trips that lasted up to two weeks; and it went about mounted and well armed.

Active in the 1730s and 1740s, the band pursued a consistent geographical strategy. Individually, men from the band rode east to villages beyond the monopoly zone in the Cambrésis to stock up on tobacco. Occasionally, they rode further north into the Austrian Netherlands, where tobacco was even cheaper. In any event, they usually paid for their merchandise in cash before meeting at their headquarters, the Silver Chain tavern in the village of Wignhies, whose owner, Pierre-Joseph Mairesse, we have already met. In the familiar setting of the bar, the gang picked leaders for its monthly trips and discussed possible itineraries. On appointed days, the crew would wait until sunset to load their horses (each of which transported two 100-pound bundles, one on each flank) and ride down to the Thon River, which they crossed with the aid of a *passeur* who stuffed their tobacco into a large, thick leather bag and pulled it across the water. (The band collectively owned the bag but individually paid the *passeur* six lt per horse load). With the river behind them, the men delved into the province of Champagne, needling their way through the Thiérache hills toward the cities of Laon and Soissons. Traveling by night and hiding the contraband by day, the gang occasionally dropped south to Reims and once, at least, rode as far west as Paris. When they neared a town, a designated gang member would leave his cargo behind and enter the city to make arrangements with local dealers for the transfer of goods. In Soissons, the smugglers climbed through a breach in the city wall, assisted by a corrupt Farm guard, to deposit their sacks in the yard of a tavern keeper. From there, the guard and his assistant moved the merchandise to a monastery, where a wholesaler distributed it to a network of retailers. Unlike the Maurepas band, the Wignhies smugglers never participated in the retail end of the trade. Having delivered their goods, they collected their money and set out on the long journey home.

Insofar as its members selected new leaders for every trip, the band was relatively democratic (like pirate crews on the high seas), but we must not romanticize the egalitarian character of the gang.[57] Its members were not equal. Like the Maurepas band, the crew was divided between hired valets who carried their boss's contraband and independent smugglers from whose ranks the leaders were chosen. For his part, Mairesse usually placed two valets in the band, each of whom was paid seventy-five lt per trip if he used his own horse or thirty to thirty-six lt if a horse had to be provided. The tavern keeper also appointed an agent whose job it was not only to carry the tavern keeper's tobacco but also to keep an eye on his two other valets and conduct the sale of their tobacco. Whereas the valets were paid fixed wages, the agent received one sixth of the profits from the sale. The remainder belonged to Mairesse, who waited safely in his tavern for the coming windfall. Such profits towered over those turned by village salt bands.

Of all the smuggling bands, those that traded in calico were the most professional or at least the most deeply integrated into larger, semilegitimate enterprises.[58] Because banned calico was far more expensive than contraband tobacco, let alone salt, the trade required capital outlays well beyond what most peasants and artisans could afford. Calico smugglers who worked independently did exist, but they were more likely to serve as agents of well-connected merchants. Take a smuggler such as Desnovalles, who in 1739 hired three valets to assist him in leading a caravan of four horses loaded with calico on a typical route from Lorraine to Paris. Insofar as one horse's load of cargo belonged personally to Desnovalles, he was acting as an independent smuggler, buying his own cloth outside the customs zone and selling it to retailers in the capital. But the three other horses' loads were the property of two Parisian merchants, one of whom had started out as a smuggler but moved into the lower ranks of the merchant class. The two merchants hired Desnovalles to deliver goods they had purchased from an unnamed merchant in Bar-le-Duc. Although Desnovalles was well paid for his services, the merchants at either end of the contraband chain—the seller in Bar-le-Duc and the buyers in Paris—drew the greatest profits.

In the calico business, smugglers like Desnovalles were bit players to a larger textile industry in which merchants and bankers amassed great fortunes while remaining above the fray of trafficking. Just like legitimate merchants, Paris calico traders paid Bar-le-Duc wholesalers in bills of exchange drawn on such prestigious banking firms as Jean Cottin and Sons. (It was no coincidence that Cottin and Sons was a Protestant bank, for the Protestant diaspora had overlapped with the calico diaspora since the prohibition was instituted a year after the revocation of the Edict of Nantes.) The Cottin banking house also lent money to Bar-le-Duc merchants to finance wholesale purchases of calicoes in the Low Countries. Similar kinds of transactions occurred in Geneva, where international merchants lent money to smugglers to underwrite the purchase of merchandise, weaponry, horses, and manpower.[59] The tobacco trade rarely operated at such levels of high finance, although larger traffickers did buy stock on credit from semilegitimate tobacco merchants. The salt trade never came close.

After 1759, the year in which the ban on calico was replaced by a stiff import duty, the professionalization of calico smuggling accelerated. Not only was there still a strong incentive to smuggle—the 25 percent duty was very much worth circumventing—but the legalization of the production, sale, and use of calico in France made it easier to retail contraband cloth within the customs zone. The adventures of smuggling kingpin Jean-Baptiste Rathier bear this out. Rathier was what was known as an "insurer" *(assureur),* a smuggler who, for a percentage of the take, "insured" the delivery of prohibited goods to merchants in the French interior. (Insurers also operated in the book trade, where licit and illicit markets interpenetrated as well.)[60] In the event that his calico was confiscated by the Farm, he and not the importers would bear the financial responsibility. Needless to say, this type of arrangement, which became quite common in the late eighteenth century, made calico smuggling only more appealing to risk-averse merchants.

Rathier was a professional. The mastermind behind one of the most sophisticated smuggling rings in eighteenth-century France, he transported calico in wagons from the interior of Lorraine to the customs border around Breuvannes and handed it off to foot smugglers, who shuttled it across the border and hid it in the woods. From the woods, the cloth was picked up by a band on horseback that moved it deeper into the customs zone to Thivet, where counterfeit seals were attached. From Thivet, it was transported by wagon to Vesaignes-sur-Marne and then carried west to the Paris calico merchants who had hired Rathier. What stands out in this operation were Rathier's impeccable contacts. In Thivet, he could count on the good offices of the Marquis de Bologne, whose château he used as a relay point. Rathier also forged ties with the Farm, taking corruption to a whole new level. Instead of bribing customs officials to look the other way on a case-by-case basis, he simply put Farm agents on his payroll, in effect doubling their annual salary. At least twenty-three agents up and down the customs border near Breuvannes received regular payments, regardless of how much calico happened to pass through their post that month. And as if that did not make his route secure enough, Rathier could depend on nests of spies prepared to inform him of any movement by local Farm brigades. Like other insurers who moved calico between Lorraine and Paris, Geneva and Montpellier, or Marseille and Aix, Rathier put the "organized" in organized crime. These were highly professional enterprises whose networks spread from bankers and merchants to corrupt Farm guards to wage-earning mules who did the physical labor and ran the risk of getting caught.

The Retail Market

Legions of smugglers in various formations, then, carried contraband across the border into the French interior. Once inside the monopoly and prohibition zone, smugglers either took it upon themselves to sell contraband directly to customers or handed it off to wholesalers and retailers who specialized in clandestine sales. At the retail end of the long commercial chain, the black market engaged with millions of consumers who routinely violated the law to get their hands on a colorful piece of fabric, a cheap ounce of tobacco, a small sack of salt, a banned book, and so on.

Smugglers who dealt directly with customers passed contraband to friends, family members, and clients; hawked it to countryfolk door to door and at rural fairs; and peddled it to townspeople in narrow streets, congested taverns, and cramped apartments. The seventeen armed smugglers who showed up at the Joyeuse fair in the Vivarais lodged at a local hotel and sold tobacco and other contraband out of their room.[61] Soldiers in Champagne took their merchandise to the streets of Laon, indiscreetly crying, "Tobacco for sale," "Who wants to buy some tobacco?"—calls heeded by townspeople eager to stock up on leaf at bargain prices.[62]

Most large-scale smugglers did not, however, take the trouble to retail the contraband they transported. They preferred to drop their cargoes outside of towns and head back to the border, leaving it to local wholesalers and retailers to market the merchandise to consumers. In small towns, retailers purchased contraband from passing smugglers and peddled it to local residents. Having purchased his supply of tobacco from regional traffickers, the wily Bernard Fontaine of Saint Jean, Savoy, flushed out potential customers at the public market, drew them into nearby alleys to make a deal, and then led them back to his place to complete the transaction.[63] An unnamed woman in the hamlet of Houllefort in the Boulonnois simply set up shop in the village cemetery, measuring out ounces of tobacco with the set of scales she brought with her.[64]

The big money was in the cities, where the majority of French tobacco was consumed. Because most large towns were walled, contraband was usually warehoused outside of town and then smuggled past city gates, over city walls, or (as in the case of Aix and Paris) through underground tunnels.[65] Farmhouses, hotels, and taverns serving as contraband depots ringed all the cities of France. Mathieu Rivoire ran one such suburban depot from his house in Ruy, conveniently located a few miles outside of Lyon on the road to Grenoble. When undercover Farm agents came to his home and asked for tobacco—there were no laws against entrapment in this period—he told them that he had just sold a large quantity to men who intended to slip it into Lyon but had two pounds left, which he would let them have for fifty sols. When the agents inquired if they could return later for more, Rivoire replied that he could provide them with 200 pounds of the same type of tobacco on a weekly basis. Clearly, this was a wholesaler with excellent connections to professional traffickers. But his clandestine operation was not to last; the agents moved in, confiscated what they could find, and arrested him.[66]

Once inside city walls, black-market goods were diffused by extensive networks of underground retailers. Thanks to intendant Fontanieu's investigations, it is possible to reconstruct the underground retail trade in the provincial capital of Grenoble in the late 1730s. At the top of a list of thirty-five individuals active in the city's illicit trade was Jeanne Leclerc, aka Big Jeanne, who lived on the street of the three cloisters. Her son, a journeyman butcher, colluded with smugglers to bring tobacco and calico into Grenoble, while she sold the merchandise "on a daily basis" to lower-level dealers and consumers. Big Jeanne was not the only source in town. Lower-level dealers could also buy from the Barthelon brothers, merchants of haberdashery and hardware, who were supplied by a gang of traffickers living near the Savoy border. Other dealers on the list included a tavern keeper, a father-and-son team of mercers who provisioned themselves with calicoes in Geneva, a smuggler who supplied corrupt Farm retailers with contraband tobacco, and a handful of artisans and widows.[67]

When it came to urban black markets, however, nothing compared to Paris. Packed with more than a half-million men, women, and children in the middle of the eighteenth century, Paris was the largest human settlement in continental Europe and a nerve center of western European consumption. Although Parisians consumed massive quantities of Farm tobacco and licit textiles, they still craved the cheap weed and bright Indian cloth that only smugglers could provide. For those willing to run the risk of moving illegal contraband into the most tightly policed city in Europe, the Paris market offered vast riches. The Farm lost an estimated six to seven million lt every year to Parisian traffic in tobacco, wine, livestock, sugar, coffee, and more.[68]

Before Parisians could lay their hands on contraband, it had to be insinuated into a city that was policed like a state within a state. All street traffic heading into the capital was channeled through designated customs gates at which the Farm posted several hundred guards. Horse-drawn coaches and carts and pedestrians carrying packages had to stop, declare their merchandise, show transport papers, and, if requested, submit cargo for inspection. Paris customs agents used special iron instruments with wooden handles to probe containers in search of contraband. Pedestrians without packages attracted less attention but were not above suspicion. It was the job of Farm officials to make sure that all goods subject to Paris customs were duly taxed and that prohibited articles were prevented from entering.[69]

Yet the Farm did not have the means to thoroughly search the mountains of merchandise and thousands of people who entered Paris each day—and even if it did, it could not have done so without completely choking the local economy. Thus many coaches and carts with hidden contraband rolled through city gates undetected on their way to appointments with retailers. François Melon ran a coach with eight-inch-wide secret compartments from Arras to Paris, where he breezed through customs and rode on to meet contacts Jean Baptiste Perret and his wife, Josephe Maillard. The tobacco, packaged in one-pound bricks and wrapped in paper, was unloaded and stored in two depots, one on rue St. Denis and the other in a room at the Silver Lion Hotel on rue Bourg l'Abbé. This was clearly a family enterprise, for the couple's thirteen-year-old daughter distributed tobacco to customers on the Ile St. Louis, hiding a few bricks at a time in the folds of her dress.[70]

Other traffickers slipped through city gates with the connivance of corrupt guards. In 1773, in one of the biggest corruption scandals ever discovered in Paris, several Farm officials stationed at the checkpoints of Conference, St. Michel, and St. Denis were charged with taking bribes and letting pass thirty to forty vehicles laden with contraband. One young guard swept up in the investigation claimed to have been blackmailed into the venture by a superior officer. He said his father, who had served the Farm faithfully for thirty years, would die of shame if he found out about his arrest. "If I am not pardoned, I'll have to take my life with my sword."[71]

While smugglers with secret compartments or allies in the Farm passed seamlessly from the provinces into Paris, those who traveled with exposed loads on horses preferred to dump their contraband in the environs and let others spirit it into the city. Consequently, much of the contraband destined for the capital pooled in the Paris basin. Indeed, the price of illicit tobacco was considerably lower outside the city perimeter, where a thriving wholesale market developed. Thanks to its sacrosanct aristocratic households, Versailles became a major hub for Paris-bound traffic. But the depots that supplied the metropolis could extend as far away as Orléans, where, for example, a "seductive woman" named Ragot stored tobacco in a secret underground cellar accessed through a hole in her yard. She "opened her house to all smugglers."[72]

From such saturated environs, contraband seeped into Paris by assorted routes. A small industry existed on the outskirts of town in which illicit traders paid pedestrians to walk through customs gates with tobacco hidden in their pockets and aprons or under their skirts and coats. Simon LeClerc, a secondhand furniture dealer, received twenty to thirty sols (the better part of a day's wage for an unskilled Parisian artisan) to carry fifteen pounds of tobacco though a Paris checkpoint.[73] Claude Ferry, a journeyman wheel maker, was solicited by a stranger on the road from La Villette to carry something into the capital in return for twenty-four sols and a drink of brandy. Ferry agreed but was stopped at the St. Martin customs gate when it appeared that he was hiding something under his clothes. The agents escorted him to their office, where they found two pounds, four ounces of tobacco sandwiched between his riding coat and clothes. Ferry claimed not to know what he was carrying, insisting that he was guilty only of needing money to buy bread for his wife and seven children. He was nevertheless thrown in the Fort-l'Évêque prison without his promised glass of liquor.[74] Meanwhile, traffickers heaved larger loads over city walls in the night, their parcels landing safely in the yards of aristocrats, ambassadors, and clergymen. Once over the wall, the contraband was received by a servant—usually a gardener or concierge—who stored it himself or passed it on to a retailer. Jacques Pachot threw his tobacco and calico over the walls of the Jardin des Plantes, the king's own gardens, to a retired gardener who carried them to a nearby house where they were warehoused for thirty sols per bundle per day.[75] Smugglers averse to scaling walls in the middle of the night could pass contraband through the doors, windows, and cracks in houses at the edge of town. It was to choke off this stream of contraband that the Farm began building a new wall around Paris in 1784.

Once inside Paris, wholesalers moved contraband to clandestine warehouses across the city. It accumulated in the courtyards of the rue St. Denis, the right bank's north–south commercial artery; in privileged neighborhoods *(lieux privilégiés)* like the Temple, where municipal regulatory power was attenuated; and in any number of clerical, aristocratic, and even royal households, including the abbey of St. Germain and the Hôtel du Petit Luxembourg on the left bank and the Palais Royal, the Louvre, the Hôtel de Sully, and the Arsenal on the right bank.[76] One of the most active depots in the city was that of the Hôtel de Soissons. Owned by indebted aristocrat Victor-Amedée de Savoie, prince of Carignan, the residence evolved from a gambling den in the 1720s to one of the capital's most important contraband clearinghouses in the 1730s and 1740s. In 1746, the finance minister informed the Paris police chief that despite previous crackdowns, snuff was still being sold "publicly" at the hôtel. The hôtel was also the likely supplier of one of the few textile shops in the city that dared to display calicoes in its front room. Both the shop owner, a certain Monsieur Charles, and Madame de Carignan, the prince's widow, were in cahoots with Paris police officers, who alerted the widow to impending police raids.[77]

Most of the retailers in Paris were, however, petty dealers who could scarcely depend on police protection. The city crawled with coffee sellers, tavern keepers, postal carriers, grocers, servants, innkeepers, and soldiers who, as one royal decree bemoaned, devoted themselves more to peddling contraband than they did to their day jobs.[78] Scales and iron weights in hand, Jean Baptiste Lemoine was one of countless coffee peddlers to weigh out tiny amounts of tobacco powder to his customers. He filled paper wrappers with half-ounces of snuff and sold it at a price ordinary Parisians could afford (six liards).[79] Joining Lemoine were soldiers like Jean Jacques, who acquired discounted army tobacco from his comrades at Invalides and hawked it by the ounce for the rock-bottom price of thirty-two sols a pound.[80] Antoine François, a domestic living outside the city walls in the faubourg Saint-Antoine, bought 200 pounds of tobacco from a local wholesaler for forty-two sols a pound, crossed through the St. Antoine checkpoint into Paris, and in the shadow of the Bastille sold it for forty-five, fifty, even sixty sols a pound.[81] Belleville tavern keeper André Baroche offered a variety of weed, rang-ing from common tobacco, which he bought for thirty-five sols and sold for thirty-eight or forty sols a pound, to higher-end St. Vincent and Dutch tobacco, which he purchased for forty-two sols but fetched fifty-five sols a pound. He conducted business in his bar or from the St. Jean cemetery off rue de Bercy.[82] Such examples could be multi-plied endlessly.

The customers of these petty dealers ranged widely in social class. Thanks to a kingdom-wide crackdown on calico consumption in the 1730s led by Philibert Orry, the finance minister who placed the French Indies Company more firmly under royal control, we know that a range of men and women—from courtiers and magistrates to professionals and artisans—dipped into the black market to procure the fashionable cloth. The majority of those arrested were common women, such as Peronnelle Masson, a poor country widow from Ambert found in pos-session of four yards of cloth, or Catherine Roybee, who happened to be standing in front of her husband's saddle shop wearing an Indian-cloth dress. Intendant Fontanieu urged the finance minister to go after people "of more elevated fortune" rather than "unfortunates who violate the law less out of disobedience than necessity, for lack of means to dress themselves otherwise."[83] Evidence about snorters and smokers of con-traband tobacco is elusive because police agents rarely pursued consum-ers, but one underground Paris peddler, Simon Lucas, a former Farm employee fired for fraud, did list his Paris clientele in 1714.[84] His cus-tomers were drawn from almost every social group, including wealthy financiers and clerics, notaries, lawyers, and merchants, common sol-diers, and laborers. His list joined men from opposite ends of the social spectrum who shared little more than their common love of tobacco: a former high-ranking financier (receiver general) not above saving a few sols in the underground market and a common water carrier who could ill afford the prices set by the state monopoly.

From the age of Louis XIV to the French Revolution, a web of illicit trade stretched from distant continents to the streets of Paris to provide multitudes of workers with their daily bread and sometimes much more. Although the indigent borderland peasant carrying an occasional sack of salt across the frontier remained a staple of the underground, countless others forged new links in long and winding global chains of underground commerce. Bankers, merchants, innkeepers, carters, soldiers, barkeeps, and urban dealers all exploited the border as a resource, working the seams between states, as did a phalanx of accessory personnel (scouts, spies, and *passeurs*) employed by organized gangs. Even corrupt agents of the Farm lived off the trade in the form of bribes. In sum, armies of people participated in moving illicit goods from sites of production to those of consumption. If we include in our tally the dockworkers who socked away tobacco on both sides of the Atlantic, merchants who diverted American leaf from official channels, laborers at Farm tobacco plants who filched weed while at work, Farm retailers who cut legitimate tobacco with contraband, sailors of the French East Indies Company who relanded Indian cloth on the Breton shore or hid it in their sea chests, "insurers" who shuttled European-made *indiennes* from the eastern frontier into the French interior, and the millions of consumers who routinely broke the law to purchase forbidden goods, it becomes clear that the so-called underground economy was anything but. It was a ubiquitous aspect of everyday life.

This parallel economy played an important role in the eighteenth-century consumer revolution. Undoubtedly, much of the boom in consumption was driven by the expansion of legitimate commerce, as retail shops opened in Paris and peddlers introduced urban consumer goods to rural folk. But smuggling also contributed to the rise in consumption by making highly regulated goods available through unofficial markets. Consumers who snorted, smoked, and chewed tobacco could purchase their leaf at local Farm shops or buy it illegally at country fairs, in village taverns, and on city streets. Opening new supply channels was even more important for calicoes, which were available exclusively on the black market until 1759. The first calico craze of the late seventeenth century, which prefigured a general turn to cotton cloth and the coming of the Industrial Revolution, would have been snuffed out by prohibition had it not been for the merchants and smugglers who circumvented the law. In both cases, ramifying illicit networks connected producers and consumers in unprecedented ways.[85]

Equally important, purveyors of contraband fueled consumption by lowering the price of popular consumer goods. Although slave-produced New World tobacco became significantly cheaper to transport over the course of the seventeenth and eighteenth centuries, in several European countries its official price, set by revenue-hungry state monopolies, remained exceedingly high. And yet tobacco became the single most widely distributed colonial good in eighteenth-century Europe. In France, the consumption of tobacco among the popular and middling classes exploded in part because of the existence of a black market that offered cheap, lesser-quality substitutes for official Farm leaf.[86] Like artisans who offered creative, low-cost imitations of high-end goods and peddlers who set their prices lower than stationary shopkeepers, smugglers put the herb within reach of ordinary consumers, undercutting Farm prices by as much as 40 percent in the provinces. And because demand for addictive substances tends to be elastic for new users—that is, the low price of drugs stimulates additional demand—the influx of cheap contraband tobacco encouraged consumption, especially among the laboring poor.[87]

Smuggling also kept Farm tobacco prices in check. On the contraband-saturated eastern edge of the monopoly, the Farm was forced to slash prices to compete with the black market.[88] But even in the interior, the Farmers General knew there was a limit to what they could charge, for any substantial price increase would inevitably lead to a commensurate escalation of illicit trade. The same held true for the calico market. After the ban was lifted in 1759 and entrepreneurs established manufactories in France, the smuggling of cheap cloth forced domestic producers to market their product at affordable prices. Competition from the underground kept prices lower throughout the market.[89]

It has been claimed that state monopolies, prohibitions, and import duties in the eighteenth century inflated the price of goods, restricting them to a mere fraction of the market they would touch in the following century.[90] But the formation of a thriving shadow economy mitigated the effects of fiscalism and protectionism to broaden the market for consumer goods. The smuggling of low-priced tobacco, calico, and other products made them widely available to consumers who might not otherwise have been willing or able to purchase them. In this way, the underground trade in cheap "colonial" goods produced in the Americas and Asia—and in Europe—helped fuel the rise in eighteenth-century consumption.

5

———◆———

Rebel Rebel

From his lair in Savoy, Louis Mandrin tapped into the great reservoir of contraband that stretched up to the North Sea and sprang into action in the summer of 1754. With a band of mounted comrades, he rode hundreds of miles across the rough terrain of southeastern France on his first major expeditions. From the pine-scented Jura Mountains of Franche-Comté in the north to the volcanic Massif Central of Auvergne in the west to the rocky plateaux of Languedoc in the south, he delivered thousands of pounds of illicit tobacco and calico to eager consumers. Even more impressive than the scale of operation were the bold methods Mandrin and his associates developed to peddle their wares. Stepping from the shadows of the underground into the full light of day, they brazenly occupied towns and carved out public spaces in which to retail contraband. More outrageously still, they cracked open the tobacco monopoly by compelling Farm agents to buy their illegal leaf. While such improvisation undoubtedly improved the gang's bottom line, it simultaneously telegraphed broader political messages to royal authorities and local spectators alike. Elaborating on traditional moral-economic forms of protest, Mandrin's methods turned the tables on the Farm to contest the legitimacy of the tobacco monopoly and further politicize an already rebellious popular culture.

Forms of Rebellion

Historians have long believed that popular revolt in early modern France followed a distinct evolution from antitax and antimilitary uprisings in the crisis-ridden seventeenth century to food and seigneurial revolts in the more stable eighteenth century.[1] But path-breaking work by Jean Nicolas exposes deep flaws in this narrative. Compiling evidence from across the kingdom, Nicolas demonstrates that from 1660 to 1789, tax rebellion remained the single most common form of French revolt, far outpacing such collective actions as bread riots, seigneurial disputes, workplace disturbances, and religious conflicts. From the age of Louis XIV to the French Revolution, fully 39 percent of all documented cases of rebellion were antifiscal, followed by subsistence riots (18 percent), attacks on nonfiscal state institutions (14 percent), and sundry other kinds of revolt. Within the predominant category of tax rebellion, moreover, the majority (65 percent) of incidents were provoked by the repression of contraband, as unruly salt smugglers were joined by rebellious calico and tobacco traffickers, the last comprising the most violent group of all.[2] Although Farm corruption lubricated relations between smugglers and their formal adversaries, more rigorous policing and an unyielding underground combined to generate active resistance in the eighteenth century. Thus, while contraband rebellion was relatively sparse in the final decades of the seventeenth century, it spiked during the economic crisis of 1709 (sixty-three rebellions), fell over the next two decades, climbed again in the 1740s and 1750s (averaging thirty rebellions a year, though jumping to fifty-six in 1754, thanks in part to Mandrin's campaigns), and peaked in the 1770s and 1780s (more than fifty incidents a year on average).[3] Far from petering out after the splendid reign of Louis XIV, fiscal revolt remained vigorous right down to the Revolution.

Tax rebellion did, however, change form. In the middle third of the seventeenth century, during the "turning of the fiscal screw" under Richelieu and Mazarin, when direct taxes soared and indirect taxes were extended to new localities, France experienced several province-wide uprisings that posed serious territorial challenges to an embattled monarchy. In the eighteenth century, by contrast, as taxes and prohibitions became regularized and large-scale uprisings subsided, resistance manifested itself through the black market, as small-scale attacks by smugglers became increasingly prevalent. The battle now took place in and over the parallel economy.[4] If the crown succeeded in relegating the furious uprisings of the *Grand Siècle* to the past, it never firmly established what German sociologist Norbert Elias claimed was a double monopoly on taxation and violence.[5] Behind the veneer of post–Louis

Quatorzian stability raged an ongoing guerrilla war between the elephantine Farm and legions of highly mobile traffickers.

In this war—and "war" was precisely the term contemporaries used to describe the conflict between Farm and smuggler[6]—three kinds of rebellion predominated. One was resistance to arrest, classified as "rebellion" by the criminal justice system. When caught red-handed with contraband, smugglers did not hesitate to use violence to escape the clutches of Farm guards, whose intrusions into their affairs they considered wholly illegitimate. Indeed, the rage engendered by such intrusions suggests that smugglers rebelled not only to defend themselves and their trade but to contest the growing presence of a despised system of policing that was associated with the depredations of the Farm rather than the legitimate extension of royal authority. With the age-old notion that the king should live off his own domain and refrain from regular taxation only recently (in historical terms) laid to rest, it was difficult enough for bona fide royal officials to collect permanent direct taxes in the eighteenth century.[7] The interventions of Farm agents, perceived as opportunistic parasites with dubious ties to the king, seemed totally unacceptable to many underground traders, who seized the opportunity to retaliate.

Consider the case of Jean-Claude Loviat, a concierge in an aristocratic Parisian household who hawked illicit tobacco from his room.[8] When three Farm agents arrived to search his premises on 16 July 1773, he shouted, "Get the hell out of here" and began throwing punches. As his wife grabbed the contraband from the cupboard and bolted, drawing two officials in pursuit, Loviat pummeled the third agent with heavy door keys until the man's face and clothing were covered in blood. Pressing his advantage, Loviat drew a sword and chased the bloodied agent through the elegant Place Royale (now known as the Place des Vosges) before making a triumphant escape. Traffickers like this, contrary to the injunctions of royal law, tended to see their stocks of contraband as legitimate property and the Farm agents who attempted to confiscate them as treacherous thieves who deserved a beating. As future customs commissioner Adam Smith observed of the British underground in 1776, the smuggler "is frequently disposed to defend with violence, what he has been accustomed to regard as his just property."[9]

A second type of contraband rebellion involved crowds of local residents who protected smugglers in their midst in the belief that they were defending basic communal values. Such values stemmed less from the paternalistic norms to which E. P. Thompson alluded when he coined the term "moral economy" to describe the logic behind eighteenth-century English food rioters than from a shared sense of economic justice that authorized villagers to resist what they took to be the Farm's illegitimate regulatory claims on the community.[10] Not that everyone in a given community subscribed to an identical vision of economic justice or participated in contraband rebellion with equal enthusiasm, but a common belief in the right to conduct state-proscribed trade was sufficiently deep to move large numbers to act collectively against Farm officials, violently if necessary. Take the rebellion that erupted in the Norman parish of St. Victor de Cretieuville in 1710, when six officials arrived to investigate a tip that a man named Vivien was openly selling contraband tobacco. As soon as villagers identified the outsiders as agents of the Farm, they cried, "Seize your weapons, the dog-buggers are here . . . let's kill them and cut them in pieces." Rifle at his side, the parish priest sounded the tocsin, which summoned a large crowd "armed with muskets, pitchforks, halberds, billhooks, axes, and metal-tipped staffs," and delivered a tirade against the Farm that invoked the name of God. The officials retorted that they represented the king, but after a tense scuffle with villagers in which one agent was struck by an iron rod, they beat a hasty retreat, promising to file a report about the entire incident.[11]

This second kind of rebellion reflected a deep normative divide between the state (or at least the state-sanctioned Farm) and the people (or at least that part of the population that supported smuggling, which, given the scale of illicit trade, was quite large). Although the monarchy attempted to taint armed and dangerous smugglers with judicial infamy in much the same way as it stigmatized murderers and thieves, an effort we will examine in a subsequent chapter, most people did not conceive of smuggling as a profound moral transgression. On the contrary, the laboring classes and many elites saw illicit trade as a perfectly legitimate way to earn money and acquire goods. And because the goods involved in such trade were perceived as benign—as a purveyor of tobacco itself, the state could hardly demonize the plant the way narcotics are demonized today—trafficking seemed like a victimless crime. These attitudes were so pervasive that even priests, the moral watchdogs of communities, did not hesitate to protect smugglers in their midst.

According to a frustrated provincial intendant in 1732, illicit tobacco trafficking was rampant "because parish priests . . . in no way make a crime of it. I discussed this with the bishop of Grenoble who, for his part, spoke strongly about it to his clergy, but to no avail."[12] Backed by centuries of church doctrine that permitted the absolution of tax evaders, priests accepted smugglers' donations, said prayers for their benefit, and intervened on their behalf with authorities outside the parish.[13] One cleric who wanted to fight this "unworthy profession" learned that a condemnation of smuggling from the pulpit would make him a "sworn enemy of the parish." You will be "well loved," warned a parishioner, so long as you do not speak "against smugglers."[14]

Given this moral environment, it is no wonder that passive resistance to the fiscal state in the form of clandestine trade was widespread. Smugglers and consumers alike had no qualms about circumventing the Farm and making a mockery of regulatory law. As the astute observer of Parisian mores, Louis-Sébastien Mercier noted of those who slipped contraband past Paris customs gates, "Every day the most honest people in the world commit an infinite number of lies. One takes pleasure in fooling fiscality, and everyone is in on the plot; people . . . pride themselves on it."[15] More than just making or saving money, smugglers and consumers relished this means of sticking it to the Farm. But the same moral environment also encouraged more violent forms of resistance, like the many communal rebellions in which crowds vigorously protected underground dealers from the perfidious "dog buggers" who worked for the Farm.

A third type of rebellion, far less common yet still more aggressive than the second, consisted of premeditated assaults on ambulatory Farm guards, customs posts, and prisons where alleged smugglers awaited trial.[16] To find an example of this rarer sort of extreme violence, we need look no further than our very own Louis Mandrin. A rebel among rebels, Mandrin improvised a kind of guerrilla warfare that involved shootings, military-style occupations, and kidnappings that went well beyond the usual skirmishes. Such aggressive violence was visible early in his career, well before the great campaigns of summer and fall 1754. Already in July 1753, as we have seen, Mandrin, Bélissard, and others shot two guards in cold blood. This blatant assault on the Farm would continue during a smuggling run in January 1754, when, with a half dozen others, the two Dauphinois preemptively ambushed the border post at Chartreuse, stealing guards' weapons and powder, destroying their duty register, and threatening to "rough up" anyone who continued to work for such an abominable institution.[17] With the post neutralized, the traffickers passed easily into France and proceeded to Curson, where, after fooling a Farm brigade into thinking they were colleagues from another post, they suddenly opened fire, killing three and wounding two.[18] Before leaving the scene of the crime, Mandrin snatched a trophy from a brigadier's corpse: the fine military hat festooned with gold trim that he would flamboyantly wear in his future exploits. Just as men in rural youth gangs carried off the hats of their rivals in symbolic expressions of dominance, so Mandrin's new chapeau represented his bloody victory over the Farm.[19]

The Curson attack had immediate repercussions. In the next town, Grand-Lemps, the smugglers learned that a Farm guard named Pierre Dutrait had boasted that, had he been at Curson, he would have made short work of the band. Although such bluster was as common among guards as it was among smugglers, Mandrin and the others did not let it go unpunished. Waiting until midnight, they sneaked into the braggart's home, seized him and his wife, and marched them outside in their nightshirts. In the darkness, they threatened to shoot Dutrait if he continued to serve the Farm and, for good measure, stole three of his rifles, a pair of pistols, a game bag, and a horse.[20]

Such bold acts of aggression, unprovoked in the sense that they were preemptive and had little to do with immediate self-defense, would define all his smuggling expeditions. Driven by vengeance, this violence reflected what William Beik calls a "culture of retribution," in which common people acted to punish or humiliate particular local officials or people of status who, in their eyes, had abused less fortunate members of the community.[21] Retribution certainly motivated Mandrin. On 9 July 1754, he would take a detour from a smuggling excursion to avenge the death of his brother Pierre. Returning to his natal village of Saint-Étienne, he hunted down Jaques Sigismond Moret, the Farm agent Mandrin blamed for denouncing his brother, and shot him in cold blood. He also murdered Moret's two-year-old granddaughter, who happened to be in her grandfather's arms when this scion of the Mandrin clan came back to settle accounts. One cannot help but see such retribution in all the battles Mandrin waged against the Farm; as his biographers like to stress, he seemed to be taking revenge on the Farmers General for ruining his life and the lives of his kin after the Italian affair. But we should refrain from interpreting the smuggler's violence through the single lens of retribution. While doing so makes for dramatic storytelling, it fails to capture the full political significance of Mandrin's violent commercial practices. Not all of his acts of rebellion occurred within the confines of a localistic culture of retribution.

Busting Monopoly

The precise meaning of any act of violence can be determined only through close analysis of the context in which it erupted, the symbolic modes by which it was expressed, and the imagined target at which it was directed.[22] To understand the full meaning of Mandrin's assaults on the Farm, it is important to move beyond his vengeful attacks on armed guards to consider the methods he used to market contraband, which evolved over the course of his career to set his band apart from others. The first significant innovation in his trading practices occurred in the summer of 1754, when, no longer content to peddle clandestinely, his gang went public, occupying whole towns in military fashion to sell contraband overtly in marketplaces. A kind of "military entrepreneur," Mandrin flagrantly defied the monopoly's security forces by opening public spaces in which to sell large quantities of cheap goods to awe-struck townspeople.[23]

Mandrin developed this daring marketing strategy over the course of three long-distance expeditions into French territory: a monthlong journey from Savoy to Languedoc between 6 June and 9 July, a jaunt out of Switzerland at the end of July (about which we know very little), and a brash campaign to Auvergne from 20 August to 5 September (Figure 5.1). Composed of thirty to sixty men, the gangs in which he traveled that summer were larger than previous ones he had joined. Besides Bélissard, the pack included a cast of picaresquely named characters with whom Mandrin would work in the months ahead, including Joseph Dhuet Saint Pierre aka the Major (from the Savoyard smuggling haven of Les Échelles), the Major's younger brother Jean-François aka Ham, Antoine Roche aka Ready-to-Drink (a French deserter from the Vivarais who now lived in Savoy), Joseph Michard aka Pug-Nose (a native of Pont-de-Beauvoisin), and Joseph Riondet aka Broc (from Les Échelles).[24] The bands of the summer of 1754 dove deep into France. Astride horses carrying two 100-pound sacks of contraband, the men

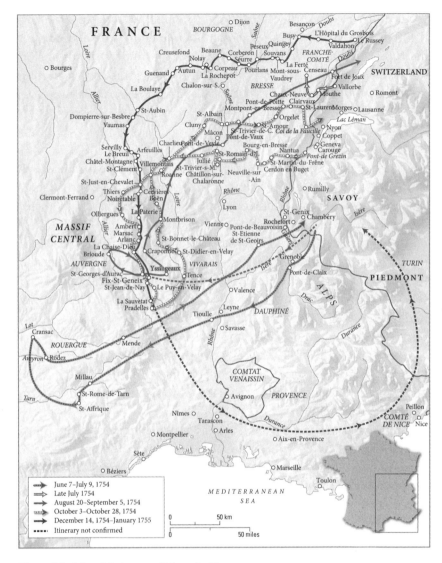

Figure 5.1. Mandrin's expeditions in France.

rode at a furious pace, rarely stopping in any town for more than a day and going far beyond the areas familiar to Mandrin from his travels as a young man. There was a certain logic to trekking so far into the kingdom. Not only did contraband fetch higher prices the further one advanced into the realm but also the interior was largely devoid of troops. After the War of Spanish Succession (1701–1714), when France ceased to be threatened by foreign invasion, the monarchy pulled regiments from the interior to post them in garrisons on the periphery.[25] The deeper a smuggling band penetrated the kingdom's core, the smaller its chances of running into soldiers.

The first large-scale expedition we know of lasted more than a month.[26] Having loaded up on calico and St. Vincent tobacco, a Euro-American blend named after the French Caribbean island, the men slipped into Dauphiné and continued west to cross the Rhône, traverse the Vivarais, and enter Languedoc, some 200 miles beyond the border. As before, the smugglers were ruthless when approaching customs posts. In a morning ambush of the Pont-de-Claix checkpoint, which overlooked the Drac River, they killed one guard and wounded others; stripped the men of their clothes, arms, and money; and destroyed their business registers. At the next river, the Rhône, they chased a Farm brigade away after killing one guard and wounding three others. They then forced local boatmen to ferry them across the water into the Vivarais. From there, the band ran southwest into the Rouergue region of Languedoc, where, from the village of Millau, came the first report of its outlandishly novel commercial methods.

What a spectacle the band must have created when it rode into town on 22 June, each man armed with a double-barreled musket, four double-barreled pistols, and sixty rounds of ammunition. The residents of Millau probably had some experience with illicit trade—who had not?—but they had never seen anything like this before. After entering the village in broad daylight, the traffickers occupied the market square, unloaded their cargo, and began to peddle their merchandise. The sheer audacity of such a maneuver was astounding. Under the old regime, town marketplaces were highly regulated spaces. One could not simply set up a stall and start hawking wares, let alone prohibited wares. Strict royal, municipal, and guild law dictated who could open shops, where they could be established, what goods of which quality could be sold at what price, how such goods were to be weighed and measured, and when vending could take place. As one historian explained, the marketplace was "the linchpin of the [state] regulatory apparatus," which is why most urban traffickers avoided it altogether.[27] Thus, when Mandrin and his comrades blithely occupied the Millau market, the sudden publicity of underground trade shocked the local subdelegate, the only representative of royal authority in town. It was not merely the presence of contraband that amazed him but the conspicuous way it was retailed. The smugglers sold prohibited tobacco and Indian cloth "more publicly than one sells spangles and rosary beads," he indignantly recounted.[28] Throwing off the cloak of secrecy that shrouded the underground market, the band forced open a space for the overt sale of contraband; they thrust illegal trade into public view in explicit violation of the prohibition and monopoly. For the rest of the summer, the gang invaded town after town, establishing illegal open markets as if operating an armed and mobile duty-free shop.

After taking in more than 3,000 lt—a successful day by any measure—the "commander" and "major" (presumably Bélissard and Mandrin or perhaps Mandrin and Saint-Pierre) regaled the good citizens of Millau with an elaborate military review. The leaders ordered their "troops" to conduct exercises in the town square like genuine royal soldiers. It must have been clear to the crowd that the traffickers were hardened and dangerous, many of them former soldiers who knew how to handle a gun. "There was not one of them," boasted a smuggler during the occupation, "who had not at least been sentenced to life in the galleys."[29] But it must have been obvious, too, that these armed traders meant no harm to their customers. Their weapons were to be used in the service of creating pockets of unofficial trade and of protecting such trade from potential incursions by the Farm.

The Moral Economy of the Gang

The brazen sale in Millau, however, was "nothing in comparison to what they did at the Rodez fair." "You will have trouble believing it," wrote the subdelegate of Vabre. Even "the people who saw it have yet to persuade themselves that it really happened."[30] The city of Rodez, capital of Rouergue, hosted one of the province's largest fairs, drawing livestock traders, textile merchants, and peddlers from the four corners of the region. Having occupied Millau, Mandrin and his flock of smugglers joined this annual migration, showing up at the festive fairgrounds on 29 June with horse loads of tobacco. Unsure of what to make of the armed band, potential buyers were skittish at first, but the traffickers reassured them that they would be protected in the event of a crackdown. Their confidence won, customers began to cash in on low-priced leaf that, sure enough, attracted the attention of one Monsieur Raynal, director of the city's Farm office. Raynal was concerned that the sudden influx of such a large quantity of contraband would crowd out local Farm sales, but he knew he did not have the firepower to stop the vending. So he approached the band with a peaceful if unusual proposition: he would buy a large portion of the contraband tobacco (roughly 1,700 pounds) at the price of thirty-five sols a pound, only five sols less than what it was going for at the fair, if the gang ceased its current sales. It was undoubtedly Raynal's intention to take this leaf out of circulation and market it under the auspices of the Farm. Enticed by the improbable prospect of selling wholesale to the Farm, Mandrin and the others accepted the terms of the offer. They closed up shop and transported the tobacco to Raynal's house, only to discover that the director had reneged on the deal and fled. Unwilling to abide this betrayal, the smugglers broke down Raynal's door, violating his private space and property, deposited the tobacco in his house, and instructed two of his neighbors to inform him that if he did not pay what he owed, "they would burn him and his house down." The 3,000 lt were paid within the hour.[31]

Prompted by an offer from the Farm itself, Mandrin and Bélissard had contrived their first forced sale. Both men had experimented with coercion before. Mandrin had extorted a 400-lt promissory note from the warehouser of Saint-Étienne but had not left any tobacco behind in exchange.[32] Bélissard had likewise compelled a notary to pay 600 lt for tobacco and horses, but this forced sale was not directed at the Farm.[33] In Rodez, the band completed a wholly new kind of transaction, and its success encouraged it to try a similar stunt in the next town. In Mende, the smugglers did not wait for the Farm director to make an offer. They forced their way into his house, took whatever funds they could find (1,052 lt in cash), and deposited a quantity of tobacco in exchange.[34] They could have easily taken the money and run—brigands did such things all the time—but they chose to close the circle of reciprocity by leaving behind what they deemed to be a commensurate amount of tobacco. Symbolically, there was a world of difference between this kind of transaction, by which the Farm was forced to pay for contraband, and that performed by men like Pierre Périssol, who simply robbed the proceeds of the wine tax in the *généralité* of Orléans.[35]

What are we to make of these forced sales? At first glance, they look a lot like "military contributions," acts of extortion committed by army officers who regularly forced occupied towns to pay taxes or provide food and lodging for troops.[36] In return for such contributions, officers promised to prevent their men from pillaging the territory. Given the prevalence of such protection rackets in war-torn early modern Europe, it is not surprising that some state officials believed Mandrin to be a demobilized officer whose forced sales constituted a species of military extortion. "Look at these people," former minister and memoirist Marquis d'Argenson noted of the band; they "exact contributions as if they were enemies."[37]

But to see Mandrin's forced sales as military contributions is to miss their larger significance. In a military contribution, money is exchanged not for goods but for protection from the harm the extortionist threatens to inflict. Although Mandrin kidnapped Farm officials, he was not in the business of selling protection. Rather, he was conducting a form of commerce in which an actual exchange of goods for money took place. It was a coercive exchange to be sure, but exchange nonetheless, and in this respect his exploits call to mind not military contributions so much as *taxations populaires,* a type of grain riot that erupted with some frequency in eighteenth-century France and Britain.[38] Hence, it is to the food riot that we must turn to unlock the meaning of the smugglers' coercive commerce.

In eighteenth-century France, the king was generally expected to shelter his people from famine and hunger. Although regional markets in grain provisioned consumers, those markets were subject to the surveillance and regulation of royal officials whose duty was to ensure an adequate supply of food for the great majority of the population. In good years, officials let the market operate according to the impersonal forces of supply and demand. But in bad years, when dearth struck and the price of grain spiked, magistrates often intervened, claiming (quite rightly in many cases) that profit-seeking merchants were colluding to force prices up, threatening the subsistence of innocent people. Denouncing such odious commercial practices as "monopolistic," officials resorted to *taxation* (price-fixing), by which they ordered grain producers and traders to sell their goods at a so-called just price, the price that prevailed under normal nonmonopolistic conditions. Derived from the Latin term *justus,* meaning "the true" or "the real," the just price was understood to be the price set spontaneously by the market without deceit or fraud and in such a way as to provide merchants with an honest profit while making food available to all but the poorest of common folk.[39]

When food prices soared and local magistrates failed to intervene, peasants, artisans, and workers assembled in crowds to fill the regulatory void and impose *taxations* themselves—hence the term *taxations populaires,* price-fixing by popular will. Driven by a set of beliefs that Thompson famously called the "moral economy of the crowd," men, women, and children assembled in large groups to demand that food sellers lower their prices to a fair level. In the face of such collective action—and the threat of violence it entailed—traders relented and sold their goods at the price fixed by the crowd. Rioters seized the food and, in compensation, left money (or IOUs) behind.[40] An exchange took place, but it did so at a price set coercively by buyers.

I suggest that we read Mandrin's forced sales as a mirror image of *taxations populaires.* Although the two modes of exchange ran in opposite directions—Mandrin was a seller forcing higher prices on his buyer, rather than a buyer eliciting lower prices from a seller—they shared certain fundamental characteristics. Both were imposed by agglomerations of ordinary people who, far from acting like unthinking mobs, conducted themselves with a surprising degree of deliberation and restraint. The smugglers could easily have plundered the Mende bureau without leaving any tobacco behind, just as food rioters could have taken grain without compensating traders. But they did not. Unlike thieves (or pirates), they chose to act under the pretext that they were engaging in a legitimate reciprocal exchange. Hence the Duc de Luynes, who followed the band's summer excursions through his contacts at court, observed that the men conducted their affairs "very honestly," although they did insist on immediate payment in cash.[41]

Further, participants in both *taxations populaires* and Mandrin's forced sales claimed that their coercive exchanges were justified by the monopolistic conditions of the market. In the case of bread, a quasi-sacred good of "prime necessity" considered vital to human existence, almost any maneuver to restrict supply and drive up prices beyond the reach of ordinary folk was perceived as monopolistic and intrinsically malicious, especially in hard times.[42] The moral economy thus authorized consumers to break "monopolies" on grain and reestablish a legitimate economic order. In the case of tobacco, no such claims to the moral imperative of subsistence provisioning could be made: no one's life depended on the leaf; no customary law regulated its price in the interests of the poor; no paternalistic economic model had been built over centuries to ensure its distribution. And yet, a similar notion about the illegitimacy of monopoly informed Mandrin's exchanges, as his next expedition would make clear.

We return to the heady exploits of the summer of 1754. Thus far I've been referring to Mandrin as if he were head of his own band, but he was probably only one of a number of independent smugglers who had joined forces. If anyone was captain of the first expedition of the summer, it was Bélissard. The second expedition at the end of July remains something of a mystery.[43] By the time of the third and final summer excursion of 20 August to 5 September, however, Mandrin had become the true leader, and it was during his tenure that the band developed the most innovative techniques for imposing its will on the Farm.[44] During this late-summer foray from Switzerland (where the band stocked up on calico and Dutch-style, St. Vincent, and Brazilian tobacco) to the rugged eastern flank of Auvergne, Mandrin came into his own, casting the mold for the great expeditions to come.

Incidents in two towns, Brioude and Craponne, reveal the band's moral economy in action. Armed with bayonet-tipped rifles and double-barreled muskets, the men reached Brioude, some 200 miles from the Savoy border, at the break of day on 26 August. The town was home to one of several thriving tobacco warehouses in the district of Clermont. In the early 1730s, the Brioude warehouse had sold roughly 10,000 pounds of tobacco annually, yielding 24,000 lt for the Farm.[45] Twenty years later, revenue would have been substantially higher. Mandrin knew that even though such entrepôts regularly shipped their profits to well-fortified cities, there was likely to be a sizable stash of coin in the warehouser's home.

After sentinels surrounded the town, the smugglers paid a visit to warehouser Angélique de la Guerre. Mandrin posted four guards at the widow's door, instructed his men to unload the tobacco in her courtyard, and went to see her. Two local magistrates and a court clerk rushed to the scene, but there was little they or anyone else could do: the armed guards watching the door would not let them pass, and the mounted police would not be arriving for another three days, by which time Mandrin would be long gone. With muskets and pistols in hand, smugglers crowded into the home to find the widow sick in bed. Undaunted by her feebleness, they spewed "a thousand curses against her," the kind of language angry young men used before resorting to violence. Then one of them, probably Mandrin, explained why they were treating her this way: "she was the reason that they were unable to conduct their profession of smuggling peaceably and in safety; and that as she caused them a lot of loss, they had come to force her, against her will, to buy all the tobacco that they presently had available or else she would not be safe and they would throw her out the window."[46]

This threatening declamation reveals two normative logics at work in the gang's forced sales. First, although violent, the perpetrators of the sales were moved by a keen sense of commutative justice, which dictates that accounts between private parties be settled fairly. A commitment to commutative justice had already manifested itself during the expedition of 6 June to 9 July. At Saint-Affrique, the band used deadly threats to force a reluctant *aubergiste* to supply food but then gave the man four louis to cover his expenses. At Saint-Rome-de-Tarn, after a smuggler accidentally shot and killed a pregnant woman, the "commander" of the band held a trial in which the accused was exculpated but forced to pay twenty-two livres to offset the costs of the burial. And in Rodez, the band took a hostage to demand the restitution of several rifles that the subdelegate had taken from fellow smugglers five years earlier. When too many guns were delivered, they consigned the surplus to the town guard and received a ticket of deposit in exchange.[47] Savoyard peddlers were known to have their own internal systems of justice, and Mandrin's band was no exception.[48]

In the case of Brioude, Mandrin held the Farm representative responsible for unspecified commercial losses. The forced sale was simply a way to settle old scores, as Mandrin himself would later intimate in a conversation with a spy who infiltrated his band. Referring to his ruinous venture into army provisioning, Mandrin complained that the Farmers General had refused to reimburse him the 40,000 lt it owed. His forced sales were simply a way of retrieving his due.[49] He would likewise claim on several occasions that the Farm had confiscated large shipments of contraband, the cost of which forced him to change his strategy from retailing tobacco directly to consumers to imposing forced sales on the Farm. He knew he was in a "bad profession," Mandrin once reportedly confessed, but he was compelled to resort to forced sales after a load of merchandise worth 50,000 livres was seized in Montpellier.[50] Examples of such fastidious accounting amid brutal violence could be multiplied. The point is that the forced sale in Brioude represented an attempt to recover money that the band believed (or claimed to believe) it was owed. The desire to compensate himself for costly confiscations would certainly explain the price premium he charged the Farm, which at three lt per pound during this expedition and five lt per pound in the next was higher than what he charged ordinary consumers. As Giovanni Levi has shown, the process by which prices were set in the early modern period often reflected an attempt to settle prior account imbalances between parties. What looks like a premium could simply be the latest attempt to settle old obligations.[51]

The wish to settle accounts does not explain everything, however. Had Mandrin been interested only in balancing his books, he could have plundered Farm coffers without leaving so much as a scrap of tobacco in exchange. But he deliberately chose to deposit the leaf, which suggests that a second, more political logic was at work in his forced sales. By compelling the Farm to purchase that which it deemed illegal, Mandrin and his band directly challenged the monopoly's claim to be the sole dealer of tobacco in the kingdom. To force the Farm to buy his contraband was to break open lines of supply and directly assert his right to engage in the trade. Hence, when the gang confronted the widow of Brioude, it cast her as an illegitimate impediment to the otherwise peaceful business of contraband, just as Mandrin had berated the warehouser of Mende for the "obstacles" the company erected to prevent him from freely selling his merchandise.[52] Such language may make Mandrin appear to be some kind of rogue free-trading capitalist, which is exactly how economic liberals in the nineteenth century portrayed him. But like those who regulated the price of grain, Mandrin was neither strictly capitalist nor anticapitalist: he was acting to correct a monopolistic form of capitalism that, he believed, unjustly blocked his access to markets. While there is no telling if Mandrin abhorred monopoly in the abstract—he was a smuggler, not a political economist—he clearly loathed the particular form in which he encountered it, a tobacco monopoly whose agents wrongfully claimed exclusive control over the French market.[53]

No matter that tobacco was not (yet) considered a good of prime necessity; the stench of monopoly was justification enough for protest. In fact, despite certain commonalities in structure, the political significance of Mandrin's forced sales was rather different from that of food riots precisely because they were *not* rooted in the cultural imperatives of subsistence provisioning. Where food protesters spontaneously filled in for absent state regulators when prices spiked, Mandrin planned his attacks well in advance—he carried a list of potential targets in his pocket—and staged them with a willfulness and aplomb that evokes modern guerrilla theater as much as early modern collective action. And whereas food rioters often attempted to remind royal authorities of their customary paternalistic obligation to respect a fundamental right to subsistence, Mandrin's men made no appeals to higher authorities, taking it upon themselves to claim the right to trade in prohibited goods and to call into question the legitimacy of an institution at the heart of the fiscal state. I am not arguing that one form of popular activism was inherently more radical than the other, for each was subversive in its own way, but when situated in a wider field of protest (from food riots to other kinds of contraband rebellions), Mandrin's physical and symbolic assaults on the Farm constituted a particularly audacious and far-reaching political challenge.[54]

The specific meaning of that challenge becomes clear when we consider the precision with which the smuggler aimed his violence. Mandrin and his fellow gang members were no angels—they would murder over a dozen Farm employees before their expeditions were through—but they rarely harmed ordinary citizens, and they refrained from harassing officials who collected direct taxes, subtleties that were not lost on observers. "He never touches the cashboxes containing direct tax receipts," noted the Marquis d'Argenson; "he only wants those belonging to the Farmers General."[55] The Duc de Luynes was likewise struck by the scrupulous modus operandi of the smugglers:

> They made a big commotion in Auvergne, where they carried a large quantity of contraband and demanded payment in silver; they did not steal from passers-by, but took all the revenue of the General Farm, invading villages, towns, and even cities, all well-armed and in possession of much ammunition and demanding immediately not only the money that the receivers admit to having but obliging them to go borrow when they say their coffers are empty. They did not kill at all, and even had a kind of *order;* they extorted *(taxoient)* the revenues and gave receipts for the money that had been remitted to them.[56]

Although such precision would become apparent to observers only during the next expedition, it was not entirely absent in Brioude, where

Mandrin and the others continued to improvise. After delivering the threatening speech to Madame de la Guerre, the smugglers seized keys from her pocket and opened her armoires, in which they found large caches of money totaling 4,350 lt, probably their biggest single take yet. But the sum still fell far short of the value of the tobacco they had already deposited in her courtyard. Using the official city scales to weigh the leaf, the smugglers determined that their tobacco was worth exactly 15,421 lt, which was 11,071 lt more than what Guerre had on hand. What to do? The warehouser tried to persuade them to take her silverware or just leave her 4,350 lt worth of tobacco, but her suggestions were met with "curses and atrocious blasphemy." The traffickers threatened that if she did not come up with the money immediately, they would set fire to the four corners of her house.

It was during this heated exchange that the smugglers conceived a new way to squeeze money out of the Farm. Having scraped up all they could find in her house, they commanded the widow to borrow from townspeople. Thanks to recent research, we know that private credit was ubiquitous in the eighteenth century, not only among the wealthy and urban but also among the poor and rural.[57] In towns and villages, merchants who had fallen on hard times often appealed to local notables, who extended them credit to keep their businesses afloat in return for interest payments (which were not always forthcoming), as well as respect, loyalty, and service—the glue that held together local social hierarchies. By insisting that Guerre borrow, the traffickers compelled her to tap into her village's credit network. Too ill to go about town herself, Guerre asked her sister-in-law, Madame Legay, to raise loans for her from the town's principal houses. Accompanied by three smugglers, Legay consulted with various notables and acquired an additional 2,310 livres, not an insignificant sum for a town the size of Brioude. About half the loan came from the direct tax receiver, but other notables, including a magistrate and a clergyman, chipped in as well. Guerre drew the loans and passed the borrowed coin on to the smugglers, who now possessed a grand total of 6,660 lt, in exchange for which they deposited twenty-two bundles (2,219 pounds) of tobacco. The remainder of the leaf was loaded back onto horses and trucked out of town. Madame de la Guerre died a week later, having suffered a blow to the chest from the butt of a smuggler's rifle.

Targeting the Farmers General

In Rodez, the band improvised its first forced sale. In Mende, it affirmed the principles behind such coercion. And in Brioude, it leveraged additional pressure against the Farm by compelling its agents to borrow from the community. The pièce de résistance of Mandrin's moral economy—the issuing of receipts—would be added in Craponne to become a distinctive feature of the gang's commercial dealings.

Craponne may not have had a major tobacco entrepôt like Brioude, but the town was large enough to sustain four licensed retailers, a fact of which Mandrin was well aware upon arrival. With forced sales becoming routine, the smugglers entered the town "in battle formation" and immediately divided into four detachments, each of which proceeded directly to a different retailer. Depositing "whatever amount pleased them," they ordered the retailers, "rifle in cheek," to make full payment within the hour.[58] The total bill came to 5,601 lt. Not having this kind of money on hand, the retailers were escorted through town to appeal to relatives, friends, and local officials. After gathering the requisite sum, much of which came from the mayor, they handed the money over to the smugglers, who, in exchange, gave them the tobacco and something new: a shred of paper with a few lines scribbled on it. It was a receipt signed by one of Mandrin's lieutenants:

> I certify that I compelled the Buraliste of Craponne by force and violence to take tobacco, Saint-Vincent as well as Bernard, for the sum of five thousand six hundred one pounds, and so that the Farm is not unaware of this I gave him the present certificate signed with my own hand to serve the Buraliste, up to the declared value. this 28 august 1754 [signed] Molet.[59]

This receipt, apparently the first of its kind, is an extraordinary document. Criminals rarely record their crimes, and yet here were Mandrin's men openly testifying to the "force and violence" they employed against the Farm. Why did they deliberately document their crime in such a way? The receipt declares that its purpose is to make the Farm aware of the forced sale. But why alert the Farm? The answer, as the military commander of the Vivarais deduced, was that the Craponne receipt would allow the tobacco retailer "to justify himself vis-à-vis his company."[60] That is, the smugglers meant for the retailer to use the receipt to prove to the Farm that he had been forced to buy the tobacco and was not, therefore, financially liable for the transaction. Not wishing to stick low-level Farm agents with the bill, Mandrin and his men shielded them from the financial consequences of the exchange. During his own venture into army provisioning, Mandrin had experienced firsthand the misfortune of being burdened with a commercial debt and abandoned by the Farm's financiers. It seems he did not want to expose warehousers and retailers to the same kind of mistreatment (Figure 5.2).

In drafting the receipt, the smugglers aimed high over the heads of local agents. The note was meant to serve as a commercial bill that would be passed up the ranks of the Farm until it reached the Farmers General, who would be obliged to honor it.[61] The Farmers would have to reimburse the unfortunate agent and themselves bear the financial brunt of the forced sale. Indeed, a receipt composed by Mandrin during the expedition of October 1754 would spell this out in no uncertain terms: "I acknowledge to have received from M. François the sum of three thousand livres for three loads of tobacco that I delivered to him, *for which sum he will be paid by MM. les fermiers-généraux.*"[62] The precision with which the receipt targeted the heads of the company illustrates the undeniably political character of the forced sales. Unlike most tax rebellions in which rioters attacked Farm agents in local acts of retribution, Mandrin's band went after lower-level agents to get at the bigwigs who ran the company. As a local Farm official in Saint Just would later recount, the smugglers did not want anything from him *"personally* but

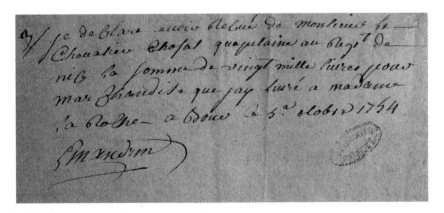

Figure 5.2. Example of a receipt signed by Mandrin, expedition of October 1754. Archives Nationales, AB XIX 793 (1).

much from the farmers general against whom [the chief] has declared an open war."[63] Of course, retribution still partially explains the use of such receipts insofar as Mandrin was attempting to humiliate the Farmers General for their ill-treatment of his family. But whatever retribution he exacted took the form of a commercial exchange that deliberately undermined the principles of the monopoly and, as we shall see, was widely interpreted as doing so. Signing receipts not only strapped the Farmers General with commercial debt. It also constituted a form of activism that, in making the tax farmers pay for the contraband the gang pumped into the monopoly, asserted the right of smugglers to conduct trade with the Farm itself.

By the time the band reached Montbrison on 29 August, all the hallmarks of the forced sale were in place. As soon as they arrived in the capital of Forez, they unloaded the tobacco at the home of the tobacco warehouser. Atypically, they also added the remaining stock of calico, which they probably wanted to get rid of before returning home. They set a price of three lt per pound of tobacco and per yard of calico and charged the official 5,532 lt. When he claimed not to possess the specie, having just forwarded his revenues to the Farm, the smugglers had a ready-made reply: "he has only to name the people at whose house there is some [money] and they would lend to him willfully or by force."[64] Once again, a tobacco dealer was forced to pass his hat around and was lucky enough to find lenders, in this case the local receiver, the official who collected the kingdom's main direct tax, the taille. The smugglers do not appear to have issued any receipts that day, but they would routinize the process of drafting receipts in expeditions to come.

After Montbrison, Mandrin put his mind to returning safely to his haven across the frontier. Since the band had crossed into France, the minister of war, the Comté d'Argenson (the marquis's brother), had deployed a special regiment of light cavalry on the French-Savoyard border and, anticipating that word of the regiment's presence might persuade Mandrin to avoid returning by way of Dauphiné, put army commanders in Franche-Comté and Burgundy on alert. As it happened, the chief did just as d'Argenson predicted, shooting north to exit France through Franche-Comté. That province's commander, the Duc de Randan, had troops posted in the area, but the band slipped by undetected, battled their way past a Farm brigade at Oye-et-Pallet, and crossed into Switzerland. From there, it was just a short hop to Savoy. D'Argenson's frustration with Randan was palpable: "We would not have gained an advantage by closing the exits on the periphery of Dauphiné," the minister rebuked, "if they found it so easy to penetrate the border by way of other provinces."[65]

The brazen killing of guards already distinguished Mandrin and the bands of which he was a part from garden-variety smugglers who hid beneath the cloak of clandestinity. But even among rebellious traffickers who resisted arrest or ran Farm agents out of town, Mandrin stood out as a bold, politically sophisticated figure. Not only did he occupy towns in military fashion to clear public space for the overt sale of contraband, directly contesting the claims of the tobacco monopoly. He also reversed relations of power with the Farm by forcing it to purchase that which it was designed to destroy, in effect wrenching open its supply lines and injecting contraband into the monopoly itself. Culminating such forced sales with a receipt (in the case of the seizure at Craponne), he lobbed his protest over the heads of provincial agents to strike the Parisian financiers at the heart of the French fiscal system.

The coercive marketing techniques developed by Mandrin and his comrades added a new layer of political meaning to contraband rebellions. Moving beyond local acts of retribution, Mandrin was in effect drawing a battle line between two competing forms of capitalism: an underground commercial capitalism of illegal (yet morally legitimate) trade and a court capitalism of legal (yet morally illegitimate) monopolistic fiscality.[66] In the summer of 1754, the fallen merchant turned smuggler was only beginning to exploit this conflict between popular economic justice and the regulatory apparatus of the fiscal state. In the expeditions to come, he would dramatize underground opposition to the Farm by performing ever more stylized forced sales on ever larger stages, drawing the attention of newspapers that would spread word of his rebellions far and wide to an international audience of readers.

6

Triumph

O F A WHOLLY DIFFERENT ORDER than his earlier ventures, Mandrin's expedition of October 1754 was larger than life. Dramatically expanding the scope of his operation, he tripled the size of his band, attacked major cities (including three provincial capitals), and sold prodigious quantities of contraband over the course of a single 600-mile run. The grand scale of the campaign certainly impressed local officials. "What do you think now, Monsieur, of our smugglers' war?" the vicar general of Valence asked the intendant of Auvergne. "We nearly laughed at their first undertakings, but this last eruption is not to be scoffed at."[1] "They have declared an open war" on the Farm, the intendant averred.[2] But more than the magnitude of the expedition, it was the methods that struck observers. The forced sales Mandrin had haphazardly improvised over the summer now became the gang's signature feature, a calling card that grew more recognizable with each repeat performance. Seeing the pattern of bold, coercive exchanges, newspaper correspondents jumped on the story, dubbing Mandrin "the General Captain of the smugglers" and launching him into the stratosphere of celebrity.[3] Having caught the media's attention, the October campaign put this once obscure smuggler on the proverbial map.

The gang Mandrin put together in October 1754 was formidable. More than a hundred strong, it was composed of several complementary elements: an officer corps, complete with a lieutenant, a major, an ensign, a secretary, and a surgeon;[4] several chiefs who had thrown their lots in with the promising young smuggler and his innovative methods;[5] a group of independent smugglers who, having been paid lump sums for enrolling in the band, would buy and sell on their own account;[6]

and scores of valets who also received lump sums but would be paid daily wages for carrying their bosses' merchandise.[7] En route, scouts contracted supplemental personnel—guides, spies, and porters—and arranged for food and lodging at inns and farmhouses.[8] Heavily armed, well mounted, and experienced, the band was nothing short of a private commercial army. Apparently, royal overseas companies were not the only organizations engaged in armed trading.

On 3 October, having stocked up on tobacco and calico, Mandrin's gang crossed the Rhône west of Carouge, entering the French province of Bugey under the cover of night (see Figure 5.1). The men stopped briefly to conduct a forced sale at Nantua, drank at Saint-Martin-du-Frêne, and rested at Pont-de-Maillat. Near Cerdon, in the morning of 5 October, the band was ambushed by a brigade of Farm guards, the first offensive ever to be launched against Mandrin. The guards killed a horse and wounded one smuggler, "Big Claude," who was forced to drop out of the pack a few days later, but they failed to slow the band's march toward its first major target: the bustling city of Bourg.

Bourg-en-Bresse

Capital of the province of Bresse, Bourg was home to some 6,000 men, women, and children, by far the largest town Mandrin had yet dared enter. Although it possessed a sizable militia, Mandrin encountered little resistance on 5 October, as his band of 112 rode into town at mid-morning, secured the city gates, and occupied the public marketplace. Mandrin's first order of business was to visit the director general of the Farm, Jean Hersmuller de la Roche, who supervised Bresse's 200 tobacco retailers.[9] Like many an agent before him, Roche had fled upon hearing of the band's arrival, leaving his "young and pretty" wife behind to conduct the negotiations.[10] Absconding was not particularly chivalrous, but it was thought that wives would not be subjected to mistreatment.

When Mandrin reached the director's home, Madame Roche was still at her morning toilette. Impatient to do business, the smuggler delivered a record-shattering thirty-eight bundles of tobacco and asked Madame Roche for 20,000 lt in exchange, a princely sum in this otherwise cash-poor society (20,000 lt constituted the annual income of a wealthy provincial noble). When the smugglers learned that Madame Roche had no money on hand, they escorted her "through the streets quite indecently in her bare feet, nightgown, and unkempt hair" to a townhouse belonging to Varenne, the region's taille receiver.[11] As they made their way across the center of town, the men called out to the citizens of Bourg to reassure them that "they wanted only agents of the Farm."[12] On his best days, and this was surely one of them, Mandrin had only the most precise targets in his sights.

As if taking a capital city and forcing a monumental transaction were not extraordinary enough, it just so happened that on 5 October a government dignitary was visiting Bourg. Jean-François Joly de Fleury, intendant of Burgundy, Bresse, and Bugey, commissioner of the king's council, and scion of a distinguished family of magistrates, was working with Varenne to distribute the taille among the towns and villages of Bresse. Joly de Fleury was by far the highest-ranking royal official with whom Mandrin ever came in contact, and their exchange would become the stuff of legend.

That morning, the intendant was basking in the glory of an elaborate reception thrown in his honor. In attendance at Varenne's townhouse were thirty gentlemen, including the city's governor, and two distinguished ladies. At 11 A.M., Mandrin and his men crowded into the tax receiver's courtyard with Madame Roche in tow. After the noisy pack of smugglers made their presence known to the highest authority in the province, a face-off between bandit and king ensued in which, according to one eyewitness, "the law of the stronger" prevailed. Frightened by the armed gang, the party of elegants fled to the Capuchin convent next door, while Joly de Fleury retreated to an apartment on the top floor and dispatched two military officers, Lieutenant Bohan and Captain Chossat, to seek out the commander of the troop and "engage him to withdraw."[13]

Striding into the courtyard, the officers introduced themselves to the band's leader, who, they now learned, was named Mandrin. Far from the brute they might have been expecting, the chief turned out to be perfectly civil, even charming. "Mandrin apologized for having to make a din at the door of an intendant," recounted Bohan, but said that he would be unable "to prevent himself from continuing his acts of hostility towards the protégés of Jean-Baptiste Bocquillon [in whose name the Farm's lease had been signed] until he was paid the sum of 20,000 livres for merchandise that he had delivered."[14] The two emissaries conveyed the smuggler's demands to Joly de Fleury, who immediately drafted a requisition order instructing Varenne to pay the 20,000 lt in question. Varenne duly dispensed the coin, which was furnished to Mandrin by Bohan and Chossat "as one presents the wine of honor to the intendant."[15] Grateful for the treasure, Mandrin promptly released Roche and penned the first receipt of the day: "I declare to have received from monsieur le chevalier Chosat captain in the Reg.t of nice the sum of twenty thousand livres for merchandise that I delivered to madame Roche[,] Bourg 5 October 1754 [signed] L. Mandrin."[16] Another receipt would be drafted in the afternoon, explicitly calling upon the Farmers General to reimburse the retailer who had been subjected to the exchange: "I acknowledge to have received from M. François the sum of three thousand livres for three loads of tobacco that I delivered to him, for which sum he will be paid by MM. les fermiers-généraux. Bourg, October 5, 1754 [signed] L. Mandrin."[17]

Money in hand, the traffickers drank and feasted in the taverns of the market district, and peddled contraband to townspeople, while Mandrin led a detachment to the prison. On their previous expedition, in Montbrison, Mandrin's men had freed all of the prisoners from jail, including seven smugglers, three thieves, and one murderer, all alleged criminals since municipal prisons were used to hold the accused before trial, not to punish convicts. Having sprung the captives, the smugglers returned the chains to the jail (for they "belonged to the King") and indiscriminately welcomed the prisoners into the band.[18] In Bourg, by contrast, Mandrin refined his methods of liberation by making distinctions between different kinds of prisoners. Announcing that he did not want "any thieves or evildoers [*malfaiteurs*] in his troop," he consulted the registers of the jail and selected ten prisoners for release: four smugglers, two counterfeiters, a deserter, a debtor, and two men whose charges are unknown.[19] Thieves, three of whom had to be thrown back in jail after slipping out with the others, were deliberately left behind.[20] Mandrin drew the line at theft.

The performance in Bourg bore all the trademarks of Mandrin's moral economy. His men remained relatively well disciplined, focusing the threat of violence (without releasing it) on the Farm. The receipts made it abundantly clear that the Farmers General were to pay for the contraband. And the chief himself was astonishingly polite, exhibiting a noble panache while dealing with the intendant and seeming to relish the part he played on this larger stage. The prison liberation was also packed with political meaning. While it was not uncommon in the heat of insurrection for crowds to free fellow protesters, Mandrin added a twist to the practice by freeing captives he did not know in a place he was not from at a time long after arrest. Depersonalizing the act of liberation, he exhibited a relatively abstract sort of solidarity with those behind bars. Like the acts of "excarceration" performed by Jack Shepard, the robber who repeatedly escaped prison to the amazement of Londoners in the 1720s, the opening of the Bourg prison countered a western European trend toward incarceration.[21] In France, where unprecedented numbers of traffickers and other convicts were being dispatched to galleys and labor camps, Mandrin's prison liberation gestured toward an alternative system of justice in which legitimate "crime" (smuggling, counterfeiting, indebtedness, desertion) and illegitimate crime (theft, "evildoing") were to be distinguished. In this respect, the moral distinctions inscribed in the forced sale and the prison liberation were of a piece.

The place of Joly de Fleury in this moral economy is not without significance. Far from mounting military resistance or even challenging Mandrin's claims, he complied with Mandrin's demands at every step. No doubt he feared for his life and that of the citizens of Bourg, but his participation went beyond mere self-preservation. First, he did everything in his power to see that Varenne was properly reimbursed by the Farmers General, as Mandrin had wished. After the smugglers left Bourg, the intendant had all of the contraband tobacco transported to Varenne's house to be methodically inventoried. Each bundle was weighed, assigned a number, and sealed: there were forty-four in all—the exact number Mandrin had written in his receipts—and the total weight was 4,918 livres. Once this information was carefully recorded, the tobacco was locked under the stairway in Varenne's home "until the reimbursement of the said sum of 23,000 livres and that of 48 livres that had been paid to those who moved, weighed, numbered, and closed the said bundles."[22] When the Farm subsequently asked Joly de Fleury to issue an order transferring possession of the contraband from Varenne to Roche so that the tobacco could be transported to a warehouse in Lyon, the intendant agreed but inserted a clause in the ordinance ensuring that such a transfer would not vitiate Varenne's claim for reimbursement.[23]

The intendant also solicited the finance minister, Moreau de Séchelles, on Varenne's behalf, but Séchelles was adamantly opposed to reimbursement. Not only did the minister believe that the royal council was in no position to make the Farmers General pay the Bourg tax receiver, but he further insisted that there was no compelling reason for it to do so. No "rule of justice" held the Farmers financially responsible: "if the smugglers intended to make [the Farmers] incur this loss, this is not a sufficient reason for the council [to act]." Instead, the minister insisted that taxpayers be forced to compensate the Farm. If tobacco-running "scoundrels" committed their crimes with the aid and support of "the peoples," he argued, then "the peoples" should pay for Mandrin's forced sales by means of a special tax. Only then will they make common cause with the Farm against "brigands and public thieves."[24] Séchelles's refusal to abide by the logic of the forced sale would not survive his fall from power, however. Two and half years later, a new finance minister found in favor of the tax receiver and ordered the Farmers General to make reimbursement, in effect validating Mandrin's receipt.[25]

It may be that in seeking reimbursement Joly de Fleury was simply concerned for Varenne's financial plight—that regardless of Mandrin's wishes, the intendant was only looking out for one of his protégés. But there is strong evidence that the intendant sympathized to some degree with Mandrin and was sincerely concerned about his fate. At the very least, he thought it more prudent to co-opt the rebel rather than attempt to exterminate him. In the days following the incursion into Bourg, Joly de Fleury took the astonishing step of asking the minister of war to grant Mandrin amnesty. We do not know the terms of the proposed arrangement. The intendant may have solicited a place for the chief in the French army, a proven way to neutralize rebels in the early modern period. (Louis XIV had co-opted Camisard leader Jean Cavalier with a command: why not do the same for Mandrin?)[26] But it was more likely that Joly de Fleury was asking for a simple truce by which Mandrin would lay down his arms in exchange for clemency. In any case, d'Argenson brusquely rejected the idea: "with regard to the amnesty you asked for Mandrin, he must not hope for a pardon as he has been condemned to death for counterfeiting, and, besides, it would set a bad example to negotiate with people of this kind."[27] The war minister had his facts wrong—Pierre Mandrin had been convicted of counterfeiting, Louis for murder—but no matter. He was not prepared to negotiate with the likes of a hardened criminal.

That Joly de Fleury had done so little to stop Mandrin on 5 October did not help his plea for amnesty. The war minister scolded the intendant, "I scarcely know a sadder circumstance than the one in which you found yourself on this occasion, which is going to make the Brigands even more enterprising and rash." (The original line of the letter was even harsher: "it is deplorable that you were obliged to yield to force at this moment.")[28] Nor was the minister of war the only government official troubled by the passivity Joly de Fleury had exhibited in Bourg. A gossipy underling of the intendant of Auvergne reported that one of the latter's esteemed colleagues (probably a fellow intendant) disapproved of the way Joly de Fleury's entourage "withdrew to the Capuchin convent, after having twice given money" to the smugglers. Instead of retreating, they should have concentrated on foiling Mandrin.[29] Such opprobrium exposed a fault line within the monarchy between officials like Joly de Fleury who viewed Mandrin sympathetically and those who had nothing but contempt for the coercive exchanges he imposed on the Farm.

The Charlieu Loop

Fresh from his triumph in Bourg, Mandrin continued his march west to the town of Charlieu. From there, the band would trace a 300-mile oval south through the mountainous eastern flank of Auvergne to the village of Langogne and then back north through the Vivarais, Lyonnais, and Beaujolais to close the circle in Charlieu. Rich in easy targets, this elongated loop formed the sweet spot of the October expedition. Auvergne was completely cut off from major trade routes, devoid of well-fortified cities (apart from its capital, Clermont), and enjoyed little protection from either the mounted police, whose paltry hundred officers were scattered across the expanse of the province, or the royal army, which had all but abandoned the central region decades ago. Mandrin chose well when he targeted this region for armed trade.

Rounding the Charlieu loop in two weeks, Mandrin standardized his methods of coercion as he conducted over a dozen rapid-fire forced sales. Each sale was composed of a series of increasingly routinized steps: securing the town, demanding payment, raising the cash, delivering the goods, documenting the sale, and liberating the prison. The first step, occupation, involved securing city gates, churches, and central marketplaces. When Roanne was taken in the afternoon of 9 October, for example, a small advance guard of twenty-five men, "mounted and armed with muskets, pistols, Bayonettes, and sabers," entered the town in battle formation and took over the square in front of the Saint-Étienne church. Blocking access to the church was an astute opening move, since church bells in preindustrial Europe were often used as early-warning systems. Bells tolled to warn residents of natural disasters, marauding armies, predatory wolves, and dangerous brigands; alerting neighboring towns and spreading a chain of alarm across the countryside. Disabling this communications system in Roanne assured that the town would remain silent. Five minutes after securing the public square, two fife players marched into town, followed by the military commander, Mandrin, a man "of great size" who rode at the head of a corps of 125 armed men, an imposing spectacle for citizens of any provincial town.[30]

Once towns were secure, the next step in imposing forced sales was to visit Farm officials and demand a lump sum of money in exchange for tobacco. In the Charlieu loop, Mandrin normally demanded 20,000 lt, the amount he had successfully solicited in Bourg and on which he would continue to insist as his opening bid. But more often than not, such a demand was far beyond the capacity of officials to fulfill. In Ambert, the Farm warehouse had in the 1730s yielded upwards of 25,000 lt a year, more than enough to cover Mandrin's far-fetched requests.[31] But when Mandrin besieged the village on 12 October 1754, by which time tobacco consumption in the district must have only increased, he found nothing close to the 20,000 lt for which he had asked. Because warehousers shipped coin to Paris every month and acted as state banks by paying local government expenses from their cash receipts, they rarely had more than a few weeks of revenue on hand. The day Mandrin arrived in Ambert, the coffers of the tobacco warehouse held only 3,000 lt.

When Farm officials came up short, Mandrin improvised. Although he frequently restated his demand, making threats and roughing up officials and their families, he often had to lower his opening bid. The case of Montbrison, the provincial capital of Forez, which Mandrin had also struck the previous summer, is particularly enlightening in this respect, because it reveals a rarely seen division between Mandrin and his men. On 23 October, the troop reached Montbrison and went immediately to the home of the salt-tax receiver Baillard du Pinet. From the outset, Baillard played his hand beautifully, barricading himself in his house at the earliest sign of the band's arrival. When the smugglers tried to break down his door, he agreed to open up only if they promised to spare his life and send in a small delegation. After Mandrin gave him his word, a small group of smugglers crossed the threshold and demanded 20,000 lt. Baillard calmly received the men, discerned which was the leader, and engaged him in conversation with his wife, sister, and mother. Mandrin said he was coming from Le Puy, where he had been shot, and asked the family to send for a surgeon to dress his wound. When it seemed that no surgeon was willing to take on such a dangerous patient—there were limits to the rebel's popularity, especially at close quarters—the receiver's wife willingly went to find a doctor. While waiting, Mandrin cleaned himself up and was fed a bowl of warm soup.

The hospitality the Baillard family lavished on Mandrin softened his initial position. The receiver invited the chief into his office to prove that his strongbox held only 5,002 lt. Normally, Baillard explained, he received about 7,000 lt a month, but there was still another week to go in October. In the seclusion of the office, Mandrin decided to cut Baillard a special deal: instead of 20,000 lt, the salt-tax receiver need pay only 6,000 lt, 5,000 of which would come from his receipts and 1,000 of which would be borrowed from the taille receiver. Aware that his men might frown on such a compromise, Mandrin suggested that they keep the deal a secret. This they did until it was time to give Baillard his tobacco. Since the men had already unloaded around forty bundles in expectation of a 20,000 lt windfall, Mandrin now instructed them to reload the extra bundles back onto their horses, "to great mutterings of protest and the dissatisfaction of his troop."[32] Rank-and-file smugglers chafed at the chief's scrupulous observance of the laws of hospitality. One man's gesture of reciprocity was another's acquiescence.

There were other times when Mandrin's attention to the moral subtleties of exchange was lost on his men. In Ambert, while Mandrin was busy imposing a tobacco sale on a warehouser, one member of his band decided to force the warehouser's wife to buy twenty-six calico handkerchiefs. The smuggler, named La Faye, demanded Madame Lussigny purchase the material for fifty-six écus (168 lt) and signed a receipt in his own name after the exchange took place. Although the band regularly sold calico to individual consumers, it did not as a rule force the textile on the Farm, an institution that did not trade in the cloth. The forced sale in this instance was the result of an overeager smuggler departing from the repertory (and logic) of his commander's coercive exchanges. While Mandrin did not annul the sale when he learned of it, he was sufficiently annoyed at its high price to give La Faye a "severe reprimand." The smuggler was ordered to return twenty-six écus to the buyer, since in Mandrin's appraisal, the handkerchiefs were "well worth 30."[33] Legend has it that the warehouser was so appreciative of Mandrin's integrity that the two sat down to share a bottle of wine.

The next step in the process of the forced sale was raising the money. After Mandrin set the payment, tobacco agents had to find coinage to cover it. Rarely able to scrape together enough money, they were almost always obliged to borrow. In fact, forcing tobacco agents to tap local credit networks became so routine during the October expedition that scouts began to survey possible targets by interrogating locals about the wealth possessed by "priests, gentlemen, and landowners" in the area, as well as warehousers.[34] The first line of lenders to which Farm agents turned was comprised of other tax officials. Although the smugglers never directly went after taille receivers and only occasionally ransomed salt-tax officials, they were more than happy to have tobacco agents tap these officials for credit. Sometimes taille and gabelle receivers could lend the full amount, as in Bourg. But when such officials were unavailable or came up short, tobacco agents had to draw on a second line of credit funded by town notables. In this case, the number and types of lenders varied considerably. At Thiers, two separate forced sales—one impressed on the warehouser's daughter, Jeanne-Thérèse Bardin, the other on the salt-tax receiver—prompted two distinct searches for credit that ultimately led to the same wealthy individual. When Bardin went looking for loans, she immediately turned to the richest man in town, seventy-five-year-old Barthélemy Riberolles, an international merchant. The tax receiver also ended up at Riberolles's home after visits with other town residents had failed to raise enough money. Barricaded in his home, Riberolles conducted negotiations through a window, agreeing to lend 4,000 lt to the tax receiver but refusing to underwrite Bardin, who, as daughter of the warehouser, could not personally guarantee repayment of the loan. This was about age, not gender. The taille receiver of Roanne had likewise refused to lend to the sons of the city's tobacco warehouser, the financial risk of lending to minors being too great. Riberolles was also angry at Bardin for having led the smugglers directly to him, "as if his home were that of a Farm treasurer where considerable sums would be found."[35]

Once a sufficient amount of coin was raised through local credit networks, Mandrin set the price of his tobacco and delivered the merchandise to the Farm. Even when a price was not explicitly stated, the practice of depositing an amount of tobacco that was commensurate to the extorted sum implicitly involved fixing a price. During the October expedition, Mandrin's pricing was relatively consistent: each bundle of tobacco was deemed to be worth 500 lt. Thus, when the band forced the retailer of Chaisse-Dieu to pay 2,000 lt, it left him four bundles of tobacco. Given that the bundles weighed around 100 pounds each, the approximate price of the tobacco was five lt per pound.[36] This became the standard price; in Pradelles, the smugglers informed Farm retailers that "they were selling [tobacco] for 100 sols [five lt] per pound."[37]

In charging roughly five lt per pound, Mandrin was imposing a high premium on the Farm. The Farm itself sold carrots of tobacco for 2.6 lt a pound.[38] When Mandrin peddled tobacco directly to consumers at "normal" black-market rates, as he had in Rodez in June, he priced it at two lt per pound, sufficiently below the official price to spark the interest of consumers.[39] Such a price was well in line with other smuggling operations at the time: in 1761, a band at the Marcenal fair sold its leaf for 1.75 lt a pound, which was "such a big difference in price compared to that of Farm retailers" that "it resulted in a very quick sale."[40] But when Mandrin forced his tobacco on the Farm, he not only raised the price well above black-market levels but exceeded the Farm's own monopolistic rates. He had set the forced-sale price at 3 or 3.5 lt a pound in the August–September expedition.[41] In October, he raised it to five lt per pound. Such a high premium may have reflected his desire to settle old scores, penalize the Farmers General for their enforcement of the monopoly, or simply make more money. Whatever the rationale, high prices were still to be distinguished from outright theft. The traffickers never failed to provide tobacco in exchange for the money they took, and they always delivered merchandise in strict accordance with the price they had set.

So committed was the chief to following through on the prices he set that the salt receiver of Roanne, who had been forced to hand over

10,000 lt, felt authorized to complain that he had not been given the correct amount of tobacco in exchange. If each bundle was worth 500 lt, as Mandrin had said, then the delivery was two bundles short. The smuggler duly acknowledged his error and had two more sacks delivered. When the extra bundles arrived, however, the gutsy receiver objected that they were not as well filled as the others, because the men guarding the bundles had sold some of their contents. In the world of day-to-day affairs, such quibbling was perfectly acceptable, for lightening the weight of fixed-price products was a common form of fraud, but Mandrin brusquely declared the haggling over. His sense of commercial justice had met its limits.[42]

Next came documentation. Not only did issuing receipts become routine while they rounded the Charlieu loop but supplementary documents were drafted as well. In Roanne, the same outspoken receiver who demanded two more bags of weed asked that the whole transaction be conducted in the presence of a judge and court clerk, who would draft an official report. Mandrin said that this request was perfectly fair; his men were "not thieves" and therefore had no objections to the presence of men of law.[43] In Ambert, documentation took another form. When the warehouser, Lussigny, asked for a receipt documenting the delivery of six bundles of tobacco in exchange for the 1,000 gold écus (3,000 lt), Mandrin replied that he would not only give him a receipt but also sign a formal statement drafted by a notary of Lussigny's choosing. It was understood that notarizing the receipt would add greater legal weight to the warehouser's claim for reimbursement. The two men went to the office of royal notary Herbuer-Laroche, who drafted a document on official stamped paper that recounted the forced sale by "Louis Mandrin, Merchant and Commander of Smugglers." The statement was signed by the warehouser, Mandrin, the notary, and two witnesses, Jean-Baptiste Ratier, a painter, and Henry Faure, a merchant.[44]

Mandrin's penchant for documentation also manifested itself in Montbrison and Boën, where local officials composed reports on the forced sales. In the first town, the "chief said that it was necessary to draw up a report of everything, as was done in other places." Although some judicial officers refused to assist in such a project, an attorney ultimately agreed to draft the document in the presence of two councilors from the presidial court.[45] Given that Mandrin and the salt-tax receiver had developed a special relationship during his visit—recall that the gang leader had already favored the receiver by lowering the amount of the forced sale—Mandrin may have wanted to provide him with extra certification to strengthen his request for reimbursement. In Boën on the same day, the tobacco retailers required an official report, and Mandrin willingly signed the document next to the signatures of municipal officers. The document stated that the tobacco bundles had been sealed with the coat of arms of a magistrate and deposited with a retailer, who "promised to present them when it will be ordained by justice."[46] The expectation of a legal settlement with the Farm could not have been clearer.

Following the documentation of the forced sale came the final visit to prison. The link between tax evasion and prison liberation seems less tenuous when we acknowledge that, in the Renaissance, French kings made a show of their beneficence by annulling taxes and pardoning prisoners in the towns they visited.[47] In purging as many as nine jails in October, Mandrin not only padded his ranks, for newly released prisoners were known to join the band,[48] but expressed a sort of royal munificence that directly challenged judicial authorities (and ultimately the kingdom's supreme judge, Louis XV) by asserting the innocence of certain alleged criminals. Every time specific types of prisoners were selected to be freed, the smuggling chief sent the message that the "crimes" of which they were accused were not really crimes at all. Indeed, the kinds of judgments he made in Bourg, where he freed smugglers, counterfeiters, a deserter, and a debtor but refused to release "thieves" and "evildoers," persisted throughout the campaign. There were, of course, moments when the band's moral conviction faltered: in Cluny, it set free two accused murderers; in Orgelet, it released one man charged with homicide and another with theft; and in Le Puy, it liberated an alleged thief. But in Roanne, the gang's moral discretion was razor sharp. After compelling the jailer's wife to throw open the prison doors, the men ordered the inmates to stand before them for questioning. Although many prisoners claimed to be smugglers, a mounted police officer observing the interrogations informed the band that some were lying and in fact were charged with homicide and highway robbery. Having been cautioned that the majority of the prisoners were "rogues who deserved to be punished," the smugglers "contented themselves with releasing two who were merely detained for fighting."[49] The method of sorting prisoners was not perfectly tidy, but the fact that a method existed at all would, as we shall see, make a strong impression on observers.

Le Puy-en-Velay

Mandrin faced little resistance rounding the Charlieu loop until he arrived in Le Puy.[50] Le Puy is the story of a forced sale gone bad. If anyone wondered what would happen if Mandrin ever encountered serious opposition, the answer came on 16 October, when Farm guards in the capital of Velay gave him a deadly run for his money. Le Puy was more than twice the size of Bourg, its walls enclosing 13,000 souls, a municipal militia, and several brigades of Farm guards and mounted police. It was a fortress of a target whose tobacco warehouse was bound to possess a small fortune in silver. Armed to the teeth, Mandrin and his men arrived in the early afternoon, filing into the city under the broken archway at the Pannessac gate. Although the smugglers called out to reassure residents that they meant no harm, as they had done in Bourg, no one was about to take any chances. "People shut their doors and closed their shops," as the town fell silent. Then, Mandrin and a detachment of twenty or thirty peeled from the pack to head down a narrow street to the home of Monsieur Dupin, Le Puy's tobacco warehouser.

Having heard rumors days before that the band was in the vicinity, Dupin had fled, turning his home over to an experienced Farm captain. Expecting the worst, Captain Le Juge prepared the stone structure for combat, reinforcing the doors and windows, stockpiling weapons, and posting two dozen guards on different floors. For once, it was Mandrin who was going to be taken by surprise. As the band eased down the narrow street toward the warehouser's home, musket fire rang out from behind the building's shuttered windows. Eighteen-year-old smuggler Michel the Blond was killed instantly while many others were wounded, including Mandrin, who took a shot in his left arm. Undaunted, the gang returned fire and pounded the house's thick front door with a battering ram while guards rained boulders down on them. (In Roanne, Mandrin's horse carried a special device for breaking down doors; is this what he used to no avail in Le Puy?) When the fortified house proved impenetrable, Jean-Baptiste Jabrin aka Binbarade led a detachment to the rooftop of a nearby structure to force their way in from above. The guards blasted them with rifle fire, crushing Binbarade's jaw and piercing the left hand of another trafficker, but the Farm could not beat back the siege. Wounded, the captain and his guards fled, leaping across neighboring rooftops to safety.

The warehouse was now in the hands of the smugglers. Furious at meeting such violent opposition, they abandoned the rituals of what should have been a relatively civil forced sale and vowed personal revenge on Le Juge and Dupin, whose heads they promised to parade on pikes through the streets of the city. Le Juge's surprise counterattack activated an intense desire for retribution that did not usually express itself in uncontested forced sales. But the conventions of war had long held that the site of a besieged enemy who had refused to surrender could, once captured, be sacked, and sack the gang did, with carnivalesque relish. After helping themselves to copious servings of Dupin's ham, sausage, and wine, they attached his wife's headscarves to their hats "as a trophy of their victory," a ritual they had performed previously in Ambert that echoed Mandrin's seizure of a brigadier's hat months before.[51] The traffickers then proceeded to move all the warehouser's furniture into the street and announced to a drum roll that a public auction would be held. Mocking the Farm's own auctions of confiscated contraband, the smugglers sold beds, tables, tapestries, mirrors, books, clothing, and, of course, tobacco to an eager crowd as local mounted police stood idly by and watched.

Prompted by deadly resistance, this act of pillaging and carnivalesque inversion recalled the fierce culture of retribution of seventeenth-century tax rebellions.[52] Farm officials had crossed a line when they attacked the band, and they were going to be held personally responsible for it. Thus, pillaging Dupin's home was not aimed at distant Farmers General in Paris but at the agents in Le Puy themselves, who were symbolically expelled from the warehouse. At the same time, however, such pillage was not devoid of the careful moral-economic distinctions evinced in previous forced sales. When his men discovered a store of grain in the attic, Mandrin wished to put it, too, up for auction, but the building's owner stepped forward to explain that the grain belonged to him, not his tenant Dupin. After weighing the circumstances of the claim, Mandrin decided against dumping the grain into the street and, instead, slapped the owner with a 600 lt fine for leasing his property to a scoundrel like Dupin. Rather than purging the grain, the smuggler imposed a moral fine on its owner, not unlike the fines that youth gangs inflicted in *charivaris* against outsiders who intruded on local marriage markets or on husbands who beat wives in excess of communal norms. The building's owner should have known better than to abet an official of the Farm, and he was now literally paying for the error of his ways. This act of penality suggests that the price premiums Mandrin imposed on the Farm may have been intended not merely to settle accounts or increase profits, but to punish the Farmers General for forcing the monopoly upon the kingdom.

After Dupin's home was pillaged and all its furnishings smashed, sold, or hauled away, a dozen band members went to the city jail, hoping to find a comrade, Jean-André Rochette, who had been locked up three weeks earlier. Rochette, it turns out, had been transferred to another prison, but the men took the opportunity to release the three prisoners (a smuggler, a perjurer, and a thief) who happened to be present. The next morning the smugglers "generously paid their hosts, gave substantial alms to the poor, and dispensed whatever was necessary to bury their comrade." A local priest consigned Michel the Blond to his grave.[53]

With the hard-fought victory in Le Puy behind them, the men rode south to Langogne and then abruptly turned back north toward Charlieu. The minister of war guessed mistakenly that after the mayhem in Auvergne the gang would hastily withdraw from France by making a direct eastern run through Dauphiné.[54] Perhaps anticipating the military buildup along the Dauphiné-Savoy border, however, Mandrin sped northeast through Bresse and Franche-Comté toward Switzerland. Near the frontier, a corps of two dozen Farm guards attempted to block the band's passage. To no avail: Mandrin's men killed one guard, sent the others fleeing, and crossed the border to safety in Switzerland.[55]

A Legend in His Own Time

The October expedition made Mandrin famous. Agitated royal officials shared reports of his misdeeds, while admiring provincials sang of his feats, initiating the formation of his legend as a "social bandit" or *justicier,* a courageous righter of wrongs.[56] One local ditty about Mandrin's incursion into Bourg contrasted his "bravery" with Joly de Fleury's cowardice.[57] But it was the medium of the newspaper that truly fanned Mandrin's notoriety across Europe. Although the kingdom's oldest newspaper, the government-sanctioned *Gazette,* refused to acknowledge his existence (or that of most rabble-rousers who threatened to upset public order), word of Mandrin's exploits crept into foreign newspapers that flourished across the border.

Established in or near the very same regions from which much French contraband originated, the biweekly *Gazettes* of Amsterdam, Utrecht, and Cologne; the twice-weekly *Courrier d'Avignon;* and the monthly *Mercure Historique et Politique* of The Hague built substantial readerships by offering material unavailable elsewhere. In addition to covering the usual news from the great European courts—the births and marriages of illustrious aristocrats, the latest twists and turns in diplomacy, and, in wartime, the pitched battles of celebrated generals—these French-language newspapers regularly commented on French domestic politics. Of course, foreign editors could not be too critical of their powerful neighbor to the west, lest they alienate the tax farmers in charge of the French postal system, whose cooperation they needed to reach subscribers in the heart of France. Yet they were far freer to treat sensitive political issues than were their counterparts in the kingdom. Not only could they provide readers with less biased reporting on war and diplomacy, but they furnished serious news on the subject of French politics. Before Mandrin burst on the scene, for example, the editors of the *Gazette d'Amsterdam* detailed the controversial disputes over Jansenism that jolted France during the reign of Louis XV. "The *Gazettes* of Amsterdam and Utrecht," wrote a frustrated director of the Royal Publishing Office, "circulate everywhere, light a fire in the kingdom, and continually give foreigners an idea of our troubles that cannot help but prove disadvantageous to the State."[58]

The readership of foreign papers was hardly universal. This was not yet the age of mass media when workers could afford to purchase a cheap newspaper on a daily basis. Subscribing to a foreign newspaper in the middle of the eighteenth century was a relatively expensive proposition. For elites, the price of subscription was well worth the news it brought, as courtiers, provincial nobles, magistrates, merchants, and lawyers were eager to be in the know about the latest political tremors in and beyond France. Judge, philosophe, and social scientist, Montesquieu tracked the history of his own age by closely reading several foreign gazettes.[59] The Marquis d'Argenson followed domestic politics—and Mandrin's itinerary—by supplementing his subscription to the official

Gazette with that of the *Gazette de Cologne*. While elites and professionals constituted the main subscribers, middling and lower groups also found ways to access the papers. Besides sharing among family and friends, Parisians and other city folk could, at little cost, peruse papers in reading rooms, purchase outdated issues from street peddlers, or rent them from booksellers. They could even listen to impromptu public readings in cafés and on street corners, which facilitated the diffusion of printed news among the illiterate. Those who wished to avoid the pricey *Gazettes* of Amsterdam and Utrecht could, moreover, subscribe to the *Courrier d'Avignon*, which, having cut special deals with the French post office, was substantially cheaper. Low postal rates allowed the *Courrier* to slash its subscription price, boosting its circulation to as many as 9,000 copies in 1757–1758, enough to rival the official *Gazette*.[60] The curious could also buy inexpensive counterfeit copies of the *Mercure historique*, which were printed in Geneva and smuggled into Lyon, or the *Gazette d'Amsterdam*, illegally reprinted in Avignon and Bordeaux, as well as in Geneva. Did French readers savor the irony of learning about Mandrin in papers that were themselves distributed clandestinely? Given the multivectored circulation of these papers and the fact that each copy passed through several hands, it is fair to say that they reached a significant fraction of the French upper and middling classes, who were becoming increasingly attuned to the idea of public opinion.

Nothing sold newspapers like war, which meant that in the peaceful age of Louis Mandrin, whose campaigns were sandwiched between the end of the War of Austrian Succession and the beginning of the Seven Years' War, editors scrambled to find substitutes for the glories of combat. Indeed, it was not so much the drama of crime or rebellion that first drew editors to his story as it was the faint echo of war. Initially, the coverage did not amount to much. The only paper to have picked up on the expeditions of the summer of 1754, the *Gazette d'Amsterdam* (11 October 1754), represented them as a simple matter of sedition and military repression: "Smugglers caused a lot of commotion in Dauphiné and Auvergne . . . : some royal troops have been ordered to march toward these areas to disperse these seditious men whose number is rather considerable." One doubts whether the story would have been printed at all had soldiers not been dispatched to rid the provinces of the traffickers. In its earliest entry on the band, the *Gazette de Cologne* (8 November 1754) reported condescendingly that "during the vacation of the parlement, & in the middle of general tranquility in Europe, we converse about the little heroic exploits by which smugglers immortalize themselves today while waiting for the noose and galleys as laurels." With no war to report, readers would have to make do with bulletins on the banal shenanigans of smugglers.

The tone of coverage changed abruptly, however, once Mandrin struck Bourg and Le Puy. The audacity of the two incursions generated a new type of reporting, at once more detailed and more dramatic. Indeed, it was only in recounting the forced sale in Bourg that newspapers personalized the story, alluding to Mandrin by name. Among vague allusions to seditious smugglers, editors now inscribed "Mandrin," a name to which, after the impressive victory in Le Puy, they attached the title "General Captain of the Smugglers," as if the entire underground was under his command.[61] Serialized by its very nature, with new expeditions to report every few weeks, the story of the "Captain" fixed Mandrin's name in print and, by extension, in the minds of thousands of readers.[62]

Not all the press Mandrin received following his October exploits was good. The man was on a rampage, after all, killing guards and extorting money from royal officials, serious crimes that even foreign Huguenot editors, natural-born enemies of French absolutism, could not condone. Remember, too, that foreign papers were dependent on the financiers who ran the postal system, many of whom had ties to the Farmers General if they were not former ones themselves. Careful not to ruffle any feathers and foreclose their only legal avenue to French readers, editors, when referring to traffickers as a group, fiercely condemned them as "brigands," a particularly reviled type of criminal in the eighteenth century.[63] The smugglers "have degenerated into thieves," reported the *Courrier d'Avignon* (3 December 1754). "It is said that the roads are infested with them. . . . We are assured that entry into Savoy is now totally closed to them by the army detachments that the King of Sardinia has posted in all the passages, having ordered at the same time to treat all those arrested as brigands." The *Gazette de Cologne* (29 November 1754) sounded a similar note of alarm: "The smugglers continue their brigandage, & no longer having any merchandise to sell, they pillage and steal everywhere so that no one is safe on the highways." Playing up the drama of an imminent clash between the French army and the traffickers, newspapers predicted that once the army prevailed, as it inevitably would, the criminals would be swiftly punished for their crimes:

> All the letters that we receive from Lyon are filled only with the unrest & brigandage committed by smugglers who, 1800 strong, roam these cantons well-armed, forcing the richest individuals to buy their goods and engaging in extreme violence. The regiments of Grassins, La Morlière, and the Breton Volunteers have been put on their tail. Those who are able to be captured will be treated like highwaymen & and as such hanged immediately without a trial. (*Gazette de Cologne,* 22 October 1754)

Undercutting such general condemnations of brigandage, however, portrayals of Mandrin himself depicted the chief in unreservedly favorable terms. In fact, the same newspapers that vaguely decried the lawlessness of seditious traffickers reported in riveting detail the full complexity of what we've been calling the smugglers' moral economy. Such detail not only made the adventures of the gang seem real to readers but showcased the moral subtleties that distinguished the gang from irredeemably lost bands of highwaymen. The Paris correspondent of the *Gazette d'Utrecht* reported on 22 November 1754 that "these smugglers, whose number and arms make them formidable, daringly travel the countryside, going from city to city, where they ransom the residents by obliging them to take a quantity of merchandise that is commensurate to the value of the sum they find suitable to require. These disturbers of the peace exhibit, however, a kind of probity, & even show a sort of generosity toward those who, for fear of mistreatment, find themselves forced to render their services. Mandrin, who is at their head, is the most determined man ever known." Copying the spry weeklies, the *Mercure historique* of November 1754 described how the smugglers asked Farm bureaus "to exchange their goods for silver coin." "They fixed the sum themselves and delivered the quantity of merchandise that they judged suitable to give. . . . Their way of asking was rather decent but was at the same time intimidating enough to make agents fear the worst if they refused to cooperate." The *Courrier d'Avignon* (29 October 1754), which had correspondents quite close to the story in Geneva and Lyon, was especially careful to accent the hero's moral acuity. Excusing Mandrin for the exorbitant rate at which he forced tobacco on the Farm in Bourg, the paper explained that the price of his contraband would fall once he was reimbursed for exactions the Farm had previously taken from him. It was also duly reported, as Mandrin would undoubtedly have wished, that his receipt was to be sent to the Farmers General, who would be held financially responsible for forced sales. Hammering this point home, the paper noted that, in Montbrison, Mandrin had required the composition of an official report to ensure that the receiver would be reimbursed. To underscore the chief's sense of decency, the *Courrier* informed readers that while liberating the Bourg jail, he refused to release four prisoners accused of theft, "saying that he did not protect these sorts of people; to the contrary, he locked them up anew with his own hand." Energetically creating a seditious but socially sensitive folk hero, newspapers neglected to report that the gang sometimes released less-savory characters.

Not unlike the gallant aristocrats newspapers described in their dispatches from royal courts, Mandrin was represented in strikingly noble terms. All the papers emphasized the graciousness with which he handled himself in Bourg, where he was respectful of Madame de la Roche, courteous toward Joly de Fleury, and honest in his dealings with Fleury's emissaries. The adjectives "eloquent," "decent," and, above all, "polite" sprinkle the coverage. According to the *Gazette d'Amsterdam* (5 November 1754), which related the Bourg incident in exquisite detail, "the chief of the smugglers received [Fleury's emissaries] very politely and told them that he was sorry that his arrival instilled so much fear in such honorable company but that he was not able to refrain from fulfilling the duties of his commission." Such politeness and grace, combined with evident martial skill, led many to assume that Mandrin was a former military officer, for it seemed far more likely that the October campaign had been conducted by a decommissioned officer than a smuggler from the ranks of the petite bourgeoisie.

Mandrin was certainly portrayed as *acting* like a distinguished officer. As the *Mercure historique et politique* (December 1754) explained, "He found the means to inspire in [his men] such a great respect for his person that they followed him blindly. He also assumed the right to accord honors to those of his troop who distinguished themselves by more or less brilliant deeds. His presumption goes so far as having imagined an order of chivalry, in which he bestows awards on those officers of his corps whose bravery commends them." The same paper recounted a spicy (if fictive) anecdote in which the smuggler cleverly outwitted a landed gentleman who had offered a 3,000 lt reward for his capture, dead or alive. Having heard rumor of the reward, Mandrin himself showed up at the nobleman's château, announcing that he had brought the chief's head. When the gentleman asked where it was, the smuggler replied, "La Voilà: I am Mandrin, & I enjoin you, Monsieur, to keep your word." When the outraged landowner balked, Louis reportedly remarked, "I pride myself on being a man of honor in my profession. Would you be so kind as to provide the 3,000 lt without delay? If not, I have my band here: one word and your castle will be pillaged." The seigneur relented and paid the reward, "after which, Mandrin took his leave in a rather decent way and withdrew with his troop."

If the polite exchanges in Bourg gave newspapers an opportunity to tout Mandrin's noble bearing, the violence in Le Puy gave them pause. A pitched battle against the Farm, complete with musket fire and casualties, had to be handled tactfully. Indeed, editors were careful to frame the narration of the event with an introduction that sharply condemned the smuggler and a conclusion that foretold certain punishment. "The expedition in Le Puy-en-Velay presents the kind of valorous conduct that we would praise in brave people who were serving a good cause but which we cannot refrain from detesting in brigands and scoundrels," the *Gazette d'Amsterdam* sanctimoniously began. Yet the substance of the report that followed undermined the introduction, offering a triumphant tale of a conquering hero, the kind of war story that encouraged readers to cheer Mandrin on. "Here is how it is said things happened." Mandrin, his lieutenant St. Pierre, and sixty-odd men "resolutely" entered the city, unaware that a hundred well-armed Farm guards were lying in wait. When the troop passed before the warehouser's home, the guards discharged a surprise volley of rifle fire, killing one smuggler and wounding others.

> Mandrain & St. Pierre, who expected nothing less than a like salute, showed in this occasion the greatest sang froid of all, & immediately led a counterattack, commanding their troop to dismount and besiege the house. For a while, shots were sporadically exchanged when the enemy came into sight, but this little, indecisive war did not at all satisfy the two chiefs, who wanted to conquer or die. Mandrin led a detachment to break down the door, while St. Pierre and others climbed on the roof. Everything came together for the two chiefs. The roof was breached, the door caved in to the blows of the battering ram; armed from head to toe, they entered and fired continuously on the guards. The action lasted nearly an hour, and the field of battle was for Man-

drin and his troop. Sixteen guards were killed and many more wounded. The smugglers lost only the one man, killed while passing in front of the house. In this incredibly bold attack the two chiefs were wounded. They captured 30 rifles, pillaged the house, and forced the rest of the Farm agents to flee. Such are the principal circumstances of this action in which bravery and temerity crowned the crime that justice will sooner or later punish.

The violence in Le Puy did not stop the editors of this *Gazette* from casting Mandrin in the familiar role of military hero: "the field of battle was for Mandrin and his troop." In fact, the single most edifying description of the kingpin was filed after the Le Puy incident by a correspondent based in Chambery, Savoy—Mandrin country—and published in the very same paper (27 December 1754). How did this bulletin get by the postal farm?

This Mandrain is a man very well known in Savoye & in Dauphiné, his homeland. He is 35 to 36 years old, has a rather handsome face, is tall, strong, robust, & very agile. To these qualities of the body he joins a keen mind, graceful and polite manners, and a natural gentleness. But he is prompt to avenge an offense, acts boldly and intrepidly in the face of any challenge, and is coolheaded with an admirable presence of mind when confronting danger. Sober & temperate, wine never seduces his reasoning. Patient & hard-working to a fault, his courage would allow him to undertake anything, bear anything, to satisfy his ambition. Perhaps he might have shone in high society & been spoken of there with honor had he not lacked an opportunity and a suitable post. Instead, he became a brigand through a chain of events the recitation of which would too much divert us.

While denouncing brigandage in principle, foreign newspapers represented Mandrin as the dashing face of the shadow economy.

The October expedition made Mandrin. The booty alone from the forced sales—an eye-popping 102,184 lt in gold and silver coin—was substantial enough to make him a very rich man.[64] Even after accounting for such costs as the original price of the merchandise, the wages of valets, and the spoils distributed to other chiefs, it is safe to say that Mandrin profited handsomely from this venture. He now possessed more wealth than most commoners and many a noble.

But more than money was at stake in a campaign that tested the authority of the Farm and, by extension, the monarchy itself. In Bourg,

Mandrin performed the most celebrated forced sale of his career, impli-
cating a distinguished royal intendant in a polite but consequential coercive exchange. In Le Puy, stunned by a surprise counterattack, he
engaged the Farm in heavy combat and prevailed over a company of
well-armed and fortified guards. In smaller towns, the constant repeti-
tion of forced sales and prison liberations made it abundantly clear that
this was no typical band of smugglers and its leader no ordinary chief.
Mandrin was directly contesting the claims of the royal tobacco monopoly (and, to a lesser extent, the calico prohibition), undermining
the regulatory authority of the Farm, and usurping the right to judge
alleged criminals—all in a way that captured the imagination of the
press. During a peacetime lull, foreign newspapers seized on his daring
exploits to craft a figure of noble bearing, moral conviction, and martial prowess, projecting Mandrin's subversive form of commerce to a
large and largely sympathetic audience.

Even before newspapers brought the story of Mandrin to their readers, the monarchy understood that the smuggler posed a political threat
of some significance. As Mandrin raced across the southeast in October
1754, Louis XV took the rare step of summoning the royal army to destroy the gang. Mandrin must have known that the forces of order were
lining up against him, but he would risk yet another expedition in December. It would be his last.

7

The Would-Be General

IN DECEMBER 1754, AFTER a few weeks of respite in Savoy and Switzerland, Mandrin launched what would be his final expedition into France. In October, French authorities had been caught off guard, allowing him to sweep through the southeast, but they now mustered the full weight of a modernizing state against him: city militias manned ramparts, the mounted constabulary patrolled roads, rising numbers of Farm brigades readied for battle, and a novel force on the scene, the royal army, prepared to give chase. Mandrin confronted an entirely new level of resistance, which he met with increasingly violent countermeasures. Indeed, whatever blood had been shed in previous expeditions paled in comparison to that spilled in the winter of 1754. Although the stiff opposition he encountered disrupted the moral economy of his coercive exchanges, the battles he fought in the last days of 1754 sealed his reputation as a brilliant if ill-fated military commander, a "general manqué" whose bravery matched that of the most illustrious officers of the day.[1]

The War on Contraband

Mandrin's triumphant October campaign stymied the French monarchy. How was it to stop the rebellious gang leader from wreaking further havoc in the southeast? One thing was certain: the crown could not count on the assistance of the court of Turin, which had neither the power nor the inclination to repress smuggling in the province of Savoy. In September 1754, as French diplomatic pressure mounted, Charles-Emmanuel III, the king of Sardinia, acknowledged that Savoy harbored violent smugglers and ordered the governor of the province to arrest fifty-four traffickers, including one Louis Mandrin.[2] None were apprehended. After the ruckus of the October expedition, the French minister of foreign affairs reclassified Mandrin's misdeeds as "atrocious crimes" in a bid to deprive him of his right to asylum and force his extradition to France. Again, Turin instructed the governor of Savoy to arrest Mandrin—again to no avail.[3] The French court now understood that if it was going to get Mandrin, it would have to do so on its own.

What was less clear was which branch of the French government had the wherewithal to do the job. Despite grandiose claims to "absolute" power, the monarchy did not possess a modern professional police force, let alone the kinds of specialized investigative units created in the twentieth century to deal with organized crime. Paris was a model of policing for the age, but vast stretches of rural France remained unmonitored by royal authorities. Indeed, the very idea of policing a kingdom of highly mobile (and therefore potentially threatening) subjects was only beginning to take root in the eighteenth century.[4] Given the rudimentary character of old-regime law enforcement, few instruments of repression were available to quash a marauder like Mandrin. At the king's disposal were four institutions: urban militias, the mounted constabulary, Farm guards, and the royal army. None was designed to destroy large bands of armed smugglers. All were thrown into the fight against Mandrin. Only one would succeed in capturing him.

Urban militias were the weakest force summoned. Before the middle of the seventeenth century, the citizens of most good-size burgs had built ramparts, constructed gates, and established militias to protect themselves from the outside world, filled with brigands, thieves, and soldiers. Militias also patrolled urban neighborhoods and added a splash of martial color to civic events. In the late sixteenth century, a Roman dignitary visiting Lyon was dazzled by the "admirable spectacle" of the city's militia, a force of some 5,000 superbly appointed citizens.[5] But after 1660, as war and civil unrest inside the kingdom abated and military engineer Vauban built a belt of fortresses along key stretches of the realm's border, towns began to dismantle their militias. Municipal authorities felt no pressing need to maintain costly arsenals and impose burdensome militia service on citizens. Many forces disappeared, and those that remained became mere shadows of their former selves, abandoned by local notables who had found ways to exempt themselves from the obligation to serve.

The decrepitude of urban defense was much in evidence by the time Mandrin appeared on the scene. The city gates of Le Puy, the largest town he struck, were in a state of total disrepair when the gang sailed past them in October 1754. The city's citizens had no interest in fortifying municipal defense, its consuls explained, since smugglers "only committed acts of violence and hostility against the retailers of tobacco."[6] Heads of families were unwilling "to risk their lives" fighting in a militia when "smugglers had not abused residents in any town."[7] Why should they stick their necks out for the Farm?

After the October expedition, however, an alarmed minister of war and anxious provincial intendants began to pressure municipal officials throughout southeastern France to shore up crumbling walls, repair dilapidated gates, and resuscitate dormant militias. The effort met with mixed success. In Ambert, townspeople showed a shameful "deficiency of zeal for the king's service and lack of courage for the defense of its own interests."[8] In the event of another raid, the intendant threatened to levy a surtax on the town to cover the Farm's losses, a warning that caused an uproar. At a town meeting on 24 December 1754, heads of household objected that they could ill afford to mount a defense or pay a surcharge, although the intendant's stern words did spur them to raise barricades and search the surrounding countryside for manpower, pitchforks, and hunting rifles. In the end, they gathered ten guns and a small crew of militiamen.

Other towns were more successful. Thiers had a raucous assembly meeting at which an unruly citizen slapped the mayor, but, despite such outbursts and the fact that the "military art" was unknown in the town, residents did mount a defense. What they lacked in rifles and powder, they made up for in personnel with a pool of 330 bourgeois and artisans who patrolled the streets night and day.[9] Other towns followed suit, reconstructing gates, closing walls, placing cannons at strategic entryways, and organizing manpower.[10] The newly raised urban militias were hardly in a position to stop Mandrin cold, but it was not unreasonable to think that vigorous resistance could impede his course through the provinces, giving stronger forces an opportunity to catch him.

One such stronger force was the *maréchaussée,* a mounted constabulary originally established to repress pillaging by soldiers, deserters, and veterans. Over the course of the eighteenth century, the *maréchaussée* evolved into a national police force whose mission was, in the words of a 1769 ordinance, to maintain "good order and public tranquility" throughout rural France.[11] In addition to keeping soldiers in line, the eighteenth-century constabulary arrested highwaymen, burglars, and thieves; policed public marketplaces and fairs; and patrolled the king's highways, escorting convicts to the galleys and tax revenues to Paris.

Above all, the *maréchaussée* was deployed to control the floating population of rural poor. From the 1750s, the French laboring classes migrated in record numbers as population increases, the "pulverization" of land into tiny parcels, and stagnant wages pushed the poverty-stricken out of their natal towns and villages.[12] Although France enjoyed robust economic growth in this period, encouraging some workers to secure better employment in distant towns, wealth did not necessarily trickle down to the working poor, forcing many to wander the roads in search of work, food, and lodging. The propertied had long tolerated the existence of the domiciled poor—neighbors who depended on charity and were more or less integrated into their communities—but they feared the throngs of allegedly rootless migrants who trudged the highways, gathered at fairs and markets, and huddled in urban squares and lodging houses. Although vagabonds did occasionally assemble into menacing bands, much of the elite's fear was a hysterical reaction to the heightened presence of indigent strangers in their midst. Jobless migrants were seen as lazy good-for-nothings whose dubious moral character impelled them to violence and crime. It was the constabulary's job to police such people by arresting all *gens sans aveu*, masterless men who lacked identification papers like letters of introduction from former employers, testimonials of good character from parish priests, or notices of leave from army officers.

Insofar as smugglers took to the roads and posed a threat to public order, their repression fell within the duties of the mounted police. In many respects, the use of the *maréchaussée* to this end had advantages over that of the Farm. Cavaliers in the constabulary had military experience, were better paid, and, like genuine military cavalry, were mounted, armed, and clothed in colorful buttoned uniforms. Nor did they elicit the same level of hostility as Farm agents, because the force was not associated with illegitimate or unfair taxes. Villagers did not always welcome police into their communities, but they were far less likely to attack them or interfere with their operations. In fact, in 1789, when rebellions against Farm agents would climax, the peasantry demanded the deployment of more, not fewer, brigades of mounted police.

Here, then, was a force that might have been able to take on the armed and dangerous smuggling bands of the north and east but for one critical drawback: it was far too small. Perpetually underfunded relative to the scale of its mission, the force amounted to a mere fraction of the Farm's army. Even after the reform of 1720, which reorganized the *maréchaussée* to extend its reach across the entire territory of the French kingdom, the force mustered fewer than 3,000 men. More brigades were added in the 1760s and 1770s as authorities attempted to crack down on theft and migrancy, but the corps never fielded more than 4,000 officers, cavalrymen, and guards.[13] As a result, whole provinces were left to depend on a mere handful of brigades. The number of mounted police in Mandrin country was paltry. In all of lawless Auvergne, there were only eighty-six men in uniform at mid-century. "The gendarmerie is fine in the best of times," wrote one subdelegate from a town raided by Mandrin, "but the insufficiency of its number makes us fear that the smugglers will try anything."[14] In Lodève, an eastern district of Languedoc where Mandrin had struck during his summer campaigns, the subdelegate had "but one brigade of *maréchaussée* composed of three cavaliers," two of which were old and sick. If armed traffickers were to reappear, the one active officer "would be obliged to capitulate and give them what they wanted."[15] Along Franche Comté's rugged eastern frontier, the two brigades in St. Claude and Pontarlier were "in no position to guard the border" with Switzerland.[16] In smuggler-infested Dauphiné, the constabulary consisted of only seventy-two men.[17]

Owing to their limited number, intendants and state ministers explicitly instructed the mounted police to avoid large armed gangs. The royal constabulary should concentrate on "purging the countryside" of vagabonds, insisted Fontanieu, the intendant of Dauphiné: "It is this to which the operations of the *maréchaussée* should be reduced because it would be unfair to wish that four or five men (of which brigades are composed) rashly confront such superior forces."[18] Finance minister Séchelles agreed. Cavaliers sent to do battle with smugglers "risked being assassinated," he warned. "By sending them against smugglers, who usually form bands of a considerable size, we would expose cavaliers pointlessly to their vengeance; it would also be dangerous to gather several brigades together for an operation against smugglers, for that would leave the province at the mercy of thieves who would not fail to profit from the opportunity."[19] Alluding to Mandrin's band, the minister of war joined the lament that the mounted police could do little against "such a considerable troop made up of resolute and seasoned men."[20]

But sparing the mounted police from the ravages of armed bands did not mean sidelining it altogether. On the contrary, cavaliers played an important role in tracking down men who allegedly participated in, or collaborated with, smuggling gangs. Essential to this task was the use of *signalements,* bulletins composed by the commission of Valence and provincial intendants that listed the names and physical descriptions (height, facial features, bodily marks) of suspected and fugitive smugglers.[21] In the absence of modern forensic instruments such as fingerprints and mug shots (let alone DNA analysis), *signalements* were all the mounted police had to go on, but the crude new tool, when combined with strong financial incentives for arrests (bonuses of fifty lt for ordinary smugglers, 150 lt for members of Mandrin's band), was sometimes enough.[22] After a fight broke out in a tavern in Les Échelles, a local official recognized one of the combatants as number thirty on his list of suspects and arrested him.[23]

In addition to hunting suspects, the mounted police assisted anti-smuggling efforts by conducting sweeps of vagabonds. In the southeast, such sweeps began immediately after Mandrin's October expedition when the stunned finance minister ordered the mounted police "to scour the roads, examine those they meet there, and arrest all who are not known or do not possess sufficient certificates and passports."[24] The minister knew that it was a common practice for foreign-based bands in the French interior to dissolve for the trip back home. He also believed that Mandrin used peddlers and men disguised as vagabonds to gather information on the deployment of troops, brigades, and police. In an effort to catch returning smugglers and roaming spies, the mounted police were ordered to arrest and interrogate as many vagabonds as possible. Information gleaned from questioning was sent to the president of the commission of Valence, who decided whether to prosecute.

Prodded by the intendant and his subdelegates, the mounted police of Franche-Comté descended mercilessly on migrants in the aftermath of the October expedition. Peddlers, artisans, agricultural laborers, deserters, beggars, petty smugglers, and discharged soldiers were swept up and thrown in prison without a shred of evidence. The interrogations of such rootless vagabonds read like a Dickens novel. Guillaume Monchemin was a thirty-one-year-old peasant farmer from Burgundy whose mother and father died when he was very young. Left with nothing to live on, he traveled the southern provinces, living hand-to-mouth as a day laborer until he joined the army at age eighteen. Shipped off to Louisiana, he fell ill with scurvy on the high seas and, after stints in the hospitals of Bordeaux and Toulouse, returned to Burgundy to eke out a living peddling brooms, the sale of which brought him to Dole, where he was arrested with no explanation.[25] Monchemin was one of scores of migrants across the southeast who were rounded up in the wake of Mandrin's fall and winter expeditions, a real show of force by the reformed constabulary. However, the overwhelming majority of suspects claimed they were innocent and, after spending days locked up in foul prisons, were released for lack of evidence.

Among those caught in the *maréchaussée*'s dragnet, only three seem to have been accused of serving in Mandrin's gang. Two were patently innocent. One was a Savoyard monk picked up on the suspicion that he was Mandrin, who was rumored to use clever disguises to foil enemies. (The image of Mandrin as trickster would be widely disseminated by popular chapbooks, as we shall see.) It turned out that the monk was just another libertine clergyman. The other innocent, a former soldier who proudly claimed to have served in the chief's gang, could not recount its itinerary and was dismissed as mentally unsound.[26] The third suspect, captured in January 1755, may well have served as a scout. André Waserbach, a Swiss, had been previously arrested for taking part in Mandrin's attack in Le Puy but was released for lack of evidence. Subsequently seen drinking with members of the band, he admitted to dining with one of Mandrin's officers, "the Major," in Orgelet on 27 October 1754, when the troop passed through on its way to Switzerland. But Waserbach protested that he was an innocent surgeon, who sold remedies and traded horses on the side. The intendant of Burgundy and the *prévôt* of Macon believed otherwise, suspecting him of serving as a scout who reconnoitered towns in advance of the gang's arrival. If the dossier on this case offers no conclusive evidence of his guilt or innocence, it does illustrate how, in its own limited way, the *maréchaussée* assisted efforts to track down members of Mandrin's band.[27]

The daunting task of confronting gangs directly was left to the Farm and army. The Farm's forces dwarfed the *maréchaussée*. Year in, year out, the Farmers General plowed a substantial proportion of their revenues (10 to 17 percent) into their police, which, if unable to eradicate smuggling altogether, could at least check the growth of the underground and partially secure enforcement of monopolies, prohibitions, and tax levies.[28] As a result, the ranks of the Farm police swelled to some 15,000 guards by mid-century and 20,000 by the end of the old regime—by far the largest and most powerful paramilitary corps in Europe. Guards were grouped into brigades of four to ten men, each headed by a brigadier and posted at points along the border. Sedentary guards watched salt and tobacco depots, manned checkpoints, and searched carts and carriages, and ambulatory units (some on horseback) patrolled roads, laid ambushes, and gave chase to fleeing suspects. In borderlands with heavy traffic, both types of brigades were deployed to form multiple lines of defense.

Eager to make the Farm profitable, the monarchy invested Farm guards with formidable police powers. The founding royal ordinances of June 1680 (salt) and July 1681 (tobacco) and a string of decrees issued over the course of the following century endowed agents with the right to search for and seize contraband anywhere in the kingdom (including the châteaux and coaches of clergymen and nobles) and to arrest, imprison, and initiate legal proceedings against suspected smugglers, their accomplices, and anyone who interfered with their work. Instead of uniforms, which were too expensive, guards were issued bandoleers inscribed with the words "Fermes du Roy" to be draped over their shoulders. Supplied with muskets, agents were also granted the right to bear arms and fire on suspects, a lethal power given the number of army veterans in the corps who knew how to handle a weapon.[29] If in the line of duty Farm agents were tempted to use excessive force, they had nothing to fear from royal or seigneurial courts, which were explicitly forbidden to prosecute them. Only specially designated (and notoriously lenient) Farm judges were allowed to hear cases of alleged misconduct.

Thanks to its extraordinary size and power, the Farm police did its job relatively well. It captured untold numbers of lone smugglers, the small fry of the underground, and occasionally took down small gangs.[30] Arresting petty traffickers and breaking up the occasional band, however, was a far cry from destroying a large and well-armed gang like Mandrin's. Stopping such an agglomeration of dangerous men was an almost impossible task for the Farm police, which suffered from two serious liabilities. First, despite its gargantuan size, it was still not large enough to protect all of the kingdom's borders, including the long eastern periphery and the confusing jumble of internal frontiers. It was simply a question of numbers. As impressive as a force of 15,000 or 20,000 was, it had to cover thousands of miles of border, protect hundreds of provincial salt and tobacco depots, man scores of checkpoints in Paris and other cities, and collect several different taxes. With their ranks spread thin over such great expanses, guards were easily outgunned by large groups of traffickers. This was especially true in the interior where "Farm brigades fixed at their posts cannot be moved around or assembled into one large corps without great difficulty."[31] The entire province of Auvergne, Mandrin's preferred place of business, had but seven brigades, roughly fifty men in all, at mid-century.[32] More agents were deployed to frontier provinces, of course, as the Farm increasingly invested in security along sensitive stretches of border, but even there security fell short. In 1738, Mandrin's natal province of Dauphiné could count no more than eighteen brigades, only ten of which were mounted.[33] The 126 men had to guard two interior lines—the western border along the Rhone and the southern border with Comtat and Provence—in addition to the mountainous eastern border that abutted the kingdom of Sardinia. In 1753 and 1754, two new brigades were posted in Chartreuse and Tullins, but the additional personnel did not come close to resolving the problem of armed smuggling. What could a brigade of seven guards do against a band of thirty, let alone an army of 100 men? No wonder one frustrated official blamed Mandrin's success on the Farmers General, whose greed and shortsightedness prevented them from doubling the size of their brigades.[34]

The other liability that weighed on the Farm related to recruitment. The average salary of a Farm guard was around 300 lt a year, a moderate sum on par with what many urban or rural day laborers earned. To make the job more appealing, the Farm offered a host of tantalizing benefits: tax exemptions, dispensation from burdensome obligations such as quartering troops, and large bonuses for arrests, confiscations, and the discovery of smuggling routes and networks.[35] The ever-modernizing Farm even created an employee pension plan in 1768, the first such scheme introduced in France. In an age when so many peasants lived precariously, a regular salary and the possibility of a pension was a powerful draw. A 1755 recruiting poster from Grenoble announced with some fanfare that salaries were being increased to 350 lt and 700 lt for guards on foot and horseback, respectively: "These increases combined with bonuses for captures and other fees can make these positions very lucrative. . . . Those who have borne arms in the King's Troops will be advantageously placed, & those who distinguish themselves by their zeal and good conduct will receive a promotion that will improve their fortune."[36]

Still, the salaries and benefits offered by the Farm were not sufficient to draw men of rank, education, or standing in their communities. On the contrary, guards were mainly recruited from the middling and lower ranks of the peasantry, the same milieu that produced many of the petty smugglers they chased.[37] The guards' common origins and limited pay not only encouraged corruption, as we have seen, but also gave little protection against traffickers of their own class who saw them as backstabbing traitors. One guard traveling alone up the Rhône Valley to Lyon stumbled on a band of smugglers in a tavern, where he was immediately frisked and interrogated. Had he not the foresight to have hidden his commission papers in the folds of his clothes and left behind his bandoleer, "he would have risked being murdered."[38] The guards' humble origins also made it difficult for them to pursue men and women of high status. The unfortunate guard who charged the coach driver of the Princesse de Conty with transporting a pound of illegal tobacco found himself out of a job after the princess lodged a complaint with the finance minister.[39] Such were the privileges of aristocrats, and there was little an ordinary police agent could do about it.

Finally, the low social standing of guards meant that many of them were illiterate and undisciplined. Indeed, the illiteracy of the brigades was so notorious that is was purportedly the subject of a wager made at a Paris café.[40] A man who claimed to have access to Farm records bet 200 gold louis that there were not ten men in all the brigades who knew how to write an official report without the help of a superior. The gambler would have lost that bet, but illiteracy ran rampant nonetheless. Only 26 percent of the Lille brigades could fill out a report, while a little more than half knew how to write.[41] Echoing a common lament among royal officials, the intendant of Dauphiné complained that he had a difficult time recruiting good men since only the "weak" enlisted.[42] To keep such men in line, the Farmers General attempted to impose strict bureaucratic procedures and severe disciplinary measures. From 1729, any guard found guilty of conspiring with smugglers was subject to the death penalty.[43] Lesser offenses like swearing, drunkenness, and laziness were declared grounds for dismissal.[44] But the reality was that the

Farm could not expect too much from a workforce yet to be disciplined by late-modern schooling and factory work.

Faced with limitations in the number and quality of its personnel, the Farm could only hope to catch a big fish like Mandrin if it resorted to spying. The idea was to gather enough good intelligence on the smuggler's itinerary to ambush him on French soil. This had worked before; in 1732, Farm spies supplied information leading to the capture of Jean Barret, leader of an infamous smuggling gang. In the summer of 1754, when authorities were first becoming aware of Mandrin, Gaspard Levet, president of the commission of Valence, asked the minister of foreign affairs to field another group of Farm-subsidized spies. The smugglers "kill and assassinate on the least suspicion and exercise violence everywhere, and they march in such great numbers and so well armed that the agents [of the Farm] can neither attack nor resist them; smugglers go search them out at their posts to assassinate them." The only thing to do, Levet reasoned, was to provide Geneva with lists of suspects who would be arrested when they visited the republic. "I feel strongly that we cannot succeed in this without employing spies."[45]

After Mandrin's October expedition rocked the southeast, the Farm took Levet's suggestion to heart. In November 1754, the director of Besançon instructed Jean François Grifon, a thirty-one-year-old army provisioner, to infiltrate Mandrin's band. In exchange for ten louis, the merchant was to win the chief's confidence, learn the time and place of his next incursion, and report back to the nearest Farm official. Grifon's mission began auspiciously enough. Posing as merchant in a tavern in Gex, a small French province northwest of Geneva, he ran across one of Mandrin's lieutenants and was invited to join the band. Grifon was offered a bonus of 100 écus for signing on, which he was expected to invest in merchandise to sell on the trail. After following the band to Carouge, however, he learned that the gang was shutting down operations for the winter, its officers selling their horses and dispersing. Apparently, the leader was "so bothered by all his racing around and the wound he had received [in Le Puy] that he no longer wanted to return to the [French] Kingdom." Not to disappoint his new comrade, Mandrin promised to write Grifon in the spring if he were to form a new band.[46]

In November 1754, another Farm official, Pierre Robert Le Roux de La Motte, *contrôleur général* and subdelegate of Pont-de-Beauvoisin, spun a more elaborate web of spies. The son of a Farm director who had literally written the book on contraband, La Motte was a zealous officer who commanded several brigades posted along the Guiers River and was on the verge of being promoted to director himself.[47] Even before Mandrin came on the scene, La Motte had taken the initiative to urge the court of Turin to arrest several smugglers residing in Savoy who had assassinated a Farm agent in cold blood.[48] After waiting in vain for assistance from across the border, La Motte went on the offensive, capturing Gabriel Degat, a member of Bélissard's band who was subsequently rescued from the controller's stables in a blaze of gunfire. In the aftermath of Mandrin's alarming October campaign, the Farm entrusted La Motte with the command of a major spying operation based in Pont-de-Beauvoisin.[49] This was a golden opportunity for the young officer, and he threw himself into the project with the utmost determination, ferreting out critical intelligence on the locations, contacts, and preferred routes of Savoyard smugglers in the hope of bringing about the "exemplary destruction" of a major gang.[50] The information he gathered was extremely valuable, too valuable for his own good, for he was ultimately gunned down by a smuggler on the banks of the Guiers, the very assassination with which this book began.

Despite its evident weaknesses, the Farm police made a formidable institution. At mid-century, the private army was surprisingly effective at patrolling borders, catching run-of-the-mill smugglers, and even disrupting the occasional gang. It also proved capable of gathering intelligence on prominent underground figures such as Mandrin. Yet all the information in the world would not be enough for the Farm to capture Mandrin without the help of the army.

Unlike urban militias, the mounted police, and the Farm's private army, the royal army had plenty of men, its ranks in 1754 nearing 120,000. Deploying the army to suppress contraband posed serious problems, however, since neither rank-and-file soldiers nor army officers saw it as their duty to fight smugglers. As we have seen, soldiers were deeply implicated in smuggling. Asking them to suppress armed bands in southeastern France was like asking pickpockets to police the streets of Paris. Nor did high-ranking officers wish to be engaged in the repression of illicit trade, for there was little glory in such an ignoble pursuit. In 1732, the last time the army was enlisted in the struggle against smuggling gangs, the Chevalier de Marcieu bristled at the idea of pursuing Barret, who had killed two Farm agents while running tobacco and calico between the Comtat and Geneva. "I quite naturally confess to you," Marcieu wrote to the Keeper of the Seals, "that I wish fervently that the Court excuse me from a commission as thankless and disgraceful as is and will be that of making the troops march against smugglers [who are] aided and abetted by a whole province."[51] As Fontanieu explained to the finance minister, "only with repugnance do [royal troops] fight bands of rogues, against which they cannot acquire the glory that animates them."[52] True glory could be won only by vanquishing worthy adversaries.

In the early 1750s, as the Farmers General grew increasingly alarmed at the loss of revenue caused by tobacco trafficking in the southeast, they once more pressed the controller general to persuade the minister of war to summon the army. War minister d'Argenson responded by alerting military governors across the region and dispatching special forces to do what Farm guards and mounted police could not: secure the border with Savoy and destroy armed trafficking. In August 1753, d'Argenson deployed the Dauphiné volunteers, a regiment of agile "light troops" who had fought in the war of Austrian Succession (1740–1748) under the command of Jean-François de Gantès. ("Volunteers" were men enlisted with more flexible service contracts than ordinary soldiers.) A force of twenty cavalry and 100 infantry, the Dauphiné volunteers were stationed in French Pont-de-Beauvoisin, where, in the town square, they conducted military exercises in plain view of their enemies across the river. Then in July 1754, after Mandrin's first major expedition, the crown sent a second larger corps of light troops to reinforce the first. Commanded by Colonel Alexis Magallon de La Morlière, a distinguished veteran of two wars, the Flanders volunteers (so named for having served in Flanders from 1744 to 1748) was composed of 140 cavalry and 240 infantry.[53] Its mission was to pursue "the smugglers of Savoy whom impunity renders bolder every day." "You know all too well how far [they] have pushed their insolence, and how important it is to repress them," d'Argenson told La Morlière, "so I must urge you to succeed in this, so that agents of the Farm cannot complain that those sent to destroy contraband are among those who facilitate it." With troops deployed in towns along the border and others stationed behind them in large clusters, the muscle of the French army was now placed at the disposal of the Farm. Nowhere was the convergence of "fiscal" and "military" branches of state more in evidence than in the war on contraband.[54]

The minister's commitment to the mission would remain halfhearted, however, until the shock of October when Mandrin's band "profited from the absence of troops" to raid tobacco warehouses throughout the southeast.[55] What at first appeared to be random attacks on Farm agents now looked like a sustained campaign organized by a single man bent on subverting the state's authority. No longer did d'Argenson see illicit trade as a strictly financial problem that concerned the Farm alone. Nothing less than the preservation of royal authority and public order was now at stake, concerns that fell squarely and honorably within the army's domain. This at least was the rhetoric d'Argenson would henceforth employ in all his correspondence on the matter. In letters to commanders in the field, he stressed that the troubles afflicting the southeast were "as contrary to public tranquility as they were injurious to the King's authority and prejudicial to the interest of his Farm." The audacity of the smugglers "has mounted to the point where it would be shameful and even dangerous to remain in inaction any longer." "They have pushed their insolence so far that the authority of the King is no less at issue than the property of the Farm."[56] This was now the army's fight.

Having been roused by the events of October, d'Argenson organized a new plan of attack. La Morlière was to remain in Pont-de-Beauvoisin, the eye of the storm, to keep the Savoy border firmly under guard, while a host of additional regiments were deployed to establish a belt of troops running from the Jura Mountains to the Mediterranean. The military governors of Burgundy, Franche-Comté, Dauphiné, Provence, and Languedoc stepped up surveillance of their provinces, while Pierre Emé, Comte de Marcieu, Commander of Dauphiné, and La Morlière whipped their troops into shape. Beyond the usual calls for discipline, they ordered all soldiers to cooperate fully and respectfully with the Farm; any soldiers suspected of engaging in contraband would be sent directly to the commission of Valence. They also drafted aggressive rules of engagement. Commanders who received reports of smuggling bands from Farm agents were to give such information the utmost attention and immediately put their troops in pursuit. Detachments were not to wait for the arrival of Farm guards before engaging in combat. They were to take the lead.[57] "Voilà," one official remarked on the army's new offensive, "in the middle of the greatest peace [arises] the whole apparatus of a little war, and our soldiers are to give chase to a bunch of rogues."[58]

Among the new deployments, one elite corps of light cavalry was particularly important: Fischer's *chasseurs*. Because Mandrin could still use scouts and spies to pilot his gang through the gaps of unguarded territory that stretched between bases, d'Argenson appointed this special strike force to chase him down the next time he shot past the border. A foreign soldier of fortune from a modest background, Lieutenant-Colonel Jean-Chrétien Fischer had made a name for himself during the War of Austrian Succession.[59] After the French army was harassed in central Europe by mobile units who had learned how to conduct small-scale attacks from the Turks, Louis XV retaliated by creating his own specialized corps of light troops. Rather than getting bogged down in heavy combat, these corps dashed in and out of battle, enjoying an unprecedented freedom of action. Fischer was given command over one such unit in 1743 and quickly distinguished himself. As his *chasseurs* grew from a pack of sixty to a regiment of 600, they engaged in espionage, scouted territory, attacked enemy cavalry, and took prisoners of war. Indeed, there are strange parallels between the careers of Fischer and Mandrin. Both developed a reputation for conducting daring maneuvers and imposing "contributions" on the vanquished, and yet the same war that made Fischer's career dashed Mandrin's hopes of becoming a military supplier, pushing him into the underground where he would develop his own style of commercial combat. The two enterprising young men—one unconventional master of special operations moving up the army ranks, the other arriving at fame circuitously through subterranean trade—would meet on a Burgundian hillside overlooking the hamlet of Guenand on 20 December 1754.

No doubt it was Fischer's reputation for lightning-fast strikes that drew the attention of d'Argenson, who, in November 1754, tapped the dashing lieutenant colonel for the job of capturing Mandrin. Who better to go after a band whose own speed resembled that of a specialized cavalry unit? Commanding a pared-down peacetime company of sixty men (twenty cavalry and forty infantry), Fischer was given a clear mission to "pursue without respite and attack smugglers anywhere he should meet them" or, in another formulation, "to dissipate and destroy gangs of armed men who have inserted themselves into [the king's] lands where they disturb the public peace."[60] Whereas most of the troops deployed against Mandrin assumed a defensive posture, guarding stretches of border or protecting assigned cities or regions, Fischer was free to go on the offensive and follow Mandrin wherever he led. A fleet strike force of this sort was just what the listless French army needed.

Having strung together an impressive intelligence network during the War of Austrian Succession, a conflict during which military espionage flourished, Fischer immediately set out to gather as much information on Mandrin as possible.[61] He traveled to Switzerland to get the lay of the land and promptly dispatched one of his captains, Georgy, to spy on Mandrin in Savoy.[62] Masquerading as a Hungarian army officer, Georgy won the confidence of a Savoyard gentleman who arranged for him to meet the smuggler in Carouge. At the meeting, Georgy flattered Mandrin by remarking that all of Vienna admired him—a plausible compliment given the rivalry between the two kingdoms—and offered to contact friends in the Austrian capital who might be able to provide the chief with a safe haven in which to retire. When Mandrin appeared interested in this proposition, Georgy replied that he would be delighted to make the necessary inquiries, buying himself some time to gain Mandrin's trust and collect the information needed to set a trap. If he had to stall for more time, he could always draft a bogus reply in German and have it mailed from Munich.[63]

Bold as it was, Georgy's infiltration of Mandrin's gang did not yield any critical intelligence. It appears that Mandrin smelled a rat and took the opportunity to feed it misinformation about the band's plans. The chief told the spy that the border was too well guarded by the French army to make a northern incursion into Franche-Comté; two weeks later, the gang would enter France by that exact route. Georgy also "discovered" that Mandrin would be crossing Lake Léman to the port of Versoix, which prompted an elaborate plan to nab the gang leader there; nothing suggests that Mandrin ever sailed into the harbor. If Mandrin seems to have exploited Georgy to throw the French army off his trail, the chief also used him to project a certain image of himself to French authorities. Swearing his love for the fatherland, he insisted that he meant no disrespect to the king, for his campaigns aimed merely to recuperate the 40,000 lt he had lost to the Farmers General in his ill-timed Italian venture. Here again, Mandrin seemed to be asserting the justice of his cause, like generations of critics blaming not the king but an intermediary, in this case the Farmers General, who had failed to reimburse him for his losses. He also intimated that he wished the king would grant him a pardon in exchange for laying down his arms, and apparently he showed Georgy a letter from d'Argenson extending just such an offer. We know that Joly de Fleury had presented the minister with a proposal along these lines, but d'Argenson denied ever having made any such overture.

The army's intelligence operation extended beyond Georgy to the diplomatic corps. D'Argenson urged his counterpart Antoine Louis Rouillé, minister of foreign affairs, to charge the king's envoy to Geneva, one Étienne-Jean Guimard, Baron de Montperoux, with establishing an intelligence bureau in the heart of the republic. As the highest representative of the French court in the city, Montperoux already had his hands full conducting diplomacy, managing commercial relations, and monitoring Voltaire, but in November 1754 he was enlisted in the war against contraband. "It has come to His Majesty's attention," d'Argenson explained to the minister of foreign affairs, that the smugglers who have recently "stolen the King's revenues, forced open prisons, and committed all sorts of violence . . . purchase their stock in the city and State of Geneva, where they find merchants who not only deliver these goods but provide the necessary aid to assure their sale by advancing loans to fund the arming and maintenance of their men as well as the purchase of horses and other beasts of burden." To block smugglers from entering the kingdom, military commanders needed to know more about their activities on the other side of the border. Thus, Montperoux should gather information on "all the smugglers' movements, the time, place, and type of cargo for each band, the name and circumstances of the chiefs who command them, the number of armed men they have with them whether on foot or mounted, the contacts they have in the kingdom, the places they deposit their arms, and finally everything that may be useful to know not only to block their passage but to assess all means that might be employed to destroy them." Once gathered, this precious intelligence should be communicated immediately to the nearest army commanders.[64]

Daunted by his new mission, Montperoux explained that there were limits to what he could do. Although merchants in Geneva were known to conduct illicit trade in calicoes, the city was hardly the tobacco haven his superiors thought it was. "From all the information I have recently gathered, I believe I can assure you that there is no merchant in Geneva who would dare sell a certain quantity of tobacco; they are watched too closely."[65] The city was doing all that its republican "form of government will allow" to repress smuggling, as the recent prosecution of illicit traders demonstrated.[66] The problem was not Geneva, the diplomat insisted, so much as the lands to its south and north. In Savoy, smugglers operated with utter impunity. After his October expedition, Mandrin and his lieutenant spent eight days in Carouge and no one attempted to arrest them. "Nothing, however, would have been easier if the Governor of Savoy had given orders."[67] Disgusted with the state of affairs to the south, Montperoux made two specific suggestions. He urged that the Savoyard who introduced Georgy to Mandrin be kidnapped and questioned; this gentleman had bragged about killing a Farm guard and was in regular contact with Mandrin. He also proposed that France wage a propaganda campaign promising amnesty for smugglers who turned themselves in and testified against their colleagues. The aim was not to cause desertion—few were expected to defect—but to sow distrust among the bandits and erode their esprit de corps. Neither suggestion was approved by superiors.

Problems lay to the north as well, Montperoux added. In the pays de Vaud, in the Swiss canton of Berne, smugglers freely bought tobacco from merchant wholesalers and transported it into France. Because the government of Berne had no interest in stopping such commerce, the French would have to track the gangs that supplied themselves there, ascertain where they intended to cross the border, and deploy troops to that exact location. Embedding spies in these gangs was, however, nearly impossible. "I uselessly sought to interest people in the job by offering rewards proportioned to services rendered," Montperoux lamented, "but I found no one willing to take on such dangerous espionage." Hardened smugglers who suspected spies in their midst would not hesitate to "break their heads." Even spies who gained their trust would have difficulty getting solid information because chiefs were constantly changing their itinerary based on what their own spies told them about the location of enemy forces. And once an itinerary was finally decided, chiefs never divulged the plan to rank-and-file gang members.[68]

Aware of such obstacles, Montperoux decided that the only way to stop Mandrin was to work with local officials in Berne. His great hope was to persuade them to seal off the Swiss coastline along Lake Léman, in effect locking the smugglers in Savoy. With both the Dauphiné and Swiss borders closed, illicit profits would dry up, and smugglers would turn their violence inward, forcing Turin to clean up the province at last. Although this plan proved far too ambitious, Montperoux did enlist two Swiss bailiffs to notify him when smugglers passed through Nyon and Morgues on the way from Savoy, an early-warning system that could be of great value to the French.

With the help of Swiss agents and the steady influx of reports from petty informers, Montperoux was able to track Mandrin's travels east of the French border in the weeks before his winter expedition. He first informed the minister of foreign affairs that the chief had been spotted with 200 men in Swiss Coppet, Nyon, and Rolle before crossing the lake to Carouge, where, wounded from the battle of Le Puy, he sent for a surgeon from Geneva. (Mandrin threatened that if Genevan authorities interfered with his search for a doctor, he would kidnap a magistrate and burn down the city's environs. When his arm remained swollen after treatment, he suspected Montperoux of bribing the surgeon to poison his wound.) After Carouge, the peripatetic smuggler was spied in several places: in Fribourg looking for another doctor; back in the outskirts of Geneva, where he and his comrades "spend money they brought back from France on expensive pleasures";[69] in Yenne at the wedding of one his partners in crime; and finally, a week before his last expedition, departing Carouge with a double-barreled shotgun to meet mounted smugglers on the northern shore of the lake. Rumor had it that the band might be taking a southerly route to Auvergne, but Montperoux suspected that the talk was an attempt to trick the French into lowering their guard in Franche-Comté. On 18 December, Montperoux reported that Mandrin would most likely enter that French province "by way of the most weakly defended places."[70] He was absolutely right, but too late: Mandrin had entered Franche-Comté three days before. Forever on the heels of Mandrin, Montperoux could never discover his point of entry into France in time to alert French troops.

Mandrin's Last Stand

Apart from Montperoux, few expected Mandrin to wage a smuggling campaign in the middle of winter. Indeed, one explanation for the severity of the October campaign was that the smugglers were pressed to reap as much treasure as possible before the cold set in. "It is to be presumed," wrote Rochebaron, commander in Lyon, in October 1754, "that they want to finish their campaign, taking all that they can before the falling of snow, which ordinarily closes the mountain passes leaving only the main highways open."[71] If any proof were needed that Mandrin was not planning to strike in wintertime, it was conveniently supplied by Grifon, the gullible Farm spy who had infiltrated Mandrin's band in Carouge only to report that it was shutting down operations until the spring.[72] Although rumors continued to fly that an incursion by way of Franche-Comté was imminent, as Montperoux duly reported, the over-confident intendant of that province assured the minister of war to put no stock in such talk. "The snow presently covering our mountains will prevent the smugglers from attempting this crossing."[73]

No sooner had the intendant penned those words, however, than news arrived that "a troop of 80 to 100 smugglers" had crossed into the province on 14 December at the village of le Russey without a single shot being fired (see Figure 5.1).[74] Two days later, it was confirmed that the band numbered "115 men, all mounted and armed with swords, rifles, and many pistols."[75] Rather than hunkering down in Savoy, Mandrin was braving the pass-clogging snow to attack in mid-December. Knowing how difficult it was to mobilize royal troops in the dead of winter—wars were usually conducted in the fair seasons—the chief probably thought his nimble gang would have the advantage. Too bad for Grifon, who, suspected of acting as a double agent, was thrown in prison, along with the mayors of the towns where Mandrin bunked his first nights in France.

The smugglers rode west to Busy, so close to Besançon, the capital of Franche-Comté, that the commander of the province took it as a personal insult, then darted southwest to la Ferté, where they slept unaware that the campaign would, the next day, enter a completely new phase. They would encounter the French army for the first time. On 16 December, near Mont-sous-Vaudrey, the gang spied a cavalry detachment from the d'Harcourt regiment en route to Dole. Sighting the men in uniform, the smugglers went on the offensive and fired forty shots, killing one soldier and wounding another before the rest of the detachment fled. Although this was nothing more than a skirmish, the band had crossed a threshold into a new arena of combat.

With no time to spare now that shots had been fired, the gang resumed its westward run into Burgundy. In the small town of Seurre, Mandrin conducted the first forced sale of the winter expedition. He was back to his old ways, injecting contraband into the Farm's supply lines. But with the army now alerted to his whereabouts, he improvised yet again, inventing a new financial instrument to expedite his transactions. Rather than simply deposit the bundles of tobacco that Seurre's warehouser was obliged to buy, he delivered a large surplus that Farm agents in nearby towns would be forced to purchase in the coming days. That is, instead of shuttling tobacco from town to town as he had done in the past, Mandrin simply dumped the bulk of his merchandise in Seurre with the intention of coercing Farm agents in proximate towns to buy coupons that entitled them to a certain amount of leaf from the main stockpile. This modification of the old receipt system would considerably lighten the troop's load, rendering it faster, more agile, and better prepared to evade royal troops.[76]

In Seurre, Mandrin and his men delivered some 146 bundles of tobacco, the lion's share of their stock. They imposed modest sales on the warehouser (2,000 lt) and salt-tax receiver (4,000 lt, of which 3,000 lt was borrowed); raided the home of the Farm captain, who was in hiding; and passed by the jail, where they interrogated the accused about their crimes, releasing them one by one until the prison was empty.[77] It looked as though the triumphs of October were repeating themselves.

After unloading their merchandise in Seurre, Mandrin and his men set their sights on the city of Beaune, which, with a population of around 8,000, was the largest town Mandrin would raid on this winter run. The stakes were high. The tobacco warehouse, serving more than 4,000 households scattered among some sixty parishes in and beyond the town, took in more than 20,000 lt a year.[78] It should have been an easy operation: secure the town, impose the sale, issue a coupon, and open the prison. But city officials had been alerted to the band's arrival and were intent on putting up a fight. If Le Puy had been the first city in which Farm guards mounted a potent defense against Mandrin, Beaune was the first town to deploy a militia for its citizens' protection. All those directives from state ministers, army commanders, and intendants to raise militias were beginning to pay off.

December 18 was market day in Beaune. A group of women from nearby Corberon, come to the city to barter, warned municipal officials that a large band of well-armed smugglers had lodged in their village the previous night. The mayor and council of Beaune swiftly readied the walled city, sounded the tocsin in the clock tower, and summoned the militia, dispatching detachments of thirty men to each of the town's four gates. Its entrances tightly closed and guarded, the city would be extremely difficult to penetrate, even for an experienced armed band. Fortunately for Mandrin, however, there was a weak link in municipal security. The official in charge of the Madeleine gate "regarded the fear of M. de Tavannes [the commander of Burgundy] as mere panic, not being able to imagine that a handful of smugglers could seize and extort money from cities." Failing to take the women of Corberon seriously, he neglected to order the sentinels to shut the gate and, instead, went to lunch, "laughing with his friends at the people's fear of the mandrins."[79]

At 11:30 A.M., the band arrived at full gallop. Finding the Madeleine gate open but defended, the "chevalier Mandrin" led a ferocious attack.[80] When Sébastien Bonvoux, a tailor in the militia who guarded the gate, impetuously fired on the smugglers, he was "drilled" with rifle shots and dropped dead in the cold mud.[81] Stripped of his weapon, sword, hat, clothes, shoes, and money, his naked corpse lay at the foot of the gate for the rest of the day. When another guard, a salt bailiff named François, rushed to push the gate closed, he took two fatal shots to the chest. As the tocsins ceaselessly rang out, the smugglers swarmed the gate, climbed the rampart, and fired their rifles. The civilian toll mounted: a soldier on leave, whose curiosity got the better of him as he watched the attack from the ramparts, was killed; a journeyman glazier was wounded in the calf; and two bakers were violently beaten. "The most fearless man was shaken," a witness to the smugglers' murderous entry observed. "I speak not with fear but with horror at the sight of their arrival; they raced across the faubourg Madeleine, rifles held high and armed, crying unanimously, 'kill, kill, set the whole city on fire.' "[82] Just as it had in Le Puy, the gang responded to violent resistance by unleashing the full force of its arms. As "alarm spread throughout the town," the *Courrier d'Avignon* reported, "everyone locked themselves in their houses, and no one dared appear at their windows."[83]

Once the gate was taken, Mandrin set up makeshift headquarters at an inn called Petite Notre Dame and sent three divisions into town, each marching 100 steps behind the other "in good order and always armed, musket at the ready."[84] Soon, the clamorous tocsin was silenced and all the streets leading to city hall put under guard. As the town fell, the initial excitement of Mandrin's arrival gave way to apprehension:

For a long time, Mandrin was heralded as a polite merchant-warrior at the head of a disciplined troop who only went after the Farm. Drawn by this image, residents appeared at their doors eager to satisfy their curiosity, but when they saw that his game was serious, that he was shooting indiscriminately, they felt unsafe and thought it prudent to shut themselves inside their houses so that he remained at this moment absolute master of the city.[85]

The town theirs, the men visited the city jail but, finding no smugglers or deserters, left the prisoners locked up. Some looted the shop of a petty tobacco and salt retailer, smashing his sign, stealing money from his coffers, and swiping merchandise, while others serviced their rifles, took potshots at people who dared leave their homes, or went drinking. Two smugglers found the mayor and brought him to headquarters to hear Mandrin's demands. Furious with the city's resistance, the chief requested 25,000 lt, the additional 5,000 lt apparently imposed as a penalty for its opposition, but he ultimately agreed to lower the sum to 20,000 lt, to be paid by the city's tobacco warehouser and salt receiver.

While awaiting the treasure, Mandrin "held court," letting in all who wanted to see him. The room, "full as an egg," was packed with admirers, the disgruntled, and the curious. "He had 5 or 6 smugglers to guard him; but if someone wanted to take him, it would have been easy, as [the smugglers] would not have been able to use their rifles, so squeezed were they; no one wanted to sacrifice himself for the farmers general, since [the smugglers] declared that they only bore a grudge against the farm and would not harm the inhabitants."[86] After Mandrin tended to the business of occupation, compensating victims of excesses committed during the siege, the warehouser and receiver arrived with the money, all 20,000 lt. When one man quipped that Mandrin could use some of the smaller coins "to make amends," Mandrin reportedly shot back, "Listen, Monsieur, I make considerably more of them than you." Stowing the gold in his purses and belt and giving the other sacks of money to one of his officers, he announced that "there is no need to count or weigh [the money]; you are decent men of good character and probity; you would not deceive me." He then drafted a note stipulating that the "farmers general will be held accountable" for the 20,000 lt received in exchange for the "bundles of tobacco that I deposited with the warehouser of Seurre."[87] As the Marquis d'Argenson noted of the Beaune raid, "This is a war waged precisely against the farmers general."[88]

After paying the tavern keepers for feeding his troop, Mandrin gave the signal to leave, tipped his hat, and announced, "See you again at Carnival."[89] This sly allusion to the pre-Lent festival suggests how much Mandrin relished turning the world upside down by forcing his contraband on the monopoly. If his earliest forced sales had been improvised without much fanfare or drama, he was now well aware of the performative dimension of his coercive exchanges and its impact on those who observed or heard stories about him. The spectacle of mischievous inversion was not lost on Beaune's street singers, who after the gang's departure seized the opportunity to ridicule the "gentlemen" of the town for lacking the courage to confront the smugglers.[90] For some, however, the violence that accompanied this political theater was no laughing matter: two weeks after his visit, the finance minister dispensed aid to widows of Beaune whose husbands had been killed in the siege.[91]

Leaving Beaune in haste, Mandrin faked a southern dive to Chalon-sur-Saône but abruptly turned west and rode toward Autun, which, although smaller than Beaune, was home to an equally impressive tobacco office. Such false leads were meant to throw off the authorities, but the town of Autun braced itself for an attack. Its governor, the Marquis de Ganay, had spent weeks preparing for the worst: the 600-strong militia had polished its weaponry, sentries searched everyone entering what city gates remained open, and innkeepers surrendered their registers for review. In the surrounding countryside, villagers watched for armed men as the *maréchaussée* patrolled the roads. On the morning of 19 December, a courier dispatched by the mayor of Beaune arrived in Autun to warn officials that Mandrin's band was in the area. All gates were immediately sealed.[92]

Having faced spirited resistance in Beaune, Mandrin must have had more than an inkling of the obstacles that awaited him in Autun. How would he defeat the walled city if all its gates were securely shut and guarded? An opportunity presented itself a few miles outside of town when the band came upon thirty-seven seminary students, many from respectable Autun families, filing to Chalon to take their orders. Mandrin instantly realized that the black-clad procession was his ticket into the fortified town. Introducing himself to the seminary's superior, abbé Hamard, he took the men hostage, ordered his band to flank the clergymen, and led them to the convent of Saint-Jean-le-Grand just outside of Autun. Hamard was instructed to persuade town officials to open the gates without delay or else the convent, "one the most beautiful buildings in the province," would be burned down.[93] The superior duly informed the authorities of the "extreme danger" in which his students found themselves.

Learning that its well-born sons were in the clutches of an armed gang, the city had no recourse but to capitulate. The militia lowered its weapons, and the mayor gave orders to open the city gates. Mandrin entered with eight men and was taken to see the mayor, whom he instructed to raise 25,000 lt from the tobacco warehouser and salt-tax receiver. Again, judging by the standards of the previous expedition, Mandrin seems to have been penalizing towns that dared resist him by exacting heavier sums. Knowing that royal troops were closing in, Farm officials played for time and, after much haggling, whittled the amount down to 9,100 lt in exchange for a commensurate share of tobacco deposited in Seurre. To seal the deal, the warehouser offered the celebrated smuggler a pinch of snuff, an act of hospitality the latter did not refuse. After exchanging a coupon for the money, he sprang six debtors from jail and recruited seven peddlers into the gang.

Guenand

Coin in hand, the smugglers left Autun around 6 P.M. on 19 December. Fischer's *chasseurs* were close on their heels, arriving at Autun only five hours after the band departed. (The soldiers crossed paths with the seminarians, who were gripped with fear at the approach of yet more armed men.) Fischer rested his troops for a few hours and then resumed pursuit before dawn, following the gang's horse hoofprints by torchlight in the snow. "The tracks," he reported, "led me first to the Montigny road, and then threw me, by way of a shortcut, into nearly inaccessible woods, whence I arrived at a mountain on the rump of which is situated the village of Guenand."[94] Halfway up the slope, Fischer spied the band. With his prey at last in his sights, he could see that Mandrin had chosen a well-protected location. Surrounded by mountains, Guenand had only one access road, which the smugglers had blocked with limbs and brush. They had also mounted four small cannons and fortified two houses, cutting slits in the walls and roof through which they leveled their muskets.

At the break of day, a smuggler exited the farmhouse, spotted some of Fischer's men in the distance, and raced back to his comrades. Like a disturbed anthill, the gang members scrambled to make a hasty escape. At this point, Fischer had to make a quick decision: should he pin the band down and wait for reinforcements to arrive to engage with maximum force, or seize the day and attack? A man of action, he chose to attack, deploying his own company as well as dragoons and grenadiers from other regiments and a handful of cavaliers from the mounted police. Descending on the village, the commander of the Beaufremont regiment later recounted, "The trumpet marched well in advance of the whole troop and sounded with all its force, because it was our plan to intimidate them by this noise of war. My drum did its best to second it by beating the charge."[95]

Seeing Fischer's men coming at him, Mandrin, too, had to make a split-second decision: retreat or stand and fight? Knowing that he was outnumbered by well-armed royal soldiers, he ordered the majority of his troop to retreat at the back of the village into the forest. To cover them, he and eighteen others stayed behind to hold off Fischer as long as they possibly could. Lending credence to the common belief that armed smugglers who faced execution if captured fought more fiercely than their opponents, they shot relentlessly and inflicted substantial casualties on the approaching soldiers.[96] Undaunted, Fischer's troops reached a building where Mandrin had posted nine men. Under heavy fire, the soldiers set the structure aflame and burned the smugglers inside. Witnessing their comrades' fiery demise, the remaining members of the band attempted to retreat as soldiers overran the hamlet. "Abandoning his arms, his horse, and even his hat"—the famous gold-trimmed chapeau taken from a fallen Farm guard—Mandrin mounted the first horse he could lay his hands on and quit the village. A subordinate officer, Arceville, wanted to go in pursuit, but Fischer instructed him to stay where he was. "Let them all go to the devil, if they want," exclaimed the commander. Arceville later told his superiors that he might have been able to kill Mandrin had he been allowed to give chase, but "such is the effect of the passive obedience to which one dedicates oneself in the exercise of the profession of arms that it is better to do harm while deferring to the orders of one's leaders than to do better while infringing them." The officer consoled himself with the knowledge that in all likelihood Mandrin would soon be caught and his fate decided by "justice."

The battle having subsided, the soldiers engaged in the time-honored art of pillage, ransacking the hamlet as they searched for smugglers' loot. Finding no more than 2,000 lt in Mandrin's mattress, the men "took possession of what legitimately belonged to [the villagers]," Arceville disapprovingly reported. "In the heart of France and the bosom of peace were revived the evils to which war inevitably leads."[97]

A "bloodbath," the battle exacted a heavy toll on both sides.[98] Fischer lost seven grenadiers, five hussards, and three officers. Ten foot soldiers were wounded, and two horses, including Fischer's own, were killed.[99] For his part, Mandrin lost the nine smugglers trapped in the fire and perhaps a dozen others (d'Arceville's claim that thirty smugglers were killed seems exaggerated).[100] Five smugglers were taken prisoner, two of whom were wounded (one fatally). The four survivors were temporarily imprisoned in Autun and then transferred to Valence to stand trial before the commission; at least three were executed. Further, crowed Fischer's officers, a number of those who got away, including Mandrin himself, had been wounded, leaving a trail in the snow "tainted with their blood."[101] The chief was also forced to abandon forty-two horses (including his own, which still carried his arms and saddle) and forty pistols and double-barreled muskets. All in all, the battle decimated the ranks of Mandrin's gang, now thrown completely on the defensive. Fischer would later boast that, according to a list found on one of the captured smugglers, he had saved at least sixty tobacco offices from attack.

Still, Fischer's *chasseurs* failed to deliver the knockout blow. Mandrin and many of his men were still at large, shaken to be sure but able to fight another day. Fischer's failure to destroy the gang at Guenand drew severe criticism from his colleagues. Arceville accused him of failing to cut off the smugglers' retreat, although Fischer claimed to have sent a detachment to the back of the village to do precisely that.[102] More damning was the lieutenant-colonel's fateful decision not to wait for reinforcements. In the first draft of a letter to Fischer, the minister of war admonished that "His Majesty" would have preferred that, instead of mounting a premature attack against the smugglers, "you had been able to hold them there to delay their movement and by this means given M. D'Espinchal the time to reach you."[103] If the "air of reproach" in this missive was finally judged too severe for Fischer's eyes—he was after all a courageous royal officer—d'Argenson sent an unedited message to d'Espinchal: "it would have been better had [Fischer] been able to contain these smugglers long enough to give you time to reinforce him."[104] Unfair or not, the general impression was that Fischer squandered an opportunity to finish Mandrin. Even the minister of war's own brother, the Marquis d'Argenson, hyperbolically noted, "Fischer was completely beaten."[105]

After Guenand, the remaining gang members made a mad dash south toward familiar territory. Casting aside all pretensions of commerce, they concentrated on getting out of France alive while avenging their fallen comrades when opportunities arose. The army was still in hot pursuit, and the smugglers knew that towns were now prepared to resist them, which was why the band did not linger in Auvergne, as was its wont.[106] After crossing the Loire at Saint-Auban on 21 December, Mandrin divided the gang of seventy into two packs: he and his lieutenant, Joseph Bertier, would lead the first group; Jacques Michard aka "Pug Nose," the second. While the second group seems to have followed the Loire south, the first dropped southwest to Dompierre, where they paused to seize the arms and horses of four mounted police. When they passed through Le Breuil, a woman roused the Farm brigade from the local tavern, but the gang was in no mood for games. It set upon the brigade with lethal force, killing two in the tavern, another two in an adjacent field, and wounding the captain, whom they "left for dead."[107] In Saint-Clément, the men took the life of a cobbler for refusing to give up the location of the town's Farm agents.

During this frantic southern sprint, a remarkable transformation in the gang's moral economy occurred as the smugglers all but abandoned the pretext of selling tobacco. On the night of 22 December, in Cervières, they extorted forty-six louis from the wife of the salt receiver "without leaving merchandise, content to give only a receipt of the sum to be drawn from what the farmers general owe them."[108] The next day at Noirétable, they took twelve louis from the taille receiver; nothing was provided in exchange save for a receipt like the one in Cervières. Such receipts registered but a modicum of the reciprocity and economic justice inscribed in previous ones. The liability of the Farmers General was still present, but no goods were mentioned and no coupons issued on the store of tobacco in the now distant town of Seurre. As the pretense of commerce ebbed, the band's violence became less discriminating. Leaving Noirétable the men shot the wife of a Farm guard who had merely come to the window of her house to see what all the fuss was about.

Although they remained violent, the smugglers—if we can still call them that—had to choose their battles carefully. They were fatigued, wounded, and still fleeing regiments of the royal army. When they approached Ambert, a town that had yielded to them on the last expedition but was now better prepared to defend itself, the smugglers dared not attack, circumventing the town on the way to Marsac (where an eyewitness noted their ragged clothing and the slings in which the wounded rested their arms). While Mandrin and two of his men stayed in Marsac, the rest of the band galloped to Chaise-Dieu where they made a mockery of the controlled exchanges of the previous expedition. After securing the city bells and lodging themselves at local inns, the smugglers pursued three tobacco retailers. The first, Joseph Richard, had locked up his home and fled. The gang smashed his windows, found his house empty, and swore they would get him next time. The second retailer, Grégoire Richard, had likewise fled with his wife. But the servant that the couple left behind was beaten with the butt of a musket and threatened with death unless she took them to her master. She promised to do so but managed to escape, prompting the frustrated smugglers to loot a neighboring shop. They had only slightly better luck with the third retailer, Jean Michaud, from whom they demanded 10,000 lt. When Michaud explained that he didn't have that kind of money on hand, they assaulted him and ransacked his furniture, only to find a measly sixty lt. The smugglers took him to their inn as a hostage and threatened his wife that they would drag him behind their horses if she did not produce the money. Borrowing from the business agent of a local count, she offered an additional fifty lt. They accepted the ransom, released the husband, and drafted a receipt with a scarcely legible signature. We don't know what the receipt said exactly, but local officials understood it to mean that a certain quantity of tobacco would be delivered, a promise never fulfilled.[109]

Mandrin showed up at Chaise-Dieu just before midnight with royal troops fast on his heels. The men fled the town and were guided south to Fix-Saint-Geneix, where they attended Christmas mass at a little church. One cannot help but wonder what thoughts passed through

Mandrin's mind as he sat in his pew that evening. He knew royal troops were only hours away, as they had been since Beaune. Did he ponder his demise? Did he reflect on his life or his prospects for salvation? Perhaps he begged God to assist in his escape. Whatever his reflections, he couldn't afford to indulge them very long, for he soon decamped to Sauvetat, site of his final showdown with the army.

Squeezing information from the smugglers' former guides, the Flanders and Dauphiné "volunteers" pursued Mandrin on his southerly plunge to Sauvetat. In fact, they took a shortcut to arrive at Sauvetat before dawn on 26 December in advance of the smugglers. Not realizing he had overtaken his prey in the night, the commander thought Mandrin's men had already come and gone. But at around 5 A.M., about an hour after troops had reached the town, thirty-six traffickers arrived in the predawn darkness. Three of them rode to a stable in the hamlet and heard a cry, "Who goes there?" One smuggler fired in the direction of the sentinel's voice. The ball missed. The soldier answered with a rifle shot that pierced the left thigh of smuggler Louis Le Vasseur aka "the Norman," who fell from his horse and dragged himself to safety. As the noise of gunfire alerted the rest of La Morlière's troop, both sides fired shots that killed two soldiers and four smugglers. Gang members withdrew to a nearby forest and fled.

Left behind, the wounded Le Vasseur tricked army Captain Diturbi de Larre into thinking that Mandrin had flown north to a château near Ambert. The deception allowed the chief to embark on a monthlong trek far from his usual theater of operations in Auvergne and Dauphiné, now swarming with soldiers and mounted police, the latter ordered to arrest all "highway adventurers and other dubious migrants."[110] From the Vivarais, the smuggler and whatever crew remained by his side dropped south into Provence and journeyed to the kingdom of Sardinia, where, safe at last, they could take the Turin road to Savoy. On 25 January, the day before Le Vasseur was to be executed by the commission of Valence, Mandrin was spotted in Carouge at his old haunt, the Silver Lion.[111]

Newspaper Heroes and Villains

In commercial terms, the December expedition was a total flop: what began with promising financial innovation in Seurre became a desperate flight to the border. But Mandrin had now done battle with the French army and lived to tell about it, a turn of events that sharpened his image as a fearless warrior. His transformation in the press from gallant adventurer to military commander, which began in November after the battle of Le Puy, accelerated dramatically with the violent events of December. Beset by international peace, editors jumped on the latest news from Beaune, Autun, and Guenand, casting the conflicts as battles between opposing armies and populating their stories with heroes and villains. But they split on the question of who was to play which role. The *Courrier d'Avignon* (or at least its correspondent from Chalon-sur-Saône) represented the battle of Guenand as a decisive victory for Fischer, a brilliant officer who crushed the enemy "bandits." The army lost some good men, the paper admitted, "but hardly anything remained of Mandrin's troop." The few "brigands" who escaped death or capture were forced to flee into a dreadful forest from which they would never escape. So many soldiers were closing in on them that "it was impossible that Mandrin and his troop would not be totally destroyed."[112]

The *Gazette d'Utrecht* took an even harder line against the smugglers. Having soured on Mandrin after Le Puy, it redoubled its efforts to discredit the chief and expose him as a criminal scoundrel. The paper acknowledged the "brisk & rather bloody battle" of Guenand but attempted to deflate the popular image of Mandrin as a formidable fighter. "The things people spout about Mandrin's fortifications and artillery are as ridiculous as the notion that he has built citadels." The fact is that "since the last defeat they suffered [in Guenand], the smugglers' courage, or rather their audacity, appears to have flagged." Weakening their morale further was the fate of two band members who had been captured and brought to justice. One trafficker was left to expire on the wheel after being broken, an excruciating punishment that "will help spread terror among these brigands," while the same fate awaited "the Norman," who would "expiate his crime by way of a public execution." Such exemplary punishments punctured the myth building up around Mandrin, or so it seemed to the paper. Woe to those "who revel in the supposed exploits of this brigand & recount with satisfaction the battles of a wretch who merits the same fate as Cartouche." The comparison to the infamous Parisian thief who ended his days on the scaffold was meant to sully the smuggling chief's moral credibility, as did offhand remarks about his character. "People already know by what means he procured so much illicit merchandise, & what they learned about this is not very edifying."[113]

While the *Courrier d'Avignon* and the *Gazette d'Utrecht* belittled Mandrin's clash with the army, other papers exploited the December battles by touting the smuggler's martial prowess. The *Gazette d'Amsterdam* printed what it claimed was a "faithful excerpt" of a leaked military report on the battle of Guenand but which was in fact a heavily embellished account that portrayed Mandrin as a heroic David going up against the Goliath of the French army. It was not that the paper disparaged the army: French officers were duly lauded for distinguished acts of valor. But the smugglers were painted as especially brave and stalwart. Facing an army of "800" men (a gross exaggeration), the smugglers "fought with extraordinary vigor." Not only did they employ a wise strategy, "prudently" establishing an impenetrable defensive position in the village, but they fought "with gallantry [and] fury . . . like wild boars who earn the respect of the hunters [*chasseurs*] who pursue them." After listing the many French officers and foot soldiers killed in action, the newspaper concluded, "Here is a battle that will be regarded as a real military marvel. One would hardly believe that 90 men could escape a corps of 800 gathered to surround them. The fact is however certain."[114]

Equally positive appraisals emanated from the *Mercure historique et politique,* which shamelessly exploited the theme of war. "After the war waged in France by the constitutional clergy against the sick & dying, there is no event that interests the curiosity of the public more than the war which the smugglers wage against the Farmers General." Although the paper introduced its account of the battle of Guenand with a lament about a rise in crime, a deplorable trend in which "this scoundrel [Mandrin] & his accomplices" were undoubtedly implicated, it inserted the exact same passage on Guenand as that printed by the fawning *Gazette d'Amsterdam,* treating readers to a courageous hero they could root for. The *Mercure historique* ended its report unambiguously on the same note of glory: the battle waged by Mandrin would forever be regarded as a "military marvel."[115]

The newspapers that favored Mandrin echoed (even as they shaped) public opinion, or at least the thin slice of opinion that can be examined. Those who followed the smuggler's exploits seem to have grown more admiring of him in the wake of Guenand, when, according to newspapers, copycat crimes began to appear. In Paris, an armed trafficker

sent five agents at the Gobelins customs checkpoint fleeing by whis-
tling to unseen accomplices and declaring, "I am Mandrin; you're
about to see some real action; my men are coming." Another prankster
borrowed the kingpin's name to send a threatening letter to the Farm
director of Nancy.[116] Even beyond newspaper reports, men and women
appear to have taken a new interest in Mandrin. In his journal, the
Burgundian abbé Boullemier noted the contrast between Fischer's strategic blunders and Mandrin's undeniable military aptitude. "Mandrin
defended himself vigorously, deploying rifle fire from the roof of the
house against [Fischer's men] with so much advantage that twenty *chasseurs* were killed including a captain and a lieutenant. Profiting from the
disorder created by his continual fire against the *chasseurs,* Mandrin and
his troop escaped with great speed through a wall that he had pierced
behind the house. He fled with so much haste that it was not possible for
the *chasseurs* to follow him."[117] In Geneva, women gossiped with delight
about Mandrin and his "victory" over Fischer, speaking of the smuggler
with "a lot of affection" as if he were a fellow citizen of the republic.[118]
Even at court, nobles like the Marquis d'Argenson had to admit that the
"so-called Mandrins . . . fought our troops bravely."[119] Perhaps the highest praise came from one of the band's principal adversaries, Diturbi de
Larre, who characterized the chief as a "général manqué," a natural-born
fighter who missed his true vocation.

During the expedition of December 1754, Mandrin encountered a state
whose powers of policing had been growing in response to the perceived challenges of an increasingly mobile population of workers, vagabonds, beggars, thieves, and smugglers. To be sure, the institutional
mechanisms put in place to control the movement of people and goods
paled in comparison to those that would be installed in the nineteenth
and twentieth centuries, but by early-modern standards they were impressive. In the middle of the eighteenth century, Mandrin's excursions
triggered a number of extraordinary security measures: towns reforti-
fied themselves, the mounted constabulary diligently swept the roads,
Farm agents conducted military-style espionage and manned posts in
unprecedented numbers, and special regiments of the royal army chased
the gang through the southeast. That such forces could be deployed
against smugglers suggests the extent to which the monarchy's power
of policing was growing in this period. And yet, the failure to capture

and destroy Mandrin, despite this coordinated onslaught, rendered his feats all the more heroic. Indeed, if the October venture had bolstered his image as an avenging merchant, Mandrin's December campaign confirmed his reputation as a brilliant military commander whose bravery and skill on the battlefield matched that of the greatest officers of his day.

Newspaper readers were left to wonder what would become of the "captain of the smugglers" now that his days of easy triumphs were behind him. Would he prudently retire, knowing that the king's army awaited him on the other side of the border, or would he valiantly fight his way back into France? For the time being, the chief paused to take refuge in Savoy, where, once again, he could depend on the generous protections of international law—or so he thought.

8

Captured

A FTER THE BLOODY EXPEDITION of December 1754, a stalemate ensued along the French-Savoyard border. Through the winter and
spring of 1755, French authorities and Savoyard smugglers eyed each
other across the Guiers, tracking each other's movements and facing off
in sporadic skirmishes. Every verbal assault, fistfight, and gunshot excited a diplomatic set-to between Versailles and Turin. The tense stand-
off would simmer until April when the assassination of a high-ranking
Farm agent excited fears among French officials that traitorous smugglers, rebellious Protestants, and belligerent Britons were forging a military alliance that posed an imminent threat to the realm's security. In
response, Louis XV would break the deadlock by launching an unprecedented covert operation to capture Mandrin on foreign soil, in direct violation of international law. In a single bold stroke, the crown hoped to get
Mandrin and end armed smuggling in the southeast once and for all.

Stalemate at the Border

During these restless months, the French state took a number of steps
to corner Mandrin in Savoy, some of which were simple extensions of
earlier strategies. The minister of war once again deployed troops along
the southeastern border and placed them on high alert. The Farm fortified cash-rich bureaus. And diplomats, military commanders, and Farmers General sent spies into Savoy and Switzerland to determine when
and where the next incursion would take place. To this end, Montperoux
now regularly corresponded with Swiss bailiffs on the northern coast of
Lake Léman and with the former spy Georgy, who had been cleared of

the charge of treason and released from prison. The Genevan envoy collected an ample supply of leads, all of whose veracity he doubted. "Mandrin spreads false rumors to conceal his plans," he explained to the minister of foreign affairs.[1] One rumor had the kingpin looking to retire in England, another planning to enter France by way of Nice, and still another killed by his confidant Saint Pierre after a squabble at the dinner table. The only thing that was clear was that the chief was constantly on the move. In early May, he was spotted in the Swiss town of Romond buying forty riding horses to be shipped across the lake to Savoy, a clue that suggested his next expedition's point of entry would be to the south, on the Dauphiné or Provence border.[2]

The most effective effort at gathering intelligence was conducted by a spy under Fischer's command named Marsin. Unlike previous moles who had fleetingly infiltrated the band only to be fed misinformation or chased away, Marsin successfully gained Mandrin's confidence in January 1755 and, after traveling with the band for several weeks (during which he oversaw shipments of tobacco from Switzerland to Savoy), provided detailed information about the major players in the gang, the merchants who supplied goods, and the innkeepers and gentlemen who safeguarded guns and money. It was Marsin who reported that Mandrin lodged regularly at the château de Rochefort, a vital piece of information that would ultimately lead to his capture. Indeed, the spy was planning to kidnap Mandrin himself but had to flee the gang when his cover was blown, escaping through a bedroom window, absconding on horseback, and killing two of his pursuers before reaching the safety of the French border.[3]

In addition to reinforcing troops and conducting espionage, the minister of war took two extraordinary steps to bring the full power of the French state to bear on the problem of armed smuggling. First, he tightened passport control on the border, instructing the army to assist the mounted police in arresting vagabonds who did not possess identity papers. The borderland dragnet begun in October intensified. Second, he imposed new measures against firearms. In the past, gun-control legislation for rural France had been designed to stop peasants from poaching game from noble estates. But in 1716, its rationale abruptly changed. Because the disorders of the War of Spanish Succession had both encouraged contraband traffic and put countless weapons in the hands of soldiers, deserters, and veterans, the regent called for the general disar-

mament of French commoners, "notably those at the border" who engaged in smuggling.[4] Yet the 1716 ordinance was never rigorously applied: poachers continued to hunt, country folk continued to bear
weapons at fairs, and traffickers continued to carry muskets to protect
their merchandise. Widespread use of arms was therefore still a problem in the winter and spring of 1755 when La Morlière, lead strategist
in the operation to capture Mandrin after Fischer's fiasco, proposed
two new measures. He urged the war minister to order army units to
arrest all gun-toting commoners in the border provinces, in effect dis-
arming the laboring classes along the frontier, and to allow soldiers to
shoot on unarmed contraband peddlers. The minister rejected the latter
suggestion out of hand but did authorize new gun-control ordinances
for Dauphiné and surrounding provinces. Henceforth, commoners were
to turn in their firearms to a designated head of community, who would
hold them until further notice.[5]

The actions taken by French authorities to police the border and seal
Mandrin in Savoy were not without effect. For months, the oversize
band remained trapped in Savoy and Switzerland, its leader unwilling
to risk a crossing. All Mandrin could do was run north to Switzerland
and south to Savoy, "fatiguing" French troops who, perpetually on alert,
mirrored his moves on the other side of the border.[6] If French forces
were able to contain Mandrin, however, they could not bring the underground to a halt. While the chief and his lieutenants holed up in
Savoy, waiting for the right moment to strike, smugglers working alone
or in small crews continued to slip across the border, nimbly circumventing Farm and army alike. Montperoux suspected that Mandrin was
organizing such foot traffic to support his dormant troop during these
difficult months.[7] In addition to this steady trickle across the border, the
occasional modest band dashed into France, such as the one that raced
through Dauphiné on its way to the Comtat Venaissin, drawing a detachment of cavalry in its wake.[8]

Thanks to the heightened presence of the royal army, the border
smoldered with firefights and brawls. As early as 24 November 1754,
smugglers in Saint Christophe, a border town divided by the Guiers River
like Pont-de-Beauvoisin, shouted "a thousand insults" at a detachment
of French troops come to the river to observe them. Verbal abuse rapidly
escalated to rifle fire, testing the patience of the French minister of war.
From the outset, d'Argenson had instructed La Morlière to avoid "doing

anything that might give rise to complaints that the King's Troops had violated the territory of the King of Sardinia," but, "as this moderation has only augmented the insolence of the smugglers," he was now prepared to allow the army to return fire if the smugglers persisted. He urged the minister of foreign affairs to bring this to the attention of the ambassador of Turin at their next meeting.[9]

In the aftermath of the December expedition, such clashes along the Guiers and Rhône rivers erupted with alarming frequency. On 15 February 1755, La Morlière's troops fired on a group of Savoyards crossing the Guiers, forcing them to abandon one of the many sacks they were carrying. As the soldiers fished the bundle out of the water, the Savoyards on the opposing riverbank hurled stones at them and shouted, "Kill, kill." The soldiers confiscated the bundle, which contained sheepskins, an import subject to customs taxes, and deposited it with La Motte.[10] Once again, the conflict quickly escalated to diplomatic levels: Turin claimed that the Savoyards were simply washing their skins in the river, as local tanners had been doing for eons; Versailles countered that the smugglers were caught red-handed crossing the river with contraband in their possession. Eventually, the affair was decided in favor of the Savoyards and the skins returned to their owners.[11]

April was the cruelest month of all. In Lucey, Savoyard "rascals" took potshots at military posts across the Rhône and kidnapped a French Farm official from a tavern.[12] Although the abducted Frenchman, La Tour, worked for an obscure Farm department that had little to do with customs enforcement, the smugglers ransomed him for 150 lt. Versailles expressed outrage at the kidnapping, but the Senate of Chambery, Savoy's highest political body, retorted that La Tour was in cahoots with the smugglers. We will never know which government was right: in June, the Frenchman failed to appear for his deposition before the senate, either because he did not want to risk his life entering Savoy (French version) or because he did not want to incriminate himself (Savoyard version). During the same month, conflict flared again in the border parish of Saint Christophe, where five French soldiers assaulted Savoyards returning home from Sunday vespers on the French side of town. Unable to deny the cracked ribs, dislocated shoulders, and debilitating bruises, French authorities threw the soldiers in jail and compensated the victims for their pain and suffering.[13]

The Assassination of La Motte

The most consequential act of violence in April 1755 was without a doubt the cold-blooded murder of Pierre Robert Le Roux de La Motte. As controller-general of the Farm in Pont-de-Beauvoisin, La Motte had received more than his fair share of abuse over the years. Like some stereotypical sheriff surrounded by outlaws in an old western, he was detested for his unstinting pursuit of smugglers and had for years been the object of scorn and mockery. On a summer night in 1752, Savoyards bathing in the river below his house sang nasty songs and hurled "all kinds of insults [against him and] all men of the Farm, threatening to slaughter him, asking for their rifles, and crying 'kill, kill.'"[14] The following summer, Bélissard and his gang stormed into French Pont-de-Beauvoisin and killed two of his guards. The band crossed back across the bridge and, adding insult to injury, taunted French customs agents from their haven in Savoy.

Such provocations seem only to have strengthened La Motte's resolve to gather intelligence that he hoped would bring Mandrin down. Receiving special funding from the Farm, the controller had for months been diligently collecting information on the gang when, on 25 March 1755, an opportunity arose that promised to break the investigation wide open. A middle-aged French tanner from Pont-de-Beauvoisin named Augustin Perrin, having traveled to Savoyard Saint-Genix on business, ran into twenty-two-year-old Louis Jarrier aka the Piedmontese, a member of Mandrin's gang. Perrin and the Piedmontese knew each other. The smuggler had seen Perrin on his way into town that morning and offered to share a bottle of wine with him after church. Later in the day, he tracked Perrin down and insisted on a drink: "You know that I once gave you some tobacco to smoke, a half dozen pipefuls. I know that you smoke. I want to give you some more, a kind that is better than that sold in [Farm] shops, but let's drink a bottle." The two sat down in a tavern where, over food, wine, and tobacco, the Piedmontese unburdened himself, broaching the subject of his criminal past and expressing a keen desire to reform. He had taken communion that very morning and wanted to turn over a new leaf:

> I want to be converted and no longer offend God; but I regard you as my friend, you have to do me the favor of pulling me out of captivity. You know M. Le Roux [de La Motte], let's drink to his health, tell him that

if he were able to get me a pardon in France . . . I would make my move: I would help him take the whole band except for four of my comrades.[15]

Perrin went straight to La Motte, who did not delay. Promising Perrin a handsome reward if the affair succeeded, he instructed the tanner to bring the smuggler a temporary passport that he could use to cross the border in security and meet La Motte at Perrin's house. In her husband's place, Madame Perrin met the trafficker at a bar in Saint-Genix, read the terms of the passport to the illiterate man, and arranged the meeting. "I would make all the captures that he should wish, be it Mandrin or others," the Piedmontese assured her, but instead of meeting at her house, he insisted on gathering in the open air of St. Martin's meadow on the French riverbank just outside of Pont-de-Beauvoisin.[16] He promised to cross the Guiers without a jacket to show that he was unarmed and suggested that the controller bring a bottle of wine so the two could drink to the success of their pact. La Motte's colleagues balked. Knowing that this fellow was "the cruelest" of bandits who had long threatened to kill the controller, La Morlière begged La Motte not to meet in an open area without a detachment of guards escorting him.[17] A seasoned Farm clerk also warned that if the controller wanted to speak to this "rogue," he should do so in a safe house after having the criminal thoroughly frisked. If La Motte had any doubts about his own safety, however, he brushed them aside. Determined not to scare off the defector, he proceeded to the meadow on 8 April with only the smallest of entourages: just the Perrins and a cavalry captain named Duverger, who served under La Morlière.

As dusk fell that spring evening, two associates of the Piedmontese, dressed in gray and armed with rifles, crossed the Guiers. As the smuggler watched from Savoy, they clambered up the riverbank, sprinted through St. Martin's meadow where the meeting was to take place, and hid behind bushes to wait for the customs agent to arrive. Soon, the Perrins appeared near a barn at the meadow's edge, the wife sitting down on a woodpile with two glasses and a bottle of wine in hand, a perversely hopeful symbol of a bargain that would run horribly amok. As Duverger hid behind a wall, La Motte and the Perrins walked through the field toward the river. Monsieur Perrin reached the bank first and called out to the Piedmontese across the water, "Come quick. Here is my wife with the Monsieur. Louis Piémontais, come on. Let's go." "Are you alone?" asked a voice from the Savoyard side of the river. "I thought I heard people talking." "Yes, we're alone," answered the husband; "there's only my wife and him." "Come then!" Madame Perrin called to La Motte.[18]

Three rifle shots rang out in rapid succession. One lead ball struck La Motte's right forearm without fracturing any bones. The second scraped his upper right thigh. But the third tore through his abdomen. Duverger charged into the meadow, firing pistol shots and barking orders to make it appear that he was at the head of a large troop. The gunmen threw themselves in the river and scrambled back across the border. Trembling, Perrin raced to his wife and asked her where La Motte was. In the dim light, they found him sitting on the ground under a large oak tree, his stomach bleeding profusely. The couple helped him up and gave him a sip of wine but it was no use. He couldn't walk. "I'm dead," he said. Soldiers who had heard the shots and run to the meadow carried the controller to La Morlière's quarters, where the following evening at 5 P.M. he died from the loss of blood.

The controller took all that he had learned about the smugglers to his grave. No one knew Mandrin's intentions and favored routes into France quite like La Motte. Without this linchpin of the operation, explained Marcieu, "it will suddenly be very difficult for the troops posted on the border with Savoy to be informed of [the bandits'] plans and maneuvers in time to make them fail."[19] The strategic loss was profound, Jacques-Raymond, comte de l'Hôpital, who served under Marcieu, agreed with a note of exasperation. "These scoundrels will seize this opportunity to attempt an incursion since we were only able to be well informed of their maneuvers by a controller whose sure and sharp knowledge of the locale and its inhabitants was matched by his intelligence and zeal."[20]

As the Piedmontese "made a trophy" of the assassination in Savoy, there was much speculation on both sides of the border as to whether Mandrin had been involved.[21] Jean-Baptiste-Joseph Damazit de Sahuguet, baron d'Espagnac, who served in Bresse, was informed that Mandrin was behind the whole affair, having paid his associate a reward of forty-five louis for a job well done. Marsin, the spy who had infiltrated Mandrin's band, reported the same, but newspapers protested the chief's innocence, defending him against all such charges. Condemning the Piedmontese for "such a cowardly assassination," the *Mercure historique et politique* reported that "Mandrin himself disavowed and openly disapproved of this detestable action, because the infamous profession that he exercises has not stifled in him certain principles of honor that he holds from nature and education."[22] It was inconceivable that the paper's hero, who had exhibited such a fine moral sensibility during his expeditions, could commit such a heinous act. Marsin's dispatch is far more trustworthy a source than the papers, but we lack conclusive evidence on this question.

Regardless of Mandrin's complicity, the French ministry of foreign affairs demanded that Turin bring the Piedmontese and his accomplices to justice, a request that, if refused, "would offend against the law of nations [*droit des gens*] . . . and the rules of humanity."[23] The government of Sardinia seemed not the least bit interested in pursuing La Motte's assassins, however. Although many local Savoyard officials were troubled by the controller's "tragic end," fearing that Farm guards would now enter Savoy to retaliate against his killers, Turin saw no need to make any arrests.[24] Rebuffing French demands for justice, the court's ambassador audaciously claimed not only that La Morlière's soldiers were responsible for La Motte's death but that the patch of land on which La Motte was shot actually belonged to the king of Sardinia. The French foreign minister showed the ambassador depositions to the contrary, but Turin could not be moved.[25]

Kidnapping Mandrin

The assassination of La Motte alarmed French authorities, who immediately associated it with two extreme threats to the kingdom's security. It was bad enough that Mandrin had prevailed over Fischer and now appeared to be behind the murder of a high-ranking Farm official. More frightening still was the prospect that the kingpin was allying himself with both internal and external enemies of the state. Internally, French officials worried that Mandrin was colluding with Huguenots, French Protestants with a long history of armed resistance to the Catholic monarchy. Externally, they fretted that he was collaborating with Great Britain, a nation on the rise that seemed intent on drawing France into another war. The fear of a triple alliance among smugglers,

Huguenots, and Britons consumed French officials at the highest levels of government.

Huguenot rebellion was not ancient history in southern France. In 1685, Louis XIV revoked the Edict of Nantes, which had permitted Protestants a degree of toleration, and set out to destroy the Reformed Church in France by executing or expelling pastors and other religious leaders. From 1702 to 1704, in the southern mountains of the Cévennes, Protestants struck back, attacking Catholic churches, killing priests, and battling the French army in a fierce guerrilla war. Frustrated by the Huguenots' unconventional tactics, the royal army went on a rampage, burning down hundreds of villages and massacring alleged Protestants throughout the area. In neighboring Vivarais, a region Mandrin was known to visit, Huguenots revived the armed struggle in 1709–1710, triggering further rounds of repression that persisted into the 1750s, when the issue of religious revolt was linked to that of contraband.[26]

Every time smugglers in the southeast resorted to deadly violence, royal officials feared that they were allying themselves with Protestants to throw the kingdom into turmoil. When contraband gangs flared in the early 1730s, the intendant of Dauphiné worried that smugglers might soon "join with the Camisards of the Cevennes." After all, traffickers who regularly passed through Huguenot villages in the Vivarais were "treated like brothers."[27] Might they be supplying the religious rebels with muskets and gunpowder? Two decades later, Mandrin's expeditions stoked the same anxieties. If gangs of smugglers could cause trouble anywhere, reasoned the distressed intendant of Languedoc, imagine what havoc they might wreak in his province, where Huguenots would join them "in the hope of reestablishing their temple."[28] After Mandrin successfully withstood the attack at Guenand in December, the intendant believed his worst fears were coming true. Not only did the smugglers appear to be supplying arms to the Huguenots but they may well have been organizing them into an army, "as they are quite capable of doing, for we have seen how they defended themselves against the king's troops."[29] The rumor that battle-hardened smugglers were arming Huguenots for joint rebellion flew through the southeast and swirled north to Paris and Versailles.[30]

Feeding fears of such a coalition was the notion that Mandrin was also conspiring with foreign powers. In a frenzy of speculation, many royal officials came to believe that the smuggler was in the pay of Great Britain, whose simmering tensions with France in North America would shortly explode into what is now known as the Seven Years' War (1756–1763). The ever paranoid intendant of Languedoc had believed all along that Mandrin was a British proxy. As he saw it, smuggling chiefs from the higher echelons of society were well acquainted with the vicissitudes of international diplomacy and regularly solicited subsidies from foreign powers in hope of raising the capital they needed to outfit their gangs.[31] D'Espagnac fanned these fears in April 1755 when he reported that Mandrin had received a *lettre de change* for 30,000 lt that could have come only from France's archenemy (a conjecture for which no evidence remains). Britain was bankrolling the gang leader's expeditions, he surmised, to sustain the latter's war against the Farm, which would in turn weaken the royal finances and exhaust French troops. "When war resumes, this gang of brigands [will] plunge into the Cevennes to foment civil war," which would distract the French army and leave the kingdom vulnerable to a British offensive.[32]

Such concerns were taken to heart at Versailles. If Britain were to declare war on France, a memoir circulating in the ministry of foreign affairs explained, the southeastern provinces "from the Rhone to the [Mediterranean] sea" would be highly susceptible to invasion. The area was inhabited not only by an "immense quantity of Protestants who have for a long time groaned under the abuse of particular laws" but also by merchants and smugglers who established "hidden and suspicious connections between these provinces and foreign countries."[33] If King Charles-Emmanuel of Sardinia were to ally himself with Britain and Austria, the smuggler-infested southeast would be exposed to occupation. As an anonymous pamphleteer warned, nothing would stop the traffickers from entering into an alliance with the English. If the "manifesto by which they declare war against the Farmers general" were any indication, they would not think twice about betraying their country.[34] Just as modern notions of patriotism were gaining purchase among French elites, the ambiguous allegiances of international smugglers sounded alarm bells in many quarters of the French monarchy.[35]

Thus took shape the threat of a triple alliance between Britons, smugglers, and Huguenots. Not everyone was convinced of the threat's reality—the military commander Lemps, for one, doubted that smugglers were arming the Huguenots since there was little money to be made in weapons trafficking—but deep concern pervaded the halls of state: the minister of war had received reports that Protestants were stockpiling weapons in underground depots in the Cevennes, royal officials could plainly see that the British were bent on war in the American colonies, and news from the provinces had just arrived that a thug in Mandrin's pay had ruthlessly assassinated a high-ranking Farm official. Something had to be done.[36]

In this tense atmosphere, a plot was hatched to kidnap Louis Mandrin from Savoy. Such a stunt would, of course, be completely illegal. The "law of nations," a loose body of international law and custom, had for centuries forbade capture of criminal suspects on foreign soil without the full consent of foreign governments,[37] hence the elaborate protocols of judicial extradition and military commanders' stern warnings to southeastern troops "never to follow the smugglers beyond the Guiers River nor beyond the lands belonging to the king" for fear of provoking an international incident.[38] But the threat emanating from across the border was such that the Farm and war ministry were willing to violate international law and run the risk of alienating a neighboring sovereign power if it meant putting an end to contraband rebellion. Besides, the foreign affairs office claimed, Sardinia had already violated the *droit des gens* when it refused to go after La Motte's assassins.

This was not the first time the idea of kidnapping Mandrin was floated. Before the new year, d'Argenson had urged Fischer "to draw Mandrin and other chiefs in some trap where they can be seized."[39] At that time, the minister had no intention of capturing the smuggler outside French borders, but in April 1755 the Marquis de Ganay proposed an elaborate plan to take Mandrin on foreign soil.[40] An obscure army colonel who had been the unlucky governor of Autun when Mandrin occupied the city in December, Ganay had harbored a "personal hatred of this brigand" ever "since he ransomed my government." To exact revenge, Ganay sketched a plan for kidnapping Mandrin in Savoy and begged d'Argenson to give it serious consideration. Not only was it impossible to capture Mandrin in France, the governor emphasized, but the shamefully "dissimulating" conduct of the king of Sardinia foreclosed any possibility of obtaining custody through judicial extradition. It was plain as day that Turin was protecting Mandrin, for the "scoundrel" had been seen dining with a Savoyard magistrate not one month prior. The only solution, therefore, was to "kidnap this bandit in his refuge." The operation would be inexpensive, requiring no more than 200 men already stationed in the area. And it would be kept "completely secret." If necessary, the French crown could deny involvement and let the governor take the fall (a policy of plausible deniability that would have a bright future in twentieth-century covert wars). Ganay asked only that he be put in charge of the mission. Although he had the good fortune to make colonel at the age of thirty, he had been languishing at that rank for ten years without hope of advancement. Capturing Mandrin would revitalize his career.

Ganay never heard back from the minister of war, but his idea did not go unheeded. In the days after La Motte's assassination, d'Argenson, L'Hôpital, La Morlière, and Farmer General Bouret d'Erigny organized their own plan. Using special couriers for communications, they hatched a plot in "the most profound secrecy." Even military officers charged with pursuing Mandrin were deliberately left in the dark, including L'Hôpital's superior, Marcieu, whom La Morlière suspected of colluding with the underground.[41] According to the plan, Captain Diturbi de Larre, the officer who had successfully captured the smuggler Le Vasseur near Sauvetat, was to command a detachment of 500 men, composed of La Morlière's troops and ninety Farm guards. La Morlière knew that Mandrin was staying a mere five miles from the border at a château in the hamlet of Rochefort. Having fallen off his horse and hurt his leg, he had been taking his convalescence at the estate since 9 May, assisted by Jean François Dhuet-Saint-Pierre, younger brother of Mandrin's confidant, the Major. The château belonged to Honoré Piolenc de Thoury, a president à mortier of the parlement of Grenoble, who had thrown it open to Mandrin and his associates. Just how deeply the parlementary magistrate was involved in contraband is not clear, but we know that certain judges from Grenoble lent money to merchants in the illicit calico trade and that Piolenc's father, a first president of the parlement, once used his influence to free a suspected smuggler from the city's prisons.[42] In any case, in the eyes of a nobleman known for his adventurous social life and mounting debts, Mandrin cut the figure of a perfect guest. La Motte's fastidious reports stated that Mandrin, Broc, and the Major stayed there regularly, spending their days in the neighboring village of Saint-Genix, where they mingled with members of another band of traffickers.[43] Knowing that Mandrin was at Rochefort, the minister of war ordered Diturbi de Larre to slip across the border into Savoy under the cover of night, kidnap Mandrin from the château, and bring him back alive so that he could stand trial before the highest smuggling court in the land, the commission of Valence.

Before midnight on 10 May 1755, soldiers assembled under an overcast sky on the French side of the Guiers north of Pont-de-Beauvoisin. Just as he had done to get Le Vasseur, Diturbi de Larre instructed his men to remove their uniforms and disguise themselves as peasants, fishermen, and smugglers so they could not be identified.[44] Their faces blackened, the soldiers and guards silently waded across the river while holding their bayonets above the water, climbed the Savoyard bank, and, avoiding the roads, advanced through wheat fields toward Rochefort. They reached the château around three in the morning.

So much at ease were the smugglers in their Savoyard lair that they had not even bothered to post guards. In the predawn darkness, the captain and his men passed undetected through an alley of walnut trees leading to an iron gate of an exterior courtyard. Laying siege to the gatehouses, they broke through to the interior courtyard to find a building flanked by two square towers, one of which, unbeknownst to the soldiers, served as Mandrin's lodging. The din of the siege woke the concierge, who, venturing out to see what was going on, was felled by a sword and interrogated, as were other domestics. "We had seriously to caress them" (read "beat them"), reported La Morlière, but the interrogators were able to learn that Mandrin's apartments were in the left tower.[45] A group of soldiers clambered up the stone steps and broke down a door to find Mandrin and Dhuet Saint-Pierre sleeping in their quarters. The chief grabbed his pistols (according to the Duc de Luynes), but neither man had time to defend himself. The soldiers seized them in their nightclothes, tied them up, dragged them downstairs, and threw them into an awaiting cart. At long last, Mandrin was in the hands of French authorities.

Pillage ensued. Soldiers and guards roughed up the château's tenant farmer and stripped his wife of her jewelry and clothing, down to the calico handkerchief tied around her neck. They stole the couple's rent money and some coin that Mandrin had stashed in their apartment, which Diturbi de Larre distributed among his men. Then, they ransacked the château, breaking into locked rooms, wardrobes, chests of drawers, and desks, taking anything and everything of value: clothing, linen, and upholstery; tapestries and paintings; crockery and silverware;

mirrors and chandeliers; weapons and tools; food; and, to the dismay of Piolenc de Thoury, bottles of his "best and oldest wines" brought from Grenoble. "These wines I will miss, because I intended them to be drunk by decent, upstanding people."[46] Whatever could not be piled on carts or stuffed in packs for the trip home was broken or destroyed. Piolenc's papers, found buried in an armoire and sealed with his family coat of arms, were ripped open and strewn in the fields. Only during a mission on foreign soil could the war on contraband have breached its customary social boundaries to destroy the property of a noble *parlementaire*.

French soldiers and guards then turned their wrath on the people of Savoy. On the march back to France, at the unsuspecting village of Avressieux, the men forced their way into the schoolmaster's house and, finding a carrot of tobacco, sacked the place and stabbed the man with bayonets. At Saint-Colombe, the marauding army shot at three peasants in front of a barn, seriously wounding one of them. Finally, "like lions," they stormed into the border town of Saint-Genix just as parishioners were getting out of church after the day's first mass.[47] Unconcerned about wounding innocent bystanders, they hunted down smugglers residing in the village. Antoine Sales aka Salomon, at whose bar Madame Perrin had met the Piedmontese, was in the street when he was approached by a group of Farm guards led by André Regard. Regard was no stranger. He had worked as a smuggler in Saint-Genix for years and, as recently as 1752, had participated in a deadly ambush of Farm agents. He had probably been arrested by the French and, turned informer, was now doing what was necessary to avoid the wheel. "Look who we have here!" he or one of his colleagues said. Sales immediately fled but, looking back to see if he was being followed, took a shot in the chest. "Oh! My God, I'm dead!" he cried as he fell to the ground. Wounded, the innkeeper could do nothing to stop Regard's younger brother from firing a second fatal charge into his body. Rejoicing over the kill, the elder Regard and another Farm agent danced around the corpse singing, "Sleep! sleep! sleep, old man!"[48]

Sales's murder was but the most ruthless of many acts of violence visited on the village that morning. As tavern keepers and suspected smugglers Pierre Tourin and his brother-in-law François Goussen, aka the "Nîmes brothers," were tied up and thrown in the cart with Mandrin, soldiers looted villagers' homes and shops, grabbing whatever they could find (hats, mirrors, books, razors, hams, and cloth). After the French departed, local officials tallied their losses and sent word to their superiors of the "diabolical carnage" the army and Farm had inflicted on their town.[49] The contrast with Mandrin's moral economy could not have been starker. Whereas in France the chief's gang preferred exchange to theft and employed the instrument of violence as precisely as possible (although exceptions to both practices did occur), in Savoy the French army acted like an occupying force, straying far beyond the confines of its mission to take the war against Mandrin to an entire village. Such a divergence in behavior would not have been lost on the outraged townspeople of Saint-Genix.

With Mandrin in tow, the soldiers left the town, marched to the tip of a peninsula jutting into the Guiers, and ferried their prisoners and bulging sacks of loot across the river to France. Back on native soil, the troop was met by La Morlière, who, after a briefing on the operation, departed for Paris to personally inform the war minister of his triumph. In a few days, d'Argenson would order the colonel to withdraw his men ever so discreetly from Dauphiné and reward him with a position among the *cordons rouges* of the royal and military order of Saint-Louis.[50]

Rightly fearing a diplomatic backlash, the minister at once began to mask the army's involvement in the kidnapping by circulating bogus cover stories. Violations of the "law of nations" were not taken lightly in the eighteenth century, but if Turin could be persuaded that the French military had not participated in the attack, the court of Louis XV could at least distance itself from the event and minimize the diplomatic damage. The first cover story floated by d'Argenson claimed that the violence in Savoy was the product of infighting among local gangs. Rumor had it that a bunch of unknown men entered the province on 10 May and killed many smugglers, La Morlière lied to Marcieu, "but those who know [the smugglers] think, Monsieur, that the truth behind this news is that these people had already quarreled among themselves a number of times and are apparently still fighting over booty stolen from the King's cashboxes as well as profits made on prohibited merchandise they sold in France. Taken with drink, they killed each other. . . ."[51] "All I can say on this subject," Diturbi de Larre further deceived the comte, "is that I learned that a troop of smugglers who ordinarily live in Saint-Genix had a falling out over the sharing of the booty they collected during their trips, so that the strongest compelled the weakest to flee to France and, in the event, finding myself with some of our troops on the border, I picked up Mandrin, four of his companions, and shot five or six who ran away. . . . It was a miracle that chance led me to the men who were fleeing."[52] This was the version of events that Marcieu passed on to his Savoyard counterpart, Sinsan, and that Mont-peroux unwittingly spread among the Swiss.

Given what many Savoyards had seen with their own eyes, this cover story could not be sustained for very long. The war minister therefore launched a second narrative, conceding that a French incursion had taken place but blaming it on rogue Farm guards. D'Argenson again misinformed Marcieu: "It appears that these were agents of the Farm who, incensed by the excesses that smugglers committed daily, wanted to exact revenge, above all for the assassination of their controller."[53] According to this false tale, the murder of La Motte provoked four Farm captains to take matters into their own hands. Without authorization from their superiors, they illegally crossed into Savoy and committed a number of infractions. Admittedly regrettable, the incursion was not a willful violation of international law by the French crown and its army. To make this cover story ring true, the finance minister ordered the arrest of four Farm officers allegedly responsible for the action. Their motive "to avenge the death of their comrades" was honorable, he explained to Marcieu, but the king could not publicly abide by their behavior. On the contrary, Louis XV had to make it clear that he personally disapproved of the kidnapping and would not tolerate such conduct from Farm brigades in the future. To this end, the Farm officials were to be led to the prisons of Lyon "with a kind of brilliance so that people are made aware of the King's true intentions."[54] So it happened that an escort of twenty cavalrymen paraded the apparent authors of Mandrin's kidnapping to Lyon and, on 25 May 1755, before a large crowd, conspicuously threw them in jail.[55]

As La Morlière took the road north to Paris to brief the war minister, Mandrin and four other captives—Saint-Pierre the younger, the brothers Nîme, and Claude Planche, a loyal servant from Rochefort— headed west toward Valence, seat of the highest smuggling court in the realm. Securely chained in a covered wagon, Mandrin and Saint-Pierre were wheeled across Dauphiné by scores of mounted cavalry officers drawn from La Morlière's regiment. As the procession made stops on its two-day journey, throngs of curious peasants, townsfolk, and nobles rushed to catch glimpses of the famous smuggler. In Voiron, on the morning of 12 May, a knight of the Order of Malta was astonished to see Mandrin sitting in the cart "with as much sangfroid as if he were going to a wedding, smoking a pipe, laughing and gently mocking himself; this was not the case with his comrade, who is a young man."[56] Also in Voiron was one of Mandrin's captors, L'Hôpital, who according to one newspaper,

> wanted to see him, and said to him while approaching: Well now, Mandrin! Here is the fruit of your magnificent exploits and your impudence. The lord [L'Hôpital] added some short reflections but they did not appear to disconcert him [Mandrin]. To the contrary, he responded with the same gay air and playful humor that he had always shown at the most frightening times. Various military officers asked him questions about his campaigns, and his answers were stated with intelligence and precision.[57]

Such newspaper reports are not entirely reliable, but similar accounts of an unshaken Mandrin appear in private correspondence. At Saint-Marcellin, not far from Mandrin's natal village of Saint-Étienne, the abbé Morel spotted Mandrin and Saint-Pierre lunching at the Petit Paris: "I was present. I saw all of their behavior. Many of his [Mandrin's] acquaintances spoke to him. He replied in a firm and resolute tone."[58] Such was Mandrin's disposition as he was escorted to prison in Valence.

As the smuggler made his way west, news of his capture spread like wildfire. Emanating from Pont-de-Beauvoisin, the first reports traveled through administrative, military, and diplomatic channels. Marcieu tipped his porter six francs when he received word of the kidnapping: "This is the least I could do for such good news."[59] D'Espagnac hoped "with all his heart" that the news was true, hailing the coming of a new era in which smuggling chiefs would be too intimidated to challenge the army.[60] Montperoux reported that all the "decent people" in Geneva rejoiced when they learned of the capture, although the calico merchants were naturally chagrined.[61] In Paris, the diligent chronicler Marquis d'Argenson was delighted to hear that Mandrin was arrested—surely this was a feather in his brother's cap—but he disapproved of the illegal *ruse de guerre* employed to catch him; the king of Sardinia was right to be upset.[62]

The wider public learned about the kidnapping from foreign newspapers, which buzzed with reports from the border. Although the press faithfully recounted the imprisonment of the Farm officers charged with illegally capturing Mandrin, it gave no credence whatsoever to the cover stories circulated by French authorities. Rather, papers splashed their pages with sympathetic portrayals of "the famous Mandrin" being taken by marauding French soldiers. If the facts were sometimes jumbled, the basic story line shone through: the army and Farm had kidnapped Mandrin at Rochefort and were handing him over to French justice. Taking liberties with the story, editors replaced the anticlimactic capture of a sleepy Mandrin in his bedroom, during which scarcely a shot was fired, with action-packed tales of the chief's heroic resistance. "Notwithstanding the superiority of the number of assailants," printed the *Gazette d'Utrecht* (27 May 1755), the smugglers defended themselves "with all the vigor imaginable." "After having killed or wounded more than 20 men," they ran out of ammunition and finally succumbed. (The same paper tantalizingly reported that the château was laden with contraband and a fortune in gold and promissory notes.) The *Gazette d'Amsterdam* (30 May 1755) and *Gazette de Cologne* (27 May 1755) not only broke news of the "excesses" committed by La Morlière's *croque-moutons* (sheep-munchers) in Saint-Genix but also provided readers with a swashbuckling account of Mandrin beating back his attackers at Rochefort: "surprised, Mandrin attacked almost instantly after being woken by the noise of his assailants; arming himself with pistols, he fired on his enemies. His three comrades shot at the same time and killed eight *argoulets* [a slang term for La Morlière's men]." Resistance proved futile, however, as soldiers fell on the smuggler from all quarters and slammed him with the butts of their rifles. "He was taken alive, tied up, and led to Grenoble" but not before troops "pillaged the château."[63]

The discrepancy between the official cover story and newspaper accounts helps to explain the variegated public perception of Mandrin's capture. Some believed the cover story; others did not.[64] One popular song about the capture disregarded the cover story altogether but made heroes out of the "soldiers of Morlière," who, "more daring than lions," had captured the "scoundrel" Mandrin.[65] More judicious, the courtier Duc de Luynes, doubted rumors that the squad that captured the smuggler "was composed of men of the Farm who acted without orders" but thought it "advisable to stick to this language since he was taken on the lands of the king of Sardinia."[66]

As rapidly as the news of Mandrin's kidnapping spread, diplomatic relations between Versailles and Turin deteriorated. On the very day of the capture, the governor of Savoy exclaimed that "one has pushed audacity to the point of not only violating the rights of sovereignty, but violently kidnapping people . . . who should possess the immunity conferred by the State of another sovereign when their extradition has not been agreed upon."[67] The governor immediately dispatched a courier to inform the king of Sardinia of the violation and sent a senator to Grenoble to reclaim Mandrin and the others. When it became clear that Mandrin would not be released, Turin, showing unexpected bravura for a second-rate power, amassed troops on the border, prompting the French to deploy their own reinforcements and shut down international trade. As the specter of war loomed, the Savoyard commander at Pont-de-Beauvoisin worried that he would be unable to stop the French with only 1,200 men but vowed "to do my duty for my honor and that of the arms of the King, my master."[68] Military tensions between France and Sardinia persisted for months, with the foreign Francophone press relating every twist and turn in diplomacy until Louis XV finally, in August 1755, dispatched a special ambassador, the illustrious Comte Philippe de Noailles, to "disavow" the king's involvement in the siege and assure France's neighbor that the guilty parties would be properly punished.[69]

Well before this diplomatic effort reached its conclusion, however, the taking of Mandrin awakened a veritable hornets' nest of criminals in Savoy. Some smugglers fled north toward Geneva, worried that the king of Sardinia had collaborated in the kidnapping and would presently be rounding up others. Many more stayed behind, eager to retaliate against the French army and Farm. Pellegrin, the Major, and le Camus flew to the border to mount a counterattack against the French, driving Diturbi de Larre into hiding. Caught in the crossfire between France and the criminal underworld, Savoy officials scrambled to prevent local gangs from taking revenge, which might induce the French to stage another invasion. The commander at Les Échelles took a number of emergency measures. He prohibited all "tolerated smugglers" from leaving town, publicly punished a recalcitrant trafficker for violating his orders, and galloped to a nearby cave to dissuade a band of smugglers from taking their revenge. He also enlisted traffickers to serve as lookouts along the border.[70]

Seething diplomatic tensions and Savoy's utter disarray raised troubling questions. Would the trial in Valence proceed as planned or would Turin intervene to secure the chief's release? If Turin's effort to halt the proceedings failed, would relations between the two countries suffer a permanent rupture? How would such a rift alter the balance of power in Europe in the run-up to the impending war? As such matters preoccupied the French, the Sardinians, and newspaper readers across western Europe, all eyes turned toward the small town of Valence, where an infamous tribunal was preparing to prosecute the most celebrated smuggler of the age.

9

The Execution of Louis Mandrin

THE COMMISSION OF VALENCE, into whose custody Mandrin was placed, was the most fearsome court in all of France. Smugglers cursed its very name. Magistrates in venerable superior courts condemned it as an oppressive "tribunal of blood." Voltaire ranked it with the Black Death and the Inquisition as one of the worst plagues ever to strike humanity. The flagship of a new fleet of antitrafficking tribunals, it was to judge the most famous smuggler in all of Europe.

The growth of illicit trade in the eighteenth century prompted significant institutional changes in the French monarchical state. As we have seen, the crown expanded the Farm police to make it the largest and most powerful paramilitary force on the continent. But it also radically restructured the criminal justice system, by hardening the penal code and creating a new institutional layer of Farm-funded extraordinary courts to prosecute smugglers on a scale never seen before. Scores of violent traffickers were sentenced to death, and tens of thousands of less aggressive smugglers were subjected to hard labor in galleys and penal camps. Indeed, the birth of the modern prison owes much to this crackdown on smuggling, a fact philosopher Michel Foucault overlooked in his celebrated work on Western incarceration.[1]

Justice Revamped

Faced with a globalizing underground economy, the monarchy could have reduced the volume of traffic by either lowering the price of state tobacco and lifting the calico prohibition, as some officials urged, or intensifying state repression. It chose, decisively, to follow the latter course and so introduced a series of measures that, unprecedented in severity, remodeled much of the criminal justice system. First, between 1680 and 1730, the crown established an antitrafficking penal code draconian even by old-regime standards. In edict after edict, the king threatened to use the most degrading punishments in the judicial arsenal: the wheel, hanging, and the galleys for serious offenders; whipping, banishment, and heavy fines for lesser ones.[2]

Penal legislation first targeted salt smugglers, who were subject to a finely graded scale of fines and galleys sentences, with the death penalty held in reserve for recidivist gang members.[3] As if such penalties were not tough enough, punishment stiffened with the introduction of the tobacco monopoly. "Tobacco fraud is much less excusable than salt fraud," argued tax farmers, whose influence in crafting penal legislation perfectly illustrated the penetration of finance into judicial affairs.[4] Peasants could be forgiven for trafficking in a necessity, a good the poor needed to survive, but such leniency could not be extended to those who traded in a state commodity that was anything but indispensable. This penal logic shaped the landmark declaration of 6 December 1707, which, claiming that previous laws were not "strong enough to rein in smugglers," set the fine for those caught buying, selling, or possessing any amount of contraband tobacco at 1,000 lt—a crippling sum five times higher than that which struck salt smugglers and three or four times the annual income of most peasants and artisans.[5] If offenders were unable to pay the fine or even make a down payment of 300 lt within a month of conviction, their financial penalty would automatically be converted to a galleys sentence (or flogging and banishment for women, who were considered too weak to endure the galleys). From the tax farmers' point of view, the conversion of fines into galleys sentences had the advantage of punishing "people of low condition" who did not have the means to pay monetary penalties.[6] Criminals who failed to pay fines had traditionally been sentenced to suffer public humiliation in the stocks, but many indigent smugglers actually preferred the stocks to fines. The same could not be said of time spent in the galleys, where convicts were forced to row Mediterranean warships at the crack of a whip, often dying before the end of their terms.

The legal implications of the 1707 declaration were far-reaching. The nonviolent trafficking practiced by the majority of smugglers had always been a simple civil offense. Fines were to be paid to the plaintiff, the

Farm, as reparation for the infringement of its monopoly rights. But by converting fines into galleys sentences, the law punished those found guilty of civil misdemeanors with the kind of "afflictive" corporal punishment traditionally reserved for felons. The galleys, the lash, and banishment were tough exemplary punishments that involved public humiliation, the deprivation of liberty, and the painful violation of the integrity of the body. It was for this reason that the foundational criminal ordinance of 1670 had stipulated that any lower-court case resulting in a sentence of corporal punishment would automatically be appealed to an appellate court for review. Royal antitrafficking statutes that authorized the automatic conversion of fines to afflictive punishments, however, gutted the appeals process. The small-time smuggler who neither resisted arrest, carried weapons, nor moved about in dangerous gangs could, if unable to scrape together enough money to cover his fine, end up in the galleys without further consideration of his case. The evolution of civil pecuniary penalties into harsh criminal punishments reveals the extent to which the crackdown on smuggling was transforming the criminal justice system.[7]

If the 1707 declaration fixed the penalties for civil smuggling violations, those of August 1729 and January 1733 set punishments for higher-order, criminal violations that threatened "the tranquility of the State and the security of our Subjects."[8] The Farmers General, who took over the tobacco monopoly from the Indies company in 1730, made it clear that they intended to pursue smuggling gangs with a vengeance. In no uncertain terms, the 1733 law declared that smugglers of tobacco who were armed and amassed in groups of three or more or who attacked Farm posts and guards "will be punished to death." Also subject to the ultimate penalty were adult males who violently resisted arrest, a stipulation that dramatically raised the stakes for those who, but for police intervention, were committing a mere civil offense. In imposing the death penalty on smugglers in this way, the monarchy extended to traffickers a punishment it had exclusively reserved for those found guilty of committing egregious crimes of political disobedience (traitors, spies, deserters, and leaders of armed uprisings) and social transgression (murderers, parricides, heretics, witches, and domestics who stole from their masters). In the penal sphere, all sorts of underground trading practices—some violent, others only potentially so—were now grouped with the most grotesque acts of criminality.

The new declarations also heavily criminalized lesser offenses. Those arrested without contraband in their possession but traveling in bands of five or more through areas of heavy traffic would be sentenced to the galleys for life, a penalty that inflicted "civil death," the confiscation of all property (to be held in trust until death, after which it reverted to the king), and the suspension of all civil rights. Like the living dead, those sentenced to life in the galleys were to be treated as though they no longer possessed a civil existence. Further down the scale of offenses, tavern keepers and others who abetted smugglers could expect to pay a 1,000 lt fine for a first offense, as if they were smugglers themselves. Villagers who failed to sound the tocsin when armed gangs passed through town would be subject to a 500 lt fine. Finally, Farm employees caught with contraband would be condemned to the galleys for five years, and those who actively collaborated with smugglers were to be executed.

The penalties against calico smugglers followed a slightly different evolution, as they were drafted by the royal council of commerce (rather than the finance minister in conjunction with tax farmers). From the outset, smugglers of the coveted fabric were to be hit with an extremely heavy fine, 3,000 lt, a sum meant to capture the windfall profits calico smugglers were suspected of making. From 1706, consumers of the fabric were also liable to fines, a provision that was enforced with some alacrity in the 1730s.[9] As for criminal violations, calico traders who worked in armed bands were at first treated less harshly than their colleagues in the tobacco business, but the declaration of 1733 assimilated the penalties for the two types of traffickers.[10]

It was one thing for the crown to proclaim a tough new penal code, quite another to enforce it. Initially, a hodgepodge of lower courts and administrators were charged with judging accused smugglers. Local salt courts *(greniers à sel)* judged salt smugglers, financial courts called "elections" tried suspected tobacco traffickers, and intendants sentenced tobacco smugglers in provinces without elections, as well as calico runners. Sometimes this system cracked down hard, as when the election of Gap adhered to the letter of the law and sentenced Disdier de Buissard, a recidivist caught leading a mare with two ballots of tobacco, to a 1,000 lt fine and life in the galleys, a severe punishment for an unarmed man who did not belong to a gang and posed no threat to Farm guards.[11] But the crown would soon discover that despite the urgent tone and precise statutes of its antitrafficking legislation, judges who were reluctant to impose draconian punishments on such morally ambiguous criminals exploited the Roman-law principle of judicial discretion to thwart royal law.

Indeed, some local officers of justice proved to be patently obstructionist, interfering with Farm investigations, delaying judicial proceedings, and freeing suspects on technicalities. The election of Rouen acquitted Marie Lenormand of tobacco trafficking because the police report on which the case hinged was misdated (the first "7" in the year 1767 was mistakenly omitted).[12] Even when lower courts did sentence offenders, they frequently imposed light fines or blocked the conversion of unpaid fines into galleys sentences. In only about a quarter of the cases did the salt court of Laval hand down sentences as harsh as the Farm had wished.[13] As for tobacco, the election of La Rochelle fined Captain André-Jacques Prevost a mere 100 lt for smuggling seventeen pounds of Caribbean leaf into France.[14] Intendants almost never slapped calico offenders with the full weight of fines, despite the persistent efforts by finance minister Orry to bolster enforcement.

When it lost cases in lower courts, the Farm appealed to the *cours des aides,* the highest financial courts in the realm. After Pierre Robin, a master tanner arrested for possessing ten and a half ounces of tobacco, was exonerated by the local election, the Farm took the case to the Paris *cour des aides,* which struck down the verdict and imposed a fine of 1,000 lt.[15] The same high court fined tavern keeper Jean Benoist 1,000 lt for possessing thirty-eight pounds of tobacco after the case was thrown out of a lower court on a technicality.[16] But *cours des aides* could not always be trusted. That of Rouen upheld a ruling that dismissed the case of a woman caught red-handed with a carrot of tobacco because it was reluctant to throw the book at a widow who possessed tobacco for personal consumption.[17] That of Bordeaux also upheld a lower-court ruling that exonerated Luc Lahens, a former Farm agent arrested for selling an ounce of contraband weed to a sailor.[18] Sharing a popular mistrust of the Farm, many appellate judges were as hesitant as their lower-court colleagues to enforce the stiff penal code spelled out in royal decrees.

What could be done when law courts both high and low impeded the prosecution of smugglers? Pushed by tax farmers, Louis XV moved to bypass recalcitrant courts in a series of bold measures that, taken together, marked the emergence of a kind of extraordinary justice that would transform the French judiciary.[19] The king was able to circumvent the courts by invoking the ancient principle of "retained justice," the margin of justice reserved for the monarch over and above that which he and his predecessors had already delegated to magistrates. The king could dispense such justice himself, through his royal council, or through the creation of special commissions.[20] In civil smuggling cases, the royal council increasingly used the principle of retained justice to overturn court decisions. When the election of Doulens, in Picardy, exonerated five peasants for possession of "false tobacco" because each of the accused had less than a pound, the royal council struck down the sentences and imposed standard fines of 1,000 lt.[21] In a similar fashion, the king's council, which since 1661 had wielded the power to overturn superior-court rulings, nullified the verdicts of *cours des aides* that upheld the lenient sentences of lower courts. Luc Lahens and many others exonerated by appeals courts were in the end sentenced by the council to pay 1,000 lt.

The royal council did not stop there. To judge criminal cases involving armed and violent smugglers and smuggling gangs, it employed the theory of retained justice to circumvent traditional tribunals and create new smuggling commissions. Like the lethal prevostial courts (quasi-military tribunals that prosecuted the migrant poor) on which they were modeled, the commissions were authorized to impose corporal punishments and the death penalty without appeal—a step that cut *cours des aides* out of the judicial loop. This was a major innovation, because heretofore all sentences of corporal punishment and death issued by lower courts were automatically transferred to appellate courts, which often softened them.[22] Now, new commissions could uphold the rulings of tough lower courts or simply take high-profile cases and issue sentences of their own.

Initially, commissions were headed by provincial intendants (and, in Paris, the chief of police) who, unlike ordinary magistrates who owned the offices they occupied, could be instantly revoked from their position and were therefore much more responsive to the will of the royal council. Having encroached on the jurisdiction of law courts since the seventeenth century, intendants were now granted authority to judge criminal cases involving armed and potentially violent smugglers.[23] Recourse to such extraordinary justice was necessary, the tax farmers argued, because "ordinary" judicial institutions had neither the will nor the capacity to stop the rise of tobacco fraud.[24] The only way to repress large gangs was to shift jurisdiction from traditional courts to special tribunals headed by intendants, who were willing to punish smugglers to the full extent of the law.

At first, intendants' tribunals were created on a case-by-case basis. For example, after a crowd in the city of Tulle attacked agents of the tobacco monopoly to free two smugglers held in custody, the finance minister committed the case to the intendant of Montauban, who judged the accused with the assistance of a former prosecutor and several local barristers. With the firm leadership of the intendant, the outcome was unequivocal: the principal assailants were sentenced to be hanged, and others were either dispatched to the galleys or banished.[25] Likewise, the intendant of Auvergne was instructed to take over a case already underway in the local election court "as it is not only a matter of contraband but of a gang and open rebellion." When the president and attorney general of the *cour des aides* of Clermont objected, the minister of finance explained that "a prompt and speedy remedy" was necessary to repress armed bands.[26]

Rather than draw up a new order for every special case that arose, the royal council soon instructed intendants to form standing courts. In the 1720s and 1730s, tribunals of this sort sprang up in many border provinces and even in interior provinces where trafficking was heavy.[27] Each tribunal was composed of an intendant and (like the prevostial courts) several *gradués,* licensed barristers who argued cases on the floor of parlements, held positions in city governments and courts, or worked for intendants as subdelegates. Drawing on this pool, intendants cherry-picked lawyers known for their "zeal and fidelity" to the crown and compensated them with funds from the Farm.[28]

In many places, the standing courts were effective enough, but in Dauphiné run-ins with a notorious gang leader, Jean Barret, exposed their ultimate weakness. Indeed, it was the failure of the intendant's court in Grenoble that led to the creation of an entirely new sort of tribunal, a supercommission that could prosecute traffickers without encumbrance. The story of the intendant's failure in Grenoble is therefore crucially important, for it prompted the establishment of the commission of Valence that, together with the sister courts it inspired, changed the face of French criminal justice.

When Mandrin was just a boy, "the most famous of all [smuggling] chiefs" was Jean Barret.[29] Based in Bresse and Gex, his gang ran calico to Provence, tobacco to Languedoc and Auvergne, and (on return trips) salt from Auvergne to the Lyonnais. In the spring of 1732, in Virville, Dauphiné, the mounted police engaged the Barret gang in a shoot-out, killing two traffickers and wounding two more. Although the chief got away, the police captured five men and retrieved an abundance of evidence, including contraband tobacco stashed in a nearby barn. After hearing the case, intendant Fontanieu and his colleagues pronounced tough sentences in strict conformity with royal legislation: three men were condemned to death and two to life terms in the galleys.[30] The intendant's court did its job, but Barret was reportedly furious with the ruling and set out to take revenge. A month after the trial, on a run from Savoy to Provence, the chief and his men broke down the door of a pub in Saint Laurent du Pont, not far from Grenoble, seized two Farm brigadiers, and hurled "atrocious insults and threats against those charged with the financial affairs of the King." In broad daylight, they tied and muzzled the guards, attached them to their horses, and, mimicking royal rituals of corporal punishment, dragged them through the streets of the village. The gang then pulled the guards into the woods, stripped them of their clothes, shot them, and repeatedly stabbed them with bayonets. After mutilating the corpses, an act of desecration that abased the memory of its victims, the band held a mock trial in which the intendant and the provincial Farm director were found guilty and executed in effigy.[31]

The wheel of revenge still spinning, royal authorities sought out Barret. A few days after the massacre in Saint Laurent du Pont, a mounted Farm brigade pursued a band of seventeen suspected of working with the murderous chief. After a bloody shoot-out at a rural tavern, the agents arrested three traffickers and gathered the smugglers' rifles, horses, and fifteen bundles of tobacco, all of which, along with one signed confession, was carefully documented in an official report to the intendant. To Fontanieu, this looked like another open-and-shut case: the smugglers had resisted arrest, fired on agents of the Farm, and were seized with weapons and contraband in hand. Indeed, so obviously guilty were they that the intendant decided to use the case to force the parlement to join his battle against the underground. Instead of judging the accused himself, he allowed the case to proceed through ordinary channels of justice, starting with the election and moving on appeal to the parlement of Grenoble (which was also a *cour des aides*). Fontanieu was betting that the election would hand down stiff sentences and the parlement would be obliged to uphold them. If the high court supported the election, as he expected, the traditional judiciary would appear every bit as eager as the intendant to rid Dauphiné of dangerous smugglers. The intendant explained, "I thought that in such a clear case the parlement would not be able to avoid issuing a judgment that [would have] conformed to my own. Its condemnation would announce to smugglers that they should expect no more mercy from this company than from me."[32] What better way to intimidate the traffickers of his province?

At first, Fontanieu's gamble seemed to pay off. The election adhered tightly to royal law and condemned the three traffickers to death. But when the case was brought before the parlement, the magistrates modified the sentence. Some *parlementaires* blamed Barret's massacre on the excessively severe punishments the intendant had inflicted on members of his gang: had the parlement instead of the intendant conducted the previous trial, they reasoned, the punishments would not have been so severe, Barret would not have felt compelled to retaliate, and the case before it would not even exist. Disregarding the sworn depositions of Farm agents and contravening the first article of the declaration of 1729, the magistrates overturned the ruling of the lower court, saved the convicts from the death penalty, and sentenced them to five years in the galleys. Galled by the Farm's intrusive reach into their province, the *parlementaires* also used the occasion of the trial to issue an unprecedented ruling that prohibited Farm officials from shooting on smugglers, undermining the company's ability to enforce antismuggling laws. Agents would now think twice before reaching for their muskets; Fontanieu lamented, "there will not be one guard on the border who will dare pull the trigger of a rifle or draft a report since such a document now possesses the least credibility." The intendant had badly miscalculated. Far from demonstrating their will to combat the underground, the magistrates of the highest court in the province were openly siding with traffickers against the Farm.[33]

The parlement's rulings galvanized public opinion against the intendant, whose tough sentencing in the Virville case now made him seem a "cruel and bloodthirsty man." "I find myself suddenly going from an object of the people's extreme attachment to one of its extreme hatred." Condemned men shouted insults as they were carted past his home, and crowds spit "vulgar language" at him. Aware that his poor reputation jeopardized his ability to act effectively as the king's man in Dauphiné, he considered tendering his resignation and withdrawing from a province in full "revolt against the authority of the King."[34]

Reassured by the finance minister, the intendant kept his post and conducted two more smuggling trials. The first involved none other than Jean Barret, who was captured in December 1732 and confessed to the brutal murders of two Farm guards. Fontanieu and his fellow judges sentenced him to be broken on the wheel.[35] However, the second trial, which judged Barret's accomplice to murder, Claude de Mure, proved more controversial. Although the intendant and his colleagues agreed that Mure was guilty, they split over the matter of sentencing. In a minority opinion, Fontanieu and the tribunal's reporter (the judge who prepared the dossier on which the verdict was based) urged that the convict be sentenced to death, as royal law dictated. The other judges, claiming that royal statutes "were too severe to be readily applied," opined in favor of a life term in the galleys. Although Fontanieu relented to the majority opinion, he was stunned by the change of heart in colleagues who had until then imposed capital punishment without hesitation. Suddenly, even "the best of all the barristers" could not be counted on to impose the death penalty.[36]

Undoubtedly, the lawyers were responding to parlementary pressure and the souring of public opinion. They could not avoid condemning Barret—the man had dragged two Farm employees to their death in front of an entire village—but the case against Mure was less clear and merited a more lenient sentence. The lawyers also worried about the possibility that smugglers would take revenge on them for handing down tough punishments; one *gradué* had already armed himself and retreated to his country house, knowing that a reprisal had recently taken place against an officer in a prevostial court.[37] In any case, the barristers no longer had the stomach to condemn violent smugglers to death. The intendant immediately suspended all capital cases and began to lobby for the creation of a completely new kind of court.[38]

As Fontanieu emphasized in his proposal to the finance minister, "a commission more general than mine" would have major advantages. First, it would be granted a much broader geographic sweep, hearing cases not only from Dauphiné but also from surrounding southern provinces. If smugglers were not restricted by provincial borders, why should the courts be? Stretching the commission's territorial jurisdiction beyond Dauphiné might also dampen parlementary resistance because, unlike the intendant's tribunal whose geographical jurisdiction perfectly matched that of the parlement, the new supercommission would appear less like a direct rival. Locating the seat of the court "anywhere but Grenoble" would have a similar effect, distancing the court from parlementary scrutiny and influence. Second, the commission would not be staffed by the intendant and local barristers but by "foreign judges who, without customs rooted in the region, would only be concerned with the disposition of the ordinances, the interest of the king and that of the public."[39] Unlike the spineless local lawyers who refused to condemn Mure to death, outside judges would apply the law as the royal council wrote it.

Orry enthusiastically endorsed Fontanieu's proposal and, on 31 March 1733, created the commission of Valence. The commission was granted territorial jurisdiction over the southern provinces of Provence and Languedoc, the central province of Auvergne, and the eastern provinces of Dauphiné, Lyonnais, and Bourgogne. Rourgue and Quercy were added in 1737, as were Limousin and Roussillon in 1766. Covering nearly half the kingdom, from the Alps to the Pyrenees, this commission was rivaled only by the parlement of Paris in its geographic reach. To head the new commission, the royal council appointed Jean-Pierre Colleau, who, as a magistrate at the châtelet (criminal court) of Melun, had experience questioning defendants, deposing witnesses, issuing sentences, and presiding over executions. He had also successfully handled a number of sensitive smuggling trials and was well prepared for the grisly work of the new commission.[40]

Like its geographical sweep, the jurisdiction of the commission steadily expanded. Created to try smugglers who were armed and amassed in gangs, the commission was soon authorized to go after individual armed smugglers, accomplices in smuggling operations, persons who acted violently toward agents of the Farm, corrupt tobacco retailers, and Farm employees suspected of fraud. To handle this heavy caseload, Colleau could count on the assistance of six judges (*assesseurs* drawn from a pool of lawyers who practiced in the parlements of Paris, Dijon, and Grenoble), a royal prosecutor, and a clerk. Also at the court's disposal were a handful of subdelegates in provincial capitals who received official reports from the Farm, initiated investigations into suspected smugglers, and transmitted the dossiers they compiled to Valence. The Farm compensated all handsomely for their work. The president earned a premium salary of 12,000 lt—an income on par with that of rich provincial nobles and parlementary magistrates—while the *assesseurs*, prosecutor, and clerk were paid between 2,400 lt and 6,000 lt, more than their peers in ordinary courts. In an age when the state was reluctant to commit resources to the criminal justice system, the Farm spent more than 40,000 lt a year on the commission of Valence alone.[41]

Orry could be forgiven for thinking in 1733 that the formidable powers of the new tribunal in Valence would intimidate traffickers and bring contraband to a halt in southeastern France.[42] As it happened, smuggling could not be so easily stamped out, and the authority of the supposedly temporary commission was repeatedly prolonged until the institution became a fixture of the old regime. It proved such a success, in fact, that sister courts were founded in Reims in 1740, Saumur in 1742, Caen in 1766, and Paris in 1771.[43] The commission of Reims covered the northeast. Saumur presided over the epicenter of the illicit salt trade in the west. Caen specialized in maritime contraband, and Paris concentrated on the voracious center of consumption that was the capital. Although special commissions had always been temporary, these five mighty tribunals became permanent features of the judicial landscape, prosecuting smugglers in almost every province in France. By the time Mandrin was imprisoned in 1755, the commission of Valence was but the flagship in a fleet of powerful courts charged with the repression of contraband.[44]

The combined effect of an expansion in Farm police, a hardening of the penal code, and the creation of new courts over which the royal council exercised greater control was striking. As the paramilitary force of the Farm captured more and more smugglers, and as newly created commissions and lower courts applied the penalties stipulated in royal legislation, the repression of trafficking expanded dramatically, soon dwarfing that of every other crime in the kingdom. The only other infraction that came close to receiving the same kind of attention was theft, the prosecution of which was also on the rise. But smuggling—in effect, theft from the state in the case of salt and tobacco—received singular attention as droves of traffickers appeared in courts designed exclusively to prosecute them. "Of all the offenses that flourished in [early] modern France," concludes one specialist of penal history, "smuggling was without a doubt the most heavily pursued 'crime.'"[45]

Given how lightly the early modern criminal justice system trod on the population at large, the sheer number of smugglers hauled before the courts was staggering. Over the century, ordinary courts and high commissions judged tens of thousands of suspected traffickers in an unprecedented blow against a highly specific form of crime. The commissions judged an estimated 30,000 traffickers from the 1730s to 1789, while hundreds of lower courts summoned countless petty smugglers to the bench.[46] The lower court of Laval, situated at ground zero of the illicit salt trade, judged as many as 4,788 smugglers between 1759 and 1793, roughly 200 cases a year. With dockets like that, it is no wonder that the elections, *juges des traites,* and *greniers à sel* sent about 13,000 smugglers to the galleys before 1748, and many more in the second half of the century.[47] And this does not even take into account the untold numbers of men and women who were fined or banished. Between 1680 to 1789, tens of thousands of smugglers passed through the judicial system. By comparison, the prevostial courts heard a total of 12,500 cases between 1758 and 1790.[48] The dockets of the dozen or so parlements who judged serious criminal cases were on par with those of the five commissions, but the former heard a wide variety of criminal cases, whereas the latter prosecuted smugglers alone.[49] More smugglers found themselves caught in the kingdom's judicial net than any other kind of criminal.

It was not just the volume of cases they handled that made smuggling courts so formidable, however. It was also the severity of their sentencing. Because the records of the commission of Valence are incomplete, we will never know the full impact of its penal punch. But of the thousands of cases it heard, a sample of 877 sentences handed down between 1733 and 1771 are extant, a sufficient number to illustrate the tribunal's prosecutorial zeal. In the sample, 162 men, roughly a fifth of the sentences, were sentenced to death, sixty-five of them to be broken on the wheel and ninety-seven to be hanged. A 19 percent death penalty rate was more than twice as high as that imposed by the parlement of Paris at the peak of its severity in the 1760s.[50] And among death sentences, a 40 percent incidence of the wheel was unheard of. The parlements of Paris and Dijon and even the notorious prevostial courts condemned no more than a fourth of their convicts to this spectacle of pain and suffering.[51] Despite the commission's apparent taste for executions, however, the majority (71 percent) of the condemned—rank-and-file members of tobacco bands, a sprinkling of salt and calico dealers, and a handful of corrupt Farm officials—were sent to the galleys for life or, more frequently, for fixed terms of three, six, or nine years. The remainder of the accused—women, lesser offenders, shady tobacco retailers—were banished from the region, whipped, temporarily imprisoned, or (in the rare case of merchants) stripped of the right to conduct business. Almost all defendants were sentenced to pay heavy fines.[52]

The figures from Valence may well be skewed toward tougher punishments, since they have been compiled from a collection of printed judgments disseminated by the commission to instill fear in the populace. A more reliable picture of the justice meted out by commissions emerges from the records of Valence's sister court in Reims. First headed by Nicolas-Pierre Colleau, son of the judge who presided over Valence in its formative years, the commission seated in the capital of Champagne enjoyed jurisdiction over all major contraband cases in northeastern France, including the provinces of Champagne, the Three Bishoprics, Soissons, Picardy, and, from 1771 to 1774, Lorraine, Bar, and much of Normandy. Like Valence, the court mainly prosecuted tobacco smugglers, although salt and calico traffickers appeared before it as well.

The commission of Reims was relentless in its pursuit of smugglers. Between 1740 and 1788, some 5,809 individuals were hauled before the court for smuggling-related crimes, 4,134 of whom received verdicts. The most egregious cases, usually involving the murder of a Farm agent, resulted in death sentences: 159 men (4 percent) were sentenced to hang or be broken in the city's public square. The majority of convicts—traffickers who worked in gangs—were spared death, but 1,404 of them (34 percent) received the next toughest punishment in the judicial arsenal: the galleys. Some were dispatched to the galleys for life, but most were sentenced to a term of three to twelve years. The commission did hand down lighter, "nonafflictive" punishments such as fines, but because unpaid fines automatically converted to galleys sentences, a good number of the 787 fined smugglers (19 percent of the total) probably ended up in the galleys just the same. An additional 7 percent of the accused were banished from the region, and the remaining 36 percent were acquitted, pardoned, or released after stints in prison. All in all, apart from the small fraction of convicts condemned to death, the commission favored incarceration and heavy fines, especially in its later years.[53]

These figures illustrate the highly repressive character of the commissions. The "booted justice" of the prevostial courts, which had the lowest acquittal rate (only 6–7 percent) and the highest death penalty rate (17 percent) of all tribunals, has long been considered the vanguard of judicial repression in the eighteenth century.[54] But it did not constitute "the only major innovation in repression to emerge in the last century before the French Revolution," as one prominent historian has claimed.[55] The smuggling courts added a whole new dimension to criminal justice in this period. In absolute terms, the five great commissions and the hundreds of lower courts dotting the kingdom condemned almost twice as many defendants to the horrors of the galleys as did prevostial courts.[56] And because all that was necessary for conviction in any given smuggling case was the written report and oral testimony of two Farm guards, a derivation of the two-witness rule formulated by the ordinance of 1670, smuggling courts were able to convict a relatively high proportion of defendants, not as high as the prevostial courts but far higher than the parlements of Paris, Rennes, Toulouse, and Grenoble. Finally, whereas the parlements released more people and subjected convicts to a wider spectrum of punishment, commissions and lower smuggling courts concentrated their sentencing on galleys or fines that often led to the galleys.[57] Smuggling courts did, of course, sentence smugglers to be hanged or broken on the wheel, but what stands out is the constant stream of convicts they sent to the galleys.[58]

Thus, the crackdown on smuggling led to a radical expansion of the penal system. Not only was the death penalty extended to a new class of criminals, as has been noted, but the heavy use of the galleys sentence brought about a historic transformation in penality. In an age when jails were not widely used to punish convicts, the expansion of the galleys and their mid-century conversion into labor camps heralded a new carceral regime. While Foucault looked to factories, slave ships, plantations, and the army to locate the origins of the modern prison, the birth of the penitentiary in France can be traced more narrowly to the galleys and camps in which more than 100,000 men were incarcerated between 1685 and 1791.[59] Because smugglers were the largest single group of convicts confined there, it is worth taking a closer look at this seminal institution.

During its heyday under the Sun King, the galley fleet in the southern port of Marseille was a powerful player in the strategic theater of the western Mediterranean. Designed for naval blockades, coastal raids, and seizures of lightly armed merchant vessels, the fleet's forty ships depended for their lightning speed on the strength and regimentation of thousands of oarsmen. Each ship required 260 men, the flagship as many as 450, all of whom had to undergo rigorous training to learn how to pull the awkward thirty-nine-foot oars in unison (Figure 9.1). "Try to imagine," wrote a former oarsman, "six men in chains, naked as a bare hand, sitting on their bench, each holding the oar . . . bodies outstretched, arms stiff to push their oar forward until it is underneath the bodies of those in front of them, who are busily moving the same way. And having thus pushed their oar forward, they raise it to plunge it into the sea; and at the same moment throw themselves, or rather hurtle themselves backwards, to fall on the bench."[60] Although exhaustion, malnutrition, and ill treatment by guards sapped the forced laborers, it was their deplorable living conditions that ultimately killed them. Disease spread like wildfire through the ships, workshops, and hospital of the Marseille arsenal. The whole environment of the galleys formed "the most vivid image of hell to be found on earth."[61]

In earlier centuries, the unfortunates who manned the fleet consisted mainly of Mediterranean slaves and destitute "volunteers" pressed into service, but during the bellicose reign of Louis XIV criminal convicts of all sorts—army deserters, Protestants, murderers, assailants, and thieves—were increasingly subject to penal servitude and exploited to power the narrow ships. It was not long before one group of convicts in particular, smugglers, overtook all others. As tobacco traffickers joined their salt-bearing colleagues in the galleys in the first half of the eighteenth century, the proportion of smugglers incarcerated in Marseille rose to more than 44 percent. During the 1740s, by which time waves of convicts from the commissions of Valence, Reims, and Saumur joined torrents of traffickers from the lower courts, 200 salt and 400 tobacco smugglers were condemned to the galleys every year.[62] It is a grim irony that with respect to this last group, the state was imposing

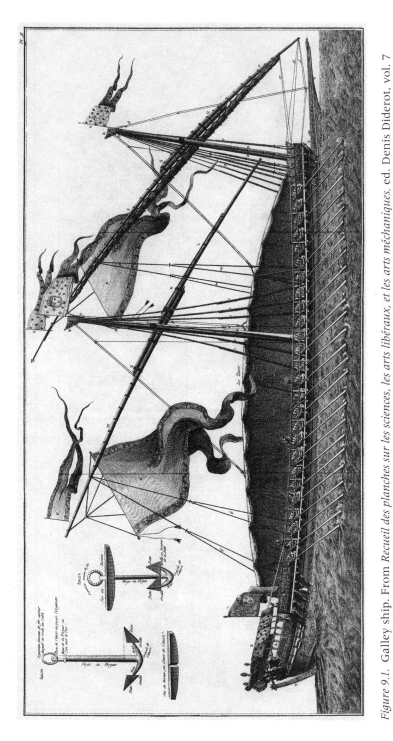

Figure 9.1. Galley ship. From *Recueil des planches sur les sciences, les arts libéraux, et les arts méchaniques,* ed. Denis Diderot, vol. 7 (Paris, 1769), "Marine," planche 2.

the punishment of forced labor on criminals who trafficked in a good that was produced by slave labor in the Americas. The violence and coercion that permeated Atlantic trade had come full circle, lending credence to the notion that the creation of that "oceanic space rendered behaviour more brutal" than before.[63]

Paradoxically, however, as ever more convicts poured into the galleys, the fleet itself became increasingly obsolete. With the French navy concentrating its resources on more powerful oceangoing ships of the line, the galleys soon became little more than floating detention centers. In 1748, Louis XV disbanded them, ordering the remaining ships to be absorbed by the royal navy, and established in their place hard-labor camps called *bagnes* at the naval bases of Toulon, Brest, and Rochefort. Henceforth, convicts sent to the "galleys" would, in fact, work in naval arsenals on the coast. The transition from fleet to penal camp did not slow the furious pace at which smugglers were incarcerated. In 1752, fully 58 percent of the Brest camp, the largest of all the new institutions, was composed of smugglers; thirty years later the proportion still held at 50 percent.[64] The origins of the modern French prison system can be traced to the eighteenth-century crackdown on illicit trade.

The advent of the galleys and work camps did not spell the end of the conspicuous exemplarity that defined the old-regime penal system.[65] Far from being spirited away under a cloak of state secrecy after receiving their sentences, smugglers were ceremoniously branded by executioners in public. In the courtyards and at the gates of tribunals across France, executioners used hot branding irons to sear the letters *GAL* onto the left shoulders of smugglers. The letters served the utilitarian purpose of identifying recidivists and escaped convicts, but they were deliberately inflicted in public to demonstrate the condition of indelible abjection into which galley convicts were thrown. (In 1744, branding was abolished for smugglers sent to the galleys for failure to pay fines, but the ritual remained in place for others.) Even more visible than branding were the chain gangs by which smugglers were transported to distant ships and camps. If passersby failed to catch sight of executioners wielding their irons, they could not help but notice the "great chains" that harnessed long lines of convicts, each burdened with thirty pounds of irons around his neck and ankle as he trudged through town and country on his way to the coast. How could a peasant laboring in a nearby field not look at such a sight and wonder about the fate of men forced to endure such a torturous odyssey?

And yet, the labor camps that succeeded the galleys did prefigure the coming of an entirely different penal system, one based not on elaborate public display but on confinement, surveillance, and labor in the service of the state.[66] Convicts were chained to their workshops during the day and fettered to their beds at night. "Even the most fearless convicts have admitted it," confessed one former prisoner at Brest; "no matter how hardened one is, the first sight of this place of misery gives a profound shock. Each hall contains twenty-eight platforms, called benches, on which 600 convicts are chained; those long lines of red uniforms, those shaved heads, those sunken eyes, those forlorn countenances, the constant rattle of chains, all combine to fill the soul with a secret terror."[67] Unlike the jails of the day, few prisoners escaped such horrific confinement. Some served their time and were released, but many succumbed to illness and died before the end of their terms. For the latter, the galleys were a death sentence.[68]

Executing Mandrin

This was the criminal justice system into which Louis Mandrin fell on the morning of 13 May 1755, as he was escorted into the town of Valence by a procession of fifty cavalrymen, sabers at the ready. The sight of a smuggler being led to his cell was nothing new in this burg. People were accustomed to seeing prisoners dragged into town, thrown in prison, led to court, marched off to the galleys, or paraded to the Place des Clercs, the large public square where smugglers were regularly executed. But the reputation of Mandrin was such that the sound of a single trumpet announcing his arrival stirred the most jaded of citizens. "The curiosity was so great that people squeezed up against each other to see him pass."[69]

They also flocked to see him after he was locked in his cell, lining up to enter the prison in small groups for a glimpse and even a chat with the "famous Chief of smugglers."[70] Those unable to elbow their way into the prison waited in the courtyard to spot Mandrin being escorted to the commission. Admirers gave him gifts of money, game, and wine, the *Courrier d'Avignon* reported, but above all they were curious, firing a barrage of questions that Mandrin handled with aplomb.

"He answers precisely all the questions put to him. He is polite toward some and loses his temper with others, which is not surprising since he is ceaselessly bombarded with a thousand different ideas about his situation and the consequences of his detention. His pride shows through in his answers."[71] "He had great presence of mind, sure and prompt answers, and a warrior-like and bold physiognomy," noted one of his biggest fans, local grocer Michel Forest. "No stranger, whatever his station, failed to stop and see him, and after having seen and conversed with him, people withdrew feeling sorry for his lot."[72] As he ate, drank, and smoked, Mandrin indulged the curiosity of the public with good humor, telling the ladies of Valence that "he would have thrown them a party if his money had not all been taken away."[73]

Mandrin was not in Valence to amuse the public, however. He was there to be judged and judged quickly before Turin could press its claim that he be returned to Savoy. With all due haste, the commission of Valence proceeded to conduct the trial according to the inquisitorial system of criminal justice that predominated on the European continent. The magistrates collected police reports, deposed witnesses, interrogated the defendant, and compiled the resulting documents into a dossier on which the verdict and sentence would be based. In inquisitorial trials, the cards were stacked heavily against the accused: judges shrouded the proceedings in secrecy, possessed the exclusive right to evaluate evidence, had recourse to torture to produce confessions, and enjoyed significant latitude in sentencing. Failing a confession, all that was needed to impose severe penalties were two incriminating depositions from witnesses, which in smuggling cases were provided by two Farm guards, not a high bar. The accused, on the other hand, was virtually defenseless. He remained ignorant of the charges until confronted by witnesses, was not permitted representation by counsel, and had no prior access to evidence used against him. Moreover, the accused in smuggling trials could challenge the all-important reports of the Farm only through an *inscription de faux,* which granted a mere two days to prove the documents false, an all but impossible task for those with few resources. And, it bears repeating, defendants before the commission of Valence had no right of appeal.

To this absurdly lopsided distribution of power must be added the social and cultural gulf that divided well-born, educated judges from poor, often illiterate rural defendants. Dramatizing the depths of this chasm, reformer Joseph Servan wrote of the first moment judges laid eyes on a defendant: "they are brought an unknown man, haggard, disfigured, white from hunger and fear, his face covered with hair like that of a wild beast. . . . Who is this being? None of his judges know—he is a shadow, a specter, appearing from the depths of a prison-cell before judges whose power terrifies him. Who can know anything of his interests, his character, his morals? Who even asks?"[74] Is this how Mandrin appeared before the commission of Valence? Probably not. We will never know in detail what passed between Mandrin and his judges, for the trial records have been lost, but the bits and pieces of the proceedings observed by or leaked to newspaper correspondents and town residents suggest he made a favorable impression on his judges. Mandrin was no rube. The educated son of a respectable merchant, he knew how to behave in polite society. The same manners, deference, and self-confidence that won over Joly de Fleury in Bourg seem to have elicited sympathy from the president of the commission. Although the judge had a reputation for ruthlessly pursuing defendants, he appeared to acknowledge that this was no ordinary smuggler.

Gaspard Levet, who had served under Colleau during the commission's opening years and assumed the presidency in 1738, went out of his way to be polite, referring to the accused as "Monsieur Mandrin." The chief reciprocated by answering the judge's questions "gaily and with a confident tone."[75] "He responded to all the interrogations with an unparalleled intrepidity and presence of mind," noted Forest.[76] And with humor as well: at one point he joked with Levet, "you should really permit me eight days leave to collect what is owed me at Guenan near Autun where I left more than 80,000 livres."[77] Although he refused to accept responsibility for the murders with which he was personally charged, he freely confessed to participating in successive armed bands and to the killings that such bands committed.[78] On top of such confessions, the commission had no problem accumulating evidence against him, since his attacks on the Farm were documented by the receipts he issued and the prison registers he signed. The commission had more than enough evidence for a conviction.

Mandrin spent his time in court sparring with hostile witnesses and exonerating those who had been inadvertently caught up in the investigation. Reacting to the damning testimony of a young man who had taken care of his horses, Mandrin impugned the credibility of the witness, a lowly valet. Would judges put stock in the word of a man of such base condition? he asked, appealing to his judge's social prejudices. Alternatively, the chief validated the depositions of witnesses for whom he had sympathy. Graciously exculpating a guide who refused to confess to accepting money for his services, Mandrin declared, "You do well to insist that you did not receive the 4 Louis; I forced you to take them, by leaving them on the table after having offered them to you twenty times to no avail. I had hired you to serve as a guide for a route I wanted to follow, and although you protested that you were not familiar with it, I kept you on."[79]

Perhaps some of the smuggler's presence of mind stemmed from a belief that his trial would not end in his death. He may have clung to the hope that the king of Sardinia would successfully reclaim the case before it was too late, but he formulated a backup plan should such a rescue fail, attempting to cut a deal with the French crown in which he pledged to serve in the army in exchange for his freedom, a possibility Joly de Fleury had raised months earlier. Mandrin now made a similar offer through the good offices of the man who captured him, Diturbi de Larre. In a letter written from his cell, Mandrin begged the captain to ask his superior officer, La Morlière, to recruit him as a soldier. Mandrin was well aware of his own reputation for military prowess: had he not repelled an attack by one of France's most distinguished commanders? Perhaps the king would seize the opportunity to bring the chief into his camp.[80] The letter reached the desk of the minister of war, just one step from the king, only to die there and dash the smuggler's last hope to save himself.

After two weeks in prison, Mandrin's prospects for freedom grew dim. The king of Sardinia was unable to persuade Versailles to extradite him to Savoy. His letter concerning military service was never dignified with an answer. And two of his valets had already perished, one by hanging and the other on the wheel. Their punishment "made some impression on Mandrin, especially at the moment he saw them delivered into the hands of the executioner."[81] On the morning of 26 May, Mandrin was officially informed of his fate. Brought before the court to hear his sentence, seated calmly on the *sellette*, a purposely demeaning low wooden stool, "he listened with a sangfroid that astonished all those present" as he heard the court declare him guilty of rebellion and armed trafficking.[82] After a long account of his misdeeds, the judgment listed his multiple punishments: he was to pay a 1,000 lt fine to the Farm and surrender the remainder of his wealth to the king, undergo torture to reveal his accomplices, kneel before the cathedral to beg forgiveness for his crimes, and mount the scaffold to be broken "face towards Heaven to finish his days there." His corpse would be carried to the city gates and exposed to arriving travelers. Mandrin accepted his sentence and signed the judgment "with all possible tranquility."[83] He was now a condemned man whose execution, according to the law, would take place that day.

An elaborately orchestrated affair, the eighteenth-century execution ceremony was designed to convey multiple meanings. Its principal function was to purge convicted criminals from the body of the community. Entrusted by God to kings and by kings to magistrates, the sword of justice did more than simply punish criminals for their misdeeds. It marked, ostracized, and expelled them. In the words of one jurist, the goal of the magistrate was "to purge society and protect it from the contagion that mixing with the wicked would not fail to spread."[84] Thus, the criminal justice system staged executions to stain convicts with infamy, subject them to public humiliation, and cast them out of the community so that its torn moral fabric could mend.

Punishment was also designed to reestablish the injured authority of the king. An awe-inspiring call to obedience, exemplary punishment was intended to instill a deep fear of transgression in would-be criminals. Because it was impossible to catch and prosecute the great majority of lawbreakers, the monarchy concentrated on the criminals it did apprehend and made a terrifying example of them. The more a populace was exposed to punishment, jurists claimed, the more it would internalize the value of obedience. Hence in 1738, the president of the commission of Valence delayed punishing several smugglers until two battalions of militia arrived. Militiamen were notorious for smuggling, so the president wanted to inflict punishment before the largest possible number of criminals or potential criminals. The same "pedagogy of fear" informed L'Hôpital's suggestion that the commission enhance the exemplarity of its punishment in this "strongly republican" region by staging executions in border towns, "well in view" of the traffickers who lived there. "These places are filled with smugglers and rebellious minds. Punishment makes an impression on men only to the extent that it is plain for all to see. . . . A few such examples would more effectively inspire terror in offenders and impart the frightening idea that people should have of the king's power than the examples made, multiplied, and hidden in Valence."[85] In an age when state authorities were wary of most public gatherings, they actively engaged crowds to bear witness to punishment.

Finally, executions had an important religious dimension. The rites of punishment provided the condemned man with ample opportunity to expiate his sins before his demise. In the final moments of his life, he was exhorted repeatedly to repent and save himself from eternal damnation. Although the political and religious elements of this ceremony were distinct, they reinforced one another. Not only did the certainty of a death sentence chase many a convict into the bosom of the Church, but criminals who repented on the scaffold embodied the exemplary character of the punishment. Who would not hesitate to embark on a life of crime after having witnessed the spectacle of a chastened convict beg forgiveness before being put to death? The theater of execution affirmed a political and moral order threatened by crime, even as it encouraged the criminal to prepare his soul for the afterlife. Ideally, contrition, divine grace, and monarchical authority would dovetail in a moving execution.

But execution ceremonies did not always go according to plan. Although highly ritualized, the script left considerable room for improvisation. How thoroughly the convict was to be degraded, how sincerely he was to repent, and how profoundly spectators were to be affected depended on the performances of executioner, confessor, condemned, and the crowd itself. Indeed, the air of contingency that hung over executions was a source of tremendous suspense. In the case of Mandrin, a rebel known for his defiance of the law, the suspense was palpable. Might members of his gang or the crowd dare attempt a rescue, allowing a man who had already dodged a death sentence and liberated dozens of prisoners to cheat justice yet again? Such perilous acts were not unheard of, and authorities prepared for the worst. Whereas most executions of the day were policed by a handful of town guards and mounted constables, Valence on the day of Mandrin's execution was teeming with police. Since the winter before his capture, when it was feared that Mandrin might attempt to liberate the municipal prison as he had famously done in Montbrison and Bourg, an army regiment had been stationed in Valence. On the day of execution, soldiers were out in force, supplemented by multiple Farm squads, two brigades of mounted police, and the municipal guard. There were enough men on hand to guard the city gates (shut for the occasion), watch the streets, and form a triple line around the scaffold.[86] Breaking through such a barrier would have been unprecedented, but Mandrin had foiled the army before and under less desperate circumstances. If royal officials thought a rescue attempt was possible, as the unusual number of bayonets suggested, then so must have many spectators standing in the crowd.

If not liberated, what would the "General Captain of the smugglers" say and do when confronted with his own death? Spectators accustomed to watching executions knew that the condemned could react to his fate in any number of ways. Would imminent death loosen the rebel's tongue, encouraging him to lash out against the Farm or the commission in a final act of defiance? Or would the looming presence of death and the prospect of eternal damnation paralyze him with fear, as it did so many others? Would he heed the exhortations of the priest and repent his crimes or turn his back on the Church and plunge into the afterlife with no sign of contrition whatsoever? All eyes were on Mandrin.

Before embarking on his final journey from prison to scaffold, the smuggler was to be tortured in a final effort to force the guilty party to reveal his accomplices. It appears that in this instance the *question préalable* was applied "only in form" and not in substance, however, because Mandrin had "previously said all that was wished of him."[87] Once the interrogation was complete, Mandrin signed the transcript "without changing expression, without trembling." He turned to Levet and said, "Monsieur, if I said something bad during the course of the lively interrogations and confrontations [with witnesses], I dare assure you that this was not my intention, and I beg your pardon."[88] Proffered perhaps in appreciation of the decision to forgo torture, this solicitation of forgiveness—resolute and sincere—foreshadowed Mandrin's performance over the next few hours.

Stepping from the confinement of his cell into the streets of Valence, Mandrin encountered the throngs of spectators who had gathered to watch him die. The city had been swelling with visitors since his arrival, but on the day of the execution 6,000 men, women, and children came from miles around, in effect doubling the size of the town. The crowd would have been even larger had the citizens of Lyon not been caught off guard by the speed of the trial and sudden announcement of his execution. "The public square was packed with people, on the rooftops, all around the houses, and platforms had even been erected, which were rented for 12 sols a person."[89] As one pamphleteer recounted, "A viper without venom from the island of Malta, a crocodile from the banks of the Rhine, a wolf from England would not have drawn more of the populace and high society around their cages at a fair."[90]

Mandrin did not face the assemblage alone. Two men accompanied him to the scaffold: his confessor and his executioner. Father Gasparini, an Italian by birth and Jesuit by vocation who resided at the nearby college of Tournon, was charged with the care of his soul. When Mandrin was committed to the prison of Valence, he rejected several overtures from priests offering spiritual guidance. At first, Mandrin would have none of it. "If I were free and had my sword, I would cut you in pieces. . . . Get out of here, you rogue," he barked at one Franciscan.[91] A Dominican who made a similar entreaty received a glass of wine in the face. But the day before the execution, after Mandrin was unofficially informed of his sentence, the bishop of Valence asked Gasparini to see the smuggler in his cell. To soften the suspicious prisoner's defenses, Gasparini conveyed the compliments of a man from Tournon whose life Mandrin had saved when smugglers mistook him for a guard and threatened to kill him. Reminding him of this good deed, Gasparini won over Mandrin: "I am condemned to death by my seven Judges, I see I no longer have any recourse, I want to confess to you."[92] Gasparini stayed for a good hour, then returned the next morning to hear the rest of the confession and grant absolution. Priests were not permitted to give communion or administer last rites to the condemned—there were limits to the partnership between church and state on such matters— but they could absolve and exhort penance, cracking open a window to salvation.

Mandrin's other escort was the executioner, come from Grenoble to do the commission's dirty work. Confined to a liminal world between life and death, between a settled honorable society and a deviant dishonorable underworld, the executioner's mere touch was enough to impart infamy.[93] Arriving at Mandrin's cell, his first task was to dress the convict in a "livery of shame."[94] After stripping the smuggler of his shoes, clothes, and trophy hat, the executioner draped a loose shirt over Mandrin's torso, leaving his head and feet humiliatingly bare, bound his hands, set a cord around his neck, and placed a placard on his back bearing the words "Chief of Smugglers, Criminals of Lèze-Majesté, Murderers, Thieves & Disturbers of the public peace."[95]

Dressed in the clothing of submission, Mandrin stepped into the street before a crowd of thousands who searched his every gesture, facial expression, and utterance for signs of his state of mind and soul. One observer noted that "he left prison with an unparalleled constancy and firmness," two cardinal masculine virtues of the period.[96] Mandrin wished no doubt to muster the manly courage and fortitude for which he was famous, preserving his reputation in the here-below while submitting himself to justice and God. Treading a double path of bravery and contrition, he advanced from the prison to the portal of Saint-Apollinaire Cathedral, where he performed an *amende honorable* (fine of honor), a penal rite usually inflicted on "atrocious" criminals (poisoners, parricides, and church robbers) that the commission imposed on smugglers guilty of lèse-majesté (Figure 9.2). His confessor nearby, Mandrin knelt on the ground before the church door, votive candle in hand, to beg forgiveness of "God, king, and justice." Three times Mandrin asked the sources of all moral and political order to pardon him. Three times his utterances radiated past Gasparini, Levet, and the cordon of guards who encircled them to reach the ears of the spectators. For an outlaw who had boasted that he would sooner kill himself than fall into the hands of justice, the ceremony was an acknowledgment of the error of his ways, an assumption of responsibility for his crimes, and an essential part of a good Christian death.[97] At the same time, by maintaining his composure during the ceremony, he kept his reputation intact. He made his amends "with a manner as

Figure 9.2. Sixteenth-century depiction of the Place des Clercs, where Mandrin was executed. The square had long been a site of exemplary punishment, indicated by the hanged man at its center. Note, too, the Saint-Apollinaire Cathedral (to the left of the scaffold), before which Mandrin performed his *amende honorable*. Detail from Sebastien Münster, *La Cosmographie universelle de tout le monde* (Paris, 1575).

proud and martial as that with which he had fought, which surprised everyone."[98]

Passing from the cathedral through the crowded Place des Clercs to the scaffold, "he was barefoot but this did not prevent him from walking with confidence."[99] As he approached the theater of his death, Mandrin noticed tears in Gasparini's eyes. "What! my father, you're crying? *I'm* not crying! So cry for both of us. It is not death that makes me sad, nor the sentence that will be executed, which will last only a moment; but I have to undergo the judgment of God, who will decide my lot for eternity."[100] The smuggler confidently mounted the scaffold and prepared to be broken. With death imminent, the crowd listened attentively for a speech of repentance, and Mandrin did not disappoint. "Youth, heed my example," he said, before making a blanket apology to agents of the Farm.[101] He sat down on the *X*-shaped cross of Saint Andrew and asked Gasparini for a drink. In a gesture of goodwill, the father handed him a flask of eau-de-vie, which would help dull the pain to come. Mandrin sniffed it, took a few swigs, and lay down on the wooden cross. He then did something noted by every eyewitness who left a record of the execution: he undid the buttons of his cuffs himself and rolled up his sleeves in preparation for the coming blows, a sign not only of his willful submission to punishment but his extraordinary sangfroid in the face of imminent death. He rolled up his shirt "with as much firmness and confidence as if it had been for something much less dangerous."[102] Like noble convicts who had the privilege of disrobing themselves before decapitation, Mandrin took the initiative to ready himself for the final punishment. "There is a man who is going to die a good Christian," encouraged the Jesuit (Figure 9.3).[103]

Once Mandrin had extended his arms and legs along the *X*-shape of the cross, the executioner tied his hands and feet. Two or three notables from the town's lay brotherhood mounted the scaffold to join Gasparini in exhorting Mandrin to suffer patiently one of the most painful ordeals the crown could impose. It was up to Gasparini and his assistants to keep the condemned from blaspheming while being broken and channel his thoughts toward God. There is no record of the exhortation at the hour of Mandrin's death, but it probably resembled that urged on a reprobate in Toulon: "I accept with all my heart the ignominy of my execution and my death . . . and I beg my God to accept it in expiation of my sins and in satisfaction of the punishment that my soul deserves to suffer in Purgatory."[104]

Le portrait de MANDRIN tiré d'après nature dans les prisons de Valence, et a été Exécuté le 26 may 1755.

Figure 9.3. Mandrin in his cell and at his execution. This engraving is a modified version of an earlier print of Cartouche. The only other extant image of Mandrin's execution is located in *Le Veritable messager boiteux* (Basle, 1756). Bibliothèque Nationale de France, N2 Mandrin.

Nine ferocious blows rained down on Mandrin. With an iron bar, the executioner struck his arms and legs eight times, shattering the bones. The ninth blow was to his stomach. Apart from Forest, who claimed that the chief suffered the pain "with matchless constancy and patience, which astonished the spectators," no chroniclers detail how the smuggler reacted to this physical assault. The same punishment applied to a German convict transformed him "into a sort of huge screaming puppet writhing in rivulets of blood . . . with four tentacles, like a sea monster of raw, slimy and shapeless flesh mixed with splinters of smashed bones."[105]

A broken man could remain suspended in a state of agony for hours before expiring; this was called—of all things—a "natural death." After the breaking of a convict, however, the magistrate could intervene and order a *retentum,* permitting the man to be mercifully strangled. It may have been a crude method of relief, but the *retentum* offered judges a mechanism by which to regulate the suffering unleashed by an executioner's blows. Strangling could be ordered at different points: before the convict was broken (to spare him all pain), immediately afterward (to limit the duration of pain), or a long time after he was broken (to inflict more pain yet still curtail the agony of a "natural death"). All depended on the magistrate's wishes. Some used the *retentum* to reward criminals for their penitence and good behavior. Frederick II of Prussia, a leading penal reformer, declared in 1749 that all criminals in his kingdom would be strangled before being broken. The infliction of excessive pain was not only inhumane, the enlightened despot argued, but risked exciting the crowd's sympathy for the condemned, an emotional response that undercut the exemplarity of the execution. Undue suffering could exasperate a crowd, arousing hostility toward the execution.

Considerations such as these had motivated the bishop and other notables of Valence to ask Levet to put Mandrin down soon after he was broken. Their pleas did not go unheeded. Precisely eight minutes after the blows were delivered, Levet instructed the executioner to strangle Mandrin. The fact that one witness (Forest again) took the trouble to count the minutes that elapsed between the moment the blows were delivered and the act of strangulation suggests that spectators were acutely aware of how much pain Mandrin was made to endure.

Following his death, Mandrin's corpse was mounted to a large coach wheel, placed horizontally atop a tall pole, and carried to the city gates, where, left to decompose or be eaten by carrion birds, it would continue to "serve as an example."[106] Moving the body to the gallows outside of town conveyed two distinct messages. First, it demonstrated that the criminal was an outcast, unworthy of Christian burial in the sacred land of the church cemetery. The denial of proper burial was merely a postmortem extension of the exclusionary dynamic of the entire execution ceremony. No other punishment "combined such a ruthless assault on the human body with a thorough-going attempt to annihilate the victim's social status."[107] Second, the exposure of Mandrin's body on the gallows marked the town of Valence as a place of law, the sight and stench of his rotting flesh serving as a grisly reminder of the monarchy's determination to enforce its prohibitions against illicit trade. The infamy emanating from a broken, unburied corpse was meant to send a powerful message to all who gazed on it.

Whether the witnesses of such punishment absorbed all that judicial and religious authorities wished to impart is a matter of debate. Some historians contend that crowds, far from passively accepting the pedagogy of executions, protested against judicial repression in carnivalesque riots.[108] Others insist that Christ-like martyrdoms staged on the scaffold edified crowds and prompted feelings of collective redemption.[109] The most recent research persuasively argues that spectators approved of harsh punishments, satisfied with a system of justice that aimed to preserve public order and rid society of disruptive malefactors.[110] How did those who witnessed Mandrin's execution react?

It should be obvious by now that many were impressed by Mandrin's courage in the face of death. Words like *constancy, fearlessness,* and *firmness* infuse chronicles of his demise. Not all convicts participated in the execution ceremony with such resolve; even the master thief Cartouche was reputed to have crumbled before the Paris executioner. By contrast, Mandrin's steadiness during his punishment seems only to have enhanced his reputation for bravery. However, it is also clear that his contrition in prison, during the *amende honorable,* and on the scaffold impressed. Mandrin may have shown courage, but he was no godless rebel, determined to defy all political and religious authority to the bitter end. Such deviancy was indeed rare.[111] Mandrin started down this road by initially rejecting clerical overtures, but he became concerned with salvation as death grew imminent, a change of heart that fulfilled the hopes of many observers. The correspondent for the *Courrier d'Avignon,* who had "wished" for a remorseful Mandrin, was delighted by this apparent change of heart. The valor for which the smuggler was so admired did not abate, the paper reported, but it "changed its objective, Religion having finally gotten the upper hand." "Consider that there is a God who leaves no crime unpunished," Mandrin was quoted telling his comrade Saint-Pierre.[112] Such apparent contrition in the rebel appears to have produced a strong emotional reaction. Even "M. Levet, who did not have a tender heart, cried."[113]

While spectators and others joined in an outpouring of sympathy for Mandrin, it should not be inferred that men and women shared a uniform opinion of his punishment. Many who felt sorry for him or were impressed by his bravery also believed his execution was wholly merited. This was the view taken by a parish priest, who wrote of

Mandrin that "many people, predisposed in his favor, regard him as a good and courageous man; but counterfeiting, the murders he committed are not excusable."[114] For this man of the cloth, murder and counterfeiting, the latter crime still clinging to Mandrin even though he was never convicted of it, was beyond the pale. Likewise, Madame de Franquières, a local noblewoman, stated flatly that the great smuggler's talents notwithstanding, "he very much deserved death."[115] She had no qualms whatsoever about his execution.

But the opinions of a priest and a noble did not necessarily reflect the thoughts of the ordinary men and women who witnessed, read, or heard about the execution. The diary of Pierre Bordier, a peasant farmer from Vendôme, recounted in gruesome detail the execution of François Damien, whose scandalous attempt on the life of Louis XV he most emphatically abhorred. Yet the farmer briefly and soberly noted the punishment of Mandrin, whose exploits he admired.[116] More to the point, Forest the grocer, who witnessed Mandrin's breaking firsthand, explicitly deplored application of the death penalty to smugglers. He had already witnessed an appalling series of executions the winter before Mandrin was captured: smugglers "are committed to our prisons every day and M. Levet, judge of the commission, scarcely lets them stay; since February 24, 25, 26, 27, 28 and March 1, 1755, three of them perished and six of them were broken. Going to execution, all had placards on their backs with the words written in capital letters: 'Smuggler, thief, murderer, criminal of lèse-majesté and disturber of the public peace.' *Never in my life have I seen such butchery.*"[117]

This characterization of executions as "butchery" suggests that, despite the normative lessons the monarchy hoped to broadcast, such punishments did not always impart infamy. Brigands, parricides, counterfeiters, and other criminals, for which ordinary people had little sympathy, may have been successfully dishonored, but Forest's journal reveals that at least some members of the crowd rejected the commission's efforts to stigmatize smugglers. Several weeks after the grocer remarked on the "butchery" in the Place des Clercs, Mandrin was broken on the wheel before his very eyes, an act that seems only to have reinforced his disgust at the commission's handiwork. After the blows of the executioner had fallen, Forest consoled himself with the idea that, far from vilifying the chief, the execution would only enhance his fame:

One never saw a brigand cause such a stir during his life and at his death. People spoke of nothing but him in all the assemblies of Germany, Spain, etc.; foreign gazettes were filled only with his deeds. After his death, a lot of people hastened to write about his expeditions and compose songs that sold for whatever they asked. Mgr our bishop had a painter from Lyon, sieur Treillat, come to do his portrait. Thus ended the life of the famous Louis Mandrin.[118]

Historians have long noted that after 1670 the French monarchy, like other early modern European states, stepped up its efforts to repress the poor and the marginal. As if criminalizing poverty itself, authorities issued tough laws against theft, migrancy, and begging, while establishing new institutions in which to incarcerate offenders. To some extent, the crackdown on smuggling was simply a part of this wider social repression. The introduction of severe antismuggling laws and the creation of new courts to impose them generated a wave of penal repression that swept over the laboring classes. Whereas contraband-dealing nobles and merchants were largely exempt from prosecution, scores of indigent smugglers were sentenced to execution, perhaps 40,000 were dispatched to the galleys, and untold numbers were banished, shackled, whipped, and fined. Using torture, the wheel, the noose, and the galleys to terrorize poor smugglers may call to mind the barbaric practices of the Middle Ages, but such repression was orchestrated by an extraordinarily modern set of financial, judicial, and penal institutions.[119] If anything, the growing numbers of smugglers incarcerated in the French labor camps of the eighteenth century evokes not the dark dungeons of medieval Europe but the well-lit prisons of the contemporary United States, where, since 1971, another battle against illicit trade—"the war on drugs"—has filled prisons with victims of poverty and racial discrimination.[120] Far from being a relic of an uncivilized past, large-scale repression of underground trade was an invention of the modern state that in many ways is still with us.

This expansion of the penal sphere was not, however, merely a reflection of a broader class war waged by the rich against the poor, as has been claimed with respect to the repression of theft.[121] The image of a society divided between the propertied and the unpropertied, capital and labor, only begins to describe the struggle between Farmers General and the shadow economy. Born not merely of commercial but court capitalism, that struggle produced a particular constellation of conflicting interests, attitudes, and practices. Those ranged on the side of the Farmers included a small but politically influential and growing subgroup of the propertied, namely, the kings, royal officials, financiers, merchants, and noble and bourgeois creditors who benefited most from state monopolies and prohibitions. Those lined up on the side of the smugglers included extensive networks of landed elites, merchants, smugglers, and consumers who participated in a sprawling illicit trade. Nor did financial interest and political position necessarily coincide. Many state creditors who profited from interest payments funded by the Farm presumably sympathized with smugglers, just as certain investors today bemoan the environmental and labor policies of corporations in which they have placed capital. Hence, the effort to repress contraband emanated from a narrower constituency than simply "the rich" or "the propertied," and it threatened to engender resentment among a much broader segment of society than simply "the poor." Produced not only by class antagonism but a fiscal state with global ambitions, the repression of smuggling affected a deep cross section of French society.

The crackdown on smuggling was, in cultural terms, more problematic than that on theft and vagabondage, because the "crime" of smuggling was steeped in moral ambiguity. In most areas of criminal justice, the monarchy defined a penal order that coincided roughly with the popular moral order of the day. When parlements meted out brutal punishment for crimes that had for centuries been considered transgressive, such as premeditated murder, grand theft, and treason, the populace generally approved or remained indifferent. Even the dreaded prevostial courts that sentenced vagabond burglars to death did not strain moral expectations, for the marginal status of migrants, their un-Christian idleness, and the fear they instilled in the settled populace justified— even encouraged—summary justice. In such cases, punishment directly reflected communal social norms, in good Durkheimian fashion. But the popular imagination did not relegate smugglers to the same ignoble status as rootless vagabonds. Smugglers were poor and mobile to be sure, but many were firmly rooted in their communities and could not be so easily scapegoated by the judiciary. Nor was the crime of smuggling so deeply stained with sin and transgression. Running a bundle of contraband across the border, joining a smuggling band, or killing a

Farm guard while resisting arrest did not bear the same moral weight as stealing, belonging to a gang of highway robbers, or committing premeditated murder. And yet punishments for the former crimes were just as severe as, if not more severe than, those for the latter. The dubious moral underpinnings of the repression of smuggling made it appear all the more cruel and, to many, unjust.

In the end, the legal struggle between Farm and smuggler was propelled by two competing normative structures. As it criminalized illicit trade, the crown attempted to stigmatize trafficking and taint smugglers with judicial infamy. But criminalizing smuggling was not like criminalizing murder, theft, or vagabondage. Smugglers and the communities that sustained them stubbornly refused to internalize the ignominious criminal status that the state imposed on them. "Among the inhabitants [of Dauphiné and Savoy] it is a title of honor to have been in the galleys or to have perished on the scaffold," wrote the chevalier Dutour in his memoir on contraband.[122] "Far from shaming [convicted smugglers]," observed the nobility of Château-Thierry, "the most infamous afflictive punishments have become the source of a kind of esteem."[123] The state could execute Louis Mandrin, but it could not remake popular culture.

10

Mandrin into Print

Vᴇʀʏ ʟɪᴛᴛʟᴇ ᴡᴀꜱ ᴡʀɪᴛᴛᴇɴ about Mandrin before his death. Song-sters scribbled ditties on scraps of paper, the literati noted thoughts in diaries, and royal officials feverishly corresponded, but no one save the editors of a few foreign newspapers actually published on Man-drin. All that changed with his execution. Mandrin's death set off an explosion in print as biographers and playwrights recounted his life story, engravers illustrated his most famous exploits, and songwriters and poets rhymed verse to eulogize his passing. In an age when the con-cept of celebrity itself was emerging, thanks to the growth of cities, the expansion of media, and the development of the idea of the sentimental self, such words and images ricocheted across western Europe to render Mandrin truly famous.[1] Even without the kind of publicity that lawyers would bring to later causes célèbres, no criminal affair in eighteenth-century France generated so much popular literature so quickly.[2] Phoe-nixlike, Mandrin was reborn as the war between Farm and people was transposed into print.

A legend was in the making to be sure, but the interlocutors who competed for the public's attention (and pocket money) did not offer identical visions of what that legend should be. The *Jugement Souverain* of the commission of Valence—the printed verdict that enumerated Man-drin's crimes and pronounced his punishment—established a basic nar-rative template. It was a moralistic tale with a beginning, middle, and end that any Hollywood scriptwriter would recognize today, but imme-diately after Mandrin's execution, the crown's version of events had to contend with a cacophony of alternative narratives, told and retold in seemingly endless permutations. Although such accounts usually concluded with the bandit perishing on the scaffold, the events leading up to that dramatic spring day diverged widely to give the stories starkly different meanings. Each narrative wound its way through a semifictionalized landscape to stamp its own ideological imprint on the story. Some reinforced the royal account by demonizing the smuggler; others posited a heroic counternarrative that excoriated the Farm; still others offered conflicting images of a man whose violence was as much to be feared as admired. A gamut of representations infused popular culture—Mandrin as brave warrior, clever trickster, honorable gentleman, bloodthirsty villain, depraved atheist, thoughtful philosopher, dangerous outlaw, and principled rebel—each of which implicitly made a larger argument about the political significance of his violent struggle with the Farm.

Historians disagree on how best to characterize popular culture in the eighteenth century. Although Peter Burke contends that it became more politically charged between the age of the Reformation and that of the French Revolution, Roger Chartier counters that France witnessed a gradual "depoliticization of folklore" from the reign of Louis XIV (1661–1715), as rebellious and carnivalesque outbursts waned.[3] Chartier's analysis relies heavily on the work of Norbert Elias, who posited that the Sun King and his successors stabilized the kingdom by instituting a double monopoly on taxation and legitimate violence.[4] As the crown built a modern fiscal state and, through the culture of the royal court, instilled an ethos of self-restraint in a once ungovernable nobility, society as a whole became increasingly compliant. Elias's claims about taxation and violence do not, however, hold up in light of recent research. As we now know, small-scale tax rebellions intensified in the last century of the old regime, even as large-scale uprisings subsided. Given the state's failure to monopolize taxation and violence, it is worth reconsidering Chartier's thesis about eighteenth-century popular culture. If the social life of ordinary people was more rebellious than once thought, can the same be said of their cultural life? The outpouring of ephemeral literature following Mandrin's execution provides an excellent opportunity to explore this question.

The Royal Narrative

The monarchy joined battle over the memory of Mandrin the moment he was executed. Of course, the execution itself spoke volumes about the crimes he had committed, but it was staged before one crowd on a single afternoon. To reach beyond the spectators who gathered at the Place des Clercs on 26 May 1755, the commission ordered that its "Sovereign judgment" be "printed, read, publicized and posted in all cities and places" mentioned within it (Figure 10.1).[5] The judgment was to be published in large format with big print, posted not only in Mandrin's place of birth, Saint-Étienne, but also every site where he was known to have committed a crime, well over fifty towns scattered across southeastern France. In each burg, the verdict would be read aloud in a public square and posted in marketplaces, courthouses, and churches for all to see. Those who lived beyond the lands where Mandrin once roamed could read the judgment in foreign newspapers and almanacs. Even the Parisian *Annonces, affiches, et avis divers* (11 June 1755), which had scarcely published a word on the smuggler during his expeditions, devoted a whole column to the verdict against him. The curious could also purchase pamphlets of the judgment that were subsidized by the Farm, an institution keenly aware of the power of the printed word.[6] In a matter of days, the royal version of Mandrin's criminal biography spread far beyond Valence to reach a large audience.

The judgment—a verdict, news bulletin, short story, and exemplary warning all in one—began with a brief biographical sketch. It described Mandrin as embroiled in counterfeiting and murder from a tender age, crimes that obliged him "to flee his home in Saint-Geoirs." After running away, he embarked on a spree of cold-blooded killings, raids, prison breaks, and attacks on Farm guards and royal soldiers. This was the vision of Mandrin as merciless brigand. To underscore his cruelty, the verdict detailed atrocities that, although incidental to the charges against him, tarnished his reputation. The bandit did not merely kill agents of the Farm, but tricked them, took them by surprise, stole from them, and murdered even those who "begged for their lives on their knees." It is thanks to the judgment that we know his festooned chapeau was stolen from a victim's corpse and that he killed both Moret, who fingered his brother for counterfeiting, and the "eighteen month old child that [Moret] held in his arms." Most important, the judgment omitted any allusions to the moral economy of the gang's forced sales, characterizing their exchanges instead as looting and common highway robbery. The reader learns nothing of the tobacco the chief consigned to warehouses or the contents of the receipts he distributed to

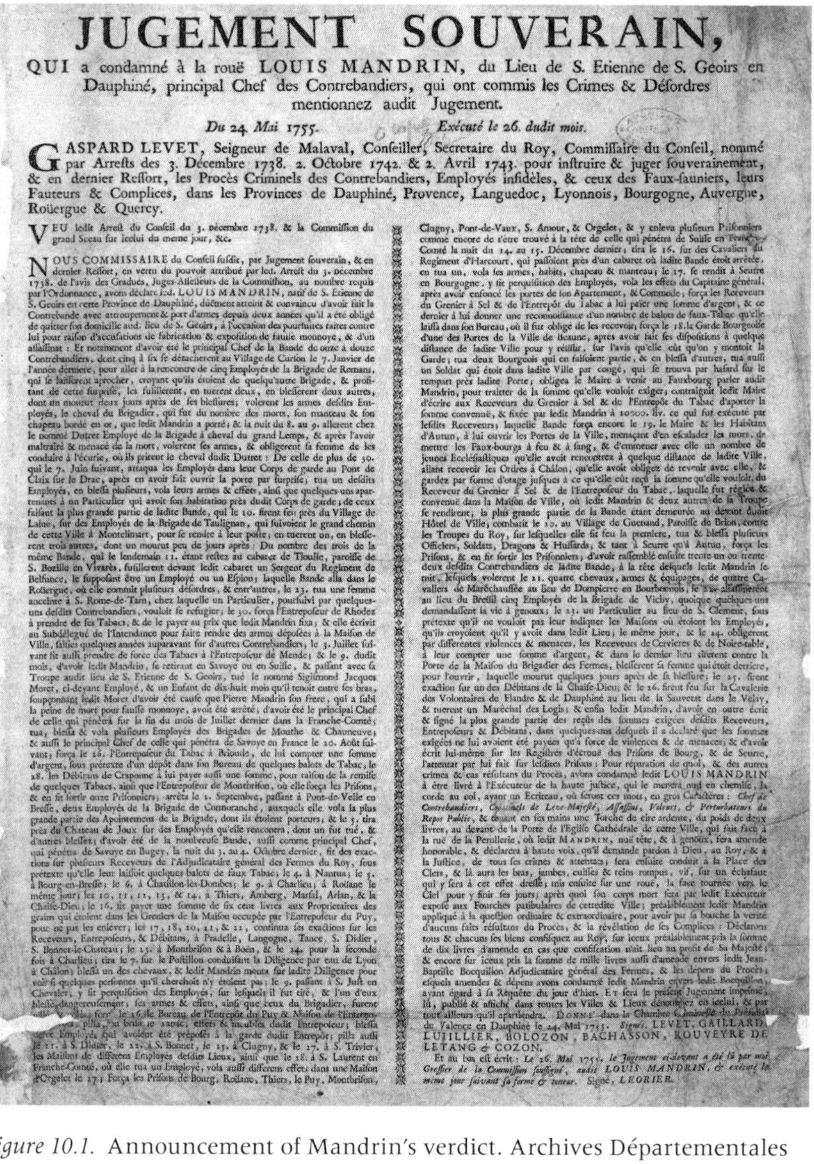
JUGEMENT SOUVERAIN,

QUI a condamné à la rouë LOUIS MANDRIN, du Lieu de S. Etienne de S. Geoirs en Dauphiné, principal Chef des Contrebandiers, qui ont commis les Crimes & Désordres mentionnez audit Jugement.

Du 24. Mai 1755. *Exécuté le 26. dudit mois.*

GASPARD LEVET, Seigneur de Malaval, Conseiller, Secretaire du Roy, Commissaire du Conseil, nommé par Arrests des 3. Décembre 1738. 2. Octobre 1742. & 2. Avril 1743. pour instruire & juger souverainement, & en dernier Ressort, les Procès Criminels des Contrebandiers, Employés infidèles, & ceux des Faux-sauniers, leurs Fauteurs & Complices, dans les Provinces de Dauphiné, Provence, Languedoc, Lyonnois, Bourgogne, Auvergne, Roüergue & Quercy.

Figure 10.1. Announcement of Mandrin's verdict. Archives Départementales de la Drôme, cliché P. Rio, B 1304.

local agents. Such receipts were introduced only as self-incriminating evidence—Mandrin impudently signing his own misdeeds—rather than certifications of commercial exchanges for which the Farmers General would be held accountable. Likewise, the judgment details the death of innocent citizens in Beaune and the killing of soldiers at

Guenand but says nothing of his polite dialogues with officials, skill on the battlefield, or support among the local population. In the final paragraph, the text turns abruptly to the punishment, as if justification for the death sentence was entirely self-evident. He who committed these crimes was to don the attire of the condemned and be broken alive on the wheel.

As it projected its own version of events, the monarchy attempted to restrict the diffusion of competing narratives. Three texts were immediately censored: a play, *La Mort de Mandrin*, and two pamphlets, *Nouveau sisteme pour s'enricher aux depens des sangsues, par Louis Mandrin* and *Le Testament politique de Louis Mandrin*.[7] But we should not make too much of this attempt to block opposing views. For one, royal censors were more adept at screening manuscripts before publication than at confiscating books already in circulation, especially in the sparsely policed provinces.[8] But there was another reason the monarchy did not aggressively police the literature on Mandrin. It so happened that in 1755 the directorship of the Royal Publishing Office, the monarchy's central censorship bureau, was occupied by none other than Chrétien-Guillaume Lamoignon de Malesherbes, a liberal-minded magistrate sympathetic to the reformist thrust of the Enlightenment. As head royal censor, Malesherbes did not seem particularly keen to shut down the discussion excited by Mandrin's execution. In fact, in June 1755, just a month after Louis perished on the wheel, the intendant of Lyon, Henri Bertin, reported that 600 copies of the anti-Farm tract *Le Testament politique de Louis Mandrin* had been shipped from a publisher in Avignon to four Lyon booksellers and that other copies were being sent to Beaucaire to be sold at the fair. Fearing that the diffusion of such a book "might have a bad effect on the spirit of the people," Bertin confiscated and destroyed the Lyon copies. But the intendant acted too hastily. Malesherbes had wanted copies of the book sent to him in Paris—and not just one or two to have on record but multiple copies, which, it may be surmised, he wished to share with friends and colleagues, many of whom were openly hostile to the Farm. No doubt he would have other opportunities to lay hands on the book, which ran through several editions in subsequent years.[9]

Given royal censors' inability and disinclination to control the Mandrin story, literature on the smuggler was left to flourish in a relatively unfettered marketplace. And flourish it did, as a mix of oral, manuscript, print, and visual media combined with an array of genres (biography, funeral oration, execution hymn, poetry, and treatise) to create a kaleidoscope of representation. So dauntingly diverse is this corpus of work that the historian's first impulse is to classify its contents according to medium and genre (popular songs here, learned treatises there). But it might be more instructive to leave intact something of the mixed quality of the corpus, treating it as eighteenth-century men and women would have experienced it. Although some scholars suggest that the culture of learned elites was at this moment breaking away from what had been a universally shared popular culture, there was still remarkable overlap between the two worlds. Elites would have been well aware of many of the works aimed at a popular audience. Thus, rather than sorting by genre and audience, it is more instructive to examine the ideological positions that cut across this heterogeneous body of work.

Mandrin as Demon

The government need not necessarily have worried about much of the postmortem literature on Mandrin. Just as most spectators at executions seem to have participated willingly in the symbolic expulsion of convicts from their earthly communities, so, too, did most authors of old-regime scaffold literature readily assist the monarchy in spreading the infamy of the condemned. In fact, unbound by jurisprudential conventions, they could go further than verdicts in dramatizing the depraved lives of criminals and the moral lessons of their punishment. This was particularly true of the *complaintes,* rhymed verses about those recently hanged or broken on the wheel. Set to familiar melodies easy to remember and share, they expeditiously carried the news of executions across cities to literate and illiterate alike. Bridging oral and written culture, such death songs were also written or printed for popular consumption. As the chronicler of Parisian life Mercier noted, "The day after—what am I saying? the very same day—a parricide, a poisoner, a murderer is executed, *complaintes* composed by singers of the Pont-Neuf are sung in all the crossroads. These gloomy couplets are hawked by even more appalling voices. Great thieves receive this kind of funeral oration too. The rabble listens to these walking Jeremiahs who slip moral lessons about the dangers of vice and debauchery into the final couplets and walk with a slow gait to suggest compunction." Thus were the executed memorialized in the capital or, for that matter, in any town large enough to boast a high criminal court and a scaffold. Such publicity was so far-reaching that Mercier could contend that "Desrues [a poisoner] is more famous in the crossroads of the capital than Voltaire."[10]

Just weeks after his execution, the first *complaintes* about Mandrin appeared in print. It is easy to understand why the publication of "Chanson sur la vie de Louis Mandrin," sung to "the tune of the hanged," was permitted in Lyon, for it closely followed the judgment, embellishing the basic narrative to add moral emphasis.[11] "Listen, young and old," it entreated, to the story of a "famous man" who violated time-honored conventions of social order to ascend "from a peasant to a Monsieur."[12] Born in Dauphiné to a good-for-nothing father, the crafty youth took flight after a run-in with the law and was "appointed chief of the smugglers." As leader of a gang, he "massacred" and "pillaged" without mercy and stole tobacco from the Farm, paying the farmers in worthless promissory notes (again, the receipts indicated theft rather than commerce). He "did not fear God nor King, / the wicked one had no faith." Yet "Sooner or later the sovereign God, / punishes a libertine man," so Mandrin was captured and taken to Valence, where he proceeded to fart before his judges—once a peasant, always a peasant—and confess his crimes under torture. Facing eternal damnation, the evil bandit repented, dropping to his knees before the cathedral of Valence. "You will supper in Paradise," his confessor reassured him before the executioner broke his arms and legs.

As if the moral of the song needed further clarification, the last two stanzas spelled it out:

> Let us pray devoutly
> to God and his saints
> that they keep us from doing evil
> as long as we remain on earth
> from fear of falling into hell
> with Judas and Lucifer.
>
> Christian people, who are listening to me
> take advantage of this example
> smuggle no longer
> cry for your great misdeeds
> and you will be able like Mandrin to make a glorious end.

The same exemplary thrust informed a song called "La Mandrinade, poème en quatre chants" (n.p., 1755), in which Mandrin makes a pact with "the demon of contraband" to trade and murder his way to fame and fortune. But his punishment is inevitable: "Sing it well, great and small / Into the ears of your children; / Because it is necessary whatever bloodline they come from, / whatever happy dispositions they bear, / To frighten them while forming them, / With the story of the evils of a wicked man."

All the main features of anti-Mandrin literature were present in these songs: his ignoble origins and early criminal record, his indiscriminate use of violence, his lack of religious faith, the inevitability of his punishment, and his last-minute repentance. Of course, songsters sensationalized the violence at the heart of these songs—theirs was a commercial enterprise, after all—but they placed Mandrin's transgression within a heavy moralizing frame. Whatever titillation deviant violence might have aroused in listeners was to be repressed quickly, which is why the hymns could claim "to frighten [children] while forming them," curbing the dangerous impulses that lurked in their souls.

Nowhere was the juxtaposition of transgressive violence and rigid morality more conspicuous than in a book called *La Mandrinade, ou L'Histoire curieuse, véritable et remarquable de la vie de Louis Mandrin* (Saint-Geoirs, 1755). Printed in a small format conducive to peddling, chopped into twenty-one easily digestible chapters, and sprinkled with proverbs, *La Mandrinade* was obviously intended for a growing popular audience.[13] Not only was literacy on the rise in the eighteenth century but also for the first time in history, criminal biographies were becoming big sellers. Such crime literature was the product of three overlapping literary genres: a Renaissance literature of roguery, which offered portraits of outcast beggars, thieves, and vagabonds; the Spanish picaresque novel, which recounted the adventures of clever rascals and tricksters; and a new form of popular biography, which divulged the private lives of famous people (kings, courtiers, and intellectuals) in an effort to shape public opinion. Drawing on these genres, biographies of such bandits as Guilleri, Cartouche, Nivet, and now Mandrin captured the imagination of a wide readership, marking the advent of a literary form that would henceforth become a staple of western popular culture.[14]

La Mandrinade added flesh to the skeletal narrative of the judgment. Before proceeding to familiar tales of Mandrin's expeditions and punishment, the text filled in a sordid back story that explained why he became such a villain in the first place, beginning with his family. Family reputation was critical in early-modern European society, as personal honor derived from the perceived worthiness of one's forebears. Hence, the indiscreet quill of the anonymous author began by slandering Louis's father as a wife-beating drunk hanged for counterfeiting and his brothers, condemned for the same crime. Apart from Mandrin's well-intentioned mother, credited with his ultimate religious conversion, the whole family reeked of criminal infamy. Any offspring of such disgraceful lineage seemed destined for a life of crime. Even before Mandrin was born, the book claimed, his poor mother suffered an excruciating pregnancy and dreamed of giving birth to a deadly snake that would be killed by a carriage wheel. More ominous still, just seconds before Mandrin's delivery, a deafening clap of thunder erupted out of the clear blue sky.

The baby born that day was not quite human. Covered in hair "more like a billy goat than a man," he conformed to what popular lore called a "wild man," a violent half-man and half-animal creature.[15] As might be expected, such a beast did not have a normal childhood. Born with a full set of teeth, so unable to suckle at his mother's breast, he nursed from cows, killing three bovines before he was old enough to eat solid food. His first word was a curse. He cheated at games, forced boys to snort tobacco, and prefigured his supposed career as a counterfeiter by stealing copper buttons and touching them up to look like coins. Mandrin's mother knew that little Louis needed to be disciplined if he was to avoid a life of crime, but she indulged him, fearful of his demonic fits of anger. "This is how parents spoil their children & turn them into rogues who go on to dishonor them," exclaimed the author in a characteristic gust of moralizing. "Our fathers had a lot more sense than we, & they always recited and lived by the proverb: 'he who loves a lot, punishes a lot.'" (230) The same sentiment echoed in songs about Mandrin: "fathers and mothers, / Strictly punish your children," admonished the *Complainte remarquable*.[16]

As Louis grew up, *La Mandrinade* continued, his moral education suffered when he took to clandestine books that challenged "King, Government, Magistrature & Religion." Feeding his mind with their "hollow observations, . . . Mandrin considered himself a Philosophe: he believed to have with the Authors he read a monopoly on knowing how to think. The people vegetate, he said, & we think." (233) Mandrin's espousal of Enlightenment philosophy is utter fabrication, but it provides insight into the ideological outlook of the author. Only a few years before *La Mandrinade* was published, the very first volumes of Diderot's *Encyclopédie* appeared, catapulting the philosophes into the public spotlight and provoking sharp debate over the implications of their new philosophy of man. Would the radical ideas disseminated by the *Encyclopédie* improve the condition of mankind or hasten its moral decline? The author of *La Mandrinade* came down on the side of counter-Enlightenment conservatives who, in the 1750s, lambasted the philosophes for their dangerously disrespectful attitudes toward religious and political authority.[17] In his eyes, the philosophes were debauched libertines whose subversive notions threatened to undermine all that was honorable, decent, and true. To make a philosophe of Mandrin was therefore to besmirch the nascent intellectual movement by associating it with a subculture of lawlessness and violence. It also made for an interesting plot device, since it was through philosophy that Mandrin lost his religious faith and embarked on a life of crime.

As told in *La Mandrinade,* Mandrin the philosopher, like so many of his ilk, found his way to the cafés and theaters of Paris, which completed his moral perversion by instilling in him the "abominable doctrine" of atheism. (234). Now "a demon incarnate" capable of the worst crimes, he returned to his native province to head a secretive and violent gang of outlaws. At this point, the book taps into a literature of roguery that had long conjured secret societies of thieves and vagabonds, parallel kingdoms hidden in underground caverns where criminals spoke their own inscrutable language.[18] An offshoot of this literature, *La Mandrinade* described the "diabolical" induction ceremony by which Mandrin was anointed ruler of this dark criminal guild. Gang members slit the throat of an innocent child, whose blood they used to swear oaths of fidelity to their new commander.

As soon as he assumed leadership over the gang, Mandrin put bounties on the heads of Farm officials and announced that he would pursue contraband by any means necessary. The band was a great success and would have remained so had the protagonist not succumbed to greed and ambition, two character flaws that recur regularly in popular biographies. As his riches made him hungrier, Mandrin abandoned selling tobacco directly to consumers in favor of a more lucrative war on the Farm, "killing, stealing from, and massacring all who resisted." (246, 250). Even a kindhearted pregnant woman who refused to surrender an agent hiding in her house did not escape his wrath. Inevitably, however, the forces of law and order catch up to the villain, who is taken to Valence to pay for his crimes. After Gasparini advances "invincible arguments to prove to him the truth of our saintly Religion," Mandrin sees the light, confesses his crimes, and expires "with sentiments that edified everyone. There is no sinner who does not put his hope in the mercy of God, however hardened by crime he may be and whatever attacks he may have committed." (253).

The onslaught of negative books like this one, and the still more readily available songs, made a strong impression on popular consciousness, as the evolution of the word "Mandrin" suggests. During his expeditions, the proper noun Mandrin, referring to the chief himself, expanded to become a common noun, applicable first to smugglers in his own gang and then to all smugglers in bands.[19] With the outpouring of media that followed the smuggler's execution, the semantic range of the word widened yet again to become one of derision for any number of tyrants, brigands, or degenerates. Hence the Comte d'Argental denigrated Frederick II of Prussia by calling him a "Mandrin."[20] The pejorative epithet joined a laundry list of nasty names, such as "Damiens" (who attempted to assassinate Louis XV), "Jansenist" (a type of Catholic vilified by the church hierarchy), and "Sodomite."[21] In 1774, one pamphleteer tarred Maupeou, the French chancellor who masterminded a controversial coup against the magistrature, as "a villain, a Mandrin, an ogre, an anthropophage, the beast of Gévaudan, a vampire."[22] The irrepressible revolutionary journalist Père Duchesne would later use the term "Mandrin" to malign counterrevolutionary "aristocrats."[23] Born of the postexecution media blitz, the negative connotations of "Mandrin" rooted themselves in French popular culture and persisted well into the nineteenth century.[24]

Mandrin as Hero

If the portrayal of Mandrin as a demon discredited his campaign against the Farm, that depiction was more than balanced by representations putting the smuggler in a favorable light. Rather than emphasizing his atrociously criminal life or his edifyingly inevitable death, many engravers, singers, and writers chose to highlight the glory of his smuggling campaigns against the Farm. Thus, to the story of a perverse demon who murdered indiscriminately was added that of a brave warrior who valiantly fought oppression, a noble bandit with a sharp wit and keen sense of justice, and an astute philosopher who relativized differences between the criminal and the heroic. Such narratives did not wholly exonerate Mandrin—he was still understood to have perpetrated criminal acts—but they significantly complicated the moral implications of his legend. In these accounts, the smuggler's violence was justified insofar as it served a higher purpose that transcended the everyday strictures of royal law. Texts that heroized the smuggling chief encouraged readers to indulge their imaginations in what were described as pardonable, even admirable transgressions. Summoning a world of liberatory rebellion, positive representations of Mandrin invited readers, viewers, and listeners to fantasize about and imaginatively join his courageous struggle against the Farm.

At the most basic level, writers depicted Mandrin as a conquering military hero. One epitaph, written in poor Latin and laid on his tomb outside Valence, told of the fearlessness with which the great "Mandrinus," "desirous of plunder, not slaughter," chased away the guards of the Farm and "devoured customs-houses."[25] Another spoke of the "valor" he exhibited while seizing "the traitants' cashboxes" and combating "the prince's troops."[26] Similarly awestruck by his military deeds, the "Song in Praise of the Great Mandrin" tells of a warrior vanquishing tax collectors who shamelessly stole from the poor. Fearless of royal troops, the "brave Mandrin" attempted to liberate France from the Farm and turn it into the "Land of Cockaigne," an earthly paradise of food, drink, and money.[27] The most extensive treatment of Mandrin as warrior can be found in the *Oraison funèbre de Messire Louis Mandrin,* which was granted permission to be published by Lyon authorities on 3 June 1755. Learned and stately funeral orations were usually reserved for men of the highest pedigree who had valorously served their kingdom. By eulogizing the lowly rebel Mandrin, this anonymous author raised the smuggler's status to that of history's greatest conqueror, Alexander the Great, *the* stock military hero of the early-modern era, with whom no less a figure than Louis XIV had identified himself.[28] Like Alexander,

Pyrrhus, and Caesar, "he wanted to conquer until death and die conquering." Every time his enemies closed in on him, "he escapes pistol in hand and sword between his teeth, he advances with the pride and intrepidity of a lion, everything bends before him, everything trails in disorder, his victorious sword fells an innumerable multitude of soldiers under its blows, it reaps them at will, it consumes, it devours everything it meets." Do not despair at the loss of this great hero, the oration intones. "He about whom you cry will have imitators. Maybe they will not resemble him in the brilliant valor that distinguishes him among heroes of his kind; but they will imitate his zeal for the public good, his wisdom and his industry."

Spread by word of mouth, the most popular poem written about Mandrin expressed a similar kind of hero worship but with an even sharper political edge. Here, at the moment of his death, the warrior speaks of his battle against the tyrannical brigands of the Farm:

> Just as Hercules was seen in the days of yore
> Traveling the universe club in hand
> To strike more than one greedy monster
> Who devastated the human race.
> So I traveled France
> To purge her of its tyrants;
> But what gratitude she shows me!
> I perish for having despoiled Brigands.
> I would have received, like them, a different reward
> If I had oppressed innocent peoples.[29]

From the Renaissance to the age of Louis XIV, French kings had used the figure of Hercules to symbolize royal power. Lynn Hunt observes that French revolutionaries would overturn this representation of the son of Zeus to make him an emblem of the strength and unity of the French people, but the transformation of Hercules from royal to popular symbol appears to have already been underway in the middle of the eighteenth century, as a new Hercules in the form of Louis Mandrin struck down oppressive tax farmers.[30] Identifying Mandrin with Hercules radically subverted a royal symbol and validated the smuggler's struggle against the Farm.

Such verse delivered especially potent messages when combined with portraiture. That the iconography surrounding Mandrin was extensive should not surprise us because portraiture as an art form was very much on the rise in eighteenth-century France. In Paris and other towns, the interiors of ordinary households were increasingly decorated with pictures, especially inexpensive engravings.[31] Most of the images featured religious figures (Christ, Mary, various saints), but profane portraits of kings, aristocrats, and even members of one's own family were becoming quite fashionable as well. One by-product of this trend was the appearance of the criminal portrait, which mirrored the development of the criminal biography.[32] Produced by the thousand and hawked by urban booksellers and traveling peddlers, criminal portraits, like songs, transmitted messages to illiterate and literate alike. It is no great stretch of the imagination to picture a young peasant or apprentice nailing a portrait of Mandrin to his wall next to an engraving of Christ on the cross or Mary holding baby Jesus in her arms. While the religious images promised to absolve the viewer's sins and bring eternal salvation, the latter offered deliverance of another kind, freedom from the oppressions of this world, chief among them the rapacious tax collector.

Images of Mandrin began to appear before his execution. In the spring of 1755, engravers in Paris and Lyon hawked a portrait that unabashedly portrayed Mandrin as a military hero taking the city of Bourg in October 1754, site of his first triumph.[33] "Putting him in the rank of the most famous figures," they sold more copies of this portrait than of those depicting the illustrious Maréchal de Saxe, who led French troops to their last great victory at the battle of Fontenoy in 1745.[34] Just days after Mandrin's execution, retailers in Valence were peddling "a great number" of portraits set in Bourg (Figure 10.2).[35]

The Bourg portraits depicted Mandrin at the glorious height of his campaigns. He appears as a dashing maverick commander without so much as a whiff of the evil bandit. If his attire falls short of that which adorned aristocrats in the portraiture of the day, it is nonetheless tidy and respectable. Flowing locks fall to his shoulder from beneath a grand military chapeau. Under a clean overcoat, he tucks a knotted cravat neatly into his vest. His bearing is manly and martial yet relaxed, as he looks confidently over his right shoulder in the kind of three-quarter turn commonly found in noble portraits of the day. He gazes into the middle distance, holding a bayonet-tipped rifle with two pistols tucked into a cloth belt (is it calico?) around his waist and a sword hanging in its scabbard from his left hip. This was "Louis Mandrin," the caption

Figure 10.2. Portrait of Mandrin in Bourg (which would be reproduced in *Histoire de Louis Mandrin*). Bibliothèque Nationale de France, collection Hennin, no. 8771.

informs the viewer, "painted and engraved in Bourg, such as he appeared there at the head of his troop, 6 October 1754."

Although we don't possess any reactions to this print, it seems to have offered viewers the thrill of experiencing Mandrin's expeditions from the safety of their own homes. One could partake vicariously in the adventure of battling the General Farm simply by gazing at Mandrin in mid-campaign. No wonder it was the most popular image of the chief ever produced, sold in Paris in sundry versions and reproduced in English, German, and Italian for an international audience. Parisians who preferred more violent images could stroll down to rue Saint-Jacques where Basset Le Jeune's shop sold engravings of the gang burning down customs offices or laying siege to towns. In one striking image that personified the spirit of underground rebellion, Mandrin grips a sword with his right hand and aims a pistol with his left as his men slay Farm officials on a battlefield strewn with corpses (Figures 10.3 and 10.4). "Here is Mandrin, the Chief of a brigand troop, / In Bourg, Autun and Baune [*sic*] he sows terror / This rash man peddles his contraband in front of the Tax Farmer, Commis, and Controller." Astonishingly, this engraving bears a permission granted by the chief of police of Paris.

The most impressive portrait of all was the engraving of Mandrin in Beaune, based on a portrait commissioned by Bishop Alexandre Milon de Mesne, the same distinguished notable credited with inviting Gasparini to talk to the imprisoned smuggler and asking Levet for a *retentum*.[36] Apparently, elites as well as commoners collected images

Figure 10.3. Mandrin, Captain of the Smugglers. Bibliothèque Nationale de France, N2 Mandrin.

Figure 10.4. Mandrin in Bourg, Autun, and Beaune. Bibliothèque Nationale de France, collection Hennin, no. 8768.

of Mandrin. The artist Jacques-André Treillard had worked for Milon before, painting the bishop's own portrait and the altar of the cathedral before which Mandrin would perform his *amende honorable* on the way to the scaffold. Treillard was now called from Lyon to paint a portrait of the famous smuggler. Whether he painted the original portrait in Mandrin's prison cell, as the engraving indicates, or at the gallows outside the city using nothing but the smuggler's remains, as the *Abrégé* and *Courrier d'Avignon* would have it, is impossible to know. The original portrait and all documentary traces of it have been lost to posterity. However, the popular engraving, which portrays the smuggler as a conquering hero, is quite suggestive. Decked out in respectable clothes, a round wig beneath his hat, and carrying the same weaponry as in the Bourg image, he is larger than life, towering over the mayor of Beaune who holds a receipt in his right hand. Going far beyond the simplistic Bourg portrait, this image not only emphasizes the military bearing of its subject but evokes the complicated moral economy of the forced sale. The deposited tobacco is shown wrapped in bundles, while the inscription explains how Mandrin, "terror" of the tax farmers and "state resister" *(réfractaire à l'état)*, "always proud and calm," "filled their warehouses with his contraband." In this image, Mandrin is an avenging merchant who forces open the tobacco monopoly as well as a military commander (Figure 10.5). Although it is impossible to say how widely this portrait circulated, we know from newspapers that it was eagerly awaited in Valence because, unlike the Bourg series, it was expected to convey a realistic rendering of Mandrin's face.[37]

While portraits offered fixed images of Mandrin in mid-campaign, books ventured deeper into his life story, creating a fuller character with distinct political views. Among the most sympathetic books to surface after the execution was, as its title suggests, a hagiographic biography, *Abrégé de la vie de Louis Mandrin* ([Dole], 1755), the authorship of which is attributed to Claude-Joseph Terrier de Cléron.[38] Terrier was a magistrate from Franche-Comté who was born into the robe nobility and acquired the position of president of the chambre des comptes of Dole in 1729, after a stint as barrister at the parlement of Besançon. From his position in the financial court, he battled what he believed were gross fiscal and administrative abuses by the monarchy, drafting judicial remonstrances against royal tax decrees. In 1761, he was thrown into the Bastille for publishing a satirical defense of the parlement of Besançon,

Louis Mandrin

Ce téméraire chef d'une troupe brigande
De meurtriers, et d'assassins,
Fut l'effroy des Traitans, et de sa contrebande
Remplit leurs magazins.

Refractaire a l'etat, toujours fier et tranquille,
Suivi partout de ses brigands,
A Baune il sçut forcer le Maire de la ville
De lui porter vingt mille francs.

gravé d'après un portrait fait dans la prison de Mau. par M. Freillard.

Figure 10.5. Mandrin's forced sale in Beaune. Bibliothèque Nationale de France, collection Hennin, no. 8772.

which was at the time combating heavy increases in taxation. It is fitting that a distinguished magistrate who would use wit to expose the fiscal abuses of the monarchy should first turn his attention to the life of Louis Mandrin, in whose exploits he reveled. Laced with so many clever turns of phrase that readers attributed the anonymous work to Voltaire, the *Abrégé* was clearly directed at an audience of the author's peers.

Terrier did not invent the stock character of the justice-seeking noble bandit—in England, such a figure had appeared as early as the first ballads about Robin Hood—but he did much to advance it in France. Earlier works on highwayman Philippe Guilleri and thief Louis Dominique Cartouche had established the type of social bandit who stole from the rich and gave to the poor.[39] Terrier cast Mandrin in a similar mold. Indeed, the Mandrin of the *Abrégé* was everything the demon-bandit of the *Mandrinade* was not. He was polite, gallant, and sharp-witted, the kind of sophisticated gentleman burglar that the presumed audience of learned readers would have appreciated.

Like the other biographies, the book opens with a description of the smuggler's family. The father is described as a talented blacksmith who practiced a respectable trade in livestock. His brother was a counterfeiter, but one does not get the sense of a family irredeemably steeped in crime. The misfortune that would lead Louis to smuggling had more to do with an external force, social discrimination, than infamous kin or innate depravity. As a young man, Louis joined the army, a profession for which he had a gift but at which he could not excel because he lacked the proper social pedigree. After the protagonist fails to climb the ranks, Terrier has him exclaim: "Gadzooks . . . I feel like I have courage and some talent but what I don't have is birth!" His career stymied, Mandrin deserts to take up a life of crime. Less than a year before Gabriel-François Coyer would launch a literary assault on a backward-looking military nobility, Terrier blamed Mandrin's turn to crime on the talented soldier's inability to advance in the socially sclerotic royal army. Victim of an eighteenth-century glass ceiling, Mandrin renounced the army and dove into the underground.

Terrier characterized Louis's smuggling career in explicitly political terms. Dubbing himself "the Farmer of the Farmers of France," Mandrin urges his gang to avenge the death of comrades fallen in Valence and "freely cast off the unbearable and bloody yoke of the Farm." This is where Terrier's Mandrin stretches far beyond the stock character of a noble bandit to become a genuine political activist. The Mandrin of the *Abrégé* is on a mission to free France from the tyranny of the Farm.

When the book turns to his expeditions, detail leaps off the page. Terrier must have used his connections as a magistrate to gain access to trial records or Farm reports to paint such a precise portrait of his subject in action. No other text came close to putting so much emphasis on Mandrin's armed trading. Whereas crimes incidental to contraband, such as the killing of Moret's eighteen-month-old child, were blithely explained away, scenes that dealt with illicit trade were carefully wrought to depict a dashing young hero. In the heat of one battle, a sentimental Mandrin is moved by the tears of a Farm agent's wife and decides to spare the man's life. To those he does wound, he provides a shirt so they "at least have some linen with which to bandage themselves; because, I have a noble soul." Such compassion was matched by a gallant masculine bearing that drew the regard of the fairer sex during commercial transactions. Far from being terrified of the chief, calico-hungry ladies and their maidservants found him a "charming figure, as appetizing as his merchandise."

But where Mandrin shines best in this account is in his forced sales. The reader is assured that the chief did not simply plunder the Farm. When forcing warehousers to buy his tobacco, he scrupulously left the correct amount of contraband at their door with a receipt discharging them of all financial responsibility; the targets here were tax farmers, not those in their employ. Indeed, more than any other biographer of the day, Terrier sensitively teased out Mandrin's moral economy from documents at his disposal and embellished what he found. Guided by a keen sense of justice, the smuggler not only paid innkeepers "exactly" what he owed but liberated prisons with the utmost discretion, allowing only smugglers to be released. "I am not your savior," the chief tells imprisoned thieves: "you well deserve to be hanged."[40]

The remainder of the story—the combat at Guenand followed by Mandrin's capture, trial, and execution—takes a more conventional line, but even here Mandrin emerges heroic. Terrier touts the chief's brilliant military stand at Guenand and punctures the royal cover story surrounding his capture: it was the royal army and not a bunch of rogue Farm guards who illegally plucked Mandrin from Savoie. Brought to trial, his lighthearted wit charms the head of the commission but cannot save him from the scaffold. Perfectly contrite at his execution, Mandrin apologizes to God, the king, and even the Farm for his crimes. "Would anyone have imagined that this was the voice of the man who so many times had caused so much such trouble for [the Farm]"? Without denying the exemplarity of the execution, Terrier gives it tragic meaning as he reminds readers that the condemned man possessed many "qualities of the soul." Like the grocer Michel Forest, the author takes solace in his hero's coolheaded courage and in his posthumous "apotheosis" into a latter-day "Hercules."

The positive representations of Mandrin in the *Abrégé* were reinforced by two plays—*Mandrin ou les effets de la vengeance, comédie, en trois actes* (La Haye, 1755) and *Mandrin, comédie nouvelle en cinq actes en prose* (London, 1755)—neither of which dwells for an instant on the smuggler's punishment. The first play, written by the prolific François Huguet, purges Mandrin of all traces of peasant origins to depict him as a polished and modestly wealthy nobleman. He courts a beautiful woman but is rebuffed by her father, a stereotypically "tyrannical" financier who "prefers money to merit." The play does not have to delve too deeply into matters of state to contrast Mandrin's worth with that of a greedy financier who understands nothing of lineage, character, or fatherhood. In the end, Mandrin must expiate his crimes, for he has attacked the Farm to save his brother, but the audience has nonetheless been treated to a delightfully polite and honorable character. The figure of Mandrin as a distinguished gentleman appears to have resonated widely, as it is also found in two engraved popular portraits, one which depicts him brandishing his saber astride a dappled rearing horse and another three-quarter portrait in which he is dressed in the richly embroidered clothing of aristocracy (Figures 10.6 and 10.7).

In the second play, Mandrin is a courageous military leader who formulates a sophisticated philosophical defense of his so-called crimes. The plot is sheer whimsy: Mandrin kidnaps the wives of six tax farmers and places them in the custody of an attorney's wife, Madame Grippe-Sol, whom they once snubbed. Grippe-Sol takes her revenge by subjecting her former tormentors to the degrading work of domestic service. The women are stripped of their jewelry (the fruits of ill-gotten tax revenue) and forced to rasp tobacco. After the audience is treated to the spectacle of social-climbing snobs getting their comeuppance, the play takes a sharp philosophical turn as Mandrin reflects on the nature of crime. All the great men of the past, including Alexander and Caesar,

Voicy MANDRIN, *le Chef d'une troupe brigan.* Ce temeraire fait valoir sa Contrebande,
Dans Bourg, Autun, et Baune, il porte la tereure, Au yeux du Partisan, Commis et Controlleur
à Paris chez Basset le Jeune rue St Jacques au coin de la rue des Mathurins

Figure 10.6. Mandrin as a gentleman-officer. Bibliothèque Nationale de
France, N2 Mandrin.

Louis Mandrin

du lieu de St. étienne, et St. gezins en dauphiné, principal Chef
des Contrebandiers, peints et gravés a
Valence. 1755

Figure 10.7. Mandrin as a gentleman. Bibliothèque Nationale de France, N2 Mandrin.

began as brigands, he explains, echoing philosophes of the day who endeavored to relativize the differences between conquerors and bandits.[41] Those who happened to succeed are memorialized as heroes, whereas those who fail are remembered as villains. It is merely an accident of history that certain rebellions are called crimes. "The crimes of which people accuse me, & for which I am going to die, exist more in the opinions of men than in the thing itself." Wholly unrepentant, the Mandrin of this comedy dismisses the notion that his rebellions constituted moral transgressions of any kind.[42]

Conflicting Images

None of the texts that portrayed Mandrin as demon or hero were free of ambiguity. The *Mandrinade,* which characterized the bandit as an atheistic monster, contains an odd chapter in which he dines at a local château "as polite and decent as a gentleman" and gallantly bestows a gift of "magnificent muslin" on his noble host. Conversely, the *Abrégé,* which justified the smuggler's forced sales, has a contrite Mandrin apologize to agents of the Farm before his execution. More than just incidentally ambiguous, however, a few key texts were contradictory at their very core. Mingling irreconcilable portraits of their protagonist, they encouraged readers to cobble together their own interpretations of the smuggler's life and death.[43]

The era's most popular work on Mandrin, the picaresque *Histoire de Louis Mandrin, depuis sa naissance jusqu'à sa mort* (Troyes, [1755]), was one such work. Appearing in at least four editions in the eighteenth century and many more in the nineteenth, the title belonged to the *bibliothèque bleue,* a vast corpus of texts that encompassed religious handbooks, bawdy comedies, and recycled chivalric romances, all hawked by urban booksellers and itinerant rural peddlers alike.[44] Identifiable by their signature blue covers, poor print quality, and diminutive peddler-friendly size, blue books were temptingly cheap: at one or two sols, they were available for purchase to all but the most destitute. These highly commodified works, cranked out in Troyes and other cities, enjoyed large press runs (on the order of 5,000 copies) and often lived on through several editions. In the first half of the eighteenth century, nearly a million blue books flooded the literary marketplace annually to reach a wider audience than any other literary form of the age.[45]

The widely diffused *Histoire de Mandrin* continued older traditions of picaresque and roguery literature insofar as it told fabulous tales of thieves, antikings, and secret treasures, but the second part of the book diverged from that tradition by adding realistic scenes that bore traces of the world in which readers actually lived.[46] In both sections, the anonymous author set out to debunk Mandrin, exposing him for the scoundrel he really was. "Brigands must not find a place in History," the first sentence of the royally sanctioned biography declares, before publicizing Mandrin's ignominious life.[47] Having dispelled the belief that the smuggler once served as a decorated army officer, the book dives into an alternate universe, a dark underground kingdom led by a sadistic prince, Mandrin, whose subjects sleep by day and counterfeit by night, laundering fake money through the contraband trade. The prince's cruelty stands fully revealed when an innocent young woman mistakenly falls into his lair and declines his offer of marriage, since she already has a husband and children in the "real" world. Not one to take rejection lightly, Mandrin throws her in prison, ties her to a post, and rapes her. When it is discovered that the same woman had earlier stumbled onto a hoard of treasure that belonged to the band, the dark prince sentences her to death. He assigns the role of executioner to the youngest gang member, in whose hand he places a dagger, but when the youth hesitates, the underworld sovereign seizes the boy's fist and fatally plunges the blade into the woman's chest.

At this point, the book pivots from the fantastical world of an antiking to a narrow account of Mandrin's campaigns. The author appears to have had a copy of the commission's verdict at hand, the use of which abruptly suffuses the book with a realism that was totally absent until then. To some extent, such realism only sharpens Mandrin's image as a cruel and heartless killer. Having determined to make war against an "odious race" of Farm agents, his band attacks Farm posts, pillages houses, and murders innocent bystanders (199). Mandrin himself bayonets a pregnant woman after she refuses to give up a suspected spy. Another child falls to his sword when he takes revenge on Moret, the agent who turned in his brother. "Perish, you and your child, may I exterminate his race," Mandrin exclaims as he fells his victims, "striking father and child indifferently and stopping only when he saw them in pieces, bathing in their own blood" (208). His wrath is so great that customers finally shun his contraband, a boycott that forces him to raid the Farm directly.

As the book promises from the very first paragraph, the guilty always pay for their crimes. "Providence" foretold that this brigand would eventually come to justice and repent his sinful ways, and so it comes to pass that, after being betrayed by one of his comrades, Mandrin is captured and condemned to death. Taking a swipe at the Enlightenment, the author asserts that just as the "so-called *philosophes*" abandon atheism on their deathbed, so did Mandrin "feel regret in his heart" at his execution. Standing on the scaffold, eyes turned to heaven and arms lifted, he delivered an edifying speech: "Here is, then, the end that you prepared me for, unfortunate passion for riches. Insane desire, it is you who leads me to the Theater of infamy. I lived in crime, I die in opprobrium. . . . Witnesses of my shame, extinguish the fires of ambition in your hearts, if you feel any horror for my unfortunate lot." The moral of the story could not have been clearer: greedy criminals die in infamy.

In many ways, the *Histoire* painted as nasty a picture of Mandrin as the *Mandrinade*. But below its surface ran a counternarrative that undercut the book's negative depictions to give favorably disposed readers something to hang on to. One merely has to look at the frontispiece, an oval reproduction of the engraving of Mandrin in Bourg, to see that the smuggler was not all bad (see Figure 10.2). The only illustration in the book, it must have had a considerable influence on readers' imaginations, particularly those who were more proficient with images than words. Corroborating the benign messages of the frontispiece is the author's description of Mandrin as a man of "some wit, an admirable deftness, & good cheer." He had "a natural eloquence that persuaded; a lively imagination; the courage to organize great undertakings, and the audacity to succeed." The protagonist was even inclined to sentiment. "Who would believe that the heart of this barbarian, who massacred with inhumanity and impudence, dared show itself sensitive to love?" (160–162). We have here the makings of a tragic figure who, despite his extraordinary personality, ended his days in infamy on the scaffold.

The plot, too, cut against the nominal portrayal of Mandrin as a bandit. In the first part of the story, when Mandrin is lording over his secret lair, he is portrayed not only as a cruel gang leader but also as a benign trickster. The trickster, an underdog who cunningly turns the tables on his superiors, had long been a stock character of popular chapbooks and fairy tales.[48] Adopting this persona, the Mandrin of the *Histoire,* a clever rogue if ever there was one, is perpetually disguising himself, deceiving people, and narrowly escaping trouble. By turns, he pretends to be a baron to court the daughter of a gentleman, a knight to seduce the women of an entire village, and a hermit to avoid a tussle with locals. After sneaking into an elegant château, he treats his men to a feast of choice meats and fine wine. What commoner finding this subtext would not cheer? There was something almost supernatural in Mandrin's physical prowess and abilities as an escape artist, not uncommon in early-modern outlaw literature.[49] The biography informs us that while some imagined that his superior strength derived from a secret herb he ingested, others believed he possessed magical powers. Whatever the source of his vigor, the *Histoire* depicted Mandrin as the kind of wily character readers delighted in rooting for.

The second part of the book on the war against the Farm abounds as well with sympathetic portrayals. Mandrin shows mercy to a Farm officer's wife, respects the lives and property of the citizens of Beaune, distributes receipts to warehousers, and refuses to admit lazy thieves to his band, liberating only smugglers from prison. Tobacco-snuffing readers must have relished the scene in which the smuggler conducts his first forced sale, stunning a dumbfounded warehouser as he shows off his merchandise. " 'Do not take this for a dream,' Mandrin assures him: 'what you see is real tobacco; your leaf is no more admirable; I'll give it to you for 40 sols a pound, and I want no buyer other than you' " (206). The moral economy that Terrier so clearly delineated is also present here, albeit embedded in a counternarrative.

Most impressively, our hero takes on the attributes of a military commander to defeat the Farm at every turn. Even a biographer determined to debunk Mandrin could not help being amazed by the rapid-fire forced sales of his last campaigns. "The speed with which he executed these [forced sales] in the Bureaux of different Provinces suggests what Mandrin could have been, had he not been a Brigand" (211). But alas, he *was* a brigand, and the positive subplot must in the end yield to the master narrative in which the formidable Mandrin is brought to justice.

The ambiguity ingrained in the *Histoire* also informed two plays: *Mandrin Pris* (Amsterdam, 1755) and *La Mort de Mandrin* (Valence, 1756). Both presented a morally-flawed man who nonetheless advanced acute critiques of the monarchy. Sold in an inexpensive unbound format, Stanislas Duplessis' *Mandrin pris* created an ethical counterpoint to Mandrin in the character of La Fleur, the chief's valet, who opens the play with a soliloquy on the moral hazards of smuggling. Is it right "to scour the countryside like werewolves, striking the innocent as well as the guilty?" Mandrin "believes that his crimes are illustrious marvels that are going to immortalize him," but "he is deceiving himself." When the valet dares raise such doubts with his boss, asserting that the latter's raids on the Farm make him a "bad Christian," Mandrin takes offense and renews his pledge of "eternal war" against the Farm. The plot turns on this moral debate, since it is La Fleur who betrays his master at Rochefort. But before the smuggler is whisked off to Valence, the play exposes the rank falsity of the cover story concocted by the monarchy to protect itself from the diplomatic fallout of the kidnapping. In the final scenes, it is made plain that the men who captured Mandrin in Savoy were not rogue Farm guards but royal soldiers sent by the French court. When a French officer arrests the chief on Savoyard soil, the latter cries, "What! the law of nations, the most sacred rights, will thus be dishonored with impunity?" In this drama, France's brigandage supersedes that of Mandrin.

The only play we know to have actually been staged in the aftermath of Mandrin's execution, *La Mort de Mandrin* by Nicolas de la Grange, presents a man who is wholly contrite through trial and execution. "Whatever my sentence is to be, I will not complain, I deserve death." Such damning self-condemnation, however, served only to heighten the tragic heroism of a character who, thanks to his "virtue" (that is, his military prowess), could lift himself from humble beginnings to pursue true "glory." Although his ambition ultimately gets the better of him, the play lauds the chief's valor and bravery, directing its opprobrium against the "detestable Tyrants" who presided over the "iniquitous" court in Valence.

The volume of words, images, and songs that materialized in the aftermath of Mandrin's execution suggests that the event constituted a critical moment in the politicization of popular media.[50] The monarchy's narrative, which justified the transgressor's punishment and, implicitly, the wider crackdown on contraband, was reinforced by a host of normative tales that demonized the smuggler. And yet, other representations sharply contested that narrative, celebrating Mandrin and his struggle to defeat the despotism of the Farm. Some texts mixed these messages in confusing cultural cocktails that simultaneously legitimated repression and liberation. The question that we must ultimately pose is not what producers meant to convey by such works but what readers, listeners, and viewers took from them. To be sure, the negative image of Mandrin gained some purchase, as the pejorative use of the word "Mandrin" attests. But given widespread hostility to the Farm, the sudden outpouring of images of Mandrin as brilliant military commander, noble bandit, political rebel, and wily prankster may well have boosted admiration for him among the popular classes and galvanized the movement against the Farm. After all, representations of Mandrin did not circulate in an ideological vacuum. Not only did cultural producers play to (and profit from) the tastes of an audience that admired as well as feared the depredations of the outlaw but cultural consumers approached words and images about Mandrin with previously conceived attitudes toward the Farm that undoubtedly shaped their interpretations.

We do not have to rely on deduction alone to assess the effects of this literary storm. After Mandrin's execution, self-styled smugglers such as "le petit Mandrin," "the children of Mandrin," and others emulated his widely publicized deeds in a rash of copycat crimes.[51] In Picardy, the chief's name was invoked by a gang of soldier-smugglers who attacked a customs post in 1757. Two decades later, protesters in Champagne hailed Mandrin in song in the midst of the largest tax uprising of pre-revolutionary France. As confrontations between Farm and traffickers flared in this eastern borderland, two songsters planted themselves in Sedan's main square to sell anthems disparaging the Farm. One of the songs, "The Catechism of the Gabelous," which slandered Farm guards as "ferocious beasts," lamented Mandrin's loss: if only "we still had Mandrin / to wage war against these crooks / and subject them to pillage."[52] Clearly, the outpouring of media after the smuggler's execution fostered a robust memory of Mandrin that underground rebels freely appropriated in their own struggles against the Farm.

One of the few extant working-class autobiographies of the period, *Journal de ma vie* by Jacques-Louis Ménétra, also reveals how printed work on Mandrin shaped popular attitudes. A Parisian glazier who toured the French provinces in search of work, Ménétra claimed to have met Mandrin in Burgundy in 1762. As this was seven years after the smuggler's execution, Ménétra, an incorrigible teller of tall tales, obviously fabricated the whole encounter. But the fictive dimension of the meeting makes it all the more interesting because the glazier, who we know to have been an avid reader of scaffold literature and criminal biography, drew on what he had culled from conversations, books, songs, and portraits. From such sources, he formed a resolutely positive opinion of Mandrin.

> As [I] took the direct route toward Dijon on the Mâcon road I saw Mandrin's advance guard of twenty men and a half hour later I saw him leading his troops. I saluted him [and] he returned my salute. And all the inhabitants of this area had nothing but good to say about him. And [I] went to sleep in the town known as Maison Neuve and slept in what I was told afterwards was the bed where Mandrin had slept. . . . The whole town was in an uproar because of Mandrin's visit during which he had asked for a stirrup cup or what they call in these parts the wine of honor, which is given to the kings of France by the provosts and aldermen on bended knee and in a cup of gold. That was one of the most serious charges and (something to do with) a poor unfortunate pregnant woman who was killed at Autun when the inhabitants closed their doors to him. Everywhere I went people said nothing but good about him and even spoke of his good deeds.[53]

Several themes stand out from this passage. Mandrin is portrayed as a military commander who expected city officials to treat him like a king. At the same time, he was a man of the people, not above returning the salute of a journeyman. Although he had committed grave crimes—the murder of a pregnant woman, told in both the *Mandrinade* and *Histoire,* crops up—the people of Burgundy nonetheless valorized his "good deeds." Any inconsistencies in the morality of his actions resolve themselves into a generally heroic conclusion: "everywhere I went people said nothing but good about him." Indeed, Mandrin was a celebrity of such stature that the ever boastful Ménétra claimed to have slept in the same bed where the smuggler himself once lay. Louis Mandrin slept here.

Ménétra's favorable impressions were formed at a time when old representations of noble knights in books of chivalry were giving way to an emerging canon of great criminals: Guilleri, Cartouche, Mandrin,

Nivet, Lescombat, and Desrues, to mention only the most famous. It has been suggested that such outlaws were particularly mythogenic because "they satisfied repressed wishes, enabling ordinary people to take imaginative revenge on the authorities to whom they were usually obedient in real life."[54] Crime literature gives readers the vicarious emotional thrill of escaping the constraints of the law, of seeing their antisocial impulses played out without having to pay the price for it.[55] Such psychoanalytic interpretations define the political limits of crime fiction, for the fantasy seems entirely escapist, but reading this literature in the middle of the eighteenth century may have had more political resonance than psychoanalytic interpretations allow. First, in an age when the monarchy was attempting to realize claims of absolute authority, any story that encouraged readers to dream of life beyond the law had potentially subversive implications.[56] More than mere escapism, the rehearsal of rebellion through media that legitimated acts of lawbreaking may have drawn listeners, viewers, and readers deeper into the conflict between Farm and smuggler. As we have seen, some smugglers actively drew from the sensationalized image of Mandrin to cover themselves and their illicit practices in the glory of the fallen hero.

Second, the pantheon of great criminals acquired new political significance when Mandrin joined its ranks. Unlike his predecessors Guilleri and Cartouche, Mandrin symbolized active rebellion against an institution that stood at the very heart of the monarchy. Cartouche, it is true, violently ridiculed the Paris police, for which he earned the eternal gratitude of the people of Paris, but he was also known as a dastardly thief who stole from other royal subjects. By contrast, Mandrin, who crusaded against the General Farm, was a hero of a rather different stripe—a rebel who dared challenge fiscal, judicial, and military authorities. In the blue pamphlet *Dialogue entre Cartouche et Mandrin* (Troyes, 1755), the executed smuggler descends to the depths of hell to be welcomed by Cartouche, who attempts to befriend him as a fellow rogue. Mandrin rebuffs the thief's overture: "Ah! miserable Crook, you have only some thefts and murders to speak of, and you dare to compare yourself to me."[57] "As long as pipes reign, as long as noses feast on tobacco, I will have my historians in the Commis of the Farm. . . . My name is written in [their] memory in letters of blood." Cartouche was grand "but a lot less so than Mandrin," added the *Mandrinade* song. Whereas the thief operated in Paris only by night, "the brave general" crossed borders to conduct his trade "under the nose of the god of light." Cartouche defeated boors; Mandrin conquered soldiers and guards. Through the figure of Mandrin, political rebellion was incorporated into popular literature on a wholly new scale to pose a direct challenge to the legitimacy of the monarchy's financial system.

11

Smuggling in the Enlightenment

O N AN EVENING IN 1764, the distinguished magistrate Chrétien Guillaume de Lamoignon de Malesherbes, former director of the Royal Publishing Office and sitting president of the highest tax court in the realm, hosted a dinner party for several luminaries of the French Enlightenment. At the table sat André Morellet, liberal economist and philosopher; Jacques Turgot, intendant of Limoges, friend of the Physiocrats, and future finance minister; and Jean le Rond d'Alembert, mathematician, member of the prestigious Académie française, and cofounder of the *Encyclopédie,* that great compendium of Enlightenment knowledge. As they dined, Malesherbes recounted how he had come into possession of a stimulating new book by an obscure Milanese writer named Cesare Beccaria. "Try to translate it," Malesherbes challenged Morellet, referring to the work's difficult opening line. Withdrawing briefly to the magistrate's private library, Morellet soon produced a perfectly clear French sentence. With the others' encouragement, he took the volume home and translated the entire work within six weeks. *Des délits et des peines (On Crimes and Punishments),* published in December 1765, was an instant success. The founding work of modern penal philosophy, it would galvanize a movement for reform of the French criminal justice system, including its treatment of smugglers.[1]

If the ephemeral literature celebrating Mandrin expressed widespread hostility to the Farm, it took the literature of the Enlightenment to transform popular resentment into a powerful movement for state reform. Having launched radical attacks on Christianity during the early phase of the Enlightenment, writers in the second half of the eighteenth century increasingly turned their attention to improving the social condition of mankind. As Cesar Chesneau Dumarsais explained in the *Encyclopédie*, "civil society" was, for the philosophe, "a divinity on earth; he burns incense to it, he honors it by his probity, by an exact attention to his duties, and by a sincere desire not to be a useless or embarrassing member of it."[2] Investing society with value once reserved exclusively for the afterlife, philosophes asserted that men and women could use the power of reason to remodel their world and better the human condition. Malesherbes, Morellet, Beccaria, and a host of other thinkers ardently believed they could solve many social ills—including the problem of smuggling—by rationalizing earthly institutions. This was no abstract academic exercise: writers threw themselves into reform movements with boundless enthusiasm, desperate to liberate society from a thicket of irrational customs and prejudices that had impeded social progress and stifled human happiness for centuries. The stakes could not have been higher.[3]

But how was reform to be instituted? The philosophes could not legislate change like members of a modern political party, nor did they wish to impose their ideas by revolutionary force, for few of them advocated a Lockean right to resistance.[4] On the contrary, they firmly believed that reform should be implemented peacefully through what educated classes of the eighteenth century were beginning to call "public opinion," a consensus forged by reasoned debate among a small but growing reading public. Morellet described the process in his pamphlet on "the freedom to write and publish on matters of administration": "When a question of political economy is submitted to the judgment of the public by way of print, the minister of state immediately obtains the judgment of learned men; not that all learned men write, but they judge the writers & their principles, & their opinion soon forms public opinion. What work, what enlightenment in a state minister can compensate for such a powerful kind of assistance?"[5] In the idealized world of the Enlightenment, men of letters published books, books were debated by the educated, the educated produced public opinion, and public opinion shaped government policy, bringing about necessary reforms.

Of course, the reality of public opinion, a vague concept more readily appealed to than consulted, was a lot messier than the theory. Men of letters did not always arrive at consensus, and the monarchy was not always keen to adopt their policy prescriptions. But in one respect, this reformist vision did come to pass: writers published increasing numbers of books on matters of state, tearing the cloak of secrecy that had enveloped financial and economic policy since the Middle Ages. From 1750 to 1789, when literary production as a whole tripled, the field of political economy expanded sevenfold to become the jewel in the crown of the high Enlightenment.[6] For the first time in French history, hundreds of books on trade, agriculture, and taxation were published every year, the most popular treatises knocking novels off the best-seller list. Adding to this effervescence, law courts published scores of "remonstrances," critical commentaries on proposed royal legislation, while magistrates, lawyers, and legal reformers produced more than a hundred treatises on the criminal justice system.[7] As texts on economics, finance, and justice proliferated, smuggling became one of a number of pressing public issues, endowing Mandrin and his shadowy comrades with a political significance far surpassing anything the chief himself might have imagined during his short life.

Political Economists

The moment Mandrin's remains were dragged to the gallows outside Valence, his memory was enlisted in Enlightenment debates on reform. But it was not the great philosophes who first took up his cause. During the smuggler's expeditions, Voltaire, who resided on the Swiss shore of Lake Léman with "the Mandrins at my door," hoped to meet the glorious "conqueror," but when the gang leader was captured and put on trial in Valence, the poet neglected to intercede on his behalf.[8] Rather, the first writers to call public attention to Mandrin and the issue of smuggling were political economists, men of letters who were beginning to study the relationship between state policy and national wealth. The vectors of this new "science," as its practitioners came to call it, ran in several directions, but one especially far-reaching line of thought pointed toward what we would today call economic liberalism, the theory that the state should withdraw from the economy in order to maximize economic growth. Although commonly associated with Adam Smith, whose *Wealth of Nations* was published in 1776, this theory first flourished in France in the third quarter of the eighteenth century, as writers campaigned against what they considered heavy-handed state policies that, since the era of Colbert, had allegedly devastated the economy and depopulated the kingdom.[9]

Liberal political economists rarely treated smuggling as a topic unto itself, but they engaged the subject while addressing higher-profile issues such as trade regulation and taxation. Indeed, as conflict between Farm and smuggler raged in the provinces from the 1750s to the 1780s, economic thinkers actively incorporated the problem of the shadow economy into their programs for reform, seeking to mediate Farm-smuggler conflict and put an end to the dreadful cycle of violence. It was the dual thrust of popular revolt from below and the demand for reform from above that fully politicized the underground.

The first economist to formulate a muscular defense of illicit trade was a Grub Street writer by the name of Ange Goudar. Goudar was perfectly situated to transform Mandrin from popular hero into poster boy for enlightened reform. A mischievous gambler who would ultimately turn spy for the French foreign ministry, Goudar held a middling position in the world of letters, perched above popular writers of the *bibliothèque bleue* who slapped together government-approved material for the broadest possible audiences, and below the clubby set of philosophes who enjoyed aristocratic patronage, contributed to the *Encyclopédie*, and attended exclusive Parisian salons. In 1754, a gambling scandal in Paris forced Goudar to flee the capital for the papal city of Avignon, where, beyond the reach of French law, he seized on the execution of Louis Mandrin to disseminate subversive principles of economic reform. His *Testament politique de Louis Mandrin* (Figure 11.1), launched within a month of the smuggler's demise, would run through five editions and more than one German translation.[10]

The success of the book stemmed from its design, which, mimicking the techniques of French fiction, was written in the putative first-person voice of Louis Mandrin. "I was collecting documents for my political Testament," the supposed Mandrin explains, when "I was arrested." His testament, completed in prison, confronted the "great crisis" gripping the kingdom in a way that those penned by eminent statesmen like "Richelieu, Colbert & Louvois" had never dared. The rebel's treatise detailed a disaster of immense proportions, in which popular violence, economic stagnation, and government corruption threatened to bring the French monarchy crashing down. "People are slitting each other's throats with the kind of furor that raged during the Wars of Religion," he declared, a shocking comparison in an age when the enlightened looked back on those wars with horror. Such fanatical mayhem could

TESTAMENT

POLITIQUE

D E

LOUIS MANDRIN,

Généraliffime des Troupes des Contrebandiers , écrit par Lui-même dans fa Prifon.

SEPTIÉME ÉDITION.

A GENEVE.

M. DCC. LVI.

Figure 11.1. Le Testament politique de Louis Mandrin. Bibliothèque Nationale de France.

not be blamed on the French people, however, for "the Frenchman is a patriot, he loves his king." Rather, "a vice has crept into the French government that has enflamed the spirit of the people and forced it to step out of its character. The vice is the system of the Farm."

Our hero then launches into a furious discourse based partly on Montesquieu's *De l'esprit des lois* (1748). A towering authority at mid-century, Montesquieu had proclaimed that the taxes most suitable to "moderate" (as opposed to "despotic") government were excise taxes on merchandise. If imposed lightly on nonsubsistence goods, such taxes would scarcely be perceptible because producers would hide them in the price of merchandise and pass the burden to consumers.[11] Psychologically, this type of levy was least likely to induce the feeling of oppression in the citizen, as proponents of taxing tobacco had long argued. At the same time, however, Montesquieu stated in no uncertain terms that such taxes were *not* to be farmed, for tax farming was fundamentally inimical to the proper functioning of a monarchy. "The history of monarchies is full of evils perpetrated by *traitants,*" he cautioned. Tax farmers reaped "immense profits" at the expense of the king, who received only a fraction of the revenue collected, and of his subjects, upon whose livelihoods farmers preyed. Worse, the wealth that tax farmers accumulated allowed them to exert "despotic" influence over the kingdom. To battle the illicit economy to which their monopolies inevitably gave rise, tax farmers forced monarchs to surrender judicial powers that allowed financiers to impose "extravagant punishments like those inflicted for the greatest crimes." Although smugglers were generally "not regarded as wicked men," they were punished "like villains, which is the most contrary thing in the world to the spirit of moderate government." Once the Roman Empire foolishly granted judicial authority to financiers, "there was no more virtue, no more police, no more laws, no more magistrature, no more magistrates."[12] In his magnum opus, Montesquieu forged a link between fiscal and judicial corruption that would serve as the basis for all subsequent discussions of smuggling.

Ignoring Montesquieu's preference for indirect taxes but elaborating on his remarks against *traitants,* Goudar developed a more explicitly economic critique of the Farm. The problem was not just that the Farm was wasteful and predatory but, as well, that it diverted money from a healthy economic cycle by which wealth passed freely from people to king and king to people. Tapping into this circular flow, greedy tax farmers siphoned large portions of treasure into their own pockets, throwing the economy into decline and putting the kingdom at risk of total collapse.[13] "The Farmers alone have more gold and silver than all the individuals in France combined." As agriculture languished and peasants were forced to abandon the land, Farmers General negotiated the terms of their contracts as if on equal footing with the king while unleashing numberless agents on the people.

As the weight of the Farm grew ever more oppressive, "Mandrin" explained, the underground economy became increasingly violent. Peasants who could no longer bear the ravages of taxation joined "to throw off the yoke of what they call the Farmers' tyranny." To add a personal dimension to such rebellion, Goudar had ordinary smugglers speak to Mandrin in fictitious letters, such as the one in which a peasant whose father had been hanged in Valence boasted, "I have killed nine tobacco guards with my own hands, held up six Farm directors, and despoiled eighteen commis." Royal ministers ignored such grassroots violence at their own peril, warned the chief, for "in certain circumstances it can contribute to the overthrow of the monarchy." "The most famous revolutions, which reduced the most powerful empires to fire and blood, always began with sparks." It was true that commissions had been established to snuff out such sparks, but unconstitutional courts only escalated the conflict and further depopulated the kingdom. There was no telling where this cycle of violence would end. Blinded by self-interest and utterly insensitive to the people's plight, the Farmers General "could witness the execution of half of France without the spectacle moving them."

The conclusion of the testament was unequivocal. "If this system [of tax farming] stops the growth of the population, if it is one of the greatest obstacles to the economy of wealth; if it diminishes the authority of the Prince, if it changes the spirit of the Nation by making a great number of subjects ferocious and rebellious; in a word if this system overturns the Constitution of the Monarchy; it must be destroyed before it destroys the State itself." It was incumbent upon Louis XV, a benevolent father to his people, to abolish the Farm, accord a general amnesty to smugglers, and come to the aid of those who, for lack of work, did not have the means to subsist.

Goudar would develop this critique the following year in his *Les intérêts de la France malentendus,* a widely read three-volume tirade against financiers, luxury, and monopoly, before embarking on a more lucrative career divulging the sordid private lives of European aristocrats. By the time Goudar moved on to scurrilous literature, however, more celebrated political economists within the republic of letters had begun to address the illicit economy. The first wave of literature emanated from a group of thinkers surrounding Jacques Claude Marie Vincent de Gournay, who promoted the slogan "laissez-faire, laissez-passer" while serving as an intendant of commerce from 1751 to 1759. Although generations of historians passed over the Gournay circle to study the ideas of the Physiocrats, we now know that the circle was absolutely essential to the development of eighteenth-century political economy. Attempting to cultivate in France the kind of commercial society that catapulted Britain to great-power status, Gournay and his associates espoused a philosophy of "egalitarian liberalism" that advocated industrial deregulation, open competition and exchange, and robust (yet still legally structured) foreign and colonial trade, all of which would stimulate the circulation of wealth and encourage social mobility.[14] To bring this "science of commerce" to the public, group members not only published their work illegally, as Goudar had, but also struck a fruitful alliance with the liberal director of the Royal Publishing Office, the ubiquitous Malesherbes. In what was still a delicate cultural climate, the director assisted them by providing special publishing privileges called "tacit permissions" that allowed works that could be construed as subversive to royal authority to be printed with the unofficial assent of his office. With Malesherbes working behind the scenes, the Gournay coterie sparked a mid-century explosion in economic literature and thought.[15]

Gournay and his friends came to the issue of smuggling through the controversy over the prohibition of calico. Although the importation and production of Indian cloth had been banned in France since 1686, the bureau of commerce began to soften the law in the 1750s, granting special privileges to produce the forbidden cloth to a handful of domestic manufacturers. When traditional manufacturers got wind of this, they flooded the council with petitions against the permissions and, astonishingly, appealed directly to the public. Opponents of the ban responded in kind, disseminating blistering criticisms of the prohibition and the logic of protectionism that underpinned it. Hence, the calico controversy was born and, with it, the first modern public debate on trafficking and its repression.[16]

Based on mercantilist assumptions about the need for state policy to protect domestic industry and labor, arguments in favor of the ban had not changed much since 1686. Manufacturers and their publicists claimed that lifting the prohibition would inundate France with cheap foreign calicoes, devastating the wool and silk industries and producing rampant unemployment. The ban was therefore essential. Smuggling had become a problem, they conceded, but only because the ban was not sufficiently enforced. Proponents of prohibition urged the Farm not only to do a better job of capturing traffickers but to go after the source of demand: the consumer. It was time for the "empire of Law" to defeat "the authority of fashion," thundered Jacob-Nicolas Moreau, staunch defender of absolutism and leading publicist for the prohibitionists.[17] Once the state suppressed consumers' desire for the fashionable cloth, smuggling would cease. The Farmers General employed the same logic when instructing its agents to burn confiscated calico publicly, believing that such a display would compel the public "to get over its taste for these kinds of clothes."[18]

The Gournay circle countered these arguments with a bold defense of free trade and consumption. Were a calico industry allowed to develop on French soil, they argued, it would successfully compete with international rivals and compensate for job losses incurred in other textile industries. Founding their arguments on a rudimentary version of what economists today call "consumer sovereignty"—the notion that it is the consumer, not the state or the producer, who ultimately decides which goods are produced and in what quantity—the circle suggested that it was pure folly to deny consumers what they wanted. Any attempt to cut them off from goods they desired, Gournay reasoned the same year Mandrin was executed, would produce illicit markets that would, in turn, generate a horrible war between smugglers and the state. "The contraband of calicoes gives rise to the daily loss of many men on both sides of the conflict; there is a continuous war on all our borders in which infinite numbers perish arms in hand, in prisons, in the galleys, & on the scaffold, & this only to force 20 million men to repudiate their inclinations, instead of adapting to these inclinations and profiting from them." "For anyone born with human sentiments," Gournay concluded, the needless destruction of otherwise useful men was "so palpable . . . that it is not possible to consider its full dimensions without shuddering."[19]

As the debate raged, a senior member of the bureau of commerce, Daniel Charles Trudaine, asked one of Gournay's protégés, Morellet, to expand his mentor's critique into a longer and potentially more persuasive work. The result was *Réflexions sur les avantages de la libre fabrication et de l'usage des toiles peintes en France,* which further developed the theory of consumer sovereignty. Adopting both utilitarian and rights-based arguments, Morellet insisted that a cabal of industrialists seeking to shore up their own profits were thwarting the interests of consumers, who composed the majority of the nation. The state should favor "the greater number over the smaller, since most certainly the general good is the good of the greater number." But it was not just their number that gave consumers the edge. Under a civilized government, every consumer had a "natural right" to dress "according to his whim and in the least expensive manner possible." The calico prohibition violated the "civil liberty" of consumers who should be free to purchase goods they found pleasing and affordable.[20] As Morellet's defenders put it, "It is not our place to prescribe [consumer tastes] but to provide for them."[21] "Our manufactures are made for the utility of our men, not our men for the utility of our manufactures."[22] Production should bend to consumer demand, not the other way around.[23]

Even if one did not subscribe to the principle of consumer sovereignty— and few merchants and policy makers in this period did[24]—there was no denying that prohibition was a complete catastrophe at a practical level. The Farm was no more capable of stopping smugglers from responding to consumer demand, Morellet observed, than it was of preventing consumers from seeking out what they wanted. No police force was large enough, no border secure enough, no judicial system cruel enough, to stanch the flow of contraband. The fruitless violence exercised by the state against the poor for profiting from such commerce mocked Enlightenment notions of progress:

> Is it not strange that an otherwise respectable order of citizens [textile producers] solicits terrible punishments such as death and the galleys against Frenchmen, & does so for reasons of commercial interest? Will our descendants be able to believe that our nation was truly as enlightened and civilized as we now like to say when they read that in the middle of the [eighteenth] century a man in France was hanged for buying in Geneva at 22 sols what he was able to sell in Grenoble for 58? Will they be able to believe that men in often dire poverty were presented with such a strong temptation as profit & were punished so severely when they succumbed to it?[25]

Morellet must have had Mandrin in mind when he wrote these words, for the latter was the only smuggler mentioned by name in the entire text. But it was the cruelty of the *system* of repression, not any single instance of it, that the author wished to emphasize. Neglecting to mention that smugglers were executed not so much for trafficking as for murdering guards and participating in armed bands, Morellet, like Montesquieu and Goudar before him, shifted readers' attention from the violence of rebellion to the inhumanity of state repression. Thousands of men were "hanged, sent to the galleys, or died arms in hand for the act of smuggling." One callous informant claimed that the local commission sent some fifty people a year to their death or to the galleys. "Oh justice is well done here!" the man boasted. "Before the creation of the commission, trials dragged on forever; today things function a lot better."[26]

Since denying consumers the right to pursue their own tastes only resulted in a cruel, wasteful, and lopsided war, it was imperative that the ban be lifted. But that did not mean that no protection was to be afforded the traditional textile industry. In place of the ban, Morellet proposed an import duty on calicoes of 10 to 12 percent, heavy enough to cushion domestic textile production against foreign competition (and yield much-needed revenue for the king) but light enough to minimize incentives for smuggling. The money that once fled the kingdom in exchange for foreign-made smuggled goods would now be put toward domestic production. Here was a solution that all "enlightened" people could support. Indeed, in 1759, a finance minister inclined toward economic liberalism took office and struck down the seventy-three-year-old prohibition, replacing it with an import duty. As Moreau and other prohibitionists predicted, lifting the ban put pressure on the older textile industries, but, as Gournay and Morellet forecast, it also gave rise to a booming domestic cotton industry. In the thirty years between the abolition of the ban and the French Revolution, no fewer than 170 calico manufactories were established on French soil.[27] Contraband did not disappear—there was still money to be made from evading the tariff—but calico smuggling became less violent as it merged with legitimate trade in the once-banned cloth.

By the time Gournay died in 1759, another school of economic thought, termed Physiocracy or "rule of nature" by one of its adherents, was on the ascendant. The Physiocrats were liberals, too, but much more rigid in their advocacy of free trade and less sympathetic to merchants and consumers. They asserted (mistakenly, we now know) that the eighteenth-century French economy was in an abysmal state of decline, because French policy had long ago deviated from "natural" economic laws by favoring industry at the expense of agriculture. Natural economic laws, which universally governed the mechanics of all production and exchange, revealed that agriculture was the sole engine of economic growth and that commerce and industry were merely "sterile" sectors whose value derived ultimately from the land. But all was not lost. The kingdom could recover from impoverishment if it followed the dictates of natural law, which, according to the "economists," as the Physiocrats were also called, required lifting the hand of government from the realm of the economy. By effacing positive law (man-made legislation) and letting the natural economic order rule through the vessel of the monarchy, France could alter course, develop large-scale agriculture, and enter a new age of prosperity.[28]

To abide by natural law would, however, require major policy reversals. First, the whole regulatory apparatus of the state, including that which structured the grain trade, the guilds, and the "mercantile system" of colonial commerce would have to go, as would all quasi-state economic institutions such as the French East Indies Company and the General Farm. Even the seemingly archaic institution of slavery in the Americas would have to be phased out in favor of wage labor.[29] Second, the laws of nature dictated a complete overhaul of the fiscal system: the odious indirect taxes that the Farm collected were to be abolished and all direct levies replaced by a single tax on the "net product" of land. All other forms of revenue, such as the excise and luxury taxes dear to Montesquieu, gouged the farmer, impeded agricultural investment, and ran up debilitating administrative costs.[30]

The founder of Physiocracy, physician François Quesnay, illustrated his theory with the *Tableau économique,* a cryptic diagram that economists now hail as the first depiction of the circular flow of income through the economy, but it fell to Quesnay's first disciple, nobleman Victor Riquetti, Marquis de Mirabeau, to transmit the doctor's ideas to the wider public. In this he succeeded brilliantly. Mirabeau's books *L'ami des hommes* (1756) and *Théorie de l'impôt* (1760), which ran through a stunning forty and eighteen editions, respectively, made the author more famous in his day than any other economist of the modern period, including Adam Smith and Karl Marx.[31] Released during the Seven Years' War, when France suffered a series of humiliating military defeats at the hands of the British, losing prized territory in North America, the Caribbean, Africa, and India, the books spoke eloquently to the apparent crisis into which the empire was plunged. That the Farmers General had the marquis thrown into the Vincennes prison for taking the trouble to expose the underlying causes of his country's ills made *Théorie de l'impôt* only that much more exciting to read.

As advocacy for economic liberalism passed from the Gournay circle to the Physiocrats, critical analyses of smuggling shifted from the
calico prohibition, understood to have violated principles of free trade
and consumer sovereignty, to the Farm's fiscal monopolies, characterized as violating something much larger: the laws of nature themselves.[32]
Whereas Quesnay's early essays merely implied that such laws demanded
the abolition of the Farm, Mirabeau made the implication explicit
with impassioned calls for the Farm's destruction, a rhetorical move
that captured widespread hostility to the institution and helps explain
the spectacular success of his work. Indeed, Physiocracy's assault on the
Farm seems to have been more in tune with prevailing economic attitudes than its dogmatic insistence on a free grain trade.[33]

According to the "friend of man," the Farm had inserted itself between king and subject to drain the realm of its wealth and throw the
economy into disarray. Nothing better illustrated how profoundly the
Farm was desolating the kingdom than the savage war the company
launched against the underground economy. The invasion of the Farm's
"armies" portended "the coming of slavery," Mirabeau declared. "Prisons, galleys, gallows and sinister tribunals are established at the cruel
whim of financiers to punish inhumanely the wretch who exercises his
natural right." Although the Farm feigns to draw blood from the capillaries, it "bleeds the people at the throat. . . . The more heated the civil
war that results from a regime insulting to natural law, the more the
Farmer profits and becomes important, & the more public order and
decency is annihilated."[34] As portrayed in such dramatic prose, the
smuggler who exercised his "natural right" was no match for the likes
of the Farmers General, "vampires" who sapped the nation and delivered it, weak and depleted, to its enemies.[35]

Not all Physiocrats were so hyperbolic. Guillaume-François Le Trosne
employed a colder, more scientific tone in his statistical analysis of the
damage done by salt and tobacco taxes: the king received 57 million lt
from the monopolies, but their real cost to the nation was calculated to
be more than double that sum. The expenses of administration and
police, not to mention the potential wealth blotted out by monopoly,
sapped the economy and provided the crown with relatively little revenue. But it made no sense to demonize the tax farmers. Compiling a
compendium of their "odious deeds" would only "give the impression
that the vice of the tax inheres in the conduct of the tax farmer: is it not

obvious that the severity of which people complain is in the nature of the tax?"[36] Indirect taxation itself was at fault.

By the same token, the moral character of smugglers was irrelevant. Le Trosne, the one Physiocrat who, as an attorney in the présidial of Orléans, had some experience with criminal law, insisted that traffickers were acting in accord with "laws of the natural order" that enshrined the liberty "to buy and sell in a condition of full competition." The imposition of fiscal monopolies had the perverse effect of turning such legitimate merchants into criminals. Although "public opinion doggedly insists on absolving" the artificial crime of smuggling, the crown "persists in condemning it."[37] All this would change once indirect taxes were abolished and the Farm dismantled. Under the rule of natural economic law, the practice of trading what was once mistakenly classified as contraband would be brought into the fold of legitimate commerce, and all repression would cease. The levies "will no longer require victims, the guilty parties will disappear, every subject will be submissive and faithful, their obedience to legal authority will no longer be compromised," and courts "will prosecute only real crimes whose punishment will be applauded by all because it will be inflicted only to assure and avenge collective security."[38] In the eyes of nature, the crime of contraband and, by implication, contraband rebellion was in fact no crime at all, Le Trosne concluded. It was the artificial by-product of a deeply flawed regime in which positive law deviated from natural law.[39]

The Physiocratic defense of smugglers is all the more striking when we recall that the "economists" were hardly friends of the common man. Although claiming to speak on humanity's behalf, they agreed with Morellet that "the bulk of the people is grossly ignorant, poor to the point of profound misery, without any real concept of public order, property, morality."[40] Little wonder that as advocates of high grain prices (which, they believed, would encourage agricultural production), the Physiocrats urged the monarchy to ignore popular demands for price controls even in times of famine. Unlike contraband rebels, construed as acting rationally according to market principles, food rioters who protested high prices were deemed irrational and blind to the ways of the natural order.[41] Further, whereas the Physiocrats sought to rescue smugglers from a false criminality imposed by positive law, they did not hesitate to use such law to crack down on other crimes of poverty. Although Quesnay wished to evacuate positive law from the realm of the economy, he nonetheless assigned it a prominent role in penality, where it was to be wielded against thieves who deviated from the natural order.[42] Le Trosne went even further, proposing harsh punishment for vagabonds, beggars, and other riffraff whom he claimed threatened the sanctity of property, refused to work, and interfered with the smooth functioning of markets. Only "the example of severe punishment"—namely, life in the galleys—could stop vagabondage, "the most contagious disorder of all."[43] And yet the same Physiocrat who denounced vagabonds and beggars set out to save smugglers from criminal infamy by reclassifying them as legitimate traders who bought and sold the fruits of nature in what should have been a free market.

Scholars have recently been invited to search the Enlightenment for underlying links that connected its paradoxical tendencies toward emancipation and domination.[44] We have certainly found one such link here. Embracing a free market based on natural law, the Physiocrats sought to decriminalize smuggling while urging the most severe repression for what were, in their eyes, less justifiable practices of the makeshift economy, namely, vagabondage, begging, and theft. The Physiocrats used a radical strain of economic liberalism to make fundamental legal distinctions between different methods by which the poor survived.

Magistrates and Lawyers

Political economists were not the only ones to bring the war on smuggling to the attention of the reading public. If the Gournay circle took aim at the calico prohibition for violating consumer sovereignty and the Physiocrats attacked the Farm's indirect taxes for defying the laws of nature, magistrates and lawyers returned to Montesquieu's conviction that tax farming itself produced despotism. During and after the Seven Years' War, as Louis XV attempted to raise taxes to cover military costs and service a swelling public debt, he met widespread opposition from parlements, the high courts that registered royal edicts. Much of that opposition was aimed at increases in direct taxes, which, when imposed without consent, magistrates claimed, despotically infringed upon national sovereignty. But magistrates in this stormy period also leveled the charge of despotism at the Farm and its repression of illicit trade. In this instance, despotism was associated less with constitutional violations of national sovereignty than with "vexations" visited upon the populace by Farm police and the draconian punishments handed down by Farm-funded commissions, both of which raised the specter of a company under royal protection subjecting the king's subjects to ferocious brutality. In terms of the history of formal political thought, the parlementary rhetoric of national sovereignty was undoubtedly more significant, but judicial discourse targeting the Farm illuminated a link between fiscal and penal tyranny as it trained a spotlight on some of the most "barbarous" practices of the monarchical state.

Magistrates in the eighteenth century tended to be socially and ideologically conservative. Propertied nobles who had received a conventional legal education and were eager to retain their privileges, they could prove quite hostile to the new philosophy of the Enlightenment. At the same time, however, they mistrusted royal authority, especially when it came to taxes. In the late 1750s and early 1760s, when Louis XV ordered the courts to approve a series of tax decrees, the magistrates erupted in an explosion of defiance.[45] Not since the great rebellion of the Fronde (1648–1652) had parlementaires mounted such a brazen challenge to the crown's fiscal encroachments. In the southeast, when the cessation of war in 1763 failed to bring expected tax relief, the parlement of Grenoble wrote extraordinarily fierce remonstrances that, echoing Goudar and the Physiocrats, tore into the tax farmers. "The luxury and pomp of these public enemies are an insult to the people's misery." Having denied access to the king, they let loose "an army of oppressors" who spread "desolation and terror" throughout the countryside. "Pallid citizens struggle against hunger, thirst, and nakedness, the turn of the seasons only augmenting their torture. Somber places of refuge scarcely suffice to hide their shame, their needs, and their hopelessness." Only the king could restore prosperity to the nation by slaying the "hydra" of the Farm.[46]

Central to the critique that the magistrates of Grenoble formulated was a blistering assault on the smuggling commissions, "sinister tribunals in which the blood of liberty runs at the whim and furor of the Traitant." The mere existence of those commissions "dishonors humanity, spreads fear and terror, and burdens with irons a free nation that might otherwise be flourishing and formidable." Of course, some of the parlement's ire stemmed from petty jurisdictional rivalry, for the commission of Valence had usurped its power to judge smugglers. But there was also a deep-seated belief among the magistrates that the commission's severity unnecessarily escalated the conflict over contraband. When contraband cases had been entrusted to the parlement, the prosecuting attorney of Grenoble recalled, both Farm agents and locals were better off. Agents were safer because "smugglers taken by surprise simply dropped their goods and fled," and residents "lived in peace without fearing the insults or excesses of [Farm] employees."[47] The introduction of repressive commissions raised the level of violence for all concerned.

What made the remonstrances of this period so subversive was not simply the confrontational language they contained but the methods by which they were diffused to the public. The parlement of Grenoble had long shown its respect for the crown by treating its remonstrances as state secrets destined for the king's eyes only. But in September 1764, following the recent practice of bolder courts, the magistrates reached beyond private lines of royal communication to take their opposition directly to the public in the form of a printed remonstrance that condemned the commission of Valence as an illegitimate "tribunal of blood."[48] In Paris, where parlementaires were closely tied to financiers through personal investments and family relations, the boldest public statements against royal fiscality emanated from rogue pamphlets rather than formal remonstrances. Two such pamphlets attracted tremendous public attention in 1763 and 1764. *Richesse de l'État* by Pierre-Philippe Roussel de la Tour took the magistrate's audacious new tax plan to the public after he failed to persuade colleagues in the Paris parlement to act on it. Simple, concise, and initially circulated free of charge, the publication became a sensation in the spring and summer of 1763. "All the public has it in hand," wrote one chronicler; "consequently even the people discuss it and wish its implementation."[49]

Roussel's reform plan involved a global recasting of the tax system whereby almost all existing levies would be replaced by one direct tax. The simplicity of the plan and its allusion to a single direct tax had a whiff of Physiocracy about it, but Roussel's tax would not be imposed exclusively on the net product of landowners. Instead, it would fall on the kingdom's two million richest subjects, grouped into twenty tax brackets based on their wealth. The advantages of this plan, its author contended, were manifold. Not only would it yield a windfall of revenue for a deeply indebted crown and simplify a convoluted and wasteful fiscal system. It would also dramatically reduce the weight of consumption taxes, which, the author observed, as had Rousseau, "the poor pay out of the necessities of life." Fiscalizing consumption was unfair because it struck the poor with devastating force. Further, once the Farm downsized, the monarchy would no longer need its "army of lowly tax agents," and jurisdiction over contraband cases would revert back to the people's "natural judges" in customary parlements and *cours des aides*.

Roussel's pamphlet excited a "flood" of at least forty tracts on tax reform.[50] The cacophony of ideas generated by opponents and proponents of reform, one historian has recently noted, produced "for the first time in France a genuine public debate on the critical theme of fiscality," just as the calico controversy had generated the first major public debate on protectionism a few years earlier.[51] Once again, the monarchy turned to royal historiographer Moreau, who had battled with Morellet over *indiennes*, but Moreau could no more control the groundswell of opinion on taxation than he had been able to direct the previous affair. Although many pamphlets that appeared in the 1763–1764 debate shared Roussel's general impulse toward reform, one work enjoyed particularly wide popularity: *L'Anti-financier, ou relevé de quelques-unes des malversations dont se rendent journellement coupables les fermiers généraux, & des vexations qu'ils commettent dans les provinces*, written by Jean Baptiste Darigrand, a firebrand of a barrister from the Paris *cour des aides*. Like Mirabeau, Darigrand would be imprisoned for his incendiary rhetoric against the Farm but not before his work hit the mark. *L'Anti-financier* endorsed Roussel's tax plan but in language that was much stronger than Roussel dared use. The barrister fearlessly hurled invective at the Farmers General, "public bloodsuckers" who amassed fortunes overnight, lived in "appalling luxury," and left gross inheritances to their children—all at taxpayer expense. The "army of agents" it commanded, some 80,000 strong, wasted public money and evaded its own fiscal obligations by exploiting the tax perquisites. The Farm was a "monster," a "scourge" that had to be stopped before it brought down the kingdom.

L'Anti-financier was more than just bluster. As a former agent of the Farm who turned on his employers to join the *cour des aides*, Darigrand knew the intricacies of the company—how it harvested taxes, guarded against contraband, and prosecuted suspected smugglers—and he used his insider knowledge to launch an attack more penetrating than any previous condemnation. Darigrand was well aware that he was piercing a veil of secrecy: "all those who are initiated in the mysteries of Finance swear on the blood of the people never to reveal its secrets."[52] But it was time to expose the intimate links between the "vexations" committed by Farm agents and the very structure of the institution. Featured in the work's title, the word *vexation* had a powerful resonance in the second half of the eighteenth century, when it alluded to any number of humiliating abuses of power inflicted on individuals by avaricious petty officials.[53] Such vexations were exasperatingly common, Darigrand explained, because the Farm offered significant financial incentives to its agents to conduct visits, pat-downs, searches, seizures, and arrests. "These little tyrants" entrapped suspects, framed the innocent, and issued false reports, as they scoured the countryside in perpetual search of pecuniary gain. How many readers did not shake with rage at the thought of "impudent" customs officials arbitrarily stopping carriages, unpacking goods, frisking suspects, and sexually abusing female travelers with utter impunity?[54] Lest readers doubt the extent of such degrading violations of personal liberty, Darigrand invited them to visit the French prisons in which innumerable innocents were falsely detained for fraud.[55]

Abuses in policing paled in comparison to those committed by the Farm's courts. According to Darigrand, as many as 30,000 cases a year passed through a labyrinth of tribunals, at the center of which lay the commissions themselves, those "burning chambers" "cemented by the blood" of their victims. The procedure of these courts was totally corrupt. Those who provided depositions that decided defendants' fates were the same Farm agents who arrested suspects and received money for their capture. And who sat in judgment? Not the "natural judges" of the *cours des aides* who traditionally heard contraband cases but special arbiters appointed and handsomely remunerated by the Farm. "Paid by the Farmers, their hands filled with gold, these judges dare to pronounce verdicts on those who have defrauded the Farm!"[56] Only financiers could have concocted a system of justice that converted fines on the poor into galleys sentences, made smugglers' families disappear without a trace, and condemned otherwise innocent men to death. To elicit readers' sympathy for the oppressed, Darigrand paused to paint a prison scene, not unlike the tableaus evoked in melodramatic lawyers' briefs, in which he stood by the side of condemned traffickers:

The trial completed, they are weighed down with chains. I help them lift their arms from the depth of their prison cells toward the Throne. I join my cries with theirs: "Oh my King! Oh well-loved King, deign turn your eyes on these unfortunates. These are your Subjects, your children. They are guilty, I admit. But when judging them, let it be remembered that they are only guilty of fraud." We are not heard. Already the whips, the hot irons, the chains, the gallows are being prepared.[57]

This exposé on the war against contraband confirmed readers' worst fears. Soon there would be only three estates in France: "the king and his august family, financiers, and slaves." The only solution was to eliminate indirect taxes and destroy the Farm.

To cap the explosion of such subversive language, controller general L'Averdy imposed his famous law of silence on works about royal finance. The declaration of 28 March 1764 prohibited all royal subjects from "publishing, selling or peddling any writings, works or projects concerning the reform of our finances, or their past, present, or future administration."[58] Although the declaration never managed to shut down public discussion, it did for several years dampen the lively debate on finance that climaxed in 1763–1764.

Criminal Law Reform

As the fury over taxation subsided, a gust of reformist thought blew into France from Milan. When Malesherbes discovered *Dei delitti e delle pene* in 1764, the magistrate could count on one hand the number of works calling for a reform of the French criminal justice system. Montesquieu had made appeals for penal leniency in *Lettres persanes* and *De l'esprit des lois,* Rousseau had come out against the death penalty in *Du contrat social,* and Voltaire had taken up his pen in defense of Jean Calas, a Protestant falsely accused of having murdered his son.[59] But it took a young Italian outlier named Cesare Beccaria to bring the pieces together into a systematic critique of European criminal law. Steeped in the works of the French Enlightenment, Beccaria adopted from Montesquieu the paradox that moderate governments ruled more effectively than authoritarian ones. From Helvétius and Condillac, he took the fundamentally secular principles of utilitarianism and human psychology. And from Rousseau, after whose heroine in *La Nouvelle Héloïse* he would name his daughter Guilia, Beccaria appropriated fierce moral conviction. A gentleman who had broken with his parents over a love affair with a woman of lesser status, he rejected his elders' world of privilege and custom in favor of a society based on humanity, rational government, and legal equality.

Des délits et des peines sounded a "melody of sentiment" to enhance its emotional appeal.[60] If Gournay, Mirabeau, and Darigrand sprinkled their treatises with sentimental turns of phrase, Beccaria saturated his book with them, hoping to elicit sympathy for those trapped in a needlessly cruel judicial system and to encourage fellow humanitarians to join the cause of radical reform. A sentimentalist, Beccaria was no less a social scientist and mathematician who founded his analysis on two bedrock principles. The first, utilitarianism, held that the behavior of human beings should not be understood in theological terms of good and evil. Rather, men and women act simply to maximize pleasure and minimize pain. From that axiom it followed that governments could raise the general level of happiness in society by aligning their legal system with man's natural utilitarian pursuits. All current legal practices should therefore be evaluated "from the point of view of whether or not they conduce to *the greatest happiness shared among the greater number*," a principle later enshrined by Jeremy Bentham.[61] The other theory on which Beccaria's manifesto was founded was that of the social contract, the notion that men had passed from a state of nature into political society through an act of association by which they yielded some measure of natural liberty in exchange for greater security. Any legal practice that violated the terms of that basic contract was illegitimate. Armed with these two powerful ideas, Beccaria laid siege to the entire coterie of practices that constituted old-regime criminal justice: the presumption of guilt over innocence, the cloak of secrecy that shrouded trials, the use of torture to elicit confessions, the arcane system of proof by which judges reached verdicts, and, above all, the cruel disproportionality between crime and punishment.

For Beccaria, no offense better illustrated rank disproportionality between crime and punishment than smuggling. The discrepancies between popular perceptions of smugglers and the punishments imposed on them were as evident as they were intolerable. Because people did not directly experience any negative effects from illicit trade—if anything, they benefited from it—they were apt to have a more favorable opinion of a smuggler than of "a thief, a forger of signatures or those who commit other offences that might affect them directly."[62] And yet the punishment of smugglers was equal to or more severe than that of criminals widely regarded as scoundrels. Such disparity between popular morality and criminal punishment violated the principle "that the disgrace inflicted by the law be the same as . . . is dictated by universal morality or the particular morality which arises from particular systems, which are the lawgivers to common opinion in any given nation."[63] Since infamy ultimately derived from common opinion and not the act of punishment itself, kings and magistrates could not ignore popular morality when setting penalties.

To restore some proportionality between the crime of smuggling and its punishment, Beccaria offered several solutions. One was to recognize at the outset that contraband was a crime "which arises from the law itself." Building on an earlier essay in which he employed differential calculus to describe the relationship between tariffs and trafficking, he analyzed the economic principle that the higher the customs duty (or more absolute the prohibition), the greater the temptation to evade it.[64] The first order of business, then, was to keep customs taxes low or, in the case of a state monopoly, to set moderate retail prices, which would sharply reduce the incidence of smuggling. Those traffickers who nevertheless persisted in plying their trade must, he believed, contrary to the Physiocrats, be caught and punished. But their punishment "should not involve dishonor since [smuggling] does not seem disgraceful in the eyes of the public." Admittedly a real crime, running contraband did not merit the infamy that current sentencing attempted to attach. Because the punishment of any crime must derive from its damage to society, traffickers should be punished relatively lightly, with confiscations of their contraband and the gear used to transport it. In serious cases, some form of "penal servitude" (hard labor) would be in order but not the kind imposed on assassins or thieves. The penal labor of a convicted tobacco smuggler, for example, "ought to be limited to toil and exertion in the excise service which he wished to defraud."[65]

Although Beccaria did not suggest a specific punishment for violent smugglers, such as those found guilty of murdering Farm agents, he made it perfectly clear that he did not believe in the death penalty. Death by the wheel was barbaric: "Can the wailings of a wretch, perhaps, undo what has been done and turn back the clock?" "The purpose of punishment is not that of tormenting or afflicting any sentient being nor of undoing a crime already committed" but rather "to prevent the offender from doing fresh harm to his fellows and to deter others from doing likewise."[66] Less painful methods of imposing capital punishment, like hanging, were no more justified by utility or the social contract. From a utilitarian perspective, hard labor was far superior to the death penalty. First, it was a more effective deterrent. Public executions were spectacular to be sure, but because they were instantaneous, they made less of an impression on the minds of spectators than did the continuous sight of hard labor, which would dissuade any would-be criminal from embarking on a life of crime. Second, penal servitude was more productive, since convict labor could be employed in public works projects of all kinds. What use was there for the corpse of an executed convict? Of scant utility, the death penalty was no more legitimate from the point of view of the social contract. No person entering into such a contract would willingly surrender to the state the power to take his or her life.

It would be difficult to overstate Beccaria's influence on the movement for French legal reform. In the final decades of the old regime, *Des délits et des peines* galvanized liberal magistrates and lawyers, emboldening them to challenge what they perceived to be a needlessly cruel and ineffectual system of punishment exemplified by the inhumane repression of smuggling.[67] In 1767, Joseph Michel Antoine Servan, the attorney-general of the parlement of Grenoble whom Voltaire dubbed the "Cicero of Dauphiné," chose to illustrate the rank disproportionality between crime and punishment with an example from the war on traffickers. "An unfortunate man, with the vain trappings of some arms, which the threat of violence perhaps forced him to take, introduces some prohibited goods, and for the modest profit he has taken from the richest men of the state one wants him to pay on the wheel." Did it make sense to subject the author of a crime which "nature" excused to the same punishment as that inflicted on parricides? "If blood is spilled for the least misdemeanors, there will not be enough of it for great crimes."[68] Parisian lawyer and future Girondin Brissot de Warville agreed completely. In a prize-winning essay that drew on what had by the 1780s become a canon of authors—political economists Goudar, Mirabeau, and Le Trosne; the magistrate Malesherbes; and philosophes Montesquieu and Beccaria—he argued that a pecuniary violation like smuggling should be punished with a pecuniary fine and nothing more, in accordance with "the Law of proportion" between crime and punishment.[69]

Beccaria's decisive intervention also opened the way for *philosophes* to join the fray over smuggling and the judicial repression it occasioned. In 1781, one of the most eminent philosophers of the late Enlightenment, the Marquis de Condorcet, declaimed against the use of the death penalty in cases of recidivist and gang-based smugglers. A few years prior, he had assailed salt and tobacco monopolies that owed their existence "to the weakness, corruption, and ignorance of the legislative power."[70] Now he narrowed his sights to the legal abuses of the Farm: "It is inconceivable that men would solicit such laws or pronounce them against their fellows; either the farmers [general] do not regard salt smugglers as beings of the same species or the farmers themselves are not men." In an extended satirical discussion, the philosopher condemned every aspect of the judicial apparatus at work in the war on smuggling: the right of Farm guards to shoot and kill smugglers who resisted arrest, the automatic conversion of fines to galley sentences, the inability of executions to deter a public that did not regard trafficking as a crime, and the procedures of commissions whose judges and witnesses were in the Farm's pocket. The whole legal infrastructure appeared to be designed according to the obscene maxim "that the weak and the poor must be sacrificed for the tranquility of the powerful and the rich."[71]

As was his wont, Diderot expressed his outrage in narrative form. *Les deux amis de Bourbonne* (1770) featured the young smuggler "Felix," arrested "arms in hand" and brought before the commission of Reims, the president of which was none other than the "terrible" Colleau, "whose temperament is perhaps the most savage that nature ever formed." After Colleau condemns Felix to the gallows, "like five hundred others who preceded him there," the latter's friend Olivier begs the president for permission to see his pal one last time. Colleau seats Olivier in a chair, calmly takes out his watch, and lets it wind down half an hour before announcing that if Olivier wants to see his dear friend alive, he'd better hurry, for Felix "will be swinging before ten minutes are up." Enraged, Olivier knocks Colleau unconscious and sprints to the site of the execution, where he proceeds to strike down the hangman and incite a riot among a populace "full of indignation at the large number of recent executions."[72] Olivier is fatally wounded by the bayonet of a mounted police officer, but Felix escapes, grief-stricken at the loss of the dear friend who saved his life. An exercise in literary naturalism, Diderot's tale contrasted the shallow heartlessness of Colleau with the deep loyalty between Olivier and Felix, putting an altogether human face on the figure of the indigent trafficker.[73]

If Diderot used narrative to blast the commissions, Voltaire characteristically employed satire. In 1768, two years after publishing his influential *Commentaire* on Beccaria, he took up the subject of smuggling. Riffing on his own *Candide,* Voltaire wrote that it was impossible, in the best of all possible worlds, for such scourges on humanity such as the pox, the plague, scrofula, the Inquisition, and the "chambre de Valence" to enter into the composition of the universe. Associating the commission of Valence with the infamous Inquisition underscored the horror of the former's secrecy and cruelty. A decade later, arguing against the death penalty, Voltaire would propose that dangerous criminals be transported to the colonies, not executed. "Mandrin, the most magnanimous of all smugglers, should have been sent to the depths of Canada to fight savages" rather than broken on the wheel in Valence.[74]

In the wake of *Des délits et des peines,* the most scathing tirade against the commissions appeared in 1775 in the form of an anonymous book entitled *Sur les finances.* Ostensibly another call to replace all taxes with a single land tax, the author shifted effortlessly in this post-Beccarian climate to judicial questions, expending most of his energy detailing the corrupt procedures and penal cruelty of the Farm's "tribunals of blood." Filling in outlines that Montesquieu had only sketched a generation earlier, the book described in lurid detail the vices inherent in the branch of justice that had been handed over to financiers. If police, witnesses, and judges "all share the spoils of the unfortunate victim who falls into their hands," convictions were forgone conclusions. And "as there is never any appeal beyond these tribunals, as everything is done there in silence & pitch-black darkness, & since the thirst for gold pronounces the verdicts, what horrible, execrable things are not committed in these dens of iniquity?" Reprising Voltaire's analogy to the Inquisition, the author targeted two judges in particular for their extreme ruthlessness: Levet, the "Torquemada" of the Farmers General who "savored the torments and pain of the wretches he executed," and his successor Colleau, whom Diderot and Condorcet had also singled out for brutality. Having executed a man for assisting a smuggler's escape, Colleau was awarded the presidency of the commission of Valence and wasted no time in his new position. "I passed through Valence eight times, & eight times I saw exposed on the highway the fresh cadavers of seven to eight hanged, & two or three wheeled." "Gaze upon your fellow man, your fellow citizen," the author beseeched, "who expires on the wheel for what in civilized states is called contraband." Humanity demanded the creation of a new system of justice to restore the balance between crime and punishment.[75]

Malesherbes

Synthesizing the ideas of political economists, conservative magistrates, and liberal reformers, Malesherbes formulated the century's most profound critique of the fiscal-judicial war on smuggling. As director of the Royal Publishing Office (1750 to 1763) and president of the *cour des aides* of Paris (1750–1771, 1774–1775), he had supported the Gournay circle in the 1750s, developed his own theory of consumer sovereignty regarding the book trade in 1758–1759, favored the publication of Mirabeau's 1760 *Théorie de l'impôt,* and asked Morellet to translate Beccaria into French in 1764.[76] During the two final decades of the old regime, Malesherbes would serve as the elder statesman of the movement for criminal law reform. Fusing Beccarian legal philosophy, an intimate knowledge of the Farm derived from his own investigations, and an incisive political theory of despotism based on Montesquieu, he used his position as head of the highest tax court in the land to sound the alarm against tyranny.

Malesherbes's attitudes toward the Farm underwent a distinct evolution. As early as 1756, he had campaigned within government circles against the "great number of bloody executions" conducted by the upstart smuggling commissions.[77] In the mid-1760s, he backed off the issue of contraband after the crown, conceding that the commissions of Reims and Saumur violated the jurisdiction of the Paris *cour des aides,* restructured the two tribunals.[78] Henceforth, three magistrates from the court would sit on the two commissions, a change that may have been responsible for slowing death-penalty rates. Although the *cour des aides* did not pass up the opportunity to instruct the king that, as long as excessive consumption taxes remained in place, no law, no matter how "terrible" or "rigorous," could stop underground trade, the court muted its objections now that the two commissions were under its influence.[79] In 1770, however, Malesherbes went back on the offensive after a shocking incident radicalized his already critical view of the Farm. It came to his attention that a tradesman by the name of Guillaume Monnerat had been falsely accused of smuggling and tossed in the Bicêtre, Paris's notorious prison-hospital. There, Monnerat was clasped in irons and confined to a dank, infested, pitch-black subterranean cell for two months before being transferred, for medical reasons, to an above-ground compartment for at least another year. Meanwhile, Farm officials attempted to dig up enough evidence to initiate a trial, all to no avail. An apparent victim of mistaken identity, Monnerat was released into the streets of Paris after having been subjected to the misery of the Bicêtre and robbed of two years of his life. He promptly filed suit.

As president of the *cour des aides,* Malesherbes jumped on the case, seeing an opportunity to investigate the pernicious practices of the war on contraband. Following a thorough examination, the court decided in the plaintiff's favor and awarded him 50,000 lt damages against the Farm, a stern warning to the company that it would henceforth pay dearly for abusing its police powers. But Monnerat would never touch the money due him. Before the judgment could take effect, the royal council, at the behest of the Farmers General, stepped in to block the damages and seize jurisdiction over the affair. The *cour des aides* responded in kind, issuing a decree of its own that nullified the action of the royal council. Malesherbes attempted to break the stalemate by negotiating with state ministers, but he was not to be heard. "If the Government wished to seize an opportunity to make a brilliant show of authority," the frustrated president wrote the chancellor, "I dare say, Monseigneur, that this occasion was very poorly chosen."[80] To end the affair once and for all, Louis XV summoned a delegation of magistrates to Compiègne and personally chastised them for disobeying him.

Malesherbes would not let it go, having learned too much from the Monnerat affair to stop now. Fresh from their visit to the royal palace, the magistrates fired off remonstrances that condemned Monnerat's barbarous treatment by the Farm. In particular, the court took aim at the use of *lettres de cachet,* sealed orders from the king that authorized the imprisonment of individuals. Such letters commonly served family members wishing to sequester mentally ill or poorly behaved relatives who threatened to dishonor the family name, but in the

1730s, controller-general Orry began to issue them for the express purpose of imprisoning suspected traffickers.[81] *Lettres* offered a way to incarcerate suspects temporarily (up to several months) while officials hunted for forensic evidence. If evidence was found, suspects were delivered to the appropriate tribunal. If not, they were released, having been taught a lesson for their alleged misdeeds. It was the use of *lettres* for precisely this purpose that Malesherbes stumbled upon when investigating the circumstances surrounding Monnerat's imprisonment. The Farm controller who arrested the unfortunate man had used a *lettre* to dispatch him to the bowels of the Bicêtre, where, as remonstrances reminded the king, he was put in "cells reserved for rogues guilty of the most atrocious crimes." "Your majesty will find it hard to believe that a man suspected of fraud was barbarously held in this abode of horror for more than a month." Even if this were not a case of mistaken identity and Monnerat was in fact a smuggler, Malesherbes reasoned (with Beccaria in mind), he did not deserve to be locked up in "these dreadful dungeons; because in the end there must be some proportion between crimes and punishments." At the very least, punishment should not be arbitrarily exacted by lower-level Farm officials entrusted with a penal tool as powerful as *lettres de cachet*. Under such conditions, our very lives and liberty "are at the mercy of a financier."[82]

Not long after the court submitted its remonstrances, the ministers of Louis XV orchestrated a coup d'état that would recast politics for the remainder of the old regime. In 1771, unwilling to brook further opposition from superior law courts, chancellor René Nicolas Charles Augustin de Maupeou introduced a sweeping reform of the judiciary, abolishing in one bold stroke three quarrelsome parlements and packing the remaining courts with a new crop of handpicked magistrates. The Paris *cour des aides* was dissolved and Malesherbes exiled to his country estate. With the courts neutralized, the crown could introduce law without having to suffer the judicial resistance that had constrained it for decades. And so the old judicial order was disbanded.

Three years later in 1774, the young Louis XVI ascended the throne and recalled the old parlements and *cours des aides* to duty. Although many chastised magistrates never recovered their fortitude, the indefatigable Malesherbes came roaring back, vigorously carrying opposition to the Farm into the new reign. If anything, the Maupeou coup further radicalized Malesherbes's vision of old-regime politics, and he seized the opportunity of his court's return to show the new sovereign how the Farm was actively perverting liberty, justice, and humanity in the midst of his seemingly tranquil kingdom. To emphasize the Farm's systematic abuse of its authority, the remonstrances of 6 May 1775, applied a word with harrowing connotations: *despotism.* That word, analyzed by Montesquieu, hurled at the crown since the religious and fiscal disputes of the 1750s and 1760s, and given fresh urgency after the Maupeou coup, was now aimed directly at the Farm.

One of the century's most important formulations of political thought, the remonstrances developed Montesquieu's association between despotism and tax farming by distinguishing royal absolutism, according to which the king legitimately held unlimited authority, from despotism, by which "each of the executors of his orders also employs a power without limits." By this definition, Malesherbes charged, no institution in France exercised despotic power quite like the Farm. At one level, as Darigrand's treatise had shown, despotism manifested itself in the myriad "vexations" committed by an "innumerable army of agents" who, goaded by financial incentives, did not hesitate to search, seize, arrest, and, Malesherbes emphasized after judging the Monnerat affair, imprison. More profoundly still, the Farmers General were reshaping the very structure of the monarchy as they violated barriers between judicial, legislative, and executive power that Montesquieu had deemed essential to liberty.[83] Over the preceding century, the financiers who ran the company had escaped oversight and established themselves as "legislators." Expelling law courts, the royal council, and even the king himself from the legislative process, tax farmers effectively wrote their own laws, which were rubber-stamped by the finance minister. Not content to dominate the legislative process, they also took over the judiciary by establishing extraordinary tribunals and a fictive royal council that, in reality, consisted only of the finance minister, the Farm's puppet.[84] In this closed circuit of judicial authority that permitted the tax farmer to serve as his own judge, procedure deteriorated rapidly, as *procès-verbaux* came to be "regarded as fixed, and fraud as proven," while punishment grew to ghastly proportions as smugglers were dispatched to galleys and scaffolds as if they had committed "great crimes." The inhumanity of imposing such penalties on mere fiscal criminals would surely not escape the king's notice: "we do not doubt that Your Majesty is moved by the account of these cruelties, and that he asks how it came to be that the death penalty was pronounced against citizens out of a financial interest."[85]

The picture painted by Malesherbes was grim but not beyond reform. The long-term solution was the convocation of the estates general, the national political body that had not been called in more than a century and a half.[86] In its absence, the magistrature had stepped in to assert the ancient right of the French "to speak to our kings and protest with liberty against the infraction of laws and national rights."[87] But it had become painfully obvious since the Maupeou coup that the courts did not have the power to defeat despotism. Only the estates general could force the crown to abolish the terrible system by which taxes were collected. While waiting for the king to convoke that national body—and who knew how long that would take—one tool of reform remained to curb fiscal, administrative, and legal abuses: state publicity. The same man who facilitated the publication of economic literature and encouraged Morellet to translate Beccaria turned once more to publicity to hasten reform. The remonstrances declared that all government acts, including Farm regulations, *lettres de cachet,* judicial memoirs, and court rulings, should be printed for public scrutiny. This was not so much an "innovation," a dirty word in old-regime politics, as a return to the halcyon days before reading and writing when government affairs had been conducted orally. After the golden age of oral publicity had passed, the written word cloaked state operations, allowing the real innovation of despotism to arise. But such was the power of print that it could usher in a new age of transparency and liberate France once and for all.[88]

It was in this spirit that, despite royal efforts to prevent their circulation, the remonstrances of 1775, like the previous anti-Maupeou remonstrances of February 1771, were themselves published in 1778, 1779, and 1789, to the acclaim of the literary world.[89] "There are few texts," opined Bachaumont, chronicler of the republic of letters, "that merit so much attention. . . . It is a masterpiece of patriotism, written with as much vigor as logic. . . . The more one discusses the remonstrances of the cour des aides, the more one finds them beautiful and admirable."[90]

In the second half of the eighteenth century, writers substantially widened the purview of the Enlightenment by exploring problems of political economy and criminal law. One of the many consequences of this conceptual shift was the vertiginous growth in public criticism of the Farm. Of course, the French literati had long vilified tax farmers. In the sixteenth and seventeenth centuries, moralists berated social-climbing financiers to found a tradition that would persist into the eighteenth century with Alain-René Lesage's 1709 play *Turcaret* and Montesquieu's 1721 *Lettres persanes,* both of which poked fun at the vulgarity of men of finance. But from the 1750s, as the high Enlightenment literatures of political economy and legal reform burgeoned—and as the Farmers General integrated themselves into the nobility[91]—critique expanded beyond questions of personal character to confront an interlocking system of tax farming, trade prohibitions, fiscal monopolies, and judicial repression. Rather than endorsing contraband rebellion on the basis of a right to resistance, writers placed the struggle between Farm and trafficker in strikingly new theoretical contexts to demand an immediate overhaul of the fiscal and judicial system. Indeed, the urgent tone of such impassioned calls contrasted with appeals for the reform of direct taxation, which evoked the specter of tyranny in far less visceral terms. Adversaries of Farm monopolies and prohibitions conjured a *crueler* form of despotism by which a nefarious fiscal-judicial complex threatened to engulf the monarchy completely if reforms were not immediately implemented.

Political economists, men of law, and legal reformers employed overlapping languages to contest the perceived tyranny of this complex. Goudar gave voice to Mandrin to claim that the Farm had violated the financial reciprocity between king and people, sapping the realm's resources. Gournay and his associates appealed to the principle of consumer sovereignty, valorizing consumer demand and the illicit traders who fed it. And the Physiocrats articulated the concept of a natural order that absolved illicit traders of their crimes; if smugglers were guilty of violating positive law, they in no way transgressed the natural laws of the economy. Although political economists often treated illicit trade as a symptom of more fundamental issues, their engagement with the underground drew them into a shockingly violent world of rebellion and repression at the center of which lay the Farm, a grotesque outgrowth of a state that heedlessly violated the dictates of reason, nature, and humanity. Less concerned with the laws of nature than with the "fundamental" laws of the kingdom, magistrates and lawyers protested against the "vexations" of Farm agents and the severity of the smuggling commissions, while more philosophically minded legal reformers inveighed against the inhumanity of French criminal justice. The draconian punishment of smugglers became a prime example of the barbarity of the penal code.

Although I sympathize with eighteenth-century efforts to decriminalize smuggling, my aim here is not to celebrate the intellectuals and jurists who, as they engaged in public debates on commercial regulation and state finance, defended smugglers against the forces of repression. To be sure, the reform movements of the high Enlightenment aimed to improve the earthly conditions of mankind, an ambitious and worthy goal, but the project to better society was not always straightforward. The same magistrates who railed against the commissions were caught up in petty professional rivalries and could be openly hostile to broader projects of reform. The same economists who invoked natural law to rehabilitate traffickers ferociously denounced jobless vagabonds and showed little compassion for the poor. And the same legal reformers who spoke of a common humanity aimed to make punishment swifter and more certain—"not to punish less, but to punish better," as Michel Foucault famously wrote.[92] If we have learned anything from the past generation of scholarship on the Enlightenment, it is that the movement was fragmented and riddled with contradictions, committing itself to lofty universalist principles while excluding various groups from the project of emancipation on the grounds of sex, skin color, and social status. Hence, the same liberal economic logic that emboldened many thinkers to defend smugglers against charges of criminality encouraged a merciless disregard for the underprivileged. In this way, the writers who reconceptualized economics and law in the eighteenth century redirected the stigma of criminality onto other lowly social groups who, in their eyes, better represented the dangerous social underworld of the old regime. They also deflected it onto the Farm itself, which, they alleged, was running the real criminal enterprise.

The sheer force of this challenge to the legitimacy of the Farm begs the question: did the literary assault on the institution tarnish the credibility of the monarchy? As the Farm became a lightning rod for criticism, did the king suffer collateral damage or was he spared by an institution that, attracting vitriol to itself, drew condemnation away from the throne? Certainly, the popular image of Louis XV did not remain unsullied in the middle decades of the century, thanks to a series of volatile religious, fiscal, and subsistence crises.[93] In the 1760s and early 1770s, as notions of kingly virtue developed among the learned, a wide gap yawned between the ideals of kingship and perceptions of the actual condition of the monarchy.[94] Louis XVI seems to have fared better, garnering popular support at the end of the old regime before squandering it in the Revolution. Yet, regardless of how subjects viewed particular monarchs, the increasingly wide circulation of the idea that the Farm was engaging in the systematic abuse of power dramatically raised expectations for imminent and thorough institutional reform. Although the notion of the Enlightenment as a single, coherent emancipatory movement is no longer tenable, its extraordinary reformist thrust cannot be denied. By the final decades of the old regime, much of the educated public had come to desire a root-and-branch reform of the state, beginning with the gargantuan Farm.

The burden to implement such reform fell squarely on the crown, and it is here that criticism of the Farm may have colored perceptions of the king. Faced with significant contraband rebellion and vociferous public debate, the monarchy could either heed criticism and shed itself of the Farm or run the risk of allowing hostility to grow to dangerous levels. As the journalist Mercier exclaimed of the contract Louis XVI signed with the Farmers General:

> What a ruinous bargain, what a disastrous and illusory contract the sovereign has signed! He consented to public misery, to be less rich himself. I would like to be able to knock down this vast and infernal machine, which seizes every citizen by the throat, drains his blood without his being able to resist, and dispenses it to two or three hundred individuals who possess the entire mass of wealth.[95]

Frustrated with the king's acquiescence to the Farm, Mercier was forced to dream of destroying the institution himself. That dream would become a reality during the French Revolution.

12

Revolution

IN 2005–2006, perched on a crag overlooking the alpine city of Grenoble, the Musée Dauphinois mounted a splendid exhibition on its native son, Louis Mandrin. Although curators carefully situated the smuggler in historical perspective, differentiating between life and legend, viewers of the exhibition had their own ideas about Mandrin, which they enthusiastically expressed in hundreds of comments, drawings, and calls to action scribbled in spiral notebooks placed at the end of the exhibition. Museumgoers from the extreme right of the political spectrum either dismissed Mandrin as just another *dealer de shit* ("drug dealer") or wished for the return of a latter-day Mandrin to cleanse the nation of criminality. Many more from the political center and left, some of whom had sung the *Complainte* in grade school or summer camp, situated Mandrin in the context of the French Revolution. Although executed a good thirty-four years before 1789, Mandrin was widely perceived as a precursor to that world-historical event. "The beginnings of the Revolution were already [present] in the actions of Louis Mandrin," wrote one viewer. "Liberté, Égalité, Fraternité!" "Vive la Révolution!" declared others, putting the smuggler squarely in a revolutionary tradition that they hoped would regenerate France once again. A revivified Mandrin would establish a new political and social order by stamping out "our present-day farmers-general": namely, IMF bankers, WTO officials, and corrupt businessmen and politicians.[1]

Mandrin was no revolutionary *avant la lettre*, however. He certainly flouted the law and attacked Farm agents, but, aside from his conspicuous method of turning the tables on the Farm, he articulated no comprehensive revolutionary program, galvanized no movement for the seizure of power, and seems not to have harbored ill will toward the king, in whose army he twice asked to serve. And yet, in the decades following his execution, as his exploits passed into the realm of legend, the illicit economy for which he stood became ever more politicized. Men of letters (including Ange Goudar, who reprised the *Testament politique* in 1789) furiously denounced the Farm and its monopolies.[2] Tax rebellions spiked in the countryside as countless of the king's subjects— smuggler and civilian alike—resisted arrest, blocked searches, attacked guard posts, pillaged residences of Farm officials, and rescued captured comrades.[3] The high incidence of contraband revolt reflected the increasingly global parameters of the underground economy, a significant historical development in its own right, but such unrest also contributed heavily to a general rise in popular rebellion. Rebellions became so widespread, in fact, that one historian suggests we see them as a "prerevolutionary" movement that set the stage for the Revolution of 1789: "It is clear that the term 'prerevolution,' widely used for the elite conflicts and crises of the last years of the Old Regime, had a plebeian counterpart, largely neglected in current accounts of revolutionary origins."[4] Just how this plebeian prerevolution fed into the conflagration of the French Revolution is the subject of this chapter.

To emphasize the significance of fiscal rebellion may seem odd in light of recent interpretations of the Revolution. Indeed, if we take in the whole sweep of the Revolution from its early years through the period of the National Convention to the First Empire, there is little doubt that the ultimate winner of the extraordinary event was the state. The abolition of what revolutionaries called "feudalism" weakened the once-dominant clergy and nobility but empowered the French government, which at the beginning of the nineteenth century enjoyed a capacity to wage war, repress social dissent, and raise revenue on a scale that surpassed that of "absolute" kings of the old regime.[5] But we should not let the outcome of the Revolution blind us to its stunning reversals and creativity. The consolidation of state power came late in the game, allowing for radical experiments in popular sovereignty that left an equally enduring legacy.

One of the earliest manifestations of the struggle for popular sovereignty was fiscal insurrection. Although tax rebellion had a major impact on the liberal revolution of 1789–1792, its consequences have largely been forgotten. This is because, in the first place, the Constituent

Assembly's overhaul of the tax system in 1791 is usually attributed to the enduring influence of the Physiocrats, who, as we know, had for decades sought to replace indirect taxes with a single tax on landed income. No less an authority than Ernest Labrousse described the financial policy of the early revolution as "but a compromise with the fiscal program of Physiocracy."[6] To root the new fiscal order in the teachings of the Physiocrats, however, is to risk exaggerating the economists' influence at the expense of popular activism. For if the new fiscal system seemed to bend to Physiocracy, it was also wrought by an actively rebellious populace. Second, social historians who have studied the great revolts of the Revolution have emphasized antiseigneurial, anticonscription, and religious uprisings, as well as particular insurrections in Paris (the taking of the Bastille, the October Days, 10 August 1792, and so on), but have virtually ignored the early fiscal revolts of 1789–1790.[7]

Neither approach is completely wrong. Physiocratic thought *was* influential during the liberal revolution, and antiseigneurial, anticonscription, and religious revolts *did* overtake fiscal rebellion to become the countryside's primary source of unrest. But few historians have noted that, at the Revolution's outset, what royal subjects yearned for above all else was the abolition of indirect taxation.[8] What most bothered ordinary people on its eve were the consumption taxes collected by the General Farm, the symbols par excellence of old-regime despotism. The destruction of those taxes by smugglers, consumers, and legislators would play a decisive role in the formation of a revolutionary state.

Revolutionary Grievances

Among the long-term causes of the French Revolution, state finance has always loomed large. The story usually told of the monarchy's financial crash is one of severe institutional constraints as global war, mounting debt, and a weak tax system conspired to paralyze the eighteenth-century state. Revenue shortfalls led to debt repudiations, debt repudiations generated high default premiums on borrowing, and high default premiums crippled the royal finances.[9] As long as the crown was unwilling to share power with elites in some kind of constitutional monarchy, genuine reform was impossible and the monarchy doomed to fail. While there is much truth to this saga of institutional fragility, it is worth remembering that France remained the premier fiscal power in Europe, enjoying revenues that were more than a third higher than those of Great Britain.[10] Although eighteenth-century France was clearly losing ground to Britain when it came to the costs of servicing public debt and the amount of revenue it raised relative to GDP and population, it was hardly the sclerotic nation of historical caricature. In fact, the financial origins of the French Revolution may lie not only in institutional weakness—what the crown was unable or unwilling to do—but institutional development—what the crown did do and the attitudes its practices generated. The dynamic growth of Farm-based court capitalism may have enriched kings, financiers, and well-connected nobles, but it appears to have deeply alienated broad swaths of society. It was this wider hostility to court capitalism, coupled with structural weaknesses in the financial system itself, that undermined the legitimacy of fiscal institutions and helped create the conditions for the French Revolution.[11]

That revolution began in the spring of 1789, when Louis XVI, his treasury burdened with debt from the American War of Independence, departed from time-honored absolutist policy and convoked the long dormant Estates General. As French men and women from all walks of life prepared for the momentous return of this ancient assembly, they were granted a rare opportunity to air their grievances. Louis XVI invited his subjects to draft *cahiers de doléances,* grievance lists that would guide the deliberations of their newly elected deputies. More than any other set of documents, the *cahiers* reveal what was bothering the French as they stepped to the threshold of revolution in 1789.

Topping the 40,000 lists was the issue of taxation. Investing taxation with constitutional significance, *cahiers* instructed deputies to wrest the power to tax from the monarchy and leverage it to secure a new constitution. If the king wanted the Estates' cooperation in raising taxes, he would have to yield authority to the nation's representatives and accept a constitutional monarchy. But the *cahiers* did not treat all taxes equally. Riddled with exemptions for elites, direct taxes would have to be thoroughly restructured. Once reformed, however, they were to be a pillar of a new constitutional order in which citizens as taxpayers possessed the right to vote and hold office.[12] Indirect taxes, by contrast, were judged much more harshly. Epitomizing all that was rotten under the old regime, they crushed the poor, saddled the kingdom with an

abusive police force, enriched parasitic financiers, and delivered the innocent to an inhumane judicial system. An appalling symbol of the
dark side of the monarchical state, indirect taxes were illegitimate to
the core. The *cahiers* demanded their abolition.[13]

Within the laundry list of indirect levies to be expunged from the
kingdom, salt and tobacco monopolies figured prominently. By far the
most scathing criticism was reserved for the gabelle, which shamelessly
exploited a good considered to be an utter necessity.[14] Because salt is a
"good of prime necessity," the clergy of Aval opined, salt taxes "singu-
larly burden the most indigent class" and should therefore be abolished
immediately.[15] What is surprising, however, is that, contrary to the as-
sertions of a long line of finance ministers, the French saw tobacco in
much the same light. Granted, some *cahiers* classified tobacco as a luxury or at least an "artificial necessity" and were thus sympathetic to the
monopoly.[16] And yet, in an age when commoners snorted or smoked
tobacco on a regular basis, many did not regard their voracious appetite
for leaf as "artificial." On the contrary, the majority of *cahiers* lumped
tobacco with salt under the rubric of necessity. In typical fashion, the
city of Pont-à-Moussan breezily called for the abolition of "all taxes on
salt, tobacco, the sale of which should be free, as well as all other
goods of prime necessity."[17] To illustrate that tobacco was indeed a necessity for the indigent, the community of Plaisir claimed that "unfortunates" who had contracted the habit of taking tobacco were known
to deprive themselves of bread to save enough money to buy Farm
leaf.[18] That the impecunious would sooner forgo bread, *the* quintessen-
tial French necessity, than tobacco proved the latter's status as an absolute necessity.

Having classified salt and tobacco as twin necessities whose exorbitant price squeezed the poor, the *cahiers* developed parallel critiques of
the two monopolies. The problem was not so much that the monopolies
violated hallowed principles of free trade but that they subjected men
and women to invasive policing and unwarranted abuse. Echoing prerevolutionary critiques by Darigrand, Malesherbes, and others, constit-
uents spoke of the "vexations" associated with searches, inspections,
and pat-downs that reduced citizens to the base condition of powerless
slaves. "How many provinces would escape daily inquisition through
the suppression of the gabelle," declared the third estate of Poitiers. "A
tax no less cruel, that on tobacco, should return to nothingness with

the fiscal genie who produced it. . . . May the abolition of these two taxes, scourges of humanity, be for their unfortunate victims the sign of liberty! May a salutary law restore their rights of citizenship!"[19] From the city of Vienne, located in Mandrin's native Dauphiné, came a declaration that only when the monopoly on tobacco was broken and the trade freed would France "be delivered from this frightening multitude of agents, bribed evildoers, whose fiscal infallibility outrages reason and justice."[20] Guards entered a house "like a band of thieves armed with sabers, hunting knives, muskets, or clubs."[21] "Are we not, with respect to salt and tobacco, the slaves of the most reviled men in public opinion?" asked the parish of Dahlain.[22] Characterizing Farm agents as "leaches," "vermin," and bearers of "plague," the *cahiers* exploited a rhetoric of physical menace that called for total eradication.[23] As if to add insult to injury, the money that such "vermin" extracted from taxpayers lined the pockets of plutocratic financiers. "The Farmers General must be suppressed," the parishioners of Buxeuil demanded, "for would it not be better that the immense sums which they gain, or rather which they extort, were sent to the royal treasury than to the hands of these avid *traitants?*"[24]

Especially damning for the salt and tobacco monopolies was the vicious war over contraband. References to "civil" or "internecine" war abound in the grievance lists. In fact, some of the longest digressions in otherwise concise *cahiers* condemned the violence of the armed conflict and the cruelty visited upon smugglers by the criminal justice system. The *bailliage* of Châteauroux complained bitterly of the "80,000 men [who] are armed against each other, some to engage in fraud, others to prevent it. . . . In the center of a civilized kingdom, citizen is armed against citizen; they cut each other's throats in the name of a financial law that . . . sacrifices the smuggler . . . to a sword of justice held by the traitaint's militia."[25] "The rabble of a numerous army," the notaries of Orléans observed, "spend their lives in pursuit of unfortunates, who, drawn by the lure of profit or forced by the most pressing need, do not hesitate to risk everything, even their lives, to procure a good that is a prime necessity for them." An indigent man brought before the law for smuggling is subjected "to the most rigorous prosecution, to fines which absorb whatever resources he had and reduce him to despair or begging, often even exposing him to punishments of infamy, which expel him from society."[26]

The galleys sentence was draconian. The third estate of Beaumont-le-Roger instructed its deputies to put an end to "the sad spectacle of seeing in the galleys those whom fiscality calls smugglers."[27] Converting fines into galleys sentences was cruel, declared the commoners of Boulonnais, who stated that "there is no proportion between the offense of a man caught with some contraband tobacco and the galleys punishment, which is inflicted on him in default of the payment of a fine. It is desperately unjust and severe to confuse simple fraud with public crimes, as the executioner does when he marks both types of offenders indiscriminately with a disgraceful brand."[28] Beccaria could not have put it better.

Such protests were often followed by explicit calls for a general amnesty of underground traders and a restructuring of the criminal justice system. Thirty-five years after Mandrin's gang liberated the prison of Puy, the city's third estate demanded that "those detained in prisons and galleys for smuggling be released and set free."[29] The punishment for trafficking ought in the future to be restricted to the confiscation of merchandise (or, at most, a modest civil fine) in order "to establish a just proportionality between the misdemeanors of contraband and the penalties attached to it."[30] The fearsome smuggling commissions would have to go, too. All too familiar with their business, the third estate of Reims forbade the government from establishing such tribunals in the future. "We demand, consequently, the abolition of commissions which presently exist, notably the one against smugglers, since it is onerous to the State and deprives citizens of the advantage of being judged by their natural judges."[31] The nobility and third estate of Vic chose more dramatic words to condemn the commissions of Reims and Valence: such "tribunals of blood, always favorable to the Farm and paid by it, can only be suspect and dangerous."[32]

On the eve of the French Revolution, the grievance lists confirmed what the ubiquity of smuggling rebellions and the language of reformist treatises had already suggested: that Farm-collected consumption taxes were the most widely detested institutions of the old regime. Although, like consumption taxes, the regulation of calico was policed by the Farm and gave rise to clashes between police and traffickers, hostility to such regulation in 1789 was minimal. The customs dues on calico imports had been so reduced in 1772 (by order of the royal council) and in 1786 (through the Eden Treaty) that the few *cahiers* that bothered to mention *indiennes* at all clamored for higher, not lower, protectionist barriers.[33] Notwithstanding the provocative rhetoric of liberal economists and the rebelliousness of calico traffickers, protectionism itself generated little resentment in the broader population. Of the two forms of state intervention that had stimulated the growth of the French underground—protectionism and fiscalism—the latter alone provoked widespread political opposition at the end of the old regime.

Tearing Down the Wall

On 17 June 1789, after the clergy and nobility proved resistant to sharing power in the Estates General, the third estate dauntlessly declared itself a National Assembly that, representing all of France, would "set out the general will of the nation" and commence the "work of national restoration."[34] Given the demands expressed in the *cahiers*, it is no surprise that the National Assembly's first act, promulgated the very day of its creation, took up taxation. The newborn Assembly boldly asserted the nation's sovereign right to consent to taxation and make fiscal law but declared a worryingly ambiguous tax policy. On the one hand, it declared all existing taxes illegal for having been established without the nation's consent. "Such as they are presently collected in the kingdom," the proclamation read, taxes "are all illegal and consequently null and void in their creation, extension, and prorogation." On the other hand, the Assembly unanimously proclaimed that "although illegally established and collected," taxes would "continue to be levied in the same way that they have been previously" until a new tax system was established.[35] Acting with the prudence one might expect of property owners, the delegates vowed to continue collecting the taxes that had long been levied under the old regime. Although patently illegal, the revenue they generated was necessary to pay interest on the public debt, for which the nation's new representatives had assumed full responsibility.

The mixed fiscal message of 17 June, when combined with Louis XVI's profound ambivalence about the Assembly and Revolution in general, would set off a wave of tax rebellions throughout France that mirrored the *cahiers* in their singular resentment of the Farm's consumption taxes. Although the surge in fiscal rebellion in 1789–1790 was the culmination of a century of violent struggle over contraband, the form

that such resistance took mutated to become part of a wider revolutionary struggle. Not that tax rebellion changed from a "prepolitical" to a
"political" form, as one historian has argued, for it had always been political, as Mandrin's career amply demonstrates.[36] Rather, the meaning
of contraband rebellion expanded as traffickers and consumers broadened the goals of collective action to connect local protests to national
political movements.

Contraband rebellion ignited during the high-stakes political drama
that followed the birth of the National Assembly. Although Louis XVI
begrudgingly tolerated the Assembly at its creation, ordering the first
two estates to join the third in the new legislature, it was not clear
whether he genuinely backed it or was merely playing for time. Parisians soon concluded that the king was stalling when he summoned
thousands of troops to the city with the apparent intention of shutting
down the capital, cutting off the Assembly in Versailles from its Parisian supporters, and nipping the Revolution in the bud. When news
reached Paris on 12 July that the king had dismissed Jacques Necker,
the popular finance minister who had curtailed the Farm and kept
bread prices low during his first administration, and more recently had
doubled the number of third-estate representatives to the Estates General, the city erupted in revolt. The tax rebellions that were endemic to
the old regime exploded once again, this time taking on revolutionary
dimensions.

Upon learning of Necker's dismissal, Parisian crowds first targeted
not the Bastille, as is commonly thought, but the customs wall recently
built around the city. The old wall, scarcely a wall at all, had been a
disjointed set of ramshackle tollgates—rolling palisades with wooden
sheds to shelter guards—installed at the city's main entrances. If they
were unconnected by any partition, that was because they were originally placed at intersections on the outskirts of town, where guards had
an unobstructed view in all directions. However, as Paris expanded over
the course of the eighteenth century, whole neighborhoods sprang up
around the tollgates, rendering the surveillance of trade and enforcement of fiscal law extremely difficult. Laws that ordered homeowners
abutting the city line to wall off their property did little to prevent the
fiscal boundary from becoming so porous that the Farm lost an estimated six million lt of revenue annually to contraband, much of it in
wine and tobacco although myriad other products were smuggled into

Paris as well.[37] What is more, cabarets called *guinguettes* appeared just beyond the city limits to provide cheap untaxed wine and food to the city's laboring classes, depriving the Farm of further revenue. Well aware that the company was failing to squeeze what it could from Paris, the sweet spot of national consumption, Farmer-General Antoine Lavoisier proposed building a new outer wall around the capital. Necker tabled the plan, but his successor, Calonne, who was on quite favorable terms with the Farm, allowed it to proceed in 1784. Hiring architect Claude-Nicolas Ledoux to design the tollgates, the Farmers General began work on the wall immediately, turning first to the left bank and then the right.

In Ledoux's hands, the new wall took on monumental proportions. The daunting partition, which would be more than ten feet high and fourteen miles long, was to ring the entire city, enclosing whole fauxbourgs (and their *guinguettes*) within the fiscal frontier. This impressive barrier was to be pierced by forty-five gateways adorned with neoclassical pavilions that imitated the stately propylaea of ancient Athens. No mere customs booths, the pavilions were to be elaborate stone complexes that would provide brigades with ample living quarters, complete with kitchens, offices, wine cellars, stables, and warehouses to store confiscated goods. This was a fiscal border whose grandiose design was bound to irk Parisians.

Even before the new wall went up, the old gates had stirred hostility. As Mercier observed, travelers had long been known to "curse high and low" the customs officials who patted them down, inspected their coaches, and opened their personal packages. Merchants were subjected to regular indignities: "While the consumer waits for his merchandise, men appear to tell you, 'unpack all this, so that I can see, examine, and weigh it, above all so that I can tax it.' . . . You may well mutter and complain that this is madness, . . . but the clerks and porters of customs do not hear you. It's as if all the packages are confiscated and belong to them, and they will only return them to you out of pure generosity."[38]

With the construction of the new "wall of the Farmers-General," long-simmering resentment boiled over. As early as October 1784, when only the foundations had been laid, the bookseller Hardy noted: "Today, everyone cries out against the realization of the farmer general's strange project to build a wall around the capital intended to check smugglers whose cunning and subterfuges lead to the apparent loss of at least half of their collections."[39] As the barrier went up, the capital buzzed with songs witty and spiteful. "Le mur murant Paris rend Paris mumurant" ("The wall walling Paris makes Paris wail") went one clever ditty. Another quatrain rhymed, "To increase its revenue / And shorten our horizon / the Farm judged it necessary / to put us all prison."[40] The most acerbic words of all were penned by Jacques-Antoine Dulaure, who asserted that the wall was the work of "tyrants." It not only interrupted promenades and blocked the circulation of fresh country air, but the "luxury" of its architecture "mocked public misery." Decorated with "porticos, baseless columns, prominent bosses, and Doric friezes," the pavilions "rivaled the most magnificent Palaces, . . . [but] these pompous obelisks, weighed down with trophies, declare only the triumph of the *traitants,* laden with the spoils of the French." Arches not of triumph but of "servitude," they recalled "the sad picture of a people continuously pursued, despoiled, and fought by armies of agents who every day renew the evils of the civil wars' anarchy and disasters." The wall humiliated the people of Paris, now forced to bear witness "to the instruments of its own misfortunes."[41]

As the partition neared completion in 1789, tensions mounted. Finding it increasingly difficult to get their goods through, tobacco and wine runners had to invent ever more sophisticated techniques of circumvention, which included burrowing underground to open tunnels or lay pipes. The walling of Paris sparked intermittent and isolated attacks on the gates, but it was not until 12 July 1789—when the news of Necker's dismissal reached the capital—that multiple rebellions exploded. Large crowds of men and women, axes and hammers in hand, stormed the newly constructed compounds to rip down iron railings, vandalize statues, smash scales and registers, and set customs houses and stables ablaze (Figures 12.1, 12.2, and 12.3). In the end, no fewer than forty of the capital's fifty-four posts were destroyed.[42]

These rebellions bore more than a passing resemblance to those of the past century. In both cases, smugglers and others with a direct interest in illicit trade were ubiquitous. Of the eighty rioters arrested in the July uprising, two groups were preponderant: wine merchants (seventeen), who traded in contraband tobacco as well as drink, and "professional" smugglers (fifteen).[43] A subsequent investigation revealed that traffickers had been instrumental in the attacks on city barriers. Some parked fully loaded carts near the gates just before they were besieged,

Figure 12.1.
Sack of the
"Bons Homes"
customs gate.
Bibliothèque
Nationale de
France, Réserve
QB-370 (23).

so they could move their merchandise into town once the guards deserted their posts. Others roused neighborhood crowds to assist them in the desolation of the checkpoints.[44]

But the scale, structure, and meaning of the July rebellion widened far beyond that of similar incidents under the old regime. Before 1789, anti-Farm rebellions had been well circumscribed in space and time. Contraband rebels and their allies committed acts of personal retribution against Farm guards, intervened locally to rescue captive traffickers and goods, or simply chased Farm agents out of town. Even Mandrin, who had a relatively sophisticated political consciousness, did not expect his

Figure 12.2. Sack of the Gobelins customs gate. Bibliothèque Nationale de France, Réserve QB-201 (118).

A BAS LES IMPÎOTS

Figure 12.3. Down with Taxes. Prerevolutionary literary descriptions of the Farm as "hydra" take visual form in this revolutionary image. Bibliothèque Nationale de France, Réserve QB-201 (120).

forced sales to effect durable political change. Those who raided the Paris customs gates in July 1789, by contrast, were acting in the midst of a constitutional struggle over national sovereignty and intended their actions to transcend the local illicit economy to influence national politics. Hence, the crowds that attacked the Paris customs gates included not only small groups of traffickers and their immediate allies but also throngs of artisans, unskilled workers, and the unemployed. The assemblage that sacked the post at the Fontainebleau road (now la place d'Italie) was two or three thousand strong. Thrilled by their participation in successful bouts of collective protest, those who joined crowds to vent their frustration with the Farm understood that they were not just temporarily displacing particular instantiations of the Farm (this agent or that gate) but forever abolishing the Farm itself. "Finally, we're going to drink 3 sous wine; we've been paying 12 sous a rather long time!" declared a locksmith destroying furniture at the Neuilly toll. "We

no longer want customs gates! We no longer want agents!" called out rioters at another site.[45] Implicit in both statements was the notion that the
rebellion in which they were participating was moving beyond a narrow
culture of retribution to claim universal and permanent institutional reforms. The idea that the storming of the customs gates in July 1789 would
bring durable change in policy was fixed in print in the pages of the *Revolutions de Paris*, a widely read revolutionary newspaper whose very first issue opened with the siege of the customs gates. Upon hearing the news of
Necker's dismissal, the paper reported with a tone of finality, "The desperate people, looking for an end to its miseries, burned many customs
posts. . . . All the customs posts . . . were burned down . . . and no goods
paid any customs dues from this moment on."[46]

The sacking of the customs gates also sent a political message that
the royal army could not shut down Paris, that Parisian citizens would
control the flow of food, arms, and people in and out of the capital, and
that the will of the people as expressed in the National Assembly could
not be denied. The timing of the rebellion certainly suggests that rioters
were responding to high political events of the day. Although the first
gate was attacked on the evening of the eleventh, the thrust of the rebellion came only after word of Necker's dismissal had got out, as the
first line of the *Revolutions de Paris* duly noted. The paper also emphasized how the event constituted an assertion of political will by which
the people of Paris seized control over the city's entryways. Their aim
was not only to free the passages for food and untaxed goods but to in-
stall a new form of revolutionary surveillance: "to avoid any surprises,
it appeared prudent to inspect carefully all the vehicles as well as the
couriers who entered and exited the capital: this precaution led to the
discovery of more than one traitor."[47] This last entry situated the customs-
gates uprising in the narrative of a larger national struggle between revolutionary and counterrevolutionary forces.

In Paris, ironically, the burning of the customs gates had limited
impact. In the end, it proved to be the storming of the Bastille on 14
July that most effectively transmitted the message that the people of
Paris would not tolerate an aristocratic plot to seize the city and dissolve the National Assembly. There are many reasons that, in the capital, the political significance of the Bastille eclipsed that of the anti-
Farm rebellion. Whereas both prison-fortress and wall had become
powerful symbols of despotism in the last decades of the old regime,

the taking of the Bastille had all the markings of a pitched military battle in which Parisians risked and sacrificed their lives in defense of the city. The loss of life on both sides dramatically raised the political stakes.[48] By contrast, the insurgency against the customs wall encountered little resistance, led to no deaths, and was perpetrated in no small part by traffickers as mindful of base profit as of honorable municipal defense. Further, whereas the new independent municipal government of Paris had everything to gain by memorializing the destruction of the Bastille, because that act led directly to its own creation, the city fathers distanced themselves from the burning of tollgates on which the city still depended for revenue. A large portion of the capital's customs taxes was earmarked for municipal expenses and hospital subsidies. It was for fear of losing that revenue that the committee of electors of Paris ruled, the day after the burning ceased on 15 July, that the collection of dues would be reestablished as soon as possible. Far from celebrating the barriers' destruction as a symbol of old-regime despotism, they pledged to rebuild an indispensable municipal resource.[49]

Overshadowed in Paris by the taking of the Bastille, the defeat of the wall had a much greater effect in the provinces. Since the calling of the Estates General in the spring of 1789, national and local politics had coalesced to provoke a rash of fiscal rebellions: on 23 March 1789, as Marseille began electing deputies to the Estates, an angry crowd attacked the home of the city's Farm director; on 29 June 1789, when Lyon was to celebrate the union of the three estates, residents sacked the city's customs gates.[50] But nothing compared to what would come to pass after Parisians burned down the capital's new wall in July. As news of the event radiated across France, peasants and artisans took their cue to rise up against the Farm.

Long a hotbed of contraband rebellion, Picardy was the first province to erupt, as crowds burned down checkpoints, destroyed company offices, chased away agents, and freed traffickers from jail throughout the remainder of the summer. As in Paris, smugglers played a vital role. In Roye, after the customs barriers were destroyed, traffickers arriving with carts of contraband salt and tobacco were welcomed by enthusiastic crowds and escorted past defunct tollgates into town.[51] Residents of Saint Quentin also cleared the way for smugglers to enter town, warning Farm guards not to interfere lest their throats be slit. As smugglers arrived in packs, they were ushered into the city and led to the main square, where they openly sold contraband. That evening, a crowd broke into the royal prison to free traffickers.[52] As the intendant of nearby Soissons informed his superiors, "Smugglers profit from the ferment that reigns in all minds; they enter towns, storm the tollgates, and, seconded by the people who find their advantage in it, publicly sell salt and tobacco. Farm agents and mounted police dare not confront these disorders, for fear that the threatening populace will knock them senseless."[53]

As in Paris, the rebellions in Picardy took on a distinctly revolutionary air as rioters broadened their claims. They not only shared a sense that this uprising was different from previous ones in that it would bring the final destruction of the Farm. They explicitly linked their rebellions to the national rise to power of the third estate. Upon hearing news of the sacking of the Paris gates, a crowd of men in the market town of Ham approached a customs checkpoint while announcing that the gate "had annoyed them long enough." Before tearing it apart and throwing the debris in the river, they interrogated the agents about their loyalty to the third estate.[54] In Jussy, rebels pursued a Farm guard into his home and tested his political allegiance. Asked what side he was on, he replied "that he supported the third estate," the right answer to be sure, even if it failed to dissuade the rebels from roughing him up.[55] Peasants from Hervilly and Roizel, marching to a fife and drum, chased a guard from his house, saying that "they no longer wanted to suffer the presence of agents, and that such was the intention of the nation."[56] Further south in Lyon, even before Necker's dismissal, crowds smashed the city's tollgates, repossessed confiscated contraband, and sold "third estate wine" for the pretax price of four sols a bottle.[57] To the townspeople and peasants of provincial France, particularly those who inhabited areas of intense trafficking (Picardy, Artois, Maine, Anjou, Languedoc, Roussillon), the coming of Revolution meant both liberation from the Farm *and* the rise to power of the Third Estate. The two ambitions were entangled.[58]

From the fall of 1789 to the spring of 1791, as tax rebellions died down and the Farm struggled to regain a measure of control, resistance took the less confrontational form of tax evasion. Much of the citizenry simply refused to pay taxes of any kind. In 1790, as the Constituent Assembly labored to craft a new financial system, direct tax receipts fell by half to two-thirds, while indirect tax revenues plummeted even further, by as much as 90 percent in some areas.[59] Having climbed to about half the budget at the end of the old regime, indirect taxes constituted but one-sixth or one-fifth of total revenue in 1790.[60] Concerned about the "dilapidation of the financial machine," the National Assembly continued to insist on the payment of such taxes, but, anticipating the fiscal liberation promised on 17 June (and again, implicitly, on 4 August when the Assembly abolished provincial privilege), taxpayers closed their purses to the Farm.[61] If the revolutionary government was about to do away with the existing tax system, which it had already declared illegitimate, why heed provisional injunctions to pay?

In the case of salt and tobacco monopolies, the refusal to pay taxes excited a surge in contraband, the market for which scarcely took the trouble to hide itself anymore. As Mandrin had done in an isolated fashion in the 1750s, smugglers and consumers drove illicit trade into the open, bringing the underground economy to the surface. In Derry-sur-Somme traffickers sold salt in front of the town hall. In Guise, a man flagrantly peddled tobacco next to a burning guard house.[62] "Expecting the [tobacco] tax soon to be suppressed or completely changed in its administration," wrote one high-ranking Farm official, "the public indulges in speculations on foreign tobaccos and on those from the former provinces of Artois, Hainault, and Flanders, which is transported, sold, and consumed almost without obstacle. The agents of the Farm who would like to stop this expose themselves to dangers all the more certain since the most favorably disposed towns, whose aid and protection they require, refuse to grant such requests until the Assembly has definitively ruled on this tax."[63]

The same thing was happening in the south. Tobacco revenue was drying up, explained an official from Puy,

> because contraband of this good is openly exchanged, even right before the eyes of the administration. Emboldened by the disorder of the moment, smugglers do not fear selling it publicly in squares, streets, and inns; its low price energizes consumers and destroys the sales of Farm retailers. . . . What is singularly astonishing is that town officials, one of whose most essential duties is to ensure that unabolished taxes are collected as in the past, set the most reprehensible and pernicious example by protecting or engaging in this prohibited trade themselves. Dreading the reactions of the distraught people, guards of the Farm do not dare show themselves and do their duty; tobacco smugglers remain unpunished and contraband grows anew each day.[64]

In many areas, local officials effectively declared the abolition of the Farm before the Constituent Assembly got around to doing so. As rebellions shook Paris and the provinces, the supply lines of an already vibrant underground economy opened further. A tide of contraband washed over France, to the delight of traders, who could now conduct business in the open, and consumers, who purchased unprecedented volumes of untaxed goods. It was as if "contraband itself, arms in hand, carried out the overthrow" of the monopolies, recalled an official in the finance ministry.[65] The nation was saturated with contraband as never before.

Reframing Rebellion

Under the old regime, the educated, property-owning classes that staffed government offices had abhorred popular violence as inherently irrational, highly contagious, and dangerously subversive.[66] Even the philosophers, economists, and legal reformers who defended smugglers against the abuses of the Farm averted their eyes from the violence of fiscal rebellion to focus instead on state repression. Not surprisingly, the propertied leaders of the Revolution also had a difficult time coming to grips with popular uprisings. The initial reaction of deputies in the National Assembly to the news of the taking of the Bastille was ambivalent in the extreme. The violence of the event was shocking, but they could not deny its far-reaching effect on national politics. Had not the fateful uprising led to the recall of Necker, the withdrawal of troops from Paris, and the strengthening of the Assembly's position vis-à-vis the potentially reactionary king? As they began to acknowledge all that the revolt had done to advance their cause, they gradually integrated it into a positive story about the Revolution's origins. In fact, according to one notable historian, the representatives' act of appropriating the Bastille created nothing less than the modern concept of revolution itself, which by definition involves an articulation between new political claims from above and violent collective action from below.[67]

To appropriate the taking of the Bastille as their own, however, revolutionary leaders had to make a distinction between two types of violence: worthy violence wielded by the people to defeat despotism in the name of liberty and unworthy violence waged by brigands to wreak havoc upon society.[68] Employing this distinction, deputies in the Assembly eventually classified the violence associated with the Bastille as legitimate, because it was instrumental in supplanting despotism with liberty. No doubt many legislators had the storming of the prison in mind when they proclaimed the right of "resistance to oppression" in the "Declaration of the Rights of Man and Citizen." The same legitimizing process would occur with the sacking of the customs gates in Paris and the provinces, although it would take longer for revolutionary leaders to legitimize fiscal rebellion. Eager to forge a durable constitutional order, newly empowered propertied elites were not inclined to condone the violence of traffickers who defied the state's demands, but they would ultimately incorporate fiscal rebellion into official narratives of the Revolution's origins in a sharply contested, two-stage process.

The first stage of this legitimizing process unfolded during the trial of those arrested for sacking Paris's customs gates. As might be expected, the judges prosecuting the case had little sympathy for the accused, bluntly declaring that to suggest that the violent destruction of the gates had anything to do with the Revolution was an "insult" to the Revolution itself.[69] In the winter and spring of 1790, the Paris election court, with the supervision of the *cour des aides,* forged ahead with the investigation, deposing witnesses, issuing arrest warrants, and rounding up eleven suspected ringleaders in nighttime raids. As soon as the trial against the eleven defendants began, however, it met with strident street protest. Raucous crowds assembled in the courtyard of the *palais de justice* to register their disapproval. Free the accused from the *conciergerie,* many demanded, or the court would be reduced to ash. As Clément de Barville, the general prosecutor of the *cour des aides,* explained, the demonstrators believed that to pursue the case against customs rebels was "to put the Revolution on trial," an allegation widely publicized in Jean-Paul Marat's radical newspaper *L'Ami du peuple.*[70]

In such a contentious atmosphere, the judges were reluctant to go forward. In a letter to the National Assembly, they lashed out at their adversaries: "attempts are made to excite the people against the ministers of justice by announcing in news sheets that plots were afoot to get rid of the best patriots and authors of the Revolution, while saying that we are violating the liberty of those who first opposed and dispersed enemies of the State and their spies, and who attempted to destroy the monuments of slavery that defiled the avenues of Paris."[71] Undermined by the claim that it was prosecuting the "authors of the Revolution," the court invited the Constituent Assembly to intervene. The affair had become so politically charged that the nation's representatives had to step in.

The Assembly's response is revealing. On 1 July 1790, as delegates discussed the upcoming Festival of the Federation, which was to celebrate the first anniversary of the storming of the Bastille, Jean-François Reubell, an Alsatian deputy who would soon press for abolition of the tobacco monopoly, shifted the subject of conversation to the other rebels of 1789: the customs-wall sackers. While you make preparations for the commemoration of the taking of the Bastille, Reubell intoned, the *cour des aides* "pursues a large number of citizens who are guilty of having extended the spirit of the revolution from the Bastille and Invalides to the customs gates." Representing the customs rebellion as an extension of the taking of the Bastille, Reubell assimilated the sackers to the now hallowed "conquerors" of the prison. Sympathetic to this reinterpretation of events, Hyacinth Muguet de Nanthou, whose committee had investigated the trial, delivered an impassioned speech in which he asked fellow legislators to remember what had happened a little more than a year earlier:

> Recall the ferment that reigned in the capital; recall how the need to be free agitated a numerous people; it considered [Farm] employees only as agents of arbitrary tax collections, of vexations of which it had for too long been the victim. It destroyed the luxurious monuments that the idiotic extravagance of a reprehensible minister appeared to have constructed in order to insult its misery; it burned down the customs gates, but with the same hand it took the Bastille and assured liberty. Without a doubt, personal interests were mixed up with this action, but they were in small number and profited from the enthusiasm that excited the love and hope of liberty . . . ; if you authorize these criminal pursuits for Paris, issue them for all the kingdom, because customs gates were burned throughout the kingdom. . . . Will the 14th of July, a day of celebration and happiness for every French citizen, for some be a day of mourning and tears? . . . It is necessary in these circumstances to veil the statue of law.[72]

Invoking Montesquieu's metaphor that republics must occasionally throw "a veil over liberty, as one hides the statues of the gods," an image that extra-legislative militants would later take up to justify popular insurgency, Muguet urged the Assembly to overlook legal violations that formed part of a broader revolutionary movement.[73] Although the sacking of the gates lacked the impeccable moral credentials of the taking of the Bastille, by this time understood to be *the* founding event of the Revolution, it was for two reasons still remissible and therefore legitimate rebellion. First, "the people" had long been the victim of tyrannical abuse and were thus understandably agitated by the need for freedom, even if some (namely, smugglers) participated in the uprising out of "personal interest"; and second, the popular violence that torched the tollgates was part and parcel of that which took the Bastille. "The same hand" committed both acts. For Muguet, rebellion was redeemable when associated with the larger cause of revolutionary liberty, which, he concluded, the customs uprising clearly was.

Not everyone in the assembly agreed. The abbé Maury, a staunch conservative, cautioned his colleagues not to confuse the defenders of liberty with "brigands" who burned public property from "personal interest." Yet his characterization of the insurgents as self-interested outlaws failed to impress. The majority of delegates were inclined to see the customs rebels as liberty-seeking revolutionaries, or at least an integral part of "a people who recovered its rights," and voted with the committee to annul the trial and free the accused. The anti-Farm rebels were exonerated as their uprising joined the pantheon of founding revolutionary acts.

With the 1 July vote, revolutionary leaders took a major step toward legitimizing the greatest tax uprising of the century, implicitly decriminalizing rebellion against the Farm and undoing decades of jurisprudence aimed at stigmatizing rebellious smugglers as infamous criminals. The following year, as a new fiscal system was erected, legislators would complete the process of assimilating the burning of the Paris customs gates into the official story line of the origins of the French Revolution.

A New Fiscal System

As the preceding chapters have illustrated, the French monarchy's efforts to stimulate, control, and fiscalize a global trade in consumer goods generated powerful opposition in the metropole. As a popular movement engaged the Farm in a protracted "war" over contraband, fueling unrest in the border provinces (and limiting what revenues the Farm could raise to plug the deficit), an elite intellectual movement pounded the Farm from above, urgently publicizing the need to abolish a "despotic" institution that had become a cornerstone of the absolute monarchy. Not completely deaf to such demands, the crown sporadically introduced reform in the last decade of the old regime. In 1780, finance minister Jacques Necker clipped the Farm's wings by placing excise taxes on alcoholic beverages (except those collected at the gates of Paris) into a separate nonfarmed administration called a _régie,_ essentially nationalizing a division within the giant private company. He also reduced the number of Farmers General from sixty to forty, attempted to reorganize how they dealt with captured smugglers, and laid out plans for restructuring the gabelle, plans also promoted by his successor, Calonne.[74] Meanwhile, customs dues on imported calico were slashed in 1772 and again in 1786, when the Eden Treaty opened trade between France and Britain, the latter in the throes of industrialization and now the world's greatest producer of "Indian" cloth. Reforms were instituted on the judicial side as well. In 1780, the French monarchy abolished the use of torture to extract confessions, and, in the edict of 1 May 1788, instituted several temporary measures "to ease the severity of punishments."[75] Although such acts remind us that the crown was very much in the process of remaking itself in the prerevolutionary era, reform was fitful and scarcely changed perceptions of the Farm, an institution from which the monarchy could never wean itself. Thus popular and elite protest against the most conspicuous forms of court capitalism—tax farming and fiscal monopolies—continued to rage right up until 1789, when the old-regime state collapsed.

During the Revolution, the pace of reform accelerated dramatically, as fiscal rebellion exploded and representatives sympathetic to institutional change took office. Adding teeth to the grievances of the _cahiers,_ the uprisings against the Farm in 1789–1790 sent the unequivocal message that there would be no room for abusive state monopolies or heavy consumption taxes in the new regime. Such a message was hardly anathema to legislators familiar with the writings of Physiocrats, who had been claiming for decades that all forms of indirect taxes were wasteful and hindered investment in agriculture. It also accorded with the views of many reformist government officials who, although unwilling to go as far as the radically free-trade Physiocrats in calling for abolition of external customs duties, wished nonetheless to efface the internal customs lines that divided the kingdom and choked domestic commerce.[76] When combined with the intellectual disposition of many a deputy, the message driven home by revolt would yield durable structural changes in fiscal policy. Although fraught with tension, the loose alliance between popular revolt and Enlightenment notions of reform was highly productive of revolutionary transformation.

The creation of a new fiscal regime did not happen overnight. At first, the National Assembly stuck to the fiscal policy it had announced the day of its creation, insisting repeatedly that citizens must pay their old taxes until new legitimate ones were created. Echoing the national legislature, the Paris government likewise proclaimed that dues would continue to be collected at the city's customs gates. Having assumed the position of the nation's corulers, elected officials were keenly aware that the success of the Revolution depended on maintaining a functioning state that paid its bills and serviced its debt, even if such expenditures had to be funded by odious taxes that, regrettably, had to remain on the books until the new fiscal order was established. "Without public revenues," explained Anne-Pierre de Montesquiou, a delegate on the finance committee, in the fall of 1790, "there can be no government or liberty. The success of the Revolution is intimately tied to the regularity of collections, and it is by the fidelity with which public charges are paid that good citizens, true friends of the Constitution, will henceforth be recognized."[77] Evading indirect taxes by buying goods on the black market was no longer excusable. "Until now," a Paris official explained, "the people unhappily bore the weight of public taxes, and fraud was not at all considered a crime; because taxation was established by the law of the strongest and because the nation had no indication of its necessity or how tax revenue was spent, it was quite natural to see subjects deftly eluding brute force. But this facile morality can no longer legitimize fraud: it is the nation, through its representatives, that henceforth decrees public contributions, that appreciates the necessity of them, and that will account for their use, and all citizens . . . will dutifully pay them with scrupulous precision."[78] Fraud could be excused when taxes were imposed illegally, but now that the nation was finally ruling itself through elected representatives, it was the duty of every citizen to pay his or her fair share.

Such idealistic announcements flew in the face of reality. Taxpayers in 1789 and 1790 had no intention of paying taxes that reeked of old-regime inequality and coercion. When authorities insisted that they pay, citizens rebelled or simply circumvented the levies by buying goods on the ubiquitous black market. The Assembly's decision on 25 June 1790 to seize the assets of the French Catholic Church and use the property to back a new paper currency, the *assignat*, bought the revolutionary government some time but did not resolve the underlying problem. The national legislature understood that it had to establish a financial system that would not only raise tax revenue but do so in a way that accorded with revolutionary principles and appeared legitimate in the skeptical eyes of the citizenry.

In the spring of 1791, after months of debate within the committees of taxation and agriculture-commerce, the Assembly finally unveiled the nation's new tax system. A testimony to just how much the Revolution could accomplish—and just how radical the supposedly "moderate" liberal revolution could be—the new tax system abruptly reversed a centuries-long trend to shift the fiscal weight of the state from indirect to direct taxes. The Assembly created three new direct taxes: the *contribution foncière* on land, the *contribution mobilière* on movable property, and the *patente* on professionals and business owners. (A fourth direct tax on doors and windows was added in 1798.) Administered by elected officials and, in theory, levied uniformly on citizens throughout France, the new taxes embodied the revolutionary principles of liberty and equality as expressed in the "Declaration of the Rights of Man and Citizen." The very term "contribution" evoked a free people consenting to taxation, rather than passively suffering "imposts" levied despotically by kings. The new contributions also grounded rights-bearing citizens in the revolutionary political system. To be eligible to vote, "active citizens" had to pay direct taxes in the amount equivalent to three days' wages. Nothing less than the political order of the nation was to rest on its taxpaying citizenry.

As legislators created direct contributions with one hand, they demolished the "gothic edifice" of indirect taxation with the other, sanctioning what had already been a partial abolition from below.[79] The first structure to be razed, not surprisingly, was the gabelle. As early as 23 September 1789, wishing to come "to the aid of taxpayers," the National Assembly implemented Necker's reform plan, slashing the price of state salt, striking down regulations compelling consumers to purchase fixed quantities of the mineral, and prohibiting Farm agents from conducting searches in homes.[80] Elaborating on the "Declaration of the Rights of Man and Citizen," which barred arbitrary arrest, permitted only "necessary" punishments, and established the presumption of innocence, the decree of 23 September dismantled the judicial apparatus that had long criminalized trafficking. Anticipating the Criminal and Customs Codes of 1791, the law prohibited courts from imposing "afflictive punishments" on convicted smugglers who failed to pay civil fines or lapsed into recidivism. The point was not merely to lighten punishment, although the measure certainly did that, but to abolish penalties that stigmatized minor traffickers. To that end, the law also struck down the smuggling commissions that had led the judicial charge against the underground. The fearsome commission of Valence was at long last abolished.

Mandrin would have cheered, but still more was to come. What remained of the gabelle was abrogated on 14 March 1790, about the same time that salt and tobacco smugglers serving time in the *bagnes* were amnestied. The internal customs lines were erased on 5 November 1790, the Paris tolls scrapped on 19 February 1791, and the excise taxes on alcoholic beverages abolished on 2 March 1791. By the spring of 1791, all that stood of the old indirect tax system were the national customs duties (there were limits to free-trade ideology even during the "liberal" revolution), registry duties that did not require "searches against citizens," and the tobacco monopoly.[81]

The big question was what to do with the monopoly. Reformers like Necker had never intended to put it on the chopping block, as they had the gabelle. On the contrary, he and Calonne wished to extend it to privileged provinces on the nation's periphery, an expansion rendered all the more practicable by the decrees of 4 August 1789, which erased geographic privileges from the map of France. And yet many *cahiers* demanded the institution's abolition in 1789, as did protesters in Paris and the provinces in 1789–1790. To complicate matters further, the monopoly yielded a steady 30 million lt a year, a substantial revenue flow that irrigated the interests of several parties. Delegates under the influence of the Farmers General teamed up with fiscal conservatives worried about deficits to demand that the monopoly be preserved and, if possible, extended to frontier provinces currently outside the Farm zone. Deputies from frontier provinces, for their part, hoped to abolish a monopoly that traded almost exclusively in colonial tobacco and establish in its place the liberty to cultivate, buy, and sell any kind of leaf throughout the kingdom. Port merchants (and their American friends) also opposed the monopoly, but they wished to maintain the prohibition against domestic cultivation in support of Atlantic trade. One can see why the taxation committee had such a difficult time reconciling conflicting interests. From the fall of 1790 to the spring of 1791, as wrangling continued within the committee, debate in the Assembly gradually bifurcated between a right-wing defense of monopoly and a left-wing opposition. As the rhetoric polarized, two questions came to the fore: how to classify tobacco as a consumer good and how to characterize the tax rebellions that opened the Revolution.

Like traditional proponents of the monopoly, right-wing deputies claimed that tobacco was a luxury purchased by consumers who voluntarily paid the tax included in its price. Advancing this line of reasoning, the abbé Maury, the same conservative who opposed an amnesty for the customs-sackers of 1789, argued that the tobacco tax was scarcely a tax at all: "it is a voluntary contribution offered to the nation by the luxury and fancy of a part of the members of the political body. Authority does not force this fiscal obligation on anyone. Each citizen imposes this tribute voluntarily on himself." Adding a constitutional twist to his argument, he declared, "You have restored, Messieurs, the French nation's right to tax itself. You would do better still by establishing a tax on the consumption of tobacco, since in this regard you would provide each individual with the means to tax himself and even the means to pay nothing." There was also the question of whether the financially strapped government could afford to forgo such a harmless revenue stream. Reproaching his colleagues for slavishly following those "fanatical economists," the Physiocrats, who thought that a single land tax would permit the systematic abolition of all indirect taxes, Maury exclaimed, "We have already abolished the gabelles . . . and prodigiously cut back the product of customs taxes, beverage excises, revenue from the king's domain, and a slew of other substantial collections, and today it is again proposed to destroy the tax on tobacco!"[82]

Such logic was countered by left-leaning deputies from Alsace, the tobacco-growing province with a keen interest in throwing off the monopoly. Politicizing the issue at every turn, the Alsatians enlisted the Jacobins to their struggle and warned that extending the monopoly to the region would turn its peasants against the Revolution. But the sharpest prong of the Alsatian campaign was the rhetoric employed on the floor of the Assembly. First, Alsatian deputies shifted the definition of tobacco from "luxury" to "necessity," a move that echoed *cahiers* and Enlightenment thinkers who had, over the course of the century, reclassified a host of nonsubsistence goods as necessities.[83] Tinkering with categories of consumption in this way had always had vague political implications, but the legislative consequences of naming necessities and luxuries became explicit during the Revolution, as the case of tobacco makes clear.[84] Tracts such as *Le financier patriote* stated flatly that tobacco "can today be put in the category of prime necessity, due to the immense number of consumers for whom it has become a real need. The deprivation of it would be disastrous for a lot of people."[85]

In the spring of 1791, the Alsatian Jacobin Charles-Louis-Victor de Broglie took this argument to the hallowed hall of the Assembly, claiming that so many common folk consumed tobacco that it had become an "object of prime necessity" that should, accordingly, be freed from the burden of excessive taxation just as salt was. "You abolished the gabelle, which you rightly called one of the greatest scourges to have afflicted the nation." The tobacco tax was "as harsh, as oppressive, as disastrous as the gabelle." It, too, must go.

Having defined tobacco as a necessity, Broglie further insisted that "the people" had already spoken on the issue of the monopoly by sacking customs gates throughout the kingdom in 1789. The memory of those fiscal insurgents had been given a boost the previous month when the Assembly voted to abolish the capital's customs dues. Now Broglie went a step further by fully embracing the fiscal rebels of 1789, portraying them as representatives of a sovereign people who had thrown off the shackles of a despotic regime at the dawn of the Revolution. "If any doubts lingered about the people's profound aversion to this dreadful regime [of tobacco], recall what happened during that remarkable moment when the Revolution began. All the customs barriers that the General Farm had erected against the circulation of tobacco in the kingdom were overthrown at once . . . [and] the fiscal chains under the weight of which the people moaned" were finally broken. Only when "all the henchmen and the inventions of the fisc" are banished, the Alsatian thundered, will "France be able to believe in its liberty." Besmirching his opponents, he exclaimed that only "enemies of the Revolution" would allow such a monstrous institution to persist. "Those members of the Assembly who have most frequently expressed regret for the destruction of the old regime, for the reform of personal privileges, for the progress of our beautiful Constitution, are also those who today are the most zealous partisans of the plan to plunge your fellow citizens once again into the degrading chains of the fisc."[86]

Throwing all his oratorical power behind the movement to abolish the monopoly, Reubell also beseeched the Assembly to side with the sovereign people against the forces of reaction. The tobacco monopoly "has been judged by the people," he declared. "Indignation arose from all sides against this regime, and fortunately for the cause of liberty, fortunately for the cause of the people, it is the apostles of the gabelle who advocate most fervently for a prohibitionist tobacco regime and openly announce that it is essential, for its maintenance, to preserve the existence of the old leeches of the people, who created and carried this regime to the last degree of cruelty."[87] The Assembly must follow the will of the "the people" and fell the tobacco monopoly.

These arguments carried the day. In February and March 1791, the Assembly voted by slim majorities to destroy the tobacco monopoly and liberalize production and sale of tobacco throughout the kingdom. After more than a century of prohibition, French farmers were free to plant the leaf and merchants to trade in it, while consumers could buy it on the open market. Although new customs regulations forbade imports of processed tobacco and imposed a moderate customs duty on foreign leaf, these were now protectionist rather than strictly fiscal measures and so failed to rile popular opinion. What mattered was the destruction of the Farm monopoly. *Père Duchesne,* the radical newspaper of Jacques-René Hébert written in the playfully vulgar voice of a pipe-smoking man of the people, rejoiced, "Long live the National fucking Assembly, which never loses sight of the foundation of decrees: liberty." The Farm agents who "searched our pockets and would have liked to seize the measly half-ounce of tobacco that we carried in our snuff-boxes" are well punished today. "I would love to put on my Sunday best and go pay my compliments to Messieurs the Farmers-General. . . . I would tell the buggers, 'you did well to build your superb palaces and castles because, if we were to start all over again, you would not be able to steal enough to build a cottage.' "[88]

The last major indirect tax destroyed, the nation's fiscal strength now rested almost entirely on new direct "contributions." This extraordinary feat, Du Pont declared to his fellow legislators, was one of the Revolution's supreme achievements. "Messieurs," he proclaimed in the name of the committee of public contributions on 29 March 1791, "the system of finances you have adopted will create, like other parts of your Constitution, a great epoch in the history of humankind. The French nation will be the first to have steadfastly rejected the advice of fiscality and made the decisions necessary to meet its public needs on the sole basis of moral principles." Such a "courageous and salutary system" reflected "the respect you vowed to the rights of man."[89]

To present the new fiscal system to wary citizens who had resisted taxation from the Revolution's outset, the Assembly circulated an "Address to the French."[90] Explaining the dramatic shift from indirect to direct taxation, the address elaborated the founding principles of the new direct contributions ("equity, equality, uniformity") and retrospectively invented three rights that the old regime had blatantly violated in fiscalizing consumption. In keeping with Enlightenment fiscal and legal rhetoric, the first "right" was to live free from the vexations of fiscal policing, to enjoy "the most intimate sweetness of your domestic life" without tax officials searching your house for contraband. The second was "to engage in the speculations of commerce." Here the antimonopolistic liberalism of Physiocracy and the early Revolution shone through: fiscality should not hinder one's freedom to trade. The third was to consume freely, to provide oneself with "useful" goods "at the best possible prices," a right derived from the consumption-oriented liberalism celebrated by Gournay and his colleagues. Far from an innocent exercise in political education, the proclamation of these three new "rights"—to household liberty, free trade, and consumption—aimed to turn French men and women into eager taxpayers by instilling an appreciation for all the Revolution had done to restore liberties lost under the old regime. Such an exercise in rights-making contradicts neo-Tocquevillian claims that the French Revolution did not concern itself with erecting protections against a potentially abusive state, reminding us yet again that the "liberal" revolution was as much about dismantling arbitrary government as about installing free-market capitalism.[91]

By 1792, the fiscal system and the judicial apparatus that supported it had been completely recast. Absent consumption taxes and the salt and tobacco monopolies, this legalizing movement produced a sharp contraction in the underground economy. Smuggling persisted principally along the national border, where it was policed by a new national customs administration that was smaller in scale, freed from tax farming, and no longer responsible for hundreds of miles of internal frontiers. Moreover, the repression of illicit trade had been thoroughly reformed. Nonviolent smugglers now appeared before elected local judges and, if convicted, were subject to relatively modest civil fines that could not be converted to corporal punishment. It is true that the new penal code prescribed heavy punishments for smugglers who undermined the integrity of the sovereign nation by aggressing customs agents, but in cases dealing with alleged threats to public order, newly established juries tended to acquit defendants rather than apply punishments perceived as too severe.[92] In two years' time, revolutionary leaders had completely unwound the fiscal-judicial complex, dissipating the violent "war" between Farm and smuggler that had appalled so many Enlightenment writers.[93]

After constitutional monarchy gave way to the Republic in 1792, as poor economic conditions and civil and foreign war heightened political tensions, the question of what to do with the Farmers General came to the fore. Their contract with the king had been annulled the day the tobacco monopoly was destroyed, but songs, broadsides, pamphlets, and newspapers continued to speak of ill-gotten gains, cooked books, delays in transmitting revenue to the treasury, a fraudulent pension system, and adulterated snuff. During the Terror (1793–1794), the claim that the Farmers were sitting on hundreds of millions of livres that belonged to the state gained purchase in the Convention. To answer such charges, the financiers worked diligently to compile a report on the company's finances, but they did not provide it quickly enough. In November 1793, after Deputy Léonard Bourdon demanded that "these public bloodsuckers be arrested" and "delivered to the blade of the law" if they did not tender their accounts within the month, nineteen Farmers were incarcerated in a former convent at Port Royal.[94] They were joined by others before being transferred to former Farm headquarters to complete their work under police surveillance. The statement they finally produced indicated that, far from owing the French state hundreds of millions, the state actually owed them. However, a rival report by the Convention's own investigative commission came to the opposite conclusion: the Farmers, having faked their accounts, owed 130 million. On 5 May 1794, the financiers were locked in the *conciergerie*, some in the same room where Marie Antoinette had awaited her demise months earlier.

The Revolutionary Tribunal dispatched them without delay, unanimously declaring twenty-eight Farmers General guilty of conspiring against the French people. Condemned to death on 8 May 1794, they were carted to the place de la Révolution, where they faced not the wheel, the noose, or any other apparatus employed by the executioners of Valence, Reims, and Saumur, but the cold blade of the guillotine. Almost forty years after Mandrin's execution, the Terror imposed its own brand of "prompt, stern, inflexible justice" to smite the Farmers General.[95]

A Contested Leviathan

Victory over the old fiscal-judicial complex proved short-lived, however, for consumption taxes, trade prohibitions, and illicit markets would come roaring back in the second half of the Revolution and under the Empire. To be sure, between 1789 and 1792, the leaders of the Revolution, pushed from below and carried by "liberal élan," had effectively resolved the problem of old-regime contraband.[96] They swept away all vestiges of fiscal monopoly and created new "contributions" that, in principle, reflected lofty values of liberty and equality. But this state of affairs did not endure. The same liberal state that smashed the Farm and proclaimed the rights of property holders and consumers failed miserably to raise revenue. Having scrapped consumption taxes, the national treasury was almost entirely dependent on a system of direct taxation that, still based on old-regime rolls, would take years to perfect. Tax revenues declined precipitously, from approximately 11 percent of GNP at the end of the old regime to 5 percent or less in the early 1790s.[97] Although abolishing consumption taxes institutionalized revolutionary ideals, it left the government with far less revenue. The fiscal state took a mighty blow for revolutionary liberty and equality.

Not that the new system was blindly utopian. Revolutionary governments might well have stuck to their principles and squeezed by with a fairer, albeit less lucrative, system of revenue had they remained at peace. In addition to raising what it could from the new "contributions," the treasury collected large proceeds from the sale of nationalized church land, which it used to underwrite the *assignats*. But the international concord of the early Revolution was fleeting. War, that implacable fact of eighteenth-century political life that helped cause the Revolution, now intervened to alter its course. Impelled by left-wing nationalist fervor and right-wing political machinations, France declared war on Austria and Prussia in 1792 and against Britain in 1793, initiating two decades of unprecedented bloodshed. Although bolstered by a citizen army, the nation's engagement in such conflict put tremendous financial pressure on the fledgling republic. As the French marched back to war, deficits sent the *assignats* into a hyperinflationary spiral, the first of its kind in the modern era, completely destabilizing the regime.

To reconstruct the fiscal-military state, the conservative governments of the Directory (1795–1799), Consulate (1799–1804), and Empire (1804–1815) abandoned revolutionary commitments to liberty and equality as they refiscalized consumption.[98] City customs dues reappeared in 1798, taxes on alcoholic beverages in 1804, an excise tax on salt in 1806, and the tobacco monopoly in 1810. As consumption taxes soared, political leaders once more hailed them as the backbone of the state. "The public treasury's fortune," proclaimed Imperial legislator Montesquiou in 1808, "depends less on the aid that property-owners furnish than on what it receives from consumers. . . . Indeed, all direct contributions tire the taxpayer and require the use of force and frequent seizures; but the same man whose faculties are exhausted by the least monetary tribute pays taxes daily on salt, tobacco, drinks, and duties, and pays each day as a consumer more than is asked of him annually as a property-owner."[99] The emancipatory fiscal logic of the early Revolution had been completely turned on its head as poor and middling consumers once again found themselves carrying a heavy burden. With consumption taxes rising (and levies from occupied territories flowing in), state revenues under the Empire reached and perhaps even surpassed old-regime levels.[100]

War not only prompted late revolutionary governments to reintroduce indirect taxes but led them to implement an increasingly aggressive customs regime. Although the Constituent Assembly had, in the spirit of the Eden Treaty, instituted only moderately protectionist tariffs in 1791, the Convention in 1793 banned the importation of all British manufactured goods, a policy reinforced by the Directory with the law of 10 Brumaire Year V (31 October 1796). But it was Napoleon who took this policy to the extreme. In 1806, the emperor developed a "Continental System" that combined high customs duties on British colonial imports (sugar, coffee, cotton, chocolate, tobacco) with prohibitions against British textiles (yarn, cloth, printed calicoes) in an attempt to ruin Albion by blocking its export markets and depriving it of specie needed to wage war.

Napoleon's blockade shifted the French economy away from Atlantic-based ports on the west coast to industrial towns in the north and east.[101] Combined with Haitian independence in 1804, which precipitated the sale of Louisiana to the United States, the Continental System ended an era of official French trade in the Atlantic. I say "official" because the other consequence of the Continental System was the reemergence of massive black markets, especially in British colonial goods and textiles. With government support, British merchants set up depots on the periphery of the French empire, in Heligoland, Jersey, Spain, Sardinia, and Sicily, from which they smuggled goods across the frontier with the connivance of customs agents. "Neutral" ships delivered British cotton yarn and cloth to northern European ports—Antwerp, Amsterdam, Rotterdam, Hamburg—whence professional *assureurs* relayed them across the Rhine, outfitted them with false origination tags, and delivered them to retailers throughout France. In short, smuggling came back with a vengeance under Napoleon. "At no moment in modern history (with the possible exception of prohibition in the United States)," hazards one historian, "did this activity constitute as numerous a profession and put into play such heavy capital."[102]

With the return of the underground came familiar modes of repression. The Fontainebleau decree on 18 October 1810 created thirty-six smuggling courts along the border; established nine high courts to prosecute gang leaders, *assureurs,* and corrupt customs agents; and raised the penalty for such criminals to ten years of hard labor and branding with the letters *VD* ("customs thief"). Armed smugglers who operated in gangs or attacked customs agents once again faced the death penalty without appeal.[103] If the resurgence of consumption taxes and protectionism betrayed the Constituent Assembly's fiscal and commercial reforms, the revival of extraordinary justice violated its commitment to a fairer criminal justice system that protected defendants' rights. Although that judicial vision was first undermined by the radical politics of the Convention, which created special courts during the Terror to judge those accused of counterrevolutionary crimes, the conservative years of the Directory and Consulate further renounced the founding principles of revolutionary justice by establishing military tribunals reminiscent of old-regime prevostial courts to repress rampant highway robbery and banditry, a by-product of military mobilization. Armed smugglers and gang members were now to be brought before special courts. By the time Napoleon issued the antismuggling Fontainebleau decree of 1810, much of the "modern security state" had already been set in place.[104]

Consumption taxes, trade prohibitions, extraordinary justice: these developments suggest a return to an old regime that was kingless but even more centralized. And yet, such a conclusion would be hasty, for many of the institutions created in this period were, in fact, strange hybrids of late revolutionary centralization *and* early revolutionary defenses against state abuse.[105] Hence the new salt tax was not a gabelle but an excise tax on producers that minimized contact between fiscal agents and the consumer.[106] The new tobacco monopoly nationalized tobacco sales, an arrangement that would last until the very end of the twentieth century, but renounced importation of American leaf and was never again relinquished to a tax farm. If high customs tariffs on textiles remained in place during the Restoration, provoking yet another "war" between smugglers and agents, the borders of France shrank to those of 1792, and the repressive apparatus of the continental blockade was partially disassembled.[107] This struggle between revolutionary traditions is responsible for the apparent "immobilism" of the nineteenth-century French tax system, as the fear of "fiscal inquisition" delayed attempts to convert the *quatre vieilles*—the four old direct taxes—into a modern income tax, just as it imposed limits on the policing and repression of the underground.

Most important, the dramatic transformations of the early Revolution set the terms of future contestation. If state power was a prime beneficiary of the Revolution, it never fully prevailed over such countervailing forces as liberalism and popular activism. In the late 1820s and 1830s, reacting against the Continental System and the protectionist regime that succeeded it under the Restoration, novelists, political theorists, and historians adopted a romantic view of liberalism. The narrator of Stendhal's *Mémoires d'un touriste* (1838), who claimed that Mandrin, "this brave smuggler [who] lacked neither audacity nor intelligence . . . had a hundred times more military talent than all the generals of his day" and who sang the praises of prerevolutionary liberals like Jacques Turgot, bemoaned the customs laws of his own day.[108] Nor did the laboring classes acquiesce to financial or protectionist policies that raised the price of consumer goods. Endowed with a revolutionary pedigree, protestors expressed fiscal discontent during every major political crisis from 1814–1815 to 1848.[109] To cry "Long live liberty! No more customs!" in 1830, as rioters on the Rhine border did, was to invoke a revolutionary tradition with tremendous ideological weight.[110] The politicization of fiscal and mercantile policy that began with Mandrin and his comrades and accelerated through the Revolution would drive a national debate on the political and economic identity of France in the nineteenth century.

Conclusion

WRAPPED INSIDE the large canvas bags that Mandrin's gang transported were two goods—tobacco and calico—which, with a number of other global commodities, bolstered the growth of European consumption in the eighteenth century. From Asia came not only brilliant cotton calico but blue and white porcelain, shiny lacquerware, and aromatic tea, as well as the pungent spices and fine silks that had been flowing west for centuries. Another basket of delectable products arrived from the Americas: tobacco, of course, but also sugar, coffee, and chocolate, psychoactive substances that, like tea, enlivened the mind, encouraged socializing, and kept workers on the move. Together with the many goods produced on the European continent itself—furniture, books, earthenware, clothing, and so on—these products effected a profound change in the material lives of millions of Europeans. Although the age of mass consumption was still two centuries away, a more diverse assortment of goods began to fill the material worlds of elites, middling sorts, and, to some extent, even laboring classes.

For the most part, accounts of this so-called consumer revolution have been sanguine. Folded into emancipatory narratives about the age of Enlightenment, it has been associated with the emergence of new forms of individuality, comfort, privacy, sociability, taste, and fashion that loosened the constraints of a rigidly traditional society. In this respect, historians have taken to heart Michel de Certeau's dictum that all consumption is production—that human beings do not merely absorb but actively create meaning through the practice of consumption. Hence, most portrayals of consumer culture in late-seventeenth- and eighteenth-century Europe depict "a rainbow of creativity, self-fashioning, exotic novelty, and (yes) pleasure," as the liberatory intellectual forces of the Enlightenment remade its material culture as well.[1]

This rosy picture of Enlightenment consumption has not gone wholly unchallenged. John Brewer, coauthor of *The Birth of a Consumer Society,* which pioneered the field of early modern consumption, has called for broader contextualization of the subject. Disturbed by myopic interpretations of consumer society that treat consumption "as an almost totally autonomous realm devoid of economic and social context," he admonishes us that "any remotely plausible account of consumer society cannot overlook the role of institutions—from the firm to the state—the topographies of consumption, questions of access and exclusion, and the complex chains that link production and consumption."[2] Indeed, if we widen the field to examine commodity production, we see that the rise of consumption in eighteenth-century Europe was predicated on rapidly changing labor conditions in many parts of the world. In Europe, an "industrious revolution" appears to have been unfolding, in which some families worked harder to increase household income so they could purchase more goods.[3] In Asia, European trading companies profited not only from superior indigenous technology but also from the low labor costs found in fertile regions, notably south India.[4] In the Americas, colonists established protoindustrial slave plantations that produced the perishable groceries Europeans eagerly integrated into their daily lives. This last transformation in the mode of production gives the lie to any narrative of unproblematic Enlightenment progress. The same willful blindness that many eighteenth-century consumers exhibited toward the social and economic conditions of production in the New World should not be excused in historians.

Taking production into account is only one way of contextualizing consumption. This study has also considered the role that states played, not only through economic or fiscal policy but by way of legal regimes and regulatory practices that reached deep into society. Early-modern globalization and the new forms of European consumption to which it gave rise did not take place in a political vacuum. Their development was coeval with and shaped by the rise of powerful fiscal-military states. Whether or not one chooses to use the term "mercantilism" to describe European rulers' interventions in this period, it is clear that, spurred by fierce geopolitical rivalry, rulers established a variety of institutions to extract resources from overseas colonies and outposts as well as from subjects closer to home. As sovereigns constructed blue-water navies, they created all manner of monopolies, trading companies, customs duties, and commercial prohibitions, rights, and privileges, not according to some coherent ideology, as critics of the term "mercantilism" rightly point out, but by adapting early modern practices of statecraft to ventures in the wider world. Casting an eye eastward toward Asia, sovereigns chartered trading companies to do commercial battle with rival European polities. They did the same in the Atlantic, but more important were the various regulatory frameworks they established for New World commerce. Spain attempted to channel its American trade through the single port of Seville, all the better to control and tax the influx of gold and silver. The English codified the terms of their commercial empire in navigation acts that strengthened the power of the navy and assured that colonial trade would redound to the benefit of the mother country. France established a similar collection of trade laws known as "the exclusive," which regulated commerce between designated ports on the French Atlantic coast and colonies in New France and the Caribbean. Although such regulatory frameworks were tailored to the particular priorities of different empires, all were crafted on the basis of the widely held principle that colonies and their settlers existed to serve the fiscal, commercial, and military interests of metropolitan rulers.

The recent groundswell in early-modern colonial history has focused mainly on Europe's impact on the world rather than the world's impact on Europe, but the effects of commercial empire often rebounded back to the metropole.[5] Many historians have stressed how empire gave rise to a plantation complex in the Americas that depended on the forced migration and enslavement of Africans and their descendants on a scale unprecedented in human history. Based on increasingly racialized human taxonomies, slavery not only shaped the social and political life of the New World but also contributed in myriad ways to metropolitan economic and cultural development.[6] Others emphasize the cascading effects of warfare. Once a strictly continental concern, European warfare spread to far-flung colonies considered ever more essential to military and diplomatic power. Defending colonies became costly, however, putting greater fiscal pressure on central states, which they, in turn, tried to relieve by further exploitation of their ultramarine holdings, heightening the kinds of tensions between local colonial elites and metropolitan rulers that would eventually lead to independence movements.[7]

I have emphasized yet another effect of the state navigation laws, prohibitions, and trading monopolies inherent in early-modern globalization: they produced relative scarcities in desirable consumer goods even as they heightened and exploited demand for them. Attempts by European rulers to stimulate and control the flow of overseas imports through fiscal, mercantile, and protectionist institutions often restricted access to, and raised the prices of, commodities. As Maxine Berg argues, such regulations encouraged metropolitan producers to manufacture import substitutes, paving the way for new modes of production associated with the Industrial Revolution.[8] But the darker consequence of state-produced scarcities was the growth of enormous underground markets. Illicit trade thrived in the colonies of the Western Hemisphere, especially in the Caribbean, and this contraband zone was connected to a sprawling parallel economy in western Europe that reached from the North Sea and English Channel across the Atlantic coasts of France and Iberia to the Mediterranean seaboards of Spain, France, and Italy. What the itineraries of Mandrin and other smugglers show is that goods produced in distant American and Asian colonies but regulated by various European rulers did not merely graze the European littoral. They penetrated deep into the continent's core, thanks to a surfeit of illegal traders who exploited customs borders to meet (and stimulate) fervent consumer demand. In the French case, black markets proliferated throughout the kingdom, providing an excellent vantage point from which to view the impact of globalization on metropolitan economy, society, politics, and culture.

The French monarchy's engagement with world trade inadvertently transformed the kingdom's underground economy. Two royal institutions in particular—the tobacco monopoly and the calico prohibition—contributed to this change. Created by Louis XIV, the French tobacco monopoly sought to raise revenue by marketing tobacco grown in France's American colonies to royal subjects in the metropole, a program that accorded perfectly with commonsensical notions of statecraft in the period. The colonies would provide a raw good at low prices, and the monarchy would market it domestically at high prices to generate a windfall in revenue. In the event, however, the Farmers General, to whom the monarchy subcontracted the monopoly, abandoned French colonial tobacco for cheaper and more savory British colonial leaf from the Chesapeake. Financiers chose to profit from British tobacco rather than subsidize their own empire, allowing fiscalism to triumph over (French) colonialism. In an age when the monarchy desperately sought new sources of revenue, fiscalizing a foreign colonial import through a royal monopoly yielded new riches for the state and its moneyed creditors.

The calico prohibition also had its roots in French commercial empire. It is worth emphasizing that the prohibition was not a protectionist reaction to the growth of global free trade but a response to the commercial success of a state-sponsored enterprise, the French East Indies Company, which introduced Indian cotton textiles to French consumers. The sale of the vivid, colorfast cloth became so brisk that traditional textile manufacturers in the metropole lobbied for protection and persuaded Louis XIV to prohibit the sale and consumption of calico in France. Although the prohibition allowed the company to continue its lucrative reexport trade, it attempted to seal off the domestic economy from importation of the coveted fabric. To enforce the ban, the monarchy turned once again to the General Farm.

Royal attempts to stimulate and control world trade had the unintended consequence of globalizing the French underground in the final century of the old regime. Contraband tobacco (American in origin but often blended with homegrown European leaf) and Indian cloth (both the original textile produced on the Asian subcontinent and European imitations) flooded all quarters of the French kingdom. Although noncolonial products (salt and books, among others) continued to play a fundamental role in the informal economy, the introduction of new colonial goods invigorated the underground as smugglers tapped commodity circuits that were now global in scale. We have seen how Louis Mandrin entered this market. A young man from a small town near the southeastern border, he struggled to keep the family business afloat in the wake of the premature death of his father. After a venture in war provisioning failed, he abandoned his hometown, slipped across the border into Savoy, and turned to smuggling. Ambitious, literate, and at home in the world of trade, Mandrin excelled in the underground, eventually leading a large gang of traffickers on a series of daring expeditions that would make him far wealthier than his family business ever could have. Not that all smugglers followed such a meteoric trajectory (or met such a grisly end); most stuck to the shadows, kept their heads down, and evaded the Farm, hoping to supplement what little they reaped from legal work with some extra cash on the side. But even the pettiest trafficker participated in an illicit economy that linked producers and consumers in long and winding commodity chains that stretched, in some cases, from Asia or the Americas to towns and villages in the heart of France.

The growth of the underground economy illuminates the paradoxical relationship between two understandings of the eighteenth century: one optimistic, filled with light and progress; the other pessimistic, haunted by darkness and misery. The happy eighteenth century, in which Enlightenment sociability leavened the public sphere, metropolitan war declined, regional and overseas commerce expanded, landed income increased, and consumption rose, was not unrelated to the sad eighteenth century, in which food prices climbed, peasant holdings disintegrated, theft mounted, begging and vagabondage became widespread, colonial war raged, and Atlantic slavery intensified. Smuggling demonstrates some of the ways in which the two sides of the century were connected, for many of the same indigent laborers who were squeezed by demographic pressure acted as conduits in the shadow economy that brought colonial goods to avid consumers in the French interior. Those excluded from the fruits of the century's economic growth proved to be essential links in the commodity chains that buttressed consumption during the Enlightenment. This is not to suggest that all smugglers were impoverished; as we have seen, some were quite wealthy and respectable, already able to participate in the century's burgeoning consumption. Nor were all consumers of illicit goods well-off; traffickers provided cheap prohibited goods to plebeian consumers, widening the circle of consumption in crucial ways. But it is interesting to note that the era's social ills seem to have pushed workers into the lower echelons of an informal economy that furnished new "colonial" products to men and women across the social spectrum. Such an observation is not meant to tip the scales toward an optimistic or pessimistic version of the eighteenth century—each reflects a basic truth about the age—but to underscore the intimate relationship between them.

As striking as its economic effects, the globalizing illicit economy had even more profound political ramifications. It prompted institutional changes in the French metropolitan state that had no analogue in the Americas, where police remained thin and (apart from the brutal enforcement of slavery) legal regimes less repressive.[9] Not only did the crown attempt to roll back the metropolitan underground by investing the Farm with extensive police powers (search, seizure, and arrest). Under pressure from tax farmers, whose reach now extended beyond finance into the judiciary, it also hardened the criminal justice system, stiffening the penal code against smuggling and creating extraordinary courts of law. Although corruption was widespread, blunting the Farm's capacity to bring smugglers to justice, it was not so pervasive as to preclude a sharp crackdown on the shadow economy in which scores of traffickers were publicly executed (many on the wheel) and tens of thousands summarily dispatched to grueling and often deadly galleys and labor camps.

The other violent political consequence of a globalizing underground was rebellion. Simply trading in or consuming prohibited goods defied the law, but, as Mandrin's career reveals, the repression of illicit trade also provoked active resistance. Whereas seventeenth-century resistance to the state exploded in twenty or thirty province-wide uprisings, in the eighteenth century it was manifested in hundreds of small-scale attacks by smugglers and their allies. Mandrin was no typical underground rebel, if such a creature can be said to have existed at all, but his extraordinary case allows us to see in microscopic detail how a smuggling chief and his associates negotiated the underworld to develop a distinct set of rebellious commercial practices. Departing from the conventions of clandestine exchange, his gang initially shocked spectators by clearing public spaces for the open sale of contraband tobacco and calico. Not content to sell their goods under cover of darkness or in the hidden spaces of homes, taverns, and back-country roads, the band marched into towns, occupied public squares, and peddled contraband in the full light of day. The audacity of such a marketing strategy posed an overt challenge to the Farm's enforcement of the monopoly and prohibition.

But that was only the beginning. Improvising yet again, Mandrin forced the sale of contraband tobacco directly on the Farm in carnivalesque exchanges that cracked open the monopoly's supply lines. Coercive yet conducted under the pretext of commercial reciprocity (like many food riots of the day), his forced sales contrasted the rank illegitimacy of the monopoly with the moral validity of the parallel economy. By signing receipts at the conclusion of his transactions, the chief ensured that the Farmers General would personally pay for his contribution to their inventory. To place financial liability for the exchanges squarely on the heads of the Farm was to take direct aim at the powerful Parisian financiers at the core of French court capitalism.

Mandrin's political theater drew widespread public attention, as audiences relished the panache with which he turned the tables on the Farm. Newspapers, the first print medium to exploit his story, publicized the gang's forced sales and noted the polite and methodical way in which its chief conducted himself. Newspaper editors also fed readers starved for war news spicy tales of a dashing Mandrin courageously defending himself against the forces of order. And yet, the publicity Mandrin garnered during his lifetime paled before what followed his trial and execution. Although the commission of Valence attempted to defame Mandrin, it could not control the story of his life and career. Hastily produced songs, poems, portraits, chapbooks, pamphlets, and plays gave their own versions of events, some demonizing the smuggler, others heroizing him, and still others balancing uneasily between. In an age when printed word and image increasingly informed popular culture, Mandrin's story added a distinctly political edge to the genre of the criminal biography. Many readers, viewers, and listeners came to believe that the chief had acted valiantly in the name of all who suffered under the yoke of the Farm.

Thus, the full political impact of the struggle between Farm and smuggler cannot be measured by the number of rebellions alone, for the conflict had far-reaching cultural ramifications. Whatever benefits in revenue and credit accrued to the monarchical state came at the symbolic cost of widespread hostility to the Farm and the system of court capitalism it exemplified. What fully politicized the shadow economy, however, was not just the rich ephemeral literature that followed Mandrin's death but the interventions of various Enlightenment writers who, disturbed by violent cycles of rebellion and repression, incorporated the problem of illicit trade into rapidly developing rhetorics of reform. Indeed, the vicious cycle of repression and rebellion might have remained a mere political distraction had it not drawn the attention of public critics who increasingly subjected state institutions to scrutiny. The literature of political economy was crucial in this respect. In the immediate aftermath of Mandrin's execution, when no philosophe dared condemn the grisly spectacle, political economist Ange Goudar assumed the smuggler's voice to implore Louis XV to avert revolution by abolishing the nefarious Farm and pardoning all underground traders. After Goudar, two different groups of learned economic thinkers seized on the problem of illicit trade. The Gournay circle, which hoped to promote in France the kind of commercial culture that had launched England to great-power status, argued that the calico prohibition violated the "natural right" of consumers to dress how they wished. Disseminating an innovative theory of consumer sovereignty, they condemned the harsh repression of smugglers who were guilty of nothing but answering the call of consumer demand. More dogmatic in their espousal of free trade, the Physiocrats directed their criticism against the Farm's fiscal monopolies, which, they claimed, violated universal laws of nature and wreaked utter havoc with the economy. Further challenging the legitimacy of the Farm, legal reformers exposed the judicial side of Farm tyranny to protest the cruel punishments imposed on smugglers by a "despotic" fiscal-judicial complex.

Ultimately, popular rebellion combined with elite demands for reform to help bring down the old-regime state. At the plebeian level, more than a century of contraband rebellion culminated in the uprisings of 1789–1790, which took on a distinctly revolutionary air as rioters went beyond contesting the Farm's local authority to demand its complete abolition. They also linked their protest to a larger movement for a new political order based on the principle of popular sovereignty. However, the burning of the Paris customs gates, the overthrow of Farm police in many provincial towns, and the resulting deluge of open contraband put revolutionary leaders in a quandary. Like most propertied men of the day, delegates to the National Assembly abhorred popular violence, but, steeped in the literature of economic, fiscal, and legal reform and confronted with what was in many areas the de facto abolition of the Farm, they ultimately proved receptive to popular protest. From 1789 to 1791, legislators valorized the revolutionary significance of the fiscal uprisings, razed the institution of the Farm, and demolished the monopolies and consumption taxes it had managed. Henceforth, the fiscal state was to be based on direct taxes—"contributions"— which, in conformity with the Declaration of the Rights of Man, were to be distributed by elected officials and levied equally on all property owners. The old-regime penchant for regressive consumption taxes was temporarily overthrown in favor of a new fiscal system that enshrined consumers' rights and embodied revolutionary ideals of liberty and equality.

It would be rash to conclude that globalization caused the French Revolution in any simple or direct way. The relationship between the two phenomena is necessarily complicated, because globalization is often understood to be an economic process, whereas the French Revolution was above all a political event. But one of globalization's effects—the growth of a thriving and rebellious underground—penetrated the metropolitan political sphere to generate severe prerevolutionary conflict and debate. Such discord did more than simply put stress on the monarchical state and heighten the demand for structural reform. It contributed directly to the outbreak and course of the Revolution, as laboring classes and elites forged intersecting movements to tear down old-regime institutions and build a new sociopolitical order. Thus, the study of illicit trade, fiscal rebellion, and Enlightenment debate illuminates heretofore hidden connections between long-term transformations in consumption and the stormy events of the revolutionary decade.

By shifting the scale of observation and alternating among global, national, and local perspectives, this account of the rise and fall (and rise) of Louis Mandrin reveals the processes, contingencies, and conflicts inherent in the history of global capitalism. The growth of world trade in the seventeenth and eighteenth centuries did not merely integrate distant markets, create new circuits of exchange, and raise levels of European consumption. It produced protracted contestation, as state-sponsored trading companies, royal monopolies, commercial prohibitions, border control, judicial repression, and incarceration incited illicit trade, popular rebellion, crime literature, and reformist debate in a seemingly endless cycle of conflict. Like countless others in eighteenth-century Europe, Mandrin, a down-on-his-luck petty merchant, adapted to and exploited the forces of transcontinental change that had penetrated the land-locked province of his youth, but he was finally crushed by the powerful institutions that activated, profited from, and sought to control those very forces.

Lest we think that this dark side of globalization pertains only to a past age of mercantilism in which state intervention in the global economy was particularly heavy-handed, it is instructive to remember how much of that world is still with us today, albeit in a new guise. "Welcome to the seventeenth century," sociologist Charles Tilly bid his readers at the dawn of the third millennium. For Tilly, the forces of contemporary globalization had so undermined the bounded nation-state that they raised the specter of an imminent return to an early-modern dystopia in which the vacuum created by failed states and international strife would be filled with unaccountable private militias and proliferating transnational organized crime. We are half the way there, he suggested, pointing to the mafias, drug cartels, arms dealers, and other rogue firms that, assisted by money-laundering corporate banks, insert themselves into formal global markets, blurring the lines between legitimate and illegitimate trade and posing grave challenges to the planet's democracies.[10]

It is curious, however, that Tilly chose to draw an analogy with the early-modern period. For all that period's chaos—wars, religious conflict, armed trading, and extortion—it was an age of rising, not declining, state power. Indeed, many of the sinister forces to which Tilly alluded were in one way or another associated with the expansion, not contraction, of European states. International trading companies, arms dealers, war financiers, venal officeholders, mercenaries, pirates, and smugglers came to the fore in an era of pitched battles among fast-developing yet far from omnipotent fiscal-military states. If Louis Mandrin and his present-day analogues illustrate anything, it is that violent illicit trade—as well as the media attention and political debate it arouses—stems not from the erosion of state authority but from its uneven and fitful growth. Rather than attributing the ills of globalization to a narrative of state decline, we would do better to consider how states and transnational criminal enterprises are "intrinsically connected, indeed dialectically involved in shaping each other."[11] Although the modern nation-state and contemporary global capitalism promise greater stability than their early-modern antecedents, they nonetheless generate forms of exploitation, repression, criminality, and revolt that echo the strife of an earlier age.

The solution to these persistent problems is not the neoliberal panacea of retreat, for the modern welfare state has proven that, if properly funded and implemented, it can attenuate the gross inequalities of industrial (and postindustrial) capitalism. Rather, recent history suggests that citizens of the world's democracies (especially those in the United States) need to reflect further on how to raise public revenues more equitably, how to regulate trade in such a way as to foster healthy economies, how to determine which financial and commercial practices should be criminalized, and how to punish violators. In sum, they need to think harder about the future of their states in a global economy that will continue to unsettle the modern world.

Notes

Abbreviations

AAE	Archives du Ministère des Affaires Etrangères
AB	*Annales de Bretagne et des pays de l'Ouest*
ADCO	Archives Départementales de la Côte-d'Or
ADD	Archives Départementales du Doubs
ADDR	Archives Départementales de la Drôme
ADH	Archives Départementales de l'Hérault
ADI	Archives Départementales de l'Isère
ADPD	Archives Départementales du Puy-de-Dôme
ADS	Archives Départementales de la Savoie
AESC	*Annales: Economie, Sociétés, Civilisations*
AHR	*American Historical Review*
AHRF	*Annales historiques de la Révolution française*
AHSS	*Annales: Histoire, Sciences Sociales*
AM	*Annales du Midi*
AMN	Archives Municipales de Nantes
AN	Archives Nationales de France
AP	J. Madival and E. Laurent, eds., *Archives parlementaires de 1787 à 1860* (Paris, 1879–), première série
BA	Bibliothèque de l'Arsenal
BMD	Bibliothèque Municipale de Dijon
BMG	Bibliothèque Municipale de Grenoble
BMV	Bibliothèque Municipale de Valence
BN	Bibliothèque Nationale de France
BN MS	Bibliothèque Nationale de France, Manuscript Collection
BSHP	*Bulletin de la Société de l'Histoire de Paris et de l'Île de France*
CA	*Courrier d'Avignon*
EHR	*Economic History Review*
GA	*Gazette d'Amsterdam*

GC   *Gazette de Cologne*
GU   *Gazette d'Utrecht*
JEH   *Journal of Economic History*
JWH   *Journal of World History*
MHP   *Mercure historique et politique*
PP   *Past and Present*
RHMC   *Revue d'histoire moderne et contemporaine*
SHAT   Service Historique de l'Armée de Terre
SVEC   *Studies on Voltaire and the Eighteenth Century*

Introduction

1. Neil McKendrick, John Brewer, and J.H. Plumb, *The Birth of a Consumer Society: The Commercialization of Eighteenth-Century England* (Bloomington, IN, 1982); John Brewer and Roy Porter, eds., *Consumption and the World of Goods* (London, 1993). For France, see Daniel Roche, *A History of Everyday Things: The Birth of Consumption in France, 1600–1800,* trans. Brian Pearce (Cambridge, 2000); Annik Pardailhé-Galabrun, *The Birth of Intimacy: Privacy and Domestic Life in Early Modern Paris,* trans. Jocelyn Phelps (Cambridge, 1991); and Cissie Fairchilds, "The Production and Marketing of Populuxe Goods in Eighteenth-Century Paris," in *Consumption and the World of Goods,* 228–248. For challenges to the thesis, see John Brewer, "The Error of Our Ways: Historians and the Birth of Consumer Society," Cultures of Consumption Workshop (Economic and Social Research Council–Arts and Humanities Research Board) working paper no. 12 (June 2004), 1–19; Jan de Vries, *The Industrious Revolution: Consumer Behavior and the Household Economy, 1650 to the Present* (Cambridge, 2008); and Frank Trentmann, "Introduction," in *The Oxford Handbook of the History of Consumption,* ed. Frank Trentmann (Oxford, 2012), 1–19. The term "consumer revolution" exaggerates the speed and social depth of the evolution to which it refers. I therefore use it with the following caveats: (1) large swaths of the population did not necessarily experience a significant increase in consumption, even though elites, the middling sort, and, strikingly, some in the laboring classes undoubtedly did; (2) the transformation was more evolutionary than revolutionary, occurring over several decades; and (3) the growth of consumption and fashion were not unique to Europe. I discuss the social limits of the French consumer revolution in greater detail in this Introduction and in Chapter 1.

2. The drift of this argument appears in a number of recent surveys: Roy Porter, *The Creation of the Modern World: The Untold Story of the British Enlightenment* (New York, 2000); John Brewer, *The Pleasures of the Imagination: English Culture in the Eighteenth Century* (Chicago, 1997); Daniel Roche, *France in the Enlightenment,* trans. Arthur Goldhammer (Cambridge, MA, 1998); and Co-

lin Jones and Dror Wahrman, eds., *The Age of Cultural Revolutions: Britain and France, 1750–1820* (Berkeley, CA, 2002).

3. Herbert Marcuse, *One-Dimensional Man: Studies in the Ideology of Advanced Industrial Society* (London, 2002), 11.

4. Roche, *France in the Enlightenment*, 550; and idem, "Apparences révolutionnaires ou révolution des apparences," in *Modes & Révolutions, 1780–1804* (Paris, 1989), 111. Michel de Certeau, *The Practice of Everyday Life*, trans. Steven Rendall (Berkeley, CA, 1984), encouraged historians to consider consumption as a creative act that is productive of meaning, hence the appearance of studies on the invention of new consumer values in this period. See Michael Kwass, "Big Hair: A Wig History of Consumption in Eighteenth-Century France," *AHR* 111 (June 2006), 631–659 and the works cited therein.

5. For a recent plea to repair this problem, see Lynn Hunt, "The French Revolution in Global Context," in *The Age of Revolutions in Global Context, c. 1760–1840*, eds. David Armitage and Sanjay Subrahmanyam (New York, 2010), 20–36.

6. Pioneered by Roche, *Peuple de Paris: essai sur la culture populaire au XVIII siècle* (Paris, 1981), after-death inventories have been used by several historians of Paris: Pardailhé-Galabrun, *Birth of Intimacy;* Cissie Fairchilds, "Production and Marketing"; and Roche (again), *The Culture of Clothing: Dress and Fashion in the Ancien Régime*, trans. Jean Birrell (Cambridge, 1994). For a provincial study that artfully exploits them, see Michel Figeac, *La douceur des Lumières: Noblesse et art de vivre en Guyenne au XVIII siècle* (Bordeaux, 2001). For two works that have skillfully plumbed inventories to detail the material lives of artisans, see Steven Laurance Kaplan, *The Bakers of Paris and the Bread Question, 1770–1775* (Durham, NC, 1996); and Clare Haru Crowston, *Fabricating Women: The Seamstresses of Old Regime France, 1675–1791* (Durham, NC, 2001).

7. Notable exceptions include Colin Jones, "Bourgeois Revolution Revivified: 1789 and Social Change," in *Rewriting the French Revolution*, ed. Colin Lucas (Oxford, 1991), 69–118; William H. Sewell Jr., "The Empire of Fashion and the Rise of Capitalism in Eighteenth-Century France," *PP* 206 (2010), 118; and Paul Cheney, *Revolutionary Commerce: The Globalization of the French Monarchy* (Cambridge, MA, 2010). For the American case, see T.H. Breen, *The Marketplace of Revolution: How Consumer Politics Shaped American Independence* (New York, 2004).

8. Braudel, "Histoire et sciences sociales: La longue durée," *AESC* 13 (1958), 729.

9. For the Marxist-Revisionist debate, see William Doyle, *Origins of the French Revolution* (Oxford, 1988), part I. For the turn toward political culture, see the seminal works of François Furet, *Interpreting the French Revolution*, trans. Elborg Forster (Cambridge, 1981); Lynn Hunt, *Politics, Culture and Class in the*

French Revolution (Berkeley, CA, 1984); and Keith Baker, _Inventing the French Revolution_ (Cambridge, 1990).

10. Sewell, "Empire of Fashion," 118. See also Jones, "Bourgeois Revolution Revivified"; and Suzanne Desan, "What's after Political Culture? Recent French Revolutionary Historiography," _French Historical Studies_ 23 (Winter 2000), 163–196.

11. Jack A. Goldstone, "The Social Origins of the French Revolution Revisited," in _From Deficit to Deluge: The Origins of the French Revolution_, eds. Thomas E. Kaiser and Dale K. Van Kley (Stanford, CA, 2011), 67–103 (quotation on 91). The pessimistic interpretation is also outlined in William Beik, _A Social and Cultural History of Early Modern France_ (Cambridge, 2009), 345–347. De Vries, _Industrious Revolution_, chapter 3, offers a possible explanation for the paradox of rising consumption and falling wages: that households worked longer and harder to increase their purchasing power. But clearly some households were laboring harder just to scrape by rather than to increase their consumption.

12. I prefer the neutral term "early modern globalization" to other formulations such as "proto-globalization" (A. G. Hopkins, ed., _Globalization in World History_ [New York, 2002]), "first globalization" (Geoffrey C. Gunn, _First Globalization: The Eurasian Exchange, 1500–1800_ [London, 2003]), or "primitive globalization" (Cheney, _Revolutionary Commerce_).

13. David Harvey, _A Brief History of Neoliberalism_ (Oxford, 2005).

14. Paul Ganster and David E. Lorey, eds., _Borders and Border Politics in a Globalizing World_ (Lanham, MD, 2005); Vera Pavlakovich-Kochi, Barbara J. Morehouse, and Doris Wastl-Walter, eds., _Challenged Borderlands: Transcending Political and Cultural Boundaries_ (Burlington, VT, 2004); and Anatole Kaletsky, _Capitalism 4.0: The Birth of a New Economy in the Aftermath of Crisis_ (New York, 2010). For critiques of facile understandings of globalization, see Frederick Cooper, "What Is the Concept of Globalization Good for? An African Historian's Perspective," _African Affairs_ 100 (2001), 189–213; and Chloé Maurel, "La World/Global History: questions et débats," _Vingtième Siècle_ 104 (Oct.–Dec. 2009), 153–166.

15. The scale of the global shadow economy is notoriously difficult to estimate. Using the work of economist Friedrich Schneider, Robert Neuwirth (_The Stealth of Nations: The Global Rise of the Informal Economy_ [New York, 2011], 27) estimates the value of the global informal economy, including widespread unofficial labor, at "close to $10 trillion." For more conservative estimates that exclude informal labor, see Willem van Schendel and Itty Abraham, _Illicit Flows and Criminal Things: States, Borders, and the Other Side of Globalization_ (Bloomington, IN, 2005), 2; Misha Glenny, _McMafia: A Journey through the Global Criminal Underworld_ (New York, 2008), xv; and Raymond Baker and Eva Joly, "Illicit Money: Can It Be Stopped?" _New York Review of Books_ (December 3, 2009), 61–63.

16. Moisés Naím, *Illicit: How Smugglers, Traffickers, and Copycats Are Hijacking the Global Economy* (New York, 2005), 68; "For Lesser Crimes, Rethinking Life behind Bars," *New York Times,* December 11, 2012; and Michelle Alexander, *The New Jim Crow: Mass Incarceration in the Age of Colorblindness* (New York, 2010). The United States may be at a turning point in the war on drugs as several states have recently permitted the growth, sale, and possession of marijuana.

17. For England, see Patrick K. O'Brien, "Inseparable Connections: Trade, Economy, Fiscal State, and the Expansion of Empire, 1688–1815," in *The Oxford History of the British Empire: Volume 2: The Eighteenth Century,* ed. P. J. Marshall (Oxford, 1998), 53–78; and Nuala Zahedieh, "Economy," in *The British Atlantic World, 1500–1800,* ed. David Armitage and Michael J. Braddick (London, 2002). For continental and global perspectives, see François Crouzet, *La guerre économique franco-anglaise au XVIIIe siècle* (Paris, 2008); Guillaume Daudin, *Commerce et prosperité: La France au XVIIIe siècle* (Paris, 2005); Kenneth Pomeranz, *The Great Divergence: China, Europe, and the Making of the Modern World Economy* (Princeton, NJ, 2000); Ronald Findlay and Kevin H. O'Rourke, *Power and Plenty: Trade, War, and the World Economy in the Second Millennium* (Princeton, NJ, 2007), chapter 5; and Jane Burbank and Frederick Cooper, *Empires in World History: Power and Politics of Difference* (Princeton, NJ, 2010), chapter 6. For the intellectual history of economic rivalry, see Sophus A. Reinert, *Translating Empire: Emulation and the Origins of Political Economy* (Cambridge, MA, 2011); Istvan Hont, *The Jealousy of Trade: International Competition and the Nation-State in Historical Perspective* (Cambridge, MA, 2005); and Cheney, *Revolutionary Commerce.*

18. In *Bandits* (London, 1969), Eric Hobsbawm argued that Robin Hood–style "social banditry" constituted an archaic form of social protest, but his methodology was criticized for conflating practices of banditry with the mythical representations that grew up around them. I have sought to avoid this problem by treating Mandrin's life and legend as two distinct historical phenomena whose relationship is to be interrogated. Further, I do not see Mandrin's rebellions as an archaic form of precapitalist protest. Many smuggling gangs in this period tapped into global commodity chains to exploit rising European consumer demand. For recent assessments of Hobsbawm and early modern European banditry, see Anton Blok, *Honour and Violence* (Cambridge, 2001), chapter 1; Nicholas Curott and Alexander Fink, "Bandit Heroes: Social, Mythical or Rational?" *American Journal of Economics and Sociology* 71 (2012), 470–497; Gherardo Ortalli, ed., *Bande armate, banditi, banditismo e repressione di giustizia negli stati europei di antico regime* (Rome, 1986); Florike Egmond, *Underworlds: Organized Crime in the Netherlands 1650–1800* (Cambridge, 1993). For banditry in eighteenth-century France, see Xavier Rousseau, "Espaces de désordres, espace d'ordre: Le banditisme aux frontières Nord-Est de la France (1700–1810)," in Catherine

Denys, ed., *Frontière et criminalité 1715–1815* (Artois, 2000), 131–174; Lise Andries, ed., *Cartouche, Mandrin et autres brigands du XVIIIe siècle* (Paris, 2010); and Valérie Sottocasa, *Les Brigands: Criminalité et protestation politique (1750–1850)* (Rennes, 2013).

19. Kalifa, *L'encre et le sang: Récits de crimes et société à la Belle Époque* (Paris, 1995); idem, *Crime et culture au XIXe siècle* (Paris, 2005).

20. See Valérie Huss, "La postérité de Mandrin: variations sur un thème," in *Louis Mandrin, malfaiteur ou bandit au grand cœur?* ed. Valérie Huss (Grenoble, 2005). On the transition from novel to film, see Jacques Migozzi, ed., *De l'écrit à l'écran: littératures populaires: mutations génériques, mutations médiatiques* (Limoges, 2000). The 1972 TV series was directed by Philippe Fourastié.

21. Mandrin has also been used by contemporary activists to protest the use of genetically modified food and to promote a redistributive "Robin Hood" tax on financial transactions.

22. In this I follow in the footsteps of Octave Chenavas, who conducted the first extensive historical research on Mandrin at the end of the nineteenth century. Burdened by his duties as deputy from the Isère, Chenavas entrusted his notes to Frantz Funck-Brentano, who published *Mandrin, capitaine général des contrebandiers de France* (Paris, 1908). Funck-Brentano's book was subsequently streamlined, but not significantly altered, by René Fonvieille, *Mandrin* (Grenoble, 1975). Although I have found both works tremendously helpful, my approach seeks to go beyond traditional biography.

23. Levi, "On Microhistory," in *Microhistory and the Lost Peoples of Europe*, ed. Edward Muir and Guido Ruggiero, trans. Eren Branch (Baltimore, 1991), chapter 5. See also William H. Sewell, *Logics of History: Social Theory and Social Transformation* (Chicago, 2005), chapter 4. Gabrielle M. Spiegel, "Comment on *A Crooked Line*," *AHR* 113 (2008), 411–412, labels this approach "neo-phenomenology."

24. Carlo Ginzburg and Carlo Poni, "The Name and the Game: Unequal Exchange and the Historiographic Marketplace," in *Microhistory*, ed. Muir and Ruggiero, 7–8; and Carlo Ginzburg, *The Cheese and the Worms: The Cosmos of a Sixteenth-Century Miller*, trans. John and Anne Tedeschi (Baltimore, 1992), 21.

25. Jacques Revel, ed., *Jeux d'Échelles: La micro-analyse à l'expérience* (Paris, 1996). Emma Rothschild, "Late Atlantic History," in *The Atlantic World c. 1450–1850*, ed. Nicholas Canny and Philip Morgan (Oxford, 2011), 634–647.

1. The Globalization of European Consumption

1. Lorena Walsh, *From Calabar to Carter's Grove: The History of a Virginia Slave Community* (Charlottesville, VA, 1997), 115, 119–120, 159, and 238.

2. *The Private Diary of Ananda Ranga Pillai,* ed. J. Frederick Price and K. Rangachari (New Delhi, 1985), 1:vii–x and 1:104; Jean Boudriot, *Compagnie des Indes, 1720–1770* (Paris, 1983), 245.

3. ADH C 1978, Nayac to Bonefon, 18 July 1754.

4. For the sake of convenience, I use "calico" like the French used the word *indiennes* to refer to all Indian cotton textiles, including muslins, painted and printed chintz, and Guinea cloth.

5. For a summary of literature on the rise of consumption, see Jan de Vries, *The Industrious Revolution: Consumer Behavior and the Household Economy, 1650 to the Present* (Cambridge, 2008), chapter 4. Just how far down the social hierarchy new forms of consumption spread is a matter of debate. In northwestern Europe—the Netherlands, England, and the Paris basin—some of the laboring poor (small farmers, shopkeepers, artisans, and laborers) undoubtedly expanded their consumption. Even in the southern provincial town of Avignon, the range of goods acquired by the laboring poor appears to have widened. See Madeleine Ferrières, *Le bien des pauvres: La consommation populaire en Avignon (1600–1800)* (Seyssel, 2004). But we should guard against overly optimistic interpretations of consumption, even for England. For a judicious assessment of clothing consumption that avoids optimistic and pessimistic extremes, see John Styles, *The Dress of the People: Everyday Fashion in Eighteenth-Century England* (New Haven, CT, 2007).

6. Carole Shammas, "Changes in English and Anglo-American Consumption from 1550–1800," in *Consumption and the World of Goods,* ed. John Brewer and Roy Porter (London, 1994), 199, applies the term "mass" consumption in the English context only to "tobacco, sugar products, and caffeine drinks." By her definition, products consumed regularly by at least 25 percent of the adult population fall into the category of mass consumption.

7. For a point of entry into the historiography on the luxury debate, see Istvan Hont, "The Early Enlightenment Debate on Commerce and Luxury," in *The Cambridge History of Eighteenth-Century Political Thought,* eds. Mark Goldie and Robert Wokler (Cambridge, 2006), 377–418.

8. See Ronald Findlay and Kevin H. O'Rourke, *Power and Plenty: Trade, War, and the World Economy in the Second Millennium* (Princeton, NJ, 2007), chapter 6; and P. C. Emmer, O. Pétré-Grenouilleau, and J. V. Roitman, eds., *A Deus ex Machina Revisited: Atlantic Colonial Trade and European Economic Development* (Leiden, 2006).

9. Neil McKendrick, John Brewer, and J. H. Plumb, *The Birth of Consumer Society: The Commercialization of Eighteenth-Century England* (Bloomington, IN, 1982); de Vries, *Industrious Revolution,* chapter 4; William H. Sewell Jr., "The Empire of Fashion and the Rise of Capitalism in Eighteenth-Century France," *PP* 206 (2010), 81–120; Carlo Poni, "Fashion as Flexible Production: The Strategies of the Lyons Silk Merchants in the Eighteenth Century," trans. Patrick Leech, in *World of Possibilities: Flexibility and Mass Production in Western Industrialization,* eds. Charles F. Sabel and Jonathan Zeitlin

(Cambridge, 1997), 37–74; and Natacha Coquery, *Tenir boutique à Paris au XVIIIe siècle* (Paris, 2011).

10. De Vries, *Industrious Revolution.*

11. Guillaume-Thomas-François Raynal, *Histoire philosophique et politique des établissements et du commerce des Européens dans les deux Indes* (Amsterdam, 1770), 1:1–2. Adam Smith borrowed from this passage in *An Inquiry into the Nature and Causes of the Wealth of Nations,* eds. R. H. Campbell and A. S. Skinner (Indianapolis, IN, 1981), 2:626.

12. Jan de Vries, "Connecting Europe and Asia: A Quantitative Analysis of the Cape-Route Trade, 1497–1795," in *Global Connections and Monetary History, 1470–1800,* eds. Dennis O. Flynn, Arturo Giraldez, and Richard Von Glahn (Aldershot, 2003), 36.

13. The importance of American silver in the development of world trade is underlined by Dennis O. Flynn and Arturo Giráldez, "Born with a Silver Spoon: The Origin of World Trade in 1571," *JWH* 6 (1995), 201–221; idem, "Cycles of Silver: Global Economic Unity through the Mid-Eighteenth Century," *JWH* 13 (2002), 391–427; Michel Morineau, *Incroyables gazettes et fabuleux métaux: Les retours des trésors américains d'après les gazettes hollondaises* (Cambridge, 1985); and de Vries, "Connecting Europe and Asia." There was a direct silver route across the Pacific to Asia, but it did not match the one that ran through Europe.

14. Quoted in Madeleine Dobie, *Trading Places: Colonization and Slavery in Eighteenth-Century French Culture* (Ithaca, NY, 2010), 93.

15. Herbert S. Klein, *The Atlantic Slave Trade* (Cambridge, 1999), 86–89; Joseph E. Inikori, "English versus Indian Cotton Textiles: The Impact of Imports on Cotton Textile Production in West Africa," in *How India Clothed the World: The World of South Asian Textiles, 1500–1800,* ed. Giorgio Riello and Tirthankar Roy (Leiden, 2009), 85–114; Colleen E. Kriger, "Guinea Cloth: Production and Consumption of Cotton Textiles in West Africa before and during the Atlantic Slave Trade," in *The Spinning World: A Global History of Cotton Textiles, 1200–1850,* ed. Giorgio Riello and Prasannan Parthasarathi (Oxford, 2011), 105–126. For the French case, in which the exchange of calicoes for captives was especially pronounced, see Jean Tarrade, *Le commerce colonial de la France à la fin de l'Ancien Régime* (Paris, 1972), I, 125–126; Jean Boudriot, *Compagnie des Indes, 1720–1770* (Paris, 1983), 240–245; Richard Drayton, "The Globalization of France: Provincial Cities and French Expansion," *History of European Ideas* 34 (2008), 429; Olivier Raveux, "Spaces and Technologies in the Cotton Industry in the Seventeenth and Eighteenth Centuries," *Textile History* 36:2 (2005), 135; Philippe Haudrère, *La Compagnie française des Indes au XVIIIe siècle* (Paris, 2005), 273–285; and Robert Harms, *The Diligent: A Voyage through the Worlds of the Slave Trade* (New York, 2002), 81.

16. In this vein, Peter Coclanis, "Atlantic World or Atlantic/World," *William and Mary Quarterly* 63:4 (October 2006), 725–742, argues for a global rather

than Atlantic approach to the early modern period. But K. H. O'Rourke and J. G. Williamson, *Globalization and History: The Evolution of a Nineteenth Century Atlantic Economy* (Cambridge, MA, 1999), while acknowledging some degree of global integration (as measured by price convergence) during the early modern period, stress that full-scale integration would occur only with the great transformations in transportation and industry in the nineteenth century.

17. Carole Shammas, "The Revolutionary Impact of European Demand for Tropical Goods," in *The Early Modern Atlantic Economy,* ed. John J. McCusker and Kenneth Morgan (Cambridge, 2000), 163–185; Maxine Berg, "In Pursuit of Luxury: Global History and British Consumer Goods in the Eighteenth Century, *PP* 182 (2004), 85–142; John E. Wills, "European Consumption and Asian Production in the Seventeenth and Eighteenth Centuries," in *Consumption and the World of Goods,* ed. John Brewer and Roy Porter (London, 1994), 133–147; C. A. Bayly, *The Birth of the Modern World 1780–1914* (Malden, MA, 2004), chapters 1–3; Anne E. C. McCants, "Exotic Goods, Popular Consumption, and the Standard of Living: Thinking about Globalization in the Early Modern World," *JWH* 18 (2007), 433–462; and idem, "Poor Consumers as Global Consumers: The Diffusion of Tea and Coffee Drinking in the Eighteenth Century," *EHR* 61 (2008), 172–200.

18. Jordan Goodman, "Excitantia: Or, How Enlightenment Europe Took to Soft Drugs," in *Consuming Habits: Drugs in History and Anthropology,* ed. Jordan Goodman, Paul E. Lovejoy, and Andrew Sherratt (London, 1995), 126. For sugar imports, see Robin Blackburn, *The Making of New World Slavery: From the Baroque to the Modern, 1492–1800* (London, 1997), 403. These figures are based on official statistics, which, given the amount of fraud and smuggling, means that real levels of importation were even higher.

19. On Indian cloth, see later in this chapter. On porcelain, see Peter Wilhelm Meister and Horst Reber, *European Porcelain of the Eighteenth Century* (Ithaca, NY, 1983), 18; and Geoffrey A. Godden, *Oriental Export Market Porcelain and Its Influence on European Wares* (London, 1979).

20. Roy Porter, *The Creation of the Modern World: The Untold Story of the British Enlightenment* (New York, 2000), 260. For a similar interpretation, see Daniel Roche, *France in the Enlightenment,* trans. Arthur Goldhammer (Cambridge, MA, 1998).

21. David T. Courtwright, *Forces of Habit: Drugs and the Making of the Modern World* (Cambridge, MA, 2001).

22. Ibid., 4. See also Goodman, "Excitantia."

23. David J. Linden, *The Compass of Pleasure: How Our Brains Make Fatty Foods, Orgasm, Exercise, Marijuana, Generosity, Vodka, Learning, and Gambling Feel So Good* (New York, 2011), 50–51.

24. Ironically, the term "commodity indigenization" was coined by Marshall Sahlins ("Cosmologies of Capitalism: The Trans-Pacific Sector of the 'World-System,'" *Proceedings of the British Academy* 74 [1988], 1–51) to explain how

non-Western cultures integrated novel European goods but is now being used to explain how non-Western goods were incorporated into European consumer culture. For studies that use the concept, see Ina Baghdiantz McCabe, *Orientalism in Early Modern France: Eurasian Trade, Exoticism, and the Ancient Regime* (Oxford, 2008); and Goodman, "Excitantia." For a critique of this approach, see Marcy Norton, *Sacred Gifts, Profane Pleasures: A History of Tobacco and Chocolate in the Atlantic* (Ithaca, NY, 2008), 7–9.

25. Igor Kopytoff, "The Cultural Biography of Things: Commoditization as Process, in *The Social Life of Things: Commodities in Cultural Perspective,* ed. Arjun Appadurai (Cambridge, 1986), 67.

26. Peter T. Furst, "Shamanism," in *Tobacco in History and Culture: An Encyclopedia,* ed. Jordan Goodman (Detroit, 2005), 2:517–522; Alexander von Gernet, "Nicotian Dreams: The Prehistory and Early History of Tobacco in Eastern North America," in *Consuming Habits: Drugs in History and Anthropology,* ed. Jordan Goodman, Paul E. Lovejoy, and Andrew Sherratt (London, 1995), 67–87.

27. Jordan Goodman, *Tobacco in History: The Cultures of Dependence* (London, 1994), chapter 2.

28. This paragraph draws from Norton, *Sacred Gifts,* chapter 1; and von Gernet, "Nicotian Dreams."

29. Quoted in Norton, *Sacred Gifts,* 45–46.

30. Marc et Muriel Vigié, *L'herbe à Nicot: Amateurs de tabac, fermiers généraux et contrebandiers sous l'Ancien Régime* (Paris, 1989), 15–16.

31. *Don Juan,* act 1, scene 1.

32. Quoted in E. Gondolff, *Le Tabac sous l'ancienne monarchie: La ferme royale, 1629–1791* (Vesoul, 1914), 139.

33. Gondolff, *Tabac,* 217. One of the most celebrated objects in eighteenth-century literature was the snuffbox in Laurence Sterne's *A Sentimental Journey through France and Italy.* Cheap snuffboxes were fabricated from the pulp of confiscated books.

34. David Garrioch, *The Making of Revolutionary Paris* (Berkeley, CA, 2004), 40 and 276. Such behavior was imitated in 1730 by a poor drunk Parisian who asked neighbors and passersby if they wanted some tobacco from her stolen mother-of-pearl snuffbox. Déborah Cohen, *La nature du peuple: Les formes de l'imaginaire sociale (XVIIIe–XXIe siècles)* (Seyssel, 2010), 269. Tobacco would not be gendered masculine until the nineteenth century, a trend reversed the following century with the introduction of the cigarette.

35. Woodruff D. Smith, *Consumption and the Making of Respectability 1600–1800* (New York, 2002), chapter 5.

36. Sidney Mintz, *Sweetness and Power: The Place of Sugar in Modern History* (New York, 1986), 180.

37. Norton, *Sacred Gifts,* chapter 5; Jordan, "Excitantia."

38. Quoted in Gondolff, *Tabac,* 219.

39. Quoted in Mary Lindemann, *Medicine and Society in Early Modern Europe* (Cambridge, 1999), 89. Although the *Encyclopédie, ou dictionnaire raisonné des sciences, des arts et des métiers*, ed. Denis Diderot and Jean le Rond d'Alembert, vol. 15 (Neufchastel, 1765), "tabac," 785, was skeptical of its physiological benefits, tobacco never lost its reputation as a potent medicinal remedy. See BN MS 8378, fol. 401; *AP*, 2:365, art. 36; and Gondolff, *Tabac*, 524–525.

40. Goodman, "Excitantia," 126. Per capita, western Europeans consumed around 1.2 pounds of tobacco a year at the end of the eighteenth century, much of it in the potent form of snuff. Goodman, *Tobacco in History*, 73.

41. This social emulation model was first formulated by Thorstein Veblen and Norbert Elias but has now been challenged. See Michael Kwass, "Big Hair: A Wig History of Consumption in Eighteenth-Century France," *AHR* 111 (June 2006), 631–659.

42. Goodman, *Tobacco in History*, 146; and Jacob Price, "Tobacco Use and Tobacco Taxation: A Battle of Interests in Early Modern Europe," in *Consuming Habits: Drugs in History and Anthropology*, ed. Jordan Goodman, Paul E. Lovejoy, and Andrew Sherrat (London, 1995), 166.

43. Richard Dunn, "After Tobacco," in *The Early Modern Atlantic Economy*, ed. John J. McCusker and Kenneth Morgan (Cambridge, 2000), 345. By 1790, the slave population of Maryland and Virginia would reach 395,663 (Historical Census Bureau, University of Virginia Library).

44. Allan Kulikoff, *Tobacco and Slaves: The Development of Southern Cultures in the Chesapeake, 1680–1800* (Durham, NC, 1986); and Jeffrey R. Kerr-Ritchie, "Slavery and Slave Trade," in *Tobacco in History and Culture: An Encyclopedia*, ed. Jordan Goodman (Detroit, 2005), 525–532.

45. Giorgio Riello and Tirthankar Roy, "Introduction," in *How India Clothed the World: The World of South Asian Textiles, 1500–1800*, ed. Giorgio Riello and Tirthankar Roy (Leiden, 2009), 6.

46. John E. Wills Jr., "Maritime Asia, 1500–1800: The Interactive Emergence of European Domination," *AHR* 98 (February 1993), 83–105. The term "armed trading" was coined by K. N. Chaudhuri, *The Trading World of Asia and the English East India Company 1660–1760* (Cambridge, 1978), 110–116. But see also Janice E. Thomson, *Mercenaries, Pirates, and Sovereigns: State-Building and Extraterritorial Violence in Early Modern Europe* (Princeton, NJ, 1994), chapter 2.

47. Quoted in John C. Rule, "Louis XIV, Roi-Bureaucrate," in *Louis XIV and the Craft of Kingship*, ed. John C. Rule (Columbus, OH, 1969), 59. For the history of the French company, see Haudrère, *La Compagnie française*. For the early history of the company, see Paul Kaeppelin, *Les origines de l'Inde française: La Compagnie des Indes Orientales et François Martin* (Paris, 1908); Glenn Ames, *Colbert, Mercantilism, and the French Quest for Asian Trade* (Dekalb, IL, 1996); and Catherine Manning, *Fortunes à faire: The French in Asian Trade, 1719–1748* (Aldershot, 1996).

48. Louis Dermigny, "Le fonctionnement des Compagnies des Indes: East India Company et Compagnie des Indes," in *Sociétés et compagnies en Orient et dans l'Océan Indien*, ed. M. Mollat (Paris, 1970), 459–462.

49. For a superb analysis of this kind of dialogue in the French silk industry, see Poni, "Fashion as Flexible Production." For the brokerage mechanism in the English case, see Chaudhuri, *Trading World of Asia;* idem, "European Trade with India," in *The Cambridge Economic History of India, Volume 1, c. 1200–1750* (Cambridge, 1982), 382–407; and John Irwin and Katherine B. Brett, *Origins of Chintz* (London, 1970), 4–5. For the French case, see Philippe Haudrère, "The French India Company and Its Trade in the Eighteenth Century," in *Merchants, Companies, and Trade: Europe and Asia in the Early Modern Era*, ed. Sushil Chaudhury and Michel Morineau (Cambridge, 1999), 202–211. The La Fontaine handkerchief is in the Asian collection of the Victoria and Albert Museum (T. 173–1921).

50. Giorgio Riello, "The Globalization of Cotton Textiles: Indian Cottons, Europe, and the Atlantic World," in *The Spinning World: A Global History of Cotton Textiles, 1200–1850*, ed. Giorgio Riello and Prasannan Parthasarathi (Oxford, 2011), 265, table 13.1. For the French company, see Haudrère, *La Compagnie française*, 286–299.

51. There is some debate over how quickly cotton cloth overtook wools and linens. Beverly Lemire, *Fashion's Favorite: The Cotton Trade and the Consumer in Britain, 1660–1800* (Oxford, 1992), and Daniel Roche, *The Culture of Clothing: Dress and Fashion in the Ancien Régime*, trans. Jean Birrell (Cambridge, 1994), emphasize the dramatic rise of cotton, whereas Styles, *Dress,* argues for a more gradual progression as linen continued to be valued for its durability.

52. See Annik Pardailhé-Galabrun, *The Birth of Intimacy: Privacy and Domestic Life in Early Modern Paris,* trans. Jocelyn Phelps (Oxford, 1991); and Raffaella Sarti, *Europe at Home: Family and Material Culture 1500–1800,* trans. Allan Cameron (New Haven, CT, 2002), 119–126. For the emergence of comfort, see Joan Dejean, *The Age of Comfort: When Paris Discovered Casual—and the Modern Home Began* (New York, 2009); and John E. Crowley, *The Invention of Comfort: Sensibilities and Design in Early Modern Britain and Early America* (Baltimore, 2001). Calicoes had been used to decorate domestic interiors in India.

53. Quoted in Prasannan Parthasarathi, "Rethinking Wages and Competitiveness in the Eighteenth Century: Britain and South India," *PP* 158 (February 1998), 79. Defoe was exaggerating, of course, as demand for cotton only gradually eclipsed that for more durable cloths such as linen. For a nuanced discussion of the advance of cotton, see Styles, *Dress,* chapter 7.

54. G. S. Rousseau and Roy Porter, "Introduction: Approaching Enlightenment Exoticism," in *Exoticism in the Enlightenment,* ed. G. S. Rousseau and Roy Porter (Manchester, 1990), 9.

55. Dobie, *Trading Places*, chapters 2 and 3; McCabe, *Orientalism*; Morag Martin, *Selling Beauty: Cosmetics, Commerce, and French Society, 1750–1830* (Baltimore, 2009), chapter 7; and Julia Anne Landweber, "Turkish Delight: The Eighteenth-Century Market in *Turqueries* and the Commercialization of Identity in France," *Proceedings of the Western Society for French History* 30 (2004), 202–211. For the literary and philosophical dimensions of early Orientalism in France, see Sylvia Murr, *L'Inde philosophique entre Bossuet et Voltaire* (Paris, 1987); and Nicholas Dew, *Orientalism in Louis XIV's France* (Oxford, 2009).

56. Edgard Depitre, *La toile peinte en France au XVIIe et au XVIIIe siècles: industrie, commerce, prohibitions* (Paris, 1912), 105; Perrin Stein, "Madame Pompadour and the Harem Imagery at Bellevue," *Gazette des Beaux Arts* 123 (1994), 29–44.

57. Beverly Lemire, "Domesticating the Exotic: Floral Culture and the East India Calico Trade with England, c. 1600–1800," *Textile History* 1 (2003), 69. The fashion for flowers in France is analyzed by Elizabeth Hyde, *Cultivated Power: Flowers, Culture, and Politics in the Reign of Louis XIV* (Philadelphia, 2005).

58. P. J. Marshall, "Taming the Exotic: The British and India in the Seventeenth and Eighteenth Centuries," in *Exoticism in the Enlightenment*, ed. G. S. Rousseau and Roy Porter (Manchester, 1990), 61; and Lemire, "Domesticating the Exotic."

59. C. A. Bayly, "The Origins of Swadeshi (Home Industry): Cloth and Indian Society, 1700–1930," in *The Social Life of Things: Commodities in Cultural Perspective* (Cambridge, 1986), 291; K. N. Chaudhuri, *Asia before Europe: Economy and Civilization of the Indian Ocean from the Rise of Islam to 1750* (Cambridge, 1990), 182–190.

60. Roche, *Culture of Clothing*, chapter 6, quotations from 137 and 145; and Styles, *Dress*, 118–122.

61. Other Indian methods of production included brushing color onto cotton cloth or "reserving" white areas of fabric by covering them with wax before plunging the cloth in dye. Raynal, *Histoire philosophique*, 1:322–333, acknowledged the "brilliant and indelible colors" of calico but refused to credit Indian producers with superior knowhow. Voltaire was more generous in *La Princesse de Babylone* (1768). For production methods, see G. P. Baker, *Calico Painting and Printing in the East Indies in the 17th and 18th Centuries* (London, 1921).

62. Georges Vigarello, *Concepts of Cleanliness: Changing Attitudes in France since the Middle Ages*, trans. Jean Birrell (Cambridge, 1988); Styles, *Dress*, 77–83.

63. Quoted in Styles, *Dress*, 114.

64. *Encyclopédie, ou dictionnaire raisonné des sciences, des arts et des métiers*, ed. Denis Diderot and Jean le Rond d'Alembert, vol. 16 (Neufchastel, 1765), "toile peinte des Indes," 370.

65. Quoted in V.-L. Bourilly, "La Contrebande des toiles peintes en Provence au XVIIIe siècle," *AM* 26 (1914), 59. François Véron Duverger du Forbonnais, *Examen des avantages et des désavantages de la prohibition des toiles peintes* (Marseille, 1755), 10, also emphasized the washability of cheap calicoes.

66. Quoted in Depitre, *Toile peinte*, 106. See also S. D. Chapman and S. Chassagne, *European Textile Printers in the Eighteenth Century* (London, 1981), 105.

67. Roche, *Culture of Clothing*, 144–145, n. 61.

68. All quotations in this paragraph are from Forbonnais, *Examen*, Part 1.

69. AN F-12 54, fol. 231.

70. AMN, HH 252–256 and 266, which lists a range of middling consumers from architects and lawyers to bakers and saddlers.

71. Madeleine Ferrières, *Le bien des pauvres: La consommation populaire en Avignon (1600–1800)* (Seyssel, 2004), 238–239.

72. Robert S. DuPlessis, "Cottons Consumption in the Seventeenth- and Eighteenth-Century North Atlantic," in *The Spinning World: A Global History of Cotton Textiles, 1200–1850*, ed. Giorgio Riello and Prasannan Parthasarathi (Oxford, 2011), 227–246; Marta Vicente, *Clothing the Spanish Empire: Families and the Calico Trade in the Early Modern Atlantic World* (New York, 2006), chapters 4 and 5.

73. Parthasarathi, "Rethinking Wages."

74. Molière, *Le bourgeois gentilhomme*, act 1, scene 2, in *Oeuvres completes*, ed. E. Despois (Paris, 1873).

2. The King Intervenes

1. For the various permutations of the fiscal-military state, see Christopher Storrs, ed., *The Fiscal-Military State in Eighteenth-Century Europe* (Surrey, 2009).

2. I am aware that "mercantilism" is a highly problematic term. Coined in the late nineteenth century and applied retrospectively to early modern states, it should be used only to invoke what was a loose political-economic framework rather than a strict set of policies; mercantilism took different forms in different places. Further, any notion that the "mercantilist state" was of a radically different order than its predecessors has to be balanced by the fact that its characteristic use of monopolies, charters, and privileges to secure colonial trade was an outgrowth of medieval and early modern state formation. The idea of a distinct "age of mercantilism" is also complicated by the persistence of protectionism in the putatively "liberal" nineteenth century and by the existence of authoritarian capitalism in China and elsewhere today. For a superb analysis of mercantilist doctrine, see Philippe Steiner, "Marchands et princes: Les auteurs dits 'mercantilistes,'" in *Nouvelle histoire de la pensée économique*, ed. Alain Béraud and Gilbert Faccarello (Paris, 1992), 1:95–130. For recent reappraisals, see Philip Stern and Carl Wennerlind, eds., *Mercantilism Reimagined: Political Economy in Early Modern*

England and Its Empire (Oxford, 2013); and "Forum: Rethinking Mercantilism," *William and Mary Quarterly* 69 (January 2012).

3. Ronald Findlay and Kevin H. O'Rourke, *Power and Plenty: Trade, War, and the World Economy in the Second Millennium* (Princeton, NJ, 2007), 228–229.

4. Quoted in William J. Ashworth, *Customs and Excise: Trade, Production, and Consumption in England 1640–1845* (Oxford, 2003), 22.

5. Patrick K. O'Brien, "The Political Economy of British Taxation, 1660–1815," *EHR* 41 (1988), 1–32; John Brewer, *The Sinews of Power: War, Money, and the English State, 1688–1783* (Cambridge, MA, 1990); and Ashworth, *Customs and Excise*. In return for paying high excise taxes, British brewers received valuable customs protections against French wines. See John V. C. Nye, *War, Wine, and Taxes: The Political Economy of Anglo-French Trade, 1689–1900* (Princeton, NJ, 2007), 78–84.

6. Although France remained the premier fiscal power of Europe in nominal terms, it failed to keep pace with British per capita taxation and could not service its public debt as cheaply as its rival, leaving it vulnerable to fiscal crises.

7. A number of studies have noted this shift: R. J. Bonney, "The Failure of the French Revenue Farms, 1600–1660," *EHR* 32 (February 1979), 11–32; Yves Durand, *Les fermiers généraux au XVIIIe siècle* (Paris, 1971), 57; François Crouzet, *La Grande Inflation: La Monnaie en France de Louis XVI à Napoléon* (Paris, 1993), 62–65, 87–89; James C. Riley, *The Seven Years War and the Old Regime in France* (Princeton, NJ, 1986), chapter 2; Joël Félix, *Finances et politiques au siècle des Lumières: Le ministère L'Averdy, 1763–1768* (Paris, 1999), chapter 2; and Philip T. Hoffman, "Early Modern France, 1450–1700," in *Fiscal Crises, Liberty, and Representative Government 1450–1789*, ed. Philip T. Hoffman and Kathryn Norberg (Stanford, CA, 2001), 226–252. Emmanuel Le Roy Ladurie, "Révoltes et contestations rurales en France de 1675 à 1788," *AESC* 29 (1974), 8, claimed that the move to indirect taxation was a deliberate attempt to pacify a rebellious countryside fed up with direct taxes.

8. Michel Morineau, "Budget de l'état et gestion des finances royales en France au dix-huitième siècle," *Revue historique* 264 (1980), 314.

9. The vast majority of indirect tax revenue was spent on servicing government bonds that had been floated to raise money for war. See Charles Joseph Mathon de la Cour, ed., *Collection de comptes rendus* (Lausanne, 1788), 93; and Jean-Claude Hocquet, "Qui la gabelle du sel du Roi de France a-t-elle enrichi?" in *Genèse de l'Etat moderne: prélèvement et redistribution,* ed. Jean-Philippe Genet and Michel Le Mené (Paris, 1987).

10. For the volume and impact of French foreign trade, see Guillaume Daudin, *Commerce et prospérité: La France au XVIIIe siècle* (Paris, 2005).

11. Jacob M. Price, "The Imperial Economy," in *Oxford History of the British Empire: vol. 2: The Eighteenth Century* (Oxford, 1998), 78–104. France crafted a comparable reexportation policy for its colonial sugar and coffee. See Paul Butel, *Les négociants bordelais, l'Europe et les îles au XVIIIe siècle* (Paris, 1974).

12. AN AD XI 48, no. 3.
13. Jan Rogozinski, *Smokeless Tobacco in the Western World 1550–1950* (New York, 1990), 63. The transnational emulation evident in the creation of tobacco monopolies and, as we shall see, calico prohibitions was part of a broader culture of European emulation examined by Sophus A. Reinert, *Translating Empire: Emulation and the Origins of Political Economy* (Cambridge, MA, 2011).
14. AN AD XI 48, no. 15, déclaration of 27 September 1674.
15. Spain had used a similar justification for its monopoly, claiming that tobacco was a luxury rather than a necessity. Marcy Norton, *Sacred Gifts, Profane Pleasures: A History of Tobacco and Chocolate in the Atlantic* (Ithaca, NY, 2008), chapter 9.
16. Although the crown had taxed salt since 1342, it did not fully monopolize its sale in the *pays de grande gabelle* until 1547. Daniel Dessert, *L'Argent du sel: le sel de l'argent* (Paris, 2012), 14–18.
17. AN AD XI 51, no. 112, déclaration of 24 August 1758.
18. AN G-1 106, doss. 1, "Fermes générales, 3e division, Tabac."
19. Quoted in E. Gondolff, *Le Tabac sous l'ancienne monarchie: La ferme royale, 1629–1791* (Vesoul, 1914), 390.
20. Moreau de Beaumont, *Mémoires concernant les impositions et droits en Europe* (1769), 4:680.
21. Jacques Necker, *De l'administration des finances de la France* (1784), 2:104.
22. George T. Matthews, *The Royal General Farms in Eighteenth-Century France* (New York, 1958), 262; Noel D. Johnson, "Banking on the King: The Evolution of the Royal Revenue Farms in Old Regime France," *JEH* 66 (December 2006), 981 and 987; and John Bosher, *French Finances, 1770–1795: From Business to Bureaucracy* (Cambridge, 1970), chapter 5.
23. Jean-Yves Grenier, *L'économie d'ancien régime* (Paris, 1996), 95; Daniel Dessert, *Argent, pouvoir et société au Grand Siècle* (Paris, 1984); idem, *L'Argent du sel*; and Hocquet, "Qui la gabelle du sel du Roi de France a-t-elle enrichi?" For further analyses of French court capitalism, see George V. Taylor, "Types of Capitalism in Eighteenth-Century France," *EHR* 79 (1964), 478–497; Gail Bossenga, "Markets, the Patrimonial State, and the Origins of the French Revolution," *1650–1850: Ideas, Aesthetics, and Inquiries in the Early Modern Era* 11 (2005), 443–510; and Laurence Fontaine, *L'économie morale: pauvreté, crédit et confiance dans l'Europe préindustrielle* (Paris, 2008), chapter 4.
24. In this respect, the Farm was much like the highly professional excise administration in England. For a reappraisal of the French Farm, see Eugene N. White, "From Privatized to Government-Administered Tax Collection: Tax Farming in Eighteenth-Century France," *EHR* 57 (2004), 636–663.
25. Quoted in Durand, *Fermiers généraux*, 57. There were sixty Farmers General from 1756 to 1780.
26. Vida Azimi, *Un Modèle administratif de l'ancien régime* (Paris, 1987), 32–33 and 37. Necker estimated the number of guards at 23,000 in *De l'administration*, vol. 1, 106.

27. AN 29 AP 85, Observations sur . . . la ferme du tabac. The remaining 10 percent came from Holland.

28. For a contemporary critique of this slippage, see Vincent de Gournay, *Remarques inédits sur Traités sur le commerce de Josiah Child* (1754; reprint, Tokyo, 1983), 304. James Pritchard, *In Search of Empire: The French in the Americas, 1670–1730* (Cambridge, 2004), 187 and 235–236, notes this slippage, too, but we should be careful not to overemphasize it. The French sugar and coffee industries were geared toward reexportation (rather than fiscality), much like British tobacco. See Butel, *Les négociants bordelais.*

29. The Farm concentrated production in the north, where consumption was highest. The city of Paris consumed so much tobacco that it had its own manufactory.

30. This was the method for producing the most common form of tobacco, which was ultimately ground by the consumer. In the 1770s and 1780s, the Farm sometimes took the additional step of grinding the tobacco into snuff before sending it to warehouses.

31. Gondolff, *Tabac,* 325.

32. *Etat par Directions des Entrepôts du Tabac tant de la France que de la Lorraine* (Paris, 1774). Based on the number of French parishes, the commonly held estimate of 43,000 retailers (Jacob M. Price, *France and the Chesapeake* [Ann Arbor, MI, 1973], 434; Marc et Muriel Vigié, *L'herbe à Nicot: Amateurs de tabac, fermiers généraux et contrebandiers sous l'Ancien Régime* [Paris, 1989], 201; and Hidemi Uchida, *Le tabac en Alsace aux XVIIe et XVIIIe siècles: Essai sur l'histoire d'une économie régionale frontalière* [Strasbourg, 1997], 25) may be too high. Necker's estimate of 10,000 (cited in Matthews, *Royal General Farms,* 121) is probably too low, however. In Champagne, there was on average 1 retailer for every 1.3 parishes in 1738. AN 129 AP 29, procès-verbal of Helvétius, 1737–1738.

33. AN AD XI 48, no. 63, arrêt du conseil, 13 July 1683.

34. AN AD XI 51, no. 17; Jean Clinquart, *Les services extérieures de la ferme générale à la fin de l'Ancien Régime* (Paris, 1996), 202–205.

35. AN G-7 1291, memoir of 1708; Gondolff, *Tabac,* 132–133. The Burgundian capital of Dijon had forty sellers (Georges Pitre, *La ferme générale de Bourgogne* [Dijon, 1908], 130), while the Atlantic boomtown of Nantes drafted grocers and mercers to join full-time tobacconists in order to meet demand (AN G-1 109, doss. 3, État des débitants, 1778).

36. ADDR C 1069, register for department of Valence, 1760s.

37. Price, *France,* 377. Marcel Marion, *Histoire financière de la France depuis 1715* (Paris, 1919), 2:232, indicates that the gross revenue of the tobacco monopoly in 1788 was 51 million lt, from which 10 million was deducted for the purchase of the leaf and another 7 million for administrative costs.

38. Price, *France,* 38, 373–375.

39. Moreau de Beaumont, *Mémoires,* 4:581 and 4:680. Turgot is quoted in Gondolff, *Tabac,* 257–258.

40. Quoted in Philippe Haudrère, *L'Empire des rois, 1500–1789* (Paris, 1997), 137.

41. Quoted in Charles Woolsey Cole, *French Mercantilism, 1682–1700* (New York, 1943), 167.

42. Cole, *French Mercantilism,* 166.

43. Chassagne, *La manufacture de toiles imprimées de Tournemine-lès-Angers: Étude d'une entreprise et d'une industrie au XVIIIe siècle* (Paris, 1971), 48; Beverly Lemire, *Fashion's Favorite: The Cotton Trade and the Consumer in Britain, 1660– 1800* (Oxford, 1992), 34–42; John E. Wills, "European Consumption and Asian Production in the Seventeenth and Eighteenth Centuries," in *Consumption and the World of Goods,* ed. John Brewer and Roy Porter (London, 1994), 137.

44. Quoted in Philippe Haudrère, "The French India Company and Its Trade in the Eighteenth Century," in *Merchants, Companies, and Trade: Europe and Asia in the Early Modern Era,* ed. Sushil Chaudhury and Michel Morineau (Cambridge, 1999), 202–211.

45. Arrêt du conseil of 26 October 1686, published in Chassagne, *Manufacture,* 36.

46. *Dictionnaire universel de commerce* (Paris, 1741), 2:1152–1153.

47. See the assessments by Michel Morineau, "The Indian Challenge: Seventeenth to Eighteenth Centuries," in *Merchants, Companies, and Trade: Europe and Asia in the Early Modern Era,* ed. Sushil Chaudhury and Michel Morineau (Cambridge, 1999); and Chassagne, *Manufacture,* 38–49.

48. The 1759 tariff was substantially reduced in 1772 and again in the Eden Treaty of 1786.

49. "In Pursuit of Luxury: Global History and British Consumer Goods in the Eighteenth Century," *PP* 182 (2004), 85–142.

50. S.D. Chapman and S. Chassagne, *European Textile Printers in the Eighteenth Century* (London, 1981), 215.

51. Wim Klooster, "Inter-Imperial Smuggling in the Americas, 1600–1800," in *Soundings in Atlantic History: Latent Structures and Intellectual Currents, 1500– 1825,* ed. Bernard Bailyn and Patricia L. Denault (Cambridge, MA, 2009), 141–180. For the French Empire, see Jean Tarrade, *Le Commerce Colonial de la France à la fin de l'ancien régime* (Paris, 1972), vol. 1, chapters 3–4; James Pritchard, *In Search of Empire: The French in the Americas, 1670–1730* (Cambridge, 2004), 201–208; and Shannon Lee Dawdy, *Building the Devil's Empire: French Colonial New Orleans* (Chicago, 2008). For the Dutch empire, see Klooster, *Illicit Riches: Dutch Trade in the Caribbean, 1648–1795* (Leiden, 1998); Linda M. Rupert, *Creolization and Contraband: Curaçao in the Early Modern Atlantic World* (Athens, GA, 2012). For the British Empire, Christian J. Koot, *Empire at the Periphery: British Colonists, Anglo-Dutch Trade, and the Development of the British Atlantic, 1621–1713* (New York, 2011); Michael Jarvis, *In the Eye of All Trade: Bermuda, Bermudans, and the Maritime Atlantic World, 1680– 1783* (Chapel Hill, NC, 2010), chapter 3; and Thomas M. Truxes, *Defying*

Empire: Trading with the Enemy in Colonial New York (New Haven, CT, 2008). For the Spanish Empire, see Stanley J. Stein and Barbara H. Stein, *Silver, Trade, and War: Spain and America in the Making of Early Modern Europe* (Baltimore, 2000); and J. H. Elliott, *Empires of the Atlantic World: Britain and Spain in America 1492–1830* (New Haven, CT, 2006), 224–234.

52. For the masterless Atlantic, see Peter Linebaugh and Marcus Rediker, *The Many-Headed Hydra: Sailors, Slaves, Commoners, and the Hidden History of the Revolutionary Atlantic* (Boston, 2000).

53. Hoh-Cheung Mui and Lorna Mui, "Smuggling and the British Tea Trade before 1784," *AHR* 74 (1968), 44–73. Illicit tobacco was also rampant. See W. A. Cole, "Trends in Eighteenth-Century Smuggling," *EHR* 10 (1958), 395–410; and R. C. Nash, "English and Scottish Tobacco Trades in the 17th and 18th Centuries: Legal and Illegal Trade," *EHR* 35 (1982), 354–372. In Spain, about half the tobacco consumed in the seventeenth century was purchased on the black market. Norton, *Sacred Gifts,* 163.

54. For discussions of illicit salt and other noncolonial goods, see Chapter 4.

55. Arthur Pierce Middleton, *Tobacco Coast: A Maritime History of Chesapeake Bay in the Colonial Era* (Newport News, VA, 1953), 188–189; Koot, *Empire,* 208.

56. Peter Linebaugh, *The London Hanged: Crime and Civil Society in the Eighteenth Century* (London, 2003), chapter 5.

57. Nash, "English and Scottish Tobacco"; Renaud Morieux, *Une mer pour deux royaumes. La Manche, frontière franco-anglaise XVIIe–XVIIIe siècles* (Rennes, 2008), chapter 8.

58. AN G-7 1294, letter of 9 July 1715.

59. Antoine Lavoisier, *Oeuvres de Lavoisier: Correspondance* (Paris, 1955), vol. 7, part 1, 231, letter to Paulze, 7 November 1769. For Parisian retailers cutting tobacco with additives, see AN Y 9512, 9512b, and 10929/b. For the adulteration or imitation of heavily taxed consumables in this period, see Reynald Abad, *Le grand marché: L'approvisionnement alimentaire de Paris sous l'Ancien Régime* (Paris, 2002); Ashworth, *Customs and Excise,* 23–24, 308, and 314; and Norton, *Sacred Gifts,* 166.

60. This and the following discussion draw from Price, *France,* in addition to the works cited later.

61. Flanders, Artois, Franche-Comté, along with Brittany, Hainault, Cambrésis, and several southern provinces were known as the *provinces réputées étrangères,* which were not subject to Colbert's tariff of 1664. Alsace, Trois Evêchés (Metz, Toul, and Verdun), Comtat de Venaissin, and later Lorraine and Gex, in addition to the free ports of Marseille and Dunkirk and later Bayonne and Lorient, were known as the *provinces traitées à l'instar de l'étranger effectif,* which were not subject to Colbert's tariff of 1667. Some but not all of these "foreign" provinces lay outside the zone of the tobacco monopoly. Note that the islands of Jersey and Guernsey, transshipment points in the English Channel, had similarly wrung special trading privileges from Britain.

62. The southern papal enclave of Comtat de Venaissin, which was the largest and most heavily populated of all, was home to a thriving tobacco and calico industry. In 1734, the Farm blockaded the enclave's food supply to force Pope Clement VII to prohibit the production and exportation of contraband. The pope conceded, but the ban was never strictly enforced. See Madeleine Ferrières, "'Au coeur du royaume': Avignonnais et Comtadins," in *Les enclaves territoriales aux temps modernes (XVIe–XVIIIe siècles),* ed. Paul Delsalle and André Ferrer (Besançon, 2000), 39–58. See also André Ferrer, "Enclaves et contrebande: l'exemple de la Franche-Comté au XVIIIe siècle," in *Les enclaves territoriales aux temps modernes (XVIe–XVIIIe siècles),* ed. Paul Delsalle and André Ferrer (Besançon, 2000), 143–160. For the consolidation of French borders, see Peter Sahlins, *Unnaturally French: Foreign Citizens in the Old Regime and After* (Ithaca, NY, 2004), chapter 7; and John Bosher, *The Single Duty Project* (London, 1964).

63. AN 29 AP 85, Observations sur la constitution et le régime de la ferme du tabac.

64. Uchida, *Le tabac en Alsace;* André Ferrer, *Tabac, sel, indiennes: douane et contrebande en Franche-Comté au XVIIIe siècle* (Besançon, 2002), 131–164; Anne Radeff, *Du café dans le chaudron: Économie globale d'ancien régime: Suisse Occidentale, Franche-Comté et Savoie* (Lausanne, 1996), 339; David Todd, *L'Identité économique de la France: Libre-échange et protectionnisme,* 92; Klooster, *Illicit Riches,* 189.

65. BN MS 8390, Fontanieu to Orry, 17 July 1732.

66. Ferrer, *Tabac, sel, indiennes,* 137.

67. Uchida, *Tabac,* 56–73. Acknowledging defeat, the crown revoked the 1749 levy in 1774.

68. Le Trosne, *Les effets de l'impôt indirect, prouvés par les deux exemples de la Gabelle & du Tabac,* 257; AN 129 AP 29 (Dupin); Forbonnais, *Recherches et considérations sur les finances de France* (Liège, 1758), 3:228. For estimates in secondary works, see Price, *France,* 407; Durand, *Fermiers généraux,* 437; David T. Courtwright, *Forces of Habit: Drugs and the Making of the Modern World* (Cambridge, MA, 2001), 17; and Jordan Goodman, *Tobacco in History: The Cultures of Dependence* (London, 1994), 220–222. The Vigiés claim that under Colbert the black market provided nearly two-thirds of the tobacco consumed but, despite an absolute rise in contraband tobacco in the eighteenth century, the *proportion* of illicit tobacco leveled off to around one-third (Vigié, *L'herbe à Nicot,* 62 and 316).

69. Morgane Vary, "Les multiples facettes de l'économie parallèle dans les villes maritimes au XVIIIe siècle," in *Justice et argent: Les crimes et les peines pécuniaires du XIIIe au XXIe siècles,* ed. Benoît Garnot (Dijon, 2006), 82.

70. AMN HH 221, Ferrand to Mellier, January 1722. On 20 December 1752, a package from Lorient, containing *indiennes* and addressed to the intendant of Rouen, was confiscated en route in the city of Caen. See Philippe Haudrère, *La Compagnie française des Indes au XVIIIe siècle* (Paris, 2005), 305.

71. René Louis de Voyer de Paulmy, Marquis d'Argenson, *Journal et mémoires du marquis d'Argenson* (Paris, 1866), 8:130 and 8:199. This rumor is doubtful, but Madame de Pompadour did upholster the furniture in her Bellevue château with illegal cloth.

72. Patrick K. O'Brien, Trevor Griffiths, and Philip Hunt, "Political Components of the Industrial Revolution: Parliament and the English Cotton Textile Industry, 1660–1774," *EHR* 44 (1991), 395–423; Maxine Berg, *Luxury and Pleasure in Eighteenth-Century Britain* (Oxford, 2005).

73. Quoted in Olivier Raveux, "The Birth of a New European Industry: L'Indiennage in Seventeenth-Century Marseilles," in *The Spinning World: A Global History of Cotton Textiles, 1200–1850,* ed. Giorgio Riello and Prasannan Parthasarathi (Oxford, 2011), 300. Ina Baghdiantz McCabe, *Orientalism in Early Modern France: Eurasian Trade, Exoticism, and the Ancient Regime* (Oxford, 2008), 196, shows that Armenians acted as cross-cultural agents in the nascent French coffee industry as well.

74. Olivier Raveux, "Spaces and Technologies in the Cotton Industry in the Seventeenth and Eighteenth Centuries: The Example of Printed Calicoes in Marseilles," *Textile History* 36:2 (2005), 131–145; V.-L. Bourilly, "La Contrebande des toiles peintes en Provence au XVIIIe siècle," *AM* 26 (1914), 52–75; Katsumi Fukasawa, "Commerce et contrebande des indiennes en Provence dans la deuxième moitié du XVIIIe siècle," *AM* 99 (1987), 175–192.

75. Morineau ("Indian Challenge") and Chassagne *(Manufacture)* convincingly argue that the revocation was not intended to go after *indienneurs*. Edgard Depitre (*La toile peinte en France au XVIIe et au XVIIIe siècles: industrie, commerce, prohibitions* [Paris, 1912]) and Anne-Marie Piuz (*L'économie genevoise de la Réforme à la fin de l'Ancien Régime XVIe–XVIIIe siècles* [Geneva, 1990]) insist that it was.

76. Piuz, *L'économie genevoise,* 455–465.

77. Ulrich Pfister, "Cotton Manufacture in Switzerland and Germany, 15th–18th Centuries," GHEN, University of Padua, 17–19 November 2005, 4; Serge Chassagne, *Le Coton et ses patrons: France, 1760–1840* (Paris, 1991), avant-propos.

78. Pierre Caspard, *La Fabrique-Neuve de Cortaillod* (Paris, 1979). The contraband routes emanating from Bar-le-Duc are documented in AN Z1a 990, 992, 1076; and AN Y 10929/b. See also Isabelle Ursch-Bernier, "Mulhouse, l'enclave des indiennes au XVIIIe siècle," in *Les enclaves territoriales aux Temps Modernes (XVIe–XVIIIe siècles),* ed. Paul Delsalle and André Ferrer (Besançon, 2000), 161–168.

79. The estimate by Véron de Forbonnais is cited in Depitre, *Toile peinte,* 105. *Le Journal Oeconomique* (April 1755), 91–93, approximated the annual volume at 14 to 15 million lt, claiming that the French had spent more than a 100 million lt on contraband calico since the ban.

80. Chassagne, *Coton.*

3. The Making of a Smuggler

1. ADS C 1, signalements of 24 September 1754 and November 1754. For the development and use of such descriptions, see Vincent Denis, *Une Histoire de l'identité: France, 1715–1815* (Seyssel, 2008), chapter 2.
2. ADCO G 2550, Délibérations de Chapitre de Notre-Dame de Beaune, fol. 49.
3. This and the previous paragraph are based on Corinne Townley, *La véritable histoire de Mandrin* (Montmélian, 2005), 253.
4. This according to the parlement of Grenoble, quoted in René Fonvieille, *Mandrin: d'après de nombreux documents inédits* (Grenoble, 1975), 33.
5. BMG, De la Porte, Mémoire Général du Dauphiné, 1754 (R 5766).
6. René Favier, *Les villes du Dauphiné aux XVIIe et XVIIIe siècles* (Grenoble, 1993), 254–301; A.-P. Simian, *Histoire de St-Étienne-de-St-Geoirs* (Paris, 1989); and Bernard Bligny, *Histoire du Dauphiné* (Toulouse, 1973), 286–287.
7. My account of Mandrin's youth draws from Frantz Funck-Brentano, *Mandrin: Capitaine Général des Contrebandiers de France* (Paris, 1908); and René Fonvieille, *Mandrin* (Grenoble, 1975).
8. Funck-Brentano, *Mandrin*, 94–95; and Fonvieille, *Mandrin*, 38–39. Land disputes and fights were far too common in this era to be taken as signs of desperation. Indeed, physical assault was so banal that it was usually settled out of court, unless accompanied by more serious crimes against property. Nicole Castan, *Les Criminels de Languedoc* (Toulouse, 1980), chapter 6. For Mandrin's brawl with his lender, see BMG Chenavas (hereafter Ch.) 137 (16).
9. André Corvisier and Jean Delmas, *Histoire militaire de la France* (Paris, 1992), vol. 2, 49.
10. BMG Ch. 137 (2), fol. 160, deliberation of 2 January 1747.
11. François R. Velde, "French Public Finance between 1683 and 1726," in *Government Debts and Financial Markets in Europe,* ed. Fausto Piola Caselli (London, 2008), 136–137.
12. For details on the Italian affair, see Funck-Brentano, *Mandrin,* chapter 10.
13. And prostitution for women. Olwen H. Hufton, *The Poor of Eighteenth-Century France 1750–1789* (Oxford, 1974).
14. "Notes de M. Morel, curé de Montrigand," *Bulletin de la société départementale d'archéologie et de statistique de la Drôme* 15 (1881), 115. For crime, see Nicole Castan, *Justice et répression en Languedoc à l'époque des lumières* (Paris, 1980); idem, *Criminels de Languedoc;* and Benoît Garnot, ed., *Histoire et criminalité de l'antiquité au XXe siècle: nouvelles approches* (Dijon, 1992). Mandrin's biographer Funck-Brentano was stunned by Louis's apparently sudden rise to the top of a smuggling band in 1754, but we now know that he had been schooled in the arts of criminality and illicit trade. See Marion Douzet, "Mandrin, Saint-Étienne-de-Saint-Geoirs et le faux monnayage: Les origines criminelles du contrebandier," *La Pierre et l'Écrit* 13 (2002), 131–140.

15. Marie-France Brun-Jansen, "Criminalité et répression pénale au siècle des Lumières. L'exemple du parlement de Grenoble," *Revue d'histoire du droit* 76 (1998), 349.

16. Alan Forrest, *Conscripts and Deserters: The Army and French Society during the Revolution and Empire* (New York, 1989), 13.

17. Pierre Chaunu's thesis that the eighteenth century witnessed an evolution from violent crime to property crime has been largely discredited. Property crimes were on the rise, but violent crime did not abate. See Xavier Rousseau, "Existe-t-il une criminalité d'Ancien Régime? Réflexions sur l'histoire de la criminalité en Europe (XVIe–XVIIIe siècle)," in *Histoire et criminalité de l'antiquité au XXe siècle: nouvelles approches,* ed. Benoît Garnot (Dijon, 1992), 123–166.

18. ADI B 2197, fols. 108–109.

19. Douzet, "Mandrin"; Funck-Brentano, *Mandrin,* 112; and ADS C 13. Laurence Brissaud, "La Contrebande dans le Nord-Dauphiné au 18ème siècle" (Mémoire, Université Pierre Mendès France, 1995) demonstrates that many Savoyard smugglers hailed from St. Étienne and neighboring Cote St. André.

20. Townley, *Véritable histoire,* 57–58 and 115.

21. ADS 2B 10009; ADDR B 1314, f. 312; AAE Sardaigne 222, de la Porte to Machault d'Arnouville, 17 June 1754; and ADPD 1C 1645, Deauvelle to Michodière, 9 November 1754.

22. Abel Poitrineau, *Remues d'hommes: essai sur les migrations montagnardes en France aux XVII et XVIIIe siècles* (Paris, 1983); Jean Nicolas, *La Savoie au dix-huitième siècle: noblesse et bourgeoisie* (Paris, 1978); Laurence Fontaine, *History of Pedlars in Europe,* trans. Vicki Whittaker (Cambridge, 1996); Anne Radeff, *Du café dans le chaudron: économie globale d'ancien régime: Suisse occidentale, Franche-Comté et Savoie* (Lausanne, 1996); Chantal and Gilbert Maistre, *L'émigration marchande savoyarde aux XVIIe et XVIIIe siècles* (Annecy, 1986).

23. Radeff, *Du café;* Fontaine, *History of Pedlars;* and Hufton, *Poor,* chapter 3.

24. Willem van Schendel, "Spaces of Engagement," in *Illicit Flows and Criminal Things: States, Borders, and the Other Side of Globalization,* ed. Willem van Schendel and Abraham Itty (Bloomington, IN, 2005), 61; and Paul Gootenberg, "Talking Like a State: Drugs, Borders, and the Language of Control," in *Illicit Flows and Criminal Things: States, Borders, and the Other Side of Globalization,* ed. Willem van Schendel and Abraham Itty (Bloomington, IN, 2005), 109.

25. I borrow "borderland mentality" from Xavier Rousseau, "Espaces de désordres, espace d'ordre: Le banditisme aux frontières Nord-Est de la France (1700–1810)," in *Frontière et criminalité 1715–1815,* ed. Catherine Denys (Artois, 2000), 131–174. For the play of national identity in borderlands, see Renaud Morieux, *Une mer pour deux royaumes: La Manche, frontière franco-Anglaise (xviie–xviiie siècles)* (Rennes, 2008), chapter 8; and Peter Sahlins, *Boundaries: The Making of France and Spain in the Pyrenees* (Berkeley, CA, 1989).

26. AAE CP Genève 66, fols. 204–207, Montperoux to Rouillé, 13 November 1754. Montperoux believed that the "inaction" of Turin stemmed from the economic "interest" the court had in maintaining smuggling. AAE CP Genève 66, fols. 244–245, Montperoux to Rouillé, 6 December 1754.

27. Julius R. Ruff, *Violence in Early Modern Europe* (Cambridge, 2001), 49. Guns were also to be had at the Beaucaire fair, a popular destination point for Savoyard smugglers.

28. BN MS 8476. La Morlière estimated that 120 full-time smugglers operated in the three Savoyard border towns of Saint-Genix, Pont-de-Beauvoisin, and Les Échelles. SHAT A1 3406, no. 92, La Morlière to d'Argenson, 9 April 1755. In 1753, Charles Goyet, who worked at the White Cross tavern in Pont-de-Beauvoisin, testified that "80 or more" major smugglers worked the border from Saint Genix to Les Échelles, fifteen of whom he named.

29. Favier, *Villes du Dauphiné*, annexe 8.

30. Town officials arrested a smuggler named La Fourma for kicking a peasant in the stomach, stealing the cherries he had brought to market, and threatening to kill a witness, but they did not bother smuggler Saint Pierre who got into a fight at the White Cross tavern. ADS C 13, letters of 30 June 1750 and 14 January 1751.

31. AN G-7 248; and Jean Descotes-Genon, *Les douanes françaises et la contrebande sur le Guiers, en Chartreuse et à Miribel-les-Echelles* (Neuilly, 1994), 9–12. One merchant shuttled textiles to a shop he owned on the French side of town, where customers would lodge at the Golden Lion while awaiting shipments.

32. SHAT 1A 3406, no. 147, Marsin's journal.

33. On the Cretet family, see Nicolas, *Savoie*, 90–92.

34. SHAT 1A 3406, no. 147, Marsin's journal; and Herbert Lüthy, *La banque protestante en France de la révocation de l'Édit de Nantes à la Révolution* (Paris, 1959), 2:107, 439–441, and 677. Rousseau claimed that the fortune of Genevan merchant François-Henri d'Ivernois originated in the money he held for Mandrin. Jacques Berchtold, "Rousseau et Cartouche," in *Cartouche, Mandrin et autres brigands du XVIIIe siècle*, ed. Lise Andries (Paris, 2010), 348.

35. SHAT 1A 3406, no. 147, Marsin's journal. According to the same document, a nobleman residing in Pont-de-Beauvoisin, Marc Antoine de Passerat de Saint-Severin, also guarded a portion of Mandrin's fortune.

4. The Shadow Economy

1. By shadow economy, I do not mean Fernand Braudel's "shadowy zone" of the economy, by which he alluded to a primordial nonmarket economic base upon which markets stood (*Structures of Everyday Life*, trans. Siân Reynolds [Berkeley, CA, 1992], 23–24), but the illegal economy also known as the "parallel," "unofficial," "illicit," or "informal" economy.

2. The million-person estimate, from James R. Farr, *The Work of France: Labor and Culture in Early Modern Times, 1350–1800* (Lanham, MD, 2008), 49, does not include the multitudes (perhaps hundreds of thousands) of urban workers who illegally produced and sold goods outside the guild system. See Steven Kaplan, *La fin des corporations* (Paris, 2001), chapter 10; Alain Thillay, *Le Faubourg Saint-Antoine et ses 'faux ouvriers': La liberté du travail à Paris aux XVIIe et XVIIIe siècles* (Paris, 2002); Daryl M. Hafter, "Women in the Underground Business of Eighteenth-Century Lyon," *Enterprise and Society* 2 (March 2001), 11–40; and Cissie Fairchilds, "The Production and Marketing of Populuxe Goods in Eighteenth-Century Paris," in *Consumption and the World of Goods,* ed. John Brewer and Roy Porter (London, 1994), 228–248.

3. Ambroise-Marie Arnould, *De la balance du commerce et des relations commerciales extérieures de la France,* 3 vols. (Paris, 1791–1795), 1:173, estimate for the year 1784.

4. Robert Darnton, *The Forbidden Best-Sellers of Pre-Revolutionary France* (New York, 1996); Thierry Rigogne, *Between State and Market: Printing and Bookselling in Eighteenth-Century France* (Oxford, 2007); André Ferrer, *Tabac, sel, indiennes: douane et contrebande en Franche-Comté* (Besançon, 2002), 165–181; Elizabeth L. Eisenstein, *Grubb Street Abroad: Aspects of the French Cosmopolitan Press from the Age of Louis XIV to the French Revolution* (Oxford, 1992); Robert Dawson, *Confiscations at Customs: Banned Books and the French Booktrade during the Last Years of the Ancien Régime* (Oxford, 2006).

5. From 1759 to 1788, the lower salt court of Laval, situated just east of the Breton border, heard 4,788 cases, while from 1765 to 1789 the commission of Saumur, a high court whose jurisdiction covered cases involving bands of salt smugglers in the west, judged some 6,878 infractions. Yves Durand, "La contrebande du sel au XVIIIe siècle aux frontières de Bretagne, du Maine et de l'Anjou," *Histoire Sociale* 7 (1974), 227–269; Micheline Huvet-Martinet, "La répression du faux-saunage dans la France de l'Ouest et du Centre à la fin de l'Ancien Régime (1764–1789)," *AB* 84 (1977), 423–443.

6. At all the edges of the grandes gabelles, smugglers secreted salt into the French interior, while those in southern France moved it laterally from lightly to moderately taxed provinces. Borders between provinces with less dramatic variations in price may not have generated the same profit margins, but, less well policed, they attracted throngs of smugglers just the same. Anne Montenach, "Le faux-saunage en Haut-Dauphiné au XVIIIe siècle: entre économie parallèle et pluriactivité," *Histoire des Alpes* 14 (2009), 149–163.

7. For the social origins of smugglers, see Ferrer, *Tabac, sel, indiennes,* 214; Micheline Huvet-Martinet, "Faux-saunage et faux-sauniers dans l'Ouest et du Centre à la fin de l'Ancien Régime (1764–1789), *AB* 85 (1978), 377–400 and 573–594; Durand, "La contrebande du sel"; Nicolas Schapira, "Contrebande et contrebandiers dans le nord et de l'est de la France 1740–1789"

(mémoire, Université de Paris, 1991), table II.5; Nils Liander, "Smuggling Bands in Eighteenth-Century France" (PhD diss., Harvard University, 1981), table 21; and Laurence Brissaud, "La Contrebande dans le Nord-Dauphiné au 18ème siècle" (mémoire d'histoire moderne, Université Pierre Mendès, 1995), chapter 2.

8. Olwen Hufton, *The Poor of Eighteenth-Century France 1750–1789* (Oxford, 1974). Worsening conditions for the laboring poor are analyzed by Jack A. Goldstone, "The Social Origins of the French Revolution Revisited," in *From Deficit to Deluge: The Origins of the French Revolution,* ed. Thomas E. Kaiser and Dale K. Van Kley (Stanford, CA, 2011), 67–103.

9. Jean Nicolas, *La Rébellion française: Mouvements populaires et conscience sociale 1661–1789* (Paris, 2002), 56–60. André Zysberg, *Les Galériens: Vies et destins de 60,000 forçats sur les galères de France 1680–1748* (Paris, 1987), 95 (graph 5); and Liander, "Smuggling Bands," 485.

10. AN G-1 106, doss. 1, "Fermes générales, 3e division, Tabac." See later for examples of smuggling profits.

11. ADH C 1696, dossier on Antoine Garnier.

12. Quoted in Jean Clinquart, *Les services extérieurs de la Ferme générale à la fin de l'Ancien Régime* (Paris, 1995), 233.

13. Quoted in Schapira, "Contrebande," 134.

14. Liana Vardi, *The Land and the Loom: Peasants and Profit in Northern France, 1680–1800* (Durham, NC, 1993); and Stephen Miller, *State and Society in Eighteenth-Century France: A Study of Political Power and Social Revolution in Languedoc* (Washington, DC, 2008).

15. Jan de Vries, *The Industrious Revolution: Consumer Behavior and the Household Economy, 1650 to the Present* (Cambridge, 2008), chapters 1–4.

16. ADS C 662, Matton to Capris de Castellamont, 8 August 1761.

17. Schapira, "Contrebande," table II.5, shows that 17.4 percent of his sample worked in such mobile trades. See also Liander, "Smuggling Bands," table 20. After mobility professionals came soldiers, artisans, and textile workers.

18. BN MS 8372, Orry to Fontanieu, 12 January 1733; and 8390, Fontanieu to Orry, 5 February 1733. For peddlers, see Laurence Fontaine, *History of Pedlars in Europe,* trans. Vicki Whittaker (Cambridge, 1996).

19. AN AD XI 49, no. 18, arrêt du conseil, 2 January 1714.

20. BA Bastille, 11127, Machault to Feydeau de Marville, 2 July 1746.

21. BA Bastille 11127. Although authorities originally intended to send a message by dispatching Boyard to the galleys, the merchants bailed him out with a large fine. On a smaller scale, Louis Pierre Prevost, a vegetable farmer from Bonneuil, was instructed by his landlord to deliver four bags of contraband, buried in a cart under a bed of legumes, to a merchant just outside Paris. He was to be paid a healthy twelve lt—six up front, six when he returned (AN Y 9512/B). This method of trafficking was especially common in the calico trade. Instead of running the risk of moving illegal merchandise themselves, merchants hired drivers for nominal fees to truck

cloth across the border. On 27 March 1740, a carter named Jean-Pierre Begat, paid to drive a three-horse cart carrying 1,087 aunes of cloth into Paris, was arrested east of the city in Meaux. An unwitting underling, Begat was eventually exonerated, but his boss, who had loaded the cart and neglected to inform him what he would be transporting, was put on trial. BA Bastille, 11127.

22. AN Y 9512, Jean Baptiste Vast, 18 November 1772; and AN V-7 493, liasse 1771–1772. Hiding tobacco in large tubs of butter was a relatively common method of smuggling. See AN Y 9513, case of Nicolas Virion, 29 March 1774.

23. AN Y 9513, case of Marie Jeanne Laurent, femme d'Antoine Boudier, 4 November 1774.

24. AN Y 10929/b. See also Ferrer, *Tabac, sel, indiennes*, 150–151.

25. Jean Nicolas, "Cabarets et sociabilité populaire en Savoie au XVIIIe siècle," in *Les intermédiaires culturels* (Aix-en-Provence, 1981), 305–321; idem, *La Savoie au XVIIIe siècle: Noblesse et bourgeoisie* (Montmélian, 2003), 862–865; Nicole Castan, *Les criminels de Languedoc* (Toulouse, 1980), chapter 6; Liander, "Smuggling Bands," chapter 7; Schapira, "Contrebande," 83–85; and Anne Radeff, *Du café dans le chaudron: économie globale d'ancien régime: Suisse occidentale, Franche-Comté et Savoie* (Lausanne, 1996), 236.

26. AN Z1a 991, jugement of 17 March 1756.

27. AN AD XI 51B, arrêt de la cour des comptes, aydes et finances du Languedoc, 9 February 1718; AN AD XI 51C, sentence de l'élection de Reims, 2 December 1747; and AN Z 1a 989, jugement of 14 March 1754.

28. AN AD XI 48, no. 126, arrêt de la cour du parlement de Rennes, 23 April 1699. For further discussions of the clergy's role in smuggling, see Hufton, *Poor*, 294–297; and Liander, "Smuggling Bands," 126–127.

29. BA Bastille, 11127, letter of 21 July 1740; AN AD XI 51, no. 141, arrest du conseil of 14 June 1768.

30. Daniel Roche, *The Culture of Clothing: Dress and Fashion in the Ancien Régime*, trans. Jean Birrell (Cambridge, 1994), 40–41, 78, 100, 106, 144, 173, and 185.

31. AN Y 10929/b, report of 16 July 1763. For similar cases, see AN Y 9512/B; BA Bastille 11127. Domestics who did not want to be directly involved in the trade simply leased their masters' space to smugglers. See AN Y 10929/b, case of 26 July 1763. For the illegal book trade in Versailles, see Robert Darnton, *Devil in the Holy Water or the Art of Slander from Louis XIV to Napoleon* (Philadelphia, 2010), 132.

32. AN Y 9512/B, case of Joseph Pithon.

33. Quoted in V.-L. Bourilly, "La Contrebande des toiles peintes en Provence au XVIIIe siècle," AM 26 (1914), 68–70.

34. ADH C 1678, procès verbal of 17 February 1730.

35. For further discussion of the nobility in illicit trade, see Liander, "Smuggling Bands," 127–130; and Nicolas, *Rébellion française*, 96–101; René Favier,

"Une province face à la contrebande," in *Louis Mandrin: malfaiteur ou bandit au grand cœur* (Grenoble, 2005), 16. The participation of Grenoble magistrates in the province's contraband trade had been reported by the intendant as early as the 1730s. BN MS 8390, Fontanieu to Orry, 6 July and 3 August 1732.

36. AN G-7 1294, Mémoire sur l'affaire Adigard, 18 December 1714. For smuggling by Breton nobles, see also AN V-7 506, doss. 3; and J. Darsel, "Gentilshommes contrebandiers: l'affaire de la Hunaudeye," *Société d'Émulation des Côtes-du-Nord* 87 (1959), 22–31.

37. BN MS 8476, f. 80; and SHAT 1A 3406, no. 276, d'Espagnac to d'Argenson, 28 May 1755.

38. SHAT, 1A 3406, no. 161, letter of 28 April 1755.

39. SHAT 1A 3406, no. 239, mémoire.

40. SHAT 1A 3406, no. 261, La Morlière to d'Argenson, 23 May 1755.

41. Ferrer, *Tabac, sel, indiennes,* 209–219; Schapira, "Contrebande," table II.2; Liander, table 18; Durand, "La contrebande du sel"; Huvet-Martinet, "Faux-saunage"; Brissaud, "La contrebande"; and Corinne Townley, *La véritable histoire de Mandrin* (Montmélian, 2005), 49–50. Although highly mobile, smugglers generally were born or resided within ten or fifteen miles of the border and did not venture too far from home. Smugglers plying their trade in Franche-Comté came from that province or its neighbors (Lorraine, Alsace, Montbéliard, Switzerland, Burgundy, Champagne). Those who had traveled the greatest distances hailed from the southeast (Savoie, Dauphiné, Auvergne—Mandrin country) or from Paris. The same held true in the north, where most were born and resided near the fiscal border along the outer edge of Picardy and Champagne. Dauphiné smugglers likewise lived in Grenoble or near the Savoy border in the Grésivaudan Valley and along the Guiers River. In western France, the salt smugglers working the Brittany-Maine/Anjou border lived along the eastern edge of that fiscal line.

42. Durand, "La contrebande du sel."

43. Laurence Fontaine, *L'économie morale: pauvreté, crédit et confiance dans l'Europe préindustrielle* (Paris, 2008); Anne Montenach, "Femmes des montagnes dans l'économie informelle: les 'faux-sauniers' en Haut-Dauphiné aux XVIIIe siècle," in *Donne e lavaro: prospettive per une storia delle montagne europee, XVIII–XX secc,* ed. Luigi Lorenzetti and Nelly Valsangiacomo (Milan, 2010), 68–83; Hafter, "Women in the Undergound."

44. Huvet-Martinet, "Faux-saunage."

45. Schapira, "Contrebande," 88 and tables II.1 and III.14; Liander, "Smuggling Bands," tables 16 and 19. Schapira's tables shows that 41 percent of the commission's cases involved tobacco exclusively, 24 percent involved salt exclusively, and 19 percent involved both (though tobacco tended to be the primary cargo). Liander's tables indicate that 46 percent of the cases involved tobacco only and 11 percent involved salt only. The discrepancies stem from differences in the years they sampled; Schapira's higher incidence

of salt smuggling is due to his inclusion of the late 1780s, when agricultural crisis forced more peasants into artisanal salt smuggling. One point on which the two studies agree is that males dominated the higher levels of smuggling.

46. BN MS 8476, mémoire concernant les contrebandiers. On the growth of the Farm police in this period, see chapter 7; Ferrer, *Tabac, sel, indiennes,* part 1; and Schapira, "Contrebande," 1–14, 245, 355, and 463.

47. Liander, "Smuggling Bands," 291.

48. BN MS 8476 and 8390. A similar report (SHAT 1A 3406, no. 181) numbered the "scoundrels" working in bands in Savoy and Switzerland at "more than 4 to 500."

49. BN MS 8375, fol. 335, Orry to Fontanieu, 8 October 1736; ADH C 1697, Orry to Bernage, 29 March 1731, and Bernage to Orry, 31 December 1732; and SHAT 1A 3385, no. 475.

50. ADS C 13, Saraceni to Sinsan, 10 July 1755. This may have been a double wedding. According to Guy Peillon, *Sur les traces de Louis Mandrin* (Lyon, 2005), 245, Louis's sister Marianne married Jacques Delaucourt aka Coconier the same month.

51. For the tobacco-filled northeast, see Schapira, "Contrebande," tables III.8 and III.12; and Liander, "Smuggling Bands," tables 16 and 17. For the salt-dominated west, see Huvet-Martinet, "Faux-saunage."

52. Because the archives of the commission of Valence are not intact, it is impossible to explore in detail the gangs that worked in southeastern France, where Mandrin waged his campaigns. However, conditions in the northeast, well documented in the archives of the commission of Reims (AN Z1a 964–1080) closely resembled those in the southeast in that tobacco coming from east of the customs zone dominated the underground markets of both regions.

53. AN Z1a 988–991; and Liander, "Smuggling Bands," chapter 8.

54. AAE CP Genève 66, fol. 313, Montperoux to Rouillé, 9 April 1755.

55. AN Z1a 990, interrogation of Guilain Degrés, 28 July 1753.

56. My discussion of the Wignhies band draws from Liander, "Smuggling Bands," chapter 7.

57. Marcus Rediker, *Villains of All Nations: Atlantic Pirates in the Golden Age* (Boston, 2004), emphasizes the egalitarian life of pirates, whereas Kris Lane, *Pillaging the Empire: Piracy in the Americas, 1500–1750* (London, 1998), provides a less romantic view. For opposing arguments on the relationship between pirates and smugglers, see Niklas Frykman, "Pirates and Smugglers: Political Economy in the Red Atlantic," in *Mercantilism Reimagined: Political Economy in Early Modern Britain and Its Empire,* ed. Philip Stern and Carl Wennerlind (Oxford, 2013); and Alan L. Karras, *Smuggling: Contraband and Corruption in World History* (Lanham, MD, 2010), chapter 2.

58. My discussion of calico bands is drawn from Liander, "Smuggling Bands," chapters 6 and 9; and AN G-7 248, on the bande d'Orange, which smuggled textiles between Geneva and Beaucaire.

59. AAE CP Genève 66, fols. 189–190, mémoire of 5 November 1754.

60. Darnton, *Forbidden Best-Sellers,* 18. For a rare example of an insurance contract involving a tobacco smuggler, see Harald Deceulaer, "Violence, magie populaire et contrats transfrontaliers," in *Fraude, contrefaçon et contrebande de l'Antiquité à nos jours,* ed. Gérard Béaur, Hubert Bonin, and Claire Lemercier (Geneva, 2006), 81.

61. ADH C 1981, Letter to St. Priest, 13 May 1756.

62. AN G-7 1291, letter of 1708.

63. ADS C 428, Casasque to Ferraris, 2 February 1755.

64. AN G-7 1292, letter of 28 July 1711.

65. Bourilly, "La Contrebande," 68–70; and Jean-Marc Peysson, "Le mur d'enceinte des fermiers-généraux et la fraude à la fin de l'ancien régime," *BSHP* 109 (1982), 233 and 238.

66. AN G-7 1293, dossier on Mathieu Rivoire, 1713.

67. BN MS 8392, fol. 40–43 and 75–78, Fontanieu to Orry, 19 January 1737 and 9 March 1737.

68. E. Gondolff, *Le Tabac sous l'ancienne monarchie: La ferme royale, 1629–1791* (Vesoul, 1914), 284; V. de Clercq, "L'incendie des barrières de Paris en juillet 1789," *BSHP* (1938), 31; Reynald Abad, *Le Grand marché: L'approvisionnement alimentaire de Paris sous l'ancien régime* (Paris, 2002), 77–83 and 93–99, estimates that 15 percent of Paris wine and livestock was contraband.

69. *Encyclopédie Méthodique: Finances* (Paris, 1784), 1:92, "Barrières"; Abad, *Grand marché,* 94.

70. AN Y 9512 and V-7 493.

71. AN Y 9512/B, case of 6 May 1773. For another case in which scores of Farm employees were implicated, see AN Y 9513, case of Martin Rousseau, 5 February 1774.

72. AN Y 10929/b, case of Étienne Lemesle, 28 June 1763.

73. AN Y 9512/B.

74. AN Y 9512, case of Claude Ferry, 5 June 1772. Some wage-earning smugglers made substantial sums, particularly those who transported calicoes. Claude Coté, a mason from Arbois in the border province of Franche-Comté, was paid fifteen lt (over a week of normal wages) for smuggling calicoes from Switzerland to France. The fee was high, but he would be paid nothing if he got caught. ADD 1C 426.

75. Liander, "Smuggling Bands," 262–263. Gardeners from Vaugirard were also responsible for smuggling sacks of tobacco from the household of Madame la Mareschalle de Duras into Paris. AN Y 10929/b, case of Leonard Gadaine, 26 July 1763.

76. AN Y 10929/b; AN Z1a 1076; AN Y 9512, case of Jean Baptiste Perret and Josephe Maillard, 18 November 1772; Schapira, "Contrebande," 83; Liander, "Smuggling Bands," 263.

77. BA Bastille 11127; Liander, "Smuggling Bands," 263–264 and 272–273.

78. AN AD XI 51, no. 39, arrest du conseil, 28 May 1743.

79. AN AD XI 51, no. 112; AN V-7 493, dossier 1.

80. AN G-7 1292, procès verbal of 8 March 1710. See also AN Y 9512, case of Pierre Fougues, 10 July 1772.

81. AN Y 9513, case of Antoine François, 29 March 1774. See also AN Y 9512, case of Nicolas Vallet, 24 August 1772.

82. AN Y 10929/b, cases handled by Pierre Thiéron, commissaire au Châtelet, 1762–1772.

83. BN MS 8392, fol. 32–40, Fontanieu to Orry, 17 January 1737. See also ADPD 1C 1627.

84. AN G-7 1294, letter to Desmaretz, 19 August 1714.

85. Anne E. C. McCants, "Exotic Goods, Popular Consumption, and the Standard of Living: Thinking about Globalization in the Early Modern World," *JWH* 18 (2007), 443–444, makes a similar point about tea consumption in England. Kaplan (*Fin,* 361) and Fairchilds ("Populuxe Goods") likewise suggest that illicit French workers helped to expand networks of distribution.

86. Though certainly not a new phenomenon, the bifurcation of the market into high and low ends, the latter imitating the former but offering a lesser-quality and cheaper product, seems to have become a major feature of consumer culture in the eighteenth century. Low-end markets were often (but not always) tinged with illicit trade, as retailers of contraband, stolen goods, and informally fabricated products offered tantalizing bargains.

87. Gianluca Fiorentini and Sam Peltzman, eds., *The Economics of Organized Crime* (Cambridge, 1995), 20–21; Friedrich Schneider and Dominik H. Enste, *The Shadow Economy: An International Survey* (Cambridge, 2002), 171; Ronald Findlay and Kevin H. O'Rourke, *Power and Plenty: Trade, War, and the World Economy in the Second Millennium* (Princeton, NJ, 2007), 259.

88. Along the eastern border, the Farm cut the price of its "superior" tobacco from fifty sols to thirty-three sols a pound, while its "inferior" product was lowered from twenty-five sols to sixteen sols a pound (AN AD XI 50, no. 90). The Farm was also forced to provide soldiers with inexpensive "tabac de cantine" to wean them from contraband.

89. Serge Chassagne, *Le Coton et ses patrons: France, 1760–1840* (Paris, 1991), 16.

90. Kenneth Pomeranz, *The Great Divergence: China, Europe, and the Making of the Modern World Economy* (Princeton, NJ, 2000), 196.

5. Rebel Rebel

1. The classic statement regarding this shift was formulated by Emmanuel Le Roy Ladurie, "Révoltes et contestations rurales en France de 1675 à 1788," *AESC* 29 (1974), 6–22. Disseminated by Roger Chartier, *The Cultural Origins of the French Revolution,* trans. Lydia G. Cochrane (Durham, NC, 1991), 141–45, Ladurie's thesis was based on the work of Yves-Marie Bercé, *Histoire des Croquants,* 2 vols. (Geneva, 1974), which failed to consider the persistence of small-scale fiscal rebellions into the eighteenth century.

2. Jean Nicolas, *La Rébellion française: Mouvements populaires et conscience sociale 1661–1789* (Paris, 2002), table I.3 and annex 2. See also Nicolas Schapira, "Contrebande et contrebandiers dans le nord et de l'est de la France, 1740–1789 (mémoire, Université de Paris I, 1991), tables III.14 and III.15; and Nils Liander, "Smuggling Bands in Eighteenth-Century France" (PhD diss., Harvard University, 1981), table 16.

3. Nicolas, *Rébellion française,* figures 3 and 4. These figures are undoubtedly low. Liander, "Smuggling Bands," tables 15 and 22, shows that in the 1740s, in the north alone (Picardy, Soissonais, and Champagne), the commission of Reims prosecuted on average twenty-three cases of violent rebellion and rioting every year. This figure does not include cases prosecuted by lower courts in the same region or instances in which rebellions went unreported or in which rebels escaped unidentified. Whatever the absolute numbers, both Nicolas and Liander demonstrate that contraband rebellion was on the rise in the 1770s and 1780s. In per capita terms, such rebellion was heaviest in the north (Artois and Picardy), where tobacco smuggling predominated; in the west (Maine and Anjou), where salt smuggling held sway; and in the far south (Roussillon), where both salt and tobacco smuggling was common.

4. Jean-Claude Hocquet, *Le sel et le pouvoir* (Paris, 1985), 404, suggested a similar hypothesis, that smuggling was "the new form of struggle" after the failure of the great antifiscal revolts under Richelieu and Mazarin.

5. Norbert Elias, *Power and Civility: The Civilizing Process,* trans. Edmund Jephcott (New York, 1982), 91–225. Elias's concept of a state monopoly of violence derived from Max Weber, *Politics as a Vocation.*

6. Administrators, economists, and newspaper correspondents regularly applied the term "war" to both the Farm's offensive against smugglers and the smugglers' rebellions against the Farm. See Chapter 11 and, for a similar use of the war metaphor during the Restoration, David Todd, *L'Identité économique de la France: Libre-échange et protectionnisme (1814–1851)* (Paris, 2008), chapter 3.

7. Alain Guéry, "Le roi dépensier: Le don, la contrainte et l'origine du système financier de la monarchie française d'Ancien Régime," *AESC* 39 (1984), 1241–1269; and Jean Meuvret, "Comment les Français du XVIIe siècle voyaient l'impôt?," in *Études d'histoire économique* (Paris, 1971), 295–308.

8. AN Y 9512/B, report of 27 July 1773.

9. Adam Smith, *An Inquiry into the Nature and Causes of the Wealth of Nations,* ed. R.H. Campbell and A.S. Skinner (Indianapolis, IN, 1981), 2:898.

10. E.P. Thompson, "The Moral Economy of the English Crowd in the Eighteenth Century," *PP* 50 (1971), 76–136. In emphasizing communal ideas of economic justice, I follow James C. Scott, *The Moral Economy of the Peasant: Rebellion and Subsistence in Southeast Asia* (New Haven, CT, 1976) and *Weapons of the Weak: Everyday Forms of Peasant Resistance* (New Haven, CT, 1985). On the current state of the moral economy paradigm, see Dominique Margairaz

and Philippe Minard, "Marché des subsistances et économie morale: ce que "taxer" veut dire," *AHRF* 352 (2008), 53–99; Didier Fassin, "Les économies morales revisitées," *AHSS* 64 (December 2009), 1237–1266; and my later discussion.

11. AN G-7 1292.

12. BN MS 8390.

13. Vincenzo Lavenia, "L'Église, juge du fisc: Théologie et impôt aux XVIe et XVIIe siècles," in *Philosophie de l'impôt*, ed. Thomas Berns et al. (Brussels, 2006), 37–68; Liander, "Smuggling Bands," 126–127 and 417.

14. Quoted in Anne Radeff, *Du café dans le chaudron: Économie globale d'ancien régime: Suisse Occidentale, Franche-Comté et Savoie* (Lausanne, 1996), 236.

15. Louis-Sébastien Mercier, *Tableau de Paris* (Amsterdam, 1782), vol. 1, chapter 123.

16. Whereas 80 percent of rebellions against the Farm were either collective in nature or occurred as a reaction to an ambush, arrest, or investigation by Farm agents, only 7 percent were the kind of premeditated aggressive attacks that Mandrin was inclined to lead. (The remaining 13 percent of rebellions were collective or individual resistance to searches, citations, or arrests occurring inside a house or tavern.) Nicolas, *Rébellion française*, 44–45.

17. AAE CP Sardaigne 222, de la Porte to Machault d'Arnouville, 17 June 1754. The assailants were not named in this attack, but the modus operandi and the fact that Mandrin passed through this post just a few days later suggest that he was behind it.

18. ADDR B 1304, jugements of Mandrin and Bélissard; Guy Peillon, *Sur les traces de Louis Mandrin* (Lyon, 2005), 17.

19. Fédérique Pitou, "Jeunesse et désordre: les coureurs de nuit à Laval au XVIIIe siècle," *RHMC* 47 (2000), 82.

20. AAE CP Sardaigne 222, de la Porte to Machault d'Arnouville, 17 June 1754; Corinne Townley, *La véritable histoire de Mandrin* (Montmélian, 2005), 60.

21. William Beik, *Urban Protest in Seventeenth-Century France: The Culture of Retribution* (Cambridge, 1997); and "The Violence of the French Crowd from Charivari to Revolution," *PP* 197 (November 2007), 75–110.

22. For overlapping approaches to early modern French popular violence, see Natalie Davis, "The Rites of Violence: Religious Riot in Sixteenth-Century France," *PP* 59 (May 1973), 51–91; Colin Lucas, "The Crowd and Politics between Ancien Régime and Revolution in France," *Journal of Modern History* 60 (September 1988), 421–457; Arlette Farge and Jacques Revel, *The Vanishing Children of Paris: Rumor and Politics before the French Revolution*, trans. Claudia Miéville (Cambridge, MA, 1991), 61; and Beik, "Violence." For useful theorizations of violence, see Charles Tilly, *The Politics of Collective Violence* (Cambridge, 2003); and Fernando Coronil and Julie Skurski, eds., *States of Violence* (Ann Arbor, MI, 2006).

23. The term "military entrepreneur" is borrowed from Thomas W. Gallant, "Brigandage, Piracy, Capitalism, and State-Formation: Transnational Crime from a Historical World-Systems Perspective," in *States and Illegal Practices*, ed. Josiah McC. Heyman (Oxford, 1999), 26.
24. The most complete list of band members is in Peillon, *Sur les traces*, 241–253.
25. André Corvisier, *Armies and Societies in Europe, 1494–1789* (Bloomington, IN, 1979), 15.
26. In addition to sources cited later, my account of this expedition is based on AAE CP Sardaigne 222, de la Porte to Machault d'Arnouville, 17 June 1754; ADDR B 1304, jugement of Mandrin; Peillon, *Sur les traces*, 27–31; and BMG Chenavas, 144.
27. Steven L. Kaplan, *Provisioning Paris: Merchants and Millers in the Grain and Flour Trade during the Eighteenth Century* (Ithaca, NY, 1984), 27.
28. ADH C 1978, letter from Nayac to Bonefon, 18 July 1754. Similarly, in Yssingeaux on 26 August, the band was reported to have "sold their merchandise publicly and with arms in hand." ADH C 1978, De Rachat to St. Priest, 29 August 1754.
29. ADH C 1978, Nayac to Bonefon, 18 July 1754. The band would conduct a similar military exercise in Saint-Affrique on 24 June, shooting rifles in the air in honor of St. Jean, their commander's patron saint.
30. ADH C 1978, Nayac to Bonefon, 18 July 1754.
31. ADH C 1978, letter from the subdelegate of Vabre, 18 July 1754.
32. AAE CP Sardaigne 222, de la Porte to Machault d'Arnouville, 17 June 1754. The extortion of the promissory note took place on 9 January 1754.
33. ADDR B 1304, no. 312.
34. ADH C 1978, Barenton to St. Priest, 7 July 1754. The troop said it would be back in a month, by which time the director should be prepared to purchase 10,000 lt of contraband tobacco.
35. Olwen Hufton, "Begging, Vagrancy, Vagabondage and the Law," *European History Quarterly* 2 (1972), 118; Nicole Castan, "La justice expéditive au XVIIIe siècle," *AESC* 31 (1976), 334. For the robbery of revenue convoys, see Daniel Dessert, *Argent, pouvoir, et société au Grand Siècle* (Paris, 1984), 38.
36. John Lynn, *The Giant of the Grand Siècle: The French Army, 1610–1715* (Cambridge, 1997), 211. They also bear a resemblance to the gabelle, the royal monopoly that forced subjects to buy a fixed allotment of salt every year. But, as we shall see, Mandrin understood himself to be breaking a monopoly rather than creating one.
37. René-Louis de Voyer, Marquis d'Argenson, *Journal et mémoires du marquis d'Argenson* (Paris, 1866), 8:396. See also AAE CP Sardaigne 222, fols. 261–264, de la Porte to Machault d'Arnouville, 17 Juin 1754; SHAT 1A 3397, no. 432, d'Argenson to d'Espagnac, 28 February 1755; Charles-Philippe d'Albert, Duc de Luynes, *Mémoires du duc de Luynes sur la cour de Louis XV (1735–1758)* (Paris, 1863), 13:356.

38. Work on *taxations populaires* is voluminous, but see George Rudé, "La taxation populaire de mai 1775 à Paris et dans la région parisienne," *AHRF* 143 (1956), 139–179; Louise Tilly, "The Food Riot as a Form of Political Conflict in France," *Journal of Interdisciplinary History* 2 (1971), 23–57; Steven L. Kaplan, *Bread, Politics and Political Economy in the Reign of Louis XV* (London, 2014); idem, *Provisioning Paris;* Cynthia Bouton, *The Flour War: Gender, Class, and Community in Late Ancien Régime French Society* (University Park, PA, 1993); and Margairaz and Minard, "Marché des subsistances."

39. Raymond de Roover, "The Concept of the Just Price," *JEH* 18 (1958), 420–421 (and comment by David Herlihy, 437–438); and John W. Baldwin, *The Medieval Theories of the Just Price* (Philadelphia, 1959), 80.

40. Bouton, *Flour War,* 96–97 and 123–124. Those who paid nothing sometimes explained that they had no money to give, a verbal gesture meant to distinguish their actions from sheer theft. Déborah Cohen, *La nature du peuple: Les formes de l'imaginaire social (XVIII–XXIe siècles* (Seyssel, 2010), 323. In the same vein, judicial and police authorities did, in certain circumstances, exercise a degree of leniency toward destitute food thieves. Arlette Farge, *Le vol d'aliments à Paris au XVIIIe siècle* (Paris, 1974).

41. Luynes, *Mémoires,* 13:356. Alan Karras, *Smuggling: Contraband and Corruption in World History* (Lanham, MD, 2010), chapter 2, argues that smugglers' preference for trade over robbery distinguished them from pirates, but Niklas Frykman, "Pirates and Smugglers: Political Economy in the Red Atlantic," in *Mercantilism Reimagined,* ed. Philip Stern and Carl Wennerlind (Oxford, 2013), emphasizes the similarities between the two groups. Following Charles Tilly, "War Making and State Making as Organized Crime," in *Bringing the State Back In,* ed. Peter Evans and Dietrich Rueschemeyer (Cambridge, 1985) and Alejandro Colás and Bryan Mabee, eds, *Mercenaries, Pirates, Bandits, and Empires: Private Violence in Historical Context* (New York, 2010), I would suggest that a continuum of exchange existed between the strictly voluntary and coercive.

42. Kaplan, *Bread,* 60–62. It is worth noting, however, that practices of *taxation* did occasionally extend beyond grain and flour to other basic goods, such as meat, candles, and wood. Margairaz and Minard, "Marché des subsistances," 62–63.

43. All we know is that with royal troops from the border provinces of Dauphiné, Bugey, and Bresse on high alert, Mandrin opted to forgo the usual southerly route from Savoy into Dauphiné in favor of a northern passage across Lake Léman, through Switzerland, and into Franche-Comté. Having grown to about fifty or sixty men, the band attacked Farm brigades in Mouthe and Chaux-Neuve but does not seem to have conducted any forced sales.

44. ADDR B 1304, jugement of Mandrin. My account of this expedition is based on ADD 1C 1310; and Peillon, *Sur les traces,* 37–44. Funck-Brentano and other biographers follow the itinerary given in *Abregé de la vie de Louis Mandrin* (1755), which is inaccurate.

45. AN 129 AP 20, procès-verbal of 1734.

46. ADPD 1C 1635, procès-verbal of 26 August 1754.

47. ADH C 1978, letter from the subdelegate of Vabre, 18 July 1754.

48. Laurence Fontaine, *History of Pedlars in Europe*, trans. Vicki Whittaker (Cambridge, 1996), 33.

49. AAE CP Genève 66, fols. 236–237, Montperoux to Rouillé, 2 December 1754. His claim of 40,000 lt seems exaggerated, given the limited scale of his Italian venture.

50. ADPD 1C 1639, suite des nouvelles; and ADH C 6877, Saulx Tavannes to Moncan, 12 October 1754. Justifications of this sort were also reported in d'Argenson, *Journal*, 8:435–436, and in such newspapers as the *GA* (5 November 1754), *CA* (29 October 1754 and 15 November 1754), and the *GC* (1 November 1754).

51. Giovanni Levi, *Inheriting Power: The Story of an Exorcist*, trans. Lydia G. Cochrane (Chicago, 1988), chapter 3.

52. ADH C 1978, St. Priest to d'Argenson and Séchelles, no date.

53. My stress on market correction is consistent with recent work on food provisioning. Steven Kaplan notes that price-fixing authorities did not intend "to throttle commerce but to domesticate it and moralize it, not to obliterate the market principle but to *correct* it." So engrained was the fear of market collusion in the mental framework of French consumers that when royal officials attempted to provision grain markets during subsistence crises, they, too, were accused of acting as a "monopoly." Kaplan, *Provisioning Paris*, 28; and idem, *The Famine Plot Persuasion in Eighteenth-Century France* (Philadelphia, 1982). Similarly, in an explicit critique of Thompson, Adrian Randall and Andrew Charlesworth argue: "The moral economy market model was therefore not an *alternative* to a capitalist market but a model of a capitalist market subject to careful regulation." Adrian Randall and Andrew Charlesworth, "The Moral Economy: Riot, Markets and Social Conflict," in *Moral Economy and Popular Protest: Crowds, Conflict and Authority*, ed. Adrian Randall and Andrew Charlesworth (London, 2000), 17. John Bohstedt, "The Moral Economy and the Discipline of Historical Context," *Journal of Social History* 26 (Winter 2002), 267, also argues that food rioters were "provoked by abuses of trade," notably cheating and extortionate prices, "not simply by capitalist trade in itself."

54. The political implications of food riots are subject to debate. For the radicalism of such riots, see Kaplan's works cited previously. For limits to that radicalism, see Bouton, *Flour War*, 167–75; and Nicolas, *Rébellion française*, 286–289.

55. D'Argenson, *Journal*, 8:436.

56. Luynes, *Mémoires*, 13:417, 23 December 1754.

57. Laurence Fontaine, *L'économie morale, pauvreté, crédit et confiance dans L'Europe préindustrielle* (Paris, 2008); and Philip T. Hoffman, Gilles Postel-Vinay, and Jean-Laurent Rosenthal, *Priceless Markets: The Political Economy of Credit in Paris, 1660–1870* (Chicago, 2000).

58. ADH C 1979, letter from Petit, 28 August 1754; see also C 1978, letter from Rachat, 29 August 1754.

59. ADH C 6828, Reynaud to St. Priest, 31 August 1754. As in Mende, the band warned the residents in Craponne that it would return in a few weeks for another sale, the money for which best be available or the town would be destroyed in a torrent of "fire" and "blood."

60. ADPD 1C 1635, Lemps to Michodière, 6 September 1754.

61. For debate on the worth of such notes, see Chapter 6.

62. Adolphe Rochas, *Biographie du Dauphiné* (Geneva, 1971), 103 (emphasis mine). In the margin of another receipt, Mandrin wrote "valid for 2501 [lt]," indicating that the receipt was to be honored as a financial note. ADPD 1C 1639, relation.

63. ADPD 1C 1639, Relation. My emphasis.

64. ADPD 1C 1635, letter from Rochebaron, 1 September [misdated 1 August] 1754.

65. SHAT 1A 3385, no. 153, d'Argenson to Randan, 17 September 1754.

66. *Capitalism* is a fraught word, of course. My definition of "underground commercial capitalism" is rather capacious, encompassing not only large smuggling ventures that required heavy capital outlays and employed wage labor but less organized forms of illicit trade as well. I define "court capitalism" in Chapter 2.

6. Triumph

1. ADPD 1C 1645, Daurelle to Michodière, 17 October 1754.

2. ADPD 1C 1638, Michodière to d'Ormesson, 27 October 1754. Only days earlier a letter from the intendancy of Lyon spoke of "a war declared against the Farm" (ADH C 1699).

3. *GA*, 29 November 1754.

4. AAE CP Genève 66, fol. 182, Montperoux to Rouillé, 1 November 1754.

5. A spy who infiltrated the band in the winter of 1755 listed around a half dozen chiefs. SHAT 1A 3406, no. 147, Marsin's journal. See also SHAT 1A 3386, no. 339, d'Argenson to d'Espagnac, 16 December 1754; ADD 1C 1310, Boynes to d'Argenson and Séchelles, 18 December 1754.

6. ADD 1C 1310, interrogation of François Griffon, 17 and 18 December 1754.

7. Valets received a hefty lump sum for signing up (100 to 300 lt) and a daily wage (twenty to sixty sols) during the expedition. See AAE CP Genève 66, fols. 216–217, Montperoux to Rouillé, 17 November 1754; René Louis de Voyer, Marquis d'Argenson, *Journal et mémoires du marquis d'Argenson* (Paris, 1866), 8:365; *GC*, 31 December 1754; Charles-Philippe d'Albert, Duc de Luynes, *Mémoires du duc de Luynes sur la cour de Louis XV (1735–1758)* (Paris, 1863), 13:356; ADH C 6877, Saulx Tavannes to Moncan, 12 October 1754, and C 1979, St. Florentin to d'Argenson, 28 October 1754.

8. Sizing up a potential target, one scout asked a local cart driver from Gamat how wealthy the town's tobacco warehouser was and how many guards were stationed there. He instructed the driver to alert tavern keepers to the smugglers' impending arrival and offered him six lt a day (and a pinch of tobacco from his silver snuffbox) for his services. ADPD 1C 1640, procès-verbal of 1 November 1754.

9. *Etrennes historiques à l'usage de la Bresse* (1755).

10. Adolphe Rochas, *Biographie du Dauphiné* (Geneva, 1971), 102–103, report of M. de Bohan.

11. Ibid.

12. AN AB XIX 793 (1), report by Joly de Fleury, 5 October 1754.

13. Rochas, *Biographie,* 102–103; and *GA* (5 November 1754).

14. Rochas, *Biographie,* 102–103.

15. Ibid.

16. AN AB XIX 793 (1).

17. There are conflicting accounts of this second forced sale. According to Bohan, it was initiated by Mandrin, who stated that he was unable "in good conscience to pass through a city such as Bourg without leaving some tobacco with the warehouser." According to Saulx Tavannes, military commander of Burgundy, a subordinate chief was responsible for the forced sale, and Mandrin had neither the power nor the inclination to stop him. The fact that Joly de Fleury's report does not refer to Mandrin when describing the second forced sale lends credence to Saulx-Tavanne's version. ADH C 6877, Saulx Tavannes to Moncan, 12 October 1754.

18. ADPD 1C 1635, Rochebaron to Joly de Fleury, misdated 1 August 1754; and Guy Peillon, *Sur les traces de Louis Mandrin* (Lyon, 2005), 46–47. The *CA* reported that these Montbrison prisoners left with the troop.

19. AN AB XIX 793 (1); Peillon, *Sur les traces,* 68.

20. Rochas, *Biographie,* 102–103.

21. Peter Linebaugh, *The London Hanged: Crime and Civil Society in the Eighteenth Century* (London, 2006), chapter 1. Foucault's notion of a "Great Confinement" in which the restless poor were subject to heavy carceral repression in the eighteenth century has been contested, but it is clear that the growth of the mounted constabulary, municipal hospitals, and, above all, the *dépôts de mendicité* did represent a step toward greater surveillance. We will take up the question of policing in Chapter 7.

22. AN AB XIX 793, nos. 1 and 5.

23. AN AB XIX 793, nos. 4, 6, and 7.

24. ADCO C 322, Séchelles to Joly de Fleury, 21 October and 14 November 1754. "When the taxpayers know that they must bear these exactions and all the damage that results from them," the minister explained, "they will be driven by their own self-interest to prevent them."

25. ADCO C 322, Trudaine to Joly de Fleury, 19 March 1757.

26. Such a proposal was advanced in *Reflexions sur les contrebandiers en France* (Leipsic, 1755). In the 1690s, the Sun King had also granted naval commissions to pirate captains in the Caribbean to induce them to disband their crews.

27. SHAT 1A 3385, no. 403, d'Argenson to Joly de Fleury, 20 October 1754. D'Argenson's rejection of the amnesty request is also mentioned in AAE CP Genève 66, fol. 247 bis, Séchelles to Rouillé, 8 December 1755. The *GA* (15 November 1754) reported that an amnesty was under discussion.

28. SHAT 1A 3385, no. 332, letter to Joly de Fleury, 11 October 1754.

29. ADPD 1C 1645, Daurelle to Michodière, 5 December 1754.

30. ADPD 1C 1639, Relation de ce que les contrebandiers ont fait dans la province d'Auvergne (hereafter "Relation").

31. AN 129 AP 20, Thiers (20,038 lt) and Brioude (24,480 lt).

32. ADPD 1C 1639, Suite des nouvelles touchant les contrebandiers (hereafter "Suite"), 22 to 29 October 1754. *CA*, 15 November 1754. Another example of hospitality leading to protection occurred in Saint-Didier, where the house of a Farm official was spared because he had furnished the troop with wine in his tavern. ADPD 1C 1639, Suite, 20–25 October 1754.

33. ADPD 1C 1637, procès-verbal of 12 October 1754.

34. ADPD 1C 1640, procès-verbal of 1 November 1754.

35. ADPD 1C 1637, Mignot to Michodière, 14 October 1754. If in Thiers the money trail led to a single lender, it was more often the case that a broader communal effort was made to raise funds for kidnapped tobacco agents. When, at Saint-Bonnet-le-Château, Monsieur Gaudin, the tobacco warehouser and salt-tax receiver, could provide only a fraction of the 12,000 lt demanded by Mandrin, he was "tormented violently" and sent around town to solicit loans. After two hours of begging, he raised 2,184 lt from six individuals who were "touched by his situation and the danger he was in." Two of the six were Farm officials, as would be expected, but among the other four were two merchants, a notary, and a priest. Adding the borrowed funds to his own, he was able to raise 4,000 lt which, though far below the amount initially imposed, satisfied the smugglers. BMG Chenavas 139 (215), procès-verbal of 22 October 1754.

36. ADPD 1C 1639, Relation.

37. Prices varied slightly, as not all the bundles weighed exactly 100 pounds. In Pradelles, the effective price was 4.8 lt because the bundles were slightly heavier than 100 pounds. ADH C 6877, letter of de Frenal de la Coste, 18 October 1754. The price at Bourg had been 4.7 lt per pound for the same reason. At Chaisse-Dieu, the bundles were somewhat lighter, and so the price rose to 5.9 lt. The price at Ambert was the highest of all at 6.4 lt per pound. ADPD 1C 1638, procès-verbal on Chaise-Dieu, 14 October 1754; and ADPD 1C 1645.

38. AN 29 AP 85, Observations sur la constitution et le régime de la ferme du tabac.

39. ADH C 1978, subdelegate of Vabre to subdelegate of Lodève, 18 July 1754.

40. ADPD 1C 1651, Mallessaigne to Michodière, 26 May 1761.

41. ADPD 1C 1635 (Brioude and Montbrison); ADH C 1982 (Craponne).

42. ADPD 1C 1639, Relation.

43. Ibid.

44. Antoine Vernière, "Courses de Mandrin dans l'Auvergne, le Velay et le Forez (1754)," *Revue d'Auvergne* 6 (1889), 263.

45. ADPD 1C 1639, Suite, 22 to 29 October 1754.

46. Vernière, "Courses de Mandrin," 305.

47. Natalie Zemon Davis, *The Gift in Sixteenth-Century France* (Madison, WI, 2000), 90–95.

48. In Cluny, for example. Peillon, *Sur les traces,* 116.

49. ADPD 1C 1639, Relation; BMG Chenavas 158, procès-verbal of 9 October 1754; and Vernière, "Courses de Mandrin," 253.

50. This reconstruction of Mandrin in Le Puy is based on ADH C 1699; C 1979; C 6877; and C 6828; ADPD 1C 1638 and 1639; and *GU* (29 November 1754).

51. ADPD 1C 1638.

52. William Beik, *Urban Protest in Seventeenth-Century France: The Culture of Retribution* (Cambridge, 1997).

53. ADH C 6877, Serphanion to Lemps, 16 October 1754.

54. SHAT, 1A 3385, no. 454, letter to Randon, 27 October 1754.

55. ADD 1C 1310, Varod to Boynes, 1 November 1754.

56. Only in October do we begin to see the kinds of positive cultural representations that Eric Hobsbawm describes as "social banditry" in *Bandits* (New York, 2000).

57. "Histoire de l'arrivée de cent contrebandiers à Bourg le 5 octobre 1754," in Peillon, *Sur les traces,* 73–74.

58. Quoted in Pierre Grosclaude, *Malesherbes: Témoin et interprète de son temps* (Paris, 1961), 73. This and the following paragraph draw from Gilles Feyel, *L'annonce et la nouvelle: La presse d'information en France sous l'ancien régime (1630–1788),* chapters 9 and 12. See also idem, "La Diffussion des gazettes étrangères en France et la révolution postale des années 1750," in *Les gazettes européennes de langue française (XVIIe–XVIIIe siècles),* ed. Henri Duranton, Claude Labrosse, and Pierre Rétat (St. Étienne, 1992), 81–98; and Henri Duranton and Pierre Rétat, eds., *Gazettes et information politique sous l'Ancien Régime* (St. Étienne, 1999).

59. Robert Favre, "Montesquieu et la presse périodique," *Etudes sur la presse au XVIIIe siècle* 3 (1978), 39–60; Feyel, *L'annonce,* 538–541.

60. René Moulinas, *L'Imprimerie, la libraire et la presse à Avignon au XVIIIe siècle* (Grenoble, 1974), 349. In 1755, when the paper was covering Mandrin, its circulation reached 7,000.

61. In early reports, the name Mandrin itself had not yet hardened into a formalized spelling; the *GC* and *GA* called him "Mandrieu" and "Mandrain," respectively, on 8 and 12 November 1754. (Saulx Tavannes wrote of "Manderin" in his early military correspondence.) The *CA*, whose savvy founding editor, François Morénas, would exploit Mandrin's story to the hilt, used italicized letters to introduce readers to the head of the band on 29 October 1754: "A few days ago we received from Lyon the following details with regard to the chief of these smugglers who is named *Mandrin*." On Morénas, see Moulinas, *L'Imprimerie*; and Jay M. Smith, *Monsters of the Gévaudan: The Making of a Beast* (Cambridge, MA, 2011), 63–75.

62. Anne-Marie Mercier-Faivre, "Le Feuilleton de Mandrin dans la *Gazette d'Amsterdam*," in *Cartouche, Mandrin et autres brigands du XVIIIe siècle*, ed. Lise Andries (Paris, 2010), 310–311, also notes the serial quality of reporting on Mandrin.

63. Lise Andries, ed., *Cartouche, Mandrin et autres brigands du XVIIIe siècle* (Paris, 2010).

64. ADPD 1C 1645, Route tenue par une bande de contres, October 1754.

7. The Would-Be General

1. The expression was that of Captain Diturbi de Larre (SHAT 1A 3406, no. 227 bis).

2. ADS C 1, Emannuel to Sinsan, 24 September 1754.

3. ADS C 1, St. Laurent to Sinsan, 13 and 20 November 1754; and AAE CP Genève 66, fol. 242, Rouillé to Séchelles, 5 December 1754.

4. Vincent Denis, *Une histoire de l'identité: France, 1715–1815* (Paris, 2008), chapter 8. For Paris, see Vincent Milliot, "Paris, une ville sans brigands? Un regard sur le 'triomphe' de la police parisienne à la fin du XVIIIe siècle," in *Cartouche, Mandrin et autres brigands du XVIIIe siècle*, ed. Lise Andries (Paris, 2010), 175–195.

5. Albert Babeau, *La vie militaire sous l'ancien régime* (Paris, 1890), 4.

6. ADH C 6828, consuls of Le Puy to St. Priest, 2 October 1754.

7. ADH C 6828, consuls of Le Puy to St. Priest, 5 November 1754.

8. ADPD 1C 1643, Michodière to consuls of Ambert, 25 December 1754.

9. ADPD 1C 1643, Mignot to Michodière, 22 and 24 December 1754, and Noyer to Michodière, 24 December 1754.

10. ADPD 1C 1643, Vixouse to Michodière, 23 December 1754; ADPD 1C 1643, Cobat and Dupuy to Michodière, 28 December 1754; Antoine Vernière, "Courses de Mandrin dans l'Auvergne, le Velay et le Forez (1754)," *Revue d'Auvergne* 6 (1889), 315–319.

11. Quoted in Jacques Lorgnier, *Les juges bottés* (Paris, 1994), 297.

12. Jack A. Goldstone, "The Social Origins of the French Revolution Revisited," in *From Deficit to Deluge: The Origins of the French Revolution*, ed. Thomas E. Kaiser and Dale K. Van Kley (Stanford, CA, 2011), 67–103.

13. Ian A. Cameron, *Crime and Repression in the Auvergne and the Guyenne, 1720–1790* (Cambridge, 1981), chapter 1; Jean-Noël Luc, *Histoire de la maréchaussée et de la gendarmerie* (Maisons-Alfort, 2004), 194.

14. ADPD 1C 1643, Madur to Michodière, 24 December 1754.

15. ADH C 1978, Bonafonds to St. Priest, 21 July 1754.

16. ADD 1C 1310, Boynes to Séchelles, 6 and 22 November 1754; and Séchelles to Boynes, 7 November 1754; and Boynes to Randan, 20 November 1754. As usual, the problem came down to a lack of funding: the intendant was reluctant to impose a new tax on the province to pay for additional brigades.

17. Cameron, *Crime and Repression,* chapter 1; Bernard Bligny, *Histoire du Dauphiné* (Toulouse, 1973), 308.

18. BN MS 8476, Mémoire sur la contrebande.

19. ADPD 1C 1636, Séchelles to Michodière, 9 September 1754; and quotation in Cameron, *Crime and Repression,* 90.

20. SHAT 1A 3385, no. 413, d'Argenson to Bernage de Vaux, 21 October 1754.

21. For *signalements* and their use by the *maréchaussée,* see Denis, *Une histoire de l'identité,* chapters 2 and 8.

22. BN MS. 8390, Fontanieu to Orry, 28 September 1732; ADH C 1698, Orry to Bernage, 20 May 1743; ADCO C 255, Trudaine to Joly de Fleury, 11 May 1757. In theory (but not always in practice), mounted police were not entitled to profit from seizures of contraband, a right Farmers General jealously guarded for their own agents. ADPD 1C 1628, memoir and letter of 21 September 1733; and BN MS 8376, f. 286, Orry to Fontanieu, 1 July 1737.

23. ADS C 13, Sclarandi to Sinsan, 20 January 1755.

24. ADD 1C 1310, Séchelles to Boynes, 27 October 1754. For similar orders, see ADH C 1979, Séchelles to St. Priest, 27 October 1754; ADPD 1C 1638, Séchelles to Michodière, 27 October 1754; and ADD 1C 426, Varod to Boynes, 10 April 1755. For earlier sweeps, see AN AD XI 48, no. 189, Ordonnance du roy, 1 August 1711; AN AD XI 49, no. 62, Ordonnance du roy, 10 November 1718.

25. ADD 1C 426, Signalements and interrogations.

26. ADPD 1C 1645, Daurelle to Michodière, 10 December 1754.

27. ADD 1C 426, interrogation of 27 January 1755. The mounted police also confiscated guns that Mandrin's band had deposited in Tannière while fleeing from Guenand. "Procès-verbal de tournée de la maréchaussée d'Autun," in *Rendre la justice en Dauphiné,* ed. Olivier Cogne (Grenoble, 2003), 387.

28. Marie-Hélène Bourquin and Emmanuel Hepp, *Aspects de la contrebande au XVIIIe siècle* (Paris, 1969), part II, chapter 2. George T. Matthews, *The Royal General Farms in Eighteenth-Century France* (New York, 1958), 129–130, notes costs of 3,779,868 lt, most of which went to guards' salaries. Jacob M. Price,

France and the Chesapeake (Ann Arbor, MI, 1973), 1121, note 231, gives estimate of 4 million in total costs.

29. André Corvisier, *L'armée française de la fin du XVIIe siècle au ministère de Choiseul* (Paris, 1964), 936.

30. For an example in which a brigade successfully captured several members of a band, see AN Z1a 991, jugement of 17 February 1755.

31. ADCO 322, Bertin to Villeneuve, 4 June 1762.

32. ADPD 1C 1638, memoir on brigades in Auvergne.

33. BN MS 8372, Orry to Fontanieu, 14 April 1732; 8360, Mémoires généraux sur toutes les fermes du Roy en Dauphiné; and 8390, Fontanieu to Orry, 17 July 1732. See also Jean Descotes-Genon, *Les douanes françaises et la contrebande sur le Guiers en Chartreuse et à Miribel-les-Echelles* (Neuilly, 1994), 23–25.

34. ADPD 1C 1645, Daurelle to Michodière, 21 December 1754.

35. High-ranking personnel (directors, controller generals, and captains) received the lion's share of bonuses, but guards who participated in seizures could substantially supplement their income. See AN AD XI 51C, Devoirs des entreposeurs, 7 December 1730, and Deliberation de messieurs les fermiers generaux, 20 April 1731; BN MS 8376, fol.172, Orry to Fontanieu, 1 April 1737; and AN AD XI 51, no. 35, deliberations of 1 February 1743. Benefits for Farm employees are listed in AN AD XI 51B, arrêt du conseil of 23 July 1720; and AN G-1 105.

36. ADPD 1C 1647, Monticourt to Michodière, 15 July 1755.

37. Jean-Claude Boy, *L'Administration des douanes en France sous l'Ancien régime* (Neuilly, 1976), 104; André Ferrer, *Tabac, sel, indiennes: douane et contrebande en Franche-Comté au XVIIIe siècle* (Besançon, 2002), 71–73; Earl Robisheaux, "The 'Private Army' of the Tax Farms: The Men and Their Origins," *Histoire Sociale* 6 (1973), 262–269.

38. BN MS 8390, Fontanieu to Orry, 24 August 1732.

39. AN G-7 49, letters from Orry of 24 February 1733. The Paris customs officials who searched Madame de Sénac's person at the Saint-Victor gate were similarly investigated. Arlette Farge, *Subversive Words: Public Opinion in Eighteenth-Century France*, trans. Rosemary Morris (University Park, PA, 1995), 176.

40. *Projet pour la suppression des douanes dans l'intérieur du royaume* (Avignon, 1763), 116.

41. Boy, *L'Administration des douanes*, 103; Ferrer, *Tabac, sel, indiennes*, 69–70; Robisheaux, "Private Army."

42. BN MS 8392, fol. 324–332, Fontanieu to Orry, 28 August 1738.

43. AN AD XI 50, no. 31, Declaration of 2 August 1729.

44. AN AD XI 51C, Ferme generale du tabac, devoirs des entreposeurs . . . 7 December 1730.

45. AAE CP Genève, f. 76–77, Levet to Saint-Contest, 29 June 1754.

46. ADD 1C 1310, Boynes to d'Argenson, 18 December 1754, and interrogation of Grifon, 17 and 18 December 1754.

47. *Projet pour la suppression des douanes*, 61–64. The father's manual, *Le Guide des employées* (1751), is located in AN G-1 63.

48. ADI 2 B, letter of 16 July 1753, reproduced in Olivier Cogne, ed., *Rendre la justice en Dauphiné* (Grenoble, 2003), 385–386; Corinne Townley, *La véritable histoire de Mandrin* (Montmélian, 2005), 57–58.

49. SHAT 1A 3386, no. 14, d'Argenson to La Morlière, 4 November 1754.

50. SHAT 1A 3406, no. 94, report of April 1755.

51. Quoted in Edmond Esmonin, *Études sur la France des XVIIe et XVIIIe siècles* (Paris, 1964), 420.

52. BN MS 8392, fol. 324–332, Fontanieu to Orry, 28 August 1738.

53. ADH C 6877, Marcieu to Moncan, 12 October 1754. This was a stripped-down version of the corps he commanded at the end of the war. André Corvisier, *Histoire militaire de la France* (Paris, 1992), 2:42–43.

54. SHAT 1A 3384, no. 46, d'Argenson to Marcieu, 18 July 1754; SHAT 1A 3384, no. 45, d'Argenson to La Morlière, 18 July 1754. This convergence manifested itself in the sharing of the mission's costs among the Farmers General, who provided wages for soldiers; the war ministry, which paid for soldiers' wood and candles; and the taxpayers of affected provinces, whom authorities suspected of being complicit in the trafficking. BN MS 8372, Orry to Fontanieu, 17 October 1732; ADD 1C 1310, d'Argenson to Randan, 23 September 1754.

55. SHAT 1A 3386, no. 12, d'Argenson to Moncan, 4 November 1754.

56. ADH C 1978, d'Argenson to St. Priest, 17 September 1754; and SHAT 1A 3385, no. 394, d'Argenson to Tavannes, 20 October 1754. The president of the commission of Valence had long been using the language of "public security" in his correspondence with the minister of foreign affairs. AAE CP Genève 66, fols. 76–77, Levet to Saint-Contest, 29 June 1754.

57. ADH C 1655, Ordre générale, 13 September 1754.

58. ADPD 1C 1645, Daurelle to Michodière, 21 December 1754.

59. E. de Ribaucourt, *La Vie militaire et les exploits de J.-C. Fischer* (Paris, 1928).

60. ADH C 6877, Saulx Tavannes to Moncan, 16 November 1754; ADCO 322, Ordonnance du Roy, 12 November 1754; Quoted in Guy Peillon, *Sur les traces de Louis Mandrin* (Lyon, 2005), 147.

61. Stéphane Genêt, *Les Espions des Lumières* (Paris, 2013), chapter 6.

62. AAE CP Genève 66, fol. 241, Séchelles to Rouillé, 5 December 1754.

63. AAE CP Genève 66, fols. 236–237 and 244–245, Montperoux to Rouillé, 2 and 5 December 1754.

64. AAE CP Genève 66, fols. 189–190, Mémoire pour M. Rouillé. The curious position of "resident" of Geneva is explored in Fabrice Brandli, *Le nain et le géant: La République de Genève et la France au XVIIIe siècle* (Rennes, 2012).

65. AAE CP Genève 66, fols. 204–207, Montperoux to Rouillé, 13 November 1754.

66. AAE CP Genève, fols. 107–110, 129, 262, and 267.

67. AAE CP Genève, f. 204–207, Montperoux to Rouillé, 13 November 1754.

68. AAE CP Genève 66, fols. 204–207 and 224–225, Montperoux to Rouillé, 13 and 22 November 1754.

69. AAE CP Genève 66, f. 202, Montperoux to Rouillé, 9 November 1754.

70. AAE CP Genève 66, f. 260–261, Montperoux to Rouillé, 18 December 1754.

71. ADPD 1C 1639, Rochebaron to Michodière, 5 October 1754. The minister of war and the intendant of Auvergne also doubted that the "war" against the Farmers General would continue into winter. René-Louis de Voyer, Marquis d'Argenson, *Journal et mémoires du marquis d'Argenson* (Paris, 1866), 8:405; and ADPD 1C 1641, Michodière to Imbert, 14 December 1754; and 1C 1645, Daurelle to Michodière, 21 December 1754.

72. D'Argenson admitted to being "fooled" by Grifon's report. SHAT 1A 3386, no. 407, to Boynes, 26 December 1754.

73. ADD 1C 1310, Boynes to d'Argenson, 16 December 1754.

74. Ibid.

75. ADD 1C 1310, Boynes to d'Argenson, 18 December 1754.

76. BMG Chenavas (hereafter Ch.) 142, copy of letter from Bertrand de Chalon, 23 December 1754.

77. BMG Ch. 142, copy of letter from Raudas, 18 December 1754.

78. AN 129 AP 29, procès verbal by Helvétius, 1738–1739.

79. ADCO G 2550, Délibérations de Chapitre de Notre-Dame de Beaune, 1753–1760, fols. 49–51. My account of Beaune is based on ADCO 2550; BN MS 8698, fols. 284–285, "Mémoire du passage de mandrin en Bourgogne"; BMG Ch. 142 (letter from M. de la Rue, 19 December 1754; and Tavaux, 20 December 1754); and BMD fonds Baudot, Ms. 939, Abbé Boullemier, "Notes sur la Bourgogne et sur Dijon," 419–423.

80. BN MS 8698, fols 284–285, Mémoire.

81. ADCO G 2550, Délibérations, fols. 49–51.

82. BN MS 8698, fols 284–285, Mémoire.

83. *CA*, 31 December 1754.

84. ADCO G 2550, Délibérations, fols. 49–51.

85. BN MS 8698, fols. 284–285, Mémoire.

86. ADCO G 2550, Délibérations, fols. 49–51.

87. AD Haute-Saône C 208, cited in E. Gondolff, *Le Tabac sous l'ancienne monarchie: La ferme royale, 1629–1791* (Vesoul, 1914), 237.

88. D'Argenson, *Journal*, 8:397, 25 December 1754.

89. BMG Ch. 142, letter from de la Rue, 19 December 1754.

90. BN MS 8698, fols. 286–287, "Pot Pourri sur les gentils hommes de Beaune."

91. ADCO C2, Saint-Florentin to Joly de Fleury, 1 January 1755; SHAT, 1A 3397, nos. 7 and 9, d'Argenson to Tavannes, 1 January 1755.

92. Harold de Fontenay, "Mandrin et les contrebandiers à Autun," *Mémoires de la société Eduenne* (1875), 133–172.

93. BMD fonds Baudot, Ms. 939, Boullemier, "Notes," 419–423.

94. *Motifs et conduite de M. Fischer dans l'attaque des contrebandiers a Gunan,* quoted in Frantz Funck-Brentano, *Mandrin: Capitaine générale des contrebandiers de France* (Paris, 1908), 305.

95. Arceville's account, "Mémoires pour servir à l'histoire de la campagne de Mandrin," was published by Frantz Funck-Brentano, *Mandrin et les contrebandiers* (Paris, 1910), 127–145.

96. *Réflexions sur les contrebandiers en France* (Leipsic, 1755).

97. Quoted in Funck-Brentano, *Mandrin et les contrebandiers,* 141. *L'Intermédiaire des chercheurs et curieux* 20 (10 June 1887), 351.

98. D'Argenson, *Journal,* 8:398.

99. Funck-Brenano, *Mandrin: Capitaine,* 308, and René Fonvieille, *Mandrin: d'après de nombreux documents inédits* (Grenoble, 1975), 115, misstate the number of wounded at fifty-seven. See ADH C 1979, letter of 22 December 1754.

100. At the end of the campaign, the smugglers told officials that they had lost twenty men, thirty horses, and their treasure. ADPD 1C 1643, Gros to Michodière, 26 December 1754.

101. ADH 1979, Relation du combat, 20 December 1754. We know that Mandrin was wounded because, according to Voltaire, after the expedition the smuggler traveled to a small town on the northern shore of Lake Léman to have his wounds bandaged "by the most famous surgeon in the country." Theodore Besterman, ed., *Voltaire's Correspondence* (Geneva, 1953–1965), no. 5438, Voltaire to Cideville, 23 January 1755.

102. Funck-Brentano, *Mandrin et les contrebandiers,* 127–145. The joint report by Fischer, Arceville, and two other officers is located in ADD 1C 1310. Another officer, Joly, confirmed that Fischer did not adequately cut off the retreat, but he put it down to the small number of troops Fischer had on hand. Had so many of his infantrymen not stayed behind in Beaune to rest, "few [smugglers] could have fled because we would have guarded the rear" of the village. ADD 1310, Joly to Tavannes, 20 December 1754. Fischer later claimed that no smuggler would have escaped "if the terrain had not been so favorable for their retreat" and if his men "had not traveled 17 leagues the same day and put three rivers behind them. Besides, if I had not attacked them, I would have risked my reputation vis-à-vis the court and the public." Fischer's account is published in Ribaucourt, *Vie militaire,* 62–65.

103. SHAT 1A 3397, no. 90, d'Argenson to Fischer, 10 January 1755.

104. SHAT 1A 3397, no. 5, d'Argenson to Espinchal, 1 January 1755. The sentiments of the minister of war were echoed by others who believed that the first real chance the monarchy had of destroying Mandrin had been squandered. "If [Fischer] had been completely unaware that help was on

the way," one tobacco warehouser fulminated, "it would be forgivable, but his excessive ambition is the cause of our misfortune." *L'Intermédiaire des chercheurs et curieux* 20 (10 June 1887), 351, letter of 26 December 175[4]. The abbé Boullemier agreed that Fischer's failure to wait for reinforcements was attributable to his selfish desire "to have all the glory for himself or to have the booty and Mandrin's treasure chest." BMD Ms. 939, fonds Baudot, Boullemier, "Notes," 421.

105. D'Argenson, *Journal,* 8:435–436.
106. ADPD 1C 1644, d'Argenson to Michodière, 4 January 1755.
107. ADPD 1C 1643, Marlet to Michodière, 23 December 1754; ADPD 1C 1642, Brinsat to Veytard, 24 October 1754.
108. ADPD 1C 1643, Gros to Michodière, 26 December 1754.
109. ADPD 1C 1644, procès verbal of 25 December 1754.
110. ADPD 1C 1644, d'Argenson to Michodière, 7 January 1755. See also ADH C 1979, letter by Poujol, 30 December 1754; and ADPD 1C 1646, St. Priest to Michodière, 24 January 1755.
111. What little we know of Mandrin's post-Sauvetat itinerary comes from the deliberations of the town of Gex and a report from Chambéry posted in the *GA* of 14 February 1755. Although corroborating, such sources are not definitive.
112. *CA*, 31 December 1754.
113. *GU*, 7 and 24 January and 18 and 21 February 1755.
114. *GA*, 17 January 1755.
115. *MHP*, January and February 1755. Lest readers doubt the vigor of these "sworn enemies of the Farmers," a subsequent edition of the paper added that the band was growing bigger every day as deserters joined its ranks in search of glory and booty.
116. Both incidents were reported in the *CA*, 17 and 24 January 1755, and the *MHP* of February 1755.
117. BMD Ms. 939, fonds Baudot, Boullemier, "Notes," 421.
118. ADD 1C 1310, letter of 24 January 1755.
119. D'Argenson, *Journal* 8:396–398, entry of 24–30 December 1754.

8. Captured

1. AAE CP Genève 66, fol. 291, Montperoux to Rouillé, 9 February 1755.
2. SHAT 1A 3406, no. 162, Georgy to d'Argenson, 28 April 1755; no. 186, Saulx Tavannes to d'Argenson, 3 May 1755; AAE CP Genève 66, fol. 321, Montperoux to Rouillé, 12 May 1755; and ADD, 1C 1310, Séchelles to Boynes, 25 January 1755.
3. SHAT 1A 3406, no. 147, Journal de la conduitte du Sr. Marsin. Marsin's report was written in Bourg under the protection of d'Espagnac and then sent to the minister of war. See also AAE CP Genève, fol. 314, Montperoux to Rouillé, 23 April 1755.

4. AN AD XI 49, no. 37, ordinance of 14 July 1716.

5. SHAT 1A 3406, nos. 51, 72, and 86; and SHAT 1A 3397–3399.

6. SHAT 1A 3406, nos. 80, 127, and 145, letters from d'Espagnac to d'Argenson, 4 and 20 April 1755, and Saulx Tavannes to d'Argenson, 24 April 1755.

7. AAE CP Genève 66, fol. 313, Montperoux to Rouillé, 9 April 1755.

8. The French town of Taulignan allowed the gang to pass but shut the city gates on the cavalry, the outraged captain of which seized the town and threw its leaders in jail. SHAT 1A 3406, nos. 191 and 220, Marcieu to d'Argenson, 4 and 12 May 1755.

9. SHAT 1A 3386, no. 325, d'Argenson to Rouillé, 9 December 1754. Border conflicts ran in the other direction, too, with French officials acting as aggressors. On 22 July 1754, five Farm guards, "pistols and sword in hand," crossed to the Savoyard side of Pont-de-Beauvoisin, seized Pierre Fauche, and carried him over to the French side of town. Fauche, who had calicoes in his possession, had not been breaking any law, for such trade was perfectly legal in Savoy. His only mistake—or was it a provocation?—was to walk so close to the borderline that he could be kidnapped by Farm guards. "We are no longer safe in this country," fumed the indignant Marquis de Saint Severin, a town notable who, according to Marsin, looked after Mandrin's fortune. Such an act of aggression constituted a "formal attack on the rights of His Majesty," the king of Sardinia. ADS C 2, letter to Sinsan, 22 July 1754. In March, French soldiers buying livestock at the Pont de Bellegrade fair in Savoy brawled with locals. SHAT 1A 3406, no. 61, Saulx Tavannes to d'Argenson, 27 March 1755.

10. AAE Turin 224, fol. 186–189, interrogations by La Motte, 24 March 1755.

11. SHAT 1A 3406, no. 110, Rouillé to d'Argenson, 14 April 1755.

12. SHAT 1A 3406, no. 130 bis, d'Espagnac to Rochebaron, 23 April 1755, and nos. 312 and 330, Saulx Tavannes to d'Argenson, 10 and 17 June 1755. Around the same time, a gang of smugglers from Saint-Genix attacked a Farm brigade that had crossed into Savoy. SHAT 1A 3406, nos. 75 and 98, letter to d'Espagnac, 2 April 1755, and from Saulx Tavannes to d'Argenson, 10 April 1755.

13. ADS C 2, Chanal to Sinsan, 29 April 1755.

14. ADS C 661, Mémoire and procès verbal, 6 July 1752.

15. SHAT 1A 3406, no. 95, deposition of Augustin Perrin, 12 April 1755. See also SHAT 1A 3406, no. 101.

16. SHAT 1A 3406, no. 95, deposition of Madame Perrin, 12 April 1755.

17. SHAT 1A 3406, no. 95, de la Tour to Marcieu, 10 April 1755; AAE Turin 224, fols. 259–260, La Morlière to d'Argenson, 9 April 1755.

18. This and the following paragraph are drawn from depositions in SHAT 1A 3406, no. 101. An unlikely alternative version of events is told in ADS C 2, Orsini to Sinsan, 9 April 1755.

19. SHAT 1A 3406, no. 93, Marcieu to d'Argenson, 10 April 1755.

20. SHAT 1A 3406, no. 96, L'Hôpital to d'Argenson, 10 April 1755.

21. SHAT 1A 3406, no. 95, de la Tour to Marcieu, 10 April 1755.

22. The *GA* (16 May 1755) and *Le Véritable messager boiteux de Basle* (Basle, 1756) published the same report, which was filed from Chambéry, Savoie.

23. AAE CP Sardaigne 224, fols. 277–278, mémoire of 17 April 1755.

24. ADS C2, Bonne to Sinsan, 9 April 1755, and Balbian to Sinsan, 16 May 1755.

25. SHAT 1A 3398, no. 329, d'Argenson to La Morlière, 19 April 1755; and 1A 3399, no. 25, d'Argenson to Rouillé, 8 May 1755.

26. AAE Mémoires et Documents, France 1347, fols. 251–262, Saint-Priest to St. Florentin, 17 January 1755.

27. BN MS 8476. A Farm inspector in Languedoc shared similar concerns that the Huguenots would assemble "following the example of the gangs of smugglers who cross their area." ADH C 1696, letter of 15 October 1729. In 1747, the intendant thought that another "famous smuggler," Droguet dit La Noblesse, was an emissary of the Huguenots. AN H-1 1459.

28. ADH C 1979, St. Priest to St. Florentin, d'Argenson, Richelieu, and Séchelles, 28 October 1754.

29. AAE Mémoires et Documents, France 1347, fols. 251–262, Saint-Priest to St. Florentin, 17 January 1755.

30. René-Louis de Voyer, Marquis d'Argenson, *Journal et mémoires du marquis d'Argenson* (Paris, 1866), 8:399–400, entry of 31 December 1754, in which he claims to have heard the news from a letter from Lyon.

31. ADH C 1979, St. Priest to Séchelles, 28 October 1754; and d'Argenson to St. Priest, 4 November 1754.

32. SHAT 1A 3406, no. 80, d'Espagnac to d'Argenson, 4 April 1755. See also nos. 49 and 52.

33. AAE CP Angleterre 439, fols. 291–298, Mémoire politique et militaire sur la situation présente de la France.

34. *Reflexions sur les contrebandiers en France* (Leipsic, 1755).

35. For patriotism in this period, see Edmond Dziembowski, *Un Nouveau patriotisme français, 1750–1770: la France face à la puissance anglaise à l'époque de la guerre de Sept Ans* (Oxford, 1998); David A. Bell, *The Cult of the Nation in France: Inventing Nationalism, 1680–1800* (Cambridge, MA, 2001), chapter 3; and Jay M. Smith, *Nobility Reimagined: The Patriotic Nation in Eighteenth-Century France* (Ithaca, NY, 2005). For the loose play of national identity among English Channel smugglers, see Renaud Morieux, *Une mer pour deux royaumes: La Manche, frontière franco-anglaise (XVIIe–XVIIIe siècles)*, chapter 8.

36. For Lemps's skepticism, see ADH C 6877, letter of 17 January 1754. For weapons stockpiling, see ADH C 440, d'Argenson to St. Priest, 3 December 1754; ADH C 441, d'Argenson to St. Priest, 19 April 1755, and Tavannes to d'Argenson, 12 April 1755.

37. Dan Edelstein, *The Terror of Natural Right: Republicanism, the Cult of Nature, and the French Revolution* (Chicago, 2009), 36–40.

38. ADH C 1655, Ordre générale, 13 September 1754.

39. SHAT 1A 3386, d'Argenson to Fischer, 16 December 1754, and d'Argenson to d'Espagnac, 16 December 1754. The trick was to find "a suitable place" to which to draw the chief. Further, Montperoux reported that Geneva would provide prison space if Turin agreed to "kidnap Mandrin at night in Carouge." AAE CP Genève, fols. 216–17 and 235, Montperoux to Rouillé, 17 and 29 November 1754.

40. SHAT 1A 3406, no. 178, "Projet pour enlever Mandrin et ses contrebandiers," April 1755. D'Espagnac also devised a plan to capture Mandrin in Savoy; the idea was to kidnap a Savoyard smuggler and force him to lead a "disguised detachment" of Fischer's troops to Mandrin. But d'Argenson forbade him from capturing any smuggling chiefs on Sardinian lands. SHAT 1A 3406, no. 141, d'Espagnac to d'Argenson, 23 April 1755; and 1A 3399, no. 11, d'Argenson to d'Espagnac, 4 May 1755.

41. SHAT 1A 3406, no. 135, L'Hôpital to d'Argenson, 22 April 1755, and no. 261, La Morlière to d'Argenson, 23 May 1755.

42. Edgard Depitre, *La toile peinte en France au XVIIe et au XVIIIe siècles: industrie, commerce, prohibitions* (Paris, 1912), 141; BN MS 8376, fol. 316, Orry to Fontanieu, 15 July 1737.

43. SHAT 1A 3406, no, 69, L'Hôpital to d'Argenson, 29 March 1755.

44. Olivier Cogne, ed., *Rendre la justice en Dauphiné* (Grenoble, 2004), 388.

45. SHAT 1A 3406, no. 261, La Morlière to d'Argenson, 23 May 1755; see also the report by the senate of Chambéry published in René Fonvieille, *Mandrin: d'après de nombreux documents inédits* (Grenoble, 1975), 313–319.

46. Quoted in Fonvieille, *Mandrin,* 313. For a complete list of damages to the château, see ADS 2B 12148.

47. ADPD 1C 1647, Desgranges to Malard, 11 May 1755.

48. ADS 2B 12148, depositions on the pillage of Saint-Genix. See also Corinne Townley, *La véritable histoire de Mandrin* (Montmélian, 2005), 67–71, 318–319, and 340; and Frantz Funck-Brentano, *Mandrin: Capitaine générale des contrebandiers de France* (Paris, 1908), 415–418.

49. All told, two people were killed and at least nine wounded, but tallies vary. See ADPD 1C 1647, Desgranges to Malard, 11 May 1755; ADS C 127, letter from intendant of Savoie to Saint-Laurent, 14 May 1755; SHAT 1A 3406, no. 216, report by officers of Saint-Genix, 11 May 1755; and the Chambéry senate report published in Fonvieille, *Mandrin,* 313–319.

50. SHAT 1A 3406, no. 238, La Morlière to d'Argenson, 12 May 1755.

51. SHAT 1A 3406, no. 212, La Morlière to Marcieu, 11 May 1755.

52. SHAT 1A 3406, no. 225, Diturbi de Larre to Marcieu, 13 May 1755, and no. 217, La Morlière to Marcieu, 12 May 1755. D'Argenson would later secretly inform Marcieu of the true events concerning Mandrin's capture. SHAT 1A 3406, no. 237, Marcieu to d'Argenson, 19 May 1755.

53. SHAT 1A 3399, no. 136, d'Argenson to Marcieu, 17 May 1755.

54. SHAT 1A 3406, no. 231 bis, Séchelles to Marcieu, 17 May 1755.

55. SHAT 1A 3406, no. 266, Bory to d'Argenson, 25 May 1755. To sustain the cover-up, the minister of war publicly ordered L'Hôpital to report any soldiers who took part in the raid because "nothing is more contrary to the intentions of the king." SHAT 1A 3399, no. 138, d'Argenson to L'Hôpital, 17 May 1755.

56. Quoted in Funck-Brentano, *Mandrin,* 423.

57. *GU* (3 June 1755).

58. BMG Chenavas 140 (7), notes of Morel, curé de Montrigand.

59. SHAT 1A 3406, no. 206, Marcieu to de la Tour, 11 May 1755.

60. SHAT 1A 3406, no. 224 bis, d'Espagnac to d'Argenson, 14 May 1755.

61. AAE CP Genève 66, f. 322, Montperoux to Rouillé, 14 May 1755.

62. D'Argenson, *Journal,* 9:8–15, entries for 17, 22, and 27 May 1755.

63. Because newspapers relied on reports from correspondents in different places, they sometimes sent mixed messages about Mandrin's capture. The *MHP* (4 June 1755) mentioned Mandrin's resistance but did not report the pillaging of the château and the village of Saint-Genix. Normally sympathetic to Mandrin, the *CA* (23 May 1755) nonetheless printed a letter purportedly signed by the Piedmontese that suggested that the chief hid cowardly in the attic at Rochefort rather than resist. The authenticity of this letter is to be doubted since it also states that the people of Saint-Genix were impressed by the courage of French troops.

64. The abbé Boullemier believed the cover story to be true (BMD ms. 939, abbé Boullemier, "Notes sur la Bourgogne et sur Dijon"), but the anonymous author of a letter from Valence did not (Cogne, ed., *Rendre,* 388).

65. BMG, *Complainte nouvelle sur la prise de Louis Mandrin.*

66. Charles-Philippe d'Albert, Duc de Luynes, *Mémoires du duc de Luynes sur la cour de Louis XV (1735–1758)* (Paris, 1864), 14:154.

67. SHAT 1A 3406, no. 216, Sinsan to Marcieu, 11 May 1755. Newspapers were quick to report that "the French violated the territory" of the kingdom of Sardinia. *GC* (27 May 1755).

68. ADS C 2, St. Juille to Sinsan, 12 May 1755.

69. *GA* (September 1755). The diplomatic fallout created by Mandrin's capture is narrated in Fonvieille, *Mandrin,* 147–175. Although some French courtiers believed that sending such a high-ranking gentleman to Turin was a needlessly humiliating capitulation on the part of Louis XV, Noailles charmed his hosts and settled the stormy affair once and for all.

70. ADS C 2, Balbian to Sinsan, 13 May 1755. For disorder in Savoy in the wake of Mandrin's arrest, see ADS C 2 and 127; AAE CP Genève 66, fol. 337; and SHAT 1A 3406.

9. The Execution of Louis Mandrin

1. Michel Foucault, *Discipline and Punish: The Birth of the Prison,* trans. Alan Sheridan (New York, 1979) was written before the publication of major

studies on the galleys and thus failed to account for the role played by smuggling in the genesis of the modern French prison system.

2. In England, too, smuggling provoked draconian measures, culminating in numerous executions in 1749. See Niklas Frykman, "Pirates and Smugglers: Political Economy in the Red Atlantic," in *Mercantilism Reimagined: Political Economy in Early Modern Britain and Its Empire,* ed. Philip Stern and Carl Wennerlind (Oxford, 2013); and Cal Winslow, "Sussex Smugglers," in *Albion's Fatal Tree: Crime and Society in Eighteenth-Century England,* ed. Douglas Hay, Peter Linebaugh, and E. P. Thompson (New York, 1975), 119–166.

3. The ordinance of May 1680 threatened salt peddlers with a 200-lt fine for a first offense and a whipping if the fine was not paid. Recidivists would be punished with a 300-lt fine and six years in the galleys (or banishment for women). Those transporting illicit salt with a horse or cart would be subject to a 300-lt fine or, if payment was not forthcoming, three years in the galleys or nine years for recidivists. Salt smugglers who operated in armed gangs would receive a 500-lt fine and nine years in the galleys or death in the case of repeat offenders. The declaration of 5 July 1704 raised the penalty on first-offense gang members to death.

4. AN G-7 1290, "Reglement contre les fraudeurs de tabac, 19 sept 1717."

5. AN AD XI 48, declaration of 6 December 1707. For previous antismuggling decrees, see the declaration of 27 September 1674 and the ordinance of 21 August 1681.

6. AN G-7 1290, reglement of 19 September 1717. Such conversions had precedents in the salt ordinance of 1680 and the tobacco declaration of 21 August 1681. The declaration of 25 January 1689 claimed that the deposit rule was designed only to reduce the Farm's legal expenses by minimizing the number of appeals, but it was clearly used as a means to strengthen penalties against trafficking violations.

7. This movement from fines to punishments reversed a medieval trend from punishments to fines. See Dominique Gonnard, "La peine et son évolution," in *Rendre la justice en Dauphiné,* ed. Olivier Cogne (Grenoble, 2003), 159–166; and Paul Freidland, *Seeing Justice Done: The Age of Spectacular Capital Punishment in France* (Oxford, 2012), 29–32.

8. AN AD XI 50, no. 31, Declaration of 2 August 1729, and no. 85, Declaration of 27 January 1733. These decrees built on the Declaration of 17 October 1720, which first imposed the death penalty on armed tobacco smugglers in groups of three or more.

9. Philibert Orry, who had close ties to the French East India Company and tended to favor industrial regulation, encouraged intendants to fine consumers during his long tenure as finance minister (1730–1745), but doing so proved difficult. See AN F-12 54, 65, 58, 73, 74–75, 77, 82; BN MS 8375–8379 and 8392; ADPD 1C 1627; ADH C 1663, 1678–1679; AMN HH 252–256, 266; and V.-L. Bourilly, "La Contrebande des toiles peintes en Provence

au XVIIIe siècle," *AM* 26 (1914), 52–75. Apart from this crackdown, the French state generally pursued traffickers, rather than consumers, a critical distinction. During U.S. prohibition in the 1930s, only the production, transport, and sale of alcoholic beverages were barred, whereas in the contemporary war on drugs, prison sentences are imposed for possession of controlled substances. See John Paul Stevens, "Our 'Broken System' of Criminal Justice," *New York Review of Books* (10 November 2011), 59.

10. Edgard Depitre, *La Toile peinte en France au XVIIe et au XVIIIe* siècles (Paris, 1912), chapters 1–3. Among the scores of decrees aimed at enforcing the calico ban, the key ones were the *arrêt* of 26 October 1686 (which set a fine of 3,000 lt for smugglers), the *arrêt* of 24 August 1706 (which established penalties for consumers), the edict of July 1717 (which added corporal punishments for armed bands), the arrêt of 8 July 1721 (which invoked the death penalty for smugglers who crossed into France), and the edict of October 1726 (which extended the death penalty to armed gangs of three or more). The declarations of 2 August 1729 and 27 January 1733 set common penalties for smugglers of calico and tobacco who were armed or participated in bands.

11. Baptiste Bessière, "Le Tribunal de l'élection des trois bailliages des montagnes au XVIIIe siècle," in *Rendre la justice en Dauphiné,* ed. Olivier Cogne (Grenoble, 2003), 27–33. For other examples of cooperative election courts, see ADDR C 728 and 974.

12. AN AD XI, no. 140, *arrêts* of 31 May 1768 and 13 June 1769.

13. Yves Durand, "La contrebande du sel au XVIIIe siècle aux frontières de Bretagne, du Maine et de l'Anjou," *Histoire Sociale* 7 (1974), 227–269.

14. AN AD XI 51, *arrêts du conseil* of 31 May 1768 and 13 June 1769; and AN AD XI 51b, *arrêt* of 11 March 1727. Examples of obstruction and leniency abound in AN AD XI 49–51c. See also André Ferrer, *Tabac, sel, indiennes: douane et contrebande en Franche-Comté* (Besançon, 2002), 277–278.

15. AN AD XI 51, no. 55, *arrest de la cour des aydes,* 16 March 1745.

16. AN AD 51c, *arrest de la cour des aydes,* 19 June 1736.

17. AN AD XI 50, no. 63, *arrêts du conseil* of 19 February and 22 April 1732.

18. AN AD XI 51, no. 82, *arrêt du conseil* of 11 June 1748.

19. This was part of a broader process of an expansion of extraordinary justice under Louis XV. See Bernard Barbiche, "Les attributions judiciaires du Conseil du roi," *Histoire, Economie et Société* 29 (Septembre 2010), 9–19.

20. For the principle of retained justice, see Jacques Richou, *Histoire des commissions extraordinaires sous l'ancien régime* (Paris, 1905).

21. AN AD XI 51, *arrêt* of 14 August 1745.

22. For the tendency of parlements to ease sentences on appeal, see Marie-France Brun-Jansen, "Criminalité et répression pénale au siècle des Lumières: L'exemple du Parlement de Grenoble," *Revue d'histoire du droit* 76 (July–September 1998), 358–359; and Nicole Castan, *Justice et répression en Languedoc à l'époque des lumières* (Paris, 1980), 247.

23. Intendants in Languedoc and Brittany, where there were no election courts, had been judging tobacco smugglers all along.

24. ADPD 1C 1627, Orry to Trudaine, 29 March 1729.

25. AN AD XI 49, judgment of 4 December 1723. See also AN G-7 1292 and 1294.

26. ADPD 1C 1626, Le Peletier to Grandville, 6 and 24 July 1729. See also AN AD XI 50, no. 154; and Charles Godard, *Les pouvoirs des intendants sous Louis XIV* (Paris, 1901), 276.

27. The intendant of Brittany was granted such jurisdiction concerning the tobacco monopoly as early as 1713. The intendants of Franche-Comté, Auch, Burgundy, and Moulin received their commissions in 1721, 1723, 1734, and 1738, respectively. The chief of Paris police began hearing cases in 1729.

28. BN MS 8372, Orry to Fontanieu, 10 August 1732. See also Ferrer, *Tabac, sel, indiennes*, 251–256.

29. BN MS 8476, first memoir.

30. AN E 2126, *arrêt* of 4 March 1732; BN MS 8390, Fontanieu to Orry, 3 July 1732.

31. BN MS 8390, Fontanieu to Orry, 6 July 1732; ADH C 1697, Fontanieu to Maurice, 8 July 1732. Punitive violence was "mutually referential" insofar as it "traveled back and forth between lower-class rebels and upper-class enforcers of state authority," suggests Paul Freedman, "Atrocities and the Executions of Peasant Rebel Leaders in Late Medieval and Early Modern Europe," *Medievalia et Humanistica* 31 (2005), 101–113.

32. BN MS 8390, Fontanieu to Orry, 3 August 1732.

33. BN MS 8467, 8390, 8372.

34. BN MS 8390, Fontanieu to Orry, 3 and 13 August 1732.

35. BN MS 8390, Fontanieu to Orry, 15 February 1733.

36. Not that the intendant was immune to all doubt when it came to smuggling jurisprudence. He worried about enforcing the declaration of 1729, which, contrary to basic legal maxims, allowed for the conviction of smugglers arrested without any material evidence of contraband. In place of such evidence, Fontanieu was willing to accept witness testimony, but *gradués* were reluctant to prosecute without evidence of seized merchandise. BN MS 8476, memoir 9, and 8390, Fontanieu to Orry, 10 December 1732.

37. BN MS 8476.

38. BN MS 8372, Orry to Fontanieu, 23 February 1733.

39. BN MS 8390 and 8391, Fontanieu to Orry, 26 March and 10 May 1733.

40. *Encyclopédie Méthodique: Finances* (Paris, 1784), 1:334–338, "Commission." Colleau's official title at the châtelet of Melun was lieutenant criminel.

41. It would spend around a quarter million livres a year on the five principal commissions. AN G-1 56–60.

42. ADH C 1698, Orry to St. Maurice, 24 August 1734.

43. The commission of Besançon fell somewhere between intendants' commissions and the five principal supercommissions. See Ferrer, *Tabac, sel, indiennes,* 245–298.

44. In their personnel, funding, and duration, the smuggling commissions differed significantly from earlier criminal commissions such as the *Grands Jours* of 1665, which had acted under the auspices of the parlement of Paris.

45. André Zysberg, *Les Galériens: vies et destins de 60,000 forçats sur les galères de France, 1680–1748* (Paris, 1987), 102.

46. The commission of Reims heard around 6,000 individual cases between 1740 and 1788 (Nils Liander, *Smuggling Bands in Eighteenth-Century France* [PhD diss., Harvard University, 1981]). The Saumur commission reached 6,878 decisions between 1765 and 1789; see Micheline Huvet-Martinet, "La répression du faux-saunage dans la France de l'Ouest et du Centre à la fin de l'Ancien Régime (1764–1789), *AB* 84 (1977), 423–443. If we apply the same rate of judgment to its earlier years between 1742 and 1765, that would add another 6,500 cases. The junior commission of Franche-Comté judged over 1,200 smugglers during its tenure from 1735 to 1789 (Ferrer, *Tabac, sel, indiennes,* 251–98). We know less about the caseloads of other commissions. That of Valence probably heard at least as many cases as Reims. Although incomplete, the Paris commission records are littered with trials of petty dealers. And the Caen commission handled numerous cases of maritime contraband.

47. Zysberg, *Les Galériens,* 100–101. By the end of the old regime, an average of 3,437 men, women, and children were arrested annually for salt smuggling alone, according to Guillaume-François de Mahy, Baron de Corméré, *Recherches et considérations nouvelles sur les finances,* 2 vols. (London, 1789), 2:187.

48. Nicole Castan, "La justice expéditive au XVIIIe siècle," *AESC* (1976), 335.

49. Castan, "Justice expéditive," 347; Benoît Garnot, "Les peines corporelles en Bourgogne au XVIIIe siècle," in *Beccaria et la culture juridique des lumières,* ed. Michel Porret (Geneva, 1997), 215–222.

50. Dominique Müller, "Magistrats français et la peine de mort au XVIIIe siècle," *Dix-huitième siècle* 4 (1972), 90.

51. Garnot, "Peines corporelles"; Pascal Bastien, *L'exécution publique à Paris au XVIIIe siècle* (Paris, 2006), 107; Castan, "Justice expéditive," 347.

52. Bernard Balsan, "La Commission du Conseil de Valence et la répression de la contrebande au XVIIIe siècle," *Revue drômoise* 85 (1988), 473–478, which is based on ADDR B 1304. We know that this archival source is incomplete because additional cases exist in ADI 7 B 59.

53. AN 603 Mi 1; Liander, "Smuggling Bands," Appendix A; and Nicolas Schapira, *Contrebande et contrebandiers dans le nord et de l'est de la France 1740–1789* (mémoire, Université de Paris I, 1991), tables IV.1–IV.8.2.

54. Castan "Justice expéditive," 348.

55. Howard G. Brown, "Domestic State Violence: Repression from the Croquants to the Commune," *Historical Journal* 42 (1999), 608. There is some debate over the degree of repression exerted through old-regime criminal justice. In emphasizing its repressive characteristics, I side with Nicole Castan ("Justice expéditive") over both Howard G. Brown, *Ending the French Revolution: Violence, Justice, and Repression* (Charlottesville, VA, 2006), 66–70, which posits an "organic" old-regime society, and Richard M. Andrews, *Law, Magistracy, and Crime in Old Regime Paris, 1735–1789* (Cambridge, 1994), which attempts to rehabilitate the 1670 criminal ordinance.

56. Zysberg, *Les Galériens,* 78–79 and 100–101.

57. For parlements, see Andrews, *Law,* 491–492; Brun-Jansen, "Criminalité"; Garnot, "Peines corporelles," 215–222; idem, "L'historiographie de la criminalité en histoire moderne," in *Histoire et criminalité de l'antiquité au XXe siècle: nouvelles approches,* ed. Yann Le Bohec, Jean-Claude Farcy, Françoise Gasparri, and Xavier Rousseaux (Dijon, 1992), 25–30; and Castan, *Justice et répression.*

58. This trend was even more pronounced in the case of the junior commission of Franche-Comté, which judged 897 people between 1735 and 1769, the vast majority for tobacco smuggling. More than half were sent to the galleys. Ferrer, *Tabac, sel, indiennes,* 280–284.

59. André Zysberg, "La Société des galériens au milieu du XVIIIe siècle," *AESC* 30 (1975), 43–67.

60. André Zysberg, "From the Galleys to Hard Labor Camps: Essay on a Long Lasting Penal Institution," in *The Emergence of Carceral Institutions: Prisons, Galleys and Lunatic Asylums 1550–1900,* ed. Pieter Spierenburg (Rotterdam, 1984), 99–100.

61. Roger Daon, *Conduite des âmes dans la voie du salut* (Paris, 1753), 320, quoted in Bastien, *L'exécution publique,* 167.

62. Zysberg, *Les Galériens,* 100–101; Nicole Castan and André Zysberg, *Histoire de galères, bagnes et prisons en France de l'Ancien Régime* (Toulouse, 2002), 112. Initially, the overwhelming number of smugglers in the galleys had been put there by lower-level courts, but that would change with the rise of commissions in the middle third of the century.

63. Jean-Frédéric Schaub, "Violence in the Atlantic," in *The Oxford Handbook of the Atlantic World 1450–1850,* ed. Nicholas Canny and Philip Morgan (Oxford, 2011), 114. Of course, the coercion of plantation slavery, which was based on the ownership of human beings as property, differed in fundamental ways from the penal servitude of the galleys.

64. Frédérique Joannic-Seta, *La bagne de Brest: L'émergence d'une institution carcérale au siècle des Lumières* (Rennes, 2000), 181–183.

65. In *Discipline and Punish,* Michel Foucault postulated a seamless transition from a penal system based on exemplarity to one based on confinement and surveillance, but, in fact, the two regimes coexisted in the eighteenth century.

66. To be sure, the *bagnes* lacked the reformatory dimension of the prisons, asylums, and hospitals of the 1790s that Foucault studied, but the disciplinary regime of the camps did anticipate certain contemporary forms of incarceration.

67. Quoted in Andrews, *Law,* 336.

68. Zysberg, *Les Galériens,* chapter 12.

69. Michel Forest, *Chroniques d'un bourgeois de Valence au temps de Mandrin* (Grenoble, 1980), 41.

70. *CA,* 19 May 1755.

71. *CA,* 20 May 1755.

72. Forest, *Chroniques,* 43.

73. Antole de Gallier, ed., *La vie de province au XVIIIe siècle* (Paris, 1877), 115; Franquières to Bressac, 19 May 1755.

74. Quoted in Sarah Maza, *Private Lives and Public Affairs: The Causes Célèbres of Prerevolutionary France* (Berkeley, CA, 1993), 239–240.

75. *CA,* 25 May 1755.

76. Forest, *Chroniques,* 43.

77. Anonymous letter from Valence, 27 May 1755, in *Rendre la justice,* 389.

78. SHAT 1A 3406, no. 287, de la Porte to d'Argenson, 1 June 1755.

79. *CA,* 28 May 1755. The chief also absolved a barber whom he had pressed into service. *Abrégé de la vie de Mandrin* ([1755]; Paris, 1991), 38.

80. SHAT 1A 3406, no. 227 bis, Diturbi de Larre to La Morlière, 16 May 1755; and no. 228 bis, Mandrin to Diturbi de Larre, no date. Diturbi de Larre was already working on a deal for St. Pierre in which the convict would be spared death if his parents turned in his older brother.

81. *CA,* 25 May 1755.

82. GU, 17 June 1755; *CA,* 28 May 1755; and SHAT 1A 3406, no. 287.

83. SHAT 1A 3406, no. 287, de la Porte to d'Argenson, 1 June 1755.

84. P. F. Muyart de Vouglans, *Les Lois criminelles de France dans leur ordre naturel* (Paris, 1780), 54, quoted in Müller, "Magistrats français," 86.

85. SHAT 1A 3406, nos. 86 and 187, L'Hôpital to d'Argenson, 8 April and 4 May 1755. "Pedagogy of fear" is from Robert Muchembled, *Les temps des supplices: de l'obéissance sous les rois absolus, XVe–XVIIIe siècle* (Paris, 1992), 82.

86. *CA,* 28 May 1755.

87. Gallier, ed., *Vie de province,* 115, Franquières to Bressac, 19 May 1755. *CA,* 28 May 1755.

88. *GA,* 17 June 1755; *CA,* 28 May 1755.

89. Forest, *Chroniques,* 43.

90. *Abregé,* 37.

91. "Lettre," in *Rendre la justice,* 388.

92. *CA,* 28 May 1755.

93. Freidland, *Seeing Justice Done,* chapter 3.

94. Bastien, *L'exécution publique,* 193.

95. BMV D 13020, *Jugement souverain qui a condamné à la roue Louis Mandrin,* 26 May 1755.

96. "Lettre," in *Rendre la justice.*

97. This interpretation of the execution is found in "Notes de M. Morel, curé de Montrigrand," *Bulletin de la société départementale d'archéologie et de statistique de la Drôme* 15 (1881), 111 and 115–117; and *CA,* 19 May 1755, 168.

98. Forest, *Chroniques,* 43.

99. *CA,* 28 May 1755. "Lettre," in *Rendre la justice,* also notes that he walked "very quickly with a sure step."

100. Forest, *Chroniques,* 43.

101. "Lettre," in *Rendre la justice.* Most eyewitnesses attest to this speech, although Madame de Franquières told her daughter that Mandrin asked Gasparini to give a speech after the smuggler's own voice failed him. Gallier, ed., *Vie de province,* 139, Franquières to Bressac, 19 May 1755. According to the *Précis de la vie de Louis Mandrin* [1755], 3, his speech was one line: "Youth, heed my example, and you, agents, I beg your pardon."

102. Forest, *Chroniques,* 43. See also "Lettre," in *Rendre la justice.*

103. "Lettre," in *Rendre la justice.*

104. Régis Bertrand, "L'exécution et l'inhumation des condamnés en Provence," in *Histoire et criminalité de l'antiquité au XXe siècle: nouvelles approches,* ed. Benoît Garnot (Dijon, 1992), 82.

105. Quoted in Mitchell B. Merback, *The Thief, the Cross, and the Wheel: Pain and the Spectacle of Punishment in Medieval and Renaissance Europe* (Chicago, 1999), 160–161.

106. *CA,* 28 May 1755.

107. Merback, *Thief,* 215.

108. Thomas W. Laqueur, "Crowds, Carnival and the State in English Executions, 1604–1868," in *The First Modern Society,* ed. A.L. Beier, David Cannadine, and James M. Rosenheim (Cambridge, 1989), 305–356.

109. Michel Bée, "Le Spectacle de l'exécution dans la France d'ancien régime," *AESC* 38 (1983), 843–862. Freidland, *Seeing Justice Done,* chapters 4–7, subscribes to Bée's thesis for the pre-modern period, but argues that from the sixteenth to the eighteenth century detached spectatorship increasingly took precedence over communal redemption.

110. Bastien, *L'exécution publique;* and Robert A. Schneider, *The Ceremonial City: Toulouse Observed, 1738–1780* (Princeton, NJ, 1995), chapter 3. See also Peter Spierenburg, *The Spectacle of Suffering: Executions and the Evolution of Repression* (Cambridge, 1984); Richard J. Evans, *Rituals of Retribution: Capital Punishment in Germany, 1600–1987* (Oxford, 1996); and V.A.C. Gatrell, *The Hanging Tree: Execution and the English People, 1770–1868* (Oxford, 1994).

111. For an example, see Bastien, *L'exécution publique,* 238.

112. *CA,* 25 and 28 May 1755.

113. Gallier, ed., *Vie de province,* 139, Franquières to Bressac, 19 May 1755.

114. "Notes de M. Morel," 116.

115. Gallier, ed., *Vie de province,* 139, Franquières to Bressac, 19 May 1755.

116. Jean Vassort, *Les papiers d'un laboureur au siècle des lumières. Pierre Bordier: Une culture paysanne* (Seyssel, 1999), chapter 5. Scribe Pierre Prion reacted similarly to the news that "Sr Mandrin[,] famous land corsair," had been executed. See Sylvie Mouysset, "Mandrin au miroir des écrits de son temps: intrépide contrebandier ou brigand scélérat?," in *Les Brigands: Criminalité et protestation politique (1750–1850),* ed. Valérie Sottocasa (Rennes, 2013), 25–26.

117. Forest, *Chroniques,* 40. My emphasis.

118. Ibid., 44.

119. Jean Tarrade, *Le commerce colonial de la France à la fin de l'ancien régime* (Paris, 1972), 1:332, was shocked to find vestiges "of a medieval character" in the antismuggling laws of the "century of Enlightenment."

120. Michelle Alexander, *The New Jim Crow: Mass Incarceration in the Age of Colorblindness* (New York, 2010).

121. Arlette Farge, *Le vol d'aliments à Paris au XVIIIe siècle* (Paris, 1974). For England, see Douglas Hay, "Property, Authority and the Criminal Law," in *Albion's Fatal Tree: Crime and Society in Eighteenth-Century England* (New York, 1975), 17–63; and Peter Linebaugh, *The London Hanged: Crime and Civil Society in the Eighteenth Century* (London, 2006), xxii.

122. ADS C 431, memoir of 15 September 1780. This explains why convicted smugglers wore the mark of the galleys as a badge of honor and preferred to do time in the stocks rather than pay heavy fines. AN G-7 1290.

123. *AP,* vol. 2, 662. Smugglers who "passed before the hand of the executioner" did not experience ignomiy, a Sardinian official similarly noted, because it was widely believed that "they did not do any harm to anyone." Quoted in Jean Nicolas, *La Rébellion française: Mouvements populaires et conscience sociale 1661–1789* (Paris, 2002), 91.

10. Mandrin into Print

1. Fred Inglis, *A Short History of Celebrity* (Princeton, NJ, 2010), chapter 3; and Leo Braudy, *The Frenzy of Renown: Fame and Its History* (New York, 1997), chapter 5.

2. Hans-Jürgen Lüsebrink, "Images et représentations sociales de la criminalité au XVIIIe siècle: l'exemple de Mandrin," *RHMC* 26 (1979), 345. In criminal cases, unlike the civil cases studied by Sarah Maza in *Private Lives and Public Affairs: The Causes Célèbres of Prerevolutionary France* (Berkeley, CA, 1993), lawyers were not allowed to make presentations in court or publish on trials.

3. Peter Burke, *Popular Culture in Early Modern Europe* (New York, 1978), 259–270; Roger Chartier, *The Cultural Origins of the French Revolution,* trans. Lydia G. Cochrane (Durham, NC, 1991), 136–141 (quotation on 140).

4. Norbert Elias, *The Civilizing Process*, trans. Edmund Jephcott (Oxford, 2000); and idem, *The Court Society*, trans. Edmund Jephcott (New York, 1983).

5. ADDR B 1304. For law courts' inclination toward publishing, see Thierry Rigogne, *Between State and Market: Printing and Bookselling in Eighteenth-Century France* (Oxford, 2007), 199–200; and Pascal Bastien, *L'exécution publique à Paris au XVIIIe siècle* (Paris, 2006), 29–31.

6. BMV D 13020. For the Farm's use of print, see Marcel Juillard, "La Brigandage et la contrebande en Haute-Auvergne au XVIIIe siècle," *Revue de la Haute-Auvergne* (1936), 458; and David Adams, *Book Illustration, Taxes and Propaganda: The Fermiers Généraux Edition of La Fontaine's Contes et Nouvelles en Vers of 1762* (Oxford, 2006).

7. Hans-Jürgen Lüsebrink, ed., *Histoires curieuses et véritables de Cartouche et de Mandrin* (Paris, 1984), 38. Frantz Funck-Brentano, *Mandrin: Capitaine générale des contrebandiers de France* (Paris, 1908), 531, mistakenly claims that the *Abrégé de la vie de Louis Mandrin* ([Dole], 1755) was banned, based on a misreading of Ange Goudar, *Analyse du testament politique de Mandrin* (1789), 3.

8. Rigogne, *Between State and Market*, 38–48.

9. BN MS 22151, nos. 173–176, Bertin to Malesherbes, 27 June and 11 July 1755. Confiscated books were often found on the bookshelves of royal officials and their friends. Robert L. Dawson, *Confiscations and Customs: Banned Books and the French Book Trade during the Last Years of the Ancien Régime* (Oxford, 2006), 17 and 121.

10. Louis-Sébastien Mercier, *Tableau de Paris*, vol. 1 (Paris, 1994), chapter 463, and vol. 2 (Paris, 1994), chapter 828.

11. *Chanson sur la vie de Mandrin augmentée de sa mort sur l'air des pendus* (Lyon, 1755).

12. Déborah Cohen, *La nature du peuple: Les formes de l'imaginaire social (XVIII–XXIe siècles)* (Seyssel, 2010), 285–288, stresses how representations of Mandrin expressed a social fantasy to escape one's low-born status.

13. Although not formally part of the *bibliothèque bleue*, the appearance of the *La Mandrinade* made a big enough splash to be noted by Friedrich Melchior Grimm in his *Correspondance littéraire* on 15 July 1755. Designating a verbal assault, the term *Mandrinade* alluded to the *Mazarinades*, pamphlets attacking Cardinal Mazarin from 1648 to 1653, and the more recent *Poissonnades* written against Madame de Pompadour in the late 1740s.

14. For literacy and the expansion of the book trade, see Chartier, *Cultural Origins*, 69–70. For crime literature, see idem, *The Cultural Uses of Print in Early Modern France*, trans. Lydia G. Cochrane (Princeton, NJ, 1987), chapter 8; Lise Andries, ed., *Cartouche, Mandrin et autres brigands du XVIIIe siècle* (Paris, 2010); Hans-Jürgen Lüsebrink, *Les Représentations sociales de criminalité en France au XVIII siècle* (Thèse de doctorat, EHESS, 1983); and Dominique Kalifa, *L'encre et le sang: récits de crimes et société à la Belle époque* (Paris, 1995).

For popular biography, see Olivier Ferret, Anne-Marie Mercier-Faivre, and Chantal Thomas, *Dictionnaire des vies privées (1722–1842)* (Oxford, 2011).

15. *La Mandrinade, ou L'Histoire curieuse, véritable et remarquable de la vie de Louis Mandrin* (Saint-Geoirs, 1755), reproduced in *Histoires curieuses et véritables de Cartouche et de Mandrin,* ed. Hans-Jürgen Lüsebrink (Paris, 1984), 228. Page references to this text will henceforth be given in parentheses in the chapter.

16. Reproduced in Éloise Antzamidakis, "Les Complaintes de Mandrin," in *Louis Mandrin: malfaiteur ou bandit au grand cœur,* ed. Valérie Huss (Grenoble, 2005), 108–109.

17. Darrin M. McMahon, *Enemies of the Enlightenment: The French Counter-Enlightenment and the Making of Modernity* (Oxford, 2001), chapter 1.

18. Chartier, *Cultural Uses,* "The Literature of Roguery in the *Bibliothèque bleue*"; and Lise Andries, *La Bibliothèque bleue au dix-huitième siècle: une tradition éditoriale* (Oxford, 1989), 47–51. See also Jacques Berchtold, "De la thésaurisation à la mise en circulation: les usages du 'trésor du brigand' dans la littérature narrative des XVIIe et XVIIIe siècles," in *Être riche au siècle de Voltaire,* ed. Jacques Berchtold and Michel Porret (Geneva, 1996), 311–329.

19. René-Louis de Voyer, Marquis d'Argenson, *Journal et mémoires du marquis d'Argenson* (Paris, 1866), 8:386, entry of 16 December 1754; and *GC,* 21 January 1755.

20. Theodore Besterman, ed., *Voltaire's Correspondence,* vol. 23 (Geneva, 1958), nos. 6924, 6955, and 7029, letters to Comte d'Argental of 5 and 25 February and 8 May 1758.

21. Nicole Castan, *Les criminels de Languedoc* (Toulouse, 1980), 255.

22. *Journal historique de la Révolution* (London, 1774), 40.

23. Frédéric Braesch, ed., *Le Père Duchesne d'Hébert* (Paris, 1938), 242 and 585.

24. See, for example, the nineteenth-century broadside *Histoire du célèbre brigand Louis Mandrin,* reprinted in Madeleine Sorensen, "Le Thème des brigands à travers la peinture, le dessin et la gravure," in *Cartouche, Mandrin et autres brigands du XVIIIe siècle,* ed. Lise Andries (Paris, 2010), 90. It was precisely this negative image of Mandrin that historians such as Funck-Brentano attempted to counter at the turn of the twentieth century.

25. *CA,* 17 June 1755 (report from Valence, 14 June 1755).

26. Michel Forest, *Chroniques d'un bourgeois de Valence au temps de Mandrin* (Grenoble, 1980), 44–45.

27. BMG Chenavas (hereafter Ch.), 139.

28. He was also compared to contemporary warrior-princes such as Charles XII of Sweden and Frederick the Great of Prussia. *Dialogue entre Charles XII, roi de Suède, et Mandrin, contrebandier* (La Haye, 1760); and BN MS 12721, fol. 179, "Vers sur le Roy Prusse," December 1756. Cohen, *La nature,* 288–299, analyzes other parallels drawn between Louis XIV and Mandrin to argue that such confusion challenged the sacred character of the king's body.

29. BMD Ms. 939, fonds Baudot, abbé Moullemier, "Notes sur la Bourgogne," 423. Rhymed in the original French, slightly different versions of this epitaph appear in BN MS 12721, fol. 35 and the parish registers of St.-Médard-en-Forez in 1755 (BMG Ch. 139). See Sylvie Mouysset, "Mandrin au mirroir des écrits de son temps: intrépide contrebandier ou brigand scélérat?" in *Les Brigands: Criminalité et protestation politique (1750–1850)*, ed. Valérie Sottocasa (Rennes, 2013), 27, for another admiring eulogy written by a man of the cloth.

30. For royal uses of Hercules, see Peter Burke, *The Fabrication of Louis XIV* (New Haven, CT, 1992), passim. For revolutionary transformations, see Lynn Hunt, *Politics, Culture, and Class in the French Revolution* (Berkeley, CA, 1984), chapter 3.

31. Annik Pardailhé-Galabrun, *The Birth of Intimacy: Privacy and Domestic Life in Early Modern Paris*, trans. Jocelyn Phelps (Philadelphia, 1991), 153–164.

32. David Kunzle, *The Early Comic Strip: Narrative Strips and Picture Stories in the European Broadsheet from c. 1450–1825* (Berkeley, CA, 1973), 187–196; and Bastien, *L'exécution publique*, 47–56.

33. The minister of war disapproved of the image, exclaiming that the only spectacle in which such a "brigand" should appear was "the execution that sooner or later awaits him." SHAT 1A 3398, no. 415, d'Argenson to d'Espagnac, 24 April 1755. See also SHAT, 1A 3406, nos. 78 and 88, d'Espagnac and Saulx Tavannes to d'Argenson, 4 and 8 April 1755.

34. *MHP*, May 1755, 573–574.

35. *CA*, 30 May 1755. My discussion of the portraits owes much to Valérie Huss, "Les Portraits de Louis Mandrin au XVIIIe Siècle," in *Louis Mandrin: malfaiteur ou bandit au grand cœur*, ed. Valérie Huss (Grenoble, 2005), 83–90.

36. Marianne Clerc, *Jacques-André Treillard (1712–1794)* (Grenoble, 1995), 32–37.

37. *CA*, 28 and 30 May 1755.

38. See the "Notice," in *Abrégé de la vie de Louis Mandrin* (reprint: Paris, 1991), 139–145.

39. Chartier, *Cultural Uses*, chapter 8; Patrice Peveri, "De Cartouche à Poulailler: l'héroïsation du bandit dans le Paris du XVIIIe siècle," in *Être parisien*, ed. Claude Gauvard and Jean-Louis Robert (Paris, 2004), 135–150; and Christian Biet, ed., *Cartouche ou les voleurs* (Vijon, 2003). On social banditry the world over, see Eric Hobsbawm, *Bandits* (New York, 2000).

40. The epitaph quoted by Forest, *Chroniques*, 45, also highlighted his prison liberations: "Snatching from justice its victims, he alone opened prisons and judged crimes."

41. Jacques Berchtold, "Rousseau et Cartouche," in *Cartouche, Mandrin et autres brigands du XVIIIe siècle*, ed. Lise Andries (Paris, 2010), 338–357.

42. *Dialogue entre Charles XII, roi de Suède, et Mandrin, contrebandier* (La Haye, 1760), 20, made a similar argument. Comparing the great conquerors of antiquity to present-day smugglers who provide "necessities and comforts

at low prices," the character of Mandrin asks: "Am I not right to say that the former . . . whose names become illustrious are in fact great Brigands, while my kind hardly merit this ignominious name." In 1759, a philosophically minded Jesuit was censured by the parlement of Rouen for inviting his class to consider how crimes of brigandage were judged differently in various historical epochs. Was he thinking of Mandrin? BN MS 12721, fol. 353; BMG Ch. 139.

43. For ambiguity in legal literature in general, see Christian Biet, *Droit et littérature sous l'Ancien Régime: le jeu de la valeur et de la loi* (Paris, 2002), 167–171.

44. To the three eighteenth-century editions cited in Lüsebrink, ed., *Histoires,* 376–377, must be added the Amsterdam edition of 1755 held by BMV.

45. Chartier, *Cultural Uses,* chapter 7; and Lise Andries, *Bibliothèque bleue au dix-huitième siècle: une tradition éditoriale* (Oxford, 1989).

46. Berchtold, "Thésaurisation."

47. *Histoire de Louis Mandrin, depuis sa naissance jusqu'à sa mort* (Troyes, [1755]), reproduced in *Histoires curieuses et véritables de Cartouche et de Mandrin,* ed. Hans-Jürgen Lüsebrink (Paris, 1984), 159. Page references to this text will henceforth be given in parentheses in the chapter.

48. Robert Darnton, *The Great Cat Massacre and Other Episodes in French Cultural History* (New York, 1984), chapter 1; Michel de Certeau, *The Practice of Everyday Life,* trans. Steven Rendall (Berkeley, CA, 1984), 23.

49. Burke, *Popular Culture,* 172; Peter Linebaugh, *The London Hanged: Crime and Society in the Eighteenth Century* (London, 2006), chapter 1.

50. Cohen, *La nature,* 413–414, also argues that this is a decisive moment in popular culture, because representations of Mandrin challenged the "irreplaceable character of the king."

51. For "le petit Mandrin," see SHAT 1A 3406, no. 54, Saulx Tavannes to d'Argenson, 25 March 1755; and AAE CP Genève 66, fol. 309, Montperoux to Rouillé, 21 March 1755. For "the children of Mandrin," see BMG Ch. 140 and 144; and ADS C2, Marcieu to Sinsan, 18 September 1755. For other bands that mimicked his techniques, see SHAT 1A 3406, nos. 118, 126, and 154; ADCO C 322; ADS C 13, 127 and 662; and Antole de Gallier, *La vie de province au XVIIIe siècle* (Paris, 1877), 116.

52. Nils Liander, "Smuggling Bands in Eighteenth-Century France" (PhD diss., Harvard University, 1981), 529–530.

53. Jacques-Louis Ménétra, *Journal of My Life,* trans. Arthur Goldhammer (New York, 1986), 82–83. Later in the text (104), Ménétra claims he ran into Mandrin's sister and Broc leading a large band of smugglers. Mouysset, "Mandrin au mirroir," also remarks that ordinary people drew a favorable opinion of Mandrin from all they had read, seen, and heard.

54. Burke, *Popular Culture,* 166.

55. Slavoj Zizek, *Looking Awry: An Introduction to Jacques Lacan through Popular Culture* (Cambridge, MA, 1992), 59.

56. De Certeau, *Practice of Everyday Life,* 23.
57. The epitaph noted by Forest, *Chroniques,* 55, drew a similar distinction: "greater than Cartouche, [Mandrin] was not guided by a fierce character ..; he was always horrified by crime and carnage."

11. Smuggling in the Enlightenment

1. André Morellet, *Mémoires de l'abbé Morellet* (Paris, 1821), 157.
2. *Encyclopédie, ou dictionnaire raisonné des sciences, des arts et des métiers,* ed. Denis Diderot and Jean le Rond d'Alembert, vol. 12 (Neufchastel, 1765), 510.
3. My emphasis on reform is consonant with recent comparative work on the Enlightenment, such as John Robertson, *The Case for the Enlightenment: Scotland and Naples 1680–1760* (Cambridge, 2005); and Gabriel Paquette, ed., *Enlightened Reform in Southern Europe and Its Atlantic Colonies, c. 1750–1830* (Farnham, 2010).
4. Jean Goldzink, "Le droit de résistance dans les Lumières françaises," in *Le Droit de résistance XIIe–XXe siècle,* ed. Jean-Claude Zancarini (Fontenay, 1999), 227–245.
5. André Morellet, *Réflexions sur les avantages de la liberté d'écrire et d'imprimer sur les matières de l'administration* (1764; published in London, 1775), 22.
6. Christine Théré, "Economic Publishing and Authors, 1566–1789," in *Studies in the History of French Political Economy: From Bodin to Walras,* ed. Gilbert Faccarello (New York, 1998), 21; Joël Félix, *Finances et politique au siècle des Lumières: Le ministère L'Averdy, 1763–1768* (Paris, 1999), chapter 1; and Robin J. Ives, "Political Publicity and Political Economy in Eighteenth-Century France," *French History* 17 (2003), 1–18.
7. Bernard Schnapper, "La diffusion en France des nouvelles conceptions pénales dans la dernière décennie de l'ancien régime," in *Voies nouvelles en histoire du droit,* ed. Bernard Schnapper (Paris, 1991), 187–205; and David Jacobson, "The Politics of Criminal Law Reform in Pre-Revolutionary France" (PhD diss., Brown University, 1976), chapter 7. For the publication of judicial *mémoires,* see Sarah Maza, *Private Lives and Public Affairs: The Causes Célèbres of Prerevolutionary France* (Berkeley, CA, 1993).
8. Theodore Besterman, ed., *Voltaire's Correspondence,* vol. 25 (Geneva, 1957), no. 5372, Voltaire to Gauffecourt, 15 December 1754; and vol. 26 (Geneva, 1957), no. 5417, Voltaire to Duport, 7 January 1755, and no. 5427, Voltaire to Dorothea, 14 January 1755. It would take a case of overwhelming religious intolerance to lure Voltaire into judicial politics.
9. This retrospective vision of Colbert was grossly exaggerated. See Philippe Minard, *La fortune du Colbertisme: État et industrie dans la France des Lumières* (Paris, 1998).
10. Gianfranco Dioguardi, *Ange Goudar contre l'Ancien Régime* (Castelnau-le-Lez, 1994); Jean-Claude Hauc, *Ange Goudar: un aventurier des Lumières* (Paris,

2004). See the favorable review of the *Testament* in Élie-Catherine Fréron, *L'Année littéraire* (Amsterdam, 1756), 7:165–168.

11. *De l'esprit des lois,* book 13, chapters 7 and 14. Montesquieu's preference for excise taxes on articles of consumption was widely shared by members of the Gournay circle, proluxury writers such as Melon and Hume, encyclopedists like Jaucourt, and Adam Smith. The Physiocrats would directly challenge this position. See Catherine Larrère, "Impôts directs, impôts indirects: Économie, politique, droit," *Archives de philosophie du droit* 46 (2002), 117–130; and Arnaud Orain, "Progressive Indirect Taxation and Social Justice in Eighteenth-Century France: Forbonnais and Graslin's Fiscal System," *European Journal of the History of Economic Thought* 17:4 (October 2010), 659–685.

12. *De l'esprit des lois,* book 11, chapter 18; and book 13, chapters 8, 19, and 20.

13. Of course, as Chapter 2 suggests, the Farm was far more efficient than critics believed. See James C. Riley, *The Seven Years War and the Old Regime in France* (Princeton, NJ, 1986), 62–67; and Eugene N. White, "From Privatized to Government-Administered Tax Collection: Tax Farming in Eighteenth-Century France," *EHR* 57 (2004), 636–663.

14. The term "egalitarian liberalism" is from Simone Meyssonnier, *La balance et l'horloge: La genèse de la pensée libérale en France au XVIIIe siècle* (Paris, 1989). For the Gournay circle, see, most recently, Fréderic Lefebvre, Loïc Charles, and Christine Théré, eds., *Le cercle de Vincent de Gournay—Savoirs économiques et pratiques administratives en France au milieu du XVIIIe siècle* (Paris, 2011). With respect to overseas trade, the Gournay circle assailed state-chartered trading companies but advocated laws that subordinated colonial interests to that of the metropole. See Alain Clément, "L'Europe ouverte au monde colonial: Les "premiers économistes" et l'utilité des colonies dans la France du XVIIIe siècle," in *La croissance en économie ouverte (XVIIIe–XXIe siècles),* ed. Bertrand Blancheton and Hubert Bonin (Brussels, 2009), 43–68.

15. Antoine Murphy, "Le développement des idées économiques en France, 1750–1756," *RHMC* 33 (1986), 521–541; Félix, *Finances et politique,* chapter 1; and Ives, "Political Publicity."

16. Loïc Charles notes that by appealing to the public and making economic as opposed to merely juridical arguments, the Gournay circle's engagement in the calico controversy marked a new place for economics in the public sphere. See his "Le cercle de Gournay: usages culturels et pratiques savantes," in *Le cercle de Vincent de Gournay,* ed. Fréderic Lefebvre, Loïc Charles, and Christine Théré (Paris, 2011), 84–86.

17. *Examen des effets que doivent produire dans le commerce de France l'usage et la fabrication des toiles peintes* (1759), chapter 4. See also *Observations sommaires et dernières des marchands & fabriquans de Lyon, Rouen & Tours, & des six corps des marchands de la ville de Paris* (n.p, n.d.).

18. AN F-12 88, 42.

19. Jacques Vincent de Gournay, "Observations sur l'examen des avantages et désavantages de la prohibition des toiles peintes," in *Examen des avantages et des désavantages de la prohibition des toiles peintes* (Marseille, 1755), 75–76. Enlightenment writers frequently used the metaphor of war to describe the conflict between Farm and smuggler. Jacques Necker blamed "inept and barbarous" fiscal laws for a "war" that pitted one part of society against the other. *De l'administration des finances* (1784), 2:57–58. Guillaume-François de Mahy, Baron de Corméré spoke of "a muted and continuous war which deprives society of a considerable part of citizens." *Recherches et considérations nouvelles sur les finances* (London, 1789), 1:100.

20. André Morellet, *Réflexions sur les avantages de la libre fabrication et de l'usage des toiles peintes en France* (Geneva, 1758), 51, 54, 168.

21. *Refléxions sur différens objets du commerce, et en particulier sur la libre fabrication des toiles peintes* (Geneva, 1759), 102.

22. Pierre Samuel Du Pont *Ephémérides du citoyen* (1769), 2:xiii.

23. Minard, *Fortune*, 337–350, describes a similar conceptual shift to a "new economy of demand."

24. See Edgard Depitre, *La toile peinte en France au XVIIe et au XVIIIe siècles: industrie, commerce, prohibitions* (Paris, 1912), 195–231.

25. Morellet, *Réflexions*, 37.

26. Ibid., 174 (reference to "Mandrin and his troop" on 178).

27. Serge Chassagne, *Le Coton et ses patrons: France, 1760–1840* (Paris, 1991), 93.

28. Catherine Larrère, *L'invention de l'économie au XVIIIe siècle: du droit naturel à la physiocratie* (Paris, 1992); Philippe Steiner, *La science nouvelle de l'économie politique* (Paris, 1998); and Paul Cheney, *Revolutionary Commerce: The Globalization of the French Monarchy* (Cambridge, MA, 2010), chapter 5.

29. Madeleine Dobie, *Trading Places: Colonization and Slavery in Eighteenth-Century French Culture* (Ithaca, NY, 2010), chapter 6. With regard to empire, the economic liberalism of the Physiocrats went much further than that of the Gournay circle. See Clément, "L'Europe ouverte."

30. Bernard Delmas, "Les Physiocrates, Turgot et 'le grand secret de la science fiscale,'" *RHMC* 56 (2009), 79–103.

31. Kenneth Carpenter, "The Economic Bestsellers before 1850," *Bulletin of the Kress Library* (May 1975), 18.

32. I do not mean to imply that this shift was seamless or complete. Just as Forbonnais, a Gournay ally, argued, like the Physiocrats, that salt smugglers "in no way violated natural law" (*Recherches et considérations sur les finances de France* [Basle, 1758], 508), Du Pont, a Physiocrat, belatedly celebrated Morellet's 1758 consumerist tract against the calico prohibition (*Ephémérides du citoyen* [1769] 3:180). Nor did the Gournay circle vanish after the Physiocrats took the stage; Turgot, Trudaine de Montigny, Morellet, Butel-Dumont, and others continued to publish influential works.

33. John Shovlin, *The Political Economy of Virtue: Luxury, Patriotism, and the Origins of the French Revolution* (Ithaca, NY, 2006), chapter 3, makes a similar point.

34. Mirabeau, *Théorie de l'impôt* (1760), 141–144. Similarly, Du Pont would write that the real criminals were not the smugglers but the tax farmers who imposed a "fiscal or monopolistic inquisition detrimental to the natural rights of citizens, to their property, to their civil liberty." *Ephémérides du Citoyen* 3 (1769), 180–181.

35. Mirabeau, *Théorie,* 151.

36. Guillaume-François Le Trosne, *Les effets de l'impôt indirect prouvés par les deux exemples de la gabelle et du tabac* (1770), 307–308.

37. Guillaume-François Le Trosne, *De l'administration provinciale, et de la réforme de l'impôt* (Basel, 1779), 81.

38. Le Trosne, *Les effets,* 326–327.

39. Echoing the Physiocrats, Adam Smith described the smuggler as "a person who, though no doubt highly blameable for violating the laws of his country, is frequently incapable of violating those of natural justice, and would have been, in every respect, an excellent citizen, had not the laws of his country made that a crime which nature never meant to be so." Adam Smith, *An Inquiry into the Nature and Causes of the Wealth of Nations,* ed. R.H. Campbell and A.S. Skinner (Indianapolis, IN, 1981), II, 898.

40. Quoted in Colin Lucas, "Talking about Urban Popular Violence in 1789," in *Reshaping France: Town, Country and Region during the French Revolution,* ed. Alan Forrest and Peter Jones (Manchester, 1991), 123.

41. Physiocrats therefore assimilated food rioters to the pejorative category of "the people." See Déborah Cohen, *La nature du peuple: Les formes de l'imaginaire social (XVIII–XXIe siècles)* (Seyssel, 2010), 179–184.

42. Mirabeau elaborated, "[t]hose who stray from the rule [of nature] are sick or corrupted limbs that must be cured or amputated." *Philosophie rurale* (Amsterdam, 1763), xviii–xix. In the twentieth century, Richard Posner of the Chicago school would build on this idea, defining crimes such as theft as "market bypassing." Bernard Harcourt, *The Illusion of Free Markets: Punishment and the Myth of Natural Order* (Cambridge, 2011), chapters 4 and 6.

43. Le Trosne, *Mémoire sur les vagabonds* (Soissons, 1764), 50.

44. William Max Nelson, "Making Men: Enlightenment Ideas of Racial Engineering," *AHR* 115 (December 2010), 1392.

45. In addition to the doubling and tripling of certain direct taxes, such decrees called for increases in salt and tobacco taxes. In 1758, the price of retail tobacco was hiked 20 percent, and in 1760 and 1763, the gabelle and other levies were raised 5 percent. Judges in the provinces led this opposition, in part because they possessed fewer state bonds than their Parisian counterparts and were therefore less troubled by the possibility that public opposition might trigger a bankruptcy. Michael Kwass, *Privilege and the Politics of Taxation in Eighteenth-Century France* (Cambridge, 2000), 182; David

Stasavage, *Public Debt and the Birth of the Democratic State* (Cambridge, 2003), 132–138.

46. ADI B 2325, remonstrances of 17 August 1763.

47. SHAT 1A 3406, no. 188, Moydieu to d'Argenson, 4 May 1755.

48. *Objets de remontrances du parlement du Dauphiné, du 7 Septembre 1764.*

49. Edmond Barbier, *Chronique de la régence et du règne de Louis XV* (Paris, 1858), 8:77.

50. Louis Petit de Bachaumont, *Mémoires secrets pour servir à l'histoire de la république des lettres en France* (Paris, 1777), 1:254 and 1:268; René Stourm, *Bibliographie historique des finances de la France au dix-huitième siècle* (Paris, 1896), 106.

51. Arnaud Decroix, *Question fiscale et réforme financière en France (1749–1789)* (Aix-en-Provence, 2006), 275.

52. Jean Baptiste Darigrand, *L'Anti-financier* (Amsterdam, 1764), 3.

53. See Emma Rothschild, *Economic Sentiments: Adam Smith, Condorcet, and the Enlightenment* (Cambridge, MA, 2001), 27–28, 110–111.

54. Darigrand, *L'Anti-financier,* 96. Charges of sexual harassment were common. See AN G-7 1293; AN Z1a 990; Reynald Abad, *Le Grand marché: L'approvisionnement alimentaire de Paris sous l'ancien régime* (Paris, 2002), 94; Jean Clinquart, *L'administration des douanes en France sous la révolution* (Neuilly, 1989), 40.

55. *Projet pour la suppression des douanes dans l'intérieur du royaume* (Avignon, 1763) also detailed the incompetence of Farm guards, whose unprovoked violence was protected by the commissions. The resulting public hatred of the Farm, the book argued, facilitated the rise of smuggling gangs such as the one headed by Mandrin.

56. Darigrand, *L'Anti-financier,* 32.

57. Ibid., 69. Recall that the *mémoires judiciaires* were allowed to be published only in civil cases so that Darigrand's text had to be published as a pamphlet, with all the risks that involved.

58. *Déclaration du Roi* (28 March 1764), 2–3.

59. Montesquieu, *Lettres persanes* (Paris, 2006), letter 102; *De l'esprit des lois,* books 6 and 12; Rousseau, *Du contrat social* (Paris, 1996), book 2, chapter 5. For Voltaire's role in the Calas affair, see Peter Gay, *Voltaire's Politics: The Poet as Realist* (New York, 1965), chapter 6.

60. Denis Diderot, quoted in Peter Gay, *The Enlightenment: An Interpretation, vol. 2: The Science of Freedom* (New York, 1969), 438.

61. Cesare Beccaria, *On Crimes and Punishments and Other Writings,* ed. Richard Bellamy (Cambridge, 2003), 7.

62. Ibid, 88.

63. Ibid, 54.

64. "Tentative analytique sur les contrebandes," in Cesare Beccaria, *Recherches concernant la nature du style,* trans. Bernard Pautrat (Paris, 2001), 179–183.

65. Beccaria, *Crimes,* 87–88.

66. Ibid, 31.

67. Although Beccaria remained isolated in his position against the death penalty, his influence on virtually all other matters of criminal law was phenomenal. See Schnapper, "Diffusion," 187–205; Jacobson, "Politics of Criminal Law Reform," chapter 7.

68. Joseph Michel Antoine Servan, *Oeuvres choisies de Servan* (Paris, 1825), 2:86–87. See Christiane Mervaud, "Voltaire et le Beccaria de Grenoble: Michel-Joseph-Antoine Servan," *SVEC* 10 (2008), 171–181.

69. Brissot de Warville, *Les moyens d'adoucir la rigueur des loix pénales en France* (Châlons-sur-Marne, 1781), 59 (see also 9–11, 57–58, 139–140).

70. Marquis de Condorcet, "Monopole et monopoleur," in *Oeuvres de Condorcet,* ed. A. Condorcet O'Connor and M.F. Arago (Paris, 1847), 11:38. The critique of the Farm's monopolies was part of a larger attack on monopoly in general, as evidenced by the article "Monopoly" in the *Encyclopédie, ou dictionnaire raisonné des sciences, des arts et des métiers,* ed. Denis Diderot and Jean le Rond d'Alembert (Neufchastel, 1765), 10:668. For the condemnation of monopoly as a form of trade, see Anoush Fraser Terjanian, *Commerce and Its Discontents in Eighteenth-Century French Political Thought* (Cambridge, 2012), chapter 4.

71. Condorcet, "Réflexions sur la jurisprudence criminelle," in *Œuvres complète de Condorcet* (Paris, 1804), 11:8 and 11:32.

72. Diderot, *The Two Friends from Bourbonne,* in *Rameau's Nephew and Other Works,* trans. Jacques Barzun and Ralph H. Bowen (Indianapolis, IN, 2001), 232–233.

73. In consistent fashion, Diderot highlighted intolerable divergences between positive criminal law and natural law in his *Encyclopédie* article on "natural law," his *Supplément au voyage de Bougainville,* and his contributions to the *Histoire des deux Indes.*

74. Voltaire, *L'Homme aux quarante écus* (Paris, 1768), 82; idem, *Prix de la justice et de l'humanité,* in *Oeuvres complètes de Voltaire* (Garnier, 1880), 30:545.

75. *Sur les finances* (London, 1775), 27–32 and 66. Stung by this public indictment, Colleau printed a pamphlet in his own defense in which he called *Sur les finances* "the most furious, atrocious, & seditious libel which has appeared yet against the Farm." *Pièce importante à joindre à l'ouvrage. . . . Sur les Finances* (n.p., n.d.), in ADH C 1650. Colleau's rejoinder and the extensive commentary on the pamphlet in the *Encyclopédie Méthodique: Finances* (Paris, 1784), 1:334–338, "Commission," suggest that *Sur les finances* was widely read.

76. In 1788–1789, Malesherbes elaborated on the argument he had articulated in the late 1750s that the consumer demand for books was too strong to be constrained by royal censorship. His ideas on the subject were finally published in *Mémoires sur la librairie et sur la liberté de la presse* in 1809.

77. Claude Josse Auger, *Mémoires pour servir à l'histoire du droit public de la France en matières d'impôts* (Bruxelles, 1779), 13, remonstrances of 14 September 1756.

78. The Valence commission was never remodeled, despite the objections of the *cours des aides* of Paris, Grenoble, Montpellier, and Dijon.

79. Auger, *Mémoires*, 370–388.

80. Ibid., 501; Malesherbes to Maupeou, 28 July 1770.

81. BN MS 8476, 8379, 8376, 8392, 8372, 8390, 8391; ADH C 1697; AN Y 10929b.

82. Auger, *Mémoires*, 504–517, remonstrances of 14 August 1770.

83. Here my analysis intersects with that of Julian Swann, "Malesherbes et la critique parlementaire du despotisme, de la bureaucratie et de la monarchie administrative," in *Le Cercle de Vincent de Gournay: Savoirs économiques et pratiques administratives en France au milieu du XVIIIe siècle*, ed. Loïc Charles, Frédéric Lefebvre, and Christine Théré (Paris, 2011), 111–129; and idem, "Les parlementaires, les lettres de cachet et la campagne contre l'arbitraire de la justice au XVIIIe siècle," in *Les parlements et les Lumières*, ed. Olivier Chaline (Paris, 2012), 179–196.

84. Malesherbes' suspicion that many of the rulings of the royal "council" were but the decisions of the finance minister alone has been documented by Michel Antoine, *Le Conseil du roi sous le règne de Louis XV* (Paris, 1970), 377–431. This was one reason why the superior courts argued that the justice delegated to them was superior to that retained by the council. Olivier Chaline, "Cassations et évocations dans les remontrances des parlements au XVIIIe siècle," *Histoire, Economie, et Société* 29 (Septembre 2010), 67.

85. Elisabeth Badinter, ed., *Les "remontrances' de Malesherbes 1771–1775* (Paris, 1985), 174–202.

86. Malesherbes had alluded to the estates general in the remonstrances of 1763 and 1770, but his calls became more urgent after the Maupeou coup.

87. Badinter, ed., *"Remontrances" de Malesherbes*, 172.

88. Keith Michael Baker, *Inventing the French Revolution* (Cambridge, 1990), 117–120.

89. *Très-humbles & très-respectueuses Remontrances que présent au Roi, notre très-honoré & souverain Seigneur, les Gens tenants sa Cour des Aides de Paris* [1778]; Auger, *Mémoires*, which contained three decades of previously unpublished remonstrances; and *Manuel pour les députés aux États-généraux, relativement aux impôts* [1789]. The royal prosecutor of the Paris *cour des aides* was right to fear that the 1778 publication would "cause a public sensation." *Extrait des registres de la cour des aides du 29 Avril 1778* (Paris, 1778). For the publishing history and influence of the 1775 remonstrances, see Decroix, *Question fiscale*, 311–315; and Swann, "Malesherbes," 121–123.

90. Quoted in Badinter, ed., *"Remontrances" de Malesherbes*, 138.

91. Yves Durand, *Les fermiers généraux au XVIIIe siècle* (Paris, 1971), book 2.

92. Michel Foucault, *Discipline and Punish: The Birth of the Prison*, trans. Alan Sheridan (New York, 1979), 82.

93. Steven L. Kaplan, *The Famine Plot Persuasion in Eighteenth-Century France* (Philadelphia, 1982); Dale K. Van Kley, *The Damiens Affair and the Unravel-*

ing of the Ancien Régime (Princeton, NJ, 1984); Jeffrey Merrick, *The Desacralization of the French Monarchy in the Eighteenth Century* (Baton Rouge, LA, 1990); Arlette Farge, *Subversive Words: Public Opinion in Eighteenth-Century France,* trans. Rosemary Morris (University Park, PA, 1995); and Kwass, *Privilege,* chapter 4.

94. Marisa Linton, *The Politics of Virtue in Enlightenment France* (New York, 2001), 145.

95. Louis-Sébastien Mercier, *Tableau de Paris* (Amsterdam, 1782), vol. 1, chapter 261.

12. Revolution

1. Many thanks to Valérie Huss for allowing me to examine the exhibit's *cahiers.*

2. Ange Goudar, *Analyse du Testament politique de Mandrin* (1789).

3. Jean Nicolas, *La Rébellion française: Mouvements populaires et conscience sociale 1661–1789* (Paris, 2002), 57, figure 3.

4. John Markoff, *The Abolition of Feudalism: Peasants, Lords, and Legislators in the French Revolution* (University Park, PA, 1996), 265, which analyzes Jean Nicolas's preliminary data. Nicolas Schapira, "Contrebande et contrebandiers dans le nord et de l'est de la France, 1740–1789 (mémoire, Université de Paris, 1991), 108, found that crimes associated with contraband peaked during the economic crisis of 1786–1789.

5. Of course, the continuity of state power was a main theme of Tocqueville's *The Old Regime and the Revolution.* For war, see David A. Bell, *The First Total War: Napoleon's Europe and the Birth of Warfare as We Know It* (Boston, 2007). For repression, see Howard G. Brown, *Ending the French Revolution: Violence, Justice, and Repression from the Terror to Napoleon* (Charlottesville, VA, 2006). For finance, see D. M. G. Sutherland, "Peasants, Lords, and Leviathan: Winners and Losers from the Abolition of Feudalism, 1780–1820," *JEH* 62 (2002), 1–24; Eugene White, "The French Revolution and the Politics of Government Finance, 1770–1815," *JEH* 55 (1995), 230 (Figure 1); and Michel Bruguière, *Gestionnaires et profiteurs de la Révolution* (Paris, 1986).

6. Ernest Labrousse, *Esquisse du mouvement des prix et des revenues en France au XVIIIe siècle* (Paris, 1933), 2:631. More recently, Nicolas Delalande, *Les Batailles de l'impôt: Consentement et résistances de 1789 à nos jours* (Paris, 2011), 38, has suggested that the new fiscal system excluded "a priori" any recourse to indirect taxes.

7. Anne Conchon, *La péage en France au XVIIIe siècle* (Paris, 2002), 440, makes the same observation.

8. One has to go back to the work of nineteenth-century republican historian Michelet to find an overview of the Revolution that stresses this essential point. The Farm's "organized war" against the people of France, wrote Michelet in *Histoire de la Révolution française* (Paris, 1979), 1:86, was one of the "evils" that incited the Revolution.

9. For an excellent synthesis of recent work, see Gail Bossenga, "Financial Origins of the French Revolution," in *From Deficit to Deluge: The Origins of the French Revolution,* ed. Thomas E. Kaiser and Dale K. Van Kley (Stanford, CA, 2011), 37–66.

10. See Joël Félix's comment in "Retour sur les origines financières de la Révolution française," *AHRF* 356 (2009), 189.

11. For a parallel argument, see John Shovlin, *The Political Economy of Virtue: Luxury, Patriotism, and the Origins of the French Revolution* (Ithaca, NY, 2006).

12. Michael Kwass, *Privilege and the Politics of Taxation in Eighteenth-Century France* (Cambridge, 2000), chapter 6.

13. Gilbert Shapiro and John Markoff, *Revolutionary Demands: A Content Analysis of the Cahiers de Doléances of 1789* (Stanford, CA, 1998), chapter 20. Some *cahiers* urged the creation of new luxury taxes, but most eschewed indirect taxation altogether.

14. Ibid. The most widespread grievance was that against the registry taxes collected by the Farm, perhaps a reflection of the mediation of lawyers in the composition of local *cahiers,* but the grievance that topped the list in terms of both its incidence and the level of hostility it aroused was the gabelle.

15. *AP,* 2:139, art. 58. See also P. Grateau, " 'Nécessité réelle et nécessité factice': doléances et culture matérielle dans la sénéchaussée de Rennes en 1789," *AB* 100 (1993), 303.

16. Citing no less an authority than Jacques Necker, the third estate of Beauvais had "to admit that this tax [on tobacco] is not offensive, since it strikes an object intended to satisfy artificial needs, and that of all the contributions it is the softest and most imperceptible; as the great administrator, the hope of France said, it is to be ranked in the category of clever fiscal inventions." *AP,* 2:304. The nobility of Saint-Mihiel grouped tobacco with playing cards and wig powder as objects of superfluity and luxury. *AP,* 2:240. See also *AP,* 6:238; and Grateau, " 'Nécessité réelle,' " 305.

17. *AP,* 2:232.

18. *AP,* 5:27. Likewise, the villagers of Erbévillier explained that they could not work without tobacco. E. Gondolff, *Le Tabac sous l'ancienne monarchie: La ferme royale, 1629–1791* (Vesoul, 1914), 335.

19. *AP,* 5:418.

20. *AP,* 3:85.

21. Quoted in Jean Clinquart, *L'administration des douanes en France sous la Révolution* (Neuilly, 1989), 40.

22. Gondolff, *Tabac,* 341.

23. Quoted in Shapiro and Markoff, *Revolutionary Demands,* 613, n. 48.

24. Quoted in George T. Matthews, *The Royal General Farms in Eighteenth-Century France* (New York, 1958), 278. See also *AP,* 6:22.

25. *AP,* 2:326.

26. *AP,* 6:683.

27. *AP,* 3:307. See also 4:750, for an attempt to assert an amoral reading of smuggling.

28. *AP,* 2:441.

29. *AP,* 5:469. See also 2:326 and 6:36.

30. *AP,* 3:275. See also 1:696, 2:99, 2:435, 3:27, and 5:588.

31. *AP,* 5:531. See also 2:304, 3:85, and 3:679.

32. *AP,* 6:19 and 6:22. See also 6:24, 6:131, and 6:719.

33. For declining rates of import taxes on calico, see Pierre Caspard, *La Fabrique-Neuve de Cortaillod* (Paris, 1979), 108.

34. Quoted in Laura Mason and Tracey Rizzo, eds., *The French Revolution* (Boston, 1999), 59.

35. Camille Bloch, ed., *Les contributions directes* (Paris, 1915), 60.

36. R.B. Rose, "Tax Revolt and Popular Organization in Picardy, 1789–1791," *PP* 43 (1969), 93.

37. Victor de Clercq, "L'incendie des barrières de Paris en Juillet 1789," *BSHP* (1938), 31.

38. Louis-Sébastien Mercier, *Tableau de Paris* (Amsterdam, 1782), vol. 1, chapter 123.

39. Quoted in E. Frémy, "L'enceinte de Paris construite par les fermiers généraux," *BSHP* 39 (1912), 119.

40. Gondolff, *Tabac,* 286.

41. *Réclamation d'un citoyen contre la nouvelle enceinte de Paris* (1787), 3 and 20–27. Hawked by a book peddler on the Pont-Neuf, this pamphlet was banned by the Paris police. Rumor had it that a tax farmer was offering 20,000 lt to anyone who could furnish the name of its author.

42. Jacques Godechot, *The Taking of the Bastille: July 14, 1789,* trans. Jean Stewart (New York, 1970), 192–194; Roger Dion, *Histoire de la vigne et du vin en France des origines au XIXe siècle* (Paris, 1959), 518–523; Frémy, "L'enceinte de Paris"; de Clercq, "L'incendie des barrières."

43. The rest were artisans, unskilled workers, and the unemployed. George Rudé, *The Crowd in the French Revolution* (Oxford, 1972), 49, 180–181, and Appendix IV; and Godechot, *The Taking of the Bastille,* 194; Dion, *Histoire de la vigne,* 521. As Lafayette would observe, the crowds that continued to attack the tollgates through 1790 were composed of smugglers "in great numbers," aided by the general populace. Quoted in Anthony Vidler, *Claude-Nicolas Le Doux: Architecture and Social Reform at the End of the Ancien Régime* (Cambridge, MA, 1990), 215.

44. Dion, *Histoire de la vigne,* 521.

45. Ibid., 522.

46. *Revolutions de Paris,* no. 1, 1 and 6.

47. Ibid., no. 1, 1, 6, and 12.

48. Hans-Jürgen Lüsebrink and Rolf Reichardt, *The Bastille: A History of a Symbol of Despotism and Freedom,* trans. Norbert Schürer (Durham, NC, 1997), chapter 2.

49. The attempt to reinstitute Paris customs was met with violent resistance. As late as January 1791, a month before the customs barriers were abolished, an investigation into a wine merchant caught with illicit tobacco provoked a battle at the La Chapelle post that left more than fifty dead and wounded.

50. Gail Bossenga, "City and State: An Urban Perspective on the Origins of the French Revolution," in *The Political Culture of the Old Regime,* ed. Keith Michael Baker (Oxford, 1987), 135.

51. Rose, "Tax Revolt," 98. Duty-free wine was also served in taverns.

52. Nils Liander, "Smuggling Bands in Eighteenth-Century France" (PhD diss., Harvard University, 1981), 213.

53. AN F-11, 210; Quoted in Clay Ramsay, *The Ideology of the Great Fear: The Soissonnais in 1789* (Baltimore, 1992), 177–179.

54. Liander, "Smuggling Bands," 211.

55. Ibid., 223–224.

56. Quoted in Schapira, "Contrebande," 110.

57. Bossenga, "City and State," 135.

58. For the indirect-tax rebellions of 1789–1790, see John Markoff, *The Abolition of Feudalism: Peasants, Lords, and Legislators in the French Revolution* (University Park, PA, 1996), 233–240, 275–277, 344–354; Bryant T. Ragan Jr., "Rural Political Activism and Fiscal Equality in the Revolutionary Somme," *Re-Creating Authority in Revolutionary France,* ed. Bryant T. Ragan and Elizabeth A. Williams (New Brunswick, NJ, 1992), 36–56; Ramsay, *Ideology,* 177–179; Stephen Miller, *State and Society in Eighteenth-Century France: A Study of Political Power and Social Revolution in Languedoc* (Washington, DC, 2008), 155, 190, 196–198; J.F. Bosher, *The Single Duty Project* (London, 1964), 152; Marcel Marion, "Le Recouvrement des impôts en 1790," *Revue Historique* 121 (1916), 1–47; and Rose, "Tax Revolt."

59. Marion, "Recouvrement," 1–47.

60. Bosher, *Single Duty Project,* 150. Jacob M. Price, *France and the Chesapeake* (Ann Arbor, MI, 1973), 797, charts the precipitous decline of the Farm's tobacco sales in 1789 and 1790.

61. Camille Bloch, ed., *Procès-Verbaux du comité des finances de l'assemblée constituante* (Rennes, 1922), 1:33. Conchon, *La péage,* 440–444, tells a similar story about seigneurial tolls.

62. Liander, "Smuggling Bands," 229.

63. Quoted in Marion, "Recouvrement," 35.

64. Quoted in Gondolff, *Tabac,* 347. See also Bloch, ed., *Procès-Verbaux,* 1:192.

65. François-Nicolas Mollien, *Mémoires d'un ministre du trésor public, 1780–1815* (Paris, 1898), 1:144. See also the documents in Clinquart, *L'administration des douanes,* 40–45. That the Farm was buckling under pressure from below was evidenced in the steep decline of "insurance" rates—the rates merchants paid smugglers to guarantee the transport of their illicit goods—

from 15–20 percent of the merchandise's value to 5–6 percent. Bosher, *Single Duty Project,* 160.

66. Déborah Cohen, *La nature du peuple: Les formes de l'imaginaire social (XVIII–XXIe siècles)* (Seyssel, 2010), chapter 1.

67. William H. Sewell Jr., *Logics of History: Social Theory and Social Transformation* (Chicago, 2005), chapter 8. See also Sophie Wahnich, "Résistance à l'oppression et devoir d'insurrection pendant la Révolution française," in *Le Droit de résistance XIIe–XXe siècle,* ed. Jean-Claude Zancarini (Fontenay, 1999), 247–264.

68. Colin Lucas, "Talking about Urban Popular Violence in 1789," in *Reshaping France: Town, Country, and Region during the French Revolution,* ed. Alan Forrest and Peter Jones (Manchester, 1991), 122–136. Applied to insurgents and tyrants who violated natural right, "brigand" became a potent term of denunciation in the Revolution. Dan Edelstein, *The Terror of Natural Right: Republicanism, the Cult of Nature, and the French Revolution* (Chicago, 2010).

69. Quoted in Dion, *Histoire de la vigne,* 526.

70. Quoted in de Clercq, "L'incendie des barrières," 47; and Frémy, "L'enceinte de Paris," 131.

71. Quoted in de Clercq, "L'incendie des barrières," 47–48.

72. *AP,* 16:605–606.

73. Montesquieu, *De l'esprit des lois* (Paris, 1979), vol. 1, book 12, chapter 19, 345. This is to my knowledge the earliest revolutionary appeal to veiling law.

74. J. F. Bosher, *French Finances 1770–1795: From Business to Bureaucracy* (Cambridge, 1970), chapter 8.

75. Preamble of May edict, quoted in Bernard Schnapper, "La diffusion en France des nouvelles conceptions pénales dans la dernière décennie de l'ancien régime," in *Voies nouvelles en histoire du droit,* ed. Bernard Schnapper (Paris, 1991), 197.

76. Bosher, *Single Duty Project.*

77. Marion, "Recouvrement," 2.

78. Ibid., 5.

79. Deputy Aubry du Bochet, quoted in Marcel Marion, *Histoire financière de la France depuis 1715* (Paris, 1919), 2:227.

80. J. B. Duvergier, ed., *Collection complète des lois* (Paris, 1834), 1:40–41; and Bloch, ed., *Procès-Verbaux,* 1:33. Necker thought that the loss in revenue from lower salt prices would be compensated by higher levels of consumption and a reduction in policing costs.

81. Bloch, ed., *Contributions directes,* 266.

82. *AP,* 20:444–446. For similar promonopoly arguments, see also the speeches by the abbé Coulmiers (*AP,* 12:559–562), Louis Charrier (*AP,* 20:404–405), and Mirabeau (*AP,* 22:556–557). Under the apparent influence of Farmer-General Lavoisier, Mirabeau spoke on behalf of the monopoly but conceded

that reforms were necessary to deal with the problem of smuggling. The price of state tobacco would have to be cut, household searches restricted, and the "too rigorous" penal code eased.

83. Michael Kwass, "Ordering the World of Goods: Consumer Revolution and the Classification of Objects in Eighteenth-Century France," *Representations* 82 (2003), 87–117.

84. Colin Jones and Rebecca Spang, "Sans-Culottes, sans Café, sans Tabac: Shifting Realms of Necessity and Luxury in Eighteenth-Century France," in *Consumers and Luxury: Consumer Culture in Europe 1650–1850,* ed. Maxine Berg and Helen Clifford (Manchester, 1999), 37–62; and Rebecca Spang, "What Is Rum? The Politics of Consumption in the French Revolution," in *The Politics of Consumption: Material Culture and Citizenship in Europe and America,* ed. Martin Daunton and Mathew Hilton (Oxford, 2001), 33–49.

85. Charles Nicolas Roland, *Le financier patriote; ou, La nation éclairée sur ses vrais intérêts* (London, 1789), 92.

86. *AP,* 20:411–414. For some, the status of the customs rioters rose to equal that of the conquerors of the Bastille. In 1795, an official in the department of the Seine declared that it was only at the moment when Parisians sacked the customs gates that "they felt freed from the chains that weighed on them. The overthrow of the wall and that of the Bastille are two deeds tied together in the annals of the Revolution; they will be inseparable." Quoted in Dion, *Histoire de la vigne,* 529.

87. *AP,* 20:461.

88. *Le Père Duchesne d'Hébert,* ed. F. Braesch (Paris, 1938), 1:583–584.

89. *AP,* 24:446.

90. In Bloch, ed., *Contributions directes,* see "Décret et adresse aux Français sur le payement des contributions," (24 June 1791), 269–270. The "Address" was drafted by the committee on public contributions.

91. Samuel Moyn, *The Last Utopia: Human Rights in History* (Cambridge, MA, 2010), 1–20, makes neo-Tocquevillian claims about the Revolution's failure to protect rights. My counteremphasis on the political motivations behind liberal economic reform is supported by Emma Rothschild, *Economic Sentiments: Adam Smith, Condorcet, and the Enlightenment* (Cambridge, MA, 2001), chapter 3; and David Todd, *L'identité économique de la France: libre-échange et protectionnisme, 1814–1851* (Paris, 2008), chapter 1.

92. Robert Allen, *Les Tribunaux criminels sous la Révolution et l'Empire, 1792–1811* (Rennes, 2005), 71–72, 221–222.

93. Ironically, in the west, the erasure of fiscal borders between Brittany and provinces to its east deprived salt-smuggling peasants of an important source of income, drawing them into opposition to the Revolution. See Jean-Clément Martin, "The Vendée, *Chouannerie,* and the State, 1791–99," in *A Companion to the French Revolution,* ed. Peter McPhee (Chichester, 2013), 246–259.

94. Quoted in Matthews, *Royal General Farms,* 281.

95. Maximilien Robespierre, "Report on the Principles of Political Morality" (5 February 1794), in Mason and Rizzo, eds., *French Revolution*, 257.

96. Philippe Minard, *La fortune du Colbertisme: État et industrie dans la France des Lumières* (Paris, 1998), 363, uses this phrase in reference to industrial deregulation in 1791, a story with striking similarities to the one told here. In both cases, lawmakers instituted liberal reforms that created institutional vacuums, which produced new problems in turn.

97. François Crouzet, *La grande inflation: la monnaie en France de Louis XVI à Napoléon* (Paris, 1993), 122.

98. The Convention (1792–1795) introduced progressive direct taxes more in line with revolutionary principles but only on a limited scale. See Jean-Pierre Gross, "Progressive Taxation and Social Justice in Eighteenth-Century France," *PP* 140 (1993), 79–126.

99. Quoted in Marion, *Histoire financière*, 4:299–300.

100. Sutherland, "Peasants, Lords, and Leviathan"; White, "French Revolution," 230 (Figure 1).

101. François Crouzet, "Le Système continental, antécédent de l'Union européenne (1806–1813)," in *La croissance en économie ouverte (XVIIIe–XXIe siècles)*, ed. Bertrand Blancheton and Hubert Bonin (Brussels, 2009), 69–86; and Ronald Findlay and Kevin H. O'Rourke, *Power and Plenty: Trade, War, and the World Economy in the Second Millennium* (Princeton, NJ, 2007), 369–371. But see Silvia Marzagalli, "The Failure of a Transatlantic Alliance? Franco-American Trade, 1783–1815," *History of European Ideas* 34:4 (2008), 456–464.

102. Jean Clinquart, *L'administration des douanes en France sous le Consulat et l'Empire* (Neuilly, 1979), 212. See Sylvia Marzagalli, *Les Boulevards de la fraude: le négoce maritime et le Blocus continental, 1806–1813* (Villeneuve d'Ascq, 1999); Roger Dufraisse, "La contrebande dans les départements réunis de la rive gauche du Rhin à l'époque napoléonienne," *Francia* 1 (1973), 508–536; Gavin Daly, "Napoleon and the 'City of Smugglers,'" *Historical Journal* 50 (2007), 333–352; idem, "English Smugglers, the Channel, and the Napoleonic Wars, 1800–1814," *Journal of British Studies* 46 (2007), 30–46; and James Ellis, *Napoleon's Continental Blockade: The Case of Alsace* (Oxford, 1981).

103. Clinquart, *L'administration des douanes en France sous le Consulat et l'Empire*, part II, chapter 5.

104. Brown, *Ending the French Revolution*.

105. Delalande, *Batailles de l'impôt*, part 1; Bernard Gainot, "La République comme association de citoyens solidaires: Pour retrouver l'économie politique républicaine (1792–1797)," in *Pour quoi faire la Révolution*, ed. Jean-Luc Chappey et al. (Marseille, 2012), 149–180.

106. The revolutionary "right" to live free from fiscal-judicial repression shaped the tax from the beginning. Emmanuel de Crouy Chanel, "La définition de l'impôt idéal sous le Directoire: la question de l'établissement d'un

impôt sur le sel," in *L'impôt en France aux XIXe et XXe siècles,* ed. Maurice Lévy-Leboyer, Michel Lescure, and Alain Plessis (Paris, 2006), 119–140.

107. Todd, *L'identité économique,* part 2.

108. *Mémoires d'un touriste* (Paris, 1854), 200.

109. Robert Schnerb, *Deux siècles de fiscalité française* (Paris, 1973); Todd, *L'identité économique;* Delalande, *Batailles de l'impôt,* part 1.

110. Quoted in Todd, *L'identité économique,* 171.

Conclusion

1. Frank Trentmann, "Introduction," in *The Oxford Handbook of the History of Consumption,* ed. Frank Trentmann (Oxford, 2012), 7.

2. John Brewer, "The Error of Our Ways: Historians and the Birth of Consumer Society," Cultures of Consumption Workshop (Economic and Social Research Council–Arts and Humanities Research Board) working paper no. 12 (June 2004), 11 and 18.

3. Jan de Vries, *The Industrious Revolution: Consumer Behavior and the Household Economy, 1650 to the Present* (Cambridge, 2008).

4. Prasannan Parthasarathi, "Rethinking Wages and Competitiveness in the Eighteenth Century: Britain and South India," *PP* 158 (1998), 79–109.

5. For this dynamic in France, see Richard Drayton, "The Globalization of France: Provincial Cities and French Expansion c. 1500–1800," *History of European Ideas* 34 (2008), 424–430; Laurent Dubois, "An Atlantic Revolution," *French Historical Studies* 32 (2009), 659–660; Allan Potofsky, "The One and the Many: The Two Revolutions Question and the 'Consumer-Commercial' Atlantic, 1789 to the Present," in *Rethinking the Atlantic World: Europe and America in the Age of Democratic Revolutions,* ed. Manuela Albertone and Antonino De Francesco (New York, 2009), 17–45. For an incisive reconceptualization of the relationship between colonial and metropolitan history that seeks to dissolve disciplinary boundaries between them, see Jean-Frédéric Schaub, "La catégorie 'études coloniales' est-elle indispensable?" *AHSS* 63 (2008), 625–646.

6. Robin Blackburn, *The Making of New World Slavery: From the Baroque to the Modern, 1492–1800* (London, 1998); Kenneth Pomeranz, *The Great Divergence: China, Europe, and the Making of the Modern World* (Princeton, NJ, 2000); Ronald Findlay and Kevin H. O'Rourke, *Power and Plenty: Trade, War, and the World Economy in the Second Millennium* (Princeton, NJ, 2007), chapter 6; and P. C. Emmer, O. Pétré-Grenouilleau, and J. V. Roitman, eds., *A Deus ex Machina Revisited: Atlantic Colonial Trade and European Economic Development* (Leiden, 2006).

7. Jane Burbank and Frederick Cooper, *Empires in World History: Power and the Politics of Difference* (Princeton, NJ, 2010), chapters 6 and 8; Findlay and O'Rourke, *Power and Plenty,* chapter 5. For the French Empire, see Jean Tarrade, *Le commerce colonial de la France à la fin de l'Ancien Régime,* 2 vols.

(Paris, 1972). For the British Empire, see Thomas Truxes, *Defying Empire: Trading with the Enemy in Colonial New York* (New Haven, CT, 2008). For interesting comparisons between the Spanish and British empires in this regard, see J. H. Elliott, *Empires of the Atlantic World: Britain and Spain in America 1492–1830* (New Haven, CT, 2006), chapter 10.

8. Maxine Berg, "In Pursuit of Luxury: Global History and British Consumer Goods in the Eighteenth Century," *PP* 182 (2004), 85–142; and Serge Chassagne, *Le Coton et ses patrons: France, 1760–1840* (Paris, 1991).

9. The limits of French imperial administration have been stressed by James Pritchard, *In Search of Empire: The French Colonies in the Americas, 1670–1730* (Cambridge, 2004); and Kenneth J. Banks, *Chasing Empire across the Sea: Communications and the State in the French Atlantic, 1713–1763* (Montreal, 2003); Tarrade, *Le Commerce colonial de la France*; and Shannon Lee Dawdy, *Building the Devil's Empire: French Colonial New Orleans* (Chicago, 2008).

10. Charles Tilly, "Welcome to the Seventeenth Century," in *The Twenty-First Century Firm: Changing Economic Organization in International Perspective*, ed. Paul DiMaggio (Princeton, NJ, 2001), 200–209; and idem, *The Politics of Collective Violence* (Cambridge, 2003), 59. Tilly's concerns are shared by others who fear that the rising power of illicit actors threatens to plunge the world into a kind of neomedievalism in which decentralized and privatized forms of power—from city-states, multinational corporations, and sovereign wealth funds to private military contractors and gated communities—have usurped the position once occupied by proper public authority. Parag Khanna, "The Next Big Thing: Neomedievalism," *Foreign Policy*, April 15, 2009.

11. Renate Bridenthal, "Introduction," in *The Hidden History of Crime, Corruption and States*, ed. Renate Bridenthal (Oxford, 2013), 2.

Acknowledgments

In this age of austerity, it is more important than ever to acknowledge the material support that makes scholarship possible. Research for this book was generously funded by the American Philosophical Society, the American Council of Learned Societies, and the Willson Center for Humanities and Arts at the University of Georgia. I would also like to thank the staffs of the French state archives and libraries where my research was conducted, in particular the wonderfully rich departmental archives of central, eastern, and southern France, where traces of Mandrin and his world have been carefully conserved.

I am profoundly grateful to the many people who collectively shaped this book. I benefited from conversations (and e-mail exchanges) with Robert Allen, David Bell, David Bien, Loïc Charles, Stephen Clay, Jim Collins, Jesse Cromwell, Clare Crowston, André Ferrer, Dena Goodman, Carla Hesse, Tony Hopkins, Jeff Horn, Lynn Hunt, Valérie Huss, Andrew Jainchill, Tom Kaiser, Tim Le Goff, Marcy Norton, Arnaud Orain, Prasannan Parthasarathi, Laurent Perillat, Jeremy Popkin, Allan Potofsky, Daniel Roche, Emma Rothschild, Jay Smith, Miranda Spieler, Corinne Townley, and Charles Walton. Suzanne Desan, Steve Kaplan, and Laura Mason offered invaluable feedback on various chapters. Peter Sahlins and Bill Sewell graciously read a draft of the whole manuscript, providing me with an abundance of insightful suggestions for strengthening my argument. The readers for Harvard University Press—Paul Cheney and Colin Jones—offered salutary advice that saved me from many an error and deepened my thinking on a wide range of questions. Finally, Laura Mason's skillful editing sharpened the manuscript's prose and (once again) taught me a lesson in writing.

I thank Mike Aronson, my editor at Harvard University Press, for his unwavering support of this project. I'm also grateful to Kathleen Drummy for easing the manuscript into production, to Isabelle Lewis for creating two absolutely essential maps, and to Claudio Saunt for setting up note-taking and photography software that allowed me to make the most of my time in provincial archives.

I have had the opportunity to present portions of this work to audiences at several conferences and workshops. Thanks go to organizers and participants at the American Philosophical Society, the Institute for Historical Studies (University of Texas at Austin), the Johns Hopkins history seminar, Queen's University history department, the American Historical Association, the Western Society for French History, and the Society for French Historical Studies. Three thematic conferences were particularly important in helping me clarify my argument: "Questioning 'Credible Commitment': Rethinking the Glorious Revolution and the Rise of Financial Capitalism" (Cambridge University), "Enlightenment 2.1" (University of California at Berkeley), and "L'impact du monde atlantique sur les 'Anciens Mondes' Africain et Européen du XVe au XIXe siècle" (EHESS and University of Nantes).

This project began at the University of Georgia and ended (as much as any project can truly end) at Johns Hopkins. I would like to thank my dear friends at UGA, whose company, humor, and perspicacity I sorely miss, for making my years in Athens so fulfilling. Colleagues at Hopkins warmly welcomed me into the history department and introduced me to the riches of its seminar. I have already learned a great deal from them, much of which influenced this book during its final stages.

Last, I would like to acknowledge the boundless support of my parents and siblings, who gave me my bearings, and of my own family, which gives my daily life its texture and joy. This book is dedicated to Laura, Max, and Isabel as a small token of appreciation for sharing their lives with me.

Index